176647

*Prose for*
*Effective Composition*

PRENTICE-HALL INTERNATIONAL, INC., *London*
PRENTICE-HALL OF AUSTRALIA, PTY., LTD., *Sydney*
PRENTICE-HALL OF CANADA, LTD., *Toronto*
PRENTICE-HALL OF INDIA (PRIVATE) LTD., *New Delhi*
PRENTICE-HALL OF JAPAN, INC., *Tokyo*
PRENTICE-HALL DE MEXICO, S.A., *Mexico City*

WILLIAM D. BAKER

*Dean of Faculty, Rockford College*

# *Prose for*

# *Effective Composition*

PRENTICE-HALL, INC.    ENGLEWOOD CLIFFS, N.J.

Second printing ...... August, 1964

# Preface

The aim of this anthology is to teach students to read, write, and think. Students begin this interactive process by reading and discussing models of thought and expression. The process itself is the important thing. It starts with reading—a close, careful reading; it moves to discussion—an interplay of ideas; it proceeds to writing—the recording of ideas in an orderly and permanent form.

Since the process is important, the text which brings order to the process is also important. It is proper, then, to discuss here the qualities which distinguish this text. Special features are: (1) quality and length of selections, (2) the use of models and patterns, (3) the arrangement of major categories and subsections, (4) the suggestions for writing, and (5) the use of several quotations at the beginning of each subsection.

*Quality and length of the selections*

The one hundred and twenty-four readings in this text were selected because they were well written; for every selection in the text, fifty selections were read, analyzed, and abandoned. More than one hundred were tested in the college classroom.

Quality and length of the selections are especially significant because students need *models* of writing. (About half of the essays here contain less than 1200 words, and only a handful contain more than 3000 words.) The selection of materials with regard to length is a unique feature of this anthology. Too often the student is provided with a model four or five times longer than he is expected to produce. Long models are especially frustrating. They confront the student with the task of saying something significant in one-quarter the space of the model. They are, therefore, less likely to give him

176647

the self-confidence necessary to good writing. Short models, on the other hand, take the time factor into consideration. Few professionals could turn out publishable articles in the time generally available to students. Therefore the use of relatively short models makes good pedagogical sense.

Quality of writing was the primary consideration in selecting materials that would have a permanent value for students. "Permanent value" does not mean a library of essays to which students will refer several years after college. It means a value to be derived by learning the process of analytical reading and writing.

Good writing holds the imagination by a special grace or force. Most of the authors here are master craftsmen of world-wide reputation; they are professionals who represent what the best minds think and feel. Thus students are provided with the best possible examples of good writing.

*The use of models and patterns*

Some basic assumptions here are: (1) that writing is an extremely complicated human activity; (2) that learning to read and write takes time, effort, much practice, and patience; and (3) that texts and teachers must offer every known assistance to the student. The time-tested method of helping is to provide models. A coach can say, "Do it this way," and then demonstrate his point by performing the action. A teacher must say, "Look at this model and learn what you can from it." There is no standard method of looking at models, and to manufacture one artificially would be to defeat the purpose of using them. For the purpose of using a model is to learn to look. But look for what? The anthologist who provides questions and exercises for the model-selections has no definitive guide. He must rely on his teaching ability and on the knowledge that other teachers will add, delete, and modify questions and exercises to accommodate special circumstances. And, of course, there are no standard models. If there were, there would be only one standard anthology.

Many of the essay models here provide especially good professional patterns. The word *pattern* should be emphasized. A skilled craftsman takes a pattern and refines and reorders it to suit a personal taste. Students can do the same with professional patterns of prose. By doing so, they learn to use such rhetorical techniques as parallelism, special and regular uses of punctuation, repetition for emphasis, and transitions for coherent flow of thought. Students often avoid these things by their initial hesitation and lack of self-confidence. The professional pattern gives them the confidence of knowing that the model has met one important criteria of successful writing—acceptance in the publisher's marketplace.

The methods of following patterns are as various as the patterns themselves. For example, in *Part One, The University,* ten authors have been chosen for special consideration as models: Livingston, Huxley, Dewey, Wilson, Hutchins, Masefield, Whitehead, Montaigne, Counts, and Bacon. Different models have been selected for each part. Even a hurried examination will show that the method of using models depends on the special characteristics of the models. Some models provide especially effective sentence patterns; others lend themselves to organizational analysis; still others reveal an effective syntactical scheme. Whatever the method of using the model, the object—careful scrutiny of written material—remains.

*The arrangement of major categories and subsections*

The arrangement of the five main parts—*The University, The Nature of Man, The Writer at Work, The Arts,* and *The Search for Significance*—moves progressively toward more sophisticated and complex techniques. Although the materials in the first section of *Part One* are shorter and have a less complex organizational pattern than those which follow, they are neither pedestrian nor crudely utilitarian. They are philosophical and analytical, and are intended to set a tone for the rest of the book.

The second main part, *The Nature of Man,* provides a microcosm within a macrocosm—it describes the movement of human beings through childhood, adolescence, and maturity, and concludes with a section on life in the city. Here especially the student is encouraged to bring his own range of experiences to bear.

The third part, *The Writer at Work,* assumes that the student will be interested in how the professionals learned their craft. It also introduces him to several provocative comments about language and style, matters that are immediately germane to his own work in college.

*Part Four, The Arts,* is included to introduce the student to the artistic and aesthetic life and to the problems of that life. An examination of man's artistic activity calls for the kind of clear and penetrating observation and analysis which is an integral part of the writer's craft.

The final part, *The Search for Significance,* assumes that the student has a broadening range of interests and a deepening philosophical outlook, within which he may discover the beginnings of his own philosophy of life. The key exercise in this section calls for an examination of the repercussions of one modern philosophical system, existentialism; it is found on p. 502.

A second table of contents (Alternate Plan of Study) has been provided as an alternate and useful arrangement of the material, especially for those courses organized according to types of writing. The distribution of the essays under various types as well as the labeling of the types themselves is arbitrary, but it seemed sensible to include an essay under more than one category if there was a question about its pedigree. And since the naming of types of writing cuts across subject-matter categories (for example, a humorous essay may also be a definition), many essays are found under more than one heading. A reader may wish to concentrate on one type of writing, say, definition, as he attempts to sharpen his ability in this area. Or he may simply want an index for the articles on humor, for the poetry, and so forth. In either case, the alternate Plan of Study assists him by listing articles under the following heads: Observation, Process, Definition, Description, Personal Experience, Evaluation, Comparison and Contrast, Analogy, Humor, Poetry, and Analysis (by Classification, by Characterization, and by Description). The latter three categories are really subdivisions of analytical writing, arranged as are all the categories, not by virtue of a strict logic but for the convenience of those who prefer such an organizational approach.

The titles devised for the reading selections have often been chosen from the text of the essay itself. Since most of the selections are parts of longer pieces with different titles, it seemed quite proper to rename the shorter selection with a more appropriate title.

Although the chief purpose has been to provide excellent *prose* models, a number of poems have been included to augment several of the sections. Models may be used not only to suggest a pattern of thought, but also to reveal shades and variations of thought. Therefore poetry finds a natural place in this book. Furthermore, an analysis of poetry is but another way of looking at proper words in proper places. It is valuable for the student writer to discover the essential differences between prose and poetry. An appreciation of these differences results in a deeper understanding of the complexities of English word order, of the power of figurative language, of the effects to be achieved by punctuation patterns, of the use of rhythm, rhyme, imagery, and other poetic devices. An example of how this book deals with the foregoing elements may be seen in the treatment of Milton's *On Arriving at the Age of Twenty-three* (p. 91).

The devices of creative prose writing, like the devices of poetry described above, are examined throughout this anthology. Accordingly, some of the *Suggestions for Writing* give attention to such matters as an imaginative approach to the subject, the creation of characters who oppose or defend a position, and the development of situations in which "idea-carrying" events can occur. Examples of such suggestions may be seen in the treatment of the articles by Locke, Shaler, Forster, and Van Doren.

*The Suggestions for Writing*

Although the exercises which follow each selection are called *Suggestions for Writing,* they are really more than that. They contain a few lines about the author in order to provide some context both for the essay and for the assignment. From time to time are included such standard exercises as: (1) questions on vocabulary (see Newman, Huxley, Montaigne, Thoreau), (2) punctuation (Newman, Huxley, Arnold), (3) sentence analysis (Livingston, Newman, Bacon), (4) paragraph analysis (Wilson, Hutchins, Masefield, Whitehead), and (5) language usage (Whitehead, Thoreau, Bacon, Hall, Veblen. The general movement of the suggestions is from analysis of the essay to an introspective attitude which will lead to thoughtful writing. For the most part, the first questions call for an analysis of the essay, and later items offer an invitation to write.

There is a sufficient variety in the one hundred and twenty-four selections so that teachers and students may choose those which interest them. There is also enough variety in the more than four hundred and seventy questions, so that choices can be made. Normally, students are not expected to follow all of the suggestions for writing or to read all of the selections.

The writing suggestions grew out of the essays. Since the essays are chiefly descriptive, definitive, or analytical, and since they are more philosophical than utilitarian, the exercises also follow these lines. A major objective has been to provide exercises which call for rigorous use of the mind, in the hope that such mental activity will develop the other senses—seeing, listening, and the like.

Generally speaking a subjective reaction to the essays is not enough. A careful analysis has to come first. What did the author say? What were his premises? Was his point clear and fairly presented? To answer such questions requires a reasoning power, a quality of mind that is basic to further activity with the essays. After the initial task of analysis, the student is ready for a deeper exploration of the theme by the process of writing.

*The use of quotations*

The quotations at the beginning of each section—another unique feature of this anthology—are intended to start one thinking about ideas in this section. These quotations have been chosen as sort of introductory remarks by notable speakers. Often the suggestions for writing refer to these quotations and direct the student to compare or contrast the material in the reading selection with the quotations. Some instructors will find the quotations especially useful as theme topics, in the light of which the reading selections may be regarded as backgrounds, references, or points of departure. The quotations may also be used to motivate students to begin their own notebooks or journals in which pertinent statements may be recorded.

Essentially, this anthology is a book of good reading, the kind that can be dipped into to refresh the pleasures of living. If it whets the appetite for reading more works by the same authors, or more works on the same themes, and by so doing begins a liberal education for the reader, it will have served the broadest and deepest purpose for which it was created.

W.D.B.

# Table of Contents

## *Human Beings* *136*

## *Man in the City* *164*

## PART THREE   THE WRITER AT WORK

## *The Matter of Style* *204*

PART FIVE        THE SEARCH FOR SIGNIFICANCE

*Part One*

# THE UNIVERSITY

# A Liberal Education

He that increaseth knowledge increaseth sorrow.
—*Ecclesiastes* I, 18, c. 200 B.C.

I went to the woods because I wished to live deliberately, to front only the essential facts of life, and see if I could not learn what it had to teach, and not, when I came to die, discover that I had not lived.
—Thoreau, *Walden,* 1854

Travel, in the younger sort, is a part of education; in the elder, a part of experience. He that travelleth into a country before he hath some entrance into the language, goeth to school, and not to travel.
—Francis Bacon, *Of Travel,* 1625

One of the benefits of a college education is to show the boy its little avail.
—Emerson, *Culture,* 1860

Curiosity is one of the permanent and certain characteristics of a vigorous mind.
—Samuel Johnson, *The Rambler,* 1751

The knowledge of the world is only to be acquired in the world, not in a closet.
—Lord Chesterfield, *Letter to His Son,* 1746

Note, too, that a faithful study of the liberal arts humanizes character and permits it not to be cruel.
—Ovid (43 B.C.-A.D. 18), *Epistolae ex Ponto,* II, 3, 14

A liberal education is not a thing of precise definition like an isosceles triangle, nor is it a fixed list of courses. . . . It is rather a human quality and a personal achievement, which can be attained in a variety of ways.
—George P. Schmidt, *The Liberal Arts College,* 1957

2

SIR RICHARD LIVINGSTONE

# A Complete Human Being*

. . . The Greeks held that the free man, the real man, the complete man, must be something more than a mere breadwinner, and must have something besides the knowledge necessary to earn his living. He must have also the education which will give him the chance of developing the gifts and faculties of human nature and becoming a full human being. They saw clearly that men were breadwinners but also that they were, or ought to be, something more: that a man might be a doctor or a lawyer or a shopkeeper or an artisan or a clerk, but that he was also a man, and that education should recognise this and help each individual to become, so far as his capacities allowed, what a man ought to be. That was the meaning of a liberal education, and that is its aim—the making of men; and clearly it is different from a technical education which simply enables us to earn our bread, but does not make us complete human beings.

And what is a complete human being? Again I shall take the Greek answer to this question. Human beings have bodies, minds and characters. Each of these is capable of what the Greeks called "virtue" . . . or what we might call "excellence." The virtue or excellence of the body is health and fitness and strength, the firm and sensitive hand, the clear eye; the excellence of the mind is to know and to understand and to think, to have some idea of what the world is and of what man has done and has been and can be; the excellence of the character lies in the great virtues. This trinity

---

* From *The Future in Education* by Sir Richard Livingstone. (New York: Cambridge University Press, 1954). Reprinted by permission of the publishers.

of body, mind and character is man; man's aim, besides earning his living, is to make the most of all three, to have as good a mind, body and character as possible; and a liberal education, a free man's education, is to help him to this; not because a sound body, mind and character help to success, or even because they help to happiness, but because they are good things in themselves, and because what is good is worth while, simply because it is good. So we get that clear and important distinction between technical education which aims at earning a living or making money or at some narrowly practical skill, and the free man's education which aims at producing as perfect and complete a human being as may be.

This is not to despise technical education which is essential; everyone has to learn to make a living and do his job, and he cannot do it without training: technical or vocational education is as much wanted as liberal education. But they are not to be confused. They are both important, both necessary, but they are different.

## SUGGESTIONS FOR WRITING

1. Sir Richard Livingstone (1880-1960), a famous classical scholar in Britain, has written *The Legacy of Greece,* 1921, and *Some Thoughts on University Education,* 1948. Here he says, "the excellence of the mind is to know *and* to understand *and* to think, to have some idea of what the world is *and* of what man has done *and* has been *and* can be." Five "and's." Their purpose is to make each "addition" emphatic. A characteristic of good writing is that it can withstand attempts to alter its pattern. Try at least three versions of the above quotation (for example, simple sentences, reversal or alteration of order, substitution of words). Compare your version with the original by reading aloud. Select two other statements by Livingstone and do the same.

2. Note that Livingstone constantly anticipates the questions of his reader. What is a full man? He tells us. What is mind? He tells us. A characteristic of clear writing is this sense of anticipation by the author, so that the reader finds satisfaction in the solutions to those questions which inevitably arise in the process of making definitions. Define an abstract term (love, hate, loyalty, pride, beauty) in a statement similar in length to the above, so that your reader finds satisfaction in the answers to questions you anticipate and provide.

3. Before we are ready to accept Livingstone's key statement about man becoming a full human being, we need a definition of the term *full.* He provides a partial answer in his listing of mind, body, and character. But what is mind? And what is body and character? Again he provides an answer by relating the Greek conception of these things. And al-

though this may not satisfy our desire to know the "modern" answer, it is a valid approach to the question. From this foundation, Livingstone states that a liberal education, as opposed to vocational training, allows a man to become complete. Livingstone's structure is simple, yet adequate: the Greeks sought to develop the full man; the full man is defined; such a man requires a liberal education and not simply technical training. Use a similar structure and length (initial statement, definition of key term, second statement) to develop a statement of one of your personal ideals.

4. The quotation by Ovid at the beginning of the section leads to thoughts of how a liberal education should affect character. Livingstone helps us pursue these thoughts. How do *you* think a liberal education should influence character? Choose one aspect of character and write about the effect of education upon it.

5. Is a purely technical education possible? The nature of the individual's daily activities, the fullness of his past experiences, and his hopes for the future all contribute to his attitude toward each new learning experience, so that his ability to "relate" technical training to a full life is what determines the "liberalness" of education. If this is so (though you may disagree), then Livingstone is not right in saying the two educations are different. In fact, there can be no more than one kind of education. If you agree, explain how education is related to living.

JOHN HENRY NEWMAN

## The Purpose of Knowledge*

I am asked what is the end of University Education, and of the Liberal or Philosophical Knowledge which I conceive it to impart: I answer, that what I have already said has been sufficient to show that it has a very tangible, real, and sufficient end, though the end cannot be divided from that knowledge itself. Knowledge is capable of being its own end. Such is the constitution of the human mind, that any kind of knowledge, if it be really such, is its own reward. And if this is true of all knowledge, it is true also of that special Philosophy, which I have made to consist in a comprehensive view of truth in all its branches, of the relations of science to science, of their mutual bearings, and their respective values. What the worth of such an acquirement is, compared with other objects which we seek,—wealth or power or honour or the con-

* From *The Idea of a University* by John Henry Newman, 1873.

veniences and comforts of life, I do not profess here to discuss, but I would maintain, and mean to show, that it is an object, in its own nature so really and undeniably good, as to be the compensation of a great deal of thought in compassing, and a great deal of trouble in the attaining.

Now, when I say that Knowledge is not merely a means to something beyond it, or the preliminary of certain arts into which it naturally resolves, but an end sufficient to rest in and to pursue for its own sake, surely I am uttering no paradox, for I am stating what is both intelligible in itself, and has ever been the common judgment of philosophers and the ordinary feeling of mankind. I am saying what at least the public opinion of this day ought to be slow to deny, considering how much we have heard of late years, in opposition to Religion, of entertaining curious and various knowledge. I am but saying what whole volumes have been written to illustrate, viz., by a "selection from the records of Philosophy, Literature, and Art, in all ages and countries, of a body of examples, to show how the most unpropitious circumstances have been unable to conquer an ardent desire for the acquisition of knowledge." That further advantages accrue to us and redound to others by its possession, over and above what it is in itself, I am very far indeed from denying; but, independent of these, we are satisfying a direct need of our nature in its very acquisition; and, whereas our nature, unlike that of the inferior creation, does not at once reach its perfection, but depends, in order to it, on a number of external aids and appliances, Knowledge, as one of the principal of these, is valuable for what its very presence in us does for us after the manner of a habit, even though it be turned to no further account, nor subserve any direct end.

## SUGGESTIONS FOR WRITING

1. John Henry Newman (1801-1890), was an Anglican clergyman and later a cardinal in the Roman Catholic Church. He was also a writer of exceptional talent whose views on education were especially noteworthy. Here he tells us that knowledge is its own end, that it is a "reward" to the mind. As he develops his ideas he occasionally uses a word not found in an ordinary vocabulary. Define the following: impart, compassing, paradox, viz., unpropitious, ardent, accrue, re-

dound, subserve. Account for the spelling of *honour* and for the capitalization of Knowledge, Philosophy, etc.

2. Newman puts a great deal of information into each sentence. As he adds qualifications and clarifies definitions, his sentences grow quite long. The first contains 56 words, the fourth 47, the fifth 78. The second sentence, however, contains only eight words. To analyze one aspect of his style, divide the long sentences in the first paragraph into several shorter ones. Compare your version with the original by reading both aloud.

3. Account for the punctuation in the fifth sentence by indicating what might have been substituted for the dash, the semicolon, and the sixth and seventh commas. What is the purpose of the colon in the first sentence?

4. Newman says knowledge "is valuable for what its very presence in us does for us." Explain in a statement of similar length how knowledge can be "in" a person and what it "does" for him. Use as an example something you once wanted to know, and explain how you felt before and after the acquisition of this knowledge.

5. Knowledge can be anything from an understanding of atomic theory to a study of the telephone book. Both may be equally unknown before we begin, but they do not offer similar satisfactions when we attain the knowledge. Hence, some kinds of knowledge are better—offer more satisfaction—than others. A liberal education, then, consists as much in selecting knowledge as in attaining it. Write a composition on the principles by which "knowledge" is to be selected. You might begin by explaining why a study of a telephone book is not "satisfying" knowledge.

6. The quotation about curiosity by Samuel Johnson at the beginning of this section leads to the thought that such a characteristic is almost an unstated assumption in Newman's article. Knowledge cannot move to the mind; therefore the mind must move to knowledge. Describe the operations of a vigorous and inquiring mind.

THOMAS HENRY HUXLEY

## The Instruction of the Intellect*

. . . Education is learning the rules of this mighty game. In other words, education is the instruction of the intellect in the laws of

---

* From *Science and Education* by Thomas Henry Huxley. Reprinted by permission of the publishers, Appleton-Century-Crofts, Inc., an affiliate of Meredith Press.

Nature, under which name I include not merely things and their forces, but men and their ways; and the fashioning of the affections and of the will into an earnest and loving desire to move in harmony with those laws. For me, education means neither more nor less than this. Anything which professes to call itself education must be tried by this standard, and if it fails to stand the test, I will not call it education, whatever may be the force of authority, or of numbers, upon the other side. . . .

That man, I think, has had a liberal education who has been so trained in youth that his body is the ready servant of his will, and does with ease and pleasure all the work that, as a mechanism, it is capable of; whose intellect is a clear, cold, logic engine, with all its parts of equal strength, and in smooth working order; ready, like a steam engine, to be turned to any kind of work and spin the gossamers as well as forge the anchors of the mind; whose mind is stored with a knowledge of the great and fundamental truths of Nature and of the laws of her operations; one who, no stunted ascetic, is full of life and fire, but whose passions are trained to come to heel by a vigorous will, the servant of a tender conscience; who has learned to love all beauty, whether of Nature or of art, to hate all vileness, and to respect others as himself.

Such a one and no other, I conceive, has had a liberal education; for he is, as completely as a man can be, in harmony with Nature. He will make the best of her, and she of him. They will get on together rarely; she as his ever beneficient mother; he as her mouthpiece, her conscious self, her minister and interpreter.

SUGGESTIONS FOR WRITING

1. Thomas Henry Huxley (1825-1895), was a scientist and writer who used much of his skill and energy to explain the consequences of scientific advances of the nineteenth century. A student audience today might want a more complete explanation of *gossamers, ascetic,* and *come to heel.* Explain the terms. Indicate the purpose of the semicolon in the second sentence and the four dots at the end of the first paragraph. What are the four dots called? Why is Nature capitalized?
2. "Education is . . ." Huxley begins by defining one thing and then another (laws of Nature). Finally he illustrates his definition by revealing an object (man) which has the characteristics implicit in his definition. A similar structure might be used to define a word like *beauty.*

"Beauty is X. By X I mean Y and Z. An object which is beautiful has characteristics implicit in Y and Z." Define an abstract term by using a similar structure.

3. Huxley's definition pertains to an ideal example and is useful to the degree that ideals provide goals. But the absence of ideals in reality makes attainment difficult and frustrating even for the most ambitious person. Write a composition indicating the difficulties (including heredity) of attaining Huxley's ideal education.

4. The quotation by Thoreau at the beginning of this section suggests a means to an education, at least a postcollege education of the kind Thoreau had in mind. Huxley's ideal education might be attained by a man like Thoreau in his woods, but it would be necessary to enter the woods with knowledge as well as determination. What would Huxley demand? In other words, what education would Thoreau need to have *before* he went off by himself to discover life?

MATTHEW ARNOLD
## The Value of Humane Letters*

There is, therefore, really no question between Professor Huxley and me as to whether knowing the great results of the modern scientific study of nature is not required as part of our culture, as well as knowing the products of literature and art. . . .

. . . The more that men's minds are cleared, the more that the results of science are frankly accepted, the more that poetry and eloquence come to be received and studied as what in truth they really are—the criticism of life by gifted men, alive and active with extraordinary power at an unusual number of points—so much the more will the value of humane letters, and of art also, which is an utterance having a like kind of power with theirs, be felt and acknowledged, and their place in education be secured. . . .

And, therefore, to say the truth, I cannot really think that humane letters are in much actual danger of being thrust out from their leading place in education, in spite of the array of authorities against them at this moment. So long as human nature is what it is, their attractions will remain irresistible. As with Greek, so with letters generally: they will some day come, we may hope, to be studied more rationally, but they will not lose their place. What

* From *Discourse in America*, 1885.

will happen will rather be that there will be crowded into education other matters besides, far too many; there will be, perhaps a period of unsettlement and confusion and false tendency; but letters will not in the end lose their leading place. If they lose it for a time, they will get it back again. We shall be brought back to them by our wants and aspirations. . . .

### SUGGESTIONS FOR WRITING

1. Matthew Arnold (1822-1888), was a British poet, essayist, and famous educator (at Rugby). Here he assumes his reader thinks there has been an attack on humane letters by scientists, and though he denies the rift, his tone pacifies any opposition by its assurance and calmness. There is also a note of defensiveness. Select two or three words or phrases or rhetorical techniques that contribute to this tone.
2. What is the function of the colon in the second sentence of the third paragraph?
3. What does Arnold mean by "humane letters"?
4. What does Arnold mean when he says that humane letters are a *criticism* of life?
5. Humane letters, says Arnold, are attractive because of human nature, because "our wants and aspirations" bring us to them. What does he mean?
6. Arnold says humane letters "will not in the end lose their leading place." If we assume he means that more time, attention, and effort will be given to them than to, say, science and mathematics, then he would not be able to support the idea of a balanced curriculum. In a balanced curriculum a student has an opportunity to learn about a great number of academic fields. Write a composition, using Arnold as a model of length and style, arguing for or against a balanced curriculum.

JOHN DEWEY

# A Philosophy of Education*

If one attempts to formulate the philosophy of education implicit in the practices of the newer education, we may, I think, discover

---

* From *Experience and Education* by John Dewey (New York: The Macmillan Company, 1954). Reprinted by permission of Kappa Delta Pi.

certain common principles amid the variety of progressive schools now existing. To imposition from above is opposed expression and cultivation of individuality; to external discipline is opposed free activity; to learning from texts and teachers, learning through experience; to acquisition of isolated skills and techniques by drill is opposed acquisition of them as a means of attaining ends which make direct vital appeal; to preparation for a more or less remote future is opposed making the most of the opportunities of present life; to static aims and materials is opposed acquaintance with a changing world.

SUGGESTIONS FOR WRITING

1. John Dewey (1859-1952), was a philosopher whose efforts at Columbia University were devoted to a rigorous examination of educational theories. Here, in two sentences, he summarizes the concept of progressive education. The first sentence tells the method of approach; the second shows six contrasting principles. Define the following words used in this selection: implicit, imposition, acquisition. List an example for each of the following: imposition from above, expression of individuality, external discipline, free activity, acquisition of isolated skills, an end which has a direct vital appeal; preparation for a remote future, static aims.

2. Use Dewey's technique as a model for a two-sentence composition, but choose another subject (athletics, business, marriage, study methods, movie criticism, travel). Follow the structure as closely as possible: "If one attempts ———— , he may, I think, discover ————. To A is opposed B; to C is opposed D; etc." This exercise will help you discover how to express yourself concisely and teach you to make a detailed scrutiny of a prose model (examining word order, use of punctuation, and choice of diction).

3. The quotation by Lord Chesterfield at the beginning of this section, although written almost two hundred years before Dewey's works, parallels his thought. Explain the parallel and develop the Chesterfield concept by providing several illustrations of the kind of knowledge that can only be acquired in the world.

4. Choose one of the six contrasting elements of Dewey's second sentence and point out the possible dangers of misinterpretation of Dewey's philosophy because of his ambiguity. For example, if there is absolutely no imposition from above in education there can be only chaos, not order; and if there is expression of individuality completely devoid of any discipline, including self-discipline, chaos again results. If we assume Dewey wanted to avoid chaos, in what ways should his ideas be qualified, clarified, illustrated, refined, or defined?

# The Purpose of a University

One father is more than a hundred schoolmasters.
—George Herbert, *Outlandish Proverbs*, 1640

What a father says to his children is not heard by the world, but it will be heard by posterity.
—Jean Paul Richter, *Levana*, 1807

The use of a university is to make young gentlemen as unlike their fathers as possible.
—Woodrow Wilson, *Address in Pittsburgh*, October 24, 1914

Every man who rises above the common level has received two educations: the first from his teachers; the second, more personal and important, from himself.
—Edward Gibbon, *Memoirs*, 1795

A university should be a place of light, of liberty, and of learning.
—Benjamin Disraeli, *Speech, House of Commons*, 1873

If I were founding a university I would found first a smoking room; then when I had a little more money in hand I would found a dormitory; then after that, or more probably with it, a decent reading room and a library. After that, if I still had more money that I couldn't use, I would hire a professor and get some textbooks.
—Stephen Leacock, *Oxford As I See It*, 1922

The True University of these days is a Collection of Books.
—Thomas Carlyle, *Heroes and Hero-Worship*, 1841

WOODROW WILSON

# The Object of a University Is Intellect*

We get a good many men at Princeton from certain secondary schools who say a great deal about their earnest desire to cultivate character among our students, and I hear a great deal about character being the object of education. I take leave to believe that a man who cultivates his character consciously will cultivate nothing except what will make him intolerable to his fellow men. If your object in life is to make a fine fellow of yourself, you will not succeed, and you will not be acceptable to really fine fellows. Character, gentlemen, is a by-product. It comes, whether you will or not, as a consequence of a life devoted to the nearest duty, and the place in which character would be cultivated, if it be a place of study, is a place where study is the object and character the results.

Not long ago a gentleman approached me in a great excitement just after the entrance examinations. He said we had made a great mistake in not taking so and so from a certain school which he named. "But," I said, "he did not pass the entrance examinations." And he went over the boy's moral excellencies again. "Pardon me," I said, "you do not understand. He did not pass the entrance examinations. Now," I said, "I want you to understand that if the Angel Gabriel applied for admission to Princeton University and could not pass the entrance examinations, he would not be admitted. He would be wasting his time." It seemed a new idea to him. This boy had come from a school which cultivated character, and he was a nice, lovable fellow with a presentable character. Therefore, he ought to be admitted to any university. I fail to see it from this

---

* From *Yale Alumni Weekly* (March 25, 1908).

point of view, for a university is an institution of purpose. We have in some previous years had pity for young gentlemen who were not sufficiently acquainted with the elements of a preparatory course. They have been dropped at the examinations, and I have always felt that we have been guilty of an offense, and have made their parents spend money to no avail and the youngsters spend their time to no avail. And so I think that all university men ought to rouse themselves now and understand what is the object of a university. The object of a university is intellect; as a university its only object is intellect. As a body of young men there ought to be other things, there ought to be diversions to release them from the constant strain of effort, there ought to be things that gladden the heart and moments of leisure, but as a university the only object is intellect.

SUGGESTIONS FOR WRITING

1. Woodrow Wilson (1856-1924), twenty-eighth president of the United States (1913-1921), was president of Princeton before he entered federal politics. Here he argues that character is a by-product, that a university exists for intellect, and that, although men at the university may find diversions, the university itself is not part of such diversions. In such expressions as "I take leave to believe . . ." and "whether you will or not," Wilson adopts an orderly but argumentative tone. What other rhetorical devices (vocabulary, illustrations, method of development, etc.) reveal this tone?

2. Does the quotation by Gibbon at the beginning of this section suggest a thought incompatible with Wilson's thesis? In what ways is it related or unrelated?

3. In the first twelve sentences of the second paragraph Wilson uses an interesting device, a story with a point, in which men apparently failed to understand each other because they began with different sets of assumptions. Using a similar device, write a short composition about an incident in your life. Make Wilson's word order your model. "Not long ago A happened. Mr. X said A was a great mistake. 'But,' I said, '_____.' "

4. Wilson says, "I am told A is true, but I believe B is true." Then he develops his idea, not by telling *why* B is true but by reiterating his belief in a variety of ways, pointing out that several plausible arguments made for A do not shake his belief in B. Such a method of argument reveals great confidence in one's position and, in fact, implicitly assumes that power holds more force than reason. If Wilson did

not hold the power of admission to Princeton, he could not have enforced his argument. Because he does hold the power, no argument for position A will prevail. Using Wilson as a model for length, style, and organization, write a theme transferring this attitude to home or school life.

ROBERT M. HUTCHINS

## A University Is a Community of Scholars*

A university is a community of scholars. It is not a kindergarten; it is not a club; it is not a reform school; it is not a political party; it is not an agency of propaganda. A university is a community of scholars.

The scholars who compose that community have been chosen by their predecessors because they are especially competent to study and to teach some branch of knowledge. The greatest university is that in which the largest proportion of these scholars are most competent in their chosen fields.

To a certain extent the ability of a university to attract the best scholars depends on the salaries it can pay. To a certain extent it depends on the facilities, the libraries and laboratories it can offer. But great scholars have been known to sacrifice both salaries and facilities for the sake of the one thing that is indispensable to their calling, and that is freedom.

Freedom of inquiry, freedom of discussion, and freedom of teaching—without these a university cannot exist. Without these a university becomes a political party or an agency of propaganda. It ceases to be a university. The university exists only to find and to communicate the truth. If it cannot do that it is no longer a university.

SUGGESTIONS FOR WRITING

1. Robert M. Hutchins became Chancellor of the University of Chicago at the age of twenty-nine and remained at this post for more than

* From "Why Go to College?" *Saturday Evening Post* (January 22, 1938). Copyright 1938 by Curtis Publishing Company. Reprinted by permission of the author.

twenty years. One of his most drastic reforms was abolishing major intercollegiate football at the University of Chicago. At least one full generation of college students has been exposed to his defense of this action by reading his *Saturday Evening Post* article en*titled "Gate Receipts and Glory" (December 3, 1938). Read the article and write an explanation of why more colleges have not adopted his views.

2. Hutchins says, "A University is X. It is not B; not C; not D; not E; not F. It is X." Make a similar schematic analysis of the final paragraph.

3. From a student's point of view much depends on the definition of *competent* in "most competent in their chosen fields." Define the word by illustrating a person who has "competence."

4. Do you agree that a university is or ought to be a community of scholars? State your reasons in a theme.

5. Do Hutchins and Wilson (in the previous article) agree or disagree on the purpose of a university? Define *intellect* and *community of scholars* in such a way as to show their interrelationship.

JOHN  MASEFIELD

# A University Stands and Shines*

There are few earthly things more splendid than a University. In these days of broken frontiers and collapsing values, when the dams are down and the floods are making misery, when every future looks somewhat grim and every ancient foothold has become something of a quagmire, wherever a University stands, it stands and shines; wherever it exists, the free minds of men, urged on to full and fair enquiry, may still bring wisdom into human affairs.

There are few earthly things more beautiful than a University. It is a place where those who hate ignorance may strive to know, where those who perceive truth may strive to make others see; where seekers and learners alike, banded together in the search for knowledge, will honour thought in all its finer ways, will welcome thinkers in distress or in exile, will uphold ever the dignity of thought and learning and will exact standards in these things. They give

---

\* Speech by John Masefield, O.M., Poet Laureate, in reply to the Toast of the Honorary Graduands proposed by the Chancellor at Luncheon immediately before the Ceremony of Installation of The Chancellor, 25th June, 1946. Reprinted by kind permission of the University of Sheffield.

to the young in their impressionable years, the bond of a lofty purpose shared, of a great corporate life whose links will not be loosed until they die. They give young people that close companionship for which youth longs, and that chance of the endless discussion of the themes which are endless, without which youth would seem a waste of time.

There are few things more enduring than a University. Religions may split into sect or heresy; dynasties may perish or be supplanted, but for century after century the University will continue, and the stream of life will pass through it, and the thinker and the seeker will be found together in the undying cause of bringing thought into the world.

To be a member of one of these great Societies must ever be a glad distinction.

In conferring it upon us you declare, or let it be presumed, that we are qualified to teach in those ways of life which we have followed. It has been a mark of the Humanist since he began among us that "he wol gladly lerne and gladly teche"; and although all of us would more gladly learn than teach, to be counted fit to teach is something of a crown to all men.

On behalf of my fellows in this glory, on behalf of the very learned, valiant, wise and gifted men beside me here, who stand for the Law by which we live, the Air by which we breathe, the Free Enquiry by which we hope to endure, and the Art by which we shall be remembered, I thank you for this great distinction, which links us with you while we last.

SUGGESTIONS FOR WRITING

1. John Masefield (1878-    ), is responding to a toast in his honor. As England's poet laureate, he has just been granted an honorary degree by the University of Sheffield. The date is 1946. An analysis of these few paragraphs will show that he made four main points: a university shines; it is beautiful; it endures; he is proud to be part of it. With what premise did he begin? How might his premise differ from a scientist's?

2. Analyze the second paragraph (about the beauty of the university). What term might be substituted for beauty? How would you have written about the beauty of the university?

3. Using a paragraph of Masefield's prose, construct a pattern for what you yourself have to say. For example, transcribe the paragraph beginning, "There are few things more enduring than a University. . . ." By substituting key words, you may develop a paragraph based roughly on Masefield's structure. It might sound like this: "There are few things more enduring than a heroic character created by a classic author. Generals and admirals may hold sway for a time; empires may falter and wane, but for as long as man can read the heroic character of fiction will continue, and interpretations of that heroism will change, and the reflective reader and the lover of ideals will be forever bound together in the humanitarian cause of finding a noble model for the rest of the world to live by."

4. Reflect on the process of imitating the pattern of professional writing described in item #3. Consult the quotations at the beginning of the section called *The Matter of Style* (p. 204) and write a theme indicating the values—or dangers—in following the professional pattern of a master writer.

ALFRED NORTH WHITEHEAD

## Principles, Not Details*

The function of a University is to enable you to shed details in favor of principles. When I speak of principles I am hardly even thinking of verbal formulations. A principle which has thoroughly soaked into you is rather a mental habit than a formal statement. It becomes the way the mind reacts to the appropriate stimulus in the form of illustrative circumstances. Nobody goes about with his knowledge clearly and consciously before him. Mental cultivation is nothing else than the satisfactory way in which the mind will function when it is poked up into activity. Learning is often spoken of as if we are watching the open pages of all the books which we have ever read, and then, when occasion arises, we select the right page to read aloud to the universe.

Luckily, the truth is far otherwise from this crude idea; and for this reason the antagonism between the claims of pure knowledge

---

* From *The Aims of Education* by Alfred North Whitehead (New York: The Macmillan Company, 1959). Copyright 1929 by The Macmillan Company; © 1957 by Evelyn Whitehead. Reprinted by permission of the publishers.

and professional acquirement should be much less acute than a faulty view of education would lead us to anticipate. I can put my point otherwise by saying that the ideal of a University is not so much knowledge, as power. Its business is to convert the knowledge of a boy into the power of a man. . . .

The justification for a university is that it preserves the connection between knowledge and the zest of life, by uniting the young and the old in the imaginative consideration of learning. The university imparts information, but it imparts it imaginatively. At least, this is the function which it should perform for society. A university which fails in this respect has no reason for existence. This atmosphere of excitement, arising from imaginative consideration, transforms knowledge. A fact is no longer a bare fact: it is invested with all its possibilities. It is no longer a burden on the memory: it is energizing as the poet of our dreams, and as the architect of our purposes.

## SUGGESTIONS FOR WRITING

1. Alfred North Whitehead (1861-1947) was a British mathematician, philosopher, and educator. Here he says in his first paragraph, "A university exists not for B but A. By A I mean idea 1 and idea 2. Idea 1 is this. It is not that." Make a similar schematic analysis of the last paragraph.

2. Whitehead's language is a judicious mixture of formal and informal; "when it is poked up into activity" is one example of informal language. Find examples which seem either particularly formal or informal.

3. Whitehead speaks of "the antagonism between the claims of pure knowledge and professional acquirement." Explain what he means by this antagonism.

4. Whitehead speaks of "the *imaginative* considerations of learning"; later he says "the university imparts information *imaginatively*": still later, "the atmosphere of excitement, arising from *imaginative* consideration, transforms knowledge." Three emphatic references to imagination. Cite examples of imaginative approaches to learning you have encountered.

5. Cite an example of a fact "invested with all its possibilities."

6. "The justification of a university is . . . ." Using Whitehead as a model for length and style, develop your own thesis about the justification of a university.

RALPH  WALDO  EMERSON

## The Office of the Scholar*

I have . . . spoken of the education of the scholar by nature, by
books, and by action. It remains to say somewhat of his duties.
They are such as become Man Thinking. They may all be com-
prised in self-trust. The office of the scholar is to cheer, to raise, and
to guide men by showing them facts amidst appearances. He plies
the slow, unhonored, and unpaid task of observation. Flamsteed
and Herschel, in their glazed observatories, may catalogue the stars
with the praise of all men, and the results being splendid and useful, honor is sure. But he, in his private observatory, cataloguing
obscure and nebulous stars of the human mind, which as yet no
man has thought of as such—watching days and months sometimes
for a few facts, correcting still his old records—must relinquish
display and immediate fame. In the long period of his preparation
he must betray often an ignorance and shiftlessness in popular
arts, incurring the disdain of the able who shoulder him aside.
Long he must stammer in his speech, often forego the living for
the dead. Worse yet, he must accept—how often!—poverty and
solitude. For the ease and pleasure of treading the old road, accepting the fashions, the education, the religion of society, he takes
the cross of making his own, and, of course, the self-accusation, the
faint heart, the frequent uncertainty and loss of time, which are
the nettles and tangling vines in the way of the self-relying and
self-directed; and the state of virtual hostility in which he seems to
stand to society, and especially to educated society. For all this loss
and scorn, what offset? He is to find consolation in exercising the
highest function of human nature. He is one who raises himself
from private considerations and breathes and lives on public and
illustrious thoughts. He is the world's eye. He is the world's heart.
He is to resist the vulgar prosperity that retrogrades ever to barbarism, by preserving and communicating heroic sentiments, noble
biographies, melodious verse, and the conclusions of history. What-

---
* From *The American Scholar,* Phi Beta Kappa Address, 1837.

soever oracles the human heart, in all emergencies, in all solemn hours, has uttered as its commentary on the world of actions—these he shall receive and impart. And whatsoever new verdict Reason from her inviolable seat pronounces on the passing men and events of today—this he shall hear and promulgate.

These being his functions, it becomes him to feel all confidence in himself, and to defer never to the popular cry. He and he only knows the world. The world of any moment is the merest appearance. Some great decorum, some fetish of a government, some ephemeral trade, or war, or man, is cried up by half mankind and cried down by the other half, as if all depended on this particular up or down. The odds are that the whole question is not worth the poorest thought which the scholar has lost in listening to the controversy. Let him not quit his belief that a popgun is a popgun, though the ancient and honorable of the earth affirm it to be the crack of doom. In silence, in steadiness, in severe abstraction, let him hold by himself; add observation to observation, patient of neglect, patient of reproach, and bide his own time—happy enough if he can satisfy himself alone that this day he has seen something truly. Success treads on every right step. For the instinct is sure, that prompts him to tell his brother what he thinks. He then learns that in going down into the secrets of his own mind he has descended into the secrets of all minds. He learns that he who has mastered any law in his private thoughts, is master to that extent of all men whose language he speaks, and of all into whose language his own can be translated. The poet, in utter solitude remembering his spontaneous thoughts and recording them, is found to have recorded that which men in crowded cities find true for them also. The orator distrusts at first the fitness of his frank confessions, his want of knowledge of the persons he addresses, until he finds that he is the complement of his hearers—that they drink his words because he fulfils for them their own nature; the deeper he dives into his privatest, secretest presentiment, to his wonder he finds this is the most acceptable, most public, and universally true. The people delight in it; the better part of every man feels, This is my music; this is myself.

In self-trust all the virtues are comprehended. Free should the scholar be—free and brave. Free even to the definition of freedom, "without any hindrance that does not arise out of his own constitution." Brave—for fear is a thing which a scholar by his very function puts behind him. Fear always springs from ignorance. It is a shame to him if his tranquillity, amid dangerous times, arise from the presumption that like children and women his is a protected class; or if he seek a temporary peace by the diversion of his thoughts from politics or vexed questions, hiding his head like an ostrich in the flowering bushes, peeping into microscopes, and turning rhymes, as a boy whistles to keep his courage up. So is the danger a danger still; so is the fear worse. Manlike let him turn and face it. Let him look into its eye and search its nature, inspect its origin—see the whelping of this lion—which lies no great way back; he will then find in himself a perfect comprehension of its nature and extent; he will have made his hands meet on the other side, and can henceforth defy it and pass on superior. This world is his who can see through its pretension. What deafness, what stone-blind custom, what overgrown error you behold is there only by sufferance—by your sufferance. See it to be a lie, and you have already dealt it its mortal blow.

Yes, we are the cowed—we the trustless. It is a mischievous notion that we are come late into nature, that the world was finished a long time ago. As the world was plastic and fluid in the hands of God, so it is ever to so much of his attributes as we bring to it. To ignorance and sin, it is flint. They adapt themselves to it as they may; but in proportion as a man has any thing in him divine, the firmament flows before him and takes his signet and form. Not he is great who can alter matter, but he who can alter my state of mind. They are the kings of the world who give the color of their present thought to all nature and all art, and persuade men by the cheerful serenity of their carrying the matter, that this thing which they do is the apple which the ages have desired to pluck, now at last ripe, and inviting nations to the harvest. The great man makes the great thing. Wherever Macdonald sits, there is the head of the table. Linaeus makes botany the most alluring of studies, and wins it from the farmer and the herb-woman; Davy, chemistry; and Cuvier, fossils. The day is always his who works in it with serenity and great aims. The unstable estimates of men crowd to him whose mind is filled with a truth, as the heaped waves of the Atlantic follow the moon.

For this self-trust, the reason is deeper than can be fathomed, darker than can be enlightened. I might not carry with me the feeling of my audience in stating my own belief. But I have already shown the ground of my hope, in adverting to the doctrine that man is one. I believe man has been wronged; he has wronged himself. He has almost lost the light that can lead him back to his prerogatives. Men are become of no account. Men in history, men in the world of today, are bugs, are spawn, and are called "the mass" and "the herd." In a century, in a millennium, one or two men; that is to say, one or two approximations to the right state of every man. All the rest behold in the hero or the poet their own green and crude being, ripened; yes, and are content to be less, so *that* may attain to its full stature. What a testimony, full of grandeur, full of pity, is borne to the demands of his own nature, by the clansman, the poor partisan, who rejoices in the glory of his chief. The poor and the low find some amends to their immense moral capacity, for their acquiescence in a political and social inferiority. They are content to be brushed like flies from the path of a great person, so that justice shall be done by him to that common nature which it is the dearest desire of all to see enlarged and glorified. They sun themselves in the great man's light, and feel it to be their own element. They cast the dignity of man from their downtrod selves upon the shoulders of a hero, and will perish to add one drop of blood to make that great heart beat, those giant sinews combat and conquer. He lives for us, and we live in him.

Men, such as they are, very naturally seek money or power; and power because it is as good as money—the "spoils," so called, "of office." And why not? for they aspire to the highest, and this, in their sleepwalking, they dream is highest. Wake them and they shall quit the false good and leap to the true, and leave governments to clerks and desks. This revolution is to be wrought by the gradual domestication of the idea of Culture. The main enterprise of the world for splendor, for extent, is the upbuilding of a man. Here are the materials strewn along the ground. The private life of one man shall be a more illustrious monarchy, more formidable to its enemy, more sweet and serene in its influence to its friend, than any kingdom in history. For a man, rightly viewed, comprehendeth the particular natures of all men. Each philosopher, each bard, each actor has only done for me, as by a delegate, what one day I can do for myself.

SUGGESTIONS FOR WRITING

1. Ralph Waldo Emerson (1803-1882) was an American poet, essayist, lecturer, and philosopher. Here he speaks of the glory of scholarship. His speech is all the more noteworthy as a clarion call to academic industriousness and self-esteem. Summarize the duties of the scholar as Emerson conceived them.

2. What is the reward of the scholar, according to Emerson?

3. Why are all virtues "comprehended" in self-trust?

4. Emerson's tone is one of inspiration. Cite examples of rhetorical devices which produce this tone.

5. Emerson says the duties of a scholar "are such as become Man Thinking." How would he define Man Thinking?

6. "Not he is great who can alter matter, but he who can alter my state of mind." Several of the sentences here are memorable utterances, the quality of statement which, one feels, should be recorded separately and reflected upon. Make an annotated list of the statements you feel are memorable.

7. Emerson says the scholar must "defer never to the popular cry." Describe a scholar (first paragraph), invent a situation in which he is tempted by the "popular cry" (second paragraph), and reveal how he holds true (or breaks faith with) his scholarship (third paragraph).

8. "The main enterprise for the world of splendor, or extent, is the upbuilding of a man." What part does university training have in this upbuilding? What part does the individual play in his own "upbuilding"? Your answers to these questions are likely to be personal and to relate to yourself. Answer them in a carefully organized composition. Do not use Emerson as a model.

ROBERT BENCHLEY

# What College Did to Me*

My college education was no haphazard affair. My courses were all selected with a very definite aim in view, with a serious purpose

---

* From *Inside Benchley* by Robert Benchley (New York: Harper & Row, Publishers, 1942). Copyright 1927 by Harper & Row, Publishers, Incorporated. Reprinted by permission of the publishers.

in mind—no classes before eleven in the morning or after two-thirty in the afternoon, and nothing on Saturday at all. That was my slogan. On that rock was my education built.

As what is known as the Classical Course involved practically no afternoon laboratory work, whereas in the Scientific Course a man's time was never his own until four p.m. anyway, I went in for the classics. But only such classics as allowed for a good sleep in the morning. A man has his health to think of. There is such a thing as being a studying fool.

In my days (I was a classmate of the founder of the college) a student could elect to take any courses in the catalogue, provided no two of his choices came at the same hour. The only things he was not supposed to mix were Scotch and gin. This was known as the Elective System. Now I understand that the boys have to have, during the four years, at least three courses beginning with the same letter. This probably makes it very awkward for those who like to get away of a Friday afternoon for the weekend.

Under the Elective System my schedule was somewhat as follows:

Mondays, Wednesdays and Fridays at 11:00:
   Botany 2a (The History of Flowers and Their Meaning)
Tuesdays and Thursdays at 11:00:
   English 26 (The Social Life of the Minor Sixteenth Century Poets)
Mondays, Wednesdays and Fridays at 12:00:
   Music 9 (History and Appreciation of the Clavichord)
Tuesdays and Thursdays at 12:00:
   German 12b (Early Minnesingers—Walter von Vogelweider, Ulric Glannsdorf and Freimann von Stremhofen. Their Songs and Times)
Mondays, Wednesdays and Fridays at 1:30:
   Fine Arts 6 (Doric Columns: Their Uses, History and Various Heights)
Tuesdays and Thursdays at 1:30:
   French 1c (Exceptions to the verb *être*)

This was, of course, just one year's work. The next year I followed these courses up with supplementary courses in the history of lace-making, Russian taxation systems before Catharine the Great, North American glacial deposits and Early Renaissance etchers.

This gave me a general idea of the progress of civilization and a certain practical knowledge which has stood me in good stead in thousands of ways since my graduation.

My system of studying was no less strict. In lecture courses I had my notebooks so arranged that one-half of the page could be devoted to drawings of five-pointed stars (exquisitely shaded), girls' heads, and ticktacktoe. Some of the drawings in my economics notebook in the course on Early English Trade Winds were the finest things I have ever done. One of them was a whole tree (an oak) with every leaf in perfect detail. Several instructors commented on my work in this field.

These notes I would take home after the lecture, together with whatever supplementary reading the course called for. Notes and textbooks would then be placed on a table under a strong lamplight. Next came the sharpening of pencils, which would take perhaps fifteen minutes. I had some of the best sharpened pencils in college. These I placed on the table beside the notes and books.

At this point it was necessary to light a pipe, which involved going to the table where the tobacco was. As it so happened, on the same table was a poker hand, all dealt, lying in front of a vacant chair. Four other chairs were oddly enough occupied by students, also preparing to study. It therefore resolved itself into something of a seminar, or group conference, on the courses under discussion. For example, the first student would say:

"I can't open."

The second student would perhaps say the same thing.

The third student would say: "I'll open for fifty cents."

And the seminar would be on.

At the end of the seminar, I would go back to my desk, pile the notes and books on top of each other, put the light out, and go to bed, tired but happy in the realization that I had not only spent the evening busily but had helped put four of my friends through college.

An inventory of stock acquired at college discloses the following bits of culture and erudition which have nestled in my mind after all these years.

## Things I Learned Freshman Year

1. Charlemagne either died or was born or did something with the Holy Roman Empire in 800.

2. By placing one paper bag inside another paper bag you can carry home a milk shake in it.

3. There is a double l in the middle of "parallel."

4. Powder rubbed on the chin will take the place of a shave if the room isn't very light.

5. French nouns ending in "aison" are feminine.

6. Almost everything you need to know about a subject is in the encyclopedia.

7. A tasty sandwich can be made by spreading peanut butter on raisin bread.

8. A floating body displaces its own weight in the liquid in which it floats.

9. A sock with a hole in the toe can be worn inside out with comparative comfort.

10. The chances are against filling an inside straight.

11. There is a law in economics called *The Law of Diminishing Returns,* which means that after a certain margin is reached returns begin to diminish. This may not be correctly stated, but there *is* a law by that name.

12. You begin tuning a mandolin with A and tune the other strings from that.

## Sophomore Year

1. A good imitation of measles rash can be effected by stabbing the forearm with a stiff whisk-broom.

2. Queen Elizabeth was not above suspicion.

3. In Spanish you pronounce z like th.

4. Nine-tenths of the girls in a girls' college are not pretty.

5. You can sleep undetected in a lecture course by resting the head on the hand as if shading the eyes.

6. Weakness in drawing technique can be hidden by using a wash instead of black and white line.

7. Quite a respectable bun can be acquired by smoking three or four pipefuls of strong tobacco when you have no food in your stomach.

8. The ancient Phoenicians were really Jews, and got as far north as England where they operated tin mines.

9. You can get dressed much quicker in the morning if the night before when you are going to bed you take off your trousers and underdrawers at once, leaving the latter inside the former.

*Junior Year*

1. Emerson left his pastorate because he had some argument about communion.

2. All women are untrustworthy.

3. Pushing your arms back as far as they will go fifty times each day increases your chest measurement.

4. Marcus Aurelius had a son who turned out to be a bad boy.

5. Eight hours of sleep are not necessary.

6. Heraclitus believed that fire was the basis of all life.

7. A good way to keep your trousers pressed is to hang them from the bureau drawer.

8. The chances are that you will never fill an inside straight.

9. The Republicans believe in a centralized government, the Democrats in a decentralized one.

10. It is not necessarily effeminate to drink tea.

*Senior Year*

1. A dinner coat looks better than full dress.

2. There is as yet no law determining what constitutes trespass in an airplane.

3. Six hours of sleep are not necessary.

4. Bicarbonate of soda taken before retiring makes you feel better the next day.

5. You needn't be fully dressed if you wear a cap and gown to a nine o'clock recitation.

6. Theater tickets may be charged.

7. Flowers may be charged.

8. May is the shortest month in the year.

The foregoing outline of my education is true enough in its way, and is what people like to think about a college course. It has become quite the cynical thing to admit laughingly that college did one no good. It is part of the American Credo that all that the college student learns is to catch punts and dance. I had to write something like that to satisfy the editors. As a matter of fact, I learned a great deal in college and have those four years to thank for whatever I know today.

(The above note was written to satisfy those of my instructors and financial backers who may read this. As a matter of fact, the original outline is true, and I had to look up the date about Charlemagne at that.)

### SUGGESTIONS FOR WRITING

1. Robert Benchley (1889-1945) is an American humorist whose satire was effective because he laced it with broad humor and common sense. His sentences seem smooth and effortless, but they are very difficult to imitate. Try to imitate the first two paragraphs. Use Benchley's structure and approximate word length for each sentence; if possible, keep the original punctuation.
2. What is Benchley's attitude toward the elective system? How would you feel about a system that had no required courses?
3. Benchley mixes practical and academic knowledge when he lists what he learned in college. Make your own list of practical and academic "facts and comment."
4. Humor is hard to define but not impossible. What is funny about this essay?

# The Function of Education

What is the task of all higher education? To make man into a machine. What are the means employed? He is taught how to suffer being bored.

—Nietzsche, *The Twilight of the Idols,* 1889

There are many things of which a wise man might wish to remain ignorant.

—Emerson, *Demonology,* 1877

Give us a child for eight years, and it will be a Bolshevist forever.

—Lenin, *Speech to the Commissars of Education,* Moscow, 1923

The things taught in schools and colleges are not an education, but the means of education.

—Emerson, *Journal,* July 15, 1831

Education should be as gradual as the moonrise, perceptible not in progress but in result.

—G. J. Whyte-Melville, *Riding Recollections,* 1878

The direction in which education starts a man will determine his future life.

—Plato, *The Republic,* 329 A.D.

We do not know what education could do for us, because we have never tried it.

—R. M. Hutchins, *The Atomic Bomb,* 1945

It was in making education not only common to all, but in some sense compulsory on all, that the destiny of the free republic of America was practically settled.

—James Russell Lowell, *Among My Books,* 1876

The primary concern of American education today is not the development of the appreciation of the "good life" in young gentlemen . . . Our purpose is to cultivate in the largest possible number . . . an appreciation of the responsibilities and the benefits which come to them because they are Americans and are free.

—James Conant, *N.Y. Times Magazine,* February 21, 1943

MICHEL DE MONTAIGNE

# Changing Judgment and Conduct*

I gladly return to the subject of the absurdity of our education: its goal has been to make us not good or wise, but learned; it has attained this goal. It has not taught us to follow and embrace virtue and wisdom, but has impressed on us their derivation and etymology. We can give the declension of virtue, if we cannot love it; if we do not know what wisdom is by practice and experience, we know it by jargon and by rote. With our neighbors, we are not content to know their family, their kindred, and their connections; we want to have them as friends and form some association and understanding with them. Education has taught us the definitions, divisions and partitions of virtue, like the surnames and branches of a genealogy, without any further concern to form between us and virtue any familiar relationship and intimate friendship. It has chosen for our instruction not the books that have the soundest and truest opinions, but those that speak the best Greek and Latin; and amid its beautiful words, it has poured into our minds the most inane ideas of antiquity.

A good education changes your judgment and conduct, as happened to Polemo, that dissipated young Greek, who, having gone by chance to a lesson by Xenocrates, did not notice merely the eloquence and mastery of the teacher, or bring back to his house merely the knowledge of some fine matter, but reaped a more perceptible and solid fruit, which was a sudden change and amendment of his former life. . . .

* From *Selected Essays of Montaigne* translated and edited by Donald Frame (Roslyn, N.Y.: Walter J. Black, Inc., 1957). Reprinted by permission of the publishers by special arrangement with the Classics Club.

SUGGESTIONS FOR WRITING

1. Michel de Montaigne (1533-1592) was a noted French essayist. He is severely critical of education for its failures, and he uses some words which might not be in everyone's vocabulary. Define the following: absurdity, derivation, etymology, declension, jargon, rote, genealogy, inane, dissipated.

2. Montaigne says, "Education has the wrong goal. But it has attained this goal." Then he points out what is wrong with the goal. In the second paragraph he sets a different goal for education, and instead of defending the idea he illustrates it by a carefully chosen example. Use Montaigne as a model and discuss the right and wrong goals of racial equality, modern art, or some such topic. "The goal of X has been to do Y (bad) and not Z (good)."

3. "A good education changes your judgment and conduct," says Montaigne, and he lists a single example to prove his point. We are willing to agree with his idealistic goal, but we remain unconvinced that Montaigne has a practical means of attaining it, or even that change is always necessary. Must we always assume, for example, that judgment and conduct need changing? Must we always assume that a person whose conduct and judgment have not changed—note, Montaigne did not say *refined,* or *developed,* or *matured*—has not received a good education? Provide the qualifications Montaigne would need to be convincing here. Use illustrations, pro and con, to make your point.

4. Montaigne wants education to teach virtue so that we have a "familiar relationship and intimate friendship" with it. Surely this does not mean that those who elect a class in, say, the virtues of religion, will become more virtuous than those who elect, say, music appreciation. Write a composition on the true meaning of Montaigne's statement.

5. The quotation from Emerson's *Journal* at the beginning of this section might be an argument against Montaigne, but first it would be necessary to define education within the context of each author's belief. Write a dialogue between the two in which each defines education and makes clear his position about its goals.

HENRY  DAVID  THOREAU

## Colleges for Living a Life*

I . . . found that the student who wishes for a shelter can obtain one for a lifetime at an expense not greater than the rent which he

---

* From the chapter on Economy, *Walden,* 1854.

now pays annually. If I seem to boast more than is becoming, my excuse is that I brag for humanity rather than for myself; and my shortcomings and inconsistencies do not affect the truth of my statement. Notwithstanding much cant and hypocrisy—chaff which I find it difficult to separate from my wheat, but for which I am as sorry as any man—I will breathe freely and stretch myself in this respect, it is such a relief to both the moral and the physical system; and I am resolved that I will not through humility become the devil's attorney. I will endeavor to speak a good word for the truth. At Cambridge College the mere rent of a student's room, which is only a little larger than my own, is thirty dollars each year, though the corporation had the advantage of building thirty-two side by side and under one roof, and the occupant suffers the inconvenience of many and noisy neighbors, and perhaps a residence in the fourth story. I cannot but think that if we had more true wisdom in these respects, not only less education would be needed, because, forsooth, more would already have been acquired, but the pecuniary expense of getting an education would in a great measure vanish. Those conveniences which the student requires at Cambridge or elsewhere cost him or somebody else ten times as great a sacrifice of life as they would with proper management on both sides. Those things for which the most money is demanded are never the things which the student most wants. Tuition, for instance, is an important item in the term bill, while for the far more valuable education which he gets by associating with the most cultivated of his contemporaries no charge is made. The mode of founding a college is, commonly, to get up a subscription of dollars and cents, and then, following blindly the principles of a division of labor to its extreme—a principle which should never be followed but with circumspection—to call in a contractor who makes this a subject of speculation, and he employs Irishmen or other operatives actually to lay the foundations, while the students that are to be are said to be fitting themselves for it; and for those oversights successive generations have to pay. I think that it would be *better than this,* for the students, or those who desire to be benefited by it, even to lay the foundation themselves. The student who secures his coveted leisure and retirement by systematically shirking any labor necessary to man obtains but an ignoble and unprofitable leisure, defrauding himself of the experience which alone can make leisure fruitful. "But," says one, "you do not mean that the students should go to work with their hands instead of their heads?" I do not mean that exactly, but I mean something which he might think a good deal like that; I mean that they should not *play* life, or *study* it merely, while the community supports them at this expensive game, but earnestly *live* it from beginning to end. How could youths better learn to live than by at once trying the experiment of living? Methinks this would exercise their minds as much as mathematics. If I wished a boy to know something about the arts and sciences, for instance, I would not pursue the common course, which is merely to send him into the neighborhood of some professor, where anything is professed and practised but the art of life —to survey the world through a telescope or a microscope, and never with his natural eye; to study chemistry, and not learn how his bread is made, or mechanics, and not learn how it is earned; to discover new satellites to Neptune, and not detect the motes in his eyes, or to what vagabond he is a satellite himself; or to be devoured by the monsters that swarm all around him, while contemplating the monsters in a drop of vinegar. Which would have advanced the most at the end of a month—the boy who had made his own jackknife from the ore which he had dug and smelted, reading as much as would be necessary for this—or the boy who had attended the lectures on metallurgy at the Institute in the meanwhile, and had received a Rodgers penknife from his father? Which would be most likely to cut his fingers? . . . To my astonishment I was informed on leaving college that I had studied navigation! —why, if I had taken one turn down the harbor I should have known more about it. Even the *poor* student studies and is taught only *political* economy, while that economy of living which is synonymous with philosophy is not even sincerely professed in our colleges. The consequence is, that while he is reading Adam Smith, Ricardo, and Say, he runs his father into debt irretrievably.

As with our colleges, so with a hundred "modern improvements"; there is an illusion about them; there is not always a positive advance. The devil goes on exacting compound interest to the last for his early share and numerous succeeding investments in them. Our inventions are wont to be pretty toys, which distract our attention from serious things. They are but improved means to an unimproved end, an end which it was already but too easy to arrive at, as railroads lead to Boston or New York. We are in great haste to construct a magnetic telegraph from Maine to Texas; but Maine and Texas, it may be, have nothing important to communicate.

## SUGGESTIONS FOR WRITING

1. Henry David Thoreau (1804-1864) was an American philosopher, naturalist, poet, and essayist. His popular *Walden* (1854), from which this selection is taken, is a mine for themes for compositions. Define the following words from the above selection: cant, hypocrisy, devil's attorney, forsooth, circumspection, coveted leisure, ignoble leisure, defrauding himself, motes in his eyes, wont to be.

2. A great virtue of Thoreau's prose is his economy of style. Rewrite the last sentence of the above selection, testing various ways of saying the same thing. Change the word order, the diction, the phrasing, the punctuation. After you have experimented, compare your samples and try to draw a conclusion about writing style.

3. Thoreau's essays are not good examples of orderly thought, but we are willing to forgive him because his digressions are often relevant and brilliant. It is unfair to draw a conclusion about organization of thought in the above selection, because it is a selection which is in itself a digression from the whole. However, we sense that digressions were a part of Thoreau's total plan and that he never intended to limit himself to a recounting of his life at Walden Pond. As he says above, he wanted to "breathe freely and stretch myself." Something in his daily life made him recall his college experiences, so he favors us with some reflections and conclusions on education. Develop an argument (based on careful analysis) for the unity of tone, style, and concept of the above selection.

4. What, precisely, does Thoreau intend when he says, "I do not mean that exactly, but I mean something which he might think a good deal like that"?

5. If Thoreau is not exaggerating when he says students should not play life or study it but "earnestly *live* it from beginning to end," suggest changes that would be necessary in the courses you are currently studying.

6. Read the article by Swarthout (p. 119) in which a hypothetical student takes issue with Thoreau. Write a similar statement about Thoreau's position here. You may believe, for example, that how you live your life is no business of the college, that your way of life is a freedom you cherish, and that, even with Thoreau's encouragement, you don't want colleges to change on your account.

ROBERT LITTELL

## The Essential Skills of Life*

What are those abilities, skills, or accomplishments, those extracurricular proficiencies that every man should have in order to be rounded and self-sufficient, and when can he acquire them, and how? . . .

Leaving all formal subjects out of consideration, he should learn how to:

| | |
|---|---|
| Swim | Drive a car |
| Handle firearms | Dance |
| Speak in public | Drink |
| Cook | And speak at least one foreign |
| Typewrite | language well |
| Ride a horse | |

The list does not end there. There are several dozen mental and physical skills that I should like him to acquire. He will acquire some of them in the mere course of growing up; he will acquire some of them more painfully, as the result of adult pressure; there are others that he will avoid; and he will eventually be punished for their omission with not a little discomfort and social misery. Ordinary education, even high-priced education, will not guarantee him the essential skills, and some of them are better learned after "education" is over.

### SUGGESTIONS FOR WRITING

1. Robert Littell (1896-    ) is an American writer, critic, and former editor of a national magazine. In this excerpt from an article about the skills often neglected in college, he notes the essential skills of a well-rounded man. Because the article was written over twenty years ago, there may be changes in the list today. What additions or deletions would you make?

---

* From *Harper's Magazine* (March, 1933). Copyright 1933 by Robert Littell. Reprinted by permission of the author.

2. Woodrow Wilson's insistence on intellect as the purpose of a university seems to be opposed to Littell's emphasis on certain practical skills. If the debate interests you, turn to Littell's original article, "What the Young Man Should Know," *Harper's Magazine* (March, 1933). Write an essay attacking or defending intellect as the proper goal of a young man.

3. Littell is concerned with the skills of a young man. What about a young woman? What skills does she need? How shall they be attained? Are they skills which a college should teach? Why or why not?


GEORGE  S.  COUNTS

## Education in a Democracy*

We know now that the traditional notion about the relation between democracy and formal education is a myth. The contemporary despotisms, if we make allowance for the resources available, have proved themselves to be quite as generous in their support of education as the free societies. In fact I am of the opinion that the dictatorships gave far more thought to education than the democratic states. . . .

The contemporary totalitarian states have taken a leaf from the book of eighteenth- and nineteenth-century democracy. They have not the slightest fear of "education for all the people," an old liberal slogan. In fact they seem to be more interested in reaching all the people than the democracies. They have demonstrated that educational institutions can be forged into a mighty instrument or weapon to serve the purposes of despotic rule. Likewise they exhibit not the slightest fear of literacy. They know that literacy is a liberating factor in society only where the press is free or at least partly free—newspapers, journals, books, bookshops, and libraries. Where the press is under strict and efficient control, literacy can become a weapon for the support of a universal tyranny. This constitutes one of the remarkable achievements of twentieth-century despotism. . . .

We in America, in my judgment, have never given adequate

* From *Vital Speeches* (February 15, 1949). Reprinted by permission of the publishers.

thought to the question of the development of an education that is suited to our democracy, particularly in the present industrial age. If we ever do, the result will be something new in the history of education. It will express at the same time both the emphasis on knowledge, understanding, and enlightenment and the emphasis on the cultivation of the basic ethical values of democracy —devotion to equality, individual worth, intellectual freedom, political liberty, democratic processes, general welfare, and mastery of relevant knowledge. And all of this must be done in terms of the realities of the contemporary age. The major difficulty which all democracies confront here is the achievement through the democratic process of an educational program designed to strengthen democracy.

## SUGGESTIONS FOR WRITING

1. George S. Counts (1889-   ) has been an educator at eight American colleges, including Yale, Chicago, Columbia, and Michigan State. His model may be stated as follows: Paragraph 1—"We know now that the traditional notion about the relation between A and B is a myth [unstated assumption: A supports B]. C also supports B. In fact it supports it better than A" [unstated assumption: A and C are in some respects opposites]. Paragraph 2—"C has learned from A how to use B" [eight sentences of illustrations]. Paragraph 3—"We have never given adequate thought to the type of B that is suited to A." Using this framework with slight modifications (including changing the word *supports*) it is possible to substitute different ideas for A, B, and C. Possible terms are: fraternal organizations and character building, segregation laws and racial discrimination, physical geography and economics. Write a theme using Counts as a model of organization and length.

2. Assuming Counts believes college courses should be designed to teach those ethical aspects of democracy which he mentions, could such courses be taught "in terms of the realities of the contemporary age"? (Define "basic ethical values" and "realities of the age" before you answer this question.)

3. Counts suggests that the democratic process may interfere with an educational program designed to strengthen democracy. Explain this paradox.

4. In a democracy, should the government support private higher education by direct or indirect means (research grants, tax benefits, classroom or laboratory construction)?

FRANCIS BACON

# Of Studies*

Studies serve for delight, for ornament, and for ability. Their chief use for delight is in privateness and retiring; for ornament, is in discourse; and for ability, is in the judgment and disposition of business; for expert men can execute, and perhaps judge of particulars, one by one; but the general counsels, and the plots and marshaling of affairs come best from those that are learned. To spend too much time in studies is sloth; to use them too much for ornament is affectation; to make judgment wholly by their rules is the humor of a scholar. They perfect nature, and are perfected by experience; for natural abilities are like natural plants, that need pruning by study; and studies themselves do give forth directions too much at large, except they be bounded in by experience. Crafty men contemn studies, simple men admire them, and wise men use them; for they teach not their own use; but that is a wisdom without them and above them, won by observation. Read not to contradict and confute, nor to believe and take for granted, nor to find talk and discourse, but to weigh and consider. Some books are to be tasted, others to be swallowed, and some few to be chewed and digested; that is, some books are to be read only in parts; others to be read but not curiously, and some few to be read wholly, and with diligence and attention. Some books also may be read by deputy, and extracts made of them by others; but that would be only in the less important arguments and the meaner sort of books; else distilled books are, like common distilled waters, flashy things. Reading maketh a full man; conference a ready man; and writing an exact man. And, therefore, if a man write little, he had need have a great memory; if he confer little, he had need have a present wit; and if he read little, he had need have much cunning, to seem to know that he doth not. Histories make men wise; poets, witty; the mathematics, subtle; natural philosophy, deep; moral, grave;

---

* From *The Essayes or Councils, Civill and Morall* (enlarged ed., London, 1625), No. 50. The text has been somewhat modernized.

logic and rhetoric, able to contend; *Abeunt studia in mores*.[1] Nay, there is no stand or impediment in the wit but may be wrought out by fit studies; like as diseases of the body may have appropriate exercises. Bowling is good for the stone and reins, shooting for the lungs and breast, gentle walking for the stomach, riding for the head and the like. So if a man's wit be wandering, let him study the mathematics; for in demonstrations, if his wit be called away never so little, he must begin again. If his wit be not apt to distinguish or find differences, let him study the schoolmen; for they are *cymini sectores*.[2] If he be not apt to beat over matters, and to call up one thing to prove and illustrate another, let him study the lawyers' cases; so every defect of the mind may have a special receipt.

SUGGESTIONS FOR WRITING

1. Francis Bacon (1561-1626) was a scientist, philosopher, and man of letters who became Lord Chancellor of England. His chief works are: *The Advancement of Learning* (1605) and *Novum Organum* (1627). In the above essay he says that distilled books, like distilled waters, are tasteless things. Study the table of contents of this anthology to see what Bacon may have said of this "distilled" book. Put your opinion in a written commentary.

2. Select four or five sentences from Bacon's essay which qualify as aphorisms (terse sayings embodying a general truth). Then, using Bacon's pattern, devise your own aphorisms. For example, first write the Baconian sentence: "Read not to contradict and confute, nor to believe and take for granted, nor to find talk and discourse, but to weigh and consider." Then, using his word order and punctuation, write your own: "Love not to quench passion and still desire, not to be loved and stay loneliness, nor to join social custom and conformity, but to fill your heart and soul."

3. What would Bacon say about the nonacademic side of college life? Would he, for example, tolerate or condemn football? Become a modern Bacon and project his thoughts into an essay on college life.

4. Bacon's style is characterized by its economy and density. "Studies serve for delight, for ornament, and for ability," he says, and he proceeds to deliver the message without a windup or flourish. In doing so he seems to a modern reader dreadfully solemn; hence, he invites

---

[1] Studies form manners.
[2] Dividers of cuminseed, i.e., hairsplitters.

parody. If the idea of poking fun at Bacon's didactic seriousness appeals to you, try a humorous piece in which you shift the meaning of key words. For example: Studies serve for delight (delight: the fun of reading a dull book when a jazz session lures?); for ornament (yes, think of the artistic effect of a doctor's diploma on his waiting room wall); and for ability (the ability to be bored stiff?).

JOHN LOCKE

## On Injudicious Haste in Study*

The eagerness and the strong bent of the mind after knowledge, if not warily regulated, is often a hindrance to it. It still presses into further discoveries and new objects, and catches at the variety of knowledge; and therefore often stays not long enough on what is before it, to look into it as it should, for haste to pursue what is yet out of sight. He that rides post through a country may be able, from the transient view, to tell in general how the parts lie, and may be able to give some loose description of here a mountain and there a plain, here a morass and there a river, woodland in one part and savannahs in another. Such superficial ideas and observations as these he may collect in galloping over it: but the more useful observations of the soil, plants, animals, and inhabitants, with their several sorts and properties, must necessarily escape him, and it is seldom men ever discover the rich mines without some digging. Nature commonly lodges her treasures and jewels in rocky ground. If the matter be knotty and the sense lies deep, the mind must stop and buckle to it, and stick upon it with labor and thought and close contemplation, and not leave it until it has mastered the difficulty and got possession of truth. But here care must be taken to avoid the other extreme: a man must not stick at every useless nicety and expect mysteries of science in every trivial question or scruple he may raise. He that will stand to pick up and examine every pebble that comes in his way is as unlikely to return enriched and laden with jewels as the other that traveled with full speed.

---

* From the *Essay Concerning Human Understanding,* 1690.

Truths are not the better or the worse for their obviousness or difficulty, but their value is to be measured by their usefulness and tendency. Insignificant observations should not take up any of our minutes, and those that enlarge our view and give light towards further and useful discoveries should not be neglected though they stop our course and spend some of our time in a fixed attention.

There is another haste that does often, and will, mislead the mind if it be left to itself and its own conduct. The understanding is naturally forward, not only to learn its knowledge by variety— which makes it skip over one to get speedily to another part of knowledge—but also eager to enlarge its views by running too fast into general observations and conclusions, without a due examination of particulars enough thereon to found those general axioms. This seems to enlarge their stock, but it is of fancies, not realities. Such theories, built upon narrow foundations, stand but weakly, and if they fall not themselves, are at least very hardly to be supported against the assaults of opposition. And thus men, being too hasty to erect to themselves general notions and ill-grounded theories, find themselves deceived in their stock of knowledge when they come to examine their hastily assumed maxims themselves or to have them attacked by others. General observations drawn from particulars are the jewels of knowledge, comprehending great store in a little room, but they are therefore to be made with the greater care and caution, lest if we take counterfeit for true, our loss and shame will be the greater when our stock comes to a severe scrutiny. One or two particulars may suggest hints of inquiry, and they do well who take these hints; but if they turn them into conclusions and make them presently general rules, they are forward indeed, but it is only to impose on themselves by propositions assumed for truths without sufficient warrant. To make such observations is, as has already been remarked, to make the head a magazine of materials which can hardly be called knowledge, or at least is but like a collection of lumber not reduced to use or order; and he that makes everything an observation has the same useless plenty, and much more falseness mixed with it. The extremes on both sides are to be avoided, and he will be able to give the best account of his studies who keeps his understanding in the right mean between them.

SUGGESTIONS FOR WRITING

1. John Locke (1632-1704) was the dominant figure in English philosophy during the last fifty years of his life. His two famous works are *An Essay Concerning Human Understanding,* 1690, and *An Essay Concerning Civil Government,* 1690. In the selection just read, he is concerned with the qualities of the mind as they relate to human understanding. Describe the qualities of mind which you think are best suited to serious study of academic subjects. In other words, describe the best "frame of mind" for studying. Devise a fictional character and show him in the act of studying. Then comment on what is happening in the character's mind.

2. Relate your own development as a pursuer of truth to Locke's advice. Can you cite instances when your haste to find the answer led you too superficially over the path of knowledge? If so, can you also cite instances when you dwelt too long on one topic and thus missed a chance for a more general knowledge?

3. Locke's advice may be sound, but is it practical? He says "be careful not to go too fast, but don't go too slow either." Rather obvious, isn't it? If you were writing such advice to a younger brother or sister, how would you state it more forcefully?

4. Locke says the value of truths "is to be measured by their usefulness and tendency." What do you suppose he means by *tendency?* Consult the dictionary. Restate the sentence without using the words *usefulness* and *tendency.* Assuming you believe your own restatement, define it in workable terms. Show the value of truth in operation; show it being used. If you wish, devise characters and a situation and show how the characters find the usefulness of truth.


OLIVER  LA  FARGE

# The Eight-Oared Shell *

. . . I took up rowing through a series of accidents, chief among which were the fact that Groton was one of the very few preparatory schools to have crews, that I was a duffer at baseball and hated it, and that Harry Morgan, who was captain in my Fifth Form year,

---

* From *Raw Material* by Oliver La Farge (Boston: Houghton Mifflin Company, 1945). Copyright 1945 by Oliver La Farge. Reprinted by permission of the publishers.

asked me one winter's afternoon what sport I was going after in the spring. I told him high-jumping. He remarked that that wasn't much of an occupation, I should come out for rowing. I was astonished for I had never pulled an oar save in skiffs on Narragansett Bay and I still held firmly to my picture of my weedy, gawky self, the weakling with eyeglasses who had achieved, not strength, but the skill to manipulate his limbs over a bar. As a matter of fact, he was short-handed. He told me I could have a place on the second crew. . . .

It took me a few days on the rowing machine to be broken of the habits one forms rowing fisherman's style in skiffs, then apparently I caught on fast. When one has never been in a shell, the practice on the machines seems stupid, a pure grind. The more one knows about rowing, the less this is so. I worked away in the second eight, very pleased to be there and much afraid that I should be dropped to the third four. Then one day someone on the first crew fell ill and I was taken up. I was delighted but assumed that this was temporary.

I don't remember now whom I replaced. But when the warmer weather came and the ice went out of the river, it was in the first boat that for the first time in my life I laid my hands on the loom of one of those grand, long, racing sweeps. By a month later I realized that in fact I was on the first crew, not just subbing but on it, and that barring disaster I should have earned my letter by the end of my Fifth Form year. Rowing was the third major sport; it ranked below baseball and football, but it was major and it carried a letter, and here I was in on it. The thing had come gently; an oarsman is fairly sure of his place in advance of the final race although upsets do happen; you grow without half realizing it into the assurance that you know how to row and pull your weight in the boat. By gentle stages I became good, by school standards, in a major sport, gradually I was knit with the other seven oarsmen and the coxswain in the union of a crew. Without anything dramatic happening I became an Athlete, a Letter Man, I acquired Face.

More than that, I discovered rowing. For most of us there is no hope whatever of continuing after we have left college, but the love of it remains. A few weeks ago I met a Yale man who had rowed there while I was at Harvard. I don't remember how the subject came up, but we began talking about it, then we drew away from the rest of the party and lovingly, happily, rowed over our whiskeys until our wives dragged us home. This has happened to me many times. No writer has told the nature of rowing in an eight-oared shell to landsmen, none who haven't rowed understand what it is we remember, the crash of the oars in the locks, the shell leaping at the catch, the unity and rhythm and the desperate effort, so when we meet we babble with joy.

What is the nature of it? To begin with the setting—the green-banked river or the Charles Basin ringed by the city, both are beautiful. The shell swinging through open country on a fine spring day is hard to beat. Down on the Basin the water is oily, in the late afternoon it catches the deepening sunset, after dark the advertising signs over the factories are reflected on it, twisting as if the lights were darting snakes, and the swirl of one's oar is shot with color. There is the slight excitement and the echoing change of sound in shooting under a bridge, there is the fresh day on the river as you carry your shell down to the float. Rural or urban water, rowing is set in beauty to begin with.

There is the nature of the stroke itself, the most perfect combination I have ever known of skill and the full release of one's power. It takes more than a dumb ox to make a fine oarsman, the traditional "weak brain and strong back" won't serve. To my mind it begins with the "recovery," the forward reach to get ready for a stroke. You are sitting on a slide, a seat on rollers, which runs on a track about two feet long, set variously according to the type of stroke your coach favors. Your two hands are on the loom of your twelve-foot oar, balancing it neatly. If you lower them too far, you sky the blade of your oar and the shift of the center of gravity will make the boat rock and cost you precious headway; if you raise them too high your oar will touch the waves and you may cause a jolt that will throw the whole boat out of time. So your hands are balancing delicately—next time you see a good crew rowing, watch the oars moving together clear of the water on the recovery, see how narrow that long shell is and realize the miracle of balance that keeps it steady while those big men swing aft and the long sweeps reach forward. Or watch a green crew, see the oars at eight different levels and the shell wallowing from side to side.

You are moving your hands, your shoulders, and your tail aft (you are facing aft) at three different rates, to bring each to its stopping point at the same time. If you rush your slide to the end of its run, that sharp motion and possibly the abrupt stopping at the end will check the motion of the shell (you can see it happen) and you yourself will fall into the position of your maximum effort with a jerk which will put you out of balance. Hands, shoulders, slide, must move *in related time* one to another, and in perfect time with the other seven men, so that at the right moment you are leaning forward just far enough for reach and not too far for power, your slide is all the way aft, your legs and knees are ready, your back is arched, not slumped, and your balancing hands are holding firmly to the oar. In the very last part of your swing your outside hand—the one towards the blade—has turned the oar a quarter circle, so that the blade, which was parallel to the water, is perpendicular to it.

CATCH! A slight raising of your hands and arms has dropped your blade into the water, and instantaneously your shoulders take hold. That simple action is not quite so simple. If you have not done it minutely right your oar may skitter out above the water, slice too deeply into the water to help the boat, or you may catch a crab—entangle your oar in water so that you can't get it out. That last is virtual shipwreck, it may knock you out of the boat, and it will almost certainly lose a race. Once you and seven other men are driving with all your forces it is too late to attempt to turn or guide your oar. You must have dropped it into the water so accurately that it will stay with the blade just submerged all the way through your pull and come out willingly. That is part of the turn of your outside hand and the act of slightly raising your arms. This raising of your arms must be neat; you don't let your oar into the water on a diagonal after you have begun to pull (that is, you don't and stay on a good crew), nor do you succumb to the natural tendency which you will see in any fisherman's rowing, to let your hands dive slightly as you get ready to catch on hard, causing the blade first to rise slightly in the air and then to hit the water with a spanking motion.

An immeasurably short time after your shoulders, your legs start to drive. Now your arms are merely straps attaching your hands to your body, legs and shoulders and back for all they are worth are pulling on the oar, everything you've got is going into it, but you have taken care that your tail, driven by your legs, will not shoot on the slide ahead of your shoulders.

You have driven through almost to the end of the catch, your slide is almost home, your shoulders are back. Now your arms come in, and just as your knees come down locked, your hands touch your stomach. Here is the prettiest part of the stroke, the shoot of the hands to start the recovery. Remember, your oar is still deep in the water rushing powerfully past your boat; if it becomes caught in that, it turns to a wild machine. As your hands touch your belly they drop, shoot out, in a motion "as fast and smooth as a billiard ball caroming," at the same time your inside wrist turns and the blade is once more parallel to the water—feathered. The shoot of your hands and arms brings your shoulders forward and you commence your recovery once more.

All of what I have described happens in a single stroke by a good oarsman. This stroke, its predecessors and successors, is performed in a unison with seven other men which is more perfect than merely being in time, with the balance of the body maintained also in relation to the keel so that the boat shall not roll. At a moderate racing rate it is performed thirty-two to thirty-six times to the minute, all of this, nothing omitted, and in a rhythm which keeps the time of the recovery not less than double that of the catch.

This is not the whole of rowing, but it is the basic part of the individual's job in it. Unite it to another fundamental and you can have a crew.

The other fundamental is unison. I have said that a crew does not merely keep time; it does something subtler than that, it becomes one. This it cannot do if there is bad feeling between any of the men in the boat; a single antagonistic personality can keep eight oarsmen accurately following stroke's oar and the coxswain's counting from becoming a crew rowing together. Crews are not made up on a basis of personalities, but according to the coach's estimates of individual capacities, it is after they are rowing together that they become friends. My crews at Harvard contained men with whom I had nothing in common, men by whom I should naturally have been bored or antagonized, and who should have disliked me. As we rowed together we became fond of each other. It had no lasting value, but for the duration of our rowing, we esteemed each other dearly. As this feeling grew, so did our boat shake down and become one, and so did we increasingly care for the foul mouthed, brilliant little devil who was our cox and in a race the instrument, voice, and control of our unity.

You have three or four years of rowing back of you, and from them the assurance that you are a sound oarsman, a sound waterman, whether or not you are going to be good enough to win a seat in the particular boat you've set your heart on. You have spent a month or so rowing on the machines, indoors, with a tentative crew made up of four or five fellows with whom you rowed last year and some newcomers, all of merit. The ice has gone out of the river, it is raw and cold but tolerable. Today you will take to the water.

This oar is yours. No man but you will handle it from now till the end of the season, barring disaster. (I saw a Princeton crew once whose managers carried the oars down for the men. One hopes it was a rare exception.) You take it from the rack and look it over, a good, spoon blade, not too wide, a sound piece of white ash, the leather in right condition. You ask the manager to roughen the handle for you a little, and watch critically while it is being done, then you take it down to the edge of the float. The others do the same, the cox brings down his rudder and megaphone.

Here is your shell, resting upside down on its rack, a long cigar of wood so thin that it bends readily under your finger, surrounding a skeleton of wood and metal that will stand up under the force you hope to bring forth. This, too, has its attributes and properties, some visible as you look her over, some yet to be learned. You take your places, the cox gives his command. Tenderly you lift her out, she's fragile. Four men on a side you carry her down to the float, and freely curse anyone who gets in your way. (Even those Princeton men carried down their own shell.) At the edge of the float you wait. The cox shouts "Up!" The shell rises to the height of your arms, and all eight of you are standing under her. Then over— gently now—bending all together you lay her in the water. This tossing a shell is a good ritual in itself, one of the many graces of rowing. It is your first genuine act as a crew together.

You put in the oars, take your places, settle yourselves. There's a lot of arranging and adjusting to be attended to. Then you shove off, and you're out in the stream.

It's months since you've been in a boat. You are nine men who

know their business individually, but collectively you hardly exist
yet. Suddenly you feel self-conscious, almost afraid. This feeling is
as much fear of a foully bad start and an affront to your art as it
is of the mechanism of yourself and your oar, but there is a fear,
something big is coming which may go wrong, and you are stale.

You all swing forward and the boat does not lurch, a good sign.
The cox's voice is familiar, he urges you profanely to get off to a
good start in front of those heavyweight bastards who are now
coming onto the float, and you feel soothed. You start. The eight
oars get in fairly well together, the shell leaps, it keeps running
well as you swing for the next stroke, it leaps again. You had forgotten; for all your years of rowing you had forgotten the power
of those eight sweeps driven together, the initial leap and run of
the boat, the settling down to a smooth, even swing. The power
of that first stroke is always astounding, so is the way the oars crash
in the locks, and you are going, and you feel like a giant and you
want to shout.

These are parts of what the oarsman loves, along with the sunny
days and the girls who stand on the bank and stare at the near-
naked men (don't think the oarsmen don't spot them), and coming
in at night listening to the sounds of other crews and seeing the
reflections of the guiding lights under the bridges dripping off your
oars, and the increasing sense of strength and competence from
day to day, and the growing union with eight other men into something mystical and strong—values of strength, skill, physical beauty
perceived, and the spirit. There are all of these in this sport which
I loved, as there must be in those beloved of others.

But a boy weighing a hundred and fifty pounds had no future in
University rowing. I treated myself to it the fall of my Freshman
year as an indulgence, I did well, but I saw that the competition
was too stiff for me, and high-jumping offered me a gambler's
chance at my H. I went out for Freshman track. I jumped against
Andover. I had some future. There was a rumor that Harvard was
going to try out these new hundred-and-fifty-pound crews that were
having such a success at one or two other colleges.

It was raw, cold, early spring. As I walked over Anderson Bridge
I saw the first Freshman eights getting into the river. Some damn
fool stepped in the bottom of a shell and put his feet through it.
Another boat got away cleanly and started going, rolling a bit but

not doing badly. I could hear the cox's commands. Some upperclass eight came downstream from Newell Boathouse and passed right under me; those fellows could row. The coach followed in his launch, megaphone in hand. What he was saying was anciently familiar. After all, what the hell was an H?

I told the track coach I was going out for rowing. He seemed to disapprove, so I told him my family wanted me to. As a matter of fact, my family wanted me to do what I wanted, but I put on an act and lied because he was a pretty decent fellow and I could not face telling him that as far as I was concerned high-jumping was the bunk, and I'd rather row in the lowest crew on the river than win my letter leaping over little sticks. I went down and signed up for rowing, feeling like a man reborn. So it happened that I was in the first hundred-and-fifty-pound crew ever to take the water from Harvard.

I find, in writing about rowing, that I tend to concentrate rather technically upon the sport itself with the attendant danger of losing that very background of its relation to a boy's life which would give it validity. This is partly because the average man who reads this has played football, and many women have at least had the game explained to them and have learned how to watch it, while the essentials of rowing are widely unknown. Then, while I partook of the comradeship of my crews, there were no intimate friends among them, nothing compared to my relationship with Jones and football. More important, rowing became for me an occupation, something complete in itself into which I entered and from which I returned to ordinary life, it maintained its own, unbroken stream winding through the other currents of my existence. I believe you will find this true of anyone who is truly devoted to any game.

But it had to relate to all the rest. At Groton it brought a tolerable relationship with boys whom I respected and who carried much weight in the School; it brought self-assurance and a realization of strength; it brought the curious, traditional honors of athletes. There is a lot more to the preference of boys in most schools for athletic over academic honors than mere over-emphasis on athletics. The little, new boy, looking about him for gods, finds them at the outset of his first term in the football giants. He sees these big, self-confident, deep-voiced men in their daily goings and comings as well as in the games, among them are the holders of many other honors, Prefects of the School, leaders of this and that. The man who tells him to SHUT UP when he tries to whisper after dark— and refrains from reporting him—is a quick-running half-back. Those who win academic honors and prizes come to light much later in the year, they have no letters broad across their chests as they go to and fro, in many cases they are quiet boys whom ordinarily one hardly notices. One may see them receive their prizes, but one does not watch, breathless, while they earn them and fight for the School. I can name off now the gods of the Sixth Form in my First Form year and tell who threw a long, magnificent forward pass, who knocked out a triple with two men on base. I saw them "tossed"—picked up by their team-mates and half thrown in the air while the boys gave them the long cheer. And then, one spring day, with *my* letter broad upon *my* chest, I was being jounced up in the air amid laughter, and it was my name on the end of the long cheer. Those gods stood around me in my mind, those great men, and I knew I was a good oarsman, and my crew had won, and it was legitimately mine, and I knew what it was to love a game and be good at it, and here was a new strength in myself.

Rowing at School was fun, but rowing at Harvard was magnificent. There was more of it, it was more intense, and it was better rowing. The hundred-and-fifty-pound crews were stepchildren, born of hesitant concessions by doubting authorities; at first they could hope for no insignia, they accepted cast-off shells and unwanted, used oars and liked them. They were made up of boys who were perfectly willing to row in a soap box if necessary so long as they could row and count from time to time on a full-fledged race. We won recognition slowly, better boats, decent oars, a minor sports letter. Not until after my time did the lightweights get the same breaks in equipment and general treatment that less conservative colleges gave their rivals. We didn't care. For three years we rowed under the brothers, Bert and Bill Haynes, who themselves adored rowing and held it a prime part of their work to make us love it, thereby making us love them. We consciously rowed *for* them. We became a crew that could make the real Varsity stretch over a short distance, we were made use of to pace the Varsity for starts and sprints, one splendid afternoon we beat the Junior Varsity handily in a regular, two-mile race.

We loved it from the bitter, all-but-winter days when ice formed

on the oars to the long, grass-smelling spring afternoons when we
went far upriver and then, before turning back, leaned on our oars
and made the age-old jokes about going a little farther and seeing
if we could stroke the Wellesley crew. The rowing after dark I remember especially; I've tried to describe it a little, I never became
entirely used to the beauty of city-ringed water and the mystery of
the bridges.

One night in the early spring there were a great many crews out
on the Charles River Basin. We were heading upstream for home,
taking it easy, and I remember how clearly the voices of coxswains
and coaches, the sound of the oars, came to us from many sides.
Our cox was peering ahead a trifle nervously. Presently, to one side
of us, we heard a practice race coming downstream, two class crews
and the coaching launch behind them, with their coxswains making
lots of noise and the coach calling from time to time. To play safe
we lay on our oars. It was full dark, the water around us pearly
in color because of the city lights, the distance a very dark grey
haze rather than black, the sky above having the tawny quality so
common over cities. A big sign on the Cambridge bank blinked
on and off, flashing a red and yellow reflection across the basin
almost to the side of the boat. Against it we caught a glimpse of
the racing crews, the two long, ruled ink-lines of the shells and the
figures in them black, small outlines in motion, sliding across the
flash of light in an instant. There was some other race going on
somewhere, and at a safe distance behind the class crews several
more were being given a workout.

It seemed to us that the sounds of boats and of racing were getting too close together in the darkness below us. Then suddenly
we heard a coach boom out in a new kind of voice, "Easy all, there!
Easy all! Hold her all! Look out, Tech crew! Look out, you there!"
And into this the coxswains' voices shouting, and other coaches,
commands, "Hold her, Starboard! Hold her, Starboard! Hold her
all! Look out, for Chrissakes, look out!" There was miscellaneous
yelling, and then a sound as if someone had jumped on an unusually large bass viol. It was a wonderful crash, and it was almost
immediately followed by another.

Like reinforcement coming into battle the second set of Harvard
racers swept past us, going full tilt. The shouting broke out again,
more tumult even than before, and there was a third crash. Then

there were a lot of orders and questions being called in the night.
Someone said, "What the hell?"

"They ran into a bunch of Tech crews coming out from their
boathouse."

"Let's go down and pitch in."

Ridiculous of course, but one halfway felt like that. A wind from
distant, ancient seas seemed to blow across us, the sound of many
oars in their locks, the shouting, the crash of galleys ramming . . .

Cox ordered, "Forward all!" We settled into position. It was time
to row home, but the quiet paddle upstream seemed strangely tame.

In the due course of time it is given to you to row a race. Not a
practice race against one of your own, but the real article, and the
oars of the boat taking position on your port hand are painted,
not crimson, but a fine, shining blue. The feeling of it starts before
then, when you take your shell down and toss her better than you
ever did before, and you and the managers are in a different, special communion over the free running of your slide, the grease on
your oar where it passes through the lock, the comfort of the
stretcher into which your feet are laced. The love you bear each
man in the boat is stronger, warmer, than it has ever been; it is
positive, almost visible. Each man looks smilingly at his neighbor
—a curious combination, already the tension and the earnestness
is on their faces, but with it comes this affection. You shove off and
paddle along to the start taking it easily, perfecting your form, the
cox saying just what he always says, everything ordinary, everything
calming.

Starting an eight-oared race is a frightful job. There is the current, and then there will be a slight crosswind, something you
wouldn't notice if you weren't trying to hold two or more boats as
light as cigar boxes in perfect line beside each other. You jockey
and jockey, the good effect of the paddle wears off. You get into
position, the starter has asked "Are you ready Harvard? Are you
ready Yale?" and one of the shells swings, and it all has to be done
over again.

At last you are set. A racing start is entirely different from the
ordinary process of getting a shell under way. This time you want
to make her fly at full speed from the first stroke, you want to
develop speed just as fast as is humanly possible, and faster. You
have practiced many times the series of short, hard strokes and the

lengthening to the full, rhythmed swing but it remains tricky, a complex set of motions to be done so rapidly and hard that it's unreasonable to think it can happen without something going wrong.

Beyond that lies the race, the test itself. You know what a gut-wracking process it is, you are too tense about the outcome, you doubt if you can stand up to it. What's ahead of you is too much. There are many things that can postpone a start and several that can cause a race to be called back within the first ten strokes. You pray for them all to happen. You are so taut inside you twang. You are afraid, not of anything, just afraid.

The pistol cracks. You carry out those first three, scrambling strokes neatly, you begin to form the full, balanced stroke as you go on to complete the ten fast ones. All those fears and tremors are gone and you are racing. Coxswain's voice comes, intentionally soothing, carrying you over into the regular swing and beat of the long-term pace your crew must set, you are eight men and you are one, the boat is going with a sizzle, smoothly through the water, and out of the corner of your eye you can see the blue blades flashing alongside you.

The effort settles down and mounts again. There are races within the race, spurts when one crew tries to pull suddenly ahead, and the other answers, the sustained, increasing efforts, the raised beats of the crew behind, the somehow easier but intense drives of the leader. Cox tells you you are past the halfway mark, he tells you you are near the end. The start tests a good crew, the last stretch proves it. You are tired now, everything is coming to a final settlement very soon, you must row harder, faster, and still row smoothly and well. You have got your second wind and used it up, you are pooped out and you know you are at the end of your strength, you simply have nothing left in you. The beat—the rate of the stroke —goes up. Cox is yelling, pleading, advising, cursing. And you are staying with it. On the recovery the captain grunts out something unintelligible but urgent. Near the end other men may wring out cries intended to be "Come on!" "Let's go!", hardly recognizable. There's not much of that, it's against your training and besides wind is too precious, but the pent-up feeling is so strong that sometimes it must have an outlet. This is a good crew, a real one. As the beat is raised, as the reserve behind the reserves of strength is poured in, each stroke taken as if it were the last you'd ever row on earth, the crew still swings together, it is still one, that awareness of each other and merging together is still present and still effective.

Three quarters of the way through you could hear them on the referee's launch and whatever others are permitted to follow, shouting, "Come on Harvard! Come on Yale!" Now you vaguely know that they are still shouting, but you can't really hear them. There is some sort of sound around the finish line, you do know that a great many people must be making a lot of noise, but you don't hear that either. You are conscious of something arching up from the banks which, without looking at it, you *see,* and you know it's cheering. Your eyes are fixed on the shoulder of the man in front of you and (I rowed starboard side) the blade of Number Seven's oar, but the one thing you do know is exactly where the other boat is. Then here it comes, the final spurt, and you cease to hear or see anything outside your business. Faint and hardly noticeable the pistol fires, then cox says, "Easy all," and you loll forward.

Done. Like that, done, over, decided. And you are through, you are truly empty now, you have poured yourself out and for a while you can hardly stand the effort of your own breathing but your tradition despises a man who fails to sit up in the boat. You have known complete exertion, you have answered every trouble of mind, spirit, and being with skilled violence and guided unrestraint, a complete happiness with eight other men over a short stretch of water has brought you catharsis. You may find it in storms at sea, in the presence of your art, on a racing horse, in bed with a woman, but you will hardly find it better or purer than you have found it here.

SUGGESTIONS FOR WRITING

1. Oliver La Farge (1901-1963), won the Pulitzer Prize for his novel *Laughing Boy* in 1930 and was Commissioner of Indian Affairs in the early 1930's. *Laughing Boy* is the story of a Navajo lad who falls in love with one of the settler's daughters, and the novel deals with the consequences of cultural differences. No other writer has treated this subject more effectively; the novel is often cited in college classes in sociology as an illustration of the effect of culture on human beings. "The Eight-Oared Shell" can hardly aspire to such a place in American letters, but it can and does reveal the excitement of discovery—a dis-

covery by which many of us have found ourselves. What is the nature of the discovery here? Does La Farge discover rowing or himself?

2. Study the organization of this essay. It has over forty paragraphs and is one of the longest in this book. Notice how the tense changes in the sixth paragraph. La Farge has been speaking in the past tense, "I took up rowing . . ."; now he turns to the present, "You are sitting on a slide . . . ." Study the sixth paragraph carefully and, using La Farge's organization, imitate it with a description from your own experience.

3. La Farge says, "I find, in writing about rowing, that I tend to concentrate rather technically upon the sport itself with the attendant danger of losing that very background of its relation to a boy's life which would give it validity." As you reflect upon the essay, do you sense that it was too technical? To fully appreciate La Farge's problem, try explaining a "technical" skill you have learned.

# The Nature of Learning

Banish me from Eden when you will, but first let me eat of the fruit of the tree of knowledge.
—R. G. Ingersoll, *The Gods, and Other Lectures,* 1876

You do ill if you praise, but worse if you censure, what you do not rightly understand.
—Leonardo da Vinci, *Notebooks,* c. 1500

To be conscious that you are ignorant is a great step to knowledge.
—Benjamin Disraeli, *Sybil,* I, 1845

One evening, when I was yet in my nurse's arms, I wanted to touch the tea urn, which was boiling merrily. . . . My nurse would have taken me away from the urn, but my mother said, "Let him touch it." So I touched it—and that was my first lesson in the meaning of liberty.
—John Ruskin, *The Story of Arachne,* 1870

Much learning doth make thee mad.
—Acts, XXVI, 24

No man is the wiser for his learning.
—John Selden, *Table Talk,* 1689

Deign on the passing world to turn thine eyes,
And pause a while from learning to be wise.
There mark what ills the scholar's life assail—
Toil, envy, want, the patron, and the jail.
—Samuel Johnson, *The Vanity of Human Wishes,* 1749

Wear your learning, like your watch, in a private pocket: and do not pull it out and strike it, merely to show that you have one.
—Lord Chesterfield, *Letters to His Son,* 1748

ARCHIBALD MACLEISH

# Teaching: The Text and the World *

What is English?

I do not put this question to be impertinent. I put it because I should like to know. I have been—officially at least—a teacher of English for the past twelve years and I have yet to hear myself defined. I will go further than that: I have yet to be told precisely what I'm doing.

The trouble in my case may be Harvard. Certainly the trouble at the beginning was Harvard. When I was notified in the early summer of 1949 that the President and Fellows of that University had approved my appointment to the Boylston Professorship of Rhetoric and Oratory I decided to drive down to Cambridge to find out what I was supposed to teach. It seemed like a good idea at the time: my last ten years or so had been in Washington and the years before that in journalism and my real profession throughout had been the writing of verse, not teaching. I say it seemed like a good idea. It didn't turn out that way.

My first call, logically, was at the Department of English since it was a Committee of the Department of English that had approached me—"approach" in the technical sense—the year before. It was an agreeable call but brief. Chairmen of Harvard departments, I was informed, do not tell their colleagues what to do: they merely circulate the memoranda. I was back on the wooden porch

---

* From *The Saturday Review* (December 9, 1961). Reprinted by permission of the publishers.

of Warren House in something under five minutes with the impression that Harvard would be an attractive place if one could get into it.

My second call was on the only member of the English Department I knew at all well, a displaced Yale man like myself. He listened, looked at the ceiling, and replied that I could teach his course in Shakespeare if I wanted. I left with the impression, later verified, that he was not entirely enthusiastic about my presence in Cambridge.

There remained the Provost of the University, the President being in Washington in those months. (By "the President" I mean, of course, the President of Harvard.) The Provost, when I found his office, was engaged but, being desperate, I decided to sit him out and that fetched him. He popped out of his office, listened mildly while I stated my business, and popped back in again with the remark, delivered over his shoulder as the door closed, that when Harvard appointed a man to a full professorship, to say nothing of the Boylston Professorship, it expected him to *know* what he wanted to teach.

It was an enlightening afternoon. I had been told in three different ways that freedom to teach at Harvard is literally freedom— with all the penalties attached. But it was not an *instructive* afternoon. I know no more about my duties on the way back to the Franklin County Hills than I had known on the way down, and twelve years later I still know little more than I knew then. I have taught the advanced writing course which all Boylston Professors since Barrett Wendell have offered and I have invented and annually reinvented a course in the nature of poetry; but though I take, or sometimes take, a proprietary satisfaction in both of them I am not at all sure that either is the course I should have taught or would have taught had I known what "English" is. It is not always English that turns up in the novels and poems and plays of the advanced writing course, nor does the course in poetry confine itself to poems in the English tongue. It can't very well since poetry recognizes no such limitation.

In those early days—my young days as a teacher of English when I was still in my late fifties—I used to assume that I was the only member of the profession who did not know what he was doing, but as time has passed I have begun to wonder. We have, at Harvard, an institution called the Visiting Committee, one to each department, which descends annually upon the appropriate class-rooms to observe the progress of education. Our particular Visiting Committee in the Department of English ends its investigations, or always did when John Marquand was chairman, by offering a dinner to the permanent appointments. And the dinner always in-cludes, or always included, a question which seems to stir the De-partmental subconscious: Why are the graduates of Harvard Uni-versity incapable of composing simple declarative sentences? Under ordinary circumstances a question such as this might be expected to serve as the gambit to a lively exchange involving, among other things, the truth of the fact asserted, but under the circumstances of our dinner, when the questioner is a distinguished alumnus who is also a member of the Committee to Visit the English Depart-ment, and when the effectiveness of the English Department in per-forming its duties is the subject of the Visitation, the innocent words take on a different aspect. They become charged with im-plications, the most challenging of which is the implication that if graduates of Harvard University are incapable of composing simple declarative sentences the Department of English is to blame. Which, in turn, implies that the teaching of English and the teaching of the composition of simple declarative sentences are one and the same thing. It is that last implication which spills the coffee on the tablecloth. Chairs are pushed back. Throats are cleared. And a strained voice, laboring under an emotion which an ignorant ob-server might think disproportionate to the cause, protests that teachers of English have better things to do than instruct the young in the composition of simple declarative sentences. Silence falls. Time passes. Someone suggests another drink all around. And there the issue reposes for another year. No member of the annual visita-tion has ever yet been rude enough to ask: What better things? And no member of the Department within my memory has ever said.

I suppose the reason for the persistence on one side and the pas-sion on the other is historical. What our Visitors are remembering, consciously or not, is the importance of simple declarative sentences in the early days of the Republic, and the part played by Harvard College in the shaping of the minds of those who used them best. What my colleagues almost certainly remember is the importance to the growth of Harvard College of the liberation of their prede-cessors from such concerns. It was because the two Adamses and their contemporaries in Massachusetts and Virginia and Connecticut and Pennsylvania could write meaningful English that the American Revolution was not merely a defeat of England but a conquest of human liberty. But it is also true that it was not until that famous sail-maker's son, Francis J. Child, was relieved of his responsibility for the teaching of freshman composition that the Department of English at Harvard became an educational influence in the larger sense of that term.

It is, I think, this latter fact that explains the difficulty of defining "English" even today and even among those whose lives are devoted to its teaching, for the emancipation of Stubby Child took place less than a century ago. There was little "English," as we use the word, prior to 1876—at least in Cambridge. When letters were first taught in the Colonial colleges they were taught in Latin with Latin manuals and Latin and Greek examples. The teaching of composition in the vulgar tongue had begun, it is true, before the Revolution, but the extraordinary debate which preceded and accompanied that event was conducted with the classical modes and models in mind. Harvard's historian, Samuel Eliot Morison, puts it with his usual pithiness: "The classical pseudonyms with which our Harvard signers of the great Declaration signed their early communications to the press were not pen names chosen by chance, but represented a very definite point of view that every educated man recognized." And the same thing seems to have been true thirty years after the Revolution when the first chair in letters was established. John Quincy Adams, the first Boylston Professor, signalized his installation by delivering an inaugural address in which the word "English" never once occurs. It was not London to him, nor Stratford, from which the great tradition flowed but Athens and Rome. "Novelty," he told his audience, "will not be expected; nor is it perhaps to be desired. A subject which has exhausted the genius of Aristotle, Cicero, and Quintilian can neither require nor admit much additional illustration. . . ."

He was thinking, of course, of rhetoric and oratory, the two subjects attached by statute to his chair. *English* literature, in the year 1806, was something a gentleman read on his own time and for his own entertainment if he read it at all. Even a quarter of a century later instruction in this area seems to have been informal —and correspondingly pleasant. Mr. Morison quotes a member of the Harvard class of 1832 as remembering "our evenings with

Chaucer and Spenser" in the study of John Quincy Adams's successor, Edward Tyrell Channing. The account hardly evokes the meeting of a course as we understand such things: "How his genial face shone in the light of the winter's fire and threw new meaning upon the rare gems of thought and humor and imagination of those kings of ancient song." It is a charming scene and one its author obviously relishes but even so he does not forget the serious business of his association with Professor Channing. It was not for those rare gems that he sat at the great man's feet. It was to learn to write. "Who of us," he reminds himself, "does not bless him every day that we write an English sentence for his pure taste and admirable simplicity!"

All of which would seem to support the conclusion that it was not until well along in Mr. Eliot's administration that "English" began at Harvard with the beginning of those laborious studies of Francis Child's in Anglo-Saxon and Middle English and Chaucer and Shakespeare and Dryden on which our modern literary scholarship is founded. But if this is so—if "English" is as new as this— then the difficulty of discussing it with members of Visiting Committees becomes understandable. Eighty years is a short time in which to fix the character and limits of a discipline. One can learn in so brief a time what "English" isn't—as, for example, that it isn't the thing it rebelled against at its beginnings. It isn't, that is to say, the "mere" teaching of the use of the English language. But one cannot learn so quickly what "English" *is*.

Literature? The teaching of literature in English? It sounds reasonable: if "English" isn't the teaching of the writing of the language it may well be the teaching of the reading of the language— the reading of what has already been written that deserves to be read again. But what do we mean by reading? Do we mean the reading of the words as words, the recognition of the structure, the interpretation of the references—in brief, the explication, as we put it, of the text? Or do we mean the reading of the substance of the words, what the words in their combination and their structure, their sounds and their significance, are *about?* But if we mean the latter, where does "English" end? The substance of the literature of our tongue is the whole substance of human experience as that experience has presented itself to the mind, the imagination, and the most sensitive of the users of that tongue. Nothing is foreign

to it. Nothing is excluded. Everything has been touched, turned
over, nuzzled, chewed, and much has been mastered, much has been
perceived. If "English" has to do with the substance of English
literature, where will we find faculties qualified to teach it? And
how, if we found them, could they fit themselves into the academic
order? What would be left for the other faculties—for the departments of philosophy and theology and biology and history and
psychology?—above all for the departments of psychology?

Obviously "English" cannot claim so vast an empire. But what
lesser kingdom is there then? The texts as texts? It was the teaching
of the texts as texts that destroyed the classics in American education. When "The Odyssey" was assigned in the last century as so
much Greek—so many lines a day and so many days in the year,
leaving the poem to take care of itself—"The Odyssey" began to
die and Greek with it. And when, later, the magnificent scholarship
of Kittredge attached itself to English texts as texts, a generation
of graduate students was produced which itched to teach anything
else—biographies of poets, economic and sociological interpretations of novels, literary history—anything but the texts themselves.
And when this revolution had set up its barricades, it in turn produced the counterrevolution of our own time. Back-to-the-text was
the word with us—and the word became flesh in an army of brave
new critics who carried everything before them only to leave us,
when the counterrevolution subsided, where we are today; betwixt
and between. We are agreed that it was a mistake to teach the poems
of Shelley by way of the pitch of his voice and the bonfire on the
beach but we are not yet entirely persuaded that *explication de
texte* has told the truth about poetry either. "English," we think
today, is something more than the teaching of the reading of words
as words but something less also, surely less, than the teaching of
the private life the words came out of, or the public life toward
which they look.

Less and more—but how much less and how much more? That is
the question we do not answer for our newly chosen colleagues
knocking at our doors to ask us what they ought to teach. Can it be
answered? I think for myself, over boldly perhaps, that it can. It
can, that is, if we will look for the answer where answers are to be
found in such cases: not in the theory but in the practice. Percy
Bridgman once remarked of the language of physics that you can

tell the meaning of a term far better by seeing what is done *with* it than by hearing what is said *about* it. The same thing is true of the language of education. The theoretical fences will all blow down, give them time enough and wind, but the actions will stand. A colleague working in an ungrateful corner of the curriculum brings the dust to air, raises the too long familiar from its accustomedness, calls Dr. Johnson from his sepulchre and makes him walk the College Yard. This is the teaching of "English," but what has this colleague taught? Or a lecturer somewhere else, struggling with an exhausted theme, renews a poem which had lost its voice and makes it cry like the first bird in Eden. This too is "English"—but what then is it?

Take the lecturer. Take Robert Penn Warren teaching "The Rime of the Ancient Mariner" in a lecture which has been widely published and much read: a lecture which gives voice to the poem. What *happens* in this lecture? The poem is "read," yes, but is it the "reading" that happens? There have been better "readings"—"readings" which place the poem more perfectly in its dramatic setting and better reveal the necessity that drives it. What truly happens here is something else. What happens is that the relation between the poem and the world of life in which the poem exists is discovered—discovered by a stroke as brief and brilliant as the blast of light which sometimes ties the earth and sky together. Every man, says Mr. Warren quietly, kills his own albatross . . . and there, with those words, the bird, the scene, the poem all come true—come real. The metaphysical talk about symbols and symbolism which usually fogs discussions of "The Rime"—is the albatross a symbol? Isn't it? But *is* it?—chokes on its own inanity and what is left is meaning, the only kind of meaning that truly means, personal meaning, immediate meaning. That world of ice and snow becomes the world of vision we all have glimpsed—we also. The murder of the bird becomes the murder of which we also are guilty, all of us: the destruction of life, the denial of love. The horror of thirst and windlessness, motionlessness, becomes the horror of stagnation we too have sensed when our rejection of love, of life, has stilled the winds of vision that should drive us. The salvation by wonder and pity becomes a salvation we could recognize if it came. Even the little precept at the end, those lines the overeducated read with titters of embarrassment, takes power to move our hearts:

He prayeth best who loveth best
All things both great and small.

One sees, looking back, what has happened. This myth of the poetic imagination which students in colleges are called on to admire as literature has become a myth of myself which I—student, teacher, man, woman, whoever—am called on to live as life. And one sees how this miracle has been accomplished. It has been accomplished not by squeezing the pips of the text but by a perception which has one foot in the text and the other in the world so that the two, text and world, are made to march together.

But is this what the teaching of "English," in its actions, is? Is this what happens in W. J. Bate's lectures on Johnson and in all the rest of the great achievements in the discipline? I think it is. I think "English" always stands with a foot in the text and a foot in the world, and that what it undertakes to teach is neither the one nor the other but the relation between them. The greatest poem, removed from the ground of our being, is an irrelevance. The ground of our being without the poem is a desert. "English," I think, is the teaching which attempts to minister between.

SUGGESTIONS FOR WRITING

1. Archibald MacLeish was born in Illinois in 1892. He is one of the very few American men of letters in official public life, having been Librarian of Congress and Under Secretary of State. The essay you have read was originally entitled "What Is English?", and was delivered as an address to the National Council of Teachers of English on Thanksgiving Day, 1961. Thousands of English teachers sat spellbound as one of the most famous English teachers in the country explained that he wasn't sure what teaching English was all about. He was seriously propounding a deep question, for when the superficial trappings are removed, many a simple and obvious question becomes profound. What is a student? What is a professor? What is a college? Using MacLeish as a pattern of organization, strip away the obvious answers to a simple question and reveal its profundity.

2. Select a poem you have read (or find one in this book) and show how it has revealed to you something about your own life.

3. Starting with an analogy about a student's life, develop MacLeish's point by example and illustration. Using the kind of figurative language MacLeish employs when he says teaching is accomplished by a "percep-

tion which has one foot in the text and one foot in the world so that the two, text and world, are made to march together."

JACQUES BARZUN

# The Teaching Process*

It is over a quarter of a century since I first obeyed the summons to teach and I can only hope the habit has not become a compulsion. "Oh to sit next a man who has spent his life in trying to educate others!" groaned Oscar Wilde. My belief is that the last thing a good teacher wants to do is to teach outside the classroom; certainly my own vision of bliss halfway through a term is solitary confinement in a soundproof cell. But feeling this way, I often wonder what originally made the impulse to teach take root. In the lives of so many good men one reads that they "drifted into teaching." They drift out again. It is clear that teachers are born, not made, and circumstances usually permit rather than compel. It is impossible to think of William James *not* teaching or of his brother Henry consenting to give a simple explanation. For many people, doing is far easier than talking about it.

From which I conclude that the teaching impulse goes something like this: a fellow human being is puzzled or stymied. He wants to open a door or spell "accommodate." The would-be helper has two choices. He can open the door, spell the word; or he can show his pupil how to do it for himself. The second way is harder and takes more time, but a strong instinct in the born teacher makes him prefer it. It seems somehow to turn an accident into an opportunity for permanent creation. The raw material is what the learner can do, and upon this the teacher-artist builds by the familiar process of taking apart and putting together. He must break down the new and puzzling situation into simpler bits and lead the beginner in the right order from one bit to the next. What the simpler bits and

---

* From *Teacher in America* by Jacques Barzun (Boston: Little, Brown & Company—Atlantic Monthly Press, 1945). Copyright 1944, 1945 by Jacques Barzun. Reprinted by permission of the publishers.

the right order are no one can know ahead of time. They vary for each individual and the teacher must grope around until he finds a "first step" that the particular pupil can manage. In any school subject, of course, this technique does not stop with the opening of a door. The need for it goes on and on—as it seems, forever—and it takes the stubbornness of a saint coupled with the imagination of a demon for a teacher to pursue his art of improvisation gracefully, unwearyingly, endlessly.

Nor is this a purely mental task. All the while, the teacher must keep his charge's feelings in good order. A rattled student can do nothing and a muddled teacher will rattle or dishearten almost any student. The teacher must not talk too much or too fast, must not trip over his own tongue, must not think out loud, must not forget, in short, that he is handling a pair of runaway horses—the pupil and a dramatic situation.

Patience is a quality proverbially required for good teaching, but it is not surprising that many good teachers turn out to be impatient people—though not with their students. Their stock of forbearance gives out before they get home. What sustains them in class is that the situation is always changing. Three successive failures to do one thing may all seem identical to the bystander, but the good teacher will notice a change, a progression, or else the clear sign that the attempt must be postponed until some other preliminary progress has been made.

It is obvious that the relation of teacher to pupil is an emotional one and most complex and unstable besides. To begin with, the motives, the forces that make teaching "go," are different on both sides of the desk. The pupil has some curiosity and he wants to know what grownups know. The master has curiosity also, but it is chiefly about the way the pupil's mind—or hand—works. Remembering his own efforts and the pleasure of discovery, the master finds a satisfaction which I have called artistic in seeing how a new human being will meet and make his own some part of our culture —our ways, our thoughts, even our errors and superstitions. This interest, however, does not last forever. As the master grows away from his own learning period, he also finds that mankind repeats itself. Fewer and fewer students appear new and original. They make the same mistakes at the same places and never seem to go very far into a subject which, for him, is still an expanding universe. Hence young teachers are best; they are the most energetic, most intuitive, and the least resented.

For side by side with his eagerness, the pupil feels resentment arising from the fact that the grownup who teaches him appears to know it all. There is, incidentally, no worse professional disease for the teacher than the habit of putting questions with a half-smile that says "I know that one, and I will tell it you: come along, my pretty." Telling and questioning must not be put-up jobs designed to make the teacher feel good about himself. It is as bad as the Jehovah complex among doctors. Even under the best conditions of fair play and deliberate spontaneity, the pupil, while needing and wanting knowledge, will hate and resist it. This resistance often makes one feel that the human mind is made of some wonderfully tough rubber, which you can stretch a little by pulling hard, but which snaps back into shape the moment you let go.

It is exasperating, but consider how the student feels, subjected to daily and hourly stretching. "Here am I," he thinks, "with my brains nicely organized—with everything, if not in its place, at least in a place where I can find it—and you come along with a new and strange item that you want to force into my previous arrangement. Naturally I resist. You persist. I begin to dislike you. But at the same time, you show me aspects of this new fact or idea which in spite of myself mesh in with my existing desires. You seem to know the contents of my mind. You show me the proper place for your contribution to my stock of knowledge. Finally, there is brooding over us a vague threat of disgrace for me if I do not accept your offering and keep it and show you that I still have it when you—dreadful thought!—*examine* me. So I give in, I shut my eyes and swallow. I write little notes about it to myself, and with luck the burr sticks: I have learned something. Thanks to you? Well, not exactly. Thanks to you and thanks to me. I shall always be grateful for your efforts, but do not expect me to love you, at least not for a long, long time. When I am fully formed and somewhat battered by the world and yet not too displeased with myself, I shall generously believe that I owe it all to you. It will be an exaggeration on the other side, just as my present dislike is an injustice. Strike an average between the two and that will be a fair measure of my debt."

At any stage in learning, this inner dialogue between opposite feelings goes on. It should go on. Teaching is possible only because there is a dialogue and one part of the mind can be used to rearrange the other. The whole secret of teaching—and it is no secret —consists in splitting the opposition, downing the conservatives by making an alliance with the radicals. It goes without saying that I am not using these words here in their workaday sense. My meaning applies to the multiplication table as well as to anything else. The conservative part of the pupil's mind is passive, stubborn, mute; but his radical minority, that is, his curiosity and his desire to grow up, may be aroused to action. The move forward is generally short; then the conservatives return to power; they preserve, they feel pride of ownership in the new acquisition and begin to think they had it as a birthright. This rhythmical action is one reason why teaching and learning must not go on all the time, nor at an accelerated pace: time and rest are needed for absorption. Psychologists confirm the fact when they tell us that it is really in summer that our muscles learn how to skate, and in winter how to swim.

If I have dwelt on the emotions of teaching and being taught, it is because many people believe that schooling only engages the mind—and only temporarily at that. "I've forgotten," says the average man, "all I ever learned at school." And he mentally contrasts this happy oblivion with the fact that he still knows how to open oysters and ride a bicycle. But my description of teaching applies equally to physical things and to metaphysical. We may forget the substance of American History but we are probably scarred for life by the form and feeling of it as imparted by book and teacher. Why is it that the businessman's economics and the well-bred woman's taste in art are normally twenty-five years behind the times? It is that one's lifelong opinions are those picked up before maturity— at school and college.

This is why a "teacher's influence," if he does exert one, is not so big a joke as it seems. Notice in the lives of distinguished men how invariably there is a Mr. Bowles or a Dr. Tompkins or a Professor Clunk—whom no one ever heard of, but who is "remembered" for inspiring, guiding, and teaching decisively at the critical time. We can all see the mark left by a teacher in physical arts like tennis or music. The pupils of Leopold Auer or Tobias Matthay can be recognized at forty paces by their posture and even in a dark room by the sound they make. For in these disciplines the teacher usually falls back on direct imitation: "Hold your hand like this," or more simply, "Watch me." Well, much good teaching is of the "watch me" order, but the more abstract the knowledge, the less easy it is to imitate the teacher, and the genuine student wants to do the real thing in a real way *by himself.*

Consequently, the whole aim of good teaching is to turn the young learner, by nature a little copycat, into an independent, self-propelling creature, who cannot merely learn but study—that is, work as his own boss to the limit of his powers. This is to turn pupils into students, and it can be done on any rung of the ladder of learning. When I was a child, the multiplication table was taught from a printed sheet which had to be memorized one "square" at a time—the one's and the two's and so on up to nine. It never occured to the teacher to show us how the answers could be arrived at also by addition, which we already knew. No one said, "Look: if four times four is sixteen, you ought to be able to figure out, without aid from memory, what five times four is, because that amounts to four more one's added to the sixteen." This would at first have been puzzling, *more* complicated and difficult than memory work, but once explained and grasped, it would have been an instrument for learning and checking the whole business of multiplication. We could temporarily have dispensed with the teacher and cut loose from the printed table.[1]

This is another way of saying that the only thing worth teaching anybody is a principle. Naturally principles involve facts and some facts must be learned "bare" because they do not rest on any principle. The capital of Alaska is Juneau and, so far as I know, that is all there is to it; but a European child ought not to learn that Washington is the capital of the United States without fixing firmly in his mind the relation between the city and the man who led his countrymen to freedom. That would be missing an association, which is the germ of a principle. And just as a complex athletic feat is made possible by rapid and accurate co-ordination, so all valua-

---

[1] I find that General Grant complained of the same thing: "Both winters were spent in going over the same old arithmetic which I knew every word of before and repeating 'A noun is the name of a thing,' which I had also heard my Georgetown teachers repeat until I had come to believe it." (*Memoirs,* New York, 1894, p. 20.)

ble learning hangs together and *works* by associations which make sense.

Since associations are rooted in habit and habits in feelings, we can see that anything which makes school seem a nightmare or a joke, which brands the teacher as a fool, or a fraud, is the archenemy of all learning. It so happens that there is one professional disease, or rather vice, which generates precisely this feeling and whose consequences are therefore fatal. I refer to Hokum and I hasten to explain what I mean. Hokum is the counterfeit of true intellectual currency. It is words without meaning, verbal filler, artificial apples of knowledge. From the necessities of the case, nine tenths of all teaching is done with words, whence the ever present temptation of hokum.

Words should point to things, seen or unseen. But they can also be used to wrap up emptiness of heart and lack of thought. The student accepts some pompous, false, meaningless formula, and passes it back on demand, to be rewarded with—appropriately enough—a passing grade. All the dull second-rate opinions, all the definitions that don't define, all the moral platitudes that "sound good," all the conventional adjectives ("gentle Shakespeare"), all the pretenses that a teacher makes about the feelings of his students towards him and vice versa, all the intimations that something must be learned because it has somehow got lodged among learnable things (like the Binomial Theorem or the date of Magna Carta)—all this in all its forms gives off the atmosphere of hokum, which healthy people everywhere find absolutely unbreathable.

In a modern play, I think by A. A. Milne, this schoolmarm vice has been caught and set down in a brief dialogue which goes something like this:

GOVERNESS. Recite.
PUPIL. "The Battle of Blenheim." (*Long pause*).
GOVERNESS. By?
PUPIL. (*silence*).
GOVERNESS. By Robert Southey.
PUPIL. By Robert Southey.
GOVERNESS. Who was Robert Southey?
PUPIL. (*pause*). I don't know.
GOVERNESS. One of our greatest poets. Begin again.
PUPIL. The Battle of Blenheim by Robert Southey one of our greatest poets.

As this example shows, hokum is subtle and I will forbear to analyze it. It hides in the porous part of solid learning and vitiates it by making it stupid and ridiculous. I remember once giving a short quiz to a class of young women who had been reading about the Renaissance. I asked for some "identification" of names and put Petrarch in the list. One girl, who had evidently read a textbook, wrote down: "Petrarch—the vanguard of the new emphasis." I spent a good hour trying to explain why this parroting of opinion was not only not "correct" but blind hokum, hokum absolute. It was not an easy job because so many teachers and books deal exclusively in that cheap commodity. The child's instinct is first to believe the Word, spoken or printed; then with growing good sense to disbelieve it, but to trust to its hokum value for getting through by "satisfying" the teacher. Great heavens, what satisfactions!

To carry my anecdote one step further, I believe I made a life-long friend and a convert to decent learning by persuading my student that almost any honest mistake would have been truer than the absurdity she was palming off. She might better have been trivial: "Petrarch was an Italian"; or flippant: "Wrote poems to a girl named Laura"; or downright mistaken: "Also spelled Plutarch," rather than do what she did. My difficulty—and this is the important point—was in convincing her that I meant what I said, in breaking down the strongest superstition of the young, which is that everybody but themselves prefers make-believe and lives by it.

SUGGESTIONS FOR WRITING

1. Jacques Barzun, born in France in 1907, received his education from a French *lycée* and from Columbia University, where he has taught since 1937. His technique of writing clearly and forcefully puts many native born speakers of English to shame. In this essay from *Teacher in America* he most successfully puts into practice a method he implies he learned from Percy Bridgman, the physicist: the operational definition. He doesn't *explain* what a teacher does, he *shows* us. Using a similar technique, show a teacher in action and reveal the operation of teaching.

2. Barzun points out that a good teacher shows people how to learn. Write about someone (not a teacher) who showed you how to learn; describe the learning experience in detail.

3. Cite an instance in your experience when you were taught some "hokum." As you unfold the story, give attention to two questions: (1) is

teaching hokum really teaching?, and (2) when you learn hokum, are
you really learning?
4. Barzun is here using "popular" style. Examine eight or ten of his sentences closely and compare them with those of Francis Bacon. Recom-
pose Barzun's sentences in Bacon's style. Then write a paragraph or
two explaining what you have learned about popular style.


NATHANIEL S. SHALER

# Learning: A Sense of Power*

At the time of my secession from the humanities, Agassiz was in
Europe; he did not return, I think, until the autumn of 1859. I had,
however, picked up several acquaintances among his pupils, learned
what they were about, and gained some notion of his methods.
After about a month he returned, and I had my first contact with
the man who was to have the most influence on my life of any of
the teachers to whom I am indebted. I shall never forget even the
lesser incidents of this meeting, for this great master by his presence
gave an importance to his surroundings, so that the room where you
met him and the furniture stayed with the memory of him.

When I first met Louis Agassiz, he was still in the prime of his
admirable manhood; though he was then fifty-two years old, and
had passed his constructive period, he still had the look of a young
man. His face was the most genial and engaging that I had ever
seen, and his manner captivated me altogether. But as I had been
among men who had a free swing, and for a year among people
who seemed to me to be cold and superrational, hungry as I doubtless was for human sympathy, Agassiz's welcome went to my heart—
I was at once his captive. It has been my good chance to see many
men of engaging presence and ways, but I have never known his
equal. . . .

As my account of Agassiz's quality should rest upon my experiences with him, I shall now go on to tell how and to what effect he

* From *Autobiography of Nathaniel Southgate Shaler* (Boston: Houghton
Mifflin Company, 1909), with omissions. Copyright 1907 by Gabriella Shaler
Webb. Reprinted by permission of the estate of Gabriella Shaler Webb. Title
supplied by the editor.

trained me. In that day there were no written examinations on any subjects which candidates for the Lawrence Scientific School had to pass. The professors in charge of the several departments questioned the candidates, and determined their fitness to pursue the course of study they desired to undertake. Few or none who had any semblance of an education were denied admission to Agassiz's laboratory. At that time, the instructors had, in addition to their meagre salaries—his was then $2,500 per annum—the regular fees paid in by the students under his charge. So I was promptly assured that I was admitted. Be it said, however, that he did give me an effective oral examination, which, as he told me, was intended to show whether I could expect to go forward to a degree at the end of four years of study. On this matter of the degree he was obdurate, refusing to recommend some who had been with him for many years, and had succeeded in their special work, giving as reason for his denial that they were "too ignorant."

The examination Agassiz gave me was directed first to find that I knew enough Latin and Greek to make use of those languages; that I could patter a little of them evidently pleased him. He didn't care for those detestable rules for scanning. Then came German and French, which were also approved: I could read both, and spoke the former fairly well. He did not probe me in my weakest place, mathematics, for the good reason that, badly as I was off in that subject, he was in a worse plight. Then asking me concerning my reading, he found that I had read the *Essay on Classification,* and had noted in it the influence of Schelling's views. Most of his questioning related to this field, and the more than fair beginning of our relations then made was due to the fact that I had some enlargement on that side. So, too, he was pleased to find that I had managed a lot of Latin, Greek, and German poetry, and had been trained with the sword. He completed this inquiry by requiring that I bring my foils and masks for a bout. In this test he did not fare well, for, though not untrained, he evidently knew more of the *Schläger* than of the rapier. He was heavy handed, and lacked finesse. This, with my previous experience, led me to the conclusion that I had struck upon a kind of tutor in Cambridge not known in Kentucky.

While Agassiz questioned me carefully as to what I had read and what I had seen, he seemed in this preliminary going over in no wise concerned to find what I knew about fossils, rocks, animals, and plants; he put aside the offerings of my scanty lore. This offended me a bit, as I recall, for the reason that I thought I knew, and for a self-taught lad really did know, a good deal about such matters, especially as to the habits of insects, particularly spiders. It seemed hard to be denied the chance to make my parade; but I afterward saw what this meant—that he did not intend to let me begin my tasks by posing as a naturalist. The beginning was indeed quite different, and, as will be seen, in a manner that quickly evaporated my conceit. It was made and continued in a way I will now recount.

Agassiz's laboratory was then in a rather small two storied build- ing, looking much like a square dwelling-house, which stood where the College Gymnasium now stands. . . . Agassiz had recently moved into it from a shed on the marsh near Brighton bridge, the original tenants, the engineers, having come to riches in the shape of the brick structure now known as the Lawrence Building. In this primitive establishment Agassiz's laboratory, as distinguished from the storerooms where the collections were crammed, occupied one room about thirty feet long and fifteen feet wide—what is now the west room on the lower floor of the edifice. In this place, al- ready packed, I had assigned to me a small pine table with a rusty tin pan upon it. . . .

When I sat me down before my tin pan, Agassiz brought me a small fish, placing it before me with the rather stern requirement that I should study it, but should on no account talk to any one concerning it, nor read anything relating to fishes, until I had his permission so to do. To my inquiry, "What shall I do?" he said in effect: "Find out what you can without damaging the specimen; when I think that you have done the work I will question you." In the course of an hour I thought I had compassed that fish; it was rather an unsavory object, giving forth the stench of old alcohol, then loathsome to me, though in time I came to like it. Many of the scales were loosened so that they fell off. It appeared to me to be a case for a summary report, which I was anxious to make and get on to the next stage of the business. But Agassiz, though always within call, concerned himself no further with me that day, nor the next, nor for a week. At first, this neglect was distressing; but I saw that it was a game, for he was, as I discerned rather than saw, covertly watching me. So I set my wits to work upon the thing, and in the course of a hundred hours or so thought I had done much—a hundred times as much as seemed possible at the start. I got interested in finding out how the scales went in series, their shape, the form and placement of the teeth, etc. Finally, I felt full of the subject, and probably expressed it in my bearing; as for words about it then, there were none from my master except his cheery "Good morning." At length, on the seventh day, came the question, "Well?" and my disgorge of learning to him as he sat on the edge of my table puffing his cigar. At the end of the hour's telling, he swung off and away, saying: "That is not right." Here I began to think that, after all, perhaps the rules for scanning Latin verse were not the worst infliction in the world. Moreover, it was clear that he was playing a game with me to find if I were capable of doing hard, continuous work without the support of a teacher, and this stimulated me to labor. I went at the task anew, discarded my first notes, and in another week of ten hours a day labor I had results which astonished myself and satisfied him. Still there was no trace of praise in words or manner. He signified that it would do by placing before me about a half a peck of bones, telling me to see what I could make of them, with no further directions to guide me. I soon found that they were the skeletons of half a dozen fishes of different species; the jaws told me so much at a first inspection. The task evidently was to fit the separate bones together in their proper order. Two months or more went to this task with no other help than an occasional looking over my grouping with the stereotyped remark: "That is not right." Finally, the task was done, and I was again set upon alcoholic specimens—this time a remarkable lot of specimens representing, perhaps, twenty species of the side-swimmers or Pleuronectidae.

I shall never forget the sense of power in dealing with things which I felt in beginning the more extended work on a group of animals. I had learned the art of comparing objects, which is the basis of the naturalist's work. At this stage I was allowed to read, and to discuss my work with others about me. I did both eagerly, and acquired a considerable knowledge of the literature of ichthyology, becoming especially interested in the system of classification, then most imperfect. I tried to follow Agassiz's scheme of division into the order of ctenoids and ganoids, with the result that I found one of my species of side-swimmers had cycloid scales on one side and ctenoid on the other. This not only shocked my sense of the value of classification in a way that permitted of no full recovery of my original respect for the process, but for a time shook my confidence in my master's knowledge. At the same time I had a malicious pleasure in exhibiting my "find" to him, expecting to repay in part the humiliation which he had evidently tried to inflict on my conceit. To my question as to how the nondescript should be classified he said: "My boy, there are now two of us who know that."

This incident of the fish made an end of my novitiate. After that, with a suddenness of transition which puzzled me, Agassiz became very communicative; we passed indeed into the relation of friends of like age and purpose, and he actually consulted me as to what I should like to take up as a field of study. Finding that I wished to devote myself to geology, he set me to work on the Brachiopoda as the best group of fossils to serve as data in determining the Palaeozoic horizons. So far as his rather limited knowledge of the matter went, he guided me in the field about Cambridge, in my reading, and to acquaintances of his who were concerned with earth structures. I came thus to know Charles T. Jackson, Jules Marcou, and, later, the brothers Rogers, Henry and James. At the same time I kept up the study of zoology, undertaking to make myself acquainted with living organic forms as a basis for a knowledge of fossils.

## SUGGESTIONS FOR WRITING

1. Nathaniel S. Shaler (1841-1906), born in Kentucky, became a distinguished American geologist. He received his degree from the Lawrence School of Science in Harvard in 1862. It was while he was at Harvard that he worked under the great Louis Agassiz. His description of the first encounter with Agassiz reveals a great deal about himself, but it also gives us a picture of Agassiz. To test the powers of your imagination, put yourself in Agassiz's place during the encounter with Shaler, and, using the personal narrative style of Shaler, write about how things must have seemed to Agassiz.

2. Examine the psychology of the situation Shaler describes. Agassiz, so Shaler would have us believe, put on an act, playing the part of the gruff old schoolmaster. He had to force Shaler to begin to learn by himself. If Agassiz had been a sympathetic listener to his complaints,

Shaler might not have learned a most important lesson—that he had the determination to force his mind and fingers to work on that fish until it revealed something to him. Write about a person who put on an act which forced you to learn something on your own.

3. Imagine you are Shaler. Write a letter home after three or four days of working on the fish. Reveal your sense of frustration. Write a second letter home on the day Agassiz said to you, "My boy, there are now two of us who know that."

E. M. FORSTER

## The Spacious Halls of Youth*

"The cow is there," said Ansell, lighting a match and holding it out over the carpet. No one spoke. He waited till the end of the match fell off. Then he said again, "She is there, the cow. There now."

"You have not proved it," said a voice.

"I have proved it to myself."

"I have proved it to myself that she isn't," said the voice. "The cow is *not* there." Ansell frowned and lit another match.

"She's there for me," he declared. "I don't care whether she's there for you or not. Whether I'm in Cambridge or Iceland or dead, the cow will be there."

It was philosophy. They were discussing the existence of objects. Do they exist only when there is some one to look at them? Or have they a real existence of their own? It is all very interesting, but at the same time it is difficult. Hence the cow. She seemed to make things easier. She was so familiar, so solid, that surely the truths that she illustrated would in time become familiar and solid also. Is the cow there or not? This was better than deciding between objectivity and subjectivity. So at Oxford, just at the same time, one was asking, "What do our rooms look like in the vac.?"

"Look here, Ansell. I'm there—in the meadow—the cow's there. Do you agree so far?"

* From *The Longest Journey* by E. M. Forster (New York: Alfred A. Knopf, Inc., 1922). Copyright 1922 by Alfred A. Knopf, Inc. Reprinted by permission of the publishers.

"Well?'

"Well, if you go, the cow stops; but if I go, the cow goes. Then what will happen if you stop and I go?"

Several voices cried out that this was quibbling.

"I know it is," said the speaker brightly, and silence descended again, while they tried honestly to think the matter out.

Rickie, on whose carpet the matches were being dropped, did not like to join in the discussion. It was too difficult for him. He could not even quibble. If he spoke, he should simply make himself a fool. He preferred to listen and to watch the tobacco smoke stealing out past the window seat into the tranquil October air. He could see the court too, and the college cat teasing the college tortoise, and the kitchen men with supper trays upon their heads. Hot food for one—that must be for the geographical don, who never came in for Hall; cold food for three, apparently at half a crown a head, for some one he did not know; hot food, *à la carte*—obviously for the ladies haunting the next staircase; cold food for two, at two shillings—going to Ansell's rooms for himself and Ansell, and as it passed under the lamp he saw that it was meringues again. Then the bedmakers began to arrive, chatting to each other pleasantly, and he could hear Ansell's bedmaker say, "Oh dang!" when she found she had to lay Ansell's tablecloth; for there was not a breath stirring. The great elms were motionless, and seemed still in the glory of midsummer, for the darkness hid the yellow blotches on their leaves, and their outlines were still rounded against the tender sky. Those elms were dryads—so Rickie believed or pretended, and the line between the two is subtler than we admit. At all events they were lady trees, and had for generations fooled the college statutes by their residence in the haunts of youth.

But what about the cow? He returned to her with a start, for this would never do. He also would try to think the matter out. Was she there or not? The cow. There or not? He strained his eyes into the night.

Either way it was attractive. If she was there, other cows were there too. The darkness of Europe was dotted with them, and in the far East their flanks were shining in the rising sun. Great herds of them stood browsing in pastures where no man came nor need ever come, or plashed knee deep by the brink of impassable rivers. And this, moreover, was the view of Ansell. Yet Tilliard's view had a good deal in it. One might do worse than to follow Tilliard, and suppose the cow not to be there unless oneself was there to see her. A cowless world, then, stretched round him on every side. Yet he had only to peep into a field, and, click! it would at once become radiant with bovine life.

Suddenly he realized that this, again, would never do. As usual, he had missed the whole point, and was overlaying philosophy with gross and senseless details. For if the cow was not there, the world and the fields were not there either. And what would Ansell care about sunlit flanks or impassable streams? Rickie rebuked his own grovelling soul, and turned his eyes away from the night, which had led him to such absurd conclusions.

The fire was dancing, and the shadow of Ansell, who stood close up to it, seemed to dominate the little room. He was still talking, or rather jerking, and he was still lighting matches and dropping their ends upon the carpet. Now and then he would make a motion with his feet as if he were running quickly backward upstairs, and he would tread on the edge of the fender, so that the fire irons went flying and the buttered-bun dishes crashed against each other on the hearth. The other philosophers were crouched in odd shapes on the sofa and table and chairs, and one, who was a little bored, had crawled to the piano and was timidly trying the Prelude to Rhine-gold with his knee upon the soft pedal. The air was heavy with good tobacco smoke and the pleasant warmth of tea, and as Rickie became more sleepy the events of the day seemed to float one by one before his acquiescent eyes. In the morning he had read Theocritus, whom he believed to be the greatest of Greek poets; he had lunched with a merry don and had tasted Zwieback biscuits; then he had walked with people he liked, and had walked just long enough; and now his room was full of other people whom he liked, and when they left he would go and have supper with Ansell, whom he liked as well as any one. A year ago he had known none of these joys. He had crept cold and friendless and ignorant out of a great public school, preparing for a silent and solitary journey, and praying as a highest favor that he might be left alone. Cambridge had not answered his prayer. She had taken and soothed him, and warmed him, and had laughed at him a little, saying that he must not be so tragic yet awhile, for his boyhood had been but a dusty corridor that led to the spacious halls of youth. In one year he had made many friends and learnt much, and he might learn even more if he could but concentrate his attention on that cow. . . .

### SUGGESTIONS FOR WRITING

1. E. M. Forster, born in 1879 in England, is an Honorary Fellow of King's College, Cambridge. He is a well-known novelist and literary critic. This story is not concerned with the difficulty of proving the existence of things but with movement from boyhood to young manhood, from "a dusty corridor" to "the spacious halls of youth." The question of the cow's existence simply marks a signpost on Rickie's road to growing up. Can you recall a similar signpost in your life? Describe it.

2. Does anything exist? Write a conclusion to the debate begun in the story.

3. Forster also reveals the difficulty a young person has in fixing his mind on a deep philosophical problem. What would you say is the basis of this difficulty?

4. Forster's use of figurative language (the spacious halls of youth) recalls the use of the same metaphor elsewhere. The Bible (John, XIV, 1): "In my Father's house are many mansions." Henry James' Preface to *The Portrait of A Lady*, 1907: "The house of fiction, in short, has not one window, but a million." Using the idea of rooms and houses, develop four or five analogies about growing up and living a full life. Use Forster as a model when you develop your analogies.

CARL VAN DOREN

# University*

From September 1903, when I entered Illinois as a freshman, to June 1911, when I took the degree of doctor of philosophy at Columbia, and then for five years more as a teacher at Columbia, I was in the University as I might have been in the Army or the Navy. While there appear to be many universities in the United States,

* From *Three Worlds* by Carl Van Doren (New York: The Viking Press, Inc., 1936). Copyright 1936 by Carl Van Doren. Reprinted by permission of the publishers.

they are in a sense all one, more or less distinct parts of a uniform system. The students who stream through them, the raw materials of the university process, furnish the spectacle. Behind that goes on the tranquil life of the permanent communities. I have often wondered why no novelist has realized that he could find as much comedy in American universities as Trollope found in his English cathedrals.

It did not occur to me, at eighteen, that the University of Illinois was only twice as old as I. Ivy already covered the buildings which rose out of smooth lawns among quiet trees. The University had been there as far back as I could remember, and I did not look farther. Antiquity is relative. If this had been Harvard or Paris I should now and then have thought of its past, as I later did at Columbia and Oxford, but it would not have touched my present very deeply. Illinois had a past which was long enough to have given the community a set of customs by which teachers and students lived. That was enough for the present. New students accepted these young customs as quickly as if they had been ages old.

Living at home, I was never absorbed in the life of the University, at least of the undergraduates. If anything absorbed me, for the first few months, it was athletics. The gymnasium rather than my fraternity was my club. Then, random in the library, I discovered Marlowe, and the glory of great verse changed my world as if mountains had sprung up out of the prairie.

All that was aching and inarticulate in me seemed to find a voice in him. Here was a poet who did not make me feel that he was older and wiser than I, only that he had words of light and fire for my cloudy thoughts and smoky feelings. I followed the course of his dramas almost without noticing what happened or what his characters were like, hearing his words as so much music. It was really an ear I found in him, not a voice. I wrote no plays in verse, nor wanted to. But I began to read poetry, and for three or four years I suppose I read as much of it as any boy alive. If there had then been better living poets I should have read them. I read George Santayana and William Butler Yeats. I know the *Shropshire Lad* by heart. I remember the stir that Theodore Roosevelt made over Edwin Arlington Robinson. But most of the poets I read were dead poets, moving for me in a past above time and not subject to it. I hardly thought of them as living in any special day or place. They existed for me, my landscape, my melodious winds. Their rhythms beat continually in my responsive pulse.

My desire to be a poet was partly a desire to belong to the company of poets, like D'Artagnan's to belong to the Musketeers. Desire alone cannot make a poet. I had an exact ear and an exacting taste, and I always knew that the poems I wrote were not good enough. I was so jealous for the honor of poets that I would let no mediocre poet come among them, even myself. But I went on hoping for a miracle, hoping that the poetic excitement which sometimes visited me, fitfully, briefly, would sooner or later stay till it had mastered me and freed me. I cast myself in the rôle of poet, and privately wore the uniform. Meanwhile I read not only poetry but also the lives of poets with a curiosity so intense and tireless that I was, so far as this would take me, a scholar before I knew it.

The black melancholy of young men has many apparent causes, but the many are really one: that the young men wish and will more than they can do. Outwardly I had little, as an undergraduate, to complain about. At the first meeting of the freshmen, held stealthily under a hedge out of reach of the sophomores, I was chosen captain of the color rush. I was asked at once to join a fraternity. My earliest contributions to the literary monthly were accepted, and I soon became assistant editor and then editor. Indifferent to academic standing, I yet won preliminary, final, and special honors. In my last year I was president of the honorary senior society, and at commencement I was class poet. Though I had less money in my pocket than I could have used, I had as much as I needed. I was two or three times in love, not once in vain. My visible life must have looked like a cheerful success. Inwardly I was often as dejected as if I had the most valid reasons. Reading great poets, I walked day and night in the shadow of excellence. My will demanded that I be excellent too. Because I could not be, I furiously scourged myself, arrogant ambition tormenting sensitive flesh and blood.

Though I knew everybody and went everywhere, I was self-conscious and self-centered. I opened myself to none of my new friends. Even to my one close friend, Glen Mullin, whom I had met in high school and who I now found was determined to be a painter, I was never quite outspoken. But he was a reader too, particularly of Blake and Rabelais, and the two of us were a small society, forever talking, insatiable and inexhaustible. He made drawings for the magazine which I edited and for which I wrote—once the entire issue under several names—poems, stories, essays, translations. With him I was oblivious of the rest of the University. I did not think about how much its schools of engineering and agriculture were doing to civilize the state, so recently frontier and prairie. I barely realized how many students came from how far, from China and India, to study farming in Urbana. One foreign student I had been told was the son of a renowned poet, but I did not know the name of Rabindranath Tagore.

On the whole I was self-taught in a university which gave me leisure and excuse to read. At the end of five years at Illinois I knew most of the Greek and Latin writers, at least the poets, in translation, a good many French and German and a few Italian and Spanish in the original, some Scandinavian and Russian, and so nearly all the English and American that I think I have never since heard of one with whose name and qualities I was not more or less familiar. I read Middle and Old English, and even wrote verses in Anglo-Saxon. Though while still in Urbana I translated Hebbel's *Judith,* I was not a linguist. (Now when I have to speak German or French I do it badly.) Reading in a foreign language seemed to me like making love in mittens. I read as a passionate experience or not at all, and I never then, or later, read the whole of a book that bored me. But I was hard to bore, I read fast, I could get quickly at what I wanted, and at twenty-one I was as much at home in a library as on a farm.

Except for my desire to be with poets I had no motive in my reading. It was simple instinct, like hunger or love. Curiosity is a major instinct, and it can drive men to endure hunger or put love aside. My curiosity was about the life stories of the men and women whom I met in history or fiction. Inquisitive as a village gossip, feverish as an eavesdropper, I watched and studied all the ins and outs of their secret minds. I sometimes identified, always compared, myself with them. Levin in *Anna Karenina* was the man with whom I felt most in common, though I was not religious. Reading Havelock Ellis on the psychology of sex, I was troubled at the number of dark impulses with which, out of so little experience, I seemed to have so much acquaintance. Flutters of recognition ran along my nerves, healthy and fastidious as I was. Few life stories bewildered me. My curiosity was too large for me to be surprised or intolerant. I accepted all I learned as evidence that the world was as rich as I demanded.

If I became something of a scholar while living a passion, it was because I effortlessly and minutely remembered whatever I had read that interested me. Scholarship itself was not an end, and as an undergraduate I never thought about it. The nearest I came to thinking about it was in the feeling I arrived at in the year when I had Evarts Greene as my teacher in American history. His tall shyness touched me. A kind of courtliness—I can think of no other word—in his intellect moved me. Seeing and admiring the conscience with which he hunted for the truth and the justice with which he tried to make it clear, I felt that I had been helter-skelter and sluttish. Exactness in learning, I told myself, was as satisfying as in verse. Scrupulous truth was beautiful, careless error was ugly. Ugly and dirty. I told myself that it would be cheap and mean ever to pretend to know anything I was not sure of, or not to know anything I had had chance or reason to find out.

SUGGESTIONS FOR WRITING

1. Carl Van Doren (1885-1950) details a portion of his autobiography in this essay. If you wish to learn more about this sensitive and intelligent American, read his *Three Worlds*. In 1939 he won the Pulitzer Prize for his biography of Benjamin Franklin, and he earned several other honors in his lifetime. His "intense and tireless curiosity" are apparent in this essay. Study the method he uses to make the reader understand the life of a boy in college. Follow the method in an autobiographical narrative.

2. Van Doren speaks of the "tranquil life of the permanent communities" which make up the American university. Write a description of the life of someone in that "permanent community" who does not have daily contact with students. Imagine what the university must seem like to someone who is not a student or a professor.

3. Who was Christopher Marlowe? Read his life in the *Dictionary of National Biography* or the *Encyclopedia Britannica* and explain why a person like Van Doren would say: "All that was aching and inarticulate in me seemed to find a voice in him."

4. Van Doren read "not only poetry but also the lives of poets with a curiosity so intense and tireless that I was, so far as this would take

me, a scholar before I knew it." How does Van Doren's "scholar" compare with Emerson's?

5. Van Doren says, "On the whole I was self-taught in a university that gave me leisure and excuse to read." What does he mean by self-taught? Is there a special area in which you are self-taught? Explain.

EDWARD T. HALL

# Learning to Learn*

Learning really came into its own as an adaptive mechanism when it could be *extended in time and space by means of language.* A fawn can learn about men with guns by the reaction of its mother when a man with a gun appears, but there is no possible way, lacking language, for that fawn to be forewarned in the absence of an actual demonstration. Animals have no way of symbolically storing their learning against future needs.

Psychologists of late have been preoccupied with learning theory, and one anthropologist, John Gillin, has worked learning theory into his text on anthropology. What complicates matters, however, is that people reared in different cultures *learn to learn* differently. Some do so by memory and rote without reference to "logic" as we think of it, while some learn by demonstration but without the teacher requiring the student to do anything himself while "learning." Some cultures, like the American, stress doing as a principle of learning, while others have very little of the pragmatic. The Japanese even guide the hand of the pupil, while our teachers usually aren't permitted to touch the other person. Education and educational systems are about as laden with emotion and as characteristic of a given culture as its language. It should not come as a surprise that we encounter real opposition to our educational system when we make attempts to transfer it overseas.

Learning to learn differently is something that has to be faced every day by people who go overseas and try to train in local personnel. It seems inconceivable to the average person brought up in one

* From *The Silent Language* by Edward T. Hall (New York: Doubleday & Co., Inc., 1959). © 1959 by Edward T. Hall. Reprinted by permission of the publishers.

culture that something as basic as this could be done any differently from the way they themselves were taught. The fact is, however, that once people have learned to learn in a given way, it is extremely hard for them to learn in any other way.

The rest of culture reflects the way one learns, since culture is "learned and shared behavior." Learning, then, is one of the basic activities of life, and educators might have a better grasp of their art if they would take a leaf out of the book of the early pioneers in descriptive linguistics and learn about their subject by studying how other people learn. Men like Sapir revolutionized linguistic theory and ultimately language-teaching methods as the direct consequence of their having to deal with problems that arose from studying the "primitive" languages. The so-called "army method" of World War II was deeply influenced by anthropologically trained linguistic scientists. So was the current State Department language program.

The educator has much to learn about his own systems of learning by immersing himself in those that are so different that they raise questions that have never been raised before. Americans in particular have too long assumed that the U.S. educational system represents the ultimate in evolution and that other systems are less advanced than our own. Even the highly elaborated and beautifully adapted educational techniques of Japan have been looked down upon. Just why we feel so complacent and smug can be explained only by the blindness that culture imposes on its members. Certainly there is very little reason for complacency when one looks, not at others, but at ourselves. The fact that so many of our children dislike school or finish their schooling uneducated suggests that we still have much to learn about learning as a process.

As one watches one's own children grow up and learn, one reflects upon the vital role of learning as an agent of culture, to say nothing of its strategic place in the mechanism of survival. Any child, from the time it is four or five, absorbs what goes on around him at a rate which is never equaled again in his lifetime. At six to ten, children are still going strong, provided that the educational system hasn't produced blocks to learning.

Yet the schools are not the only agents responsible for education. Parents and older people in general play a part. Having learned to learn in a particular fashion, adults can communicate their prejudices or convictions in a variety of subtle and often not so subtle ways. Here is an example of this which has been experienced in one way or another by almost everyone who shares in our culture.

This story begins when a great-grandmother visits her three-year-old great-granddaughter. The child, like most three-year-olds, is toddling around and absorbing everything that's going on. Apart from eating and sleeping, one of her main concerns is to gain control of the communications taking place around her in order to be able to interact with others on their own terms. Great-grandmother watches this. Something in what she sees makes her anxious. She sits still for a moment and suddenly blurts out without warning and in a disapproving tone of voice, "Look at the little copycat. Louise, stop that! Don't be such a copycat." By withholding approval the great-grandmother was demonstrating one of the principal ways in which learning is directed away from conscious imitation, which she obviously disapproves. Children, of course, are exceedingly sensitive to this process.

In order to serve mankind, learning, like sex, cannot run wild but has to be channeled and at times directed. There is much to learn of the details of how this process works in different cultures, and it is just barely possible that by studying others we Americans, who pride ourselves on our efficiency, might actually learn things that would help us to break our educational log jam. Our current approach to the teaching of reading is one of the many obvious defects in American pedagogy. It is a symptom that something is wrong with our way of teaching. Instead of being rewarding for the child, learning has often become painful and difficult.

On Truk, the atoll in the Southwest Pacific, children are permitted to reach the age of nine or ten before anyone begins to get technical with them about what they are supposed to know. As the Trukese phrase it, "He doesn't know yet, he is only a child." Americans tend to correct children rather impatiently. With us, learning is supposed to be endowed with a certain amount of pressure so that the person who learns fast is valued over the one who learns slowly. Some cultures seem to place less emphasis on speed and perhaps a little more on learning correctly. On the other hand, the current educational mode in the United States is to tell the child to guess if he doesn't know the meaning of a word. Not very good training for future scientists.

Americans like to think that children must "understand" what they have learned. What happens, of course, is that a good deal of material that would be simple enough to learn without frills is made more difficult by the complex, and often erroneous, explanations that go with it. Somehow the fetish of explanation and logic as a process does not seem to weigh down the Arab or the Japanese, yet both have made singular contributions to the world of science.

How people learn to learn differently will continue to be an area of investigation for some time to come. As it now stands, however, these differences represent one of the barriers that have to be overcome each time two people raised in different cultures interact over any but the shortest period of time. The American will say, "Why can't the South Americans learn to be on time?" or "Why can't the Thai learn to boil the water for the ice cubes?" The answer, of course, is because no one taught them in a way which was consistent with how they learned everything else in life.

### SUGGESTIONS FOR WRITING

1. Edward T. Hall (1918-    ), is an anthropologist and scientist who studied under America's master anthropologist, the late Ralph Linton of Columbia University. He does not use the style of the academic anthropologist—though he lapses into it occasionally—but the style of someone trying to "popularize" his subject. One characteristic of such style is lack of qualification. Find evidence of this characteristic in the above essay.

2. Because some children dislike school, does it follow that our national system of learning is at fault? If so, how should the fault be corrected? If not, what *is* at fault?

3. What does Hall mean by "the fetish of explanation and logic as a process" as these pertain to our learning system?

4. In his final sentence, Hall implies that one must be taught in a way that is consistent with the way he learned everything else in life. Are you aware of a consistent method of teaching in your own formal and informal education? Characterize the method. Can you change methods of formal education without changing informal learning at home and elsewhere? Counts, in a previous essay, implies that modern despotisms

have tried to alter informal education. Can a democracy do this? If so, in what way can informal education be altered?

JOHN MILTON

## On Arriving at the Age of Twenty-three

How soon hath Time, the subtle thief of youth,
Stolen on his wing my three and twentieth year!
My hasting days fly on with full career,
But my late spring no bud or blossom shew'th.
Perhaps my semblance might deceive the truth,
That I to manhood am arrived so near;
And inward ripeness doth much less appear,
That some more timely-happy spirits endu'th.
Yet be it less or more, or soon or slow,
It shall be still in strictest measure even
To that same lot, however mean or high,
Toward which Time leads me, and the will of Heaven;
All is, if I have grace to use it so,
As ever in my great Task-Master's eye.

ROBERT HERRICK

## To the Virgins to Make Much of Time

Gather ye rose-buds while ye may,
   Old Time is still a-flying:
And this same flower that smiles today,
   Tomorrow will be dying.

The glorious lamp of heaven, the Sun,
   The higher he's a-getting
The sooner will his race be run,
   And nearer he's to setting.

That age is best which is the first,
   When youth and blood are warmer;

But being spent, the worse and worst
Times, still succeed the former.

Then be not coy, but use your time;
And while ye may, go marry:
For having lost but once your prime,
You may for ever tarry.

## SUGGESTIONS FOR WRITING

1. John Milton (1608-1674), famous English poet whose best known work is *Paradise Lost* (1667), writes in the above poem about the regret he feels upon "losing" his youth, a regret which may be shared by other college students. The poem is a sonnet (14 lines) in iambic pentameter (five stressed syllables per line) with a special rhyme scheme (*abba, abba, cde, dce*). Such a form imposes rigid patterns on the poet. Yet within it Milton has been able to express his meaning perfectly. A prose version of his thought might read: "I have become twenty-three too quickly. The days pass but I see no sign of maturity. Perhaps I look older than I feel, or perhaps I am mature and am not aware of it. In any case, Time and the Will of Heaven will determine the pace of my life." Compare the prose and poetry and comment on poetry as memorable and forceful expression.

2. Explain: hasting days, my semblance, timely-happy spirits, endu'th, great Task-Master's eye?

3. "Time, the subtle thief of youth" is an example of figurative language. The appropriateness of "subtle thief" to the theme is noteworthy. Why? Devise several other metaphors beginning, "Time is . . ."

4. Write of a time when a particular experience made you regret a not-to-be-recaptured joy of youth.

5. Robert Herrick (1591-1674) is best known for his *Hesperides* (1648), a collection of some 1,200 poems. In the above poem Herrick advises young people to make the most of their youth. Is it true that after a certain point in life one passes the "best" of his living? Are there no joys of middle age comparable to the joys of youth? Write an essay expressing your views on these questions.

6. Make a prose paraphrase of these poems and then create a situation in which two college friends discuss their youth. Use the poets' arguments as parts of the dialogue.

*Part Two*

# THE NATURE
# OF MAN

# The Experience of Childhood

Of all people children are the most imaginative. They abandon themselves without reserve to every illusion. No man, whatever his sensibility may be, is ever affected by Hamlet or Lear as a little girl is affected by the story of poor little Red Riding Hood.
—J. B. Macaulay, *Milton,* 1825

If parents would only realize how they bore their children.
—George Bernard Shaw, *Misalliance,* 1914

Children begin by loving their parents; as they grow older they judge them; sometimes they forgive them.
—Oscar Wilde, *The Picture of Dorian Gray,* 1891

You send your child to the schoolmaster, but 'tis the schoolboys who educate him.
—Emerson, *The Conduct of Life,* 1860

A boy is an appetite with a skin pulled over it.
—Author unknown.

A boy's love is water in a basket.
—Spanish proverb

There are many loving parents in the world, but no loving children.
—Chinese proverb

Suffer the little children to come unto me, and forbid them not; for of such is the kingdom of God.
—Mark X, 14

WALT WHITMAN

# There Was a Child Went Forth*

There was a child went forth every day,
And the first object he look'd upon, that object he became,
And that object became part of him for the day or a certain part of the day,
Or for many years or stretching cycles of years.

The early lilacs became part of this child,
And grass and white and red morning-glories and white and red clover,
    and the song of the phoebe-bird,
And the Third-month lambs and the sow's pink-faint litter, and the mare's
    foal and the cow's calf,
And the noisy brood of the barnyard or by the mire of the pond-side,
And the fish suspending themselves so curiously below there, and the
    beautiful curious liquid,
And the water-plants with their graceful flat heads, all became part of him.

The field-sprouts of Fouth-month and Fifth-month became part of him,
Winter-grain sprouts and those of the light-yellow corn, and the esculent
    roots of the garden,
And the apple-trees cover'd with blossoms and the fruit afterward, and
    woodberries, and the commonest weeds by the road,
And the old drunkard staggering home from the outhouse of the tavern
    whence he had lately risen,
And the schoolmistress that pass'd, and the quarrelsome boys,
And the tidy and fresh-cheek'd girls, and the barefoot negro boy and girl,
And all the changes of city and country wherever he went.
His own parents, he that had father'd him, and she that had conceiv'd him
    in her womb, and birth'd him,
They gave this child more of themselves than that,
They gave him afterward every day, they became part of him.

---

* From *Leaves of Grass*, 1871.

The mother at home quietly placing the dishes on the supper-table,
The mother with mild words, clean her cap and gown, a wholesome odor falling off her person and clothes as she walks by,
The father, strong, self-sufficient, manly, mean, anger'd, unjust,
The blow, the quick loud word, the tight bargain, the crafty lure.
The family usages, the language, the company, the furniture, the yearning and swelling heart,
Affection that will not be gainsay'd, the sense of what is real, the thought if after all it should prove unreal,
The doubts of day-time and the doubts of night-time, the curious whether and how,
Whether that which appears so is so, or is it all flashes and specks?
Men and women crowding fast in the streets, if they are not flashes and specks, what are they?
The streets themselves and the façades of houses, and goods in the windows,
Vehicles, teams, the heavy-plank'd wharves, the huge crossing at the ferries,
The village on the highland seen from afar at sunset, the river between,
Shadows, aureola and mist, the light falling on roofs and gables of white or brown two miles off,
The schooner near by sleepily dropping down the tide, the little boat slacktow'd astern,
The hurrying tumbling waves, quick-broken crests, slapping,
The strata of color'd clouds, the long bar of maroon-tint away solitary by itself, the spread of purity it lies motionless in,
The horizon's edge, the flying sea-crow, the fragrance of salt marsh and shore mud,
These became part of that child who then went forth every day, and who now goes, and will always go forth every day.


SUGGESTIONS FOR WRITING


1. Walt Whitman (1819-1892) is one of the best—and most controversial—American poets. Whitman lists and lists and lists. The thesis of the poem is stated in the first two lines, "There was a child went forth every day/And the first object he look'd upon, that object he became." All else is a simple listing. Or is it? What do you think?

2. You were once a child that went forth. What were the objects you looked upon that made you the person you are?

3. The vocabulary here is relatively unpoetic. "Third-month" is the Quaker form of the name of March—it is not a poetic name. What is the meaning of: esculent, façades, strata, aureola?

4. What is the difference between prose and poetry? Type the first two stanzas in paragraph form so that they look like prose. There is no

rhyme, no conventional meter or stanza, no use of elaborate poetic figures. Yet, this is poetry. Why?

5. What does Whitman mean by the final phrase, "will go forth every day"?

6. Walt Whitman "knew" of the experiences in the poem. Could a child have sufficient introspection to "know" these experiences? Construct an imaginative experience of a child, pointing out (in paragraphs which alternate between description of experiences and comments on the meaning of those experiences) what really happens to a child who is developing into a rational human being.

WILLIAM WORDSWORTH

# Heaven Lies About Us in Our Infancy*

Our birth is but a sleep and a forgetting:
The Soul that rises with us, our life's Star,
    Hath had elsewhere its setting
      And cometh from afar:
      Not in entire forgetfulness,
      And not in utter nakedness,
But trailing clouds of glory do we come
    From God, who is our home:
Heaven lies about us in our infancy!
Shades of the prison-house begin to close
    Upon the growing Boy,
But he beholds the light, and whence it flows
    He sees it in his joy;
The Youth, who daily farther from the east
    Must travel, still is Nature's priest,
      And by the vision splendid
Is on his way attended;
At length the Man perceives it die away,
And fade into the light of common day.

SUGGESTIONS FOR WRITING

1. William Wordsworth (1770-1850) wrote the "Ode on Intimations of Immortality from Recollections of Early Childhood" in 1803; in 1856

* From *Ode on Intimations of Immortality from Recollections of Early Childhood, 1807.*

Ralph Waldo Emerson called it the "high water mark which the intellect has reached in this age." The poem as a whole bears a close allegiance to the theory of the soul expounded by Socrates in Plato's *Phaedo* (399 B.C.). Socrates says that if beauty and good and other ideas exist, and if we refer all the objects of sensible perception to these ideas (if we relate all things we sense to abstract concepts of beauty, good, and so forth), then just as these abstract concepts exist, so must the soul exist (and must have existed before we were born). Therefore, if our souls did exist before we were born, they existed apart from our bodies possessing intelligence before they came into man's shape.

If you wish to further investigate the *Phaedo,* I refer you to pages 76 and 77 of the Stephanus edition of Plato (Paris, 1578). Most modern editions carry the pagination of the 1578 edition in the margin of the text. A readily available modern edition of the *Phaedo* was published by the Liberal Arts Press in New York in 1950.

2. Are there absolutes—concepts of beauty, truth, goodness, justice, and so forth—beyond which there is nothing else?

3. Does the soul exist as an absolute?

4. Are children born morally innocent?


JEAN JACQUES ROUSSEAU

# Childhood Cruelty*

One day I was learning my lesson by myself in the room next to the kitchen. The servant had put Mademoiselle Lambercier's combs in front of the fireplace to dry. When she came back to fetch them, she found one with a whole row of teeth broken. Who was to blame for the damage? No one except myself had entered the room. On being questioned, I denied that I had touched the comb. M. and Mademoiselle Lambercier both began to admonish, to press, and to threaten me; I obstinately persisted in my denial; but the evidence was too strong, and outweighed all my protestations, although it was the first time that I had been found to lie so boldly. The matter was regarded as serious, as in fact it deserved to be. The mischievousness, the falsehood, the obstinacy appeared equally deserving of punishment; but this time it was not by Mademoiselle

---

* From Book I of *Confessions* by Jean Jacques Rousseau, 1783.

Lambercier that chastisement was inflicted. My uncle Bernard was written to and he came. My poor cousin was accused of another equally grave offence; we were involved in the same punishment. It was terrible. Had they wished to look for the remedy in the evil itself and to deaden forever my depraved senses, they could not have set to work better, and for a long time my senses left me undisturbed.

They could not draw from me the desired confession. Although I was several times brought up before them and reduced to a pitiable condition, I remained unshaken. I would have endured death, and made up my mind to do so. Force was obliged to yield to the diabolical obstinacy of a child—as they called my firmness. At last I emerged from this cruel trial, utterly broken, but triumphant.

It is now nearly fifty years since this incident took place, and I have no fear of being punished again for the same thing. Well, then, I declare in the sight of heaven that I was innocent of the offence, that I neither broke nor touched the comb, that I never went near the fireplace, and had never even thought of doing so. It would be useless to ask me how the damage was done; I do not know, and I cannot understand; all that I know for certain is, that I had nothing to do with it.

Imagine a child, shy and obedient in ordinary life, but fiery, proud, and unruly in his passions: a child who had always been led by the voice of reason and always treated with gentleness, justice, and consideration, who had not even a notion of injustice, and who for the first time becomes acquainted with so terrible an example of it on the part of the very people whom he most loves and respects! What an upset of ideas! what a disturbance of feelings! what revolution in his heart, in his brain, in the whole of his little intellectual and moral being! Imagine all this, I say, if possible. As for myself, I feel incapable of disentangling and following up the least trace of what then took place within me.

I had not sense enough to feel how much appearances were against me, and to put myself in the place of the others. I kept to my own place, and all that I felt was the harshness of a frightful punishment for an offence which I had not committed. The bodily pain, although severe, I felt but little; all I felt was indignation, rage, despair. My cousin, whose case was almost the same, and who had been punished for an involuntary mistake as if it had been a premeditated act, following my example, flew into a rage, and worked himself up to the same pitch of excitement as myself. Both in the same bed, we embraced each other with convulsive transports: we felt suffocated; and when at length our young hearts, somewhat relieved, were able to vent their wrath, we sat upright in bed and began to shout, times without number, with all our might: Carnifex! carnifex! carnifex!*

While I write these words, I feel that my pulse beats faster; those moments will always be present to me though I should live a hundred thousand years. That first feeling of violence and injustice has remained so deeply graven on my soul, that all the ideas connected with it bring back to me my first emotion; and this feeling, which, in its origin, had reference only to myself, has become so strong in itself and so completely detached from all personal interest, that, when I see or hear of any act of injustice—whoever is the victim of it, and wherever it is committed—my heart kindles with rage, as if the effect of it recoiled upon myself. When I read of the cruelties of a ferocious tyrant, the crafty atrocities of a rascally priest, I would gladly set out to plunge a dagger into the heart of such wretches, although I had to die for it a hundred times. I have often put myself in a perspiration, pursuing or stoning a cock, a cow, a dog, or any animal which I saw tormenting another merely because it felt itself the stronger. This impulse may be natural to me, and I believe that it is; but the profound impression left upon me by the first injustice I suffered was too long and too strongly connected with it, not to have greatly strengthened it.

With the above incident the tranquillity of my childish life was over. From that moment I ceased to enjoy a pure happiness, and even at the present day I feel that the recollection of the charms of my childhood ceases there.

SUGGESTIONS FOR WRITING

1. Rousseau (1712-1778) published his *Confessions* anonymously in 1783. He began the book with these words: "I am commencing an undertaking, hitherto without precedent, and which will never find an imitator. I desire to set before my fellows the likeness of a man in all the

---

* Carnifex is a public executioner of ancient Rome.

truth of nature, and that man myself." What "truth of nature" is revealed here?

2. Recreate the scene where Rousseau was brought before his uncle and "reduced to a pitiable condition." Reveal the tragedy.

3. Write of a time when you were unjustly accused as a child. Reveal the injustice of the act and the hopelessness of your situation.

4. Rousseau tells the story from the point of view of the child, or at least the man reflecting on his own childhood. Take the side of his guardians. How were they to judge his innocence when all the evidence pointed to his guilt? If you were his guardian, how would you test for truth?

5. The outline of Rousseau's statement is as follows: (1) some mischief happened; (2) I was accused and punished; (3) I was innocent; (4) my feelings about justice changed; (5) I could not see the opposite point of view; (6) the emotion I felt then has led me to support the weak against the strong; (7) the incident ended the "purity" of my childhood. Use a similar seven-item frame to tell of your own childhood.

LEIF PANDURO

# Adults Talk Too Much*

Do you know what's the matter with adults? They talk too much. Particularly, they talk too much about how they'd like to understand you when, as a matter of fact, they don't understand a damn thing. They'd never know what you were talking about if you told them how you felt way down deep inside, because they always regard you as an enemy. And all that about not having to do anything except speak up is pure crap. It's a snare, is what I mean to say. They tempt you, and if you take them at their word there's hell to pay. It's probably because it's been too long since they were young for them to remember how anyone feels when he's eighteen.

You can't tell them that it's just that you're against things in general. You can't tell them that what they're saying doesn't mean a damn thing to you because you look at things in a different way and that things mean something else to you *personally*. Probably it isn't very clever or smart to be that way, but anyhow that's the

---

* From *Kick Me in the Traditions* by Leif Panduro (New York: Paul S. Eriksson, Inc., 1960). © 1960 by Leif Panduro. Reprinted by permission of the publishers.

way it is. You don't always use common sense when you think, even though they're always drilling it into you that common sense is absolutely the only thing.

Every single second has seventeen million possibilities but we make use of only one—never more than one. It's enough to give you apoplexy.

"Are you paying attention?" old Jacob said a little later.

"Yes," I said.

"Because it's very important that you understand it thoroughly!" It was very important to him.

Of course, it was very wrong of me to kick old Jacob in the rump, but I must say in defense of myself that I didn't kick him very hard and that I didn't do it until he began again to give me all that stuff about how important it was for me to understand him. Then I knew that we never would get to understand each other. Not by means of words, at any rate. Well then, there he stood in front of me in the summerhouse and talked and talked. And when he was through he turned to go. The bell rang for the next class, and he asked me over his shoulder if I understood everything now.

"Sure," I said, and let him have one right in the ass.

At first he stood still for a few seconds, as if he were inviting me to do it again because he couldn't believe I had done it once. Then he turned around and looked at me for a long time.

"Did you kick me?" he said.

"I guess I did," I said.

"Yes—I guess you did," he said quietly, thinking it over. "It's so strange. Why did you do it?"

"Don't know," I said.

Suddenly he flared up. "I could tell the rector," he said.

There was a big lump in my throat.

"I could, you know," he said. "And you'd be expelled."

"Yes," I said.

"If only I could understand why you did it," he said biting his lip with one of his discolored front teeth. He started in again about how he wished I'd tell him why I had done what I did, but then he gave it up. Maybe he was afraid I might kick him again.

He didn't say anything to Brøns. It was just as well he didn't, because Brøns certainly would have had me on the carpet for an hour to find out why I'd done it. And it would have been very complicated explaining that I'd done it because I'm really very fond of old Jacob.

Adults don't understand things like that. For them everything is so simple.

The trouble with my legs got worse and worse. And then the day we were to have the big reunion with the alumni drew near. . . .

I've always been a good runner, you know, and I was picked to be third man in the relay race. I thought that getting into the race would calm down my legs for a while, but it didn't work out that way at all.

The baton that's used in a relay race is really nothing but a little stick. The first man on each team starts with the stick in his hand and runs like hell for a hundred yards and then passes it to the number two man, and so on. The important thing is for both of you to be in step with each other, otherwise you'll lose several yards. In training for the race, we had practiced very carefully how to pass the stick.

I was number three on the team and Hubert was number four. The number four man should really be the best on the team, partly because he should be able to hold a lead if his team is ahead and partly because he should catch up with the other runner if it isn't.

But Hubert wasn't very good in either of these respects. To tell you the truth, he wasn't much of a runner at all. I guess I've told you how uneasy he makes people because of the way he looks— how you feel sorry for him and are afraid to hurt his feelings. Well, he takes advantage of that quite a lot. You see through it easily enough but you don't have the heart to do anything about it. It's really a pretty crummy situation.

Then too, he's always talking about what great things he can do and putting others in the shade. If you're racing him on an equal footing he either gets a pain in his groin or else loses a shoe. And then he rattles on and on, telling you what a wonderful runner he is. Finally, after he's told you six thousand times you end up believing him. It's a damn good trick.

Well, when the baton was handed to me the old students' man was something like thirteen or fourteen yards ahead. I got hold of the stick all right. It felt smooth and cool, and I sprinted off. I pulled up even with him in the first fifty yards and as we came into the turn I went by him. Naturally, all the students shouted and cheered. Then, after rounding the turn, I stepped on the gas. There's something psychological about it, you know. When the alumni man began to creep up on me again I ran even faster and put ten, fifteen yards between us. That works every time—it's very demoralizing—and I left him far behind. Hubert stood waiting for me down at the last turn. From the expression on his face I knew he was thinking, "Sure, you've done pretty well, but now I'll show you how a relay race should be run." And then when he put his paw out to take the stick I wouldn't let go of it. He took one end of it, and I kept a good grip on the other.

"Give it to me, you jackass!" he groaned.

"Damned if I will," I said, and kept on running.

And then suddenly the whole field got very quiet. I heard the church clock strike three. A rooster crowed, and down at the station a train let off steam.

"Let go now!" Hubert screamed.

But nothing doing. It was as if my life depended on keeping hold of that stick. And then people all over the field began to laugh—they were having a ball. Hubert tugged and pulled at the baton, but I gave a quick, strong jerk and yanked it away from him, and then kept right on running around the track. I ran around it twenty times while the spectators howled and screamed. The old students just about killed themselves laughing.

Old Brøns tried to get me to think better of it. He ran out onto the track and followed me for a while, but he got so out of breath that he had an awfully hard time appealing to my better nature.

Finally, I ran over into the woods and buried the baton under a tree. And then I ran home again. The tournament was over. Only a few youngsters from the first middle-school form were kicking goals down at one end of the field.

I went and took a shower, and when I got back Hubert was standing in front of the mirror squeezing pimples.

"You stupid pig!" he said.

"What's wrong?" I said.

"You should have given the baton to me, you fool!"

"I don't give to beggars," I said. Quick as a flash.

"You went and ruined everything!" he said.

"And what did you think you were going to do with it?"

He primped himself carefully and gave me a very superior look.
"We've called a meeting," he said.
"Really?" I said. "I'm scared stiff."
"And suppose," he said, "you get your ass kicked?"
"I'm shivering with fright," I said.
"You're such a privileged monkey," he said. "You think you can get away with anything just because your mother has money."
There we were—back on that subject again.
"Be good enough to wipe your pimples off my mirror," I said. "They could be contagious."
That's the worst thing anyone could say to him. He got blue in the face and came toward me.
And then I kicked him. Pretty soon both of us were rolling around on the floor and pounding each other. I can't stand to touch him because he's always sort of sweaty. And he smells a little, too. I don't know how a whale smells when it's being boiled down, but I always imagine it to be more or less the way Hubert smells. He's very strong, by the way, and besides he's repressed. It's always hard to fight with people when they blow their tops. They have a lot of extra strength then.
"I hope you've had enough now."
Then the bell rang for afternoon tea, and we scowled at each other real hard and went downstairs. Brøns stood at the doorway and he said he wanted to talk to me later.
It was strangely quiet when I walked through the dining room. The younger fellows avoided my glance, but one of the old boys —he was pretty drunk—got up and said he thought they ought to give a cheer for the victor. The old fellows nearly raised the roof yelling.

SUGGESTIONS FOR WRITING

1. Leif Panduro is a Danish author whose work was unnoticed in this country until the 1960's. His *Kick Me in the Traditions,* 1960, from which this selection is taken, is a rare story of a Copenhagen boy who, although normal in most ways, gets down on all fours and bites people when he is angry. The adults in his life don't understand him, just as the uncle in Rousseau's story (p. 98), and the Older Generation in Swarthout's (p. 119) do not understand children. Many college students think their parents (and college professors) fail to understand *them.*

Few observers, however, are able to pinpoint the difficulty as well as Panduro. Explain why old Jacob got kicked in the traditions.

2. Tell of a time you were frustrated by an adult who just wouldn't understand.

3. This is the story of an eighteen-year-old who is reluctant to enter the adult world. He and the writer of the Lucky Henry theme in the Swarthout selection are unwilling to admit that the adult world is right. What happens to such people? Write a story of such a character at the age of thirty-eight.

4. What happens if the adult world is wrong? Suppose an eighteen-year-old mathematician in the year 2000 discovered that the adult world was wrong. Write an essay which describes his findings and the results of his discovery.

ROBERT PAUL SMITH

## The Natural Enemy of the Child *

On my block, when I was a kid, there was a lot of loose talk being carried on above our heads about how a father was supposed to be a pal to his boy. This was just another of those stupid things that grownups said. It was our theory that the grownup was the natural enemy of the child, and if any father had come around being a pal to us we would have figured he was either a little dotty or a spy. What we learned we learned from another kid. I don't remember being taught how to play mumbly-peg. . . . When you were a kid, you stood around while a covey of ancients of nine or ten played mumbly-peg, shifting from foot to foot and wiping your nose on your sleeve and hitching up your knickerbockers, saying, "Lemme do it, aw come on, lemme have a turn," until one of them struck you in a soft spot and you went home to sit under the porch by yourself or found a smaller kid to torture, or loused up your sister's rope skipping, or made a collection of small round stones. . . .

One day you said, "Lemme have a turn, lemme have a turn," and some soft-hearted older brother, never your own, said, "Go-

---

* From *Where Did You Go? Out. What Did You Do? Nothing.*, by Robert Paul Smith (New York: W. W. Norton & Company, 1957). © 1957 by Robert Paul Smith. Reprinted by permission of the publishers.

wan, let the kid have a turn," and there, by all that was holy, you were playing mumbly-peg.

Well now, I taught those kids to play mumbly-peg, and for all I know, if I hadn't happened to be around that day, in another fifteen years they would have to start protecting mumbly-peg play-ers . . . —but why don't the kids teach the other kids to play mumbly-peg? What do these kids do with themselves all the time?

\* \* \* \*

It is now time to talk about clothesline.

Clothesline was to my childhood what Scotch tape is to my kids. Clothesline was the universal matter. Clothesline was what, when you decided on any project, you had to find first, unless you were indoors, when what you had to find was a hairpin. This you found by finding your mother.

Clothesline was, for girls, skipping rope. It was used by boys for tying each other, and any girls handy, up. Sometimes this was done against the tyee's will, but almost as often it was done with permission. One of us had seen Houdini, all of us had read about him. We tied each other up to see how long it would take to get free. We tied up prisoners. From time to time, and now I cannot get inside that year's head, we tied each other up just for tying each other up. No game, no revenge, no torture, no acting out. Just tying up, as sometimes we ran around and screamed just for that itself.

Clothesline was used for fastening things together, for example, fastening two kids together, back to back, as above. It was used to harness a batch of little kids together for use as horses with a delivery wagon. It was used the same way with a sled, and some-times instead of little kids we used the patient collie who lived next door.

Clothesline was used, between the clothespoles in our backyard, as a tightrope. Call me a liar, but there was a time when we thought we could learn to walk a tightrope and we tried it, although despite our best efforts, what we did not learn to walk was a very slack clothesline. It was used as a high-jump standard, and the day one of us found a bamboo pole in the center of a rolled up rug, it was used as a pole-vault standard too. It was used as a climbing rope, for the ascent of garages, it was used as a belt, as a lasso (which we pronounced then "lassoo" and I learned later is really a lariat, which I still pronounce "larri*et*"), as a part of something we called bolas, a kind of Gaucho "lassoo."

This was made by tying a couple of rocks to both ends of a piece of clothesline. This assembly was whirled around the head and let go, and it wrapped itself around the clothespole, other kids, and one's own ankles with equal force and pain.

Clothesline was a sort of natural resource, found in abundance growing in backyards, and it was The Law that when it did not have clothes on it, it was borrowable. It was not permitted to cut it, however, and once it was necessary to cut it unless it was a very long clothesline and the loss would not show, you had to steal it. Then it was all right for belts and bolas. I just remembered a game of my early childhood, which was to run through the wash, and feel the damp and clean-smelling sheets against one's face. Do *that* with an electric drier! Along with clotheslines, sort of the fruit of this freely growing vine, were clothespins, for which we had a number of uses. In my town, they were the clothespins without springs: they could be made into dolls, they were good for digging, they made fine tent stakes, they could be turned into a sort of primitive pliers, and with the aid of a few strips of wood and a couple of nails, a toy in which two figures with little wooden hammers struck alternate blows. We thought of clothespins generally as just some-thing good to have a few of stashed away. They were very good-shaped things. Once in a great while we would encounter a spring clothespin: these were real treasures, and were carried clamped on the finger until incipient gangrene set in.

SUGGESTIONS FOR WRITING

1. Robert Paul Smith (1915-     ) is an American humorist and essayist. His book, *"Where Did You Go?" Out. "What Did You Do?" Nothing.* (1957), from which this selection was taken, contains the thesis that children no longer know how to entertain themselves. Television and other mechanized recreations have robbed them of learning how to amuse themselves. Do you agree? Elaborate.

2. For Smith, "clothesline was the universal matter." Was there any "universal matter" in your childhood? Describe its uses.

3. From the perspective of a generation of living, Smith remembers his childhood with nostalgia. He romanticizes. Most of us do. Specifically; in

what sentences, phrases, and words can his romantic attitude be detected?

4. Smith's humorous force comes from a wild exaggeration. In moderation this can be effective. Select an incident from your childhood which the present generation seems to have forgotten. Try for a humorous effect by using, in moderation, a little exaggeration.

5. A certain rhetorical effect comes from adding example upon example. In the first paragraph, the final sentence ends with four examples. ". . . and you went home (1) to sit under the porch by yourself or (2) found a smaller kid to torture, or (3) loused up your sister's rope skipping, or (4) made a collection of small round stones." Consider the difference in rhetorical effect if Smith had simply said, ". . . and you went home to do such a thing as sitting under the porch by yourself." Or if he had developed each of the four examples into a narrative and allotted a separate sentence to each. A similar rhetorical effect is achieved by Whitman in the poem which begins this section—the effect of adding example to example. If Smith's prose were put into lines of verse, would there be anything poetic about it?

THELMA JONES

# I'll Show 'Em*

In the fall of my first grade year, I had a new coat, a good one of gray chinchilla cloth. As the faculty children all marched down the hill, I boasted, "It cost eight dollars." I snuggled around luxuriously in the coat. It made me feel like a dear little pampered rich girl. One faculty child said, "It's a little large, though."

"Well, of course," I retorted. "It has to last me until it's too small, then Margaret gets it—eight dollars, after all, what did you think!"

At school that day, out on the bare clay playground, a big nice girl had laid the outline of a house with rows of bricks. She was being the mother and she had several first graders in the various rooms being her little daughters. It looked like a fine game. I, sure of myself in the expensive coat, walked in to join. The big girl jumped up. She towered over me. She had a beautiful brown fur piece and muff.

---

* From *Skinny Angel* by Thelma Jones (New York: McGraw-Hill Book Company, Inc., 1946). Copyright 1946 by McGraw-Hill Book Company, Inc. Reprinted by permission of the publishers.

"Get out," she said deliberately. "Turn right around and get out of my house. I don't want you. You aren't cute. Why don't you get a coat that fits? You look like a little Dutch girl in that coat."

I turned around, confused and unbelieving. The big girl called after me. "Your coat's so big you take three steps before it takes one." All her daughters whooped over this. The coat grew and grew. I felt it growing down over my hands, down to my feet, up over my head. I was a walking coat taking careful, slow steps out of the brick house.

"Little Dutch girl, little Dutch girl," the big girl's daughters mocked.

I thought everybody on the playground was looking at me. I did not know where to turn my hot eyes, or where to go. I walked up on the front porch of the school and boosted myself up on a window ledge there. "They'll be sorry," I whispered. "I'll be the World's Greatest and show 'em."

SUGGESTIONS FOR WRITING

1. Thelma Jones, the daughter of a college president in Nebraska in the 1920's wrote a book about her childhood days and called it *Skinny Angel* (1946). She recalls a time in her life when her father was earning eight hundred dollars a year (payable in script which could be redeemed at local stores at a 5 per cent discount). She was one of several children, and the coat she speaks of was tremendously important to her. The ridicule to which she was subjected altered her concept of people "in the outside world." The ridicule of children is a fruitful topic to develop because the use of exaggeration comes naturally. Use the Thelma Jones selection as a model and reveal a child being ridiculed by others.

2. Ridicule by children is quite different from ridicule by college students, which in turn is different from ridicule by adults. As a language exercise, set down several statements and reveal how each of the three age groups would use them for ridicule. Begin with the statement: The coat is too large.

3. Write of a time when you were ridiculed. Use the method employed by Thelma Jones: choose a specific instance, center on a specific object, use dialogue, and indicate your reaction to the ridicule.

# The Threshold of Adulthood

There must always be a struggle between a father and son, while one aims at power and the other at independence.
—Samuel Johnson, Boswell's *Life of Johnson*, 1791

Men are but grown-up boys after all.
—William Dean Howells, *Literature and Life*, 1902

It is a great pity that men and women forget that they have been children. Parents are apt to be foreigners to their sons and daughters. Maturity is the gate of Paradise which shuts behind us; and our memories are gradually weaned from the glories in which our nativity was cradled.
—George W. Curtis, *Prue and I*, 1856

Turn, turn, my wheel! 'Tis nature's plan
The child should grow into the man.
—Longfellow, *Kéramos*, 1878

When I was a child, I spake as a child, I understood as a child, I thought as a child: but when I became a man, I put away childish things.
—I Corinthians, XIII, 11

If you strike a child, take care that you strike it in anger, even at the risk of maiming it for life. A blow in cold blood neither can nor should be forgiven.
—George Bernard Shaw, *Maxims for Revolutionists*, 1903

"Ye know a lot about [raising children]," said Mr. Hennessy. "I do," said Mr. Dooley. "Not bein' an author, I'm a gr-reat critic."
—Finley Peter Dunne, *The Bringing Up of Children*, 1906

LORD CHESTERFIELD

# Letter to His Son

*London, October 16, 1747*

Dear Boy:

The art of pleasing is a very necessary one to possess, but a very difficult one to acquire. It can hardly be reduced to rules; and your own good sense and observation will teach you more of it than I can. "Do as you would be done by," is the surest method that I know of pleasing. Observe carefully what pleases you in others, and probably the same things in you will please others. If you are pleased with the complaisance and attention of others to your humors, your tastes, or your weaknesses, depend upon it, the same complaisance and attention on your part to theirs will equally please them. Take the tone of the company that you are in, and do not pretend to give it; be serious, gay, or even trifling, as you find the present humor of the company; this is an attention due from every individual to the majority. Do not tell stories in company; there is nothing more tedious and disagreeable; if by chance you know a very short story, and exceedingly applicable to the present subject of conversation, tell it in as few words as possible; and even then, throw out that you do not love to tell stories, but that the shortness of it tempted you.

Of all things, banish the egotism out of your conversation, and never think of entertaining people with your own personal concerns or private affairs; though they are interesting to you, they are tedious and impertinent to everybody else; besides that, one cannot keep one's own private affairs too secret. Whatever you think your own excellencies may be, do not affectedly display them in company; nor labor, as many people do, to give that turn to the conversation, which may supply you with an opportunity of exhibiting them. If they are real, they will infallibly be discovered, without your pointing them out yourself, and with much more advantage. Never maintain an argument with heat and clamor, though you think or know yourself to be in the right; but give your opinion modestly and coolly, which is the only way to convince; and, if that does not do, try to change the conversation, by saying, with good humor, "We shall hardly convince one another; nor is it necessary that we should, so let us talk of something else."

Remember that there is a local propriety to be observed in all companies; and that what is extremely proper in one company may be, and often is, highly improper in another.

The jokes, the *bon-mots,* the little adventures, which may do very well in one company, will seem flat and tedious, when related in another. The particular characters, the habits, the cant of one company may give merit to a word, or a gesture, which would have none at all if divested of those accidental circumstances. Here people very commonly err; and fond of something that has entertained them in one company, and in certain circumstances, repeat it with emphasis in another, where it is either insipid, or, it may be, offensive, by being ill timed or misplaced. Nay, they often do it with this silly preamble: "I will tell you an excellent thing," or, "I will tell you the best thing in the world." This raises expectations, which, when absolutely disappointed, make the relator of this excellent thing look, very deservedly, like a fool.

If you would particularly gain the affection and friendship of particular people, whether men or women, endeavor to find out their predominant excellency, if they have one, and their prevailing weakness, which everybody has; and do justice to the one, and something more than justice to the other. Men have various objects in which they may excel, or at least would be thought to excel; and though they love to hear justice done to them, where they know that they excel, yet they are most and best flattered upon those points where they wish to excel, and yet are doubtful whether they do or not. As for example: Cardinal Richelieu, who was undoubtedly the ablest statesman of his time, or perhaps of any other, had the idle vanity of being thought the best poet too; he envied the great Corneille his reputation, and ordered a criticism to be written upon the *Cid.* Those, therefore, who flattered skillfully, said little to him of his abilities in state affairs, or at least but *en passant*, and as it might naturally occur. But the incense which they gave him, the smoke of which they knew would turn his head in their favor, was as a *bel esprit* and a poet. Why? Because he was sure of one excellency, and distrustful as to the other.

You will easily discover every man's prevailing vanity by observing his favorite topic of conversation; for every man talks most of what he has most a mind to be thought to excel in. Touch him but there, and you touch him to the quick. The late Sir Robert Walpole (who was certainly an able man) was little open to flattery upon that head, for he was in no doubt himself about it; but his prevailing weakness was, to be thought to have a polite and happy turn to gallantry—of which he had undoubtedly less than any man living. It was his favorite and frequent subject of conversation, which proved to those who had any penetration that it was his prevailing weakness, and they applied to it with success.

Women have, in general, but one object, which is their beauty; upon which scarce any flattery is too gross for them to follow. Nature has hardly formed a woman ugly enough to be insensible to flattery upon her person; if her face is so shocking that she must, in some degree, be conscious of it, her figure and air, she trusts, make ample amends for it. If her figure is deformed, her face, she thinks, counterbalances it. If they are both bad, she comforts herself that she has graces, a certain manner, a *je ne sais quoi* still more engaging than beauty. This truth is evident from the studied and elaborate dress of the ugliest woman in the world. An undoubted, uncontested, conscious beauty is, of all women, the least sensible of flattery upon that head; she knows it is her due, and is therefore obliged to nobody for giving it her. She must be flattered upon her understanding; which, though she may possibly not doubt of herself, yet she suspects that men may distrust.

Do not mistake me, and think that I mean to recommend to you abject and criminal flattery: no; flatter nobody's vices or crimes: on the contrary, abhor and discourage them. But there is no living in the world without a complaisant indulgence for people's weaknesses, and innocent, though ridiculous vanities. If a man has a mind to be thought wiser, and a woman handsomer, than they really are, their error is a comfortable one to themselves, and an innocent one with regard to other people; and I would rather make them my friends by indulging them in it, than my enemies by endeavoring (and that to no purpose) to undeceive them.

There are little attentions, likewise, which are infinitely engaging, and which sensibly affect that degree of pride and self-love, which is inseparable from human nature; as they are unquestionable proofs of the regard and consideration which we have for the persons to whom we pay them. As, for example, to observe the little habits, the likings, the antipathies, and the tastes of those whom we would gain; and then take care to provide them with the one, and to secure them from the other; giving them genteelly to understand, that you had observed they liked such a dish or such a room; for which reason you had prepared it: or, on the contrary, that having observed they had an aversion to such a dish, a dislike to such a person, etc., you had taken care to avoid presenting them. Such attention to such trifles flatters self-love much more than greater things, as it makes people think themselves almost the only objects of your thoughts and care.

These are some of the *arcana* necessary for your initiation in the great society of the world. I wish I had known them better at your age; I have paid the price of three-and-fifty years for them, and shall not grudge it, if you reap the advantage. Adieu.

### SUGGESTIONS FOR WRITING

1. Philip Dormer Stanhope (1694-1773), fourth Earl of Chesterfield, was a statesman and diplomat. He wrote political tracts and contributed to periodicals of his time, but he is remembered chiefly for his "Letters" to his natural son, Philip Stanhope. These were written almost daily from 1737 onwards and were designed for the education of the young man. As we read them today, they seem to be fairly sensible but stuffy. Would you like to receive such letters from your father? Why or why not?

2. "Never think of entertaining people with your own personal concerns of private affairs; though they are interesting to you, they are tedious and impertinent to everybody else . . ." What a dull life this would be if everyone followed that advice! How would you qualify it (or would you?) if you were writing to your son?

3. A difference of opinion among men of good will and a willingness to argue that difference intelligently is but knowledge in the making. Philosophers since Socrates have pleaded to have their theories subjected to penetrating criticism. How, then, can Chesterfield suggest that

the conversation be changed with, "We shall hardly convince one another; nor is it necessary that we should, so let us talk of something
else."? Describe an imaginary experience in which his advice is either
valid or invalid.
4. What do you think of Chesterfield's advice to "discover every man's
prevailing vanity"?

# Advice of an Aztec Mother to Her Daughter*

Take care that your garments are such as are decent and proper;
and observe that you do not adorn yourself with much finery, since
this is a mark of vanity and of folly. As little becoming is it, that
your dress should be very mean, dirty, or ragged; since rags are a
mark of the low, and of those who are held in contempt. Let your
clothes be becoming and neat, that you may neither appear fantastic nor mean. When you speak, do not hurry your words from
uneasiness, but speak deliberately and calmly. Do not raise your
voice very high, nor speak very low, but in a moderate tone. Neither
mince, when you speak, nor when you salute, nor speak through
your nose; but let your words be proper, of a good sound, and your
voice gentle. Do not be nice in the choice of your words. In walking, my daughter, see that you behave becomingly, neither going
with haste, nor too slowly; since it is an evidence of being puffed
up, to walk too slowly, and walking hastily causes a vicious habit
of restlessness and instability. Therefore neither walk very fast, nor
very slow; yet, when it shall be necessary to go with haste, do so—
in this use your discretion. And when you may be obliged to jump
over a pool of water, do it with decency, that you may neither appear clumsy nor light. When you are in the street, do not carry
your head much inclined, or your body bent; nor as little go with
your head very much raised, since it is a mark of ill breeding; walk
erect, and with your head slightly inclined. Do not have your mouth
covered, or your face, from shame, nor go looking like a near-
sighted person, nor, on your way, make fantastic movements with
your feet. Walk through the street quietly, and with propriety.

---

*From *History of the Conquest of Mexico* by William H. Prescott, trans.,
1843.

Another thing that you must attend to, my daughter, is, that when you are in the street you do not go looking hither and thither, nor turning your head to look at this and that; walk neither looking at the skies nor on the ground. Do not look upon those whom you meet with the eyes of an offended person, nor have the appearance of being uneasy; but of one who looks upon all with a serene countenance; doing this, you will give no one occasion of being offended with you. Show a becoming countenance; that you may neither appear morose, nor, on the other hand, too complaisant. See, my daughter, that you give yourself no concern about the words you may hear, in going through the street, nor pay any regard to them, let those who come and go say what they will. Take care that you neither answer nor speak, but act as if you neither heard nor understood them; since, doing in this manner, no one will be able to say with truth that you have said anything amiss. See, likewise, my daughter, that you never paint your face, or stain it or your lips with colors, in order to appear well, since this is a mark of vile and unchaste women. Paints and coloring are things which bad women use—the immodest, who have lost all shame and even sense, who are like fools and drunkards, and are called *rameras* [prostitutes]. But, that your husband may not dislike you, adorn yourself, wash yourself, and cleanse your clothes; and let this be done with moderation, since if every day you wash yourself and your clothes it will be said of you that you are over-nice—too delicate; they will call you *tapepetzon tinemaxoch.*

My daughter, this is the course you are to take, since in this manner the ancestors from whom you spring brought us up. Those noble and venerable dames, your grandmothers, told us not so many things as I have told you—they said but few words, and spoke thus:

"Listen, my daughters; in this world it is necessary to live with much prudence and circumspection. Hear this allegory, which I shall now tell you, and preserve it, and take from it a warning and example for living aright. Here, in this world, we travel by a very narrow, steep, and dangerous road, which is as a lofty mountain ridge, on whose top passes a narrow path; on either side is a great gulf without bottom; and if you deviate from the path you will fall into it. There is need, therefore, of much discretion in pursuing the road." My tenderly loved daughter, my little dove, keep this illustration in your heart, and see that you do not forget it—it will be to you as a lamp and a beacon so long as you shall live in this world.

## SUGGESTIONS FOR WRITING

1. We know nothing of the circumstances of this letter, except that it was probably written four or five hundred years ago. Devise a situation which would make the sending of such a letter plausible.
2. If this letter were the only remnant of an extinct civilization, what deductions could you make about the society of the country from which it came?
3. Compare the quality of advice here with the standard "Dorothy Dix" fare. What is the significant difference?
4. This letter, written in obvious sincerity, comments on a number of aspects of deportment: dress, speech, choice of words, gait, posture, countenance, make-up, cleanliness. The second paragraph gives reasons for carefully heeding the advice. Prepare a letter from a modern mother to her daughter and, using the Aztec letter as a model, comment on the same aspects of deportment.

GLENDON SWARTHOUT

# The Inscrutable Generation*

## Lucky Henry

The point I wish to make in this paper is that Thoreau wasn't. In my opinion, my generation is the luckiest that ever lived. Historically, we have missed everything draggy. We were too late for hot wars, and depressions are things the folks brag about while we bob for the cherries in their Manhattans. We have had ample allowances, cars, driver training, luxury schools which never overtaxed our intellects, indulgent parents, and the miracle of television. Our future, too, is great. Jobs are abundant and pay well. We may marry practically when we choose and hence are never frustrated sexually. I have no information concerning Henry

---

* From *Where the Boys Are* by Glendon Swarthout (New York: Random House, Inc., 1960). © 1960 by Glendon Swarthout. Reprinted by permission of the publishers.

David's libido but some winter nights in Massachusetts must have been mighty *icy*.

It is a new thing for a generation to go around feeling fortunate all the time. We have to watch ourselves; we have to be sly; because our only problem is that the world is an *Indian-giver*. It cannot decide whether it wants us to enjoy the fruits of its labors or to be contrite that we have them. Society has a schizoid notion that perhaps it should retrieve what it's given. As a consequence we are shot at and challenged and criticized and deplored and niggled perpetually and from all sides. Teachers and parents and faculty and ministers and newspaper editors have the mission of not leaving us in peace. Spare the Sputnik and spoil the child. We are not grateful enough, responsible enough, ambitious enough, individualistic enough, serious enough. We are silent and delinquent and inscrutable and we don't care a used cigarette filter about world conditions or citizenship or morality or democracy or organized religion. In other words, we are not like *you*.

You are damn right, we're not. You did not shape us in your image, you made us what you would have liked to be, and now you are not satisfied. I'm sorry. We *are*. Oh, we recognize that our experience has been limited; we have never lived in the woods; we have never had to trudge to town; and this first class, red carpet, jet prop flight through youth we regret a little. But the luggage of our discontent weighs less because we have so many other advantages. Our good fortune we accept, thank you. To it we are very well-adjusted. We refuse to rock the boat for the sake of lights and shadows on the water. If it pleases you we will pretend to be what we are not. Punch our buttons and we will produce the right answers.

But I would address myself to the older generation in this manner. We never asked to be so lucky. We did not vote to be born when we were, we were not polled at conception on our environmental preferences. If it gives you a large charge to take out on us your envy, proceed. You cannot hurt us. In our transcendental way we are thoreauly content. We are as remote, as hermetic, as untouchable, really, as a woman eight months along. The world can go to hell in a basket for all she cares. She will have her baby. We will have ours.

SUGGESTIONS FOR WRITING

1. Glendon Swarthout, a novelist in his forties, is an English professor who has written three very different books: *They Came to Cordura* (1956), *Where the Boys Are* (1960), and *Welcome to Thebes* (1962). The above selection comes from *Where the Boys Are* and is a hypothetical college theme by a student in an honors section of freshman English. Most critics felt that Swarthout was not revealing the promise of his first book when he wrote *Where the Boys Are,* but at least some college teachers knew that he was telling a not too pleasant truth about a college population. Does the above selection seem to you to be representative of the attitude of some college students you know? Describe those students.
2. Analyze the language in this selection. Set down as many words or phrases as you can which are considered college jargon.
3. Write your own theme on Henry David Thoreau. Was *he* lucky or are you?
4. Make a one-sentence summary for each of the four paragraphs. Do you feel the student's argument is merely ingenious or really valid?

THOMAS B. MORGAN

# Teen-Age Heroes*

Eighteen million American teen-agers growing older in a world they didn't make—a world overpopulated and underfed, overorganized and yet disorganized, impersonal and self-indulgent, machine tooled, purposeless, yet filled with unrealized possibility and in danger of coming to an apocalyptic end—have settled a new world of their own. They have established a colony Out There in Teen-Land, a kind of pseudo-adult world. It is not a young world, if youth means daring and imagination, idealism and individualism, skepticism and iconoclasm. But it does have such a definite identity and appearance that one can visit it as a tourist, with camera, dictionary, and sick pills. (A nice place to visit, yes; but no place to live.) Because they have to live at home, go to school, belong to

---
* From *Esquire Magazine* (March, 1960). © 1960 by Esquire, Inc. Reprinted by permission of the publishers.

clubs, shop for supplies, and appear in court, the teen-agers' colony is attached to the American mainland and carries on foreign relations with it. The hearts and minds of teen-agers, though, are usually in Teen-Land: they are totally aware of themselves as Teen-Agers, something their parents never were when they were younger. They feel and are made to feel (no doubt by articles such as this) that they are a race apart, a minority in an alien land. Thus, they cling with fierce pride to a private set of folkways that seem mysterious and confounding in the extreme to outsiders. These folkways create pressures to conform and inhibit the individual as insistently as those in the adult world, but they give the teen-ager an illusion of choice. Paralleling the adult world, Teen-Land is built on insecurity and its greatest concern is for safety. The cost of safety is uniqueness of personality and the measure of it is membership in the herd.

To understand this complex young world, one should get to know the heroes of teen-agers. Here is what prompted this inquiry: the assumption that heroes directly and indirectly reveal much about the hero-worshipers' values and that the heroes of teen-agers would contribute some understanding of those who idolize them in an era in which communication between generations has all but broken down.

This assumption isn't made because all teen-age heroes have special knowledge. Today, a young man is elected to heroship by teen-age girls who buy phonograph records without regard for his insights. The hero, after a short wait, is then accepted by teen-age boys, who buy him uncritically, perhaps to please the girls. The boys don't have feminine heroines of their own. There are girl singers who are popular with teen-agers, but none receive the adulation that the girls lavish on the males. It seems that teen-age girls, maturing faster than boys, have no interest in worshiping a member of their own sex. They are prepared to accept a male symbol long before the boys have extricated themselves from Mother. It has even been suggested that boys do not care for girl singers because the female voice reminds them of Mom and, worse, Discipline. As it works out, then, both sexes accept the choice of heroes made by one sex, and the weaker sex at that.

What makes the heroes themselves, in the flesh, a potential source of information about teen-agers is that they are, of course, more than mere show-business characters. Most of them are teen-agers and only one is out of his twenties. They not only perform; they also reflect those whom they are performing for and are approved by. They are part of Teen-Land as well as symbols of it. Some are virtually overnight sensations and none are so far from a time when they were nobodies that they cannot remember their own experiences as members of the teen world on the far side of the footlights.

Recently, some of these heroes were tarnished by the payola scandals. But in the outcry over payola, the essential nature of the idols themselves was ignored. The superficial crookedness of individuals in the record business was excoriated, leaving untouched something deeper—the irresponsibility of many who profoundly affect teen-age life.

One recent night, a nineteen-year-old boy named Frankie Avalon, a rock-and-roll ballad singer physically reminiscent of Frank Sinatra, was seen doing his turn at the Steel Pier Music Hall on the boardwalk at Atlantic City. When he stepped on the stage, about two hundred well-fed, well-enough-dressed girls in the first six rows and in the side balconies shrieked in the typically violent and mechanical way we have all come to know and love. The sound was a cross between an explosive high-school cheer and the mating call of the red squirrel. A number of the screamers were not looking at their hero, but at each other, to make sure that they were being seen screaming—i.e., belonging. In general, the Frankie Avalon fans were seated screamers, not the old dance-in-the-aisle kind of the naïve Sinatra days, which had merely been a kind of premonition of things to come. A few, however, left their seats to run up the aisle and take flashbulb pictures of Avalon, screaming a little as they went. Back of the forward wall of noise, row upon row of teen-agers applauded conventionally. This may have been because they were less enthusiastic, but more than likely they did not scream because they were outside the bright glow of the footlights. If the management had turned up the house lights, they might have achieved a more perfect pandemonium.

But perfect or not, by enabling post-pubescent girls to express themselves within the damp warmth and safety of the crowd, a modern teen-age hero, such as Avalon, fulfills his function and collects his money. The expression takes many forms. In New Haven, Connecticut, girls in summer frocks pulled the shoes off Avalon's feet in an attempt to drag him from the stage into the audience. In Buffalo, New York, a wild herd of little women trampled him and sprained his back, while in Milwaukee twenty-one girls fainted during one show. When Avalon sang *Boy Without a Girl* on a television show, the camera panned on girls sobbing in the audience. After that, wherever he appeared in person, girls who had seen him on TV sobbed while he sang this song. Avalon's merchandising business keeps the idolatry percolating at long distance: among his wares for young women are Avalon shirts, sweaters, bracelets, buttons and authentic locks of hair. The latter are collected when Avalon goes to the barbershop—which reminds one of that old boast of the hog business: "We use everything but the squeal."

Now the stimulus for all this is 5 feet 7 inches tall and weighs less than 135 pounds. On stage at the Steel Pier Music Hall, his hair was wavy, his face sweet-to-babyish, eyes sad, skin sallow under make-up, and mouth uncertain. His clothes were a careful combination of show-biz elegance and Pat Boone purity: silk suits and white buck shoes. By nature or design, his manner was gentle, a little frightened, and awesomely humble.

This humility, which is characteristic of many teen-age heroes (Fabian, Ricky Nelson, and the like), was a response to the felt need of the audience to identify with one who was celestial and yet not far out of reach. Since the aspirations of many teen-agers seem to be at the lowest level in the history of America, too much self was taboo and anyone too far away (or out) would be ignored. The cardinal principle of the successful hero would be that humbleness creates an indispensable aura of accessibility.

Fabian became a teen-age hero in spite of the fact that he was no bundle of singing talent. "Maybe I would have never made it if I could sing," Fabian has said. His appeal is similar to Ricky Nelson's, but also he elicits motherly sympathy from the girls because he is so obviously awkward and inept. It is now one of the hoary legends of Teen-Land that Fabian was discovered sitting on a doorstep in South Philadelphia by Bob Marcucci, a former waiter who is himself not yet thirty. With his partner, Peter De Angelis, Marcucci had discovered and then promoted Frankie Avalon to stardom. Having developed the magic touch, he searched for and found Fabian two years ago. Fabian was fourteen, had never sung a note in anger, and thought that the $6 a week he was earning in a drugstore was fair money. When last seen, he was getting $35,000 for acting (not badly, by Hollywood standards) in Fox's *Hound Dog Man.*

Sitting just behind the camera in one of those canvas chairs, Marcucci was watching every move his gold mine made. Marcucci is a short, swarthy man who reminds one of a nervous assistant director at a boy's camp. He has the ability to analyze precisely the demands of the teen-age public and to know what to do about it. He has found a career in exporting talent to Teen-Land. First, he selects promising raw material. Then he molds it. He indoctrinates it for three months. Then he takes it to live TV shows so that it can see what the business is like. Then he lets it make a few test records. Since it cannot sing too well without an orchestra and the electronic facilities (echo chambers, bass and treble modulators, tape splicers and the works) of a recording studio, he teaches it to pantomime while its records play over the loud-speaker during its first public appearance before an audience of two hundred. He dresses it, first in sweaters and white bucks, then in open Belafonte shirts and big belt buckles. He coifs it by modifying the ducktail and getting more of the Ricky Nelson bob. He postures it, taking advantage of good shoulders, which should bunch forward, and narrow hips, which should always be off keel. He takes it on the road, shows it to disc jockeys, and advertises it in trade papers. He decides (brilliantly) to use only its first name instead of its last. He interests Dick Clark in it, and after one shot on TV, it breaks up an audience of 24,000 in Albany, New York. It sells 300,000 copies of a record called *I'm a Man,* then 750,000 of *Turn Me Loose.*

In Fabian, Marcucci consciously or unconsciously produced a caricature that combined the sure-fire qualities of Ricky with those of his own Frankie Avalon. The mood in Teen-Land permits even such an obvious construction to become a hero. What Marcucci could not have planned, however, was the fact that Fabian's inability to sing would really be an asset. Marcucci tried to teach him; he went through four singing teachers trying. Fortunately, all efforts failed. Here was the ultimate in humbleness and teen-audience identification. Nobody in the audience could sing either, so that made . . . Fabian seem all the more accessible. Mediocrity fell in love with its own image.

Every world has means of expressing itself—a culture. Our 18,-

000,000 teen-agers (exceptions duly noted) spend $10,000,000,000 to support theirs. They have publications written in their own language (Teen-glish?) which keep them abreast of their times. *Dig, Ingenue, Seventeen, 16, Teen,* etc., instruct them in custom, ritual, propriety, sex mores, and proper-think; their goal is to inculcate group values. One magazine not long ago defined "What is a Square?" for its readers, who were told, among other things, that a square is one who refuses to go with a group to a movie he has already seen. Then there are motion pictures, television shows, and radio programs, which provide a kind of cultural game of ring-around-the-rosie. The teens influence the adults who provide the entertainments which in turn influence the teens and so on, and on. After sex and violence, the main theme of these entertainments is a kind of deadpan morality which would be funny if it did not border on madness. Thus, the producer of *I Was a Teenage Frankenstein* defended himself against an attack on his very popular picture by pointing out that none of the young villains and monsters in the movie drank or smoked. And in the basic boy-meets-girl film, scripts are adjusted to make sure that a curious kind of justice, appealing to teen-agers, triumphs. In a teen picture, after the boy gets the girl pregnant, he's got to get stabbed. Watching rock-and-roll programs, citizens of Teen-Land may learn the newest folk dances while they follow the fashions of the times. Hearing disc jockeys on radio, too, teen-agers can absorb their culture. They are infused with meaningful backbeat rhythms and simultaneously absorb the philosophies of the modern jocks, which are a mixture of Beat, Babbitt and Payola. Beyond these visual and aural items of acculturation, there is the automobile. What the frontier was to our pioneers, what Miami is to our modern adult culture, the auto is to the teen—the means of getting away.

Finally, away out on the fringe of Teen-Land, heroin takes some teen-agers where they cannot get by car.

The primary focus of the teen culture, however, is the teen-age hero who, like heroes of all cultures, represents the final expression of those values by which it lives. The . . . aforementioned heroes are the Apollos and Zeuses of Teen-Land. A few years ago, the movies supplied most of the heroes for adolescent Americans. Marlon Brando and James Dean were two, but the former's receding hairline and the latter's death disconnected them from the young. Chances are they would have faded anyway, because rock and roll was bigger than both of them. Now, except for Dick Clark, every first-class teen-age hero is a recording star. No athlete, politician, businessman, or intellectual is accorded comparable esteem, nor could he be, given the teen-agers' demand for safety. The ideal athlete is admired for courage, the politician for principles, the businessman for enterprise, and the intellectual for devotion to hard truths—all represent values that tend to separate the individual from the crowd, that expose him, and that lead him into an uncertain and dangerous future. Teen-agers make virtues of conformity, mediocrity and sincerity. It is a simple matter of survival: there's safety in the crowd. They can express themselves through their safe-sex heroes, each one of whom represents his own brand of sex—rebellious sex, sincere sex, clean sex, low-down sex, motherly sex, cool sex—at no risk. It's perfect: it's sex, but it's safe. Without leaving the warmth and security of the crowd, you can say what you want to say to the world.

You can have your cake without being eaten.

## SUGGESTIONS FOR WRITING

1. Mr. Morgan has set up an organizational scheme that is simple to hold in mind but sometimes difficult to put into effect. He wants to write a description of the teen-ager, and he has chosen to do this by describing teen-age heroes. The basic metaphor which unifies his article is that the teen-ager is a citizen of another world. Make a one-sentence summary of each paragraph. Then examine Morgan's premises. Is his method of analysis valid for this essay?

2. Do teen-agers really live in a land of their own? Does everyone else live in Squaresville? What premises are necessary for these conclusions?

3. Are teen-agers responsible for the actions of their heroes? On whom should responsibility be placed—parents, schools, government?

4. What is the average period of reign for a "king of the teen-agers"? What gives a hero "staying power," so that he can remain popular even as the public changes and matures? Robert Frost, in his book of poems *In the Clearing* (1962), has a poem entitled "How Hard It Is to Keep from Being King When It's in You and in the Situation." Do teen-age heroes face this difficulty?

EUGENE GILBERT

# Today's Teen-Agers Seem Different*

If you believe your teen-age son and daughter are causing you a good deal more trouble than you ever gave your parents, you are probably right. On the other hand, if you are under twenty, there may be good reason for you to regard your elders as a peculiarly insensitive, outmoded, and irrational tribe.

The rift between the generations, in our time, is puzzling because the age gap between them is relatively small. Many of the parents of today's high-school set were teen-agers themselves when they married during the war and have, in effect, "grown up with their children."

Perhaps this is part of the trouble. There are other elements—a few of which I have tried to sort out in the hope that this might help the generations to put up with each other more happily.

I am not a teacher or a sociologist; I am not even the parent of a teen-ager. (I am bracing myself for this event—my son, Howard, has just passed Gesell's "golden age" of ten.) But for some fifteen years I have been carrying on an intensive study of the adolescent in a role where he is most distinctly himself—as a consumer. In 1945, when I was a college student myself, I was struck with the notion that stores and manufacturers were losing a lot of money because they were largely blind to my contemporaries' real tastes and habits. I started then to become a market researcher in a virtually unexplored field. I have been at it ever since. Today the company I head is regularly called on to probe, describe, and analyze the ways of teen-age consumers and has completed more than six million interviews with them. What kind of name, we are asked, will attract the young to a new ice-cream bar? What newspapers, magazines, TV and radio programs do they prefer and why? What makes them like or dislike a particular watch, soft drink, candy, comic book, typewriter, or jacket?

In our hunt for practical, dollars-and-cents answers to such ques-

* From *Harper's Magazine* (November, 1959). © 1959 by Eugene Gilbert. Reprinted by permission of the author.

tions we inevitably find out a good deal more. For our information, we not only interview young people—we also use them to ask the questions. We have a nationwide network of some five thousand young poll-takers. They represent all social strata—children of business and professional men, farmers, white collar and manual workers. They are sharp observers and we use the techniques of opinion and market research to interpret their findings.

Our salient discovery is that within the past decade the teen-agers have become a separate and distinct group in our society. Psychologists and social scientists underline their separateness. Advertisers and merchants cater to their whims. Newspapers devote special sections to the interests of the teen-age reader, who is accepted as a special kind of customer along with the housewife and the adult sports fan. And the response of the teen-ager has been, characteristically, to match the image. I am not speaking here—or elsewhere—of the youngsters who get into trouble. Despite newspaper headlines and our well-founded concern with their problems, delinquents represent only a minute percentage of our teen-age population. I am concerned here not with why a handful of boys and girls behave badly, but with exploring why the great majority seem to their elders so odd. How different are they really?

Adolescents, ever since anyone has observed them, have been rebelling—openly or secretly—against their elders. At the same time they have always been desperately eager to keep in step with their crowd—known to the social scientists today as the peer group. Never before, however, have these phases of human development been given so much public and formal recognition. And never before has quite so young a group exercised the same kind of power —for good or ill. Today's teen-ager is a remarkably independent character. The fact is, he can afford to be.

The high-school boys and girls of 1959 are likely to have about four times as much money to spend as their counterparts in 1945 —the individual average is $10 a week compared with $2.50 fifteen years ago. Two-thirds of this is a parental dole—the allowance. But the balance is earned income. Today's teen-agers—despite contrary views from some of their teachers—are an industrious lot.

Within a decade, the number of teen-agers holding steady year-round jobs has doubled—reaching a total of 800,000 in 1956. Some of these youngsters have left school to go to work, but many manage to hold down lucrative jobs after school hours as delivery boys, newspaper route boys, baby sitters, soda jerks. About four million spend their vacations working and some 4.5 million do part-time work or odd jobs throughout the year.

Typical of most American youngsters today are the students and graduates of the Pearl River High School in Rockland County, New York. Their guidance director circulated a questionnaire last August and found that 90 per cent of the 1959 graduates had found summer jobs in fields which they hoped to pursue in college. Thirty out of seventy-five boys and girls earned more than $400 during the summer at such jobs as clerk, camp counselor, kitchen worker, stock boy, photo-offset press loader, caddie, carpenter, car-pool attendant, church organist, laboratory assistant, salesgirl, and road-maintenance worker. Sixty-five out of the seventy-five of the junior class also found summer jobs and earned an average of $250 apiece.

A good slice of such earnings is saved for college expenses. But a considerable part is also spent. Last year teen-agers had purchasing power amounting to an estimated $9.5 billion—enough to cause some major merchandising and fashion upheavals.

Today's teen-ager is a very practical youth. For example, the problem of getting good marks places higher on the list of most youngsters' conscious worries than dating, money, or parent-child problems. This is not because mother nags about homework, but because the teen-ager knows he must meet stiff competition from his peers and needs a college degree if he is to get on in the world, which he fully intends to do.

That world, however, is very different from the one in which his parents lived as children and young adults. And herein may lie an important clue to the gap between the generations. For people in their late thirties, forties, and fifties today, the two overwhelming experiences of life were the Depression and World War II. Far more than they realize, the impressions and standards formed in those days have shaped their present attitudes and thinking. But to the teen-ager these are dim, irrelevant periods.

"My, I'm tired of hearing about all those noble causes my mother worked for when she was in college," said one high-school girl. "I don't believe they were all that noble. And who cares now, anyhow?"

The difficulty, it would seem, is global.

"Today's young people don't speak the same language as we do," a middle-aged Yugoslav Communist complained the other day. "They don't feel as we do about things."

Parents from Chattanooga to China would probably agree. Possibly, however, it is the "things" as much as the "feelings" that have changed. And it may be that today's teen-agers are adapting, in their own way, to a situation very different from what any prior generation of adolescents has experienced.

Is there not, for example, a certain crude logic in hastening the growing up process in the shadow of the atom and hydrogen bomb? What meaning have "patriotism," "peace," and the other slogans of the bygone idealism when the dilemma that faces us is not a matter of winning a war but survival? To lose one's identity within the pattern of one's contemporaries, to seek the haven of a steady job rather than personal achievement, to prize material possessions above abstract principles—these may be the best available safety rafts in an insecure world.

The wiser of our politicians are learning gradually that one cannot use the old stock-in-trade of the past twenty years to appeal to young voters. Many of them have scarcely heard of the New Deal. They are not veterans of any war and don't hope to be. New issues must be defined though just what they are no one has yet figured out.

SUGGESTIONS FOR WRITING

1. Eugene Gilbert is a market researcher in his forties. He sets forth his qualifications for writing this essay in the fourth paragraph. What you see depends on where you are standing. Is Mr. Gilbert qualified from everyone's point of view? Who is best qualified? Note that this question does not suggest a weakness in his generalizations, his authority, or his statistics. Indeed, he very carefully makes his readers feel that his opinions are worth listening to—a good technique for any writer trying to be convincing. Whose word would be most convincing to you and why?

2. There are a number of items here with which it is possible to disagree. Using Gilbert's sense of orderliness in your argument, analyze the items with which you disagree.

3. Are today's teen-agers really different? How can one know? Does the pace of life have anything to do with it? Can you cite evidence that the pace of life is different today?
4. Define an American teen-ager for a visitor from Russia or China.


C. G. LUMBARD

## Big Charge out of College*


When you hear about a fraternity you might be one of those people who think about real nice guys getting blackballed and getting their entire lives ruined, or maybe you think about keeping the Jews and Negroes out. Perhaps you think of some innocent little kid getting beaten to death with a paddle. I don't know. But when I think about the fraternity, I think about sitting around out in the back yard on warm afternoons, drinking beer and talking about football or where infinity is or women or automobiles. And I think about everyone calling everyone else "babe," and I think of Friday nights at dinner. . . .

Of course I didn't go along with the sentimental idea that each fraternity member is the truest possible friend of every other. That's not the way it works. We had some real tools in our house. And there were undoubtedly guys who thought I was a fairly moldy specimen. And in ways I was.

But we used to have some real good times. I used to like walking home from football games. It's warm in California during September and October, and on those Saturday afternoons we'd walk home with our white shirts on, the ones we had to wear to sit in the rooting section, and we'd feel our faces sunburned from sitting out there in the stadium all afternoon, and our voices would be hoarse from all the cheering and yelling.

There'd be a happy feeling, too, because we were always doing something on Saturday night, even if it was only going to a movie. There would usually be a slight haze in the air, late on those fall afternoons, and it made everything seem fuzzy and friendly. Some-

---

* From *Senior Spring* by C. G. Lumbard (New York: Simon & Schuster, Inc., 1954). Copyright 1954 by C. G. Lumbard. Reprinted by permission of the publishers.

times people would be burning leaves in the gutter, and we'd walk along and smell that warm fall smell drifting up the street.

It was standard procedure to stop at Joe's Food Market down on the corner and buy a quart of beer to drink in the back yard after the game. This was frowned on in general because lots of the guys' parents would drop by the fraternity house, and there'd be mothers and little sisters and things running all around. But we'd buy the beer anyway, and four or five of us would sit out in the back yard behind the fishpond, under some great big pine trees, and drink our beer and talk. It was fine to do things like that. It made us feel like we were getting a big charge out of college.

## SUGGESTIONS FOR WRITING

1. C. G. Lumbard was in his late twenties when he published his first book, *Senior Spring* (1954), from which this selection was taken. In addition to having caught the vernacular of the American college student, Lumbard has an easy flow to his writing. A theory of communication holds that the movement of language is regulated by signals. The first paragraph here moves until it reaches a certain word (what is it?); then it flows until the second paragraph, where we go into a side issue. Indicate where in the second paragraph it begins moving again (a movement that continues to the end of the selection). What conclusion can you draw from this analysis relating to a theory of language flow?

2. The person reminiscing here is Steve Burnett, a college senior. Develop an analysis to reveal the author's awareness of this fact.

3. Follow the five-paragraph plan you see here and write a theme in which you make clear your own thoughts and feelings about a period in your life. Begin with a paragraph about what some people think (general misconceptions) and go on to point out what the situation is as you have actually experienced it.


WILLIAM MAXWELL

# A Serious Engagement*

The new dormitory for boys was opened toward the end of May. The smell of fresh plaster and new wood lingered in the corridors

---

* From *The Folded Leaf* by William Maxwell (New York: Harper & Row, Publishers, 1945). Copyright 1945 by William Maxwell. Reprinted by permission of the publishers.

of the building and on the stairways, which were bare and bright and clean. Most houses and public buildings are at their best, have more character, and beauty, before people have quite managed to take possession of them (before the last rug is unrolled, the calendar hung on the kitchen wall); and again after they have been abandoned to rats and spiders and the barrier between outside and inside has given way in a tinkle of broken glass.

Anyone walking into a certain corner room on the third floor would have found nothing in it yet but a dresser, two chairs, a desk, and an iron bed that during the daytime disappeared into the wall. There were two windows looking out over the tennis courts which were behind the library and two more facing the rear of a stone church. All four windows were wide open, and the air that blew in was warm and washed with sunshine. Near the door was a washstand with a mirror over it, and there was another door which opened into a closet. On the desk, surrounded by books and papers, was a blue bowl filled with ridiculous, long-stemmed plants grown all out of proportion and fourteen or fifteen inches tall. The old age of flowers (these were violets, mostly) is as strange and as pathetic as the old age of people.

The door that led out into the corridor was standing partly open and from down the hall came the sound of water running, of someone singing in the shower. No words, nothing but the tune—"Tales from the Vienna Woods." The voice was cheerful and confident, and had no musical quality whatever.

After a few minutes the water was turned off and there was a deep silence; then the sound of slippered feet coming down the hall. The door swung open and Lymie came into the room with a towel wrapped around his hips and his hair damp and standing on end. . . .

Lymie tossed the towel on a chair, went to the dresser, and took out a pair of white shorts, a pair of blue socks. His shoes were in the closet and they had been shined. After he had tied the laces, he stood up and worked himself into a light gray turtle-neck sweater that covered his wrists and throat. He dressed quickly but with a certain amount of care, as if he had ahead of him an engagement of some seriousness. When he had finished, he went over to the washstand and combed his hair so it lay smooth and flat on his head. . . .

Through the open windows came the sound of scoring from the tennis courts and of choir practice from the church. . . . Lymie went to the front windows and looked out; then to the desk where he picked up an envelope and took out the note that was inside. On the envelope was written: *For Lymon Peters Jr. Courtesy of bearer.* He read the note slowly, almost as if he were wanting to make sure that the words had not changed any since that morning, when Sally gave it to him. . . .

He picked up the blue bowl and listened a moment to the voices of the choir, rising in rings of sound. When he left the room this time the door was closed behind him.

SUGGESTIONS FOR WRITING

1. William Maxwell (1908-    ), an American writer, wrote *The Folded Leaf,* from which this selection was taken, in 1945. Like Salinger's *Catcher in the Rye* it tells the story of the development of a boy into a young adult. The same theme is represented in C. G. Lumbard's *Senior Spring,* W. Somerset Maugham's *Of Human Bondage,* and James Michener's *The Fires of Spring.* Human development through various stages of life often (usually?) comes in almost imperceptible changes which are difficult to set down in any kind of dramatic form. Maxwell faces this problem in the above selection. The feelings of Lymon Peters need to be revealed not by what he says but by the way he looks at things. And yet, what he sees when he looks gives us some insight into his development. What do you feel you know about him after reading this short selection?

2. What we find here is mostly a picture; first the frame (the building and the room), then the person in the frame. He does this and that, he leaves, and the episode is ended. Using the same approach, write an episode from your own observation. In the manner of Maxwell, share with the reader not only visual details but also a thought or two (judgments) to which they give rise.

3. Lymon Peters is savoring his moments of expectation. We sense this in the deliberateness of his movements. Often the way a person feels is clearly revealed by the way he acts, even though he may not be aware that he is exhibiting his feelings. Make a list of someone's actions and from the list write a composition which will reveal how the person felt at the time.

# Human Beings

A human being: an ingenious assembly of portable plumbing.
—Christopher Morley, *Human Being*, 1932

If a man could say nothing against a character but what he can prove, history could not be written.
—Samuel Johnson, Boswell's *Life of Johnson*, 1791

You can tell the character of every man when you see how he receives praise.
—Seneca (4 B.C.-65 A.D.) *Epistles*

When writing a novel a writer should create living people; people, not characters. A *character* is a caricature.
—Hemingway, *Death in the Afternoon*, 1932

Grand, gloomy, and peculiar, he sat upon the throne a sceptred hermit, wrapped in the solitude of his own originality.
—Charles Phillips, *The Character of Napoleon*, 1817

"Annyhow, I bet no wan iver took Binjamin Franklin f'r a waiter." "I wondher why?" asked Mr. Hennessy.
"I don't know," said Mr. Dooley, "onless it was that even in th' prisince iv a king Binjamin Franklin niver felt like a waiter."
—Finley Peter Dunne, *Diplomatic Uniforms*, 1906

It is in trifles, and when he is off his guard, that a man best shows his character.
—Schopenhauer, *Parerga and Paralipomena*, 1851

I am accounted by some people a good man. How cheap that character is acquired! Pay your debts, don't borrow money, nor twist your kitten's neck off, nor disturb a congregation, etc. and your business is done. I know things (thoughts or things, thoughts *are* things) of myself, which would make every friend I have fly me as a plague patient.
—Charles Lamb, *Letter to Bernard Barton*, 1824

DAVID RIESMAN, WITH NATHAN GLAZER
AND REUEL DENNEY

# "Directed" Characters*

One way to see the structural differences between the three types [of social character—tradition-directed, inner-directed, and other-directed] is to see the differences in the emotional sanction or control in each type.

The tradition-directed person feels the impact of his culture as a unit, but it is nevertheless mediated through the specific, small number of individuals with whom he is in daily contact. These expect of him not so much that he be a certain type of person but that he behave in the approved way. Consequently the sanction for behavior tends to be the fear of being *shamed*.

The inner-directed person has early incorporated a psychic gyroscope which is set going by his parents and can receive signals later on from other authorities who resemble his parents. He goes through life less independent than he seems, obeying this internal piloting. Getting off course, whether in response to inner impulses or to the fluctuating voices of contemporaries, may lead to the feeling of *guilt*.

Since the direction to be taken in life has been learned in the privacy of the home from a small number of guides and since principles, rather than details of behavior, are internalized, the inner-directed person is capable of great stability. Especially so when it turns out that his fellows have gyroscopes too, spinning at the same speed and set in the same direction. But many inner-directed in-

* From *The Lonely Crowd* by David Riesman, Nathan Glazer, and Reuel Denney (New Haven, Conn.: Yale University Press, 1950). Copyright 1950 by Yale University Press. Reprinted by permission of the publishers.

dividuals can remain stable even when the reinforcement of social approval is not available—as in the upright life of the stock Englishman isolated in the tropics.

Contrasted with such a type as this, the other-directed person learns to respond to signals from a far wider circle than is constituted by his parents. The family is no longer a closely knit unit to which he belongs but merely part of a wider social environment to which he early becomes attentive. In these respects the other-directed person resembles the tradition-directed person: both live in a group milieu and lack the inner-directed person's capacity to go it alone. The nature of this group milieu, however, differs radically in the two cases. The other-directed person is cosmopolitan. For him the border between the familiar and the strange—a border clearly marked in the societies depending on tradition-direction—has broken down. As the family continuously absorbs the strange and so reshapes itself, so the strange becomes familiar. While the inner-directed person could be "at home abroad" by virtue of his relative insensitivity to others, the other-directed person is, in a sense, at home everywhere and nowhere, capable of a rapid if sometimes superficial intimacy with and response to everyone.

The tradition-directed person takes his signals from others, but they come in a cultural monotone; he needs no complex receiving equipment to pick them up. The other-directed person must be able to receive signals from far and near; the sources are many, the changes rapid. What can be internalized, then, is not a code of behavior but the elaborate equipment needed to attend to such messages and occasionally to participate in their circulation. As against guilt-and-shame controls, though of course these survive, one prime psychological lever of the other-directed person is a diffuse *anxiety*. This control equipment, instead of being like a gyroscope, is like a radar.[1]

## SUGGESTIONS FOR WRITING

1. David Riesman (1909-    ) is a graduate of Harvard College and Harvard Law School. Since 1946 he has been a member of the social science department at the University of Chicago. The above article comes from a book he wrote with Reuel Denney and Nathan Glazer, *The Lonely*

---

[1] The "radar" metaphor was suggested by Karl Wittfogel. [Author.]

*Crowd* (1950). It is couched in the style of the social scientists, but it adopts a special tone when it brings in radar and the gyroscope. Analyze the language and style of this essay. Choose five sentences and rewrite them in non-social-scientist language and style.

2. Write a character sketch for each of the three types of persons mentioned above.

3. Prepare an argument showing that most educated persons have, at least in part, some of the attributes of each character type mentioned above. Your argument will be more effective if you reveal a multidimensional character in a variety of situations. In other words, you will *show* the character rather than *tell* about him.

4. Develop either the gyroscope or radar analogy by describing a character who behaves as if his life were controlled by one of these instruments.

D. H. LAWRENCE

# Benjamin Franklin*

Old Daddy Franklin will tell you. He'll rig him up for you, the pattern American. Oh, Franklin was the first downright American. He knew what he was about, the sharp little man. He set up the first dummy American.

At the beginning of his career, this cunning little Benjamin drew up for himself a creed that should "satisfy the professors of every religion, but shock none."

Now wasn't that a real American thing to do?

*"That there is One God, who made all things."*

(But Benjamin made Him.)

*"That He governs the world by His Providence."*

(Benjamin knowing all about Providence.)

*"That He ought to be worshiped with adoration, prayer, and thanksgiving."*

(Which cost nothing.)

*"But—"* But me no buts, Benjamin, saith the Lord.

---

* From *Studies in Classic American Literature* by D. H. Lawrence (London: Thomas Seltzer, Inc., 1923). Copyright 1923 by Thomas Seltzer, Inc.; 1951 by Frieda Lawrence. Reprinted by permission of the Viking Press, Inc.

*"But that the most acceptable service of God is doing good to men."*

(God having no choice in the matter.)

*"That the soul is immortal."*

(You'll see why, in the next clause.)

*"And that God will certainly reward virtue and punish vice, either here or hereafter."*

Now if Mr. Andrew Carnegie, or any other millionaire, had wished to invent a God to suit his ends, he could not have done better. Benjamin did it for him in the eighteenth century. God is the supreme servant of men who want to get on, to *produce*. Providence. The provider. The heavenly storekeeper. The everlasting Wanamaker.

And this is all the God the grandsons of the Pilgrim Fathers had left. Aloft on a pillar of dollars.

*"That the soul is immortal."*

The trite way Benjamin says it!

But man has a soul, though you can't locate it either in his purse or his pocketbook or his heart or his stomach or his head. The *wholeness* of a man is his soul. Not merely that nice little comfortable bit which Benjamin marks out.

It's a queer thing, is a man's soul. It is the whole of him. Which means it is the unknown him, as well as the known. It seems to me just funny, professors and Benjamins fixing the functions of the soul. Why the soul of man is a vast forest, and all Benjamin intended was a neat back garden. And we've all got to fit in to his kitchen garden scheme of things. Hail Columbia!

The soul of man is a dark forest. The Hercynian Wood that scared the Romans so, and out of which came the white-skinned hordes of the next civilization.

Who knows what will come out of the soul of man? The soul of man is a dark vast forest, with wild life in it. Think of Benjamin fencing it off!

Oh, but Benjamin fenced a little tract that he called the soul of man, and proceeded to get it into cultivation. Providence, forsooth! And they think that bit of barbed wire is going to keep us in pound forever? More fools them.

This is Benjamin's barbed wire fence. He made himself a list of virtues, which he trotted inside like a grey nag in a paddock.

1  TEMPERANCE   Eat not to fullness: drink not to elevation.

2  SILENCE   Speak not but what may benefit others or yourself; avoid trifling conversation.

3  ORDER   Let all your things have their places; let each part of your business have its time.

4  RESOLUTION   Resolve to perform what you ought; perform without fail what you resolve.

5  FRUGALITY   Make no expense but to do good to others or yourself—i.e., waste nothing.

6  INDUSTRY   Lose no time, be always employed in something useful; cut off all unnecessary action.

7  SINCERITY   Use no hurtful  deceit; think innocently and justly, and, if you speak, speak accordingly.

8  JUSTICE   Wrong none by doing injuries, or omitting the benefits that are your duty.

9  MODERATION   Avoid extremes, forbear resenting injuries as much as you think they deserve.

10  CLEANLINESS   Tolerate no uncleanliness in body, clothes, or habitation.

11  TRANQUILLITY   Be not disturbed at trifles, or at accidents common or unavoidable.

12  CHASTITY   Rarely use venery but for health and offspring, never to dullness, weakness, or the injury of your own or another's peace or reputation.

13  HUMILITY   Imitate Jesus and Socrates.

A Quaker friend told Franklin that he, Benjamin, was generally considered proud, so Benjamin put in the Humility touch as an afterthought. The amusing part is the sort of humility it displays. "Imitate Jesus and Socrates," and mind you don't outshine either of these two. One can just imagine Socrates and Alcibiades roaring in their cups over Philadelphian Benjamin, and Jesus looking at him a little puzzled, and murmuring: "Aren't you wise in your own conceit, Ben?"

"Henceforth be masterless," retorts Ben. "Be ye each one his own master unto himself, and don't let even the Lord put his spoke in." "Each man his own master" is but a puffing up of masterlessness.

Well, the first of Americans practiced this enticing list with assiduity, setting a national example. He had the virtues in columns, and gave himself good and bad marks according as he thought his behavior deserved. Pity these conduct charts are lost to us. He only remarks that Order was his stumbling block. He could not learn to be neat and tidy.

Isn't it nice to have nothing worse to confess?

He was a little model, was Benjamin. Doctor Franklin. Snuff-colored little man! Immortal soul and all!

The immortal soul part was a sort of cheap insurance policy.

Benjamin had no concern, really, with the immortal soul. He was too busy with social man.

1   He swept and lighted the streets of young Philadelphia.
2   He invented electrical appliances.
3   He was the center of a moralizing club in Philadelphia, and he wrote the moral humorisms of Poor Richard.
4   He was a member of all the important councils of Philadelphia, and then of the American colonies.
5   He won the cause of American Independence at the French Court, and was the economic father of the United States.

Now what more can you want of a man? And yet he is *infra dig*, even in Philadelphia.

I admire him. I admire his sturdy courage first of all, then his sagacity, then his glimpsing into the thunders of electricity, then his common-sense humor. All the qualities of a great man, and never more than a great citizen. Middle-sized, sturdy, snuff-colored Doctor Franklin, one of the soundest citizens that ever trod or "used venery."

I do not like him.

And, by the way, I always thought books of Venery were about hunting deer.

There is a certain earnest naïveté about him. Like a child. And like a little old man. He has again become as a little child, always as wise as his grandfather, or wiser.

Perhaps, as I say, the most complete citizen that ever "used venery."

Printer, philosopher, scientist, author and patriot, impeccable husband and citizen, why isn't he an archetype?

Pioneer, Oh Pioneers! Benjamin was one of the greatest pioneers of the United States. Yet we just can't do with him.

What's wrong with him then? Or what's wrong with us?

I can remember, when I was a little boy, my father used to buy a scrubby yearly almanac with the sun and moon and stars on the cover. And it used to prophesy bloodshed and famine. But also crammed in corners it had little anecdotes and humorisms, with a moral tag. And I used to have my little priggish laugh at the woman who counted her chickens before they were hatched, and so forth, and I was convinced that honesty was the best policy, also a little priggishly. The author of these bits was Poor Richard, and Poor Richard was Benjamin Franklin, writing in Philadelphia well over a hundred years before.

And probably I haven't got over those Poor Richard tags yet. I rankle still with them. They are thorns in young flesh.

Because although I still believe that honesty is the best policy, I dislike policy altogether; though it is just as well not to count your chickens before they are hatched, it's still more hateful to count them with gloating when they *are* hatched. It has taken me many years and countless smarts to get out of that barbed wire moral enclosure that Poor Richard rigged up. Here am I now in tatters and scratched to ribbons, sitting in the middle of Benjamin's America looking at the barbed wire, and the fat sheep crawling under the fence to get fat outside and the watchdogs yelling at the gate lest by chance anyone should get out by the proper exit. Oh America! Oh Benjamin! And I just utter a long loud curse against Benjamin and the American corral.

Moral America! Most moral Benjamin. Sound, satisfied Ben!

Man is a moral animal. All right. I am a moral animal. And I'm going to remain such. I'm not going to be turned into a virtuous little automaton as Benjamin would have me. "This is good, that is bad. Turn the little handle and let the good tap flow," saith Benjamin and all America with him. "But first of all extirpate those savages who are always turning on the bad tap."

I am a moral animal. But I am not a moral machine. I don't work with a little set of handles or levers. The Temperance-silence-order-resolution-frugality-industry-sincerity-justice-moderation-cleanliness-tranquillity-chastity-humility keyboard is not going to get me going. I'm really not just an automatic piano with a moral Benjamin getting tunes out of me.

Here's my creed, against Benjamin's. This is what I believe:

*"That I am I."*

*"That my soul is a dark forest."*

*"That my known self will never be more than a little clearing in the forest."*

*"That gods, strange gods, come forth from the forest into the clearing of my known self, and then go back."*

*"That I must have the courage to let them come and go."*

*"That I will never let mankind put anything over me, but that I will try always to recognize and submit to the gods in me and the gods in other men and women."*

There is my creed. He who runs may read. He who prefers to crawl, or to go by gasoline, can call it rot.

Then for a "list." It is rather fun to play at Benjamin.

1  TEMPERANCE   Eat and carouse with Bacchus, or munch dry bread with Jesus, but don't sit down without one of the gods.

2  SILENCE   Be still when you have nothing to say; when genuine passion moves you, say what you've got to say, and say it hot.

3  ORDER   Know that you are responsible to the gods inside you and to the men in whom the gods are manifest. Recognize your superiors and your inferiors, according to the gods. This is the root of all order.

4  RESOLUTION   Resolve to abide by your own deepest promptings, and to sacrifice the smaller thing to the greater. Kill when you must, and be killed the same: the *must* coming from the gods inside you, or from the men in whom you recognize the Holy Ghost.

5  FRUGALITY   Demand nothing; accept what you see fit. Don't waste your pride or squander your emotion.

6  INDUSTRY   Lose no time with ideals; serve the Holy Ghost; never serve mankind.

7  SINCERITY   To be sincere is to remember that I am I, and that the other man is not me.

8  JUSTICE   The only justice is to follow the sincere intuition of the soul, angry or gentle. Anger is just, and pity is just, but judgment is never just.

9  MODERATION   Beware of absolutes. There are many gods.

10  CLEANLINESS   Don't be too clean. It impoverishes the blood.

11  TRANQUILLITY   The soul has many motions, many gods come and go. Try and find your deepest issue, in every confusion, and abide by that. Obey the man in whom you recognize the Holy Ghost; command when your honor comes to command.

12  CHASTITY   Never "use" venery at all. Follow your passional impulse, if it be answered in the other being; but never have any motive in mind, neither offspring nor health nor even pleasure, nor even service. Only know that "venery" is of the great gods. An offering up of yourself to the very great gods, the dark ones, and nothing else.

13  HUMILITY   See all men and women according to the Holy Ghost that is within them. Never yield before the barren.

SUGGESTIONS FOR WRITING

1. David Herbert Lawrence (1885-1930), poet and novelist, was the author of a number of remarkable novels, among them *Sons and Lovers* (1913) and *Lady Chatterly's Lover* (1928). His *Studies in Classic American Literature* (1923) contains this essay on Franklin which, unlike Mark Twain's, which follows, is a direct thrust unsoftened by humor. Yet like Twain, Lawrence complains of the "barbed wire moral enclosure" in which Franklin's maxims imprisoned him as a boy. "They are," says Lawrence, "thorns in young flesh." Therefore he takes Franklin's list of thirteen virtues and rewrites them to suit his own creed. Analyze Lawrence's method. Is it valid in this essay? What are his premises?

2. Lawrence suggests a dialogue between Benjamin Franklin and the Lord. Write a dialogue between the portrait of Franklin as Lawrence drew it and the Mark Twain of *Huck Finn*.

3. Lawrence calls Franklin's list of virtues a "barbed wire fence." What, then, would Lawrence call the Ten Commandments? Is Lawrence simply against lists of virtues or is he making a special case of Franklin's list? The answer may lie in your interpretation of Lawrence's "Holy Ghost." Explain what he means by the term.

4. From hints throughout the essay one may draw a conclusion about Lawrence's opinion of Americans. Draw a portrait of the American as Lawrence sees him.

MARK TWAIN

## The Late Benjamin Franklin*

*"Never put off till to-morrow what you can do day after to-morrow just as well."* —B. F.

This party was one of those persons whom they call Philosophers. He was twins, being born simultaneously in two different houses in the city of Boston. These houses remain unto this day, and have signs upon them worded in accordance with the facts. The signs are considered well enough to have, though not necessary, because the inhabitants point out the two birthplaces to the stranger anyhow, and sometimes as often as several times in the same day. The subject of this memoir was of a vicious disposition, and early prostituted his talents to the invention of maxims and aphorisms calculated to inflict suffering upon the rising generation of all subsequent ages. His simplest acts, also, were contrived with a view to their being held up for the emulation of boys forever—boys who might otherwise have been happy. It was in this spirit that he became the son of a soapboiler, and probably for no other reason than that the efforts of all future boys who tried to be anything might be looked upon with suspicion unless they were the sons of soapboilers. With a malevolence which is without parallel in history, he would work all day, and then sit up nights, and let on to be studying algebra by the light of a smouldering fire, so that all other boys might have to do that also, or else have Benjamin Franklin thrown up to them. Not satisfied with these proceedings, he had a fashion of living wholly on bread and water, and studying astronomy at mealtime—a thing which has brought affliction to millions of boys since, whose fathers had read Franklin's pernicious biography.

His maxims were full of animosity toward boys. Nowadays a boy cannot follow out a single natural instinct without tumbling over some of these everlasting aphorisms and hearing from Franklin on the spot. If he buys two cents' worth of peanuts, his father says, "Remember what Franklin has said, my son—'A groat a day's a

* From *Sketches New and Old*, 1875.

penny a year,' " and the comfort is all gone out of those peanuts. If he wants to spin his top when he has done work, his father quotes, "Procrastination is the thief of time." If he does a virtuous action, he never gets anything for it, because "Virtue is its own reward." And that boy is hounded to death and robbed of his natural rest, because Franklin said once, in one of his inspired flights of malignity:

> Early to bed and early to rise
> Makes a man healthy and wealthy and wise.

As if it were any object to a boy to be healthy and wealthy and wise on such terms. The sorrow that that maxim has cost me through my parents' experimenting on me with it, tongue cannot tell. The legitimate result is my present state of general debility, indigence, and mental aberration. My parents used to have me up before nine o'clock in the morning sometimes when I was a boy. If they had let me take my natural rest where would I have been now? Keeping store, no doubt, and respected by all.

And what an adroit old adventurer the subject of this memoir was! In order to get a chance to fly his kite on Sunday he used to hang a key on the string and let on to be fishing for lightning. And a guileless public would go home chirping about the "wisdom" and the "genius" of the hoary Sabbath-breaker. If anybody caught him playing "mumble-peg" by himself, after the age of sixty, he would immediately appear to be ciphering out how the grass grew—as if it was any of his business. My grandfather knew him well, and he says Franklin was always fixed—always ready. If a body, during his old age, happened on him unexpectedly when he was catching flies, or making mud pies, or sliding on a cellar door, he would immediately look wise, and rip out a maxim, and walk off with his nose in the air and his cap turned wrong side before, trying to appear absent-minded and eccentric. He was a hard lot.

He invented a stove that would smoke your head off in four hours by the clock. One can see the almost devilish satisfaction he took in it by his giving it his name.

He was always proud of telling how he entered Philadelphia for the first time, with nothing in the world but two shillings in his pocket and four rolls of bread under his arm. But really, when you come to examine it critically, it was nothing. Anybody could have done it.

To the subject of this memoir belongs the honor of recommending the army to go back to bows and arrows in place of bayonets and muskets. He observed, with his customary force, that the bayonet was very well under some circumstances, but that he doubted whether it could be used with accuracy at a long range.

Benjamin Franklin did a great many notable things for his country, and made her young name to be honored in many lands as the mother of such a son. It is not the idea of this memoir to ignore that or cover it up. No; the simple idea of it is to snub those pretentious maxims of his, which he worked up with a great show of originality out of truisms that had become wearisome platitudes as early as the dispersion from Babel; and also to snub his stove, and his military inspirations, his unseemly endeavor to make himself conspicuous when he entered Philadelphia, and his flying his kite and fooling away his time in all sorts of such ways when he ought to have been foraging for soap fat, or constructing candles. I merely desired to do away with somewhat of the prevalent calamitous idea among heads of families that Franklin *acquired* his great genius by working for nothing, studying by moonlight, and getting up in the night instead of waiting till morning like a Christian; and that this programme, rigidly inflected, will make a Franklin of every father's fool. It is time these gentlemen were finding out that these execrable eccentricities of instinct and conduct are only the *evidences* of genius, not the *creators* of it. I wish I had been the father of my parents long enough to make them comprehend this truth, and thus prepare them to let their son have an easier time of it. When I was a child I had to boil soap, notwithstanding my father was wealthy, and I had to get up early and study geometry at breakfast, and peddle my own poetry, and do everything just as Franklin did, in the solemn hope that I would be a Franklin some day. And here I am.

SUGGESTIONS FOR WRITING

1. Samuel Langhorne Clemens (1835-1910), known as Mark Twain, was a printer, river pilot, miner, journalist, lecturer, publisher, capitalist,

novelist, and humanitarian. The above selection is from the series of humorous essays called *Sketches New and Old* (1875). Twain is chiefly concerned with Franklin's "unwholesome" influence on boys. Franklin's maxims, Twain says, "were full of animosity toward boys." One of the most enduring characters in American fiction, Huck Finn, is definitely not the type of boy that Franklin's maxims would produce. Yet both Benjamin Franklin and Huck Finn are definitive American characters. Explain the paradox.

2. Like Leif Panduro and Robert Paul Smith, Mark Twain believes that children have a world of their own. He says, "I wish I had been the father of my parents long enough to make them comprehend this truth, and thus prepare them to let their son have an easier time of it." What "truth" would you have wished to make your parents comprehend if you had been their father?

3. Study the technique Twain uses to ridicule Franklin. Following his pattern and his special way of using exaggeration, write a character sketch on a famous historical person.

CARL SANDBURG

# George W. Brown: Pioneer*

At the time I was born one pioneer stood out above all others in the town and country—the name, George W. Brown. A farm boy in Saratoga County, New York, he learned the carpenter's trade, worked on the earliest railroads of the Mohawk Valley, heard from relatives in Illinois of good land out there cheap. In 1836 he was twenty-one and with his wife rode a covered wagon west and ever west for weeks on weeks while the rains came nearly every day and the wagon wheels stuck in mud and clay and had to be lifted or pried loose. Some nine miles from Galesburg in July of 1836 he stopped and looked around, not a house in sight. He traded his team of horses for an eighty of land. His wife ran the farm while he built houses. In Galesburg, Knoxville, Henderson Grove, in later years they pointed to houses well built by Geroge W. Brown. He laid by what he could of his earnings while thinking, studying, and then studying some more. In 1846 he was seen at his small log

* From *Always the Young Strangers* by Carl Sandburg (New York: Harcourt, Brace & World, Inc., 1953). Copyright 1952, 1953 by Carl Sandburg. Reprinted by permission of the publishers.

house near Tylerville, barefooted and wearing only a straw hat, a
hickory shirt, and jeans pants. He was putting together and experimenting with a machine to plant corn. He wrestled and wrangled
with his crude materials, and in 1851 assembled a machine with
which two men and a team could plant sixteen to twenty acres of
corn in a day. Alone in the little log house, he was his own designer,
tooler, assembler, and demonstrator.

In the spring of 1852 he planted with his machine sixteen acres
of corn for himself and eight acres for a neighbor. He planned
that year, and hoped to finish, ten machines and he completed
only one. He sold livestock, sold his last horses, for means to clinch
his patents. In order to go on and produce and sell his cornplanters, he sold his farm, borrowed money at ten per cent interest, sometimes one to two per cent a month, one month paying three per
cent. In 1856 he got his shops in Galesburg going and made six
hundred cornplanters and the next year a thousand. His machines
spread far over the Midwest during the war years, 1861-1865, and
they were credited with food-production increase that helped the
North in winning the war.

Manufacturing costs ran high, however, and after the Brown
Cornplanter Works had been going for ten years, it was said in
Galesburg, "George W. Brown isn't worth a dollar." The ruthless
competition against him slowed down when the United States Supreme Court validated his patents and ordered one competitor to
pay him two hundred thousand dollars. The tide turned and his
plant produced and sold eight thousand machines a year. He had
two hundred men working for him, his shops covering all of a city
block except the corner lot he reserved for the new Methodist
Church of which he was a regularly attending member. The barefoot farmer and carpenter of 1846 enjoyed walking around from
the woodworking department to the machine and blacksmith shops,
then to the pattern rooms, the construction department, the painting and finishing rooms, the storage sheds. Also he had a massive
thronelike chair built, and it was placed on the platform near the
pulpit of his church. There on a Sabbath morning Mr. Brown sat
facing the congregation and they could see him while he saw them.

Mr. Brown was mayor of Galesburg when I was born. I saw him
driving on the streets of Galesburg and I was perhaps eight years
old at the one and only time that I am sure Mr. Brown saw me

when I saw him. It was a summer morning and I was walking alone and barefoot on a dusty road nearly two miles east of Galesburg. I was heading for a swimming hole we called "The Root" where a blowndown tree and its large root made a creek dam and we used to brag that the water was "nearly up to your belly button." I had not quite reached the front gate of Mr. Brown's large farm when I looked back, slowed down in my walk, and kept on looking back. I saw a pair of glossy black horses, a spanking team, on a slow trot, pulling a well kept, shining buggy. The man driving was stockily built, wore a black hat, a black coat, a white shirt with a lay-down collar, and a black bow tie tucked under the collar. His face was broad and pink, a straight nose, the upper lip and cheeks smooth-shaven, and a smoothly rounded, carefully trimmed white beard at his chin.

He pulled in on the reins and slowed the horses to a walk. He gave me a sidewise passing glance, looked me in the eye as he rode past. I couldn't have believed that he was going to stop the buggy and ask me in for a ride—I couldn't and didn't so believe. I was satisfied that he didn't come to a halt and ask me questions. He looked like he had the law with him and had authority to ask me questions that would bother me to answer. I was ten or fifteen feet behind him when the buggy stopped. I saw him reach up one arm and with one hand pull a rope that lifted a lever that moved up and opened the gate. Having never seen a gate open so smooth and easy for a man who didn't get out of a buggy or wagon, I enjoyed seeing it. And I especially enjoyed watching it performed by a nationally known inventor who was the founder of the Brown Cornplanter Works covering nearly one city block. I watched him close the gate by the same easy one-arm pull that had opened it. Then I walked on past the first brickyard, past Highland Park, and joined other kids in water "nearly up to the belly button."

SUGGESTIONS FOR WRITING

1. Carl Sandburg (1878-    ), born in Galesburg, Illinois, had been an itinerant laborer and a soldier in the Spanish-American War before he worked his way through Lombard College in Galesburg. A noted American poet, biographer of Lincoln, and writer of children's books, Mr. Sandburg has won two Pulitzer Prizes. His first book of poems,

*Chicago Poems* (1916), was characterized by simple, powerful utterances which depicted a crude, vital America that Sanburg knew from experience. His poetry also reveals a sensitive appreciation of the beauty of ordinary people and commonplace things. It is interesting to see similar characteristics in his later character sketches in prose, such as the sketch of George W. Brown. The five paragraphs are chronological. There are no elaborate figures of speech to distract from the business at hand. Write a character sketch, using Sandburg's pattern. Choose someone you knew during your childhood.

2. Are there special traits in George W. Brown that one might classify as peculiarly American? Are there some traits that are not American? What is it that characterizes an American?

3. Show a man in the process of *doing* something and you will reveal more about the man than paragraphs of generalized description. Reveal the dominant traits of someone you know by showing him in the process of doing something.

WALTER LIPPMANN

# Edison: Inventor of Invention*

It is impossible to measure the importance of Edison by adding up the specific inventions with which his name is associated. Far-reaching as many of them have been in their effect on modern civilization, the total effect of Edison's career surpasses the sum of them all. He did not merely make the incandescent lamp and the phonograph and innumerable other devices practicable for general use; it was given to him to demonstrate the power of applied science so concretely, so understandably, so convincingly that he altered the mentality of mankind. In his lifetime, largely because of his successes, there came into widest acceptance the revolutionary conception that man could by the use of his intelligence invent a new mode of living on this planet; the human spirit, which in all previous ages had regarded the conditions of life as essentially unchanging and beyond man's control, confidently, and perhaps somewhat naively, adopted the conviction that anything could be changed and everything could be controlled.

* From *Interpretations, 1931-1932* by Walter Lippmann (New York: The Macmillan Company, 1932). Copyright 1932 by Walter Lippmann. Reprinted by permission of the publishers.

The idea of progress is in the scale of history a very new idea. It seems first to have taken possession of a few minds in the seventeenth and eighteenth centuries as an accompaniment of the great advances in pure science. It gained greater currency in the first half of the nineteenth century when industrial civilization began to be transformed by the application of steam power. But these changes, impressive as they were, created so much human misery by the crude and cruel manner in which they were exploited that all through the century men instinctively feared and opposed the progress of machines, and of the sciences on which they rested. It was only at the end of the century, with the perfecting of the electric light bulb, the telephone, the phonograph, and the like, that the ordinary man began to feel that science could actually benefit him. Edison supplied the homely demonstrations which insured the popular acceptance of science, and clinched the popular argument, which had begun with Darwin, about the place of science in man's outlook on life.

Thus he became the supreme propagandist of science and his name the great symbol of an almost blind faith in its possibilities. Thirty years ago, when I was a schoolboy, the ancient conservatism of man was still the normal inheritance of every child. We began to have electric lights, and telephones, and to see horseless carriages, but our attitude was a mixture of wonder, fear, and doubt. Perhaps these things would work. Perhaps they would not explode. Today every schoolboy not only takes all the existing inventions as much for granted as we took horses and dogs for granted, but, also, he is entirely convinced that all other desirable things can and will be invented. In my youth the lonely inventor who could not obtain a hearing was still the stock figure of the imagination. Today the only people who are not absolutely sure that television is perfected are the inventors themselves. No other person played so great a part as Edison in this change in human expectation, and, finally, by the cumulative effect of his widely distributed inventions plus a combination of the modern publicity technique and the ancient mythmaking faculty of men, he was lifted in the popular imagination to a place where he was looked upon not only as the symbol but the creator of a new age.

In strict truth an invention is almost never the sole product of any one mind. The actual inventor is almost invariably the man who succeeds in combining and perfecting previous discoveries in such a way as to make them convenient and profitable. Edison had a peculiar genius for carrying existing discoveries to the point where they could be converted into practicable devices, and it would be no service to his memory, or to the cause of science which he serves so splendidly, to pretend that he invented by performing solitary miracles. The light which was born in his laboratory at Menlo Park fifty-two years ago was conceived in the antecedent experiments of many men in many countries over a period of nearly forty years, and these experiments in their turn were conceivable only because of the progress of the mathematical and physical sciences in the preceding two centuries.

The success which Edison finally achieved in his specific inventions demonstrated the possibility of invention as a continuing art. Mr. Hoover, in his tribute printed yesterday,[1] pointed directly to this fact as constituting the historic importance of the man, when he said that Edison "did more than any other American to place invention on an organized basis of the utilization of the raw materials of pure science and discovery." Because of Edison, more than of any other man, scientific research has an established place in our society; because of the demonstrations he made, the money of taxpayers and stockholders has become available for studies the nature of which they do not often understand, though they appreciate their value and anticipate their ultimate pecuniary benefits.

It would be a shallow kind of optimism to assume that the introduction of the art of inventing has been an immediate and unmixed blessing to mankind. It is rather the most disturbing element in civilization, the most profoundly revolutionary thing which has ever been let loose in the world. For the whole ancient wisdom of man is founded upon the conception of a life which in its fundamentals changes imperceptibly if at all. The effect of organized, subsidized invention, stimulated by tremendous incentives of profit, and encouraged by an insatiable popular appetite for change, is to set all the relations of men in violent motion, and to create overpowering problems faster than human wisdom has as yet been able to assimilate them. Thus the age we live in offers little prospect of outward stability, and only those who by an inner serenity and

---

[1] December 15, 1929.

disentanglement have learned how to deal with the continually unexpected can be at home in it. It may be that in time we shall become used to change as in our older wisdom we had become used to the unchanging. But such wisdom it is impossible to invent or to make widely and quickly available by mass production and salesmanship. It will, therefore, grow much more slowly than the inventions which ultimately it must learn to master.

### SUGGESTIONS FOR WRITING

1. Walter Lippmann (1889-     ), has been a political columnist for more than fifty years. Since 1931 he has written for the *New York Herald Tribune*. He was awarded a Pulitzer Prize in 1958. His books on politics and morals emphasize individual integrity and freedom rather than social or governmental control. Edison encouraged what Lippmann calls "organized, subsidized invention, stimulated by tremendous incentives of profit," yet his contribution is so great that it is impossible to ignore; hence he is viewed with mixed feelings. Analyze Lippmann's message. List positive ideas in one column and other ideas in a second column. Is there a balance?

2. "The actual inventor is almost invariably the man who succeeds in combining and perfecting previous discoveries in such a way as to make them convenient and profitable." Whether such a man is called an engineer or a scientific technician, he is always in demand in any society. Assume you are a responsible college educator who must devise the best possible program for producing such a man. With what basic courses would you begin, and why?

3. Using Lippmann's organizational pattern, select a businessman or scientist in America and relate his feats to a broad-scale idea, e.g., human progress, national destiny, or improved social relations.

H. L. MENCKEN

# Dempsey vs. Carpentier*

In the great combat staged there in that colossal sterilizer beneath the harsh Jersey sun there was little to entertain the fancier of

---

* From *A Mencken Chrestomathy* by H. L. Mencken (New York: Alfred A. Knopf, Inc., 1949). Copyright 1949 by Alfred A. Knopf, Inc. Reprinted by permission of the publishers.

gladiatorial delicacies. It was simply a brief and hopeless struggle between a man full of romantic courage and one overwhelmingly superior in every way. This superiority was certainly not only in weight nor even in weight and reach.

As a matter of fact, the difference in weight was a good deal less than many another championship battle has witnessed, and Carpentier's blows seldom failed by falling short. What ailed them was that they were not hard enough to knock out Dempsey or even to do him any serious damage. Whenever they landed Dempsey simply shook them off. And in the intervals between them he landed dozens and scores of harder ones. It was a clean fight, if not a beautiful one. It was swift, clear-cut, brilliant and honest.

Before half of the first round was over it must have been plain to even the policemen and Follies girls at the ringside that poor Carpentier was done for. Dempsey heaved him into the ropes, indeed, at the end of the first minute and thereafter gave him such a beating that he was plainly gone by the time he got to his corner. Blow after blow landed upon his face, neck, ribs, belly and arms. Two-thirds of them were upper cuts at very short range—blows which shook him, winded him, confused him, hurt him, staggered him. A gigantic impact was behind them. His face began to look blobby; red marks appeared all over his front.

Where was his celebrated right? Obviously he was working hard for a chance to unlimber it. He walked in boldly, taking terrific punishment with great gallantry. Suddenly the opportunity came and he let it fly. It caught Dempsey somewhere along the frontiers of his singularly impassive face. The effect upon him was apparently no greater than that of a somewhat angry slap upon an ordinary ox. His great bulk hardly trembled. He blinked, snuffled amiably and went on. Five seconds later Carpentier was seeking cover behind the barricade of his own gloves, and Dempsey was delivering colossal wallops under it, over it and headlong through it.

He fought with both hands, and he fought all the time. Carpentier, after that, was in the fight only intermittently. His right swings reached Dempsey often enough, but as one followed another they hurt him less and less. Toward the end he scarcely dodged them. More and more they clearly missed him, shooting under the arms or sliding behind his ears.

In the second round, of course, there was a moment when Carpentier appeared to be returning to the fight. The crowd, eager to reward his heroic struggle, got to its legs and gave him a cheer. He
waded into Jack, pushed him about a bit, and now and then gave
him a taste of that graceful right. But there was no left to keep it
company, and behind it there was not enough amperage to make it
burn. Dempsey took it, shook it off, and went on.

Clout, clout, clout! In the space of half a minute Carpentier
stopped twenty-five sickening blows—most of them short, and all
of them cruelly hard. His nose began to melt. His jaw sagged. He
heaved pathetically. Because he stood up to it gamely, and even
forced the fighting, the crowd was for him, and called it his round.
But this view was largely that of amateurs familiar only with rough
fights between actors at the Lambs club. Observed more scientifi-
cally, the round was Jack's. When it closed he was as good as new—
and Carpentier was beginning to go pale.

It was not in the second, but in the third round that Carpentier
did his actual best. Soon after the gong he reached Jack with a
couple of uppers that seemed to have genuine steam in them, and
Jack began to show a new wariness. But it was only for a moment.
Presently Carpentier was punching holes through the air with
wild rights that missed the champion by a foot, and the champion
was battering him to pieces with shorts that covered almost every
square inch of his upper works. They came in pairs, right and left,
and then in quartets, and then in octets, and then almost continuously.

Carpentier decayed beneath them like an Autumn leaf in Vallom-
brosa. Gently and pathetically he fluttered down. His celebrated
right by this time gave Jack no more concern. It would have taken
ten of them to have knocked out even Fatty Arbuckle. They had
the effect upon the iron champion of petting with a hot water bag.
Carpentier went to his corner bloody and bowed. It was all over
with the high hopes of that gallant France. He had fought a brave
fight; he had kept the faith—but the stars were set for Ireland and
the Mormons.

The last round was simply mopping up. Carpentier was on the
floor in half a minute. I doubt that Dempsey hit him hard in this
round. A few jabs, and all the starch was out of his neck. He got up
at nine, and tried a rush. Jack shoved him over, and gave him two

or three light ones for good measure as he went down again. He managed to move one of his legs, but above the waist he was dead. When the referee counted ten Dempsey lifted him to his feet and helped him to his stool.

With his arms outstretched along the ropes, he managed to sit up, but all the same he was a very badly beaten pug. His whole face was puffy and blood ran out of his nose and mouth. His façade was one great mass of hoof-prints. Between them his skin had the whiteness of a mackerel's belly. Gone were all his hopes. And with them, the hard francs and centimes, at ruinous rates of exchange, of all the beauty and chivalry of France. Many Frenchmen were in the stand. They took it as Carpentier fought—bravely and stoically. It was a hard and a square battle, and there was no dishonor in it for the loser.

But as a spectacle, of course, it suffered by its shortness and its one-sidedness. There was never the slightest doubt in any cultured heart, from the moment the boys put up their dukes, that Dempsey would have a walk-over.

As I say, it was not only or even mainly a matter of weight. Between the two of them, as they shook hands, there was no very noticeable disparity in size and bulk. Dempsey was the larger, but he certainly did not tower over Carpentier. He was also a bit the thicker and solider, but Carpentier was thick and solid too. What separated them so widely was simply a difference in fighting technique. Carpentier was the lyrical fighter, prodigal with agile footwork and blows describing graceful curves. He fought nervously, eagerly and beautifully. I have seen far better boxers, but I have never seen a more brilliant fighter—that is, with one hand.

Dempsey showed none of that style and passion. He seldom moved his feet, and never hopped, skipped or jumped. His strategy consisted in the bare business: (a) of standing up to it as quietly and solidly as possible; and (b) of jolting, bumping, thumping, bouncing and shocking his antagonist to death with the utmost convenient despatch.

This method is obviously not one for gladiators born subject to ordinary human weaknesses and feelings; it presents advantages to an antagonist who is both quick and strong; it grounds itself, when all is said, rather more on mere toughness than on actual skill at fighting. But that toughness is certainly a handy thing to have when one hoofs the fatal rosin. It gets one around bad situations. It saves the day when the vultures begin to circle overhead.

To reinforce his left Dempsey has a wallop in his right hand like the bump of a ferryboat into its slip. The two work constantly and with lovely synchronization. The fighter who hopes to stand up to them must be even tougher than Jack is, which is like aspiring to be even taller than the late Cy Sulloway. Carpentier simply fell short. He could not hurt Dempsey, and he could not live through the Dempsey bombardment. So he perished there in that Homeric stewpan, a brave man but an unwise one.

The show was managed with great deftness, and all the antecedent rumors of a frame-up were laid in a manner that will bring in much kudos and mazuma to Mons. Tex Rickard, the manager, hereafter. I have never been in a great crowd that was more orderly, or that had less to complain of in the way of avoidable discomforts.

Getting out of the arena, true enough, involved some hot work with the elbows; the management, in fact, put in small fry after the main battle in order to hold some of the crowd back, and so diminish the shoving in the exits, which were too few and too narrow. If there had been a panic in the house, thousands would have been heeled to death. But getting in was easy enough, the seats though narrow were fairly comfortable, and there was a clear view of the ring from every place in the monster bowl. Those who bought bleacher tickets, in fact, saw just as clearly as those who paid $50 apiece for seats at the ringside.

The crowd in the more expensive sections was well-dressed, good-humored and almost distinguished. The common allegation of professional moralists that prize fights are attended by thugs was given a colossal and devastating answer. No such cleanly and decent looking gang was ever gathered at a Billy Sunday meeting, or at any other great moral outpouring that I have ever attended. All the leaders of fashionable and theatrical society were on hand, most of them in checkerboard suits and smoking excellent cigars, or, if female, in new hats and pretty frocks.

Within the range of my private vision, long trained to esthetic alertness, there was not a single homely gal. Four rows ahead of me there were no less than half a dozen who would have adorned the "Follies." Behind me, clad in pink, was a creature so lovely that she caused me to miss most of the preliminaries. She rooted for Carpentier in the Franch language, and took the count with heroic fortitude.

## SUGGESTIONS FOR WRITING

1. H. L. Mencken (1880-1956) was a journalist and student of the American language unparalleled in the history of American newspapers. He edited *The American Mercury* from 1924 to 1933, and he was long a columnist for the Baltimore *Sun*. His six series of *Prejudices* (1919-1927) reveal his social, political and moral views, and his *The American Language* (1918—with later revisions) is a scholarly masterpiece. One tribute to his power, effectiveness, and influence on American letters is paid by Richard Wright, one of America's foremost Negro authors, in *Black Boy* (see excerpt on page 335). Mencken's interest in language is revealed in everything he wrote. For example, note the fifth sentence of the above piece, "What ailed them was that they were not hard enough to knock out Dempsey. . . ." Somehow this is Mencken and no other sports writer in America. Select a half dozen sentences which seem "somehow special" and recast them in your own words.

2. Mencken does not simply report what happened. He interprets what he saw, but above all he comes to grips with it, grapples with it, masters it. Carpentier had the sympathy of the crowd, but was not the favorite from the standpoint of betting. Heywood Broun, another reporter at the fight, said: "Jack Dempsey won fairly and squarely. He is a great fighter, perhaps the most efficient the world has ever known, but everybody came away from the arena talking about Carpentier." Taking a clue from Mencken, write a report of an event in which the crowd's favorite loses.

3. Describe the cheering section when the home team is losing.

PAUL GALLICO

# What the Human Animal Can Stand *

It all began back in 1922 when I was a cub sportswriter and consumed with more curiosity than was good for my health. I had seen my first professional prizefights and wondered at the curious

---

* From *Farewell to Sport* by Paul Gallico (New York: Alfred A. Knopf, Inc., 1938). Copyright 1937 by Paul Gallico. Reprinted by permission of the publishers.

behavior of men under the stress of blows, the sudden checking and the beginning of a little fall forward after a hard punch, the glazing of the eyes and the loss of locomotor control, the strange actions of men on the canvas after a knockdown as they struggled to regain their senses and arise on legs that seemed to have turned into rubber. I had never been in any bad fist fights as a youngster, though I had taken a little physical punishment in football, but it was not enough to complete the picture. Could one think under those conditions?

I had been assigned to my first training camp coverage, Dempsey's at Saratoga Springs, where he was preparing for his famous fight with Luis Firpo. For days I watched him sag a spar boy with what seemed to be no more than a light cuff on the neck, or pat his face with what looked like no more than a caressing stroke of his arm, and the fellow would come all apart at the seams and collapse in a useless heap, grinning vacuously or twitching strangely. My burning curiosity got the better of prudence and a certain reluctance to expose myself to physical pain. I asked Dempsey to permit me to box a round with him. I had never boxed before, but I was in good physical shape, having just completed a four-year stretch as a galley slave in the Columbia eight-oared shell.

When it was over and I escaped through the ropes, shaking, bleeding a little from the mouth, with rosin dust on my pants and a vicious throbbing in my head, I knew all that there was to know about being hit in the prize ring. It seems that I had gone to an expert for tuition. I knew the sensation of being stalked and pursued by a relentless, truculent professional destroyer whose trade and business it was to injure men. I saw the quick flash of the brown forearm that precedes the stunning shock as a bony, leather-bound fist lands on cheek or mouth. I learned more (partly from photographs of the lesson, viewed afterwards, one of which shows me ducked under a vicious left hook, an act of which I never had the slightest recollection) about instinctive ducking and blocking than I could have in ten years of looking at prizefights, and I learned, too, that as the soldier never hears the bullet that kills him, so does the fighter rarely, if ever, see the punch that tumbles blackness over him like a mantle, with a tearing rip as though the roof of his skull were exploding, and robs him of his senses.

There was just that—a ripping in my head and then sudden

blackness, and the next thing I knew, I was sitting on the canvas covering of the ring floor with my legs collapsed under me, grinning idiotically. How often since have I seen that same silly, goofy look on the faces of dropped fighters—and understood it. I held onto the floor with both hands, because the ring and the audience outside were making a complete clockwise revolution, came to a stop, and then went back again counterclockwise. When I struggled to my feet, Jack Kearns, Dempsey's manager, was counting over me, but I neither saw nor heard him and was only conscious that I was in a ridiculous position and that the thing to do was to get up and try to fight back. The floor swayed and rocked beneath me like a fishing dory in an offshore swell, and it was a welcome respite when Dempsey rushed into a clinch, held me up, and whispered into my ear: "Wrestle around a bit, son, until your head clears." And then it was that I learned what those little love taps to the back of the neck and the short digs to the ribs can mean to the groggy pugilist more than half knocked out. It is a murderous game, and the fighter who can escape after having been felled by a lethal blow has my admiration. And there, too, I learned that there can be no sweeter sound than the bell that calls a halt to hostilities.

From that afternoon on, also, dated my antipathy for the spectator at prizefights who yells: "Come on, you bum, get up and fight! Oh, you big quitter! Yah yellow, yah yellow!" Yellow, eh? It is all a man can do to get up after being stunned by a blow, much less fight back. But they do it. And how a man is able to muster any further interest in a combat after being floored with a blow to the pit of the stomach will always remain to me a miracle of what the human animal is capable of under stress.

SUGGESTIONS FOR WRITING

1. Paul Gallico (1897-      ) is an American author and newspaperman. The above selection is less than half of a longer piece called "The Feel," which appears in Gallico's *Farewell to Sport* (1939). In other sections of the article he tells of standing on a tennis court opposite Bill Tilden's booming serve, or skiing down the course of a breakneck downhill race, or trying to catch a curve thrown by a major league pitcher. In each of these instances he is after "the feel" of the thing— he wants to know what the athlete *experiences* in order to write about

it effectively. Your experiences in learning need not be as dramatic as Gallico's, but they may be as rewarding. Ask someone on the varsity to let you try your skill at the discus, javelin, broad jump, high jump, pole vault, high or low hurdles, fencing, wrestling, or tumbling. Use Gallico as a pattern and describe "the feel" of the sport.

2. Gallico's thesis is that experience deepens appreciation. Apply it to other areas. For example, has anything happened to your appreciation of the discipline of study?

3. After reading Gallico's piece, comment on the anonymous quotation: "It signifies nothing to play well if you lose."

4. Comment on the quotation: "An American university is an athletic institution in which a few classes are held for the feebleminded." (Ascribed to a Chinese student.)

# Man in the City

The larger our great cities grow, the more irresistible becomes the attraction which they exert on the children of the country, who are fascinated by them, as the birds are fascinated by the lighthouse or the moths by the candle.
> —Havelock Ellis, *The Task of Social Hygiene,* 1916

O beautiful for patriot dream
    That sees beyond the years
Thine alabaster cities gleam
    Undimmed by human tears!
> —Katherine Lee Bates, *America the Beautiful,* 1893

A great city is that which has the greatest men and women.
> —Whitman, *Song of the Broad-Axe,* 1855

God the first garden made, and the first city Cain.
> —William Cowley, *The Garden,* 1664

Not houses finely roofed or the stones of walls well-built, nay nor canals and dockyards, make the city, but men able to use their opportunity.
> —Alcaeus *On Aristides,* c. 560 B.C.

City life: millions of people being lonesome together.
> —Thoreau, *Journal,* 1906

Purple-robed and pauper-clad
Raving, rotting, money-mad
A squirming herd in Mammon's mesh,
A wilderness of human flesh;
Crazed with avarice, lust, and rum,
New York, thy name's Delirium.
> —Byron Rufus Newton, *Owed to New York,* 1903

The largest part of mankind are nowhere greater strangers than at home.
> —Coleridge, *Aids to Reflection,* 1825

SINCLAIR LEWIS

# The Usefullest City in the World *

Villages—overgrown towns—three-quarters of a million people still dressing, eating, building houses, attending church, to make an impression on their neighbors, quite as they did back on Main Street, in villages of two thousand. And yet not villages at all, the observer uneasily sees, as he beholds factories with ten thousand workmen, with machines more miraculous than the loaves and fishes, with twice the power and ten times the skill of a romantic grand duchy. They are transitional metropolises—but that transition will take a few hundred years, if the custom persists of making it a heresy punishable by hanging or even by ostracism to venture to say that Cleveland or Minneapolis or Baltimore or Buffalo is not the wisest, gayest, kindliest, usefullest city in all the world. So long as every teacher and journalist and workman admits that John J. Jones, the hustling sales manager for the pickle factory, is the standard in beauty and courtesy and justice—well, so long will they be sore stricken with a pest of J. J. Joneses.

It is not quite a new thought to submit that though admittedly Mr. Jones somewhat lacks in the luxuries of artistic taste and agreeable manners, yet he is so solid a worker, so true a friend, and so near to genius in the development of this astounding and adventurously new industrial system, that he is worthier, he is really more beautiful, than any Anatole France or [word omitted]. Are his pickle machines with their power and ingenuity a new art, com-

---

* From *The Man from Main Street: A Sinclair Lewis Reader,* edited by Melville H. Cane and Harry E. Maule (New York: Random House, Inc., 1953). Copyright 1953 by the Estate of Sinclair Lewis, Melville H. Cane and Pincus Berner, executors. Reprinted by permission of the publishers.

parable to *vers libre*, and is there not in his noisiest advertising, his billboards smeared across tranquil fields, a passion for achievement which is, to the unprejudiced discernment, a religious fervor, an esthetic passion, a genius such as inspired the crusader and explorer and poet? Is not his assailant a blind and reactionary fellow who demands in this rough glorious pioneer outworn standards and beauties dead and dry?

Only it happens that these generous inquirers who seek to make themselves comfortable by justifying their inescapable neighbor, Mr. Jones, give him somewhat too much credit. Mr. Jones, the sales manager, Mr. Brown, the general manager, Mr. Robinson, the president—all the persons in the pickle hierarchy most to be accredited with passion and daring and new beauties—are nothing in the world but salesmen, commercial demagogues, industrial charlatans, creators of a demand which they wistfully desire to supply. Those miraculous, those admittedly noble machines—they were planned and built and improved and run by very common workmen, who get no credit whatever for pioneering. Those astounding pickle formulae, they were made by chemists, unknown and unglorified. Even those far-flung billboards, the banners of Mr. Jones's gallant crusade—their text was written by forty-a-week copywriters, their pictures—their very terrible pictures—painted by patient hacks, and the basic idea, of having billboards, came not from the passionate brain of Mr. Jones but was cautiously worked out, on quite routine and unromantic lines, by hesitating persons in an advertising agency.

And it is these workmen, chemists, hacks, who are likely to be eager about beauty, courageous in politics—Moon Calves—children of the new world. Mr. Jones himself—ah, that rare and daring and shining-new creator of industrial poetry, he votes the Republican ticket straight, he hates all labor unionism, he belongs to the Masons and the Presbyterian Church, his favorite author is Zane Grey, and in other particulars noted in this story, his private life seems scarce to mark him as the rough, ready, aspiring, iconoclastic, creative, courageous innovator his admirers paint him. He is a bagman. He is a pedlar. He is a shopkeeper. He is a camp follower. He is a bag of aggressive wind.

America has taken to itself the credit of being the one pioneering nation of the world; it has thereby (these three hundred years now) excused all flabbiness of culture and harshness of manner and frantic oppression of critics. And, strangely, Europe has granted that assertion. Never an English author descends upon these palpitating and grateful shores without informing us that from our literature one expects only the burly power and clumsiness of ditch-diggers. We listen to him, and are made proud of the clumsiness and burliness—without quite going so far as to add also the power.

It is a national myth.

England has, in India, Africa, Canada, Australia, had quite as many new frontiers, done quite as much pioneering—and done it as bravely and as cruelly and as unscrupulously—as have we in pushing the western border from the Alleghenies to Honolulu. Thus France in Africa, Holland in the West Indies, Germany all over the world. And England has quite as many Rough Fellows as America. Lord Fisher criticizing the British navy in the tones of a tobacco-chewing trapper—is he so much less of a Rough Fellow and Pioneer and Innovator than the Harvard instructor reading Austin Dobson by candlelight? The silk salesman, crossing the Arizona desert—in a Pullman—is he so much bolder a ditchdigger than Ole Bill, the English Tommy?

A myth! America is no longer an isolated race of gallant Indian-slayers. It is a part of the world. Like every other nation, it is made up of both daring innovators and crusted crabs. Its literature and its J. J. Joneses are subject to the same rules as the literature and the bustling innumerous J. J. Joneses of England or Spain or Norway. Mr. Henry van Dyke is no newer or more pioneering than Mr. H. G. Wells—and subject to no more lenient rules or more provincial judgments.

Of this contradiction between pioneering myth and actual slackness, these Monarchs, these cities of 300,000 or so, are the best examples. Unfortunately American literature has discerned as types of communities only the larger or older cities—as New York, San Francisco, Richmond—and the villages, with nothing between. Yet there is a sort of community in between, an enormously important type—the city of a few hundred thousand, the metropolis that yet is a village, the world center that yet is ruled by cautious villagers. Only Booth Tarkington, with his novels flavored by Indianapolis, and a few local celebrities eager to present the opulence of their several Monarchs, have dealt with these cities which, more

than any New York, produce our wares and elect our presidents—
and buy our books. Yet they are important enough to quarrel over
—they are great enough to deserve the compliment of being told
one's perception of the truth about them.

. . . . . . . . . . . . . . . . . . .

To say that they are subject to the same rules as Munich or
Florence does not at all mean that they are like Munich or Florence.
They have grown so rapidly, they have been so innocent and so
Republican and so Presbyterian and so altogether boosting and
innocent, that they have produced a type of existence a little different from any other in the world. It may not continue to be so
different—it some time may be subject also to fine tradition and
the vision of quiet and honest work as against noisy selling of
needless things—but this fineness it will not attain without self-
study, and an admission that twenty story buildings are not necessarily nobler than Notre Dame, and that the production of 19,000
motor cars a day does not of itself prove those cars to be better
built than cars produced at one a day.

This foreshadowing of a future adoption of richer traditions does
not, of course, mean at all that in the future these Monarchs are
to be spiritually or physically like Munich or Florence. It is a paradox of psychology that it is precisely the richest philosophies, with
the largest common fund of wisdom from all ages, which produce
the most diverse and lovely products, while it is the thinner and
hastier philosophies which produce the most standardized and
boresomely similar products.

German Munich and Italian Florence are vastly and entertain-
ingly different in all that counts—in passions, wines, aspirations,
and furniture—for the reason that they have both digested and
held and brilliantly changed a common wisdom of Plato and
Shakespeare and Karl Marx. But German Milwaukee and Italian
Hartford are uncomfortably alike because they have cast off all the
hard-earned longings of mankind and joined in a common aspiration to be rich, notorious, and One Hundred Per Cent American.

It is this fact which is the second great feature of the American
cities of 300,000—and as important as their other feature of unconquerable villageness. It is this fact which makes a novel that
chanced to be local and concrete and true in regard to Omaha
equally local and concrete and true regarding twenty other cities.

Naturally, they are not all precisely alike. There is a difference resulting from situation—from a background of hills or plain, of river or seacoast; a difference from the products of the back country —iron, wheat, cotton; a distinct difference from the various ages— the difference between Seattle and Charleston.

But these differences have for a long time now tended to decrease, so powerful is our faith in standardization. When a new hotel, factory, house, garage, motion-picture theater, row of shops, church, or synagogue is erected in gray Charleston, rambling New Orleans, or San Francisco of the '49ers, that structure is precisely, to the last column of reinforced concrete and the last decorative tile, the same as a parallel structure in the new cities of Portland or Kansas City. And the souls of those structures—the hospitality of the hotels, the mechanical methods in the garages, the minutest wording of the sermons in the churches—are increasingly as standardized as the shells.

It would not be possible to write a novel which would in every line be equally true to Munich and Florence. Despite the fundamental hungers equally true to all human beings, despite the similarity of manners and conversation in the layer of society which contentedly travels all over the world, despite the like interest of kissing at Fiesole and at Gansedorf, so vast and subtle are the differences in every outward aspect, every detail of artistic aspiration and national pride and hope, that the two cities seem to belong to two different planets.

But Hartford and Milwaukee—the citizens of those two distant cities go to the same offices, speak the same patois on the same telephones, go to the same lunch and the same athletic clubs, etc., etc., etc.

.   .   .   .   .   .   .   .   .   .   .   .   .   .   .   .

The test of the sameness is in the people. If you are by magic taken instantly to any city of over 80,000 in the United States and set down in the business center, in a block, say, with a new hotel, a new motion-picture theater, and a line of newish shops, not three hours of the intensest study of the passing people—men on business errands, messenger boys, women shopping, poolroom idlers—would indicate in what city, indeed in what part of the country, you were. Only by traveling to the outskirts and discovering mountains or ocean or wheat fields, and perhaps Negro shanties, Mexican adobes, or German breweries, would you begin to get a clue—and these diverse clues lessen each year. They know it not, but all these bright women and pompous men are in uniforms, under the discipline of a belligerent service, as firmly as any soldier in khaki. For those that like it—that is what they like; but there are those of us who hesitated about being drafted into the army of complacency.

SUGGESTIONS FOR WRITING

1. Sinclair Lewis (1885-1951) won the Nobel Prize for Literature in 1930, but he had previously declined the Pulitzer Prize for his novel, *Arrowsmith* (1926) with these words: "Every compulsion is put upon writers to become safe, polite, obedient, and sterile. I protest. I declined election to the National Institute of Arts and Letters some years ago, and now I must decline the Pulitzer Prize." His essay above (from the unpublished introduction to *Babbitt*, 1922) is a protest characteristic of a man who set out to awaken America to various evils. In two carefully written paragraphs, explain just what evils Lewis was protesting.

2. Lewis's technique is to bring together the arguments of the opposition and banish them by satirical thrusts or deliberately blunt rhetorical questions. Try this technique on your favorite target. First, work to understand Lewis's method thoroughly. Copy the second and third paragraphs and then write two similar paragraphs.

3. Lewis is protesting standardization. Does he offer a substitute? Does he need to? How do you feel about the subject? State your views.

4. Lewis did not live to see the flowering of shopping centers on the outskirts of every large city in America. Write a report on these shopping centers, one which Lewis would have enjoyed reading.


JANE JACOBS

## Barbarity in the City Streets*

To build city districts that are custom-made for easy crime is idiotic. Yet that is what we do. Today barbarism has taken over many city streets—or people fear it has, which comes to much the same thing in the end.

---

* From *Harper's Magazine* (September, 1961). © 1961 by Jane Jacobs. Another version of this material appears in *The Death and Life of Great American Cities*, by Jane Jacobs. Reprinted by permission of Random House, Inc.

"I live in a lovely quiet residential area," says a friend of mine who is hunting for another place to live. "The only disturbing sound at night is the occasional scream of someone being mugged."

It does not take many incidents of violence to make people fear the streets. And as they fear them, they use them less, which makes the streets still more unsafe.

This problem is not limited to the older parts of cities. Sidewalk and doorstep insecurity are as serious in cities that have made conscientious efforts to rebuild as they are in those cities that have lagged. Nor is it illuminating to tag minority groups, or the poor, or the outcast, with responsibility for city danger. Some of the safest—as well as some of the most dangerous—sidewalks in New York, for example, are those along which poor people or minority groups live. And this is true elsewhere.

Deep and complicated social ills underlie delinquency and crime —in suburbs and towns as well as great cities. But if we are to maintain a city society that can diagnose and keep abreast of these profoundly difficult problems, the starting point must be to strengthen the workable forces that now exist for maintaining urban safety and civilization. In fact we do precisely the opposite.

First, we must understand that the public peace—the sidewalk and street peace—of cities is not kept primarily by the police, necessary though they are. It is kept primarily by an intricate, almost unconscious, network of voluntary controls and standards among the people themselves. In some city areas—notably older public housing projects and streets with very high population turnover— the keeping of public sidewalk law and order is left almost entirely to the police and special guards. Such places are jungles.

Nor can the problem be solved by spreading people out more thinly, trading the characteristics of cities for the characteristics of suburbs. If this were possible, then Los Angeles should be in good shape because superficially it is almost all suburban. It has virtually no districts compact enough to qualify as dense city. Yet Los Angeles' crime figures are flabbergasting. Among the seventeen standard metropolitan areas with populations over a million, Los Angeles stands pre-eminent in crime, especially the crimes associated with personal attack, which make people fear the streets. (Los Angeles, for example, has a forcible rape rate more than twice as high as either of the next two cities, which happen to be St.

Louis and Philadelphia, three times as high as the rate for Chicago, and more than four times the rate for New York.)

The reasons for Los Angeles' high crime rates are complex, and at least in part obscure. But of this we can be sure: thinning out a city does not insure safety from crime and fear of crime. This is demonstrable too in cities where pseudosuburbs or superannuated suburbs are ideally suited to rape, muggings, beatings, holdups, and the like. The all-important question is: How much easy opportunity does any city street offer to crime? It may be that there is some absolute amount of crime in a given city, which will find an outlet somehow (I do not believe this). In any case, different kinds of city streets garner radically different shares of barbarism.

Some city streets afford no such opportunity. The streets of the North End of Boston are outstanding examples. City planners officially consider this area a "slum" but the streets are probably as safe as any place on earth. Although most of the North End's residents are Italian or of Italian descent, the district's streets are heavily and constantly used also by people of every race and background. Some of the strangers from outside work in or close to the district; some come to shop and stroll; many make a point of cashing their paychecks in North End stores and immediately making their big weekly purchases in streets where they know they will not be parted from their money between the getting and the spending.

Frank Havey, director of the North End Union, the local settlement house, says, "In twenty-eight years I have never heard of a single case of rape, mugging, molestation of a child, or other street crime of that sort in the district. And if there had been any, I would have heard of it even if it did not reach the papers." Half a dozen times or so in the past three decades, says Havey, would-be molesters have made a try toward luring a child or, late at night, attacking a woman. In every such case the try was thwarted by passers-by, by kibitzers from windows, or shopkeepers.

Meantime, in the Elm Hill Avenue section of Roxbury, a part of inner Boston that is suburban in superficial character, prudent people stay off the streets at night because of the ever present possibility of street assaults with no kibitzers to protect the victims. For this and other related reasons—dispiritedness and dullness— most of Roxbury has run down. It has become a place to leave.

Roxbury's disabilities, and especially its Great Blight of Dullness, are all too common in other cities too. But differences like these in public safety within the same city are worth noting. The once fine Elm Hill Avenue section's basic troubles are not due to a criminal or a discriminated-against or a poverty-stricken population. Its troubles are due to the fundamental fact that it is physically unsuited to function with vitality as a city district, and so cannot function safely.

Even within supposedly similar parts of supposedly similar places, drastic differences in public safety exist. For example, at Washington Houses, a public housing project in New York, a tenants' group put up three Christmas trees in mid-December 1958. The biggest tree—a huge one—went into the project's inner "street," a landscaped central mall. Two smaller trees were placed at the outer corners of the project where it abuts a busy avenue and lively cross streets. The first night, the large tree and all its trimmings were stolen. The two smaller ones remained intact, lights, ornaments, and all, until they were taken down at New Year's. The inner mall is *theoretically* the most safe and sheltered place in the project. But, says a social worker who has been helping the tenants' group, "People are no safer in that mall than the Christmas tree. On the other hand, the place where the other trees were safe, where the project is just one corner out of four, happens to be safe for people."

Everyone knows that a well used city street is apt to be safe. A deserted one is apt to be unsafe. But how does this work, really? And what makes a city street well used or shunned? Why is the inner sidewalk mall in Washington Houses—which is supposed to be an attraction—shunned when the sidewalks of the old city just to its west are not? What about streets that are busy part of the time and then empty abruptly? A city street equipped to make a safety asset out of the presence of strangers, as successful city neighborhoods always do, must have three main qualities:

First, there must be a clear demarcation between public and private spaces. They cannot ooze into each other as they do typically in housing projects where streets, walks, and play areas may seem at first glance to be open to the public but in effect are special preserves. (The fate of Washington Houses' large Christmas tree is a classic example of what happens when the distinction between public and private space is blurred, and the area which should be under public surveillance has no clear practicable limits.)

Second, there must be *eyes* upon the street, eyes belonging to what we might call its natural proprietors. To insure the safety of both residents and strangers, the buildings on a street must be oriented to it. They cannot turn their backs or blank sides on it and leave it blind.

And third, the sidewalk must have users on it fairly continuously, both to add more effective eyes and to induce plenty of people in buildings along the street to watch the sidewalks. Nobody enjoys sitting on a stoop or looking out a window at an empty street. But large numbers of people entertain themselves, off and on, by watching street activity.

In settlements smaller than cities, public behavior (if not crime) is controlled to some extent by a web of reputation, gossip, approval, disapproval, and sanctions. All of these are powerful if people know each other and word travels. But a city's streets must control not only the behavior of city people but also of visitors who want to have a big time away from the gossip and sanctions at home. It is a wonder cities have solved such a difficult problem at all. And yet in many streets they do it magnificently.

The issue of unsafe streets cannot be evaded by trying to make some other features of a locality safe instead—for example, interior courtyards, or sheltered play spaces. The streets of a city are where strangers come and go. The streets must not only defend the city against predatory strangers. They must also insure the safety of the many peaceable strangers who pass through. Moreover no normal person can spend his life in some artificial haven, and this includes children. Everyone must use the streets.

On the surface, we seem to have here some simple aims: To try for streets where the public space is unequivocally public and to see that these public street spaces have eyes on them as continually as possible.

But it is far from simple to accomplish these things. You can't make people use streets without reason. You can't make people watch streets if they do not want to. The safety of the street works best—and with least taint of hostility or suspicion—where people are using and enjoying the city streets voluntarily.

The basic requisite for such surveillance is a substantial quantity of stores and other public places sprinkled along the sidewalks; it is especially important that places frequented during the evening and night be among them. Stores, bars, and restaurants—the chief examples—abet sidewalk safety in different and complex ways.

First, they give people concrete reasons for using the sidewalks.

Second, they draw people along the sidewalks past places which have few attractions in themselves; this influence does not carry very far geographically, so there must be many—and different— enterprises in a city district if they are to give walkers reason for crisscrossing paths and populating barren stretches on the street.

Third, small businessmen and their employees are typically strong proponents of peace and order themselves; they hate broken windows, holdups, and nervous customers. If present in sufficient abundance, they are great street watchers and sidewalk guardians.

Fourth, the activity generated by people on errands, or people aiming for food or drink, in itself attracts more people to the street.

This last point seems incomprehensible to city planners and architectural designers. They operate on the premise that city people seek emptiness, obvious order, and quiet. Nothing could be less true. The love of people for watching activity and other people is evident in cities everywhere. This trait reaches an almost ludicrous extreme on upper Broadway in New York, where the street is divided by a narrow, central mall, right in the middle of traffic. Benches have been placed at the cross-street intersections of this long mall, and on any day when the weather is even barely tolerable they are filled with people watching the pedestrians, the traffic, and each other.

Eventually Broadway reaches Columbia University and Barnard College, one to the right, the other to the left. Here all is obvious order and quiet. No more stores and the activity they generate, almost no more pedestrians—and no more watchers on the benches. I have tried them and can see why. No place could be more boring. Even the students shun it. They do their outdoor loitering, homework, and street watching on the steps overlooking the busiest campus crossing.

It is just so elsewhere. A lively street always has both its users and watchers. Last year I was in the Lower East Side of Manhattan, waiting for a bus on a street full of errand-goers, children playing, and loiterers on the stoops. In a minute or so a woman opened a third floor tenement window, vigorously yoo-hooed at me, and shouted down that "The bus doesn't run here on Saturdays!" Then

she directed me around the corner. This woman was one of thousands of New Yorkers who casually take care of the streets. They
notice strangers. They observe everything going on. If they need to
take action, whether to direct a stranger or to call the police, they
do so. Such action usually requires, to be sure, a certain self-assurance about the actor's proprietorship of the street and the support
he will get if necessary, and this raises special problems I will not
deal with here. But the fundamental thing is the watching itself.

Not everyone in cities helps to take care of the streets, and many
a resident or worker is unaware of why his neighborhood is safe.
Consider, for example, a recent incident which occurred on the
street where I live.

My block is a small one, but it contains a remarkable range of
buildings, varying from several vintages of tenements to three or
four story houses. Some of these have been converted into low
rent flats with stores on the ground floor; some, like ours, have
been returned to single-family use. Across the street are some four
story brick tenements with stores below. Half of them were converted twelve years ago into small high rent elevator apartments.

From my second story window I happened to see a suppressed
struggle going on between a man and a little girl. He seemed to be
trying to get her to go with him, by turns cajoling her, and then
acting nonchalant. The child was making herself rigid against the
wall.

I wondered whether I should intervene, but then it became unnecessary. The wife of the butcher emerged from their shop with
a determined look on her face. Joe Cornacchia came out of his
delicatessen and stood solidly to the other side. Several heads poked
out of the tenement windows above; one was withdrawn quickly,
and its owner reappeared a moment later in the doorway behind
the man. Two men from the bar next to the butcher shop came
to the doorway and waited. On my side of the street, the locksmith,
the fruit man, and the laundry proprietor came out of their shops,
and other eyes peered from windows. That man did not know it,
but he was surrounded. Nobody was going to allow a little girl to
be dragged off, even if nobody knew who she was. I am sorry—for

dramatic reasons—to have to report that the little girl turned out
to be the man's daughter.

Throughout this little drama, perhaps five minutes in all, *no
eyes appeared in the windows of the high rent apartments.* It was
the only building of which this was true. When we first moved to
our block, I used to hope that soon all the old tenements would
be rehabilitated in the same way. I know better now, and am filled
with gloom by the recent news that such a transformation is sched-
uled for the rest of the block. The high rent tenants, most of whom
are so transient we cannot even keep track of their faces, have not
the remotest idea of who takes care of their street, or how. A city
neighborhood can absorb and protect a substantial number of
these birds of passage. But if and when they *become* the neighborhood, the streets will gradually grow less secure, and if things get
bad enough they will drift away to another neighborhood which
is mysteriously safer.

### SUGGESTIONS FOR WRITING

1. Jane Jacobs (1916-    ), a resident of Greenwich Village, was born in
   Scranton, Pennsylvania. She has written about urban problems for many
   publications and is an associate editor of *Architectural Forum.* Her
   latest book is *Life and Death of Great American Cities,* 1962. Mrs.
   Jacobs argues that the people who plan, build, and police our cities
   are using a set of assumptions that are entirely incorrect. Cite these
   assumptions in a few paragraphs.

2. Describe what Mrs. Jacobs would consider an ideal city street. In order
   to make your description complete, sketch the street on paper, blocking in the stores, apartments, and other buildings so that you can easily
   see the relationship of one to the other.

3. Compare the street you live on with the ideal you have described in
   question 2. What specific improvements could you suggest for your
   street? Would such improvements require a changing of the building
   code for your area? Check the code to make sure.

4. Reveal an incident which has occurred on your street (an auto accident,
   a child wandering in the street, a fire, a police call, anything unusual).
   Use the same method as Mrs. Jacobs. Indicate where you were at the
   time, what you saw from that point, what others saw, what you heard,
   what you thought, and what conclusion can be drawn.

STEPHEN K. BAILEY

## City Politics*

Contrary to what many people seem to believe, the hard ethical issues of public life rarely concern party politics. Party decisions tend to roll according to preset patterns. Every elected executive works out a few obvious benchmarks for relationships with political leaders (for example, "consult party leaders on all appointments, but solicit their help in trading little appointments to the party for big appointments to you"). In any case, to suggest that most party officials are frequently ethical "problems" is to distort their normal role beyond recognition. For every occasion when a party leader asked me for a favor that disturbed my conscience, I can think of a dozen times when the same party leader helped me defend the public interest against the importunities of nonparty pressure groups.

Upon reflection, it is my firm belief that insofar as party politics interferes with the pursuit of the public interest, it is largely a result of the necessities of campaign finance. Most venality in public life could be abolished or reduced to insignificance if the public would assume responsibility for broadly based campaign financing and would insist upon the public auditing and disclosure of all campaign gifts and expenditures. This would not eliminate corruption entirely, for wherever power and money converge some venality will be found. But our present method of financing political campaigns is, in my estimation, the single most corrupting factor in our political life—local, national, and, especially, state.

Take 10 problems which faced me as mayor, and which are typical of perhaps 100 I faced in two years as an elected executive.

1. A peacock farm on the edge of town kept neighbors awake for a month or so a year during the peacock mating season. The city government was asked by the neighbors to see to it that the birds were quieted. Ethical question: is a temporary irritation—includ-

---

* From *The New Republic* (August 15, 1960). © 1960 by Harrison-Blaine, Inc. Reprinted by permission of the publishers.

ing loss of sleep—for 10 families worth the destruction of a hobby and a partial livelihood for one person?

2. The best detective on the chronically underpaid police force is suspected of taking protection money from some local two-bit gamblers. The evidence is too vague and unsubstantial to stand in court. Ethical question: is the *possibility* of the evidence being correct important enough to warrant a substantial investigation, with a consequent probable loss in efficiency and morale in the police department during and long after the investigation, a certain loss in public confidence in the whole force, and the ever present possibility that the rumor was planted by a crank? And out of the many pressing issues coming across the mayor's desk, how much time and effort does such an investigation warrant from the mayor himself?

3. The whole scheme of volunteer fire departments is looked upon by the chief of the city's only paid department as wasteful, inefficient and dangerous to the public safety. The volunteers claim that their firefighting record is topnotch, that they save the tax-payers money. Ethical question: if neither side can be proved incorrect, how does one weigh the values of volunteer community endeavors against marginal inefficiencies in operation of a vital service?

4. Many years ago, one department store was farsighted enough to have bought up some land for off-street parking. This off-street parking gave the store quite a competitive advantage. The city, in a new municipal parking program, needed a portion of the private parking lot assembled by the department store years before. When established, the municipal lot might destroy the store's competitive advantage. Ethical question: at what point does the public interest demand that private farsightedness be penalized?

5. Two mayors in four years happened to have lived on Wyllys Avenue. Wyllys Avenue desperately needed repaving. But so did some other streets in the city. Ethical question: should Wyllys Avenue be paved, granted a heavy presumption that many citizens would claim that the mayor had "taken care of himself"?

6. A federal grant-in-aid cut in half the city's welfare load, making a sinecure out of one of the two city welfare positions. The holder

of the sinecure was a Negro appointed by the opposition party. Ethical question: should work somehow be "made" for the Negro, or should he be dropped? For anyone who knows the problems of status, morale and upward mobility among Negroes in a largely white community, the political questions posed by this case are easy compared to the long-range ethical questions.)

7. The virulent opposition of a local printer-publicist might be tamed on a few key issues with the proper placing of a few city printing contracts. Ethical question: obvious.

8. Buying of tires in wholesale lots would save the taxpayers $300 a year—about one cent per citizen per annum. A score of little Middletown tire merchants would lose $10 or more in income. Ethical question: how does one balance one cent each for 30,000 people *versus* $10 each for 20 merchants?

9. Parents concerned with the safety of their children on the way to and from school are constantly demanding increased police protection and more sidewalks. A more legitimate demand would be hard to imagine. But there are limits. Ethical question: granted that *total* safety never can be assured, what grounds beyond obvious necessity and "the squeaky wheel gets the grease" can be found for awarding or denying protection?

10. There is a likelihood that one of the major industries in town will have to close down a sizable slice of its operations. This may mean 2,000 unemployed. A steel company is looking for a New England site for a steel mill. It finds an "ideal" location in Middletown. That "ideal" location is a stretch of the Connecticut River which is unspoiled and is deeply treasured by small-boat owners and by nature lovers. Ethical question: is the provision of employment for 2,000 people worth the destruction forever of natural beauty?

If I should be asked today how I resolved, in my own mind, the ethical dilemmas posed in the previous paragraphs, I should not know how to answer. Most of the dilemmas were not mine to resolve alone. Other people shared official power with me, and many citizens without official power assumed substantial unofficial responsibility for community decisions. But insofar as I had to make

up my mind by myself, or felt that my judgment might be determining in the minds of others, I did repair to two or three very
general propositions for ethical guidance. In practice, the propositions were never articulated, but in retrospect I know that they
were there. All of them had been woven into my life by parental,
religious, and academic influences—in most cases by all three. My
father, although never a minister, was a Professor of Religion and
a firm believer in the Social Gospel. My studies at Oxford had
brought me close to Immanuel Kant and Jean Jacques Rousseau.
Ideas like "the categorical imperative" and "the general will" were
connected in my mind with such Biblical injunctions as "Let justice
roll down as waters; and righteousness as a mighty stream."

The most helpful single question I could ask myself seemed to
be, "What do you want Middletown to be like 10 years from now?"
Against this, many things fell into place. I wanted more beauty,
fewer slums, less bigotry, more recreation, more community spirit,
a more sustained sense of public responsibility, a more dynamic and
prosperous economy, better education, a stronger and more truly
competitive two-party system, and a heightened sense of personal
dignity for all. These were some of the benchmarks against which
specific ethical issues were measured or rationalized. They were
not my marks. They were the marks of the civilization of which
I was a minuscule reflection.

SUGGESTIONS FOR WRITING

1. Stephen K. Bailey (1915-    ) was mayor of Middletown, Connecticut
   before he was chosen for his present position as dean of the Maxwell
   School of Citizenship of Syracuse University. As one of our country's
   most articulate mayors, he was ably suited to write this article. Many
   readers will be surprised that "the hard ethical issues of public life
   rarely concern party politics." What other "facts" of public life as
   here represented were surprising? Discuss.

2. "Take 10 problems which faced me as mayor . . ." Take 10 problems which face you as a student, as a brother, or as a son, and analyze
   them according to Bailey's pattern.

3. Create a situation where "neither side can be proved incorrect," and
   indicate what you, as an elected public official, would decide.

4. What would be your solution to problem number seven in the essay?
   Would you give the printer contracts? Conduct an interview with the
   printer in which you reveal your answer.

5. "What do you want Middletown to be like 10 years from now?" Apply Bailey's question to your own city.

CHARLES DICKENS

## The City of Magnificent Intentions*

We reached Washington at about half-past six that evening, and had upon the way a beautiful view of the Capitol, which is a fine building of the Corinthian order, placed upon a noble and commanding eminence. Arrived at the hotel; I saw no more of the place that night; being very tired, and glad to get to bed.

Breakfast over next morning, I walk about the streets for an hour or two, and, coming home, throw up the window in the front and back, and look out. Here is Washington, fresh in my mind and under my eye.

Take the worst parts of the City Road and Pentonville, or the straggling outskirts of Paris, where the houses are smallest, preserving all their oddities, but especially the small shops and dwellings, occupied in Pentonville (but not in Washington) by furniture brokers, keepers of poor eatinghouses, and fanciers of birds. Burn the whole down; build it up again in wood and plaster; widen it a little; throw in part of St. John's Wood; put green blinds outside all the private houses, with a red curtain and a white one in every window; plough up all the roads; plant a great deal of coarse turf in every place where it ought *not* to be; erect three handsome buildings in stone and marble, anywhere, but the more entirely out of everybody's way the better; call one the Post Office, one the Patent Office, and one the Treasury; make it scorching hot in the morning, and freezing cold in the afternoon, with an occasional tornado of wind and dust; leave a brick field without the bricks, in all central places where a street may naturally be expected: and that's Washington.

The hotel in which we live, is a long row of small houses fronting on the street, and opening at the back upon a common yard,

_____

* From *American Notes For General Circulation*, London, 1850. The title of this selection has been added by the editor.

in which hangs a great triangle. Whenever a servant is wanted, somebody beats on this triangle from one stroke up to seven, according to the number of the house in which his presence is required; and as all the servants are always being wanted, and none of them ever come, this enlivening engine is in full performance the whole day through. Clothes are drying in this same yard; female slaves, with cotton handkerchiefs twisted round their heads, are running to and fro on the hotel business; black waiters cross and recross with dishes in their hands; two great dogs are playing upon a mound of loose bricks in the centre of the little square; a pig is turning up his stomach to the sun, and grunting "that's comfortable!"; and neither the men, nor the women, nor the dogs, nor the pig, nor any created creature takes the smallest notice of the triangle, which is tingling madly all the time.

I walk to the front window, and look across the road upon a long, straggling row of houses, one story high, terminating, nearly opposite, but a little to the left, in a melancholy piece of waste ground with frowzy grass, which looks like a small piece of country that has taken to drinking, and has quite lost itself. Standing anyhow and all wrong, upon this open space, like something meteoric that has fallen down from the moon, is an odd, lopsided, one-eyed kind of wooden building, that looks like a church, with a flagstaff as long as itself sticking out of a steeple something larger than a tea chest. Under the window is a small stand of coaches, whose slave-drivers are sunning themselves on the steps of our door, and talking idly together. The three most obtrusive houses near at hand, are the three meanest. On one—a shop, which never has anything in the window, and never has the door open—is painted in large characters, "The City Lunch." At another, which looks like the back-way to somewhere else, but is an independent building in itself, oysters are procurable in every style. At the third, which is a very, very little tailor's shop, pants are fixed to order; or, in other words, pantaloons are made to measure. And that is our street in Washington.

It is sometimes called the City of Magnificent Distances, but it might with greater propriety be termed the City of Magnificent Intentions; for it is only on taking a bird's-eye view of it from the top of the Capitol, that one can at all comprehend the vast designs of its projector, an aspiring Frenchman. Spacious avenues, that begin in nothing, and lead nowhere; streets, mile-long, that only want houses, roads, and inhabitants; public buildings that need but a public to be complete; and ornaments of great thoroughfares, which only lack great thoroughfares to ornament—are its leading features. One might fancy the season over, and most of the houses gone out of town for ever with their masters. To the admirers of cities it is a Barmecide Feast; a pleasant field for the imagination to rove in; a monument raised to a deceased project, with not even a legible inscription to record its departed greatness.

Such as it is, it is likely to remain. It was originally chosen for the seat of Government, as a means of averting the conflicting jealousies and interests of the different States; and very probably, too, as being remote from mobs; a consideration not to be slighted, even in America. It has no trade or commerce of its own: having little or no population beyond the President and his establishment; the members of the legislature who reside there during the session; the Government clerks and officers employed in the various departments; the keepers of the hotels and boardinghouses; and the tradesmen who supply their tables. It is very unhealthy. Few people would live in Washington, I take it, who were not obliged to reside there; and the tides of emigration and speculation, those rapid and regardless currents, are little likely to flow at any time towards such dull and sluggish water.

SUGGESTIONS FOR WRITING

1. The Charles Dickens (1812-1870), who wrote *David Copperfield* and *A Tale of Two Cities,* was also a reporter for the world at large as he traveled in America. His report here is in diary form. Note the second sentence: "Arrived at the hotel; I saw no more of the place that night; being very tired, and glad to get to bed." This is the abbreviated narrative of a diary. Try the technique as you describe your arrival in a city. Reveal the impression a traveler would get.

2. What impression did you get of Washington (or any other large city) during your first visit?

3. The third paragraph compares Washington with certain parts of London and environs, parts which Dickens' readers would be likely to know. Clearly this paragraph is uncomplimentary to Washington. What defense might have been made on behalf of the beauty of the young capital?

4. The fourth paragraph describes a hotel at which Dickens stayed. What has that hotel to do with the city? Why is it that the place you stay affects your feelings about a city? Analyze.

5. In the final paragraph Dickens tries to predict the future of Washington. Write him a letter to tell him how far his prediction was mistaken.

WALT WHITMAN

# Give Me the Streets of Manhattan*

Keep your splendid silent sun,
Keep your woods O Nature, and the quiet places by the woods,
Keep your fields of clover and timothy, and your corn-fields and orchards,
Keep the blossoming buckwheat fields where the Ninth-month bees hum;
Give me faces and streets—give me these phantoms incessant and endless
   along the trottoirs!
Give me interminable eyes—give me women—give me comrades and lovers
   by the thousand!
Let me see new ones every day—let me hold new ones by the hand every
   day!
Give me such shows—give me the streets of Manhattan!
Give me Broadway, with the soldiers marching—give me the sound of the
   trumpets and drums!
(The soldiers in companies or regiments—some starting away, flush'd and
   reckless,
Some, their time up, returning with thinn'd ranks, young, yet very old,
   worn, marching, noticing nothing;)
Give me the shores and wharves heavy-fringed with black ships!
O such for me! O an intense life, full to repletion and varied!
The life of the theatre, bar-room, huge hotel, for me!
The saloon of the steamer! the crowded excursion for me! the torchlight
   procession!
The dense brigade bound for the war, with high piled military wagons
   following;
People, endless, streaming, with strong voices, passions, pageants,
Manhattan streets with their powerful throbs, with beating drums as now,
The endless and noisy chorus, the rustle and clank of muskets, (even the
   sight of the wounded,)

---

* From *Give Me the Splendid Silent Sun.*

Manhattan crowds, with their turbulent musical chorus!
Manhattan faces and eyes forever for me.


SUGGESTIONS FOR WRITING

1. Walt Whitman's *Leaves of Grass* (1855) set a new style in American
   poetry. His self-styled "barbaric yawp" appalled some and delighted
   others. How do you feel about it? Is it poetry?
2. Two comments on word usage: *trottoirs* are paths along which horses
   trot; *Ninth-month* bees are September bees—a Quaker locution. Ponder
   the use of punctuation here. What is the effect of the dashes, the
   parentheses, the exclamation points? Revise the punctuation and a
   word or two here and there and write the lines in regular paragraph
   order, and you have a piece of prose. Try it; then comment on what
   constitutes poetry.
3. Compare Whitman's statement about a city in the poem above with
   the quotation by Thoreau at the beginning of this section. Account
   for the different points of view.
4. The lines of verse here are actually the second stanza of a poem in
   *Leaves of Grass* called "Give Me the Splendid Silent Sun." The first
   stanza tells of the beauty of the country, so that the lines here are
   really a forceful rebuttal to Whitman's own statements. Using this
   second stanza as a model of specific descriptive statements, write a composition about the city's "intense life, full to repletion and varied."


JOHN A. KOUWENHOVEN

## Skylines and Skyscrapers*

   Those engaged in discovering America often begin by discovering the Manhattan skyline, and here as well as elsewhere they
discover apparently irreconcilable opposites. They notice at once
that it doesn't make any sense, in human or aesthetic terms. It is
the product of insane politics, greed, competitive ostentation,
megalomania, the worship of false gods. Its products, in turn, are
traffic jams, bad ventilation, noise, and all the other ills that metro-

---

* From "What Is American about America?" *Harper's Magazine* (July, 1956).
© 1956 by John A. Kouwenhoven. Reprinted by permission of the author.

politan flesh is heir to. And the net result is, illogically enough, one of the most exaltedly beautiful things man has ever made.

Perhaps this paradoxical result will be less bewildering if we look for a moment at the formal and structural principles which are involved in the skyline. It may be helpful to consider the skyline as we might consider a lyric poem, or a novel, if we were trying to analyze its aesthetic quality.

Looked at in this way, it is clear that the total effect which we call "the Manhattan skyline" is made up of almost innumerable buildings, each in competition (for height, or glamor, or efficiency, or respectability) with all of the others. Each goes its own way, as it were, in a carnival of rugged architectural individualism. And yet—as witness the universal feeling of exaltation and aspiration which the skyline as a whole evokes—out of this irrational, unplanned, and often infuriating chaos, an unforeseen unity has evolved. No building ever built in New York was placed where it was, or shaped as it was, because it would contribute to the aesthetic effect of the skyline—lifting it here, giving it mass there, or lending a needed emphasis. Each was built, all those now under construction are being built, with no thought for their subordination to any over-all effect.

What, then, makes possible the fluid and everchanging unity which does, in fact, exist? Quite simply, there are two things, both simple in themselves, which do the job. If they were not simple, they would not work; but they are, and they do.

One is the gridiron pattern of the city's streets—the same basic pattern which accounts for Denver, Houston, Little Rock, Birmingham, and almost any American town you can name, and the same pattern which, in the form of square townships, sections, and quarter sections, was imposed by the Ordinance of 1785 on an almost continental scale. Whatever its shortcomings when compared with the "discontinuous street patterns" of modern planned communities, this artificial geometric grid—imposed upon the land without regard to contours or any preconceived pattern of social zoning—had at least the quality of rational simplicity. And it is this simple gridiron street pattern which, horizontally, controls the spacing and arrangement of the rectangular shafts which go to make up the skyline.

The other thing which holds the skyline's diversity together is the structural principle of the skyscraper. When we think of individual buildings, we tend to think of details of texture, color, and form, of surface ornamentation or the lack of it. But as elements in Manhattan's skyline, these things are of little consequence. What matters there is the vertical thrust, the motion upward; and that is the product of cage or skeleton, construction in steel—a system of construction which is, in effect, merely a three-dimensional variant of the gridiron street plan, extending vertically instead of horizontally.

The aesthetics of cage, or skeleton, construction have never been fully analyzed, nor am I equipped to analyze them. But as a lay observer, I am struck by fundamental differences between the effect created by height in the RCA building at Radio City, for example, and the effect created by height in Chartres cathedral or in Giotto's campanile. In both the latter (as in all the great architecture of the past) proportion and symmetry, the relation of height to width, are constituent to the effect. One can say of a Gothic cathedral, "This tower is too high"; of a Romanesque dome, "This is top-heavy." But there is nothing inherent in cage construction which would invite such judgments. A true skyscraper like the RCA building could be eighteen or twenty stories taller, or ten or a dozen stories shorter without changing its essential aesthetic effect. Once steel cage construction has passed a certain height, the effect of transactive upward motion has been established; from there on, the point at which you cut it off is arbitrary and makes no difference.

Those who are familiar with the history of the skyscraper will remember how slowly this fact was realized. Even Louis Sullivan—greatest of the early skyscraper architects—thought in terms of having to close off and climax the upward motion of the tall building with an "attic" or cornice. His lesser contemporaries worked for years on the blind assumption that the proportion and symmetry of masonry architecture must be preserved in the new technique. If with the steel cage one could go higher than with load-bearing masonry walls, the old aesthetic effects could be counterfeited by dressing the façade as if one or more buildings had been piled on top of another—each retaining the illusion of being complete in itself. You can still see such buildings in New York: the first five stories perhaps a Greco-Roman temple, the next ten a neuter warehouse, and the final five or six an Aztec pyramid. And that Aztec pyramid is simply a cheap and thoughtless equivalent of the more subtle Sullivan cornice. Both structures attempt to close and climax the upward thrust, to provide something similar to the *Katharsis* in Greek tragedy.

But the logic of cage construction requires no such climax. It has less to do with the inner logic of masonry forms than with that of the old Globe-Wernicke sectional bookcases, whose interchangeable units (with glass-flap fronts) anticipated by fifty years the modular unit systems of so-called modern furniture. Those bookcases were advertised in the 'nineties as "always complete but never finished"—a phrase which could with equal propriety have been applied to the Model-T Ford. Many of us remember with affection that admirably simple mechanism, forever susceptible to added gadgets or improved parts, each of which was interchangeable with what you already had.

Here, then, are the two things which serve to tie together the otherwise irrelevant components of the Manhattan skyline: the gridiron ground plan and the three-dimensional vertical grid of steel cage construction. And both of these are closely related to one another. Both are composed of simple and infinitely repeatable units.

SUGGESTIONS FOR WRITING

1. John A. Kouwenhoven, formerly an associate editor of *Harper's Magazine,* is a professor at Barnard College. This excerpt was taken from an article entitled "What Is American about America?" In it Kouwenhoven discusses several other American items that are composed of infinitely repeatable units, namely, chewing gum, baseball, jazz, and comic strips. The thesis is fascinating, if not utterly convincing. Consider the repetitive elements in modern America and extend Kouwenhoven's thesis.

2. Kouwenhoven begins: "Those engaged in discovering America . . . ," and he shows us a special kind of discovery—by analysis. Use the technique of discovery by analysis in an area you know through experience.

3. Cast yourself in the role of an architect and analyze some buildings. Kouwenhoven says, "Once steel cage construction has passed a certain height, the effect of transactive upward motion has been established; from there on, the point at which you cut it off is arbitrary and makes no difference." Do you agree? The Greeks worked on a theory of the "golden oblong," which set forth as perfect a proportion which was

three units wide and two units tall. True? Until relatively recent times, architects thought you had to "close off and climax the upward movement of a tall building." Is it true that tall buildings need to be closed off and climaxed?

4. Kouwenhoven's thesis—the "Americanism" of the gridiron and the cage —has some validity for New York. Does this make Boston or Philadelphia or San Francisco non-American?

E . B . W H I T E

# New York*

On any person who desires such queer prizes, New York will bestow the gift of loneliness and the gift of privacy. It is this largess that accounts for the presence within the city's walls of a considerable section of the population; for the residents of Manhattan are to a large extent strangers who have pulled up stakes somewhere and come to town, seeking sanctuary or fulfillment or some greater or lesser grail. The capacity to make such dubious gifts is a mysterious quality of New York. It can destroy an individual, or it can fulfill him, depending a good deal on luck. No one should come to New York to live unless he is willing to be lucky.

New York is the concentrate of art and commerce and sport and religion and entertainment and finance, bringing to a single compact arena the gladiator, the evangelist, the promoter, the actor, the trader and the merchant. It carries on its lapel the unexpungeable odor of the long past, so that no matter where you sit in New York you feel the vibrations of great times and tall deeds, of queer people and events and undertakings. I am sitting at the moment in a stifling hotel room in 90-degree heat, halfway down an air shaft, in midtown. No air moves in or out of the room, yet I am curiously affected by emanations from the immediate surroundings. I am twenty-two blocks from where Rudolph Valentino lay in state, eight blocks from where Nathan Hale was executed, five blocks from the publisher's office where Ernest Hemingway hit

Max Eastman on the nose, four miles from where Walt Whitman sat sweating out editorials for the Brooklyn Eagle, thirty-four blocks from the street Willa Cather lived in when she came to New York to write books about Nebraska, one block from where Marceline used to clown on the boards of the Hippodrome, thirty-six blocks from the spot where the historian Joe Gould kicked a radio to pieces in full view of the public, thirteen blocks from where Harry Thaw shot Stanford White, five blocks from where I used to usher at the Metropolitan Opera and only a hundred and twelve blocks from the spot where Clarence Day the Elder was washed of his sins in the Church of the Epiphany (I could continue this list indefinitely); and for that matter I am probably occupying the very room that any number of exalted characters sat in, some of them on hot, breathless afternoons, lonely and private and full of their own sense of emanations from without.

When I went down to lunch a few minutes ago I noticed that the man sitting next to me (about eighteen inches away along the wall) was Fred Stone. The eighteen inches were both the connection and the separation that New York provides for its inhabitants. My only connection with Fred Stone was that I saw him in *The Wizard of Oz* around the beginning of the century. But our waiter felt the same stimulus from being close to a man from Oz, and after Mr. Stone left the room the waiter told me that when he (the waiter) was a young man just arrived in the country and before he could understand a word of English, he had taken his girl for their first theater date to *The Wizard of Oz*. It was a wonderful show, the waiter recalled—a man of straw, a man of tin. Wonderful! (And still only eighteen inches away.) "Mr. Stone is a very hearty eater," said the waiter thoughtfully, content with this fragile participation in destiny, this link with Oz.

New York blends the gift of privacy with the excitement of participation; and better than most dense communities it succeeds in insulating the individual (if he wants it, and almost everybody wants or needs it) against all enormous and violent and wonderful events that are taking place every minute. Since I have been sitting in this miasmic air shaft, a good many rather splashy events have occurred in town. A man shot and killed his wife in a fit of jealousy. It caused no stir outside his block and got only small mention in the papers. I did not attend. Since my arrival, the greatest air show ever

staged in all the world took place in town. I didn't attend and neither did most of the eight million other inhabitants, although they
say there was quite a crowd. I didn't even hear any planes
except a couple of westbound commercial airliners that habitually
use this air shaft to fly over. The biggest ocean-going ships on the
North Atlantic arrived and departed. I didn't notice them and
neither did most other New Yorkers. I am told this is the greatest
seaport in the world, with six hundred and fifty miles of water
front, and ships calling here from many exotic lands, but the only
boat I've happened to notice since my arrival was a small sloop tack-
ing out of the East River night before last on the ebb tide when I
was walking across the Brooklyn Bridge. I heard the *Queen Mary*
blow one midnight, though, and the sound carried the whole history of departure and longing and loss. The Lions have been in
convention. I've seen not one Lion. A friend of mine saw one and
told me about him. (He was lame, and was wearing a bolero.) At
the ballgrounds and horse parks the greatest sporting spectacles
have been enacted. I saw no ballplayer, no race horse. The governor
came to town. I heard the siren scream, but that was all there was
to that—an eighteen-inch margin again. A man was killed by a
falling cornice. I was not a party to the tragedy, and again the
inches counted heavily.

I mention these merely to show that New York is peculiarly constructed to absorb almost anything that comes along (whether a
thousand-foot liner out of the East or a twenty-thousand-man convention out of the West) without inflicting the event on its inhabitants; so that every event is, in a sense, optional, and the inhab-
itant is in the happy position of being able to choose his spectacle
and so conserve his soul. In most metropolises, small and large, the
choice is often not with the individual at all. He is thrown to the
Lions. The Lions are overwhelming; the event is unavoidable. A
cornice falls, and it hits every citizen on the head, every last man in
town. I sometimes think that the only event that hits every New
Yorker on the head is the annual St. Patrick's Day parade, which is
fairly penetrating—the Irish are a hard race to tune out, there are
500,000 of them in residence, and they have the police force right in
the family.

The quality in New York that insulates its inhabitants from life
may simply weaken them as individuals. Perhaps it is healthier to

live in a community where, when a cornice falls, you feel the blow; where, when the governor passes, you see at any rate his hat.

I am not defending New York in this regard. Many of its settlers are probably here merely to escape, not face, reality. But whatever it means, it is a rather rare gift, and I believe it has a positive effect on the creative capacities of New Yorkers—for creation is in part merely the business of forgoing the great and small distractions.

Although New York often imparts a feeling of great forlornness or forsakenness, it seldom seems dead or unresourceful; and you always feel that either by shifting your location ten blocks or by reducing your fortune by five dollars you can experience rejuvenation. Many people who have no real independence of spirit depend on the city's tremendous variety and sources of excitement for spiritual sustenance and maintenance of morale. In the country there are a few chances of sudden rejuvenation—a shift in weather, perhaps, or something arriving in the mail. But in New York the chances are endless. I think that although many persons are here from some excess of spirit (which caused them to break away from their small town), some, too, are here from a deficiency of spirit, who find in New York a protection, or any easy substitution.

There are roughly three New Yorks. There is, first, the New York of the man or woman who was born here, who takes the city for granted and accepts its size and its turbulence as natural and inevitable. Second, there is the New York of the commuter—the city that is devoured by locusts each day and spat out at night. Third, there is the New York of the person who was born somewhere else and came to New York in quest of something. Of these three trembling cities the greatest is the last—the city of final destination, the city that is a goal. It is this third city that accounts for New York's high-strung disposition, its poetical deportment, its dedication to the arts, and its incomparable achievements. Commuters give the city its tidal restlessness; natives give it solidity and continuity; but the settlers give it passion. And whether it is a farmer arriving from Italy to set up a small grocery store in a slum, or a young girl arriving from a small town in Mississippi to escape the indignity of being observed by her neighbors, or a boy arriving from the Corn Belt with a manuscript in his suitcase and a pain in his heart, it makes no difference: each embraces New York with the intense excitement of first love, each absorbs New York with the fresh eyes of an adventurer, each generates heat and light to dwarf the Consolidated Edison Company.

The commuter is the queerest bird of all. The suburb he inhabits has no essential vitality of its own and is a mere roost where he comes at day's end to go to sleep. Except in rare cases, the man who lives in Mamaroneck or Little Neck or Teaneck, and works in New York, discovers nothing much about the city except the time of arrival and departure of trains and buses, and the path to a quick lunch. He is desk-bound, and has never, idly roaming in the gloaming, stumbled suddenly on Belvedere Tower in the Park, seen the ramparts rise sheer from the water of the pond, and the boys along the shore fishing for minnows, girls stretched out negligently on the shelves of the rocks; he has never come suddenly on anything at all in New York as a loiterer, because he has had no time between trains. He has fished in Manhattan's wallet and dug out coins, but has never listened to Manhattan's breathing, never awakened to its morning, never dropped off to sleep in its night.

## SUGGESTIONS FOR WRITING

1. E. B. White (1899-      ) lives at North Brooklyn, Maine. Before becoming a contributing editor of *The New Yorker,* White was a frequent contributer to *Harper's.* The above article is an excerpt from a long piece especially commissioned by *Holiday Magazine.* In addition to being one of America's most revered essayists, he has written many books, the most notable of which are: *Is Sex Necessary?* (1929) in collaboration with James Thurber, *One Man's Meat* (1944), *Stuart Little* (1945), *Charlotte's Web* (1952), and *The Second Tree from the Corner* (1953). In 1941 he edited *A Subtreasury of American Humor.* The list of his books and literary contributions reveals that he usually gives us the point of view of a writer, yet the views in the above excerpt are simply those of an intelligent and sophisticated human being who is letting the impressions of the city penetrate his consciousness. He writes with apparent ease, but it is worth careful study in an attempt to master this technique. Write an impression of your home town, taking your stylistic clues from White.

2. White says there is a "quality in New York that insulates its inhabitants from life." Study his essay carefully and determine what this quality is. Try to determine whether the same quality may be present in any large city, or whether it is a quality within human beings wherever they may live. Write an essay considering these questions.

3. "There are roughly three New Yorks," says White. Choose a place you know well and write an essay describing how many different places it becomes to the various people who live or visit there. Consider the native born, the occasional visitor, and the regular visitor. Create three fictional characters and show how each reacts to the place by describing their experiences.

AUBREY MENEN

# A First Look at New York*

This is the description of what someone saw on his first visit to New York City. He was forty-seven years old at the time. He had seen most of the world, and he felt he knew what was what. He had heard about New York and he was pretty sure he wouldn't like it.

Still, there seemed to be no active harm in the trip. From all he had been told he would be warm and comfortable. Nobody would eat him, although he understood that New Yorkers would eat practically anything else that was put in front of them. He decided that the best way to face the trip was to treat it as a child treats Christmas: there would be fun, noise, perhaps gifts (he knew that Americans were generous). It might end in tears, but not if he left the party early. This he privately arranged to do.

I was the man. I live in Rome, and the first step was to get a visa. I went to the American Embassy and I was treated with every courtesy. I was asked to recall where I had lived for the last five years. The addresses were considered innocent. I was asked my weight. It was considered just right. I was given my visa.

I went aboard a plane. For a few minutes I saw the city of Rome below me, mellow and old in the September sunlight. I picked out the great buildings at which I had stared in wonder for so long: I traced the streets in which, morning and evening, I had walked with my head full of thoughts of the great heroes and unforgettable rogues who had walked there before me. As Rome sank away into the autumn mists, I was certain that whatever lay before me on my journey, I would never find another city which gave me, at every

* From *Holiday* (October, 1959). © 1959 by The Curtis Publishing Company. Reprinted by permission of the author and the William Morris Agency.

hour and at every corner, so deep a sense of excitement, the peril, and the continuing adventure of being a civilized man. But within a day I had found it.

I had flown the Atlantic thinking of Rome, I had landed at Idlewild thinking of Rome. In my hotel I had bathed, shaved, and changed, writing in my mind a letter back to Rome. Then I went out into the street. I stood, for the first time in my life on the fifth of the great avenues which traverse the city of New York.

I had long ago made up my mind what I would see. The avenue would be dark, because of the height of the buildings. The buildings would be tall because of the greed of their builders. The shadowed street would be crammed with hurrying people, and these would be chasing dollars. (I had formed, over the years, a clear picture of chasing dollars. It would be like chasing women—a dedicated pursuit, but a little furtive.)

If I looked closer into the faces of these people I would find nothing to repel me. But I would feel a certain lack of warmth. This would be because they were all materialists. They would all be pragmatically going places, like engineers on steam locomotives. If I walked down the street, I would find it devoid of poverty, and of art. If I ventured into a shop or a bar and spoke to an employee, I would find him offensively familiar, but a mass of nerves. He would call me "Mac", which is not my name, and I would have to address him as my buddy, which would not be truthful. He would try to sell me something, and if by chance or strength of will I bought nothing, I would leave him more of a mass of nerves than ever.

The road itself would be made dangerous by cars of inordinate length owned and driven by plumbers, building workers and janitors. The men would be smiling, but worried about Russia. The women would be beautiful, but being in unchallenged command of the city and the country at large would all wear the expressions of feudal lords.

I looked about me. I was puzzled. I looked about me thus for three days and then I was seized with a strong emotion. I began to feel like a schoolboy who had suddenly discovered girls: I mean that happy moment when he finds that they are not an unfortunate product of evolution but human beings like himself. Human beings, moreover, who improve on acquaintance: who are

likeable, then lovable, and finally ravishing. I felt, if you like, calf
love. I was bowled over. But I was not bowled over easily. It was
not done with one pretty face. It took a gigantic city of eight million people—I am, after all, a somewhat venerable calf. Still, over
I went.

Calf love begins, as you will all remember, with a fondness for
names. I remember that when I was a boy the girl next door was
called Muriel. As a name I saw nothing in it for years. Then one
day it sounded on my ears like a carillon of silver bells. It was the
same in New York. One side of my hotel looked on to Fifth Avenue,
while the adjacent side faced 55th Street. It is therefore described as
being "on Fifth at Fifty-fifth." On reflection, I think this must be
nearly the ugliest group of words that can be conceived in the
English language. Yet after three days I said the phrase with such
pleasure I rolled it round my tongue—that, and all the other
mathematical addresses in which New York abounds. It seemed to
me that here the problem of street addresses had found, as the
mathematicians say, an *elegant* solution.

It is a key word. Let us stand on my hotel corner and see it as I
saw it on the morning when I knew I had lost my heart to the
place.

I saw, stretching out on either hand, an avenue so wide that, had
it been made in Europe, it could only have led up to a palace. Here,
on my right hand it led, astonishingly, into what I took to be the
open country until I found that it was Central Park. I saw a vast
piazza, and then a prospect of fields and trees which seemed to have
no ending. To my left, and as far as I could see, the avenue was
lined with towers. Many of them white and shining: most had
flags that waved lazily in the October breeze. The tops of these
towers were so high that they gleamed with light from far horizons.
Cloud shadows fell on them: mists were imprisoned between them.
They seemed to catch the sky and spread it, like a banner, over
their topmost and airy balconies. I gazed at them as the traveler in
past times gazed at the triple walls of Byzantium or the marble
temples of Rome, knowing that nothing like this had ever been
seen on earth before.

I walked between the towers for a while, watching the light and
shadows change the color of their summits from moment to moment, when suddenly I found, almost it seemed at my feet, a small

shrine or chapel built in the Gothic taste. I went inside and found that it was not a chapel but a huge cathedral, St. Patrick's. I returned to the doorway, went out on the steps and looked up again at the towers. Immediately the cathedral shrank back to the size of a shrine. Then, for the first time, I realized how vast the towers really were, and how bold was the decision to build them.

At one corner of the avenue, not far from the southerly spire of the cathedral, was a hole in the ground in which men were working. I then remembered that as a boy I had been shown pictures of the first of New York's towers and had been told that there was nothing remarkable in them. By a lucky chance the whole of Manhattan Island was of solid stone. There had, therefore, been little to it save joining girder to girder and putting slab on slab until the things were built. I crossed over to the hole. I looked in it. There was the stone all right, a few inches below the pavement and indeed quite solid. But I knew that the explanation I had been given was the tedious nonsense of small minds faced with a wonder. The towers could not be explained away. The builders of medieval cathedrals might have said, "Let us pull down our homes, build many vast bell towers, and live in them." But they did not. A caliph in Bagdad might have said, "I am tired of seeing houses. Let us sweep them away and build great minarets, and let them be so vast that we can all live in them." But no caliph did. The builders of New York built their city not so much on rock, as in the air. There has been no decision so remarkable since the Venetians made up their minds to found their city on water.

I crossed the road and stood beneath the middle tower of Rockefeller Center. I have seen the Pyramids. They are not really big, but they look gigantic. St. Peter's is at the end of the road in which I live in Rome. It is a large place, and the façade looks like an enormous cliff face. The tower I was now looking up at is 850 feet high. It has seventy stories. It is one of the largest buildings on earth. Yet there is only one word to describe it and that is to say that it is slender. It is so slender as to seem frivolous. At its foot is an open-air rink with people skating to Viennese waltzes.

.    .    .

Thus far, at least for me, the finest tourist sight in New York is not within the city. It is not the Empire State Building, which is very big but getting shabby on top. It is not the Statue of Liberty, which is also very big but much too small for its site (I wish someone would move it to Central Park). It is not even Grant's Tomb, cozily domestic as that is, with Mrs. Grant sleeping beside her husband in a tomb just as big as his, just as central, and since she was nobody, much more conspicuous. The most memorable sight that New York has to offer are the roads which lead out of the city to the country districts on the mainland.

I traveled four times along the roads that lead to Westchester County. They are called parkways, and for once a fancy made-up name is justified. They are exactly that. A strip of land on either side of the roads has been left (or landscaped) as natural, unspoiled countryside. Such few houses as there are have been hidden by trees. Broad stretches of grass, growing in humps and hillocks, are set out with flowering bushes. Whole miles run through dense forests, which when I saw them, were burning with the intense colors of the New England fall. In no other major city of the world has the country been allowed to lie so close to the town. It seemed to me that such roads must have been built by men of a future century, for, without doubt, the brutal destruction of the countryside is the hallmark of our own. But here hills, forests, lakes and country paths extend in vast New World perspectives on either side. It is very quiet. And this is where the New Yorker, when he can afford it, lives.

His house is of wood, built to the design of a century and more ago. It is furnished with antique furniture. It is surrounded by copses, paddocks and lawns. The New Yorker comes home to this house every night. He brings up his family there. He confines his wife to it, and turns her, for at least five days of the week, into the wife of a gentleman farmer. It is a way of living that strikes the foreign visitor as commodious, sensible, elegant and, of course, preposterous. Of all the people of the earth, the New Yorker should not be able to go home each evening to the calm of an unspoiled countryside. But he does. He is showing the rest of us how to be civilized. He is leading the way. That, after all, has been the duty of the fortunate citizens of all the great prime cities of history, each in its day.

The date on which I had privately arranged to go back to Europe had long passed. I had stayed on, passing each day in wonderment, curiosity, and tearing high spirits. But I spent a lot of money. The day came when I felt I must leave the new Rome and go back to the old. At the airport, which I had barely deigned to notice when I arrived, I suddenly bought every picture of New York that I could find. They are pinned up before me now, as I sit at my desk. I have just got up and taken a walk through the heart of Old Rome. I have climbed the Spanish Steps. I looked at the lights come on as the evening fell. The dome of St. Peter's was a great and lovely shadow against the sky. I felt calm. I had the long, long thoughts of a man who lives in Rome. Then suddenly I knew how much I missed the towers of Manhattan. . . . I wanted to be high in the air again, above Fifth Avenue, talking about oysters. I wanted to sit for a week on a porch in Westchester County. I wanted to stand up at the right time at the ball game. I wanted to spend not three weeks, but six months in New York.

I came home. I asked a friend with a head for figures to work out, given what I had spent in three weeks, how much I would have to earn and save to make this possible. His figure, in which I have full faith, lies written on a slip of paper before me now. I should live so long.

SUGGESTIONS FOR WRITING

1. Aubrey Menen (1912-      ), half-Indian and half-Irish but Italian by preference, wrote about New York on special assignment for *Holiday* magazine. The first five paragraphs are largely autobiographical, and he doesn't get to "standing" in New York until the end of the fifth paragraph. Why the long introduction? Using the simple straightforward style of Menen, produce a similar introduction to a place you have recently visited.

2. Menen gets his effect, in part, by contrasts. His sentences flow along very easily, one piling on top of another, until the pyramid is built. Then he raises up a sweeping generalization to crown the achievement. Three examples of sweeping generalizations: "I gazed at them . . . knowing that nothing like this had ever been seen on earth before." "There has been no decision so remarkable since the Venetians made up their minds to found their city on water." "In no other major city of the world has the country been allowed to lie so close to the town." Try the technique. Build slowly and maintain control over the generalization; don't let it sweep you away.

3. Menen's final sentence, "I should live so long," is puzzling. Does he mean to end with a final light touch, not daring to try to cap his former generalizations? Or, does he mean that the expense of living in New York is absolutely prohibitive, that in fact, it is not a good city to live in, thus cancelling all he has said?

4. Menen brought his misconceptions of New York with him, and he aired them for all to view. What is your concept of a city abroad? What are the people like? the buildings? the parks? the restaurants?

*Part Three*

# THE WRITER
# AT WORK

# The Matter of Style

The writer should so write that his readers not only may but must understand.
—Quintilian, *Institutiones Oratoriae*, c. A.D. 100

No one will ever lose a reader, no matter how difficult the subject, by writing agreeably, with good humor, with an effort of informality.
—Bernard DeVoto in Munson's *The Writer's Workshop Companion*, 1951

The style is the man himself. (*Le style est l'homme même.*)
—Georges Louis Leclerc de Buffon, *Discourse*, 1853

He knew that the whole mystery of beauty can never be comprehended by the crowd, and that while clearness is a virtue of style, perfect explicitness is not a necessary virtue.
—Arthur Symons, *The Symbolist Movement in Literature*, 1899

In imitating great authors I have always excelled myself.
—Addison, *The Guardian*, September 4, 1713

Whoever wishes to attain an English style, familiar but not coarse, and elegant but not ostentatious, must give his days and nights to the volumes of Addison.
—Samuel Johnson, *Lives of the Poets*, 1781

About this time I met with an odd volume of the *Spectator* [much of which was written by Addison]. . . . I thought the writing excellent, and wished if possible to imitate it.
—Benjamin Franklin, *Autobiography*, 1791

Demosthenes felt such delight in the history of Thucydides, that to obtain a familiar and perfect mastery of his style, he copied his history eight times.
—Isaac Disraeli, *Curiosities of Literature*, 1881

Before we use either to write or speak eloquently, we must dedicate our minds wholly to follow the most wise and learned men. . . . The which when we earnestly mind to do we cannot but in time appear somewhat like them.
—Thomas Wilson, *The Arte of Rhetorique*, 1553

BEN JONSON

# Of Style*

For a man to write well there are required three necessaries: to read the best authors, observe the best speakers, and much exercise of his own style. In style, to consider what ought to be written, and after what manner, he must first think and excogitate his matter, then choose his words, and examine the weight of either. Then take care, in placing and ranking both matter and words, that the composition be comely, and to do this with diligence and often. No matter how slow the style be at first, so it be labored and accurate. Seek the best, and be not glad of the forward conceits or first words that offer themselves to us, but judge of what we invent, and order what we approve. Repeat often what we have formerly written, which beside that it helps the consequence and makes the juncture better, quickens the heat of the imagination, which often cools in the time of setting down, and gives it new strength, as if it grew lustier by the going back. As we see in the contention of leaping, they jump farthest that fetch their race largest; or in throwing a dart or javelin, we force back our arms to make our loose the stronger. Yet if we have a fair gale of wind, I forbid not the steering out of our sail, so the favor of the gale deceive us not. For all that we invent does please us in the conception or birth, else we would never set it down. But the safest is to return to our judgment and handle over again those things the easiness of which might make them justly suspected. So did the best writers in their beginnings; they imposed upon themselves care and industry. They did nothing rashly. They obtained first to write well, and then custom made it easy and

---

* From *Timber: or Discoveries Made upon Men and Matter,* 1640.

a habit. By little and little their matter showed itself to them more plentifully; their words answered, their composition followed, and all, as in a well-ordered family, presented itself in the place. So that the sum of all is, ready writing makes not good writing, but good writing brings on ready writing. Yet when we think we have got the faculty, it is even then good to resist it, as to give a horse a check sometimes with a bit, which doth not so much stop his course as stir his mettle. Again, whither a man's genius is best able to reach, thither it should more and more contend, lift, and dilate itself, as men of low stature raise themselves on their toes and so ofttimes get even, if not eminent. Besides, as it is fit for grown and able writers to stand of themselves and work with their own strength, to trust and endeavor by their own faculties, so it is fit for the beginner and learner to study others and the best. For the mind and memory are more sharply exercised in comprehending another man's things than our own, and such as accustom themselves and are familiar with the best authors shall ever and anon find somewhat of them in themselves; and in the expression of their minds, even when they feel it not, be able to utter something like theirs, which hath an authority above their own. Nay, sometimes it is the reward of a man's study, the praise of quoting another man fitly. And though a man be more prone and able for one kind of writing than another, yet he must exercise all. For as in an instrument, so in style, there must be a harmony and consent of parts.

SUGGESTIONS FOR WRITING

1. Ben Jonson (1572-1637) was a poet, player, playwright, and philosopher. His chief prose work, *Timber: or Discoveries Made upon Men and Matter* (1640), contains the above selection, "Of Style." Although he was not formally appointed the first poet laureate of England, the essentials of the position were conferred on him in 1616 when a pension was granted to him by James I. As unofficial poet laureate he was admired and respected by other writers, and was in a position to offer advice, as he does in the above essay. Note the similarity in style with Bacon's *Of Studies.* Jonson advises a writer to read the best authors. Who are some you might find helpful in perfecting your style? Transcribe a few paragraphs of your favorite author and analyze the style.
2. Rewrite Jonson's paragraph in modern style. Break it into several paragraphs if you wish.

3. How does a good writer become better? Men through the ages have asked themselves this question. If Jonson's answer does not fully satisfy you, develop your own response.
4. According to Jonson what is wrong with the writing of most beginners?


ALEXANDER POPE

## from An Essay on Criticism

In wit, as nature, what affects our hearts
Is not th' exactness of peculiar parts;
'Tis not a lip, or eye, we beauty call,
But the joint force and full result of all.
Thus when we view some well-proportioned dome,
(The world's just wonder, and even thine, O Rome!)
No single parts unequally surprise,
All comes united to th' admiring eyes;
No monstrous height, or breadth, or length appear;
The Whole at once is bold, and regular.
      Whoever thinks a faultless piece to see,
Thinks what ne'er was, nor is, nor e'er shall be.
In every work regard the writer's End,
Since none can compass more than they intend;
And if the means be just, the conduct true,
Applause, in spight of trivial faults, is due;
As men of breeding, sometimes men of wit,
T'avoid great errors, must the less commit:
Neglect the rules each verbal Critic lays,
For not to know some trifles, is a praise.
Most Critics, fond of some subservient art,
Still make the Whole depend upon a Part:
They talk of principles, but notions prize,
And all to one loved Folly sacrifice.
      Once on a time, La Mancha's Knight, they say,
A certain bard encount'ring on the way,
Discoursed in terms as just, with looks as sage,
As e'er could Dennis of the Grecian stage;
Concluding all were desperate sots and fools,
Who durst depart from Aristotle's rules.
Our author, happy in a judge so nice,

Produced his Play, and begged the Knight's advice;
Made him observe the subject, and the plot,
The manners, passions, unities; what not?
All which, exact to rule, were brought about,
Were but a Combat in the lists left out.
"What! leave the Combat out?" exclaims the Knight;
Yes, or we must renounce the Stagirite.
"Not so by Heaven" (he answers in a rage),
"Knights, squires, and steeds, must enter on the stage."
So vast a throng the stage can ne'er contain.
"Then build a new, or act it in a plain."
  Thus Critics, of less judgment than caprice,
Curious not knowing, not exact but nice,
Form short Ideas; and offend in arts
(As most in manners) by a love to parts.
  Some to *Conceit* alone their taste confine,
And glitt'ring thoughts struck out at every line;
Pleased with a work where nothing's just or fit;
One glaring Chaos and wild heap of wit.
Poets like painters, thus, unskilled to trace
The naked nature and the living grave,
With gold and jewels cover every part,
And hide with ornaments their want of art.
True Wit is Nature to advantage dressed,
What oft was thought, but ne'er so well expressed . . .

## SUGGESTIONS FOR WRITING

1. Alexander Pope (1688-1744) wrote his *Essay on Criticism* (1711) when he was only twenty-one. This remarkable poem in heroic couplets is an exposition of the rules of taste and the rules of criticism. Pope's concern for the relation between humanity and nature and his pre-occupation with perfection and beauty are revealed in a paraphrase of the first five lines of this excerpt: In human intelligence as in the natural world, what we call beautiful is not a particular part but the impact of the whole. Paraphrase the rest of the selection.

2. Write a criticism of a painting in which you attempt to point out "the joint force and full result of all."

3. Analyze one of your own imaginative writings on the basis of Pope's principles of criticism.

4. To develop an appreciation of Pope's ability, devise a system of criticism (three or four points by which a work of art should be judged). Analyze some lines of poetry to reveal and illustrate your system.

H . L . M E N C K E N

## Style Is a Living and Breathing Thing *

With precious few exceptions, all the books on style in English are by writers quite unable to write. The subject, indeed, seems to exercise a special and dreadful fascination over schoolma'ms, bucolic college professors, and other such pseudoliterates. One never hears of treatises on it by George Moore or James Branch Cabell, but the pedagogues, male and female, are at it all the time. In a thousand texts they set forth their depressing ideas about it, and millions of suffering high-school pupils have to study what they say. Their central aim, of course, is to reduce the whole thing to a series of simple rules—the overmastering passion of their melancholy order, at all times and everywhere. They aspire to teach it as bridge whist, the American Legion flagdrill and double entry bookkeeping are taught. They fail as ignominiously as that Athenian of legend who essayed to train a regiment of grasshoppers in the goose-step.

For the essence of a sound style is that it cannot be reduced to rules—that it is a living and breathing thing, with something of the devilish in it—that it fits its proprietor tightly and yet ever so loosely, as his skin fits him. It is, in fact, quite as securely an integral part of him as that skin is. It hardens as his arteries harden. It has *Katzenjammer* on the days succeeding his indiscretions. It is gaudy when he is young and gathers decorum when he grows old. On the day after he makes a mash on a new girl it glows and glitters. If he has fed well, it is mellow. If he has gastritis it is bitter. In brief, a style is always the outward and visible symbol of a man, and it cannot be anything else. To attempt to teach it is as silly as to set up courses in making love. The man who makes love out of a book is not making love at all; he is simply imitating someone else making love. God help him if, in love or literary composition, his preceptor be a pedagogue!

The schoolma'm theory that the writing of English may be taught

---

* From *Prejudices: Fifth Series* by H. L. Mencken (New York: Alfred A. Knopf, Inc., 1927). Copyright 1928 by Alfred A. Knopf, Inc. Reprinted by permission of the publishers.

is based upon a faulty inference from a sound observation. The sound observation is that the great majority of American high-school pupils, when they attempt to put their thoughts upon paper, produce only a mass of confused and puerile nonsense—that they express themselves so clumsily that it is often quite impossible to understand them at all. The faulty inference is to the effect that what ails them is a defective technical equipment—that they can be trained to write clearly as a dog may be trained to walk on its hind legs. This is all wrong. What ails them is not a defective technical equipment but a defective natural equipment. They write badly simply because they cannot think clearly. They cannot think clearly because they lack the brains. Trying to teach them is as hopeless as trying to teach a dog with only one hind leg. Any human being who can speak English understandably has all the materials necessary to write English clearly, and even beautifully. There is nothing mysterious about the written language; it is precisely the same, in essence, as the spoken language. If a man can think in English at all, he can find words enough to express his ideas. The fact is proved abundantly by the excellent writing that often comes from so-called ignorant men. It is proved anew by the even better writing that is done on higher levels by persons of great simplicity, for example, Abraham Lincoln. Such writing commonly arouses little enthusiasm among pedagogues. Its transparency excites their professional disdain, and they are offended by its use of homely words and phrases. They prefer something more ornate and complex—something, as they would probably put it, demanding more thought. But the thought they yearn for is the kind, alas, that they secrete themselves—the muddled, high-falutin, vapid thought that one finds in their own textbooks.

I do not denounce them because they write so badly; I merely record the fact in a sad, scientific spirit. Even in such twilight regions of the intellect the style remains the man. What is in the head infallibly oozes out of the nub of the pen. If it is sparkling Burgundy the writing is full of life and charm. If it is mush the writing is mush too. The late Dr. Harding, twenty-ninth President of the Federal Union, was a highly self-conscious stylist. He practiced prose composition assiduously, and was regarded by the pedagogues of Marion, Ohio, and vicinity as a very talented fellow. But when he sent a message to Congress it was so muddled in style that even the late

Henry Cabot Lodge, a professional literary man, could not understand it. Why? Simply because Dr. Harding's thoughts, on the high
and grave subjects he discussed, were so muddled that he couldn't
understand them himself. But on matters within his range of customary meditation he was clear and even charming, as all of us are.
I once heard him deliver a brief address upon the ideals of the
Elks. It was a topic close to his heart, and he had thought about it
at length and *con amore*. The result was an excellent speech—
clear, logical, forceful, and with a touch of wild, romantic beauty.
His sentences hung together. He employed simple words, and put
them together with skill. But when, at a public meeting in Washington, he essayed to deliver an oration on the subject of the late
Dante Alighieri, he quickly became so obscure and absurd that even
the Diplomatic Corps began to snicker. The cause was plain: he
knew no more about Dante than a Tennessee county judge knows
about the Institutes of Justinian. Trying to formulate ideas upon
the topic, he could get together only a few disjected fragments and
ghosts of ideas—here an ear, there a section of tibia, beyond a puff
of soul substance or other gas. The resultant speech was thus enig-
matical, cacophonous and awful stuff. It sounded precisely like a
lecture by a college professor on style.

A pedagogue, confronted by Dr. Harding in class, would have set
him to the business of what is called improving his vocabulary—
that is, to the business of making his writing even worse than it
was. Dr. Harding, in point of fact, had all the vocabulary that he
needed, and a great deal more. Any idea that he could formulate
clearly he could convey clearly. Any idea that genuinely moved
him he could invest with charm—which is to say, with what
the pedagogues call style. I believe that this capacity is possessed by all literate persons above the age of fourteen. It is
not acquired by studying textbooks; it is acquired by learning
how to think. Children even younger often show it. I have a
niece, now eleven years old, who already has an excellent style.
When she writes to me about things that interest her—in other
words, about the things she is capable of thinking about—
she puts her thoughts into clear, dignified and admirable English.
Her vocabulary, so far, is unspoiled by schoolma'ms. She doesn't try
to knock me out by bombarding me with hard words, and phrases
filched from Addison. She is unaffected, and hence her writing is

charming. But if she essayed to send me a communication on the subject, say, of Balkan politics or government ownership, her style would descend instantly to the level of that of Dr. Harding's state papers.

To sum up, style cannot go beyond the ideas which lie at the heart of it. If they are clear, it too will be clear. If they are held passionately, it will be eloquent. Trying to teach it to persons who cannot think, especially when the business is attempted by persons who also cannot think, is a great waste of time, and an immoral imposition upon the taxpayers of the nation. It would be far more logical to devote all the energy to teaching, not writing, but logic— and probably just as useless. For I doubt that the art of thinking can be taught at all—at any rate, by schoolteachers. It is not ac- quired, but congenital. Some persons are born with it. Their ideas flow in straight channels; they are capable of lucid reasoning; when they say anything it is instantly understandable; when they write anything it is clear and persuasive. They constitute, I should say, about one-eighth of one per cent of the human race. The rest of God's children are just as incapable of logical thought as they are incapable of jumping over the moon. Trying to teach them to think is as vain an enterprise as trying to teach a streptococcus the prin- ciples of Americanism. The only thing to do with them is to make Ph.D.'s of them, and set them to writing handbooks on style.

SUGGESTIONS FOR WRITING

1. H. L. Mencken, about whom comment is made on p. 160, entitled the above piece "Literature and the Schoolma'm." He says that the trouble with trying to teach style is that style cannot be reduced to rules. This seems sensible enough until you begin to work out a defini- tion of rules. If your interpretation of "rules" is broad enough, no one can teach anyone anything. The job here, then, is to define "rules" not as Mencken used the term but as a teacher of style might.

2. Mencken says students cannot write clearly "because they cannot think clearly. They cannot think clearly because they lack the brains." True? Discuss.

3. Do you share Mencken's view that most of "God's children are just as incapable of logical thought as they are incapable of jumping over the moon."? What is his premise?

4. Mencken wrote this piece in 1926. Do you have any reason to believe he would change any part of it now? Is he arguing that inability to

write (acquire a good style) is part of human nature or a part of the age? Is human nature incapable of change?
5. Mencken criticizes schoolma'ms and college professors with vehemence. From your personal experience, do they deserve it?
6. If you were hired to teach writing style, would you refuse the position on the grounds that the task was impossible? If not, what would you do?

F. L. LUCAS

# On the Fascination of Style*

When it was suggested to Walt Whitman that one of his works should be bound in vellum, he was outraged—"Pshaw!" he snorted, "—hangings, curtains, finger bowls, chinaware, Matthew Arnold!" And he might have been equally irritated by talk of style; for he boasted of "my barbaric yawp"—he would *not* be literary; his readers should touch not a book but a man. Yet Whitman took the pains to rewrite *Leaves of Grass* four times, and his style is unmistakable. Samuel Butler maintained that writers who bothered about their style became unreadable but he bothered about his own. "Style" has got a bad name by growing associated with precious and superior persons who, like Oscar Wilde, spend a morning putting in a comma, and the afternoon (so he said) taking it out again. But such abuse of "style" is misuse of English. For the word means merely "a way of expressing oneself, in language, manner, or appearance"; or, secondly, "a *good* way of so expressing oneself"—as when one says, "Her behavior never lacked style."

Now there is no crime in expressing oneself (though to try to *impress* oneself on others easily grows revolting or ridiculous). Indeed one cannot help expressing oneself, unless one passes one's life in a cupboard. Even the most rigid Communist, or Organization-man, is compelled by Nature to have a unique voice, unique fingerprints, unique handwriting. Even the signatures of the letters on your breakfast table may reveal more than their writers guess. There are blustering signatures that swish across the page like cornstalks bowed before a tempest. There are cryptic signatures, like a scrabble of lightning across a cloud, suggesting that behind is a lofty divinity whom all must know, or an aloof divinity whom none is worthy to know (though, as this might be highly inconvenient, a docile typist sometimes interprets the mystery in a bracket underneath). There are impetuous squiggles implying that the author is a sort of strenuous Sputnik streaking round the globe every eighty minutes. There are florid signatures, all curlicues and danglements and flamboyance, like the youthful Disraeli (though these seem rather out of fashion). There are humble, humdrum signatures. And there are also, sometimes, signatures that are courteously clear, yet mindful of a certain simple grace and artistic economy—in short, of style.

Since, then, not one of us can put pen to paper, or even open his mouth, without giving something of himself away to shrewd observers, it seems mere common sense to give the matter a little thought. Yet it does not seem very common. Ladies may take infinite pains about having style in their clothes, but many of us remain curiously indifferent about having it in our words. How many women would dream of polishing not only their nails but also their tongues? They may play freely on that perilous little organ, but they cannot often be bothered to tune it. And how many men think of improving their talk as well as their golf handicap?

No doubt strong silent men, speaking only in gruff monosyllables, may despise "mere words." No doubt the world does suffer from an endemic plague of verbal dysentery. But that, precisely, is bad style. And consider the amazing power of mere words. Adolf Hitler was a bad artist, bad statesman, bad general, and bad man. But largely because he could tune his rant, with psychological nicety, to the exact wave length of his audiences and make millions quarrelsome-drunk all at the same time by his command of windy nonsense, skilled statesmen, soldiers, scientists were blown away like chaff, and he came near to rule the world. If Sir Winston Churchill had been a mere speechifier, we might have lost the war; yet his speeches did quite a lot to win it.

No man was less of a literary aesthete than Benjamin Franklin; yet this tallow chandler's son, who changed world history, regarded as "a principal means of my advancement" that pungent style which he acquired partly by working in youth over old *Spectators;* but mainly by being Benjamin Franklin. The squinting demagogue, John Wilkes, as ugly as his many sins, had yet a tongue so winning that he asked only half an hour's start (to counteract his face) against any rival for a woman's favor. "Vote for you!" growled a surly elector in his constituency. "I'd sooner vote for the devil!" "But in case your friend should not stand . . . ?" Cleopatra, that ensnarer of world conquerors, owed less to the shape of her nose than to the charm of her tongue. Shakespeare himself has often poor plots and thin ideas; even his mastery of character has been questioned; what does remain unchallenged is his verbal magic. Men are often taken, like rabbits, by the ears. And though the tongue has no bones, it can sometimes break millions of them.

"But," the reader may grumble, "I am neither Hitler, Cleopatra, nor Shakespeare. What is all this to me?" Yet we all talk—often too much; we all have to write letters—often too many. We live not by bread alone but also by words. And not always with remarkable efficiency. Strikes, lawsuits, divorces, all sorts of public nuisance and private misery, often come just from the gaggling incompetence with which we express ourselves. Americans and British get at cross-purposes because they use the same words with different meanings. Men have been hanged on a comma in a statute. And in the valley of Balaclava a mere verbal ambiguity, about *which* guns were to be captured, sent the whole Light Brigade to futile annihilation.

Words can be more powerful, and more treacherous, than we sometimes suspect; communication more difficult than we may think. We are all serving life sentences of solitary confinement within our own bodies; like prisoners, we have, as it were, to tap in awkward code to our fellow men in their neighboring cells. Further, when A and B converse, there take part in their dialogue not two characters, as they suppose, but six. For there is A's real self—call it $A_1$; there is also A's picture of himself—$A_2$; there is also B's picture of A—$A_3$. And there are three corresponding personalities of B. With six characters involved even in a simple tête-à-tête, no wonder we fall into muddles and misunderstandings.

Perhaps, then, there are five main reasons for trying to gain some mastery of language:

We have no other way of understanding, informing, misinforming, or persuading one another.

Even alone, we think mainly in words; if our language is muddy, so will our thinking be.

By our handling of words we are often revealed and judged. "Has

he written anything?" said Napoleon of a candidate for an appointment. "Let me see his *style*."

Without a feeling for language one remains half blind and deaf
to literature.

Our mother tongue is bettered or worsened by the way each generation uses it. Languages evolve like species. They can degenerate;
just as oysters and barnacles have lost their heads. Compare ancient
Greek with modern. A heavy responsibility, though often forgotten.

Why and how did I become interested in style? The main answer, I suppose, is that I was born that way. Then I was, till ten,
an only child running loose in a house packed with books, and in a
world (thank goodness) still undistracted by radio and television. So
at three I groaned to my mother, "Oh, I *wish* I could read," and at
four I read. Now travel among books is the best travel of all, and
the easiest, and the cheapest. (Not that I belittle ordinary travel—
which I regard as one of the three main pleasures in life.) One
learns to write by reading good books, as one learns to talk by
hearing good talkers. And if I have learned anything of writing, it
is largely from writers like Montaigne, Dorothy Osborne, Horace
Walpole, Johnson, Goldsmith, Montesquieu, Voltaire, Flaubert and
Anatole France. Again, I was reared on Greek and Latin, and one
can learn much from translating Homer or the Greek Anthology,
Horace or Tacitus, if one is thrilled by the originals and tries, however vainly, to recapture some of that thrill in English.

.        .        .

The writer should respect truth and himself; therefore honesty.
He should respect his readers; therefore courtesy. These are two of
the cornerstones of style. Confucius saw it, twenty-five centuries ago:
"The Master said, The gentleman is courteous, but not pliable:
common men are pliable, but not courteous."

First, honesty. In literature, as in life, one of the fundamentals is
to find, and be, one's true self. One's true self may indeed be unpleasant (though one can try to better it); but a false self, sooner or
later, becomes disgusting—just as a nice plain woman, painted to
the eyebrows, can become horrid. In writing, in the long run, pretense does not work. As the police put it, anything you say may be
used as evidence against you. If handwriting reveals character, writing reveals it still more. You cannot fool *all* your judges *all* the
time.

Most style is not honest enough. Easy to say, but hard to practice. A writer may take to long words, as young men to beards—to impress. But long words, like long beards, are often the badge of charlatans. Or a writer may cultivate the obscure, to seem profound. But even carefully muddied puddles are soon fathomed. Or he may cultivate eccentricity, to seem original. But really original people do not have to think about being original—they can no more help it than they can help breathing. They do not need to dye their hair green. The fame of Meredith, Wilde or Bernard Shaw might now shine brighter, had they struggled less to be brilliant; whereas Johnson remains great, not merely because his gifts were formidable but also because, with all his prejudice and passion, he fought no less passionately to "clear his mind of cant."

Secondly, courtesy—respect for the reader. From this follow several other basic principles of style. Clarity is one. For it is boorish to make your reader rack his brains to understand. One should aim at being impossible to misunderstand—though men's capacity for misunderstanding approaches infinity. Hence Molière and Po Chu-i tried their work on their cooks; and Swift his on his menservants—"which, if they did not comprehend, he would alter and amend, until they understood it perfectly." Our bureaucrats and pundits, unfortunately, are less considerate.

Brevity is another basic principle. For it is boorish, also, to waste your reader's time. People who would not dream of stealing a penny of one's money turn not a hair at stealing hours of one's life. But that does not make them less exasperating. Therefore there is no excuse for the sort of writer who takes as long as a marching army corps to pass a given point. Besides, brevity is often more effective; the half can say the whole, and to imply things may strike far deeper than to state them at length. And because one is particularly apt to waste words on preambles before coming to the substance, there was sense in the Scots professor who always asked his pupils —"Did ye remember to tear up that fir-r-st page? . . ."

SUGGESTIONS FOR WRITING

1. Frank Laurence Lucas (1894-    ) has written novels, poems, plays, and translations. He is a Fellow and Lecturer in King's College, Cambridge, and University Reader in English. His book, *The Search for Good*

*Sense,* is a collection of essays on four eighteenth-century prose stylists. It is not an exaggeration to say that he has spent a professional lifetime thinking about writing style. Summarize his views, and indicate which of his points seems most effective and why.

2. Honesty, courtesy, brevity. These terms seem more like a set of rules for a visiting diplomat, yet Lucas uses them as "rules" for writing. Reflect on the similarity between rules for writing and rules for living. *Why* are they similar?

3. "Even signatures reveal . . . more than the writers guess." Analyze a few signatures of acquaintances. What do they tell you about the person?

4. "If Sir Winston Churchill had been a mere speechifier, we might have lost the war; yet his speeches did quite a lot to win it." A skeptic says this is exaggeration, but is it? Cite an experience when "mere speechifying" changed the course of events.

5. Devise a dialogue between Mencken and Lucas, with Mencken attacking teachers of style.


WILLIAM  HAZLITT

## Differences Between Writing and Speaking*

Some minds are proportioned to that which may be dispatched at once, or within a short return of time; others to that which begins afar off and is to be won with length of pursuit.

—Bacon

It is a common observation that few persons can be found who speak and write equally well. Not only is it obvious that the two faculties do not always go together in the same proportions, but they are not unusually in direct opposition to each other. We find that the greatest authors often make the worst company in the world, and again some of the liveliest fellows imaginable in conversation or extempore speaking seem to lose all this vivacity and spirit the moment they set pen to paper. For this a greater degree of quickness or slowness of parts, education, habit, temper, turn of mind and a variety of collateral and predisposing causes are necessary to account. The subject is at least curious and worthy of an attempt to explain it. I shall endeavor to illustrate the difference by familiar examples rather than by analytical reasonings. The

---
* From *The Plain Speaker,* 1826.

philosopher of old was not unwise who defined motion by getting up and walking.

The great leading distinction between writing and speaking is, that more time is allowed for the one than the other, and hence different faculties are required for, and different objects attained by each. He is properly the best speaker who can collect together the greatest number of apposite ideas at a moment's warning; he is properly the best writer who can give utterance to the greatest quantity of valuable knowledge in the course of his whole life. The chief requisite for the one, then, appears to be quickness and facility of perception—for the other, patience of soul and a power increasing with the difficulties it has to master. He cannot be denied to be an expert speaker, a lively companion, who is never at a loss for something to say on every occasion or subject that offers. He, by the same rule, will make a respectable writer who, by dint of study, can find out anything good to say upon any one point that has not been touched upon before, or who by asking for time, can give the most complete and comprehensive view of any question. The one must be done offhand, at a single blow; the other can only be done by a repetition of blows, by having time to think and do better.

In speaking, less is required of you, if you only do it at once with grace and spirit; in writing, you stipulate for all that you are capable of, but you have the choice of your own time and subject.

We see persons of that standard or texture of mind that they can do nothing but on the spur of the occasion; if they have time to deliberate they are lost. There are others who have no resource, who cannot advance a step by any efforts or assistance beyond a successful arrangement of commonplaces; but these they have always at command, at everybody's service. Set the same person to write a common paragraph and he cannot get through it for very weariness; ask him a question, ever so little out of the common road and he stares you in the face. What does all this bustle, animation, plausibility and command of words amount to? A lively flow of animal spirits, a good deal of confidence, a communicative turn, and a tolerably tenacious memory with respect to floating opinions and current phrases. Beyond the routine of the daily newspapers and coffeehouse criticism, such persons do not venture to think at all; or if they did it would be so much the worse for them, for they would only be perplexed in the attempt and would perform their part in the mechanism of society with so much the less alacrity and easy volubility.

The most dashing orator I ever heard is the flattest writer I ever read. In speaking, he was like a volcano vomiting out *lava;* in writing, he is like a volcano burnt out. Nothing but the dry cinders, the hard shell remains. The tongues of flame with which in haranguing a mixed assembly he used to illuminate his subject and almost scorched up the panting air, do not appear painted on the margin of his works. He was the model of a flashy, powerful demagogue— a madman blest with a fit audience.

It is not merely that the same individual cannot sit down quietly in his closet and produce the same or a correspondent effect but sit down yourself and read one of these very popular and electrical effusions (for they have been published), and you would not believe it to be the same! The thunder-and-lightning mixture of the orator turns out a mere drab-colored suit in the person of the prose writer. We wonder at the change and think there must be some mistake, some legerdemain trick played off upon us, by which what before appeared so fine now appears to be so worthless. The deception took place *before;* now it is removed. The orator's vehemence of gesture, the loudness of the voice, the speaking eye, the conscious attitude, the inexplicable dumb show and noise,—all "those brave sublunary things that made his raptures clear,"—are no longer there and without these he is nothing—his "fire and ire" turn to puddle and ditch water, and the god of eloquence and of our idolatry sinks into a common mortal, or an image of lead, with a few labels, nicknames, and party watchwords stuck in his mouth. The truth is that these always made up the stock of his intellectual wealth, but a certain exaggeration and extravagance of *manner* covered the nakedness and swelled out the emptiness of the *matter.*

An orator can hardly get beyond *commonplaces;* if he does he gets beyond his hearers. The most successful speakers, even in the House of Commons, have not been the best scholars or the finest writers. Those speeches that in general told the best at the time are not now readable. What were the materials of which they were chiefly composed? An imposing detail of passing events, a formal display of official documents, an appeal to established maxims, an echo of popular clamor, some worn-out metaphor newly vamped up,—some hackneyed argument used for the hundredth, nay thousandth time, to fall in with the interests, the passions, or prejudices of listening and devoted admirers—some truth or falsehood repeated as the Shibboleth of party time out of mind, which gathers strength from sympathy as it spreads, because it is understood or assented to by the million, and finds in the increased action of the minds of numbers the weight and force of an instinct. A *commonplace* does not leave the mind "sceptical, puzzled, and undecided in the moment of action"; "it gives a body to opinion and a permanence to fugitive belief." It operates mechanically and opens an instantaneous and infallible communication between the hearer and the speaker. A set of cant phrases, arranged in sounding sentences, and pronounced "with good emphasis and discretion," keep the gross and irritable humors of an audience in constant fermentation, and levy no tax on the understanding. To give a reason for anything is to breed a doubt of it, which doubt you may not remove in the sequel, either because your reason may not be a good one or because the person to whom it is addressed may not be able to comprehend it or because *others* may not be able to comprehend it. He who offers to go into the grounds of an acknowledged axiom risks the unanimity of the company "by most admired disorder," as he who digs to the foundation of a building to show its solidity, risks its falling. But a commonplace is enshrined in its own unquestioned evidence, and constitutes its own immortal basis.

The writer must be original or he is nothing. He is not to take up with ready-made goods, for he has time allowed him to create his own materials, and to make novel combinations of thought and fancy, to contend with unforeseen difficulties of style and execution, while we look on and admire the growing work in secret and at leisure. There is a degree of finishing as well as of solid strength in writing which is not to be got at every day, and we can wait for perfection. The author owes a debt to truth and nature which he cannot satisfy at sight, but he has pawned his head on redeeming it. It is not a string of claptraps to answer a temporary or party purpose—violent, vulgar, and illiberal—but general and lasting truth that we require at his hands. We go to him as pupils, not as partisans. We have a right to expect from him profounder views of things, finer observations, more ingenious illustrations, happier and bolder expressions. He is to give the choice and picked results of a whole life of study, what he has struck out in his most felicitous moods, has treasured up with most pride, has labored to bring to light with most anxiety and confidence of success. He can wait. He is not satisfied with a reason he has offered for something; let him wait till he finds a better reason. There is some word, some phrase, some idiom that expresses a particular idea better than any other, but he cannot for the life of him recollect it; let him wait till he does. Is it strange that among twenty thousand words in the English language the one of all others that he most needs should have escaped him? There are more things in nature than there are words in the English language, and he must not expect to lay rash hands on them all at once. You will allow a writer a year to think of a subject; he should not put you off with a truism at last. You allow him a year more to find out words for his thoughts; he should not give us an echo of all the fine things that have been said a hundred times. A person in habits of composition often hesitates in conversation for a particular word; it is because he is in search of the best word and *that* he cannot hit upon. In writing he would stop till it came. It is not true, however, that the scholar could avail himself of a more ordinary word if he chose, or readily acquire a command of ordinary language; for his associations are habitually intense, not vague and shallow, and words occur to him only as *tallies* to certain modifications of feeling. They are links in the chain of thought. His imagination is fastidious, and rejects all those that are "of no mark or likelihood."

To conclude this account with what perhaps I ought to have set out with—a definition of the character of an author. There are persons who in society, in public intercourse, feel no excitement,

> Dull as the lake that slumbers in the storm,

but who, when left alone, can lash themselves into a foam. They are never less alone than when alone. Mount them on a dinner table, and they have nothing to say; shut them up in a room to themselves, and they are inspired. They are "made fierce with dark keeping." In revenge for being tongue-tied, a torrent of words flows from their pens, and the storm which was so long collecting comes down apace. It never rains but it pours. Is not this strange, unaccountable? Not at all so. They have a real interest, a real knowledge of the subject, and they cannot summon up all that interest, or bring all that knowledge to bear while they have anything else to attend to. Till they can do justice to the feeling they have, they can do nothing. For this they look into their own minds, not in the faces of a gaping multitude. What they would say (if they could) does not lie at the orifices of the mouth ready for delivery, but is wrapped in the folds of the heart and registered in the chambers of the brain. In the sacred cause of truth that stirs them they would put their whole strength, their whole being into requisition; and as it implies a greater effort to drag their words and ideas from their lurking places, so there is no end when they are once set in motion. The whole of a man's thoughts and feelings cannot lie on the surface, made up for use; but the whole must be a greater quantity, a mightier power, if they could be got at, layer upon layer, and brought into play by the levers of imagination and reflection. Such a person then sees farther and feels deeper than most others. He plucks up an argument by the roots, he tears out the very heart of his subject. He has more pride in conquering the difficulties of a question, than vanity in courting the favor of an audience. He wishes to satisfy himself before he pretends to enlighten the public.

SUGGESTIONS FOR WRITING

1. William Hazlitt (1778-1830), English critic and essayist, studied theology and painting before turning to writing. His work may be divided into three classes: essays on art and drama, essays on literary criticism, and essays on miscellaneous subjects. In this essay, he illustrates the difference between writing and speaking, but he does not indicate why some people can perform one skill more effectively than the other. Why do you suppose this difference exists, or does it?

2. "The most dashing orator I ever heard is the flattest writer I ever read." Reverse this. Is the best writer you know also a good speaker? Are the two skills incompatible? Reveal through short character sketches people who are skillful at one or both of these disciplines.

3. Turn to *Vital Speeches* and read the speech you previously heard someone deliver. What differences, if any, do you notice in the reading? Is the difference in you or in the situation?

4. "An orator cannot get beyond *commonplaces*. . . ." Have you heard a commencement address or political speech which was full of commonplaces? Have you ever heard a speech that did *not* contain commonplaces? Defend or attack Hazlitt's thesis.

RING  LARDNER

## On  Conversation*

The other night I happened to be comeing back from Wilmington, Del. to wherever I was going and was setting in the smoking
compartment or whatever they now call the wash room and over-
heard a conversation between two fellows who we will call Mr.
Butler and Mr. Hawkes. Both of them seemed to be from the same
town and I only wished I could repeat the conversation verbatim
but the best I can do is report it from memory. The fellows evidently had not met for some three to fifteen years, as the judges say.

"Well," said Mr. Hawkes, "if this isn't Dick Butler!"

"Well," said Mr. Butler, "if it isn't Dale Hawkes."

"Well, Dick," said Hawkes, "I never expected to meet you on this
train."

"No," replied Butler. "I genally always take Number 28. I just
took this train this evening because I had to be in Wilmington
today."

"Where are you headed for?" asked Hawkes.

"Well, I am going to the big town," said Butler.

"So am I, and I am certainly glad we happened to be in the same
car."

"I am glad too, but it is funny we happened to be in the same car."

It seemed funny to both of them but they successfully concealed
it so far as facial expression was concerned. After a pause Hawkes
spoke again:

"How long since you been back in Lansing?"

"Me?" replied Butler. "I ain't been back there for twelve years."

"I ain't been back there either myself for ten years. How long
since you been back there?"

"I ain't been back there for twelve years."

"I ain't been back there myself for ten years. Where are you
headed for?"

---

* From *First and Last* by Ring Lardner. (New York: Charles Scribner's Sons,
1934). Copyright 1934 by Ellis A. Lardner; © 1962 by Ring Lardner, Jr. Reprinted by permission of the publishers.

"New York," replied Butler. "I have got to get there about once a year. Where are you going?"

"Me?" asked Hawkes. "I am going to New York too. I have got to go down there every little wile for the firm."

"Do you have to go there very often?"

"Me? Every little wile. How often do you have to go there?"

"About once a year. How often do you get back to Lansing?"

"Last time I was there was ten years ago. How long since you was back?"

"About twelve years ago. Lot of changes there since we left there."

"That's the way I figured it. It makes a man seem kind of old to go back there and not see nobody you know."

"You said something. I go along the streets there now and don't see nobody I know."

"How long since you was there?"

"Me?" said Hawkes. "I only get back there about once every ten years. By the way what become of old man Kelsey?"

"Who do you mean, Kelsey?"

"Yes, what become of him?"

"Old Kelsey? Why he has been dead for ten years."

"Oh, I didn't know that. And what become of his daughter? I mean Eleanor."

"Why Eleanor married a man named Forster or Jennings or something like that from Flint."

"Yes, but I mean the other daughter, Louise."

"Oh, she's married."

"Where are you going now?"

"I am headed for New York on business for the firm."

"I have to go there about once a year myself—for the firm."

"Do you get back to Lansing very often?"

"About once in ten or twelve years. I hardly know anybody there now. It seems funny to go down the street and not know nobody."

"That's the way I always feel. It seems like it was not my old home town at all. I go up and down the street and don't know anybody and nobody speaks to you. I guess I know more people in New York now than I do in Lansing."

"Do you get to New York often?"

"Only about once a year. I have to go there for the firm."

"New York isn't the same town it used to be neither."

"No, it is changing all the time. Just like Lansing. I guess they all change."

"I don't know much about Lansing any more. I only get there about once in ten or twelve years."

"What are you reading there?"

"Oh, it is just a little article in *Asia*. They's a good many interesting articles in *Asia*."

"I only seen a couple copies of it. This thing I am reading is a little article on 'Application' in the *American*."

"Well, go ahead and read and don't let me disturb you."

"Well I just wanted to finish it up. Go ahead and finish what you're reading yourself."

"All right. We will talk things over later. It is funny we happened to get on the same car."

SUGGESTIONS FOR WRITING

1. Ring Lardner (1885-1933) was known as a sports writer and columnist before his success with short stories. His baseball stories in *You Know Me, Al: A Busher's Letters* (1916) are, many think, written with a skill in the use of idiom second only to Mark Twain's. His later stories showed him as a sardonic humorist exposing follies and vices through his characters' conversational speech. As in this excerpt, he tried to reveal a tone and special feeling by deliberately misspelling. Write a short fictional biography of either Mr. Hawkes or Mr. Butler. Note Lardner's tone and technique and employ it in your biography.

2. Capture and illuminate, as Lardner has done, a similar conversational encounter.

3. Are Butler and Hawkes regional characters? national? international? Have they existed since the beginning of time? Two cave men meet on the path to the water hole. Is their conversation similar to the one between Butler and Hawkes?

4. Conversation does not have to be funny in itself to be amusing to the reader. Nor does it need to be "tagged" with "he said's" each time. Reverse the technique in Lardner's piece and show two *brilliant* conversationalists in action.

# Language

Take care of the sense and the sounds will take care of themselves.
—"The Dutchess" in Lewis Carroll's
*Alice in Wonderland,* 1865

The English language is a methodical, energetic, businesslike and sober language, that does not care much for finery and elegance, but does care for logical consistency and is opposed to any attempt to narrow-in life by . . . strict rules.
—Otto Jesperson, *Growth and Structure of the English Language,* 1938

I have been leading up—or down, if you like—to an extremely simple and obvious but fundamental remark: that no word can be judged as to whether it is good or bad, correct or incorrect, beautiful or ugly, or anything else that matters to a writer, in isolation.
—I. A. Richards, *Principles of Literary Criticism,* 1924

What is all wisdom save a collection of platitudes? Take fifty of our current proverbial sayings—they are so trite, so threadbare, that we can hardly bring our lips to utter them. None the less they embody the concentrated experience of the race.
—Norman Douglas, *South Wind,* 1925

The forcible writer stands bodily behind his words with his experiences. He does not make books out of books, but he has been *there* in person.
—Thoreau, *Journal,* 3 February, 1852

The thought that most thrills our existence is one
Which, before we can frame it in language, is gone.
—Edward Bulwer-Lytton, *Lucile,* 1860

The first and most important thing of all, at least for writers today, is to strip language clean, to lay it bare down to the bone.
—Ernest Hemingway, *Paris Was Our Mistress,* 1947

GILBERT  HIGHET

# The Best-Known Monument of American Prose*

*FOURSCORE and seven years ago* . . .
These five words stand at the entrance to the best-known monument of American prose, one of the finest utterances in the entire language, and surely one of the greatest speeches in all history. Greatness is like granite: it is molded in fire, and it lasts for many centuries.

Fourscore and seven years ago . . . It is strange to think that President Lincoln was looking back to the 4th of July 1776, and that he and his speech are now further removed from us than he himself was from George Washington and the Declaration of Independence. Fourscore and seven years before the Gettysburg Address, a small group of patriots signed the Declaration. Fourscore and seven years after the Gettysburg Address, it was the year 1950 (in November 1950 the Chinese had just entered the war in Korea), and that date is already receding rapidly into our troubled, adventurous, and valiant past.

Inadequately prepared and at first scarcely realized in its full importance, the dedication of the graveyard at Gettysburg was one of the supreme moments of American history. The battle itself had been a turning point of the war. On the 4th of July 1863, General Meade repelled Lee's invasion of Pennsylvania. Although he did not follow up his victory, he had broken one of the most formidable aggressive enterprises of the Confederate armies. Losses were heavy on both sides. Thousands of dead were left on the field, and thou-

---

sands of wounded died in the hot days following the battle. At first, their burial was more or less haphazard; but thoughtful men gradually came to feel that an adequate burying place and memorial were required. These were established by an interstate commission that autumn, and the finest speaker in the North was invited to dedicate them. This was the scholar and statesman Edward Everett of Harvard. He made a good speech—which is still extant: not at all academic, it is full of close strategic analysis and deep historical understanding.

Lincoln was not invited to speak, at first. Although people knew him as an effective debater, they were not sure whether he was capable of making a serious speech on such a solemn occasion. But one of the impressive things about Lincoln's career is that he constantly strove to *grow*. He was anxious to appear on that occasion and to say something worthy of it. (Also, it has been suggested, he was anxious to remove the impression that he did not know how to behave properly—an impression which had been strengthened by a shocking story about his clowning on the battlefield of Antietam the previous year.) Therefore when he was invited he took considerable care with his speech. He drafted rather more than half of it in the White House before leaving, finished it in the hotel at Gettysburg the night before the ceremony (not in the train, as sometimes reported), and wrote out a fair copy next morning.

There are many accounts of the day itself, 19 November 1863. There are many descriptions of Lincoln, all showing the same curious blend of grandeur and awkwardness, or lack of dignity, or—it would be best to call it humility. In the procession he rode horseback: a tall lean man in a high plug hat, straddling a short horse, with his feet too near the ground. He arrived before the chief speaker, and had to wait patiently for half an hour or more. His own speech came right at the end of a long and exhausting ceremony, lasted less than three minutes, and made little impression on the audience. In part this was because they were tired, in part because (as eyewitnesses said) he ended almost before they knew he had begun, and in part because he did not speak the Address, but read it, very slowly, in a thin high voice, with a marked Kentucky accent, pronouncing "to" as "toe" and dropping his final R's.

Some people of course were alert enough to be impressed. Everett congratulated him at once. But most of the newspapers paid little attention to the speech, and some sneered at it. The *Patriot and Union* of Harrisburg wrote, "We pass over the silly remarks of the President; for the credit of the nation we are willing . . . that they shall no more be repeated or thought of"; and the London *Times* said, "The ceremony was rendered ludicrous by some of the sallies of that poor President Lincoln," calling his remarks "dull and commonplace." The first commendation of the Address came in a single sentence of the Chicago *Tribune,* and the first discriminating and detailed praise of it appeared in the Springfield *Republican,* the Providence *Journal,* and the Philadelphia *Bulletin.* However, three weeks after the ceremony and then again the following spring, the editor of *Harper's Weekly* published a sincere and thorough eulogy of the Address, and soon it was attaining recognition as a masterpiece.

At the time, Lincoln could not care much about the reception of his words. He was exhausted and ill. In the train back to Washington, he lay down with a wet towel on his head. He had caught smallpox. At that moment he was incubating it, and he was stricken down soon after he re-entered the White House. Fortunately it was a mild attack, and it evoked one of his best jokes: he told his visitors, "At last I have something I can give to everybody."

He had more than that to give to everybody. He was a unique person, far greater than most people realize until they read his life with care. The wisdom of his policy, the sources of his statesmanship—these were things too complex to be discussed in a brief essay. But we can say something about the Gettysburg Address as a work of art.

A work of art. Yes: for Lincoln was a literary artist, trained both by others and by himself. The textbooks he used as a boy were full of difficult exercises and skillful devices in formal rhetoric, stressing the qualities he practiced in his own speaking: antithesis, parallelism, and verbal harmony. Then he read and reread many admirable models of thought and expression: the King James Bible, the essays of Bacon, the best plays of Shakespeare. His favorites were *Hamlet, Lear, Macbeth, Richard III,* and *Henry VIII,* which he had read dozens of times. He loved reading aloud, too, and spent hours reading poetry to his friends. (He told his partner Herndon that he preferred getting the sense of any document by reading it aloud.) Therefore his serious speeches are important parts of the long and noble classical tradition of oratory which begins in Greece, runs through Rome to the modern world, and is still capable (if we do not neglect it) of producing masterpieces.

The first proof of this is that the Gettysburg Address is full of quotations—or rather of adaptations—which give it strength. It is partly religious, partly (in the highest sense) political: therefore it is interwoven with memories of the Bible and memories of American history. The first and the last words are biblical cadences. Normally Lincoln did not say "fourscore" when he meant eighty; but on the solemn occasion he recalled the important dates in the Bible—such as the age of Abraham when his first son was born to him, and he was "fourscore and six years old" (Gen. 16:16; cf. Exod. 7:7). Similarly he did not say there was a chance that democracy might die out: he recalled the somber phrasing of the Book of Job—where Bildad speaks of the destruction of one who shall vanish without a trace, and says that "his branch shall be cut off; his remembrance shall perish from the earth" (Job 18:16-17; cf. Jer. 10:11, Micah 7:2). Then again, the famous description of our State as "government of the people, by the people, for the people" was adumbrated by Daniel Webster in 1830 (he spoke of "the people's government, made for the people, made by the people, and answerable to the people") and then elaborated in 1854 by the abolitionist Theodore Parker (as "government of all the people, by all the people, for all the people"). There is good reason to think that Lincoln took the important phrase "under God" (which he interpolated at the last moment) from Weems, the biographer of Washington; and we know that it had been used at least once by Washington himself.

Analyzing the Address further, we find that it is based on a highly imaginative theme, or group of themes. The subject is—how can we put it so as not to disfigure it?—the subject is the kinship of life and death, that mysterious linkage which we see sometimes as the physical succession of birth and death in our world, sometimes as the contrast, which is perhaps a unity, between death and immortality. The first sentence is concerned with birth:

Our *fathers brought forth a new* nation, *conceived* in liberty.

The final phrase but one expresses the hope that

this nation, under God, shall have a *new birth* of freedom.

And the last phrase of all speaks of continuing life as the triumph over death. Again and again throughout the speech, this mystical contrast and kinship reappear: "those who *gave their lives* that that nation might *live*," "the brave men *living* and *dead*," and so in the central assertion that the dead have already consecrated their own burial place, while "it is for us, the *living*, rather to be dedicated . . . to the great task remaining." The Gettysburg Address is a prose poem; it belongs to the same world as the great elegies, and the adagios of Beethoven.

Its structure, however, is that of a skillfully contrived speech. The oratorical pattern is perfectly clear. Lincoln describes the occasion, dedicates the ground, and then draws a larger conclusion by calling on his hearers to dedicate themselves to the preservation of the Union. But within that, we can trace his constant use of at least two important rhetorical devices.

The first of these is *antithesis:* opposition, contrast. The speech is full of it. Listen:

The world will little *note*
      nor long *remember*             what *we say here*
but      it can never *forget*            what *they did here.*

And so in nearly every sentence: "brave men, *living* and *dead*"; "to *add* or *detract*." There is antithesis of the Founding Fathers and the men of Lincoln's own time:

Our *fathers brought forth* a new nation . . .
now *we* are testing whether that nation . . . can *long endure.*

And there is the more terrible antithesis of those who have already died and those who still live to do their duty. Now, antithesis is the figure of contrast and conflict. Lincoln was speaking in the midst of a great civil war.

The other important pattern is different. It is technically called *tricolon*—the division of an idea into three harmonious parts, usu-

ally of increasing power. The most famous phrase of the Address
is a tricolon:

> government of the people
>            by the people
> and       for the people.

The most solemn sentence is a tricolon:

> we cannot dedicate
> we cannot consecrate
> we cannot hallow        this ground.

And above all, the last sentence (which has sometimes been criticized as too complex) is essentially two parallel phrases, with a tricolon growing out of the second and then producing another
tricolon: a trunk, three branches, and a cluster of flowers. Lincoln
says that it is for his hearers to be dedicated to the great task remaining before them. Then he goes on:

> that from these honored dead

—apparently he means "in such a way that from these honored
dead"—

> we take increased devotion to that cause.

Next, he restates this more briefly:

> that we here highly resolve . . .

And now the actual resolution follows, in three parts of growing
intensity:

that these dead shall not have died in vain
that this nation, under God, shall have a new birth of freedom

and that

   (one more tricolon)

> government of the people
>            by the people
> and       for the people
> shall not perish from the earth.

Now, the tricolon is the figure which, through division, emphasizes basic harmony and unity. Lincoln used antithesis because he was speaking to a people at war. He used the tricolon because he was hoping, planning, praying for peace.

No one thinks that when he was drafting the Gettysburg Address, Lincoln deliberately looked up these quotations and consciously chose these particular patterns of thought. No, he chose the theme. From its development and from the emotional tone of the entire occasion, all the rest followed, or grew—by that marvelous process of choice and rejection which is essential to artistic creation. It does not spoil such a work of art to analyze it as closely as we have done; it is altogether fitting and proper that we should do this: for it helps us to penetrate more deeply into the rich meaning of the Gettysburg Address, and it allows us the very rare privilege of watching the workings of a great man's mind.

## SUGGESTIONS FOR WRITING

1. Gilbert Highet (1906-    ) has degrees from Glasgow University and Oxford University. He taught at Oxford until 1938. At that time he moved to Columbia University, where he is Professor of Greek and Latin. He wrote, among other books, *The Art of Teaching* (1950) and *Man's Unconquerable Mind* (1954). The above essay, which comes from *A Clerk of Oxenford* (1954), is a model of analysis and a model of appreciation. What is the essence of good prose? Highet provides the answer in his comments on Lincoln's Gettysburg Address. Summarize Highet's concept of well-written English prose.
2. Highet attributes some of Lincoln's skill to textbooks. He says, "The textbooks he used as a boy were full of difficult exercises and skillful devices in formal rhetoric, stressing the qualities he practiced in his own speaking: antithesis, parallelism, and verbal harmony." Here is an answer to Mencken (see p. 209). Depict a debate between Highet and Mencken.
3. Commit the Gettysburg Address to memory. Say it aloud several times and then write as much of it as you can. Correct your draft and repeat the procedure until you have mastered the speech.
4. Although the Gettysburg Address is a speech, does it seem to you to lose effectiveness if read silently? If not, write a letter to Hazlitt (see p. 218) explaining that you have found an exception to his generalization about the differences between writing and speaking.
5. Analysis, Highet tells us, "allows us the very rare privilege of watching the workings of a great man's mind." If you knew nothing of Lincoln

but the Gettysburg Address, what kind of a character sketch would you draw?


GERTRUDE STEIN

## Words That Are Coming Out*

One of the things that is a very interesting thing to know is how you are feeling inside you to the words that are coming out to be outside of you.

Do you always have the same kind of feeling in relation to the sounds as the words come out of you or do you not. All this has so much to do with grammar and with poetry and with prose.

Words have to do everything in poetry and prose and some writers write more in articles and prepositions and some say you should write in nouns, and of course one has to think of everything.

A noun is a name of anything, why after a thing is named write about it. A name is adequate or it is not. If it is adequate then why go on calling it, if it is not then calling it by its name does no good.

People if you like to believe it can be made by their names. Call anybody Paul and they get to be a Paul call anybody Alice and they get to be an Alice perhaps yes perhaps no, there is something in that, but generally speaking, things once they are named the name does not go on doing anything to them and so why write in nouns. Nouns are the name of anything and just naming names is alright when you want to call a roll but is it any good for anything else. To be sure in many places in Europe as in America they do like to call rolls.

As I say a noun is a name of a thing, and therefore slowly if you feel what is inside that thing you do not call it by the name by which it is known. Everybody knows that by the way they do when they are in love and a writer should always have that intensity of emotion about whatever is the object about which he writes. And therefore and I say it again more and more one does not use nouns.

---

Now what other things are there beside nouns, there are a lot of other things beside nouns.

When you are at school and learn grammar grammar is very exciting. I really do not know that anything has ever been more exciting than diagraming sentences. I suppose other things may be more exciting to others when they are at school but to me undoubtedly when I was at school the really completely exciting thing was diagraming sentences and that has been to me ever since the one thing that has been completely exciting and completely completing. I like the feeling the everlasting feeling of sentences as they diagram themselves.

In that way one is completely possessing something and incidentally one's self. Now in that diagraming of the sentences of course there are articles and prepositions and as I say there are nouns but nouns as I say even by definition are completely not interesting, the same thing is true of adjectives. Adjectives are not really and truly interesting. In a way anybody can know always has known that, because after all adjectives effect nouns and as nouns are not really interesting the thing that effects a not too interesting thing is of necessity not interesting. In a way as I say anybody knows that because of course the first thing that anybody takes out of anybody's writing are the adjectives. You see of yourself how true it is that which I have just said.

Beside the nouns and the adjectives there are verbs and adverbs. Verbs and adverbs are more interesting. In the first place they have one very nice quality and that is that they can be so mistaken. It is wonderful the number of mistakes a verb can make and that is equally true of its adverb. Nouns and adjectives never can make mistakes can never be mistaken but verbs can be so endlessly, both as to what they do and how they agree or disagree with whatever they do. The same is true of adverbs.

In that way any one can see that verbs and adverbs are more interesting than nouns and adjectives.

Beside being able to be mistaken and to make mistakes verbs can change to look like themselves or to look like something else, they are, so to speak on the move and adverbs move with them and each of them find themselves not at all annoying but very often very much mistaken. That is the reason any one can like what verbs can do. Then comes the thing that can of all things be most mistaken and they are prepositions. Prepositions can live one long life being really being nothing but absolutely nothing but mistaken and that makes them irritating if you feel that way about mistakes but certainly something that you can be continuously using and everlastingly enjoying. I like prepositions the best of all, and pretty soon we will go more completely into that.

Then there are articles. Articles are interesting just as nouns and adjectives are not. And why are they interesting just as nouns and adjectives are not. They are interesting because they do what a noun might do if a noun was not so unfortunately so completely unfortunately the name of something. Articles please, *a* and *an* and *the* please as the name that follows cannot please. They the names that is the nouns cannot please, because after all you know well after all that is what Shakespeare meant when he talked about a rose by any other name.

I hope now no one can have any illusion about a noun or about the adjective that goes with the noun.

But an article an article remains as a delicate and a varied something and any one who wants to write with articles and knows how to use them will always have the pleasure that using something that is varied and alive can give. That is what articles are.

Beside that there are conjunctions, and a conjunction is not varied but it has a force that need not make any one feel that they are dull. Conjunctions have made themselves live by their work. They work and as they work they live and even when they do not work and in these days they do not always live by work still nevertheless they do live.

So you see why I like to write with prepositions and conjunctions and articles and verbs and adverbs but not with nouns and adjectives. If you read my writing you will you do see what I mean.

Of course then there are pronouns. Pronouns are not as bad as nouns because in the first place practically they cannot have adjectives go with them. That already makes them better than nouns.

Then beside not being able to have adjectives go with them, they of course are not really the name of anything. They represent some one but they are not its or his name. In not being his or its or her name they already have a greater possibility of being something than if they were as a noun is the name of anything. Now actual given names of people are more lively than nouns which are the name of anything and I suppose that this is because after all the name is only given to that person when they are born, there is at least the element of choice even the element of change and anybody can be pretty well able to do what they like, they may be born Walter and become Hub, in such a way they are not like a noun. A noun has been the name of something for such a very long time.

That is the reason that slang exists it is to change the nouns which have been names for so long. I say again. Verbs and adverbs and articles and conjunctions and prepositions are lively because they all do something and as long as anything does something it keeps alive.

One might have in one's list added interjections but really interjections have nothing to do with anything not even with themselves. There so much for that. And now to go into the question of punctuation.

What does a comma do.

I have refused them so often and left them out so much and did without them so continually that I have come finally to be indifferent to them. I do not now care whether you put them in or not but for a long time I felt very definitely about them and would have nothing to do with them.

As I say commas are servile and they have no life of their own, and their use is not a use, it is a way of replacing one's own interest and I do decidedly like to like my own interest in what I am doing. A comma by helping you along holding your coat for you and putting on your shoes keeps you from living your life as actively as you should lead it and to me for many years and I still do feel that way about it only now I do not pay as much attention to them, the use of them was positively degrading. Let me tell you what I feel and what I mean and what I felt and what I meant.

When I was writing those long sentences of The Making of Americans, verbs active present verbs with long dependent adverbial clauses became a passion with me. I have told you that I recognize verbs and adverbs aided by prepositions and conjunctions with pronouns as possessing the whole of the active life of writing.

Complications make eventually for simplicity and therefore I have always liked dependent adverbial clauses. I have liked dependent adverbial clauses because of their variety of dependence and independence. You can see how loving the intensity of complication of these things that commas would be degrading. Why if you want the pleasure of concentrating on the final simplicity of excessive complication would you want any artificial aid to bring about that simplicity. Do you see now why I feel about the comma as I did and as I do.

Think about anything you really like to do and you will see what I mean.

When it gets really difficult you want to disentangle rather than to cut the knot, at least so anybody feels who is working with any thread, so anybody feels who is working with any tool so anybody feels who is writing any sentence or reading it after it has been written. And what does a comma do, a comma does nothing but make easy a thing that if you like it enough is easy enough without the comma. A long complicated sentence should force itself upon you, make you know yourself knowing it and the comma, well at the most a comma is a poor period that it lets you stop and take a breath but if you want to take a breath you ought to know yourself that you want to take a breath. It is not like stopping altogether which is what a period does stopping altogether has something to do with going on, but taking a breath well you are always taking a breath and why emphasize one breath rather than another breath. Anyway that is the way I felt about it and I felt that about it very very strongly. And so I almost never used a comma. The longer, the more complicated the sentence the greater the number of the same kinds of words I had following one after another, the more the very many more I had of them the more I felt the passionate need of their taking care of themselves by themselves and not helping them, and thereby enfeebling them by putting in a comma.

So that is the way I felt punctuation in prose, in poetry it is a little different but more so and later I will go into that. But that is the way I felt about punctuation in prose.

### SUGGESTIONS FOR WRITING

1. Gertrude Stein (1874-1946), author, and friendly critic of American writers, was constantly experimenting with language. In her book *Lectures in America* (1935), based on lectures to college students in this country, she explains some of her reasons for experimentation. A

number of American soldiers visited her in France near the end of
World War II and found her a delightful, frank, and forthright woman.
Knowing she appreciates frankness, write her a letter of frank com-
ment on her theories about parts of speech and punctuation.

2. "What does a comma do." Gertrude Stein does not answer that question directly but reveals her experiences with commas (she refused them
often). Reveal your experiences with commas or other marks of
punctuation. What do they do?

3. What values are there in learning what established (or even experimental) authors think about parts of speech and punctuation? Are
these matters settled without a doubt? Do grammar books give us rigid
rules for usage? What degree of flexibility is there? If you were addressing a class of would-be authors, what would you tell them about parts
of speech and punctuation?

4. Gertrude Stein is interesting to read aloud. Reflect on your experience
of reading her aloud and write a note to others about the relation between sound and sense.

5. The writing here looks easier to imitate than it is. It is rewarding,
however, to attempt imitation of Gertrude Stein. It helps you see her
purpose. It will also reveal the uses of punctuation and the effects of
an experimental style.

ALFRED HITCHCOCK

# Freshly Coined Language*

In time the script and the sets are finished, and we are ready
to start shooting. One great problem is to get the players to adapt
themselves to film technique. Many of them, of course, come from
the stage; they are not cinema-minded at all. So, quite naturally,
they like to play long scenes straight ahead. I am willing to work
with the long uninterrupted shot: you can't avoid it altogether,
and you can get some variety by having two cameras running, one
close up and one farther off, and cutting from one to the other
when the film is edited. But if I have to shoot a long scene continuously, I always feel I am losing grip on it, from a cinematic
point of view. The camera, I feel, is simply standing there, *hoping*

---

* From "Direction," by Alfred Hitchcock, in *Footnotes to the Film,* edited by
Charles Davy (London: Peter Davies, Ltd., 1939). Reprinted by permission of the
publishers.

to catch something with a visual point to it. What I like to do always is to photograph just the little bits of a scene that I really need for building up a visual sequence. I want to put my film together on the screen, not simply to photograph something that has been put together already in the form of a long piece of stage acting. This is what gives an effect of life to a picture: the feeling that when you see it on the screen you are watching something that has been conceived and brought to birth directly in visual terms. The screen ought to speak its own language, freshly coined, and it can't do that unless it treats an acted scene as a piece of raw material which must be broken up, taken to bits, before it can be woven into an expressive visual pattern.

You can see an example of what I mean in *Sabotage*. Just before Verloc is killed, there is a scene made up entirely of short pieces of film, separately photographed. This scene has to show how Verloc comes to be killed, how the thought of killing him arises in Sylvia Sidney's mind and connects itself with the carving knife she uses when they sit down to dinner. But the sympathy of the audience has to be kept with Sylvia Sidney; it must be clear that Verloc's death, finally, is an accident. So, as she serves at the table, you see her unconsciously serving vegetables with the carving knife, as though her hand were keeping hold of the knife of its own accord. The camera cuts from her hand to her eyes and back to her hand, then back to her eyes as she suddenly becomes aware of the knife making its error. Then to a normal shot, the man unconcernedly eating; then back to the hand holding the knife. In an old style of acting, Sylvia would have had to show the audience what was passing in her mind by exaggerated facial expression. But people today in real life often don't show their feelings in their faces; so the film treatment showed the audience her mind through her hand, through its unconscious grasp on the knife. Now the camera moves again to Verloc, back to the knife, back again to his face. You see him seeing the knife, realizing its implication. The tension between the two is built up with the knife as its focus.

Now when the camera has immersed the audience so closely in a scene such as this, it can't instantly become objective again. It must broaden the movement of the scene without loosening the tension. Verloc gets up and walks round the table, coming so close to the camera that you feel, if you are sitting in the audience, almost as though you must move back to make room for him. Then the camera moves to Sylvia Sidney again, then returns to the subject: the knife.

So you gradually build up the psychological situation, using the camera to emphasize first one detail, then another. The point is to draw the audience right inside the situation instead of leaving them to watch it from outside, from a distance. And you can do this only by breaking the action up into details and cutting from one to the other, so that each detail is forced in turn on the attention of the audience and reveals its psychological meaning. If you played the whole scene straight through and simply made a photographic record of it with the camera always in one position, you would lose your power over the audience. They would watch the scene without becoming really involved in it, and you would have no means of concentrating their attention on what the characters are feeling.

One way of using the camera to give emphasis is the reaction shot. By the reaction shot I mean any close-up which illustrates an event by showing instantly the reaction to it of a person or a group. The door opens for someone to come in, and before showing who it is, you cut to the expressions of the persons already in the room. Or, while one person is talking, you keep your camera on someone else who is listening. This over-running of one person's image with another person's voice is a method peculiar to the talkies; it is one of the devices which help the talkies to tell a story faster than a silent film could tell it and faster than it could be told on the stage.

Or you can use the camera to give emphasis whenever the attention of the audience has to be focused for a moment on a certain player. There is no need for him to raise his voice or move to the centre of the stage or do anything dramatic. A close-up will do it all for him, will give him, so to speak, the stage all to himself.

In recent years I have become more commercially minded, afraid that anything at all subtle may be missed. I have learnt from experience how easily small touches are overlooked. The other day a journalist came to interview me, and we spoke about film technique. "I always remember," he said, "a little bit in one of your silent films, *The Ring*. The young boxer comes home after winning his fight. He is flushed with success, wants to celebrate. He pours out champagne all round. Then he finds that his wife is out, and he

knows at once that she is out with another man. At this moment
the camera cuts to a glass of champagne; you see a fizz of bubbles
rise off it, and there it stands untasted, going flat. That one shot
gives you the whole feeling of the scene." Yes, I said, that sort of
imagery may be quite good; I don't despise it and still use it now
and then. But is it always noticed?

There was another bit in *The Ring,* which I believe hardly anyone noticed. The scene was outside a boxing booth at a fair, with
a barker talking to the crowd. Inside the booth a professional is
taking on all comers. He has always won in the first round. A man
comes running out of the booth and speaks to the barker: something unexpected has happened. Then a cut straight to the ringside: you see an old figure 1 being taken down and replaced by
a brand new figure 2. I meant this single detail to show that the
boxer now is up against someone he can't put out in the first round.
But it went by too quickly. Perhaps I might have shown the new
figure 2 being taken out of a paper wrapping; something else was
needed to make the audience see in a moment that the figure for
the second round had never been used before.

The film always has to deal in exaggerations. Its methods reflect
the simple contrasts of black and white photography. One advantage of color is that it would give you more intermediate shades.
I should never want to fill the screen with color: it ought to be
used economically, to put new words into the screen's visual language when there's a need for them. You could start a color film
with a board room scene: sombre paneling and furniture, the
directors all in dark clothes and white collars. Then the chairman's
wife comes in, wearing a red hat. She takes the attention of the
audience at once, just because of that one note of color. Or suppose
a gangster story: the leader of the gang is sitting in a café with a
man he suspects. He has told his gunman to watch the table. "If
I order a glass of port, bump him off. If I order green chartreuse,
let him go."

This journalist asked me also about distorted sound, a device I
tried in *Blackmail* when the word "knife" hammers on the consciousness of the girl at breakfast on the morning after the murder.
Again, I think this kind of effect may be justified. There have always been occasions when we have needed to show a phantasma-
goria of the mind in terms of visual imagery. So we may want to

show someone's mental state by letting him listen to some sound—
let us say church bells—and making them clang with distorted insistence in his head. But on the whole nowadays I try to tell a story
in the simplest possible way, so that I can feel sure it will hold the
attention of any audience and won't puzzle them.

### SUGGESTIONS FOR WRITING

1. Alfred Hitchcock (1899-    ), a noted film director, is famous for his carefully devised suspense stories and movie scripts. In this essay he indicates the relation between writing and seeing: "The screen ought to
   speak its own language, freshly coined. . . ." Show how a screen director must use the same rhetorical devices (unity, coherence, emphasis)
   as a writer.
2. Write a description of an incident familiar to you for a single movie
   scene. Indicate the position of the camera (relative distance from the
   subject, angle of view) for each shot. You will probably find that you
   need at least fifty different shots to convey even a simple message.
3. Write the dialogue for a movie scene. Indicate where the camera will
   be and what it will be filming as each line is spoken.
4. Write an essay on film punctuation. A fade-out is a period. A flash-
   back is a new chapter. Continue this analogy.
5. "The film always has to deal in exaggerations." Does it? Will the film
   ever develop a sophisticated audience if it continues to cater to com-
   mercialism?

THORSTEIN VEBLEN

## Language of the Leisure Class*

. . . lately, since college athletics have won their way into a recognized standing as an accredited field of scholarly accomplishment,
this latter branch of learning—if athletics may be freely classed as
learning—has become a rival of the classics for the primacy in
leisure-class education in American and English schools. Athletics
have an obvious advantage over the classics for the purpose of
leisure-class learning, since success as an athlete presumes, not only

---

* From *The Theory of the Leisure Class,* 1899. Viking Press. Reprinted by
permission of the publisher.

a waste of time, but also a waste of money, as well as the possession of certain highly unindustrial archaic traits of character and temperament. In the German universities the place of athletics and Greek-letter fraternities, as a leisure-class scholarly occupation, has in some measure been supplied by a skilled and graded inebriety and a perfunctory duelling.

The leisure class and its standards of virtue—archaism and waste—can scarcely have been concerned in the introduction of the classics into the scheme of the higher learning; but the tenacious retention of the classics by the higher schools, and the high degree of reputability which still attaches to them, are no doubt due to their conforming so closely to the requirements of archaism and waste.

"Classic" always carries this connotation of wasteful and archaic, whether it is used to denote the dead languages or the obsolete or obsolescent forms of thought and diction in the living language, or to denote other items of scholarly activity or apparatus to which it is applied with less aptness. So the archaic idiom of the English language is spoken of as "classic" English. Its use is imperative in all speaking and writing upon serious topics, and a facile use of it lends dignity to even the most commonplace and trivial string of talk. The newest form of English diction is of course never written; the sense of that leisure-class propriety which requires archaism in speech is present even in the most illiterate or sensational writers in sufficient force to prevent such a lapse. On the other hand, the highest and most conventionalised style of archaic diction is—quite characteristically—properly employed only in communications between an anthropomorphic divinity and his subjects. Midway between these extremes lies the everyday speech of leisure-class conversation and literature.

Elegant diction, whether in writing or speaking, is an effective means of reputability. It is of moment to know with some precision what is the degree of archaism conventionally required in speaking on any given topic. Usage differs appreciably from the pulpit to the market place; the latter, as might be expected, admits the use of relatively new and effective words and turns of expression, even by fastidious persons. A discriminate avoidance of neologisms is honorific, not only because it argues that time has been wasted in acquiring the obsolescent habit of speech, but also as showing that the speaker has from infancy habitually associated with persons who have been familiar with the obsolescent idiom. It thereby goes to show his leisure-class antecedents. Great purity of speech is presumptive evidence of several successive lives spent in other than vulgarly useful occupations; although its evidence is by no means entirely conclusive to this point.

As felicitous an instance of futile classicism as can well be found, outside of the Far East, is the conventional spelling of the English language. A breach of the proprieties in spelling is extremely annoying and will discredit any writer in the eyes of all persons who are possessed of a developed sense of the true and beautiful. English orthography satisfies all the requirements of the canons of reputability under the law of conspicuous waste. It is archaic, cumbrous, and ineffective; its acquisition consumes much time and effort; failure to acquire it is easy of detection. Therefore it is the first and readiest test of reputability in learning, and conformity to its ritual is indispensable to a blameless scholastic life.

On this head of purity of speech, as at other points where a conventional usage rests on the canons of archaism and waste, the spokesmen for the usage instinctively take an apologetic attitude. It is contended, in substance, that a punctilious use of ancient and accredited locutions will serve to convey thought more adequately and more precisely than would the straightforward use of the latest form of spoken English; whereas it is notorious that the ideas of today are effectively expressed in the slang of today. Classic speech has the honorific virtue of dignity; it commands attention and respect as being the accredited method of communication under the leisure-class scheme of life, because it carries a pointed suggestion of the industrial exemption of the speaker. The advantage of the accredited locutions lies in their reputability; they are reputable because they are cumbrous and out of date, and therefore argue waste of time and exemption from the use and the need of direct and forcible speech.

SUGGESTIONS FOR WRITING

1. Thorstein Veblen (1857-1929) was a social scientist at the University of Chicago when he wrote his famous *Theory of the Leisure Class* (1899). He ridicules the snobs' use of language, keeping a straight face

all the time. What does a "straight face" mean and how can it be illustrated here?

2. "The highest and most conventionalised style of archaic diction is quite characteristically properly employed in communications between an anthropomorphic divinity and his subjects." In what book may examples of such diction be found? List some quotes from this source to reveal Veblen's point.

3. Is Veblen also making fun of his own style of writing? Why does he write in the style of "the language of the leisure class"?

4. G H O T I spells fish: The GH as pronounced in *enough,* O as in *women,* and TI as in *nation.* Veblen says "English spelling is archaic, cumbrous, and ineffective," and the illustration makes his point. Write a carefully documented composition on the difficulties of English spelling. Consult the front pages of your dictionary for material on the history of English spelling.

5. Analyze Veblen's essay to discover what characteristics—in addition to conspicuous consumption and conspicuous waste—may truly be attributed to the leisure class. Make a list of such characteristics; think of another area (not athletics or language) where such characteristics apply; then, in an essay modeled on Veblen's, apply them.

ANATOL RAPOPORT

## The Gap Between Words and Experience*

A great advantage in making definitions by *exhibiting an example* is that one cannot define fictions that way. Just try to define Jabberwock or the First Cause by pointing to something and see how sticking to definition by exhibiting an example protects you from believing in ghosts. However, this advantage becomes a disadvantage when one wishes to define something which is not immediately at hand or something more abstract than objects to which one can point. Jonathan Swift made great fun of definition by example. He describes in his satire, *Gulliver's Travels,* how the

* From "What Do You Mean?" in *Science and the Goals of Man* by Anatol Rapoport (New York: Harper & Row, Publishers, 1950). Copyright 1950 by Harper & Brothers. Reprinted by permission of the publishers.

academicians of Lagado decided to do away with spoken language altogether, arguing that

> . . . since the words are only names for things, it would be convenient for all men to carry about them such things as were necessary to express the particular business they are to discourse on . . .

Accordingly, says Swift, the learned men of Lagado

> adhere to the new scheme of expressing themselves by things, which hath only this inconvenience attending it, that if a man's business be very great, and of various kinds, he must be obliged in proportion to carry a greater bundle of things upon his back, unless he can afford one or two strong servants to attend him.

The great value of making a definition by exhibiting an example is that it does bridge the gap between words and experience. This, in fact, is the only purpose of definition. Definition by synonym and definition by classification may indirectly bridge this gap if the words used in the definition are closer to experience than the words defined. But this is not necessarily so. In the case of definition by example it is *necessarily* so, because what you exhibit is *not* a word. Still a difficulty remains, quite aside from Swift's objections, to this kind of definition. Many words refer to real things, and these may not be at hand to point to, or one may not point to them at all. Here are a few examples:

| | |
|---|---|
| electric current | hydrogen |
| standard deviation | habeas corpus |
| the French language | mumps |
| acrophobia | sonata |
| chiaroscuro | taxes |

The *operational definition* succeeds most effectively in connecting such *abstract* words with experience.

In discussing operational definitions of abstract physical concepts, Philipp Frank says:

> These sentences [operational definitions] contain the abstract words of the physical principles like "current" . . . also the words of the everyday English language. Obviously, they contain words like "wire"

and other words which describe the apparatus by which the intensity of a current is actually measured.[1]

Note how the operational definition works. One cannot point to an ampere of electric current (the most one could point at would be the wire that carries it). But one does not dodge the issue by defining a word with other words without bothering to determine whether they are any closer to experience. One gives a set of *directions*, in words, to be sure, but words almost certainly closer to experience than the word defined (wire, magnet, etc.). If one follows these directions, one has the experience summarized by the words "one ampere of electric current."

Sometimes a definition that sounds like an Aristotelian one performs the job of an operational definition. If I say "Acrophobia is a mental disturbance characterized by a fear of high places" I seem to be making an Aristotelian definition. But it can easily be translated into an operational one: "Question a great many people on how they feel about high places, and you will find that a certain percentage of them will declare that they are 'afraid' of high places. Furthermore, if such a person happens to be on a roof or a mountaintop, he usually exhibits a quickening of heart beat and expresses a desire to get down. Such people are said to suffer from acrophobia."

Let us see what happens when we apply an operational definition to a fiction. A vampire, for example, can be defined by a good Aristotelian definition: "A vampire is a person who habitually sucks other people's blood." If we attempted to translate this definition into an operational one, we would have to say something like this: "Have a great many persons watched at night, and you will find that some go abroad and suck blood out of sleeping people, usually from a small lesion in the neck. Such people are called vampires." This operational definition is formally as good as the one of acrophobia except for one thing: you will probably not find any people with bloodsucking habits.

So it appears from the operations prescribed by the operational definition that if any "meaning" is to be attached to the word "vampire," it cannot refer to a person (since no such persons are observed). The operations have revealed that the Aristotelian defi-

---

[1] Philipp Frank, "Science Teaching and the Humanities."

nition of a "vampire," although formally flawless, is meaningless.

Practically all operational definitions say in fact "Do so-and-so, and you will find . . ." They *predict* an experience. They may also be called definitions by prediction.

In modern semantic literature, definitions by synonym and by classification are often called "intensional definitions," while those by enumeration, example, and operation are called "extensional definitions." From the standpoint of bridging the gap between words and experiences, extensional definitions are to be preferred. As a matter of fact, if that gap is bridged at all, somewhere a definition by example or an operational definition is involved.

The definition by example need not involve language at all. The syntactic structure of an operational definition involves an imperative form of a verb (do so-and-so) and a predictive assertion (you will find . . .). This structure is sometimes clumsy and may be discarded for the elegant structure of the Aristotelian definition (a so-and-so is a such-and-such which is characterized by a this-and-that); but if a definition is to serve its purpose (sharing experience), an indication of experience must be involved.

"The stockyards are an area where animals are processed into meat" is a short, elegant definition of the stockyards. But the *reality* of the stockyards is implied in another, clumsier definition, which I would give to a visitor in Chicago if I wanted to bring the stockyards within the range of his experience.

"Take the Halsted Street car to 39th St., etc. . . ."

"Hell is the place where the wicked go when they die" also looks like a definition. But when you try to translate it into operational terms you will immediately get into difficulties. You will be at a loss to indicate a proper procedure in order to experience hell.

Just as assertions about things must be traced to the experiences that gave rise to them, the meanings of words must also be traced in this way.

Words which fail to show an ancestry of experience may nevertheless be well "defined" by intensional definitions, that is, by other words. But they usually cannot be defined by extensional definitions, especially by exhibiting an example and by the operational definition, because these, by their very nature, imply connection with experience.

Extensional definitions, therefore, especially the operational ones, are more generally valuable for the purpose for which definitions are intended—to bridge the gap between words and experience. An operational definition can do everything all the others can do and often more. In some cases only an operational definition can bridge the gap between words and experience. Its drawback is that grammatically it is not very elegant. Therefore, if one is concerned with literary style, one might avoid the operational definition; but if one is concerned with communicating meaning, one should use it at the slightest indication that the meaning is otherwise not clear.

Granted that a way can be found to map experience on language, how can the infinite variety of experience to which we are subject be mapped on a language of only a few thousand words, to which the vocabulary of most people is limited?

### SUGGESTIONS FOR WRITING

1. Anatol Rapoport (1911-    ) is a scientist who is seriously concerned with the function of a special set of scientific instruments: words. He says: "From the standpoint of bridging the gap between words and experiences, extensional definitions are to be preferred." Define, *a la* Rapoport, *extensional definitions* and then conceive of circumstances in which it would not be best to "bridge the gap between words and experiences."

2. Rapoport reveals the syntactic structure of Aristotelian and operational definitions. In so doing he emphasizes a point made throughout this book—the effectiveness of models as a means of conveying thoughts. He finds that two models will adequately convey the two chief methods of defining. "A so-and-so is a such-and-such which is characterized by a this-and-that." Aristotelian. "Do so-and-so and you will find . . ." Operational. Prepare a list of various models which could be substituted for Rapoport's model of an operational definition.

3. Intensional definitions are definitions by (1) synonym or (2) classification. Extensional definitions are definitions by (3) enumeration, (4) example, (5) operation (or prediction). Which of the above five would be most acceptable for defining each of the following: black, vampire, the Black Sea, hate, Uncle Sam, my uncle Sam, stock exchange, stork, the Iron Curtain, tyranny, the Ten Commandments, man, general semantics, symbol.

4. Write a composition in which you provide an operational definition of a concept you have felt most keenly in the past few months.

BERNARD DEVOTO

# The World's Most Intricate Skill *

Skill develops from controlled, corrected repetitions of an act for which one has some knack. Skill is a product of experience and criticism and intelligence. Analysis cannot much transcend those truisms. Between the amateur and the professional, between the duffer and the expert, between the novice and the veteran there is a difference not only in degree but in kind. The skillful man is, within the function of his skill, a different integration, a different nervous and muscular and psychological organization. He has specialized responses of great intricacy. His associative faculties have patterns of screening, acceptance and rejection, analysis and sifting, evaluation and selective adjustment much too complex for conscious direction. Yet as the patterns of appraisal and adjustment exert their automatic and perhaps metabolic energy, they are accompanied by a conscious process fully as complex. A tennis player or a watchmaker or an airplane pilot is an automatism but he is also criticism and wisdom.

It is hardly too much to say that a mountain man's life was skill. He not only worked in the wilderness, he also lived there and he did so from sun to sun by the exercise of total skill. It was probably as intricate a skill as any ever developed by any way of working or living anywhere. Certainly it was the most complex of the wilderness crafts practiced on this continent. The mountains, the aridity, the distances, and the climates imposed severities far greater than those laid on forest-runners, rivermen, or any other of our symbolic pioneers. Mountain craft developed out of the crafts which earlier pioneers had acquired, and like its predecessors, incorporated Indian crafts, but it had a unique integration of its own. It had specific crafts, technologies, theorems and rationales and rules of thumb, codes of operating procedure—but it was a pattern of total behavior.

---

* From *Across the Wide Missouri* by Bernard DeVoto (Boston: Houghton Mifflin Company, 1947). Copyright 1947 by Houghton Mifflin Company. Reprinted by permission of the publishers.

Treatises could be written on the specific details; we lack space even for generalizations. Why do you follow the ridges into or out of unfamiliar country? What do you do for a companion who has collapsed from want of water while crossing a desert? How do you get meat when you find yourself without gunpowder in a country barren of game? What tribe of Indians made this trail, how many were in the band, what errand were they on, were they going to or coming back from it, how far from home were they, were their horses laden, how many horses did they have and why, how many squaws accompanied them, what mood were they in? Also, how old is the trail, where are those Indians now, and what does the product of these answers require of you? Prodigies of such sign reading are recorded by impressed greenhorns, travelers, and army men, and the exercise of critical reference and deduction which they exhibit would seem prodigious if it were not routine. But reading formal sign, however impressive to Doctor Watson or Captain Frémont, is less impressive than the interpretation of observed circumstances too minute to be called sign. A branch floats down a stream—is this natural, or the work of animals, or of Indians or trappers? Another branch or a bush or even a pebble is out of place—why? On the limits of the plain, blurred by heat mirage, or against the gloom of distant cottonwoods, or across an angle of sky between branches or where hill and mountain meet, there is a tenth of a second of what may have been movement—did men or animals make it, and, if animals, why? Buffalo are moving downwind, an elk is in an unlikely place or posture, too many magpies are hollering, a wolf's howl is off key—what does it mean?

Such minutiae could be extended indefinitely. As the trapper's mind is dealing with them, it is simultaneously performing a still more complex judgement on the countryside, the route across it, and the weather. It is recording the immediate details in relation to the remembered and the forecast. A ten mile traverse is in relation to a goal a hundred miles, or five hundred miles away: there are economies of time, effort, comfort, and horseflesh on any of which success or even survival may depend. Modify the reading further, in relation to season, to Indians, to what has happened. Modify it again in relation to stream flow, storms past, storms indicated. Again in relation to the meat supply. To the state of the grass. To the equipment on hand. . . . You are two thousand miles from depots of supply and from help in time of trouble.

All this (with much more) is a continuous reference and checking along the margin or in the background of the trapper's consciousness while he practices his crafts as hunter, wrangler, furrier, freighter, tanner, cordwainer, smith, gunmaker, dowser, merchant. The result is a high-level integration of faculties. The mountain man had mastered his conditions—how well is apparent as soon as soldiers, goldseekers, or emigrants come into his country and suffer where he has lived comfortably and die where he has been in no danger. He had no faculties or intelligence that the soldier or the goldseeker lacked; he had none that you and I lack. He had only skill. A skill so effective that, living in an Indian country, he made a more successful adaptation to it than the Indian—and this without reference to his superior material equipment. There was no craft and no skill at which the mountain man did not come to excel the Indian. He saw, smelled, and heard just as far and no farther. But there is something after all in the laborious accretion that convolutes the forebrain and increases the cultural heritage, for he made more of it.

SUGGESTIONS FOR WRITING

1. Bernard De Voto (1897-1956), born in Utah, spent most of his life in New York and Massachusetts. He was editor of the *Saturday Review* and conducted the monthly "Easy Chair" column of *Harper's*. His passions were literature, social justice, and conservation of natural resources. He spent a good deal of time in the mountains and forests of our national parks. He also devoted himself to the history of the opening of our western frontiers (*Across the Wide Missouri*—from which this excerpt is taken; *1846, Year of Decision*). Thus he is well qualified to discuss the intricate skill of the mountain man. But he would be the first to admit that the matter of intricate skill is also germane to the writer. He would not have had to change a word in the first two paragraphs if the key word in the first sentence of the third paragraph had been "writer" instead of "mountain man." As a matter of fact, let the key word be "writer" and, changing as few words as possible, continue the rest of the essay. What you write is likely to be humorous, but don't let that deter you.
2. A good deal of a writer's success depends upon his skill as an observer. Reread some of the things a mountain man had to observe skillfully

(check especially paragraph four) and indicate what a writer would see
that a mountain man would miss—and vice versa.

3. The value of observation is as important to writers as any other skill
   they possess. Guy de Maupassant, in his preface to *Pierre et Jean* (1887),
   tells us that Flaubert once said to him: "When you pass . . . before
   a grocer seated at his door, before a janitor who smokes his pipe, before
   a stand of coaches, show me this grocer and this janitor, their pose, their
   whole physical appearance, including also—indicated by the ingenuity
   of the picture—their whole moral nature, in such fashion that I cannot
   confuse them with any other grocer, or any other janitor; and make me
   see, by a single word, in what respect one coach horse differs in appearance from fifty others that follow him or precede him." Describe a short
   scene in such detail that even Flaubert would have been satisfied with it.


MAX   BEERBOHM

# How Shall I Word It? *

It would seem that I am one of those travellers for whom the
railway bookstall does not cater. Whenever I start on a journey, I
find that my choice lies between well-printed books which I have no
wish to read, and well-written books which I could not read without permanent injury to my eyesight. The keeper of the bookstall,
seeing me gaze vaguely along his shelves, suggests that I should
take "Fen Country Fanny" or else "The Track of Blood" and have
done with it. Not wishing to hurt his feelings, I refuse these works
on the plea that I have read them. Whereon he, divining despite
me that I am a superior person, says "Here is a nice little handy
edition of More's 'Utopia' " or "Carlyle's 'French Revolution' " and
again I make some excuse. What pleasure could I get from trying
to cope with a masterpiece printed in diminutive greyish type on a
semitransparent little greyish page? I relieve the bookstall of nothing but a newspaper or two.

The other day, however, my eye and fancy were caught by a
book entitled "How Shall I Word It?" and sub-entitled "A Complete Letter Writer for Men and Women." I had never read one

---

* From *And Even Now* by Max Beerbohm (New York: E. P. Dutton & Co.,
Inc., 1921). Copyright 1921 by E. P. Dutton & Co., Inc. Reprinted by permission
of the publishers.

of these manuals, but had often heard that there was a great and constant "demand" for them. So I demanded this one. It is no great fun in itself. The writer is no fool. He has evidently a natural talent for writing letters. His style is, for the most part, discreet and easy. If you were a young man writing "to Father of Girl he wishes to Marry" or "thanking Fiancée for Present" or "reproaching Fiancée for being a Flirt," or if you were a mother "asking Governess her Qualifications" or "replying to Undesirable Invitation for her Child," or indeed if you were in any other one of the crises which this book is designed to alleviate, you might copy out and post the specially provided letter without making yourself ridiculous in the eyes of its receiver—unless, of course, he or she also possessed a copy of the book. But—well, can you conceive any one copying out and posting one of these letters, or even taking it as the basis for composition? You cannot. That shows how little you know of your fellow creatures. Not you nor I can plumb the abyss at the bottom of which such humility is possible. Nevertheless, as we know by that great and constant "demand," there the abyss is, and there multi-tudes are at the bottom of it. Let's peer down . . . No, all is dark-ness. But faintly, if we listen hard, is borne up to us a sound of the scratching of innumerable pens—pens whose wielders are all trying, as the author of this handbook urges them, to "be original, fresh, and interesting" by dint of more or less strict adherence to sample.

Giddily you draw back from the edge of the abyss. Come!—here is a thought to steady you. The mysterious great masses of helpless folk for whom "How Shall I Word It?" is written are sound at heart, delicate in feeling, anxious to please, most loth to wound. For it must be presumed that the author's style of letter writing is informed as much by a desire to give his public what it needs, and will pay for, as by his own beautiful nature; and in the course of all the letters that he dictates you will find not one harsh word, not one ignoble thought or unkind insinuation. In all of them, though so many are for the use of persons placed in the most trying circum-stances, and some of them are for persons writhing under a sense of intolerable injury, sweetness and light do ever reign. Even "yours truly, Jacob Langton," in his "letter to his Daughter's Mercenary Fiancé," mitigates the sternness of his tone by the remark that his "task is inexpressibly painful." And he, Mr. Langton, is the one writer who lets the post go out on his wrath. When Horace Masterton, of Thorpe Road, Putney, receives from Miss Jessica Weir, of Fir Villa, Blackheath, a letter "declaring her Change of Feelings," does he upbraid her? No; "it was honest and brave of you to write to me so straightforwardly and at the back of my mind I know you have done what is best. . . . I give you back your freedom only at your desire. God bless you, dear." Not less admirable is the behaviour, in similar case, of Cecil Grant (14, Glover Street, Streatham). Suddenly, as a bolt from the blue, comes a letter from Miss Louie Hawke (Elm View, Deerhurst), breaking off her betrothal to him. Haggard, he sits down to his desk; his pen traverses the notepaper—calling down curses on Louie and on all her sex? No; "one cannot say good-bye for ever without deep regret to days that have been so full of happiness. I must thank you sincerely for all your great kindness to me. . . . With every sincere wish for your future happiness," he bestows complete freedom on Miss Hawke. And do not imagine that in the matter of self-control and sympathy, of power to understand all and pardon all, the men are lagged behind by the women. Miss Leila Johnson (The Manse, Carlyle) has observed in Leonard Wace (Dover Street, Saltburn) a certain coldness of demeanour; yet "I do not blame you; it is probably your nature"; and Leila in her sweet forbearance is typical of all the other pained women in these pages: she is but one of a crowd of heroines.

Face to face with all this perfection, the not perfect reader begins to crave some little outburst of wrath, of hatred or malice, from one of these imaginary ladies and gentlemen. He longs for—how shall he word it?—a glimpse of some bad motive, of some little lapse from dignity. Often, passing by a pillar box, I have wished I could unlock it and carry away its contents, to be studied at my leisure. I have always thought such a haul would abound in things fascinating to a student of human nature. One night, not long ago, I took a waxen impression of the lock of the pillar box nearest to my house, and had a key made. This implement I have as yet lacked either the courage or the opportunity to use. And now I think I shall throw it away . . . No, I shan't. I refuse, after all, to draw my inference that the bulk of the British public writes always in the manner of this handbook. Even if they all have beautiful natures they must sometimes be sent slightly astray by inferior impulses, just as are you and I.

And, if err they must, surely it were well they should know how to do it correctly and forcibly. I suggest to our author that he should sprinkle his next edition with a few less righteous examples, thereby both purging his book of its monotony and somewhat justifying its subtitle. Like most people who are in the habit of writing things to be printed, I have not the knack of writing really good letters. But let me crudely indicate the sort of thing that our manual needs. . . .

*Letter from Poor Man to Obtain Money from Rich One*

(The English law is particularly hard on what is called blackmail. It is therefore essential that the applicant should write nothing that might afterwards be twisted to incriminate him.—Ed.)

Dear Sir,

Today, as I was turning out a drawer in my attic, I came across a letter which by a curious chance fell into my hands some years ago, and which, in the stress of grave pecuniary embarrassment, had escaped my memory. It is a letter written by yourself to a lady, and the date shows it to have been written shortly after your marriage. It is of a confidential nature, and might, I fear, if it fell into the wrong hands, be cruelly misconstrued. I would wish you to have the satisfaction of destroying it in person. At first I thought of sending it on to you by post. But I know how happy you are in your domestic life; and probably your wife and you, in your perfect mutual trust, are in the habit of opening each other's letters. Therefore, to avoid risk, I would prefer to hand the document to you personally. I will not ask you to come to my attic, where I could not offer you such hospitality as is due to a man of your wealth and position. You will be so good as to meet me at 3.00 A.M. (sharp) tomorrow (Thursday) beside the tenth lamp post to the left on the Surrey side of Waterloo Bridge; at which hour and place we shall not be disturbed.

I am, dear Sir,
Yours respectfully
*James Gridge.*

*Letter from Young Man Refusing to Pay His Tailor's Bill*

Mr. Eustace Davenant has received the half-servile, half-insolent screed which Mr. Yardley has addressed to him. Let Mr. Yardley cease from crawling on his knees and shaking his fist. Neither this posture nor this gesture can wring one bent farthing from the pockets of Mr. Davenant, who was a minor at the time when that series of ill made suits was supplied to him and will hereafter, as in the past, shout (without prejudice) from the housetops that of all the tailors in London Mr. Yardley is at once the most grasping and the least competent.

*Letter to Thank Author for Inscribed Copy of Book*

Dear Mr. Emanuel Flower,

It was kind of you to think of sending me a copy of your new book. It would have been kinder still to think again and abandon that project. I am a man of gentle instincts, and do not like to tell you that "A Flight into Arcady" (of which I have skimmed a few pages, thus wasting two or three mintes of my not altogether worthless time) is trash. On the other hand, I am determined that you shall not be able to go around boasting to your friends, if you have any, that this work was not condemned, derided, and dismissed by your sincere well-wisher, *Wrexford Cripps.*

*Letter to Member of Parliament Unseated at General Election*

Dear Mr. Pobsby-Burford,

Though I am myself an ardent Tory, I cannot but rejoice in the crushing defeat you have just suffered in West Odgetown. There are moments when political conviction is overborne by personal sentiment; and this is one of them. Your loss of the seat that you held is the more striking by reason of the splendid manner in which the northern and eastern divisions of Odgetown have been wrested from the Liberal Party. The great bulk of the newspaper-reading public will be puzzled by your extinction in the midst of our party's triumph. But then, the great mass of the newspaper-reading public has not met you. I have. You will probably not remember me. You are the sort of man who would not remember anybody who might not be of some definite use to him. Such, at least, was one of the impressions you made on me when I met you last summer at a dinner given by our friends the Pelhams. Among the other things in you that struck me were the blatant pomposity of your manner, your appalling flow of cheap platitudes, and your hoggish lack of ideas. It is such men as you that lower the tone of public life. And I am sure that in writing to you thus I am but expressing what is felt, without distinction of party, by all who sat with you in the late Parliament.

The one person in whose behalf I regret your withdrawal into private life is your wife, whom I had the pleasure of taking in to the aforesaid dinner. It was evident to me that she was a woman whose spirit was well-nigh broken by her conjunction with you. Such remnants of cheerfulness as were in her I attributed to the Parliamentary duties which kept you out of her sight for so very many hours daily. I do not like to think of the fate to which the free and independent electors of West Odgetown have just condemned her. Only, remember this: chattel of yours though she is, and timid and humble, she despises you in her heart.

I am, dear Mr. Pobsby-Burford,

Yours very truly,

*Harold Thistlake.*

*Letter from Young Lady in Answer to Invitation from
old Schoolmistress*

My dear Miss Price,

How awfully sweet of you to ask me to stay with you for a few days but how *can* you think I may have forgotten you for of course I think of you so very often and of the three years I spent at your school because it is such a joy not to be there any longer and if one is at all down it bucks one up directly to remember that *thats* all over atanyrate and that one has enough food to nurrish one and not that awful monottany of life and not the petty fogging daily tirrany you went in for and I can imagin no greater thrill and luxury in a way than to come and see the whole dismal grind still going on but without me being in it but this would be rather beastly of me wouldn't it so please dear Miss Price dont expect me and do excuse mistakes of English Composition and Spelling and etcetra in your affectionate old pupil,

*Emily Therese Lynn-Royston.*

ps, I often rite to people telling them where I was edducated and highly reckomending you.

*Letter in Acknowledgment of Wedding Present*

Dear Lady Amblesham,

Who gives quickly, says the old proverb, gives twice. For this reason I have purposely delayed writing to you, lest I should appear to thank you more than once for the small, cheap, hideous present you sent me on the occasion of my recent wedding. Were you a poor woman, that little bowl of ill-imitated Dresden china would convict you of tastelessness merely; were you a blind woman, of nothing but an odious parsimony. As you have normal eyesight and more than normal wealth, your gift to me proclaims you at once a Philistine and a miser (or rather did so proclaim you until, less than ten seconds after I had unpacked it from its wrappings of tissue paper, I took it to the open window and had the satisfaction of seeing it shattered to atoms on the pavement). But stay! I perceive a possible flaw in my argument. Perhaps you were guided in your choice by a definite wish to insult me. I am sure, on reflection, that this was so. I *shall not forget.*

Yours, etc.,

*Cynthia Beaumarsh.*

P.S. My husband asked me to tell you to warn Lord Amblesham to keep out of his way or to assume some disguise so complete that he will not be recognized by him and horsewhipped.

PPS. I am sending copies of this letter to the principal London and provincial newspapers.

*Letter from . . .*

But enough! I never thought I should be so strong in this line. I had not forseen such copiousness and fatal fluency. Never again will I tap these deep dark reservoirs in a character that had always seemed to me, on the whole, so amiable.

SUGGESTIONS FOR WRITING

1. Max Beerbohm (1872-1961) is an English caricaturist, essayist, novelist, and parodist. His *Zuleika Dobson* (1911) is a classic of deft irony. Here he pretends to make fun of a letter writing manual, but he is really satirizing "genteel" manners, which foster pretense and hypocrisy instead of genuine expression of feeling. Of the six letters, which seems to you to reveal the harshest criticism?

2. Beerbohm obviously enjoys himself in this piece. He gives one a feeling that he is on an outing and full of glee. Analyze his style to reveal why.

3. Write a letter (after one of Beerbohm's models) to an acquaintance who has just done one of the following: stolen something from you, defeated you in a contest, insulted you in public. The object is to reveal your great injury but also to display the sense of glee with which you write.

# Learning to Write

Elliott Nugent would say, "Well, Thurber, we've got our problem, we've got all these people in the living room. Now what are we going to do with them?" I'd say that I didn't know and couldn't tell him until I'd sat down at the typewriter and found out.*

—Interview with James Thurber, *The Paris Review*

Let the writer take up surgery or bricklaying if he is interested in technique. There is no mechanical way to get the writing done, no short cut.*

—Interview with William Faulkner, *The Paris Review*

Writing is considered a profession, and I don't think it is a profession. I think that everyone who does not *need* to be a writer, who thinks he can do something else, ought to do something else. Writing is not a profession but a vocation of unhappiness. I don't think an artist can ever be happy.*

—Interview with Georges Simenon (author of 400 novels)

No man but a blockhead ever wrote except for money.

—Samuel Johnson, in Boswell's *Life of Johnson,* 1791

How can a man sit down to write until he has stood up to live?

—Thoreau, *Walden,* 1854

I never knew what I thought about anything until I had written about it. To write an essay was to find out what I thought; for I did not know at the beginning how or where it would end.

—Allen Tate, *The Man of Letters in the Modern World,* 1955

The one great rule of composition—and if I were a professor of rhetoric I should insist on this—is to *speak the truth*. This first, this second, this third. This demands earnestness and manhood chiefly.

—Thoreau, *Journal,* 6 December, 1859

---

* From *Writers at Work:* The Paris Review Interviews, Malcolm Cowley, ed. © 1957 by The Paris Review, Inc. Reprinted by permission of the Viking Press, Inc.

MARK TWAIN

# Training and Experience in Writing*

From old experience I know that amateur productions, offered
ostensibly for one's honest cold judgment, to be followed by an
uncompromisingly sincere verdict, are not really offered in that
spirit at all. The thing really wanted and expected is compliment
and encouragement. Also, my experience has taught me that in almost all amateur cases compliment and encouragement are impossible—if they are to be backed by sincerity.

I have this moment finished reading this morning's pair of offerings and am a little troubled. If they had come from strangers I
should not have given myself the pain of reading them, but should
have returned them unread, according to my custom, upon the plea
that I lack an editor's training and therefore am not qualified to
sit in judgment upon any one's literature but my own. But this
morning's harvest came from friends and that alters the case. I have
read them and the result is as usual: they are not literature. They
do contain meat but the meat is only half cooked. The meat is certainly there and if it could pass through the hands of an expert
cook the result would be a very satisfactory dish indeed. One of
this morning's samples does really come near to being literature,
but the amateur hand is exposed with a fatal frequency and the exposure spoils it. The author's idea is, in case I shall render a favorable verdict, to offer the manuscript to a magazine.

There is something about this naive intrepidity that compels admiration. It is a lofty and reckless daring which I suppose is ex-

* From *The Autobiography of Mark Twain* edited by Charles Nieder (New
York: Harper & Row, Publishers, 1958). © 1958 by The Mark Twain Company.
Reprinted by permission of the publishers.

hibited in no field but one—the field of literature. We see something approaching it in war, but approaching it only distantly. The untrained common soldier has often offered himself as one of a forlorn hope and stood cheerfully ready to encounter all its perils —but we draw the line there. Not even the most confident untrained soldier offers himself as a candidate for a brigadier-generalship, yet this is what the amateur author does. With his untrained pen he puts together his crudities and offers them to all the magazines, one after the other—that is to say, he proposes them for posts restricted to literary generals who have earned their rank and place by years and even decades of hard and honest training in the lower grades of the service.

I am sure that this affront is offered to no trade but ours. A person untrained to shoemaking does not offer his services as a shoemaker to the foreman of a shop—not even the crudest literary aspirant would be so unintelligent as to do that. He would see the humor of it; he would see the impertinence of it; he would recognize as the most commonplace of facts that an apprenticeship is necessary in order to qualify a person to be tinner, bricklayer, stonemason, printer, horse doctor, butcher, brakeman, car conductor, midwife—and any and every other occupation whereby a human being acquires bread and fame. But when it comes to doing literature, his wisdoms vanish all of a sudden and he thinks he finds himself now in the presence of a profession which requires no apprenticeship, no experience, no training—nothing whatever but conscious talent and a lion's courage.

We do not realize how strange and curious a thing this is until we look around for an object lesson whereby to realize it to us. We must imagine a kindred case—the aspirant to operatic distinction and cash, for instance. The aspirant applies to the management for a billet as second tenor. The management accepts him, arranges the terms and puts him on the payroll. Understand, this is an imaginary case; I am not pretending that it has happened. Let us proceed.

After the first act the manager calls the second tenor to account and wants to know. He says:

"Have you ever studied music?"

"A little—yes, by myself, at odd times, for amusement."

"You have never gone into regular and laborious training, then, for the opera, under the masters of the art?"

"No."

"Then what made you think you could do second tenor in Lohengrin?"

"I thought I could. I wanted to try. I seemed to have a voice."

"Yes, you have a voice, and with five years of diligent training under competent masters you could be successful, perhaps, but I assure you you are not ready for second tenor yet. You have a voice; you have presence; you have a noble and childlike confidence; you have a courage that is stupendous and even superhuman. These are all essentials and they are in your favor but there are other essentials in this great trade which you still lack. If you can't afford the time and labor necessary to acquire them leave opera alone and try something which does not require training and experience. Go away now and try for a job in surgery."

## SUGGESTIONS FOR WRITING

1. Mark Twain, about whom comment is made on p. 148, was a man of vigorous opinions. He was and remains a figure of enduring popularity in American letters. Although his steamboat days provided him with the experiences which enriched his books, it is as a man of letters that he was best known in his lifetime. Consequently many people wrote to him asking for advice, as the second paragraph of the above piece indicates. As he says, he usually returns "offerings" unread, pleading that he lacks an editor's training. But he is still begging the question. For if, as Mencken insists, writing cannot be taught, how is an editor to do what a teacher cannot?

Paul Reynolds, whose book *The Writer and His Markets* (1959) offers sound advice on what to do with a piece of writing after it is written, confesses that not much can be done before that. "Our heritage of the written word," Reynolds says, "is more than two thousand years old. Yet no effective technique has been developed to teach writing."

Gorham Munson, whose *Writer's Workshop Companion*, 1951, is also useful to a beginning writer, offers sound advice which, if it had been taken by Mark Twain's acquaintance, would have saved Twain the trouble of writing the essay. Munson says, "Don't query. Write the piece. Write it for readers. Even if it doesn't place in the end, you still have gained something: practice. You are a more experienced craftsman than if you had queried, been turned down, and not written the proposed piece."

The above paragraphs notwithstanding, suppose you found yourself on a convenient deserted island—deserted except for your favorite author or one of the country's most influential publishers—what would you want to ask (to learn, to understand) about writing?

2. In opera, as Mark Twain points out, one can get many years of competent training before performing in public. Strangely enough, the same opportunity is not generally available for the would-be writer. Colleges and universities offer courses in writing, but even the most aspiring student could take only a few courses in four years of undergraduate work. Most graduate programs have nothing to do with writing and make the assumption that training in the history and bibliography of literature—or even the analysis of literature—will help a person in writing. Finally, even those few graduate programs in writing (where a publishable novel is acceptable for a dissertation) do not provide full-time "training in writing." Write an outline of a curriculum which provides full-time training in writing. You have four years, 120 credits, good teachers; what courses should be taught?

3. Most successful authors have not credited college courses for their success. If college is not the answer, what is? Suggest a plan for learning how to become a successful author.


E.  B.  WHITE

## Too Busy to Write? *

A course in ghostwriting opens this month at American University, Washington, D. C., and youngsters whose dream is to put words in somebody else's mouth may further their ambition by enrolling. Theirs is a queer dream, but these are queer times. Some university was bound, sooner or later, to make an honest woman out of a ghostwriter, and it's probably no worse than spring football, at that. Dr. Walter P. Bowman, who will teach the course at American, points out that ghostwriters are indispensable today—"indispensable artisans," he calls them. If the course is to face up to realities, Dr. Bowman presumably will not make the mistake of preparing his lectures himself but will locate a behind-the-scenes man on the faculty to get up his stuff for him. The students, for their part, will not waste their own valuable time studying for their

* From *The Second Tree from the Corner* by E. B. White (New York: Harper & Row, Publishers, 1954). Copyright 1952 by E. B. White. Originally appeared in *The New Yorker*. Reprinted by permission of Harper & Row, Publishers.

exams but will get some bright freshman to come up with the answers. We've been wondering what sort of final examination would be suitable for a course in ghostwriting. Cyrano de Bergerac, an early ghost, is probably the model to go by. If we were running the shop, we'd require every student, as a condition for passing the course, to compose a ballade while fighting a duel.

"Most of the great speeches we hear," said Dr. Bowman, "are written in whole or in part by someone backstage. It is time we recognized the fact." Well, everyone recognizes the fact that public men receive help in writing speeches, but whether the speeches are "great" is something else again. Roosevelt was a great man and an accomplished actor, but his speeches rarely seemed great to us; they seemed exactly what they were—smooth, carefully contrived, and bravely spoken, right up to the studied reference to God in the final sentence. Because of the nature of radio and television, virtually all public utterances nowadays are prefabricated, and while this tends to raise the general level of expression and gets rid of windbags, it also diminishes the chance of greatness. Great speeches are as much a part of a man as his eyeballs or his intestines. If Lincoln had had help on his Gettsyburg speech, the thing would almost certainly have started "Eighty-seven years ago . . ."—showing that the ghost was right on the job.

We did a couple of short hitches, years ago, in the ghost world. A fellow who was trying to interest a syndicate in buying a column patterned after O. O. McIntyre turned the job of writing the sample column over to us. He said he was too busy to do it himself. (Imagine being too busy to imitate O. O. McIntyre!) We had plenty of leisure, and we wrote the column, and the other fellow signed it. We felt ghostly but not unhappy, and in no time at all the syndicate itself became too busy to write checks, and the enterprise blew up, as it well deserved to do. Another time, working for an adman who had motor accounts, we were told that the president of one of the motorcar companies was too busy to write a Christmas piece for the house organ, so we wrote it and he signed it. Here, too, nature took its course. The innocent forgery, so out of keeping with the spirit of Bethlehem, was presumably discovered by the American public— which is extremely sensitive to such things—and people stopped buying that make of car, and it is now out of existence, as it deserves to be, despite our effort to save it with a poem containing the lines:

Together we sally at top of the morn,
With frost on the fender and toots on the horn.

American University, if it is bent on adding ghost training to its curriculum, may soon have to decide how far into the shadowy jungles to proceed. An advertisement appeared in the Washington *Post* recently, reading as follows:

Too Busy To Paint? Call On The Ghost Artists. We Paint It— You Sign It. Why Not Give An Exhibition?

It turned out that the man behind this enterprise was Hugh Troy, veteran of many a satirical mission. But let no one be fooled. Mr. Troy's jokes go to the heart of the matter; the sober carry on in earnest what he indicates in fun. Essentially, the thing we find discouraging about the ghost world is not its areas of candid dishonesty but that the whole place smells of the American cult of busyness. Too busy to write. Lincoln probably had as much on his mind as the president of the motorcar company, but when an occasion arose, he got out a pencil and went to work alone. His technique is as good today, despite electronics, as it was then. Few men, however, have that kind of nerve today, or that kind of loneliness. They're all too busy taking their ghost to lunch and filling him in.

SUGGESTIONS FOR WRITING

1. E. B. White, about whom comment is made on p. 194, admits in this essay that he once was a ghostwriter. He still works with the staff of *The New Yorker* producing the "Talk of the Town" column, which some think is the most sophisticated writing in America. What do you think about ghostwriting? Was E. B. White too harsh on it, or not harsh enough?
2. There is something more to the matter than being too busy to write. What about ability? Lincoln was not too busy to write, but he also had the ability. If a man cannot write well should he be forced to compose his own speeches? What is the solution?
3. If your college offered a course in ghostwriting, would you enroll? What would you expect to learn in such a course?
4. It is not ghostwriting that E. B. White finds discouraging, but the cult of busyness. Analyze this "cult." Why does it exist? Is it a product of the times or a problem of human nature? Will an increase of leisure

time for both labor and business in the years ahead make a change in this cult?

5. Too busy to write? What do you really mean when you tell someone you are too busy to write? Your analysis of this question may lead you to discourse on a theory of inspiration—"I can't write unless I am inspired." Make an honest evaluation of this theory. Finally, let your analysis lead you to the question of motivation (note the quotation by Samuel Johnson at the beginning of this section).

GEORGE ORWELL

# Why I Write*

Putting aside the need to earn a living, I think there are four great motives for writing, at any rate for writing prose. They exist in different degrees in every writer, and in any one writer the proportions will vary from time to time, according to the atmosphere in which he is living. They are:

(1) Sheer egoism. Desire to seem clever, to be talked about, to be remembered after death, to get your own back on grown-ups who snubbed you in childhood, etc., etc. It is humbug to pretend that this is not a motive, and a strong one. Writers share this characteristic with scientists, artists, politicians, lawyers, soldiers, successful businessmen—in short, with the whole top crust of humanity. The great mass of human beings are not acutely selfish. After the age of about thirty they abandon individual ambition—in many cases, indeed, they almost abandon the sense of being individuals at all—and live chiefly for others, or are simply smothered under drudgery. But there is also the minority of gifted, wilful people who are determined to live their own lives to the end, and writers belong in this class. Serious writers, I should say, are on the whole more vain and self-centered than journalists, though less interested in money.

(2) Aesthetic enthusiasm. Perception of beauty in the external world, or, on the other hand, in words and their right arrange-

---

* From *Such, Such Were the Joys* by George Orwell (New York: Harcourt, Brace & World, Inc., 1953). Copyright 1945, 1952, 1953 by Sonia Brownell Orwell. Reprinted by permission of the publishers and Brandt & Brandt.

ment. Pleasure in the impact of one sound on another, in the firmness of good prose or the rhythm of a good story. Desire to share an experience which one feels is valuable and ought not to be missed. The aesthetic motive is very feeble in a lot of writers, but even a pamphleteer or a writer of textbooks will have pet words and phrases which appeal to him for nonutilitarian reasons; or he may feel strongly about typography, width of margins, etc. Above the level of a railway guide, no book is quite free from aesthetic considerations.

(3) Historical impulse. Desire to see things as they are, to find out true facts and store them up for the use of posterity.

(4) Political purpose—using the word "political" in the widest possible sense. Desire to push the world in a certain direction, to alter other people's idea of the kind of society that they should strive after. Once again, no book is genuinely free from political bias. The opinion that art should have nothing to do with politics is itself a political attitude.

It can be seen how these various impulses must war against one another, and how they must fluctuate from person to person and from time to time. By nature—taking your "nature" to be the state you have attained when you are first adult—I am a person in whom the first three motives would outweigh the fourth. In a peaceful age I might have written ornate or merely descriptive books, and might have remained almost unaware of my political loyalties. As it is I have been forced into becoming a sort of pamphleteer. First I spent five years in an unsuitable profession (the Indian Imperial Police, in Burma), and then I underwent poverty and the sense of failure. This increased my natural hatred of authority and made me for the first time fully aware of the existence of the working classes, and the job in Burma had given me some understanding of the nature of imperialism: but these experiences were not enough to give me an accurate political orientation. Then came Hitler, the Spanish civil war, etc. By the end of 1935 I had still failed to reach a firm decision. I remember a little poem that I wrote at that date, expressing my dilemma:

> A happy vicar I might have been
> Two hundred years ago,
> To preach upon eternal doom
> And watch my walnuts grow;

But born, alas, in an evil time,
I missed that pleasant haven,
For the hair has grown on my upper lip
And the clergy are all clean shaven.

And later still the times were good,
We were so easy to please,
We rocked our troubled thoughts to sleep
On the bosoms of the trees.

All ignorant we dared to own
The joys we now dissemble;
The greenfinch on the apple bough
Could make my enemies tremble.

But girls' bellies and apricots,
Roach in a shaded stream,
Horses, ducks in flight at dawn,
All these are a dream.

It is forbidden to dream again;
We maim our joys or hide them;
Horses are made of chromium steel
And little fat men shall ride them.

I am the worm who never turned,
The eunuch without a harem.
Between the priest and the commissar
I walk like Eugene Aram;

And the commissar is telling my fortune
While the radio plays,
But the priest has promised in Austin Seve,
For Duggie always pays.

I dreamed I dwelt in marble halls,
And woke to find it true;
I wasn't born for an age like this;
Was Smith? Was Jones? Were you?

The Spanish war and other events in 1936-7 turned the scale and thereafter I knew where I stood. Every line of serious work that I have written since 1936 has been written, directly or indirectly, *against* totalitarianism and *for* democratic socialism, as I understand it. It seems to me nonsense, in a period like our own, to think that one can avoid writing of such subjects. Everyone writes of them in one guise or another. It is simply a question of which side one takes and what approach one follows. And the more one is conscious of one's political bias, the more chance one has of acting politically without sacrificing one's aesthetic and intellectual integrity.

What I have most wanted to do throughout the past ten years is to make political writing into an art. My starting point is always a feeling of partisanship, a sense of injustice. When I sit down to write a book, I do not say to myself, "I am going to produce a work of art." I write it because there is some lie that I want to expose, some fact to which I want to draw attention, and my initial concern is to get a hearing. But I could not do the work of writing a book, or even a long magazine article, if it were not also an aesthetic experience. Anyone who cares to examine my work will see that even when it is downright propaganda it contains much that a full-time politician would consider irrelevant. I am not able, and I do not want, completely to abandon the world view that I acquired in childhood. So long as I remain alive and well I shall continue to feel strongly about prose style, to love the surface of the earth, and to take a pleasure in solid objects and scraps of useless information. It is no use trying to suppress that side of myself. The job is to reconcile my ingrained likes and dislikes with the essentially public, nonindividual activities that this age forces on all of us.

It is not easy. It raises problems of construction and of language, and it raises in a new way the problem of truthfulness. Let me give just one example of the cruder kind of difficulty that arises. My book about the Spanish civil war, *Homage to Catalonia,* is, of course, a frankly political book, but in the main it is written with a certain detachment and regard for form. I did try very hard in it to tell the whole truth without violating my literary instincts. But among other things it contains a long chapter, full of newspaper quotations and the like, defending the Trotskyists who were accused of plotting with Franco. Clearly such a chapter, which after a year or two would lose its interest for any ordinary reader, must ruin the book. A critic whom I respect read me a lecture about it. "Why did you put in that stuff?" he said. "You've turned what might have been a good book into journalism." What he said was true, but I could not have done otherwise. I happened to know what very few people in England had been allowed to know, that innocent men were being falsely accused. If I had not been angry about that I should never have written the book.

In one form or another this problem comes up again. The problem of language is subtler and would take too long to discuss. I will only say that of late years I have tried to write less picturesquely and more exactly. In any case I find that by the time you have perfected any style of writing, you have always outgrown it. *Animal Farm* was the first book in which I tried, with full consciousness of what I was doing, to fuse political purpose and artistic purpose into one whole. I have not written a novel for seven years, but I hope to write another fairly soon. It is bound to be a failure, every book is a failure, but I do know with some clarity what kind of book I want to write. Looking back through the last page or two, I see that I have made it appear as though my motives in writing were wholly public-spirited. I don't want to leave that as the final impression. All writers are vain, selfish, and lazy, and at the very bottom of their motives there lies a mystery. Writing a book is a horrible, exhausting struggle, like a long bout of some painful illness. One would never undertake such a thing if one were not driven on by some demon whom one can neither resist nor understand. For all one knows that demon is simply the same instinct that makes a baby squall for attention. And yet it is also true that one can write nothing readable unless one constantly struggles to efface one's own personality. Good prose is like a windowpane. I cannot say with certainty which of my motives are the strongest, but I know which of them deserve to be followed. And looking back through my work, I see that it is invariably where I lacked a *political* purpose that I wrote lifeless books and was betrayed into purple passages, sentences without meaning, decorative adjectives and humbug generally.

### SUGGESTIONS FOR WRITING

1. Eric Blair (1903-1950) used the pen name of George Orwell. His *Animal Farm* (1946) and *Nineteen Eighty-Four* (1949) are his most widely read books. After graduating from Eton, Orwell spent five years in Burma as a policeman and then returned to England where, after a period spent doing odd jobs and being unemployed (see *Down and Out in*

*Paris and London*), he began to write articles, reviews, and then books. For the larger part of his adult life, then, he was a writer. He suggests in the above essay that there are four great motives for writing. At the present time what seems to be the strongest of the four for you?

2. Samuel Johnson said, "No man but a blockhead ever wrote except for money." Orwell begins by saying, "Putting aside the need to earn a living . . ." Can it be put aside? What do you think? Must not money be a strong motive for writing?

3. Taking your organizational clues from Orwell, explain why you write.

4. Orwell says, "Writing a book is a horrible, exhausting struggle, like a long bout of some painful illness." Have you ever felt that way about writing? Or is this feeling reserved for someone immersed in writing long enough (several months) to produce a book?

W. SOMERSET MAUGHAM

## How to Write Perfectly*

I have continued with increasing assiduity to try to write better. I discovered my limitations and it seemed to me that the only sensible thing was to aim at what excellence I could within them. I knew I should never write as well as I could wish, but I thought with pains I could arrive at writing as well as my natural defects allowed. On taking thought it seemed to me that I must aim at lucidity, simplicity and euphony. I have put these three qualities in the order of the importance I assigned to them.

I have never had much patience with the writers who claim from the reader an effort to understand their meaning. You have only to go to the great philosophers to see that it is possible to express with lucidity the most subtle reflections. You may find it difficult to understand the thought of Hume, and if you have no philosophical training its implications will doubtless escape you; but no one with any education at all can fail to understand exactly what the meaning of each sentence is. There are two sorts of obscurity that you find in writers. One is due to negligence and the other to wilfulness. People often write obscurely because they have never taken the

* From *The Summing Up* by W. Somerset Maugham (London: William Heinemann, Ltd., 1938). Copyright 1938 by W. Somerset Maugham. Reprinted by permission of the publishers and Doubleday & Co., Inc.

trouble to learn to write clearly. This sort of obscurity you find too often in modern philosophers, in men of science, and even in literary circles. Here it is indeed strange. You would have thought that men who passed their lives in the study of the great masters of literature would be sufficiently sensitive to the beauty of language to write if not beautifully at least with perspicuity. Yet you will find in their works sentence after sentence that you must read twice to discover the sense. Often you can only guess at it, for the writers have evidently not said what they intended.

Another cause of obscurity is that the writer is himself not quite sure of his meaning. He has a vague impression of what he wants to say, but has not, either from lack of mental power or from laziness, exactly formulated it in his mind and it is natural enough that he should not find a precise expression for a confused idea. This is due largely to the fact that many writers think, not before, but as they write. The pen originates the thought. But this sort of obscurity merges very easily into the wilful. Some writers who do not think clearly are inclined to suppose that their thoughts have a significance greater than at first sight appears. It is flattering to believe that they are too profound to be expressed so clearly that all who run may read, and very naturally it does not occur to such writers that the fault is with their own minds which have not the faculty of precise reflection. It is very easy to persuade oneself that a phrase that one does not quite understand may mean a great deal more than one realizes. From this there is only a little way to go to fall into the habit of setting down one's impressions in all their original vagueness. Fools can always be found to discover a hidden sense in them. There is another form of wilful obscurity that masquerades as aristocratic exclusiveness. The author wraps his meaning in mystery so that the vulgar shall not participate in it. His soul is a secret garden into which the elect may penetrate only after overcoming a number of perilous obstacles. But this kind of obscurity is not only pretentious; it is shortsighted. For time plays it an odd trick. If the sense is meagre time reduces it to a meaningless verbiage that no one thinks of reading.

Simplicity is not such an obvious merit as lucidity. I have aimed at it because I have no gift for richness. Within limits I admire richness in others, though I find it difficult to digest in quantity. I can read one page of Ruskin with delight, but twenty only with weariness. The appeal is sensuous rather than intellectual, and the beauty of the sound leads you easily to conclude that you need not bother about the meaning. But words are tyrannical things, they exist for their meanings, and if you will not pay attention to these, you cannot pay attention at all. Your mind wanders. This kind of writing demands a subject that will suit it. It is surely out of place to write in the grand style of inconsiderable things. No one wrote in this manner with greater success than Sir Thomas Browne, but even he did not always escape this pitfall. In the last chapter of *Hydriotaphia* the matter, which is the destiny of man, wonderfully fits the baroque splendor of the language, and here the Norwich doctor produced a piece of prose that has never been surpassed in our literature; but when he describes the finding of his urns in the same splendid manner the effect (at least to my taste) is less happy. When a modern writer is grandiloquent to tell you whether or no a little trollop shall hop into bed with a commonplace young man you are right to be disgusted.

To my mind King James's Bible has been a very harmful influence on English prose. I am not so stupid as to deny its great beauty. It is majestical. But the Bible is an oriental book. Its alien imagery has nothing to do with us. Those hyperboles, those luscious metaphors, are foreign to our genius. I cannot but think that not the least of the misfortunes that the secession from Rome brought upon the spiritual life of our country is that this work for so long a period became the daily, and with many the only, reading of our people. Those rhythms, that powerful vocabulary, that grandiloquence, became part and parcel of the national sensibility. The plain, honest English speech was overwhelmed with ornament. Blunt Englishmen twisted their tongues to speak like Hebrew prophets. . . . ever since, English prose has had to struggle against the tendency to luxuriance.

The dictum that the style is the man is well known. It is one of those aphorisms that say too much to mean a great deal. I suppose that if a man has a confused mind he will write in a confused way, if his temper is capricious his prose will be fantastical, and if he has a quick, darting intelligence that is reminded by the matter in hand of a hundred things he will, unless he has great self-control, load his pages with metaphor and simile. I can read every word that

Dr. Johnson wrote with delight, for he had good sense, charm and wit. No one could have written better if he had not wilfully set himself to write in the grand style. He knew English when he saw it. No critic has praised Dryden's prose more aptly. He said of him that he appeared to have no art other than that of expressing with clearness what he thought with vigor. And one of his *Lives* he finished with the words: "Whoever wishes to attain an English style, familiar but not coarse, and elegant but not ostentatious, must give his days and nights to the volumes of Addison." But when he himself sat down to write it was with a very different aim. He mistook the orotund for the dignified. He had not the good breeding to see that simplicity and naturalness are the truest marks of distinction. For to write good prose is an affair of good manners. It is, unlike verse, a civil art. It has been said that good prose should resemble the conversation of a well-bred man (and have we not also been told that good prose should be like the clothes of a well-dressed man, appropriate but unobtrusive?).

Whether you ascribe importance to euphony, the last of the three characteristics that I mentioned, must depend on the sensitiveness of your ear. A great many readers, and many admirable writers, are devoid of this quality. Poets as we know have always made a great use of alliteration. They are persuaded that the repetition of a sound gives an effect of beauty. I do not think it does so in prose. It seems to me that in prose alliteration should be used only for a special reason; when used by accident it falls on the ear very disagreeably. But its accidental use is so common that one can only suppose that the sound of it is not universally offensive. Many writers without distress will put two rhyming words together, join a monstrous long adjective to a monstrous long noun, or between the end of one word and the beginning of another have a conjunction of consonants that almost breaks your jaw. These are trivial and obvious instances. I mention them only to prove that if careful writers can do such things it is only because they have no ear. Words have weight, sound and appearance; it is only by considering these that you can write a sentence that is good to look at and good to listen to.

I have read many books on English prose, but have found it hard to profit by them; for the most part they are vague, unduly theoretical, and often scolding. But you cannot say this of Fowler's *Dictionary of Modern English Usage*. It is a valuable work. Fowler liked simplicity, straightforwardness and common sense. He had a sound feeling that idiom was the backbone of a language and he was all for the racy phrase. He was no slavish admirer of logic and was willing enough to give usage right of way through the exact demesnes of grammar. English grammar is very difficult and few writers have avoided making mistakes in it. It is necessary to know grammar, and it is better to write grammatically than not, but it is well to remember that grammar is common speech formulated. Usage is the only test. I would prefer a phrase that was easy and unaffected to a phrase that was grammatical. I have given the matter of style a great deal of thought and have taken great pains. I have written few pages that I feel I could not improve and far too many that I have left with dissatisfaction. I cannot say of myself what Johnson said of Pope: "He never passed a fault unamended by indifference, nor quitted it by despair." I do not write as I want to; I write as I can.

Anything is better than not to write clearly. There is nothing to be said against lucidity, and against simplicity only the possibility of dryness. This is a risk that is well worth taking when you reflect how much better it is to be bald than to wear a curly wig. But there is in euphony a danger that must be considered. It is very likely to be monotonous. I do not know how one can guard against this. I suppose the best chance is to have a more lively faculty of boredom than one's readers so that one is wearied before they are. One must always be on the watch for mannerisms and when certain cadences come too easily to the pen ask oneself whether they have not become mechanical.

If you could write lucidly, simply, euphoniously and yet with liveliness you would write perfectly; you would write like Voltaire. And yet we know how fatal the pursuit of liveliness may be: it may result in the tiresome acrobatics of Meredith. Macaulay and Carlyle were in their different ways arresting; but at the heavy cost of naturalness. Their flashy effects distract the mind. They destroy their persuasiveness; you would not believe a man was very intent on ploughing a furrow if he carried a hoop with him and jumped through it at every other step. A good style should show no sign of effort. What is written should seem a happy accident.

SUGGESTIONS FOR WRITING

1. W. Somerset Maugham (1874-    ) is a novelist, playwright, and short-story writer. College students for more than two generations have found his semiautobiographical novel, *Of Human Bondage* (1915) worth reading and worth remembering. Maugham has fifty years of success as a writer to support his theories. Summarize his essay and add a paragraph indicating precisely what a man must do to write "perfectly."
2. Maugham says, "I have never had much patience with the writers who claim from the reader an effort to understand their meaning." When William Faulkner was asked what readers might do who had failed to understand his novels after two readings, he said, "Read them a third time." Who is correct? To what degree may an author be demanding of his reader? In your answer be sure to define "the average man."
3. Maugham thinks the King James Bible has had a harmful influence on English prose. He admits its great beauty, but complains of the "alien imagery." What is imagery? Does the imagery seem alien to you? Examine a few passages and report.
4. "Good prose should resemble the conversation of a well-bred man." What do you suppose Maugham means by this, and how would he define "well-bred man"? Indicate what you think he means by "conversation." When? Under what circumstances? How many present? Topics under discussion?
5. "Words have weight, sound and appearance; it is only by considering these that you can write a sentence that is good to look at and good to listen to." Find some sentences that look and sound good and set them beside their opposites. What conclusions do you draw?

BERTRAND RUSSELL

# How I Write*

I cannot pretend to know how writing ought to be done, or what a wise critic would advise me to do with a view to improving my own writing. The most that I can do is to relate some things about my own attempts.

Until I was twenty-one, I wished to write more or less in the style

---

* From *Portraits from Memory* by Bertrand Russell (London: George Allen & Unwin, Ltd., 1951). Copyright 1951, 1952, 1953, © 1956 by Bertrand Russell. Reprinted by permission of the publishers and Simon & Schuster, Inc.

of John Stuart Mill. I liked the structure of his sentences and his manner of developing a subject. I had, however, already a different ideal, derived, I suppose, from mathematics. I wished to say everything in the smallest number of words in which it could be said clearly. Perhaps, I thought, one should imitate Baedeker rather than any more literary model. I would spend hours trying to find the shortest way of saying something without ambiguity, and to this aim I was willing to sacrifice all attempts at aesthetic excellence.

At the age of twenty-one, however, I came under a new influence, that of my future brother-in-law, Logan Pearsall Smith. He was at that time exclusively interested in style as opposed to matter. His gods were Flaubert and Walter Pater, and I was quite ready to believe that the way to learn how to write was to copy their technique. He gave me various simple rules, of which I remember only two: "Put a comma every four words," and "never use 'and' except at the beginning of a sentence." His most emphatic advice was that one must always rewrite. I conscientiously tried this, but found that my first draft was almost always better than my second. This discovery has saved me an immense amount of time. I do not, of course, apply it to the substance, but only to the form. When I discover an error of an important kind, I rewrite the whole. What I do not find is that I can improve a sentence when I am satisfied with what it means.

Very gradually I have discovered ways of writing with a minimum of worry and anxiety. When I was young each fresh piece of serious work used to seem to me for a time—perhaps a long time—to be beyond my powers. I would fret myself into a nervous state from fear that it was never going to come right. I would make one unsatisfying attempt after another, and in the end have to discard them all. At last I found that such fumbling attempts were a waste of time. It appeared that after first contemplating a book on some subject, and after giving serious preliminary attention to it, I needed a period of subconscious incubation which could not be hurried and was if anything impeded by deliberate thinking. Sometimes I would find, after a time, that I had made a mistake, and that I could not write the book I had had in mind. But often I was more fortunate. Having, by a time of very intense concentration, planted the problem in my subconsciousness, it would germinate underground until, suddenly, the solution emerged with blinding clarity, so that it only remained to write down what had appeared as if in a revelation.

The most curious example of this process, and the one which led me subsequently to rely upon it, occurred at the beginning of 1914. I had undertaken to give the Lowell Lectures at Boston, and had chosen as my subject "Our Knowledge of the External World." Throughout 1913 I thought about this topic. In term time in my rooms at Cambridge, in vacations in a quiet inn on the upper reaches of the Thames, I concentrated with such intensity that I sometimes forgot to breathe and emerged panting as from a trance. But all to no avail. To every theory that I could think of I could perceive fatal objections. At last, in despair, I went off to Rome for Christmas, hoping that a holiday would revive my flagging energy. I got back to Cambridge on the last day of 1913, and although my difficulties were still completely unresolved, I arranged, because the remaining time was short, to dictate as best I could to a stenographer. Next morning, as she came in at the door, I suddenly saw exactly what I had to say, and proceeded to dictate the whole book without a moment's hesitation.

I do not want to convey an exaggerated impression. The book was very imperfect, and I now think that it contains serious errors. But it was the best that I could have done at that time, and a more leisurely method (within the time at my disposal) would almost certainly have produced something worse. Whatever may be true of other people, this is the right method for me. Flaubert and Pater, I have found, are best forgotten so far as I am concerned.

Although what I now think about how to write is not so very different from what I thought at the age of eighteen, my development has not been by any means rectilinear. There was a time, in the first years of this century, when I had more florid and rhetorical ambitions. This was the time when I wrote *The Free Man's Worship,* a work of which I do not now think well. At that time I was steeped in Milton's prose, and his rolling periods reverberated through the caverns of my mind. I cannot say that I no longer admire them, but for me to imitate them involves a certain insincerity. In fact, all imitation is dangerous. Nothing could be better in style than the Prayer Book and the Authorized Version of the Bible, but they express a way of thinking and feeling which is different from that of our time. A style is not good unless it is an intimate and almost involuntary expression of the personality of the writer, and then only if the writer's personality is worth expressing. But although direct imitation is always to be deprecated, there is much to be gained by familiarity with good prose, especially in cultivating a sense for prose rhythm.

There are some simple maxims—not perhaps quite so simple as those which my brother-in-law Logan Pearsall Smith offered me—which I think might be commended to writers of expository prose. First: never use a long word if a short word will do. Second: if you want to make a statement with a great many qualifications, put some of the qualifications in separate sentences. Third: do not let the beginning of your sentence lead the reader to an expectation which is contradicted by the end. Take, say, such a sentence as the following, which might occur in a work on sociology: "Human beings are completely exempt from undesirable behavior patterns only when certain prerequisites, not satisfied except in a small percentage of actual cases, have, through some fortuitous concourse of favourable circumstances, whether congenital or environmental, chanced to combine in producing an individual in whom many factors deviate from the norm in a socially advantageous manner." Let us see if we can translate this sentence into English. I suggest the following: "All men are scoundrels, or at any rate almost all. The men who are not must have had unusual luck, both in their birth and their upbringing." This is shorter and more intelligible, and says just the same thing. But I am afraid any professor who used the second sentence instead of the first would get the sack.

This suggests a word of advice to such of my hearers as may happen to be professors. I am allowed to use plain English because everybody knows that I could use mathematical logic if I chose. Take the statement: "Some people marry their deceased wives' sisters." I can express this in language which only becomes intelligible after years of study, and this gives me freedom. I suggest to young professors that their first work should be written in a jargon only to be understood by the erudite few. With that behind them, they can ever after say what they have to say in a language "understanded of the people." In these days, when our very lives are at the mercy of the professors, I cannot but think that they would deserve our gratitude if they adopted my advice.

## SUGGESTIONS FOR WRITING

1. Bertrand Russell (1872-   ) is an English essayist, philosopher, and mathematician. His *Principia Mathematica* (1913), written with A. N. Whitehead, is an outstanding treatise on mathematical theory. But it is as an essayist, and philosopher that Bertrand Russell is best known. He received the Nobel Prize for Literature in 1950. In this essay he admits what almost all other writers have confessed, "I cannot pretend to know how writing ought to be done. . . . The most that I can do is to relate some things about my own attempts." In another part of *Portraits from Memory* (from which this excerpt was taken), Russell speaks of the value of a writing technique he stumbled on as a young man when he found a need to copy "almost word for word, into a notebook" a work by the German philosopher Georg Cantor. It became, he says, "more intelligible." Perhaps such stumbling and such fortuitous periods of learning are the best anyone can hope for in the complex business of writing. Citing Russell as an illustration, write an essay defending or attacking the "lucky stumble" theory of learning to write.
2. Russell lists three rules which "might be commended to writers of expository prose." His rules are based on a long career of writing. If you were to devise a set of rules for writing, it would seem reasonable to use as a background your reading instead of your own writing. In an essay similar to Russell's, indicate not "How I Write" but "How I Would Like to See Writing Written."
3. Russell advocates the use of plain English. Under what circumstances would this be inadvisable? What about law? What about theory? He allows "a jargon only to be understood by the erudite few" for special occasions, but is his argument convincing?

BENJAMIN FRANKLIN

# How I Learned to Write*

From a child I was fond of reading, and all the little money that came into my hands was ever laid out in books. Pleas'd with the *Pilgrim's Progress,* my first collection was of John Bunyan's works, in separate little volumes. I afterward sold them to enable me to buy R. Burton's Historical Collection; they were small chapmen's

* From the *Autobiography of Benjamin Franklin,* 1816. The text has been somewhat modernized.

books and cheap, 40 or 50 in all. My father's little library consisted chiefly of books in polemic divinity, most of which I read, and have since often regretted that, at a time when I had such a thirst for knowledge, more proper books had not fallen in my way, since it was now resolv'd I should not be a clergyman. *Plutarch's Lives* there was, in which I read abundantly, and I still think that time spent to great advantage. There was also a book of Defoe's, called an *Essay on Projects,* and another of Dr. Mather's, called *Essays to do Good* which perhaps gave me a turn of thinking that had an influence on some of the principal future events of my life.

This bookish inclination at length determin'd my father to make me a printer, tho' he had already one son [James] of that profession. In 1717 my brother James return'd from England with a press and letters to set up his business in Boston. I lik'd it much better than that of my father, but still had a hankering for the sea. To prevent the apprehended effect of such an inclination, my father was impatient to have me bound to my brother. I stood out some time, but at last was persuaded, and signed the indentures, when I was yet but 12 years old. . . . I was to serve as an apprentice till I was 21 years of age, only I was to be allow'd journeyman's wages during the last year. In a little time I made great proficiency in the business, and became a useful hand to my brother. I now had access to better books. An acquaintance with the apprentices of booksellers, enabled me sometimes to borrow a small one, which I was careful to return soon and clean. Often I sat up in my room reading the greatest part of the night, when the book was borrow'd in the evening and to be return'd early in the morning, lest it should be miss'd or wanted. And after some time an ingenious tradesman Mr. Matthew Adams who had a pretty collection of books, and who frequented our printing house, took notice of me, invited me to his library, and very kindly lent me such books as I chose to read. I now took a fancy to poetry, and made some little pieces. My brother, thinking it might turn to account encourag'd me, and put me on composing occasional ballads. One was called the *Lighthouse Tragedy,* and contained an account of the drowning of Capt. Worthilake, with his two daughters: the other was a sailor song on the taking of *Teach* or Blackbeard the pirate. They were wretched stuff, in the Grubstreet ballad stile, and when they were printed he sent me about the town to sell them. The first sold wonderfully, the event being recent, having made a great noise. This flatter'd my vanity. But my father discourag'd me, by ridiculing my performances, and telling me verse-makers were generally beggars; so I escap'd being a poet, most probably a very bad one. But as prose writing has been of great use to me in the course of my life, and was a principal means of my advancement, I shall tell you how in such a situation I acquir'd what little ability I have in that way.

There was another bookish lad in the town, John Collins by name, with whom I was intimately acquainted. We sometimes disputed, and very fond we were of argument, and very desirous of confuting one another. Which disputacious turn, by the way, is apt to become a very bad habit, making people often extremely disagreeable in company, by the contradiction that is necessary to bring it into practice, and thence, besides souring and spoiling the conversation, productive of disgusts and, perhaps enmities where you may have occasion for friendship. I had caught it by reading my father's books of dispute about religion. Persons of good sense, I have since observ'd, seldom fall into it, except lawyers, university men, and men of all sorts that have been bred at Edinburgh. A question was once, some how or other, started between Collins and me, of the propriety of educating the female sex in learning, and their abilities for study. He was of opinion that it was improper, and that they were naturally unequal to it. I took the contrary side, perhaps a little for dispute['s] sake. He was naturally more eloquent, had a ready plenty of words, and sometimes as I thought bore me down more by his fluency than by the strength of his reasons. As we parted without settling the point, and were not to see one another again for some time, I sat down to put my arguments in writing, which I copied fair and sent to him. He answer'd, and I reply'd. Three or four letters of a side had pass'd, when my father happen'd to find my papers and read them. Without ent'ring into the discussion, he took occasion to talk to me about the manner of my writing, observ'd that, tho' I had the advantage of my antagonist in correct spelling and pointing (which I ow'd to the printing house) I fell far short in elegance of expression, in method and in perspicuity, of which he convinc'd me by several instances. I saw the justice of his remarks, and thence grew more attentive to the *manner* in writing, and determin'd to endeavour at improvement. . . .

About this time I met with an odd volume of the *Spectator*. It was the third. I had never before seen any of them. I bought it, read it over and over, and was much delighted with it. I thought the writing excellent, and wish'd if possible to imitate it. With that view, I took some of the papers, and, making short hints of the sentiment in each sentence, laid them by a few days, and then, without looking at the book, try'd to complete the papers again, by expressing each hinted sentiment at length, and as fully as it had been express'd before, in any suitable words, that should come to hand.

Then I compared my Spectator with the original, discover'd some of my faults, and corrected them. But I found I wanted a stock of words or a readiness in recollecting and using them, which I thought I should have acquir'd before that time, if I had gone on making verses, since the continual occasion for words of the same import but of different length, to suit the measure, or of different sound for the rhyme, would have laid me under a constant necessity of searching for variety, and also have tended to fix that variety in my mind, and make me master of it. Therefore I took some of the tales and turn'd them into verse: And after a time, when I had pretty well forgotten the prose, turn'd them back again. I also sometimes jumbled my collections of hints into confusion, and after some weeks, endeavour'd to reduce them into the best order, before I began to form the full sentences and complete the paper. This was to teach me method in the arrangement of thoughts. By comparing my work afterwards with the original, I discover'd many faults and amended them; but I sometimes had the pleasure of fancying that in certain particulars of small import, I had been lucky enough to improve the method or the language and this encourag'd me to think I might possibly in time come to be a tolerable English writer, of which I was extremely ambitious.

My time for these exercises and for reading was at night, after work or before it began in the morning; or on Sundays, when I contrived to be in the printing house alone, evading as much as I could the common attendance on public worship, which my father used to exact of me when I was under his care: And which indeed I still thought a duty, tho' I could not, as it seemed to me, afford the time to practise it.

SUGGESTIONS FOR WRITING

1. Benjamin Franklin (1706-1790), taken to task by Mark Twain (p. 146) and D. H. Lawrence (p. 139), had little formal education, but read widely. He was particularly influenced by Locke, Shaftesbury, Xenophon, *The Spectator,* and some of Cotton Mather's works. In this essay he tells of his early efforts to write, and notes that his father caused him to pay more attention to the *manner* of writing. Although the particular method he used (proximate memorizing) was not a new technique, it is Franklin who gave it a favorable reputation. To test the effectiveness of Franklin's method, select a passage in which you think the writing excellent and follow Franklin's plan step by step.

2. "My time for these exercises," says Franklin, "was at night." In other words he learned to write in his spare time and with no formal instruction. As a printer's apprentice he must have worked long hours and under standards which he would today call severe, yet he took time to learn to write. It is a fascinating picture and we have no reason to doubt its authenticity. Write a description of a typical week in Franklin's life at this time. Use your imagination to fill in the details.

3. Franklin says he took the positive side in the debate "on the propriety of educating the female sex in learning." His friend, John Collins, took the negative. Write out the debate, pretending first to be Franklin and then Collins.

4. Franklin was encouraged to write by his self-taught method of learning. Have you taught yourself something by a "common sense" method? If so, write about it.

WALLACE STEGNER

# To a Young Writer*

The moment you start consciously writing for an audience you begin wondering if you are saying what the audience wants or expects. The peculiar virtue of this audience is that it leaves up to you what should be said. You have heard Frank O'Connor speak of the difference between the private and the public arts. Unless it is being dramatized or read aloud over the radio, fiction is one of the private ones. The audience has nothing to do with its making

---

* From *The Atlantic Monthly* (November, 1959). © 1959 by The Atlantic Monthly Company. Reprinted by permission of Brandt & Brandt, agents for the author.

or with the slant it takes. You don't discover what should go into your novel by taking a poll or having a trial run in Boston or Philadelphia. You discover it by thinking and feeling your way into a situation or having it feel its way into you. From inside a web of relationships, from the very heart of a temperament, your imagination creates outward and forward.

You write to satisfy yourself and the inevitabilities of the situation you have started in motion. You write under a compulsion, it is true, but it is the compulsion of your situation, not of a private hatred or envy or fear; and you write to satisfy yourself, but you write always in the remote awareness of a listener—O'Connor's man in the armchair. He responds to what you respond to and understands what you understand. Above all, he listens. Being outside of you, he closes a circuit, he is an ear to your mouth. Unless at least one like him reads you, you have written uselessly: your book is as hypothetical as the sound of the tree that falls in the earless forest.

Nevertheless, I repeat, except for vaguely imagining him and hoping he is there, ignore him, do not write what you think he would like. Write what you like. When your book is published you will have a letter from at least one of him, perhaps from as many as twenty or thirty of him. With luck, as other books come on his numbers will grow. But to you he will always be a solitary reader, an ear, not an audience. Literature speaks to temperament, Conrad says. Your books will find the temperaments they can speak to.

And I would not blame you if you still asked, Why bother to make contact with kindred spirits you never see and may never hear from, who perhaps do not even exist except in your hopes? Why spend ten years in an apprenticeship to fiction only to discover that this society so little values what you do that it won't pay you a living wage for it?

Well, what goes on in your novel—the affectionate revelation of a relationship, the unraveling of the threads of love and interest binding a family together, the tranquil and not so tranquil emotions surrounding the death of a beloved and distinguished grandfather—this is closer to what happens in church than to what happens in the theater. Fiction always moves toward one or another of its poles, toward drama at one end or philosophy at the other. This book of yours is less entertainment than philosophical meditation presented in terms of personalities in action. It is serious, even sad; its colors and lights are autumnal. You have not loved Chekhov for nothing—maybe you imagined him as your reader in the armchair. He would listen while you told him the apparently simple thing you want to say: how love lasts, but changes, how life is full of heats and frustrations, causes and triumphs, and death is cool and quiet. It does not sound like much, summarized, and yet it embodies everything you believe about yourself and about human life and at least some aspects of the people you have most loved. In your novel, anguish and resignation are almost in balance. Your people live on the page and in the memory because they have been loved and therefore have been richly imagined.

Your book is dramatized belief: and because in everyday life we make few contacts as intimate as this with another temperament and another mind, these scenes have an effect of cool shock—first almost embarrassment, then acknowledgment. Yes, I want to say. Yes, this is how it would be.

I like the sense of intimate knowing that your novel gives me. After all, what are any of us after but the conviction of belonging? What does more to stay us and keep our backbones stiff while the world reels than the sense that we are linked with someone who listens and understands and so in some way completes us? I have said somewhere else that the aesthetic experience is a conjugal act, like love. I profoundly believe it.

The worst thing that could happen to the ferocious seekers after identity is that they should find it and it only. There are many who do their best to escape it. Of our incorrigible and profound revulsion against identity, I suppose that physical love is the simplest, most immediate, and for many the only expression. Some have their comfort in feeling that they belong to the world of nature, big brother to the animals and cousin to the trees; some commit themselves to the kingdom of God. There is much in all of them, but for you, I imagine, not enough in any. For you it will have to be the kingdom of man, it will have to be art. You have nothing to gain and nothing to give except as you distill and purify ephemeral experience into quiet, searching, touching little stories like the one you have just finished, and so give your uncommon readers a chance to join you in the solidarity of pain and love and the vision of human possibility.

But isn't it enough? For lack of the full heart's desire, won't it serve?

SUGGESTIONS FOR WRITING

1. Wallace Stegner (1909-    ) is an Iowa-born author and educator. He graduated from the University of Utah and taught at Harvard and Stanford. His books include *Remembering Laughter* (1937), *On a Darkling Plain* (1940), *Fire and Ice* (1941), *Mormon Country* (1942), *The Big Rock Candy Mountain* (1943), and *One Nation* (1945). For such a man to offer advice to a young writer is indeed appropriate. One imagines that he follows his own advice. Summarize Stegner's accumulated wisdom about writing and comment on the point or points which seem most valuable.

2. "Write what you like," says Stegner. But he warns the would-be author to have an awareness of "the man in the armchair." Each of us probably have "a man in an armchair." Describe yours.

3. "Your people live on the page and in the memory," Stegner tells his young friend, "because they have been loved and therefore have been richly imagined." What character in fiction is most lifelike? We all have our favorites. Why does yours live? What makes him come to life? Is it simply the author's skill or is it, in part, your full participation in the act of reading?

ROBERT BENCHLEY

# How I Create*

In an article on How Authors Create, in which the writing methods of various masters of English prose like Conrad, Shaw, and Barrie are explained (with photographs of them in knickerbockers plaguing dogs and pushing against sundials), I discover that I have been doing the whole thing wrong all these years. The

---

* From *No Poems or Around the World Backwards and Sideways* by Robert Benchley (New York: Harper & Row, Publishers, 1932). Copyright 1932 by Robert Benchley. Reprinted by permission of the publishers.

interviewer in this case hasn't got around to asking me yet—doubtless because I have been up in my room with the door shut and not answering the bell—but I am going to take a chance anyway and tell him how I do my creative work and just how much comes from inspiration and how much from hashish and other perfumes. I may even loosen up and tell him what my favorite hot weather dishes are.

When I am writing a novel I must actually live the lives of my characters. If, for instance, my hero is a gambler on the French Riviera, I make myself pack up and go to Cannes or Nice, willy-nilly, and there throw myself into the gay life of the gambling set until I really feel that I *am* Paul De Lacroix, or Ed Whelan, or whatever my hero's name is. Of course this runs into money, and I am quite likely to have to change my ideas about my hero entirely and make him a bum on a tramp steamer working his way back to America, or a young college boy out of funds who lives by his wits until his friends at home send him a hundred and ten dollars.

One of my heroes (Dick Markwell in "Love's How-do-you-do"), after starting out as a man-about-town in New York who "never showed his liquor" and was "an apparently indestructible machine devoted to pleasure," had to be changed into a patient in the Trembly Ward of a local institution, whose old friends didn't recognize him and furthermore didn't want to.

But, as you doubtless remember, it was a corking yarn.

This actually living the lives of my characters takes up quite a lot of time and makes it a little difficult to write anything. It was not until I decided to tell stories about old men who just sit in their rooms and shell walnuts that I ever got around to doing any work. It doesn't make for very interesting novels, but at any rate the wordage is there and there is something to show the publishers for their advance royalties. (Publishers are crotchety that way. They want copy, copy, copy all the time, just because they happen to have advanced a measly three hundred dollars a couple of years before. You would think that printing words on paper was their business.)

And now you ask me how I do my work, how my inspiration comes? I will tell you, Little Father. Draw up your chair and let me put my feet on it. Ah, that's better! Now you may go out and play!

Very often I must wait weeks and weeks for what you call "inspiration." In the meantime I must sit with my quill pen poised in air over a sheet of foolscap, in case the divine spark should come like a lightning bolt and knock me off my chair on to my head. (This has happened more than once.) While I am waiting I mull over in my mind what I am going to do with my characters.

Shall I have Mildred marry Lester, or shall Lester marry Evelyn? ("Who is Evelyn?" I often say to myself, never having heard of her before.) Should the French proletariat win the Revolution, or should Louis XVI come back suddenly and establish a Coalition Cabinet? Can I afford to let Etta clean up those dishes in the sink and get them biscuits baked, or would it be better to keep her there for another year, standing first on one foot and then on the other?

You have no idea how many problems an author has to face during those feverish days when he is building a novel, and you have no idea how he solves them. Neither has he.

Sometimes, while in the throes of creative work, I get out of bed in the morning, look at my writing desk piled high with old bills, odd gloves, and empty gingerale bottles, and go right back to bed again. The next thing I know it is night once more, and time for the Sand Man to come around. (We have a Sand Man who comes twice a day, which makes it very convenient. We give him five dollars at Christmas.)

Even if I do get up and put on a part of my clothes—I do all my work in a Hawaiian straw skirt and a bow tie of some neutral shade—I often can think of nothing to do put pile the books which are on one end of my desk very neatly on the other end and then kick them one by one off on to the floor with my free foot.

But all the while my brain is work, work, working, and my plot is taking shape. Sometimes it is the shape of a honeydew melon and sometimes a shape which I have never been quite able to figure out. It is a sort of amorphous thing with two heads but no face. When this shape presents itself, I get right back in bed again. I'm no fool.

I find that, while working, a pipe is a great source of inspiration. A pipe can be placed diagonally across the keys of a typewriter so that they will not function, or it can be made to give out such a cloud of smoke that I cannot see the paper. Then, there is the process of lighting it. I can make lighting a pipe a ritual which has not been equaled for elaborateness since the five-day festival to the God of the Harvest. (See my book on Rituals: the Man.)

In the first place, owing to twenty-six years of constant smoking without once calling in a plumber, the space left for tobacco in the bowl of my pipe is now the size of a medium body pore. Once the match has been applied to the tobacco therein, the smoke is over. This necessitates refilling, relighting, and reknocking. The knocking out of a pipe can be made almost as important as the smoking of it, especially if there are nervous people in the room. A good, smart knock of a pipe against a tin wastebasket and you will have a neurasthenic out of his chair and into the window sash in no time.

The matches, too, have their place in the construction of modern literature. With a pipe like mine, the supply of burnt matches in one day could be floated down the St. Lawrence River with two men jumping them. . . .

When the novel is finished, it is shipped to the Cutting and Binding Room, where native girls roll it into large sheets and stamp on it with their bare feet. This accounts for the funny look of some of my novels. It is then taken back to the Drying Room, where it is rewritten by a boy whom I engage for the purpose, and sent to the publishers. It is then sent back to me.

And so you see now how we creative artists work. It really isn't like any other kind of work, for it must come from a great emotional upheaval in the soul of the writer himself; and if that emotional upheaval is not present, it must come from the works of any other writers which happen to be handy and easily imitated.

SUGGESTIONS FOR WRITING

1. Robert Benchley (1889-1945)—drama critic, humorist, and actor—graduated from Harvard and wrote for New York newspapers and magazines. He was drama critic for the *New Yorker* from 1929 to 1940. His most notable works are sketches of the tribulations of the average man. He never wrote a novel about the French Riviera, nor did he do most of the other things that he speaks of in this essay. It is, of course, a delightful parody of an interview with a novelist. Try your hand at

parody. In your imagination, interview someone with an unusual occupation, say a tree surgeon, and attribute to him the same steps to
success which would be noted by a movie star.

2. If Benchley had a serious purpose in writing this piece, what was it?
   For what audience was it intended?

*Part Four*

# THE ARTS

# Poetry

I have said that poetry is the spontaneous overflow of powerful feelings: it takes its origin from emotion recollected in tranquillity.
—Wordsworth, *Lyrical Ballads, Second Edition,* 1800

No poet, no artist of any art, has his complete meaning alone. His significance, his appreciation is the appreciation of his relation to the dead poets and artists. You cannot value him alone; you must set him, for contrast and comparison, among the dead.
—T. S. Eliot, *The Sacred Wood,* 1920

The poet is he that hath fat enough, like bears and marmots, to suck his claws all winter. He hibernates in this world, and feeds on his own marrow.
—Thoreau, *Walden,* 1854

All lyrical work must, as a whole, be perfectly intelligible, but in some particulars a little unintelligible.
—Goethe, *Elective Affinities,* 1808

Poetry should surprise by a fine excess and not by singularity. It should strike the reader as a wording of his own highest thoughts, and appear almost as a remembrance.
—Keats, *Letter to John Taylor,* 1818

Experience has taught me, when I am shaving in the morning, to keep watch over my thoughts, because, if a line of poetry strays into my memory, my skin bristles so that the razor ceases to act.
—A. E. Housman, *The Name and Nature of Poetry,* 1933

The poet's function is to describe, not the thing that has happened, but a kind of thing that might happen. . . . Poetry is something more philosophic and of graver import than history, since its statements are of the nature rather of universals, whereas those of history are singulars.
—Aristotle, *Poetics,* 330 B.C.

JOHN CIARDI

# Robert Frost: The Way to the Poem*

*Stopping by Woods on a Snowy Evening†*

Whose woods these are I think I know.
His house is in the village though;
He will not see me stopping here
To watch his woods fill up with snow.

My little horse must think it queer
To stop without a farmhouse near
Between the wood and frozen lake
The darkest evening of the year.

He gives his harness bells a shake
To ask if there is some mistake.
The only other sound's the sweep
Of easy wind and downy flake.

The woods are lovely, dark and deep.
But I have promises to keep,
And miles to go before I sleep,
And miles to go before I sleep.

    The School System has much to say these days of the virtue of
reading widely, and not enough about the virtues of reading less
but in depth. There are any number of reading lists for poetry,
but there is not enough talk about individual poems. Poetry,

---

  * From *The Saturday Review* (April 12, 1958). © 1958 by John Ciardi. Reprinted by permission of the publishers.
  † From *Complete Poems of Robert Frost* (New York: Holt, Rinehart and
Winston, Inc., 1923). Copyright 1923 by Holt, Rinehart and Winston, Inc.; 1951
by Robert Frost. Reprinted by permission of the publishers.

finally, is one poem at a time. To read any one poem carefully is the ideal preparation for reading another. Only a poem can illustrate how poetry works.

Above, therefore, is a poem—one of the master lyrics of the English language, and almost certainly the best-known poem by an American poet. What happens in it?—which is to say, not *what* does it mean, but *how* does it mean? How does it go about being a human re-enactment of a human experience? The author—perhaps the thousandth reader would need to be told—is Robert Frost.

Even the TV audience can see that this poem begins as a seemingly simple narration of a seemingly simple incident but ends by suggesting meanings far beyond anything specifically referred to in the narrative. And even readers with only the most casual interest in poetry might be made to note the additional fact that, though the poem suggests those larger meanings, it is very careful never to abandon its pretense to being simple narration. There is duplicity at work. The poet pretends to be talking about one thing, and all the while he is talking about many others.

Many readers are forever unable to accept the poet's essential duplicity. It is almost safe to say that a poem is never about what it seems to be about. As much could be said of the proverb. The bird in the hand, the rolling stone, the stitch in time never (except by an artful double-deception) intend any sort of statement about birds, stones, or sewing. The incident of this poem, one must conclude, is at root a metaphor.

Duplicity aside, this poem's movement from the specific to the general illustrates one of the basic formulas of all poetry. Such a grand poem as Arnold's "Dover Beach" and such lesser, though unfortunately better known, poems as Longfellow's "The Village Blacksmith" and Holmes's "The Chambered Nautilus" are built on the same progression. In these three poems, however, the generalization is markedly set apart from the specific narration, and even seems additional to the telling rather than intrinsic to it. It is this sense of division one has in mind in speaking of "a tacked-on moral."

There is nothing wrong in itself with a tacked-on moral. Frost, in fact, makes excellent use of the device at times. In this poem, however, Frost is careful to let the whatever the moral is grow out of the poem itself. When the action ends the poem ends. There is no epilogue and no explanation. Everything pretends to be about the narrated incident. And that pretense sets the basic tone of the poem's performance of itself.

The dramatic force of that performance is best observable, I believe, as a progression in three scenes.

In scene one, which coincides with stanza one, a man—a New England man—is driving his sleigh somewhere at night. It is snowing, and as the man passes a dark patch of woods he stops to watch the snow descend into the darkness. We know, moreover, that the man is familiar with these parts (he knows who owns the woods and where the owner lives), and we know that no one has seen him stop. As scene one forms itself in the theater of the mind's eye, therefore, it serves to establish some as yet unspecified relation between the man and the woods.

It is necessary, however, to stop here for a long parenthesis: Even so simple an opening statement raises any number of questions. It is impossible to address all the questions that rise from the poem stanza by stanza, but two that arise from stanza one illustrate the sort of thing one might well ask of the poem detail by detail.

Why, for example, does the man not say what errand he is on? What is the force of leaving the errand generalized? He might just as well have told us that he was going to the general store, or returning from it with a jug of molasses he had promised to bring Aunt Harriet and two suits of long underwear he had promised to bring the hired man. Frost, moreover, can handle homely detail to great effect. He preferred to leave his motive generalized. Why?

And why, on the other hand, does he say so much about knowing the absent owner of the woods and where he lives? Is it simply that one set of details happened in whereas another did not? To speak of things "happening in" is to assault the integrity of a poem. Poetry cannot be discussed meaningfully unless one can assume that everything in the poem—every last comma and variant spelling—is in it by the poet's specific act of choice. Only bad poets allow into their poems what is haphazard or cheaply chosen.

The errand, I will venture a bit brashly for lack of space, is left generalized in order the more aptly to suggest *any* errand in life and, therefore, life itself. The owner is there because he is one of the forces of the poem. Let it do to say that the force he represents is the village of mankind (that village at the edge of winter) from which the poet finds himself separated (has separated himself?) in his moment by the woods (and to which, he recalls finally, he has promises to keep). The owner is he who lives in his village house, thereby locked away from the poet's awareness of the time the snow tells as it engulfs and obliterates the world the village man allows himself to believe he "owns." Thus, the owner is a representative of an order of reality from which the poet has divided himself for the moment, though to a certain extent he ends by reuniting with it. Scene one, therefore, establishes not only a relation between the man and the woods, but the fact that the man's relation begins with his separation (though momentarily) from mankind.

End parenthesis one, begin parenthesis two.

Still considering the first scene as a kind of dramatic performance of forces, one must note that the poet has meticulously matched the simplicity of his language to the pretended simplicity of the narrative. Clearly, the man stopped because the beauty of the scene moved him, but he neither tells us that the scene is beautiful nor that he is moved. A bad writer, always ready to overdo, might have written: "The vastness gripped me, filling my spirit with the slow steady sinking of the snow's crystalline perfection into the glimmerless profundities of the hushed primeval wood." Frost's avoidance of such a spate illustrates two principles of good writing. The first, he has stated himself in "The Mowing": Anything *more* than the truth would have seemed too weak" (italics mine). Understatement is one of the basic sources of power in English poetry. The second principle is to let the action speak for itself. A good novelist does not tell us that a given character is good or bad (at least not since the passing of the Dickens tradition): he shows us the character in action and then, watching him, we know. Poetry, too, has fictional obligations: even when the characters are ideas and metaphors rather than people, they must be *characterized in action*. A poem does not *talk about* ideas; it *enacts* them. The force of the poem's performance, in fact, is precisely to act out (and thereby to make us act out empathically, that is, to *feel out,* that is, to *identify with*) the speaker and why he stopped. The man is the principal actor in this little "drama of why" and in scene one he is the only character, though as noted, he is somehow related to the absent owner.

End second parenthesis.

In scene two (stanzas two and three) a *foil* is introduced. In fiction and drama, a foil is a character who "plays against" a more important character. By presenting a different point of view or an opposed set of motives, the foil moves the more important character to react in ways that might not have found expression without such opposition. The more important character is thus more fully revealed—to the reader and to himself. The foil here is the horse.

The horse forces the question. Why did the man stop? Until it occurs to him that his "little horse must think it queer" he had not asked himself for reasons. He had simply stopped. But the man finds himself faced with the question he imagines the horse to be asking: what *is* there to stop for out there in the cold, away from bin and stall (house and village and mankind?) and all that any self-respecting beast could value on such a night? In sensing that other view, the man is forced to examine his own more deeply.

In stanza two the question arises only as a feeling within the man. In stanza three, however (still scene two), the horse acts. He gives his harness bells a shake. "What's wrong?" he seems to say. "What are we waiting for?"

By now, obviously, the horse—without losing its identity as horse—has also become a symbol. A symbol is something that stands for something else. Whatever that something else may be, it certainly begins as that order of life that does not understand why a man stops in the wintry middle of nowhere to watch the snow come down. (Can one fail to sense by now that the dark and the snowfall symbolize a death wish, however momentary, *i.e.*, that hunger for final rest and surrender that a man may feel, but not a beast?)

So by the end of scene two the performance has given dramatic force to three elements that work upon the man. There is his relation to the world of the owner. There is his relation to the brute world of the horse. And there is that third presence of the unownable world, the movement of the all-engulfing snow across all the orders of life, the man's, the owner's, and the horse's—with the difference that the man knows of that second dark within the dark of which the horse cannot, and the owner will not, know.

The man ends scene two with all these forces working upon him simultaneously. He feels himself moved to a decision. And he feels a last call from the darkness: "the sweep/Of easy wind and downy flake." It would be so easy and so downy to go into the woods and let himself be covered over.

But scene three (stanza four) produces a fourth force. This fourth force can be given many names. It is certainly better, in fact, to give it many names than to attempt to limit it to one. It is social obligation, or personal commitment, or duty, or just the realization that a man cannot indulge a mood forever. All of these and more. But, finally, he has a simple decision to make. He may go into the woods and let the darkness and the snow swallow him from the world of beast and man. Or he must move on. And unless he is going to stop here forever, it is time to remember that he has a long way to go and that he had best be getting there. (So there is something to be said for the horse, too.)

Then and only then, his question driven more and more deeply into himself by these cross-forces, does the man venture a comment on what attracted him: "The woods are lovely, dark and deep." His mood lingers over the thought of that lovely dark and deep (as do the very syllables in which he phrases the thought), but the final decision is to put off the mood and move on. He has his man's way to go and his man's obligations to tend to before he can yield. He has miles to go before his sleep. He repeats that thought and the performance ends.

But why the repetition? The first time Frost says "And miles to go before I sleep," there can be little doubt that the primary meaning is: "I have a long way to go before I get to bed tonight." The second time he says it, however, "miles to go" and "sleep" are suddenly transformed into symbols. What are those "something elses" the symbols stand for? Hundreds of people have tried to ask Mr. Frost that question and he has always turned it away. He has turned it away *because he cannot answer it.* He could answer some part of it. But some part is not enough.

For a symbol is like a rock dropped into a pool: it sends out ripples in all directions, and the ripples are in motion. Who can say where the last ripple disappears? One may have a sense that he knows the approximate center point of the ripples, the point at which the stone struck the water. Yet even then he has trouble marking it surely. How does one make a mark on water? Oh, very well—the center point of that second "miles to go" is probably

approximately in the neighborhood of being close to meaning, perhaps, "the road of life"; and the second "before I sleep" is maybe
that close to meaning "before I take my final rest," the rest in darkness that seemed so temptingly dark and deep for the moment of
the mood. But the ripples continue to move and the light to change
on the water, and the longer one watches the more changes he sees.
Such shifting and being at the same instant is of the very sparkle
and life of poetry. One experiences it as one experiences life, for
every time he looks at an experience he sees something new, and
sees it change as he watches it. And that sense of continuity in
fluidity is one of the primary kinds of knowledge, one of man's
basic ways of knowing, and one that only the arts can teach, poetry
foremost among them.

Frost himself certainly did not ask what that repeated last line
meant. It came to him and he received it. He "felt right" about it.
And what he "felt right" about was in no sense a "meaning" that,
say, an essay could apprehend, but an act of experience that could
be fully presented only by the dramatic enactment of forces which
is the performance of the poem.

Now look at the poem in another way. Did Frost know what he
was going to do when he began? Considering the poem simply as
an act of skill, as a piece of juggling, one cannot fail to respond to
the magnificent turn at the end where, with one flip, seven of the
simplest words in the language suddenly dazzle full of never-ending
waves of thought and feeling. Or, more precisely, of felt thought.
Certainly an equivalent stunt by a juggler—could there be an
equivalent—would bring the house down. Was it to cap his performance with that grand stunt that Frost wrote the poem?

Far from it. The obvious fact is that *Frost could not have known
he was going to write those lines until he wrote them.* Then a second fact must be registered: *he wrote them because, for the fun of
it, he had got himself into trouble.*

Frost, like every good poet, began by playing a game with himself. The most usual way of writing a four line stanza with four
feet to the line is to rhyme the third line with the first, and the
fourth line with the second. Even that much rhyme is so difficult
in English that many poets and almost all of the anonymous ballad
makers do not bother to rhyme the first and third lines at all, settling for two rhymes in four lines as good enough. For English is

a rhyme-poor language. In Italian and in French, for example, so many words end with the same sounds that rhyming is relatively easy—so easy that many modern French and Italian poets do not bother to rhyme at all. English, being a more agglomerate language, has far more final sounds, hence fewer of them rhyme. When an Italian poet writes a line ending with "vita" (life) he has literally hundreds of rhyme choices available. When an English poet writes "life" at the end of a line he can summon "strife, wife, knife, fife, rife," and then he is in trouble. Now "life-strife" and "life-rife" and "life-wife" seem to offer a combination of possible ideas that can be related by more than just the rhyme. Inevitably, therefore, the poets have had to work and rework these combinations until the sparkle has gone out of them. The reader is normally tired of such rhyme-led associations. When he encounters "life-strife" he is certainly entitled to suspect that the poet did not really want to say "strife"—that had there been in English such a word as, say, "hife," meaning "infinite peace and harmony," the poet would as gladly have used that word instead of "strife." Thus, the reader feels that the writing is haphazard, that the rhyme is making the poet say things he does not really feel, and which therefore the reader does not feel except as boredom. One likes to see the rhymes fall into place, but he must end with the belief that it is the poet who is deciding what is said and not the rhyme scheme that is forcing the saying.

So rhyme is a kind of game, and an especially difficult one in English. As in every game, the fun of the rhyme is to set one's difficulties high and then to meet them skillfully. As Frost himself once defined freedom, it consists of "moving easy in harness."

In "Stopping by Woods on a Snowy Evening" Frost took a long chance. He decided to rhyme not two lines in each stanza, but three. Not even Frost could have sustained that much rhyme in a long poem (as Dante, for example, with the advantage of writing in Italian, sustained triple rhyme for thousands of lines in "The Divine Comedy"). Frost would have known instantly, therefore, when he took the original chance, that he was going to write a short poem. He would have had that much foretaste of it.

So the first stanza emerged rhymed a-a-b-a. And with the sure sense that this was to be a short poem, Frost decided to take an additional chance and to redouble: in English three rhymes in four

lines is more than enough; there is no need to rhyme the fourth
line. For the fun of it, however, Frost set himself to pick up that
loose rhyme and to weave it into the pattern, thereby accepting the
all but impossible burden of quadruple rhyme.

The miracle is that it worked. Despite the enormous freight of
rhyme, the poem not only came out as a neat pattern, but managed
to do so with no sense of strain. Every word and every rhyme falls
into place as naturally and as inevitably as if there were no rhyme
restricting the poet's choices.

That ease in difficulty is certainly inseparable from the success of
the poem's performance. One watches the skill-man juggle three
balls, then four, then five, and every addition makes the trick more
wonderful. But unless he makes the hard trick seem as easy as an
easy trick, then all is lost.

The real point, however, is not only that Frost took on a hard
rhyme trick and made it seem easy. It is rather as if the juggler,
carried away, had tossed up one more ball than he could really
handle, and then amazed himself by actually handling it. So with
the real triumph of this poem. Frost could not have known what a
stunning effect his repetition of the last line was going to produce.
He could not even know he was going to repeat the line. He simply
found himself up against a difficulty he almost certainly had not fore-
seen and he had to improvise to meet it. For in picking up the
rhyme from the third line of stanza one and carrying it over into
stanza two, he had created an endless chain link form within
which each stanza left a hook sticking out for the next stanza to
hang on. So by stanza four, feeling the poem rounding to its end,
Frost had to do something about that extra rhyme.

He might have tucked it back into a third line rhyming with the
*know-though-snow* of stanza one. He could thus have rounded the
poem out to the mathematical symmetry of using each rhyme four
times. But though such a device might be defensible in theory, a
rhyme repeated after eleven lines is so far from its original rhyme
sound that its feeling as rhyme must certainly be lost. And what
good is theory if the reader is not moved by the writing?

It must have been in some such quandary that the final repetition
suggested itself—a suggestion born of the very difficulties the poet
had let himself in for. So there is that point beyond mere ease in
handling a hard thing, the point at which the very difficulty offers

the poet the opportunity to do better than he knew he could. What, aside from having that happen to oneself, could be more self-delighting than to participate in its happening by one's reader-identification with the poem?

And by now a further point will have suggested itself: that the human insight of the poem and the technicalities of its poetic artifice are inseparable. Each feeds the other. That interplay is the poem's meaning, a matter not of *What Does It Mean,* for no one can ever say entirely what a good poem means, but of *How Does It Mean,* a process one can come much closer to discussing.

### SUGGESTIONS FOR WRITING

1. John Ciardi (1915-    ) was born in Boston. He graduated from Tufts College and the University of Michigan and has taught English at the University of Kansas City and Harvard. He is poetry editor of the *Saturday Review* and a respected poet in his own right. His analysis of Robert Frost's "Stopping By Woods on a Snowy Evening" is calculated to increase one's appreciation not only of one poem but of poetry in general. To what extent did Ciardi succeed with you? Will you ever read or listen to Frost's poem with the same impressions? If not, in what way are they different?

2. Archibald MacLeish once said, "A poem should not mean, but be." Is this what Ciardi intends when he says we should be concerned not with *what* the poem means but with *how* it means? If it is not the same thing, make the distinction clear.

3. Apply Ciardi's "rules" for analyzing poetry to his article. Analyze it from the *how* instead of the *what*. Divide his article into parts, as Ciardi does for Frost's poem, and discuss the *how*.

4. Choose a poem you like and analyze it according to the model that Ciardi has provided.

5. Does a detailed analysis harm a poem and destroy one's pleasure in it? Is Ciardi here "pulling the wings off a butterfly"? Is beauty as a concept capable of being dissected and put under a microscope?

ARCHIBALD MACLEISH

# Why Do We Teach Poetry? *

There is something about the art of poetry which induces a de-
fensive posture. Even in the old days when the primacy of poetry
was no more challenged than the primacy of Heaven, which is now
also challenged, the posture was habitual. If you published your
reflections on the art in those days you called them a *Defense*. Today, when the queen of sciences is Science, you do not perhaps employ that term but you mean it. It is not that the gentlemen at the
long table in the Faculty Club whose brains have been officially
cleared to serve as depositories of scientific secrets of the eighth and
thirteenth classes are patronizing in their manner. They are still
gentlemen and therefore still modest no matter how great their distinction or how greatly certified. But one knows one's place. One
knows that whereas the teachers of science meet to hear of new triumphs which the newspapers will proudly report, the teachers of
poetry meet to ask old questions—which no one will report: such
questions as, why teach poetry anyway in a time like this?

It is a relief in this general atmosphere to come upon someone
who feels no defensiveness whatever: who is perfectly certain that
poetry ought to be taught now as at any other time and who is perfectly certain also that he knows why. The paragon I have in mind
is a young friend of mine, a devoted teacher, who was recently made
headmaster of one of the leading American preparatory schools,
and who has been taking stock, for some time past, of his curriculum and his faculty. Poetry, as he sees it, ought to be taught "as a
most essential form of human expression as well as a carrier
throughout the ages of some of the most important values in our
heritage." What troubles him is that few teachers, at least in the
schools he knows, seem to share his conviction. He is not too sure
that teachers themselves have "an abiding and missionary faith in
poetry" which would lead them to see it as a great clarifier—a

---

* From *The Atlantic Monthly* (March, 1956). © 1956 by Archibald MacLeish.
Reprinted by permission of the author.

"human language" capable of competing with the languages and mathematics and science.

But though teachers lack the necessary faith, the fault, as my young friend sees it, is not wholly theirs. The fault is the fault of modern criticism, which has turned poetry into something he calls "poetry itself"—meaning, I suppose, poetry for poetry's sake. "Poetry itself" turns out to be poetry with its meanings distilled away, and poetry with its meanings distilled away is difficult if not impossible to teach in a secondary school—at least *his* secondary school. The result is that secondary school teachers have gone back, as to the lesser of two evils, to those historical and anecdotal practices sanctified by American graduate schools in generations past. They teach "poets and not poetry." With the result that "students become acquainted with poets from Homer to MacLeish" (quite a distance no matter how you measure it!) "but the experience doesn't necessarily leave them with increased confidence in what poetry has to offer." I can well believe it.

The reason why modern criticism has this disastrous effect, the reason why it produces "an almost morbid apathy toward 'content' or 'statement of idea,'" is its excessive "preoccupation with aesthetic values." Modern criticism insists that poems are primarily works of art; and when you insist that poems are primarily works of art you cannot, in my friend's view, teach them as carriers "throughout the ages of some of the most important values in our heritage." What is important about Homer and Shakespeare and the authors of the Bible is that they were "realists with great vision . . . whose work contains immensely valuable constructions of the meaning of life"; and if you talk too much about them as artists, those constructions of the meaning of life get lost.

Now this, you will observe, is not merely another walloping of the old horse who was once called the New Criticism. It goes a great deal farther. It is a frontal attack upon a general position maintained by many who never accepted the New Criticism or even heard of it. It is an attack upon those who believe—as most poets, I think, have believed—that a poem *is* primarily a work of art and must be read as a work of art if it is to be read at all. It is a high-minded and disinterested attack delivered for the noblest of purposes, but an attack notwithstanding—and an effective one. What it contends is that an approach to poetry which insists that a poem is a work of art blocks off what the poem has to say, whereas what the poem has to say is the principal reason for teaching it. What the argument comes down to, in other words, is the proposition that it is a mistake, in teaching poetry, to insist that poetry is art, because, if you do so insist, you will not be able to bring your students to the meaning of the poem, the idea of the poem, what the poem has to tell them about man and world and life and death—and it is for these things the teaching of the poem is important.

Now, I can understand this argument and can respect the reasons for making it. Far too many of those who define poetry in exclusively artistic terms use their definition as a limiting and protective statement which relieves them of all obligation to drive the poem's meanings beyond the meanings of the poem: beyond the mere translation of the symbols and metaphors and the classical or other references—the whole apparatus of *explication de texte*. Far too many, indeed, of those who have to do with literature generally in our time, and particularly with modern literature, consider that meanings in any but a literary (which includes a Freudian) sense are not only outside, but beneath, their proper concern—that the intrusion of questions of morality and religion into the world of art is a kind of trespass and that works of literary art not only should but *can* be studied in a moral vacuum. Literature in the hands of such teachers is well on the way to becoming again that "terrible queen" which the men of the nineties raised above life and which Yeats, when he outgrew the men of the nineties, rejected.

But although I can understand this argument, and although I can respect its reasons, and although I believe it raises a true issue and an important issue, I cannot accept it; for it rests, or seems to me to rest, on two quite dubious assumptions. The first is the assumption, familiar in one form or another to all of us, that the "idea" of a work of art is somehow separable from the work of art itself. The most recent—and most egregious—expression of this persistent notion comes from a distinguished Dean of Humanities in a great institution of learning who is reported by the New York *Times* to have argued in a scholarly gathering that "the idea which the reader derives from Ernest Hemingway's *The Old Man and The Sea* comes after the reader has absorbed some 60,000 words. This takes at least an hour. . . . A similar understanding could come after a few minutes study of a painting by a skillful artist." Precisely, one imagines, as the Doré illustrations gave one the "idea" of the *Inferno* in a few easy looks! . . .

But all this is a negative way of saying what a defender of poetry should not be afraid of saying positively. Let me say it. We have lost our concern with ends because we have lost our touch with reality and we have lost our touch with reality because we are estranged from the means to reality which is the poem—the work of art. To most members of our generation this would seem an extravagant statement but it is not extravagant in fact and would not have seemed so in another time. In ancient China the place of poetry in men's lives was assumed as matter of course; indeed, the polity was based on it. The three hundred and five odes or songs which make up the Song-word Scripture survived to the fourth century B.C., when Confucius is said to have collected them because they were part of the government records preserved in the Imperial Archive. For thousands of years the examinations for the Chinese civil service were examinations in poetry, and there is no record that the results were more disappointing to the throne than examinations of a different character might have been. Certainly there is no record that a Chinese civil servant ever attempted to deny an honor student in a military academy his commission in the imperial army *or* navy because he was friendly with his own mother! Idiocies which the study of science and of other abstractions in contemporary institutions of naval education in the United States seem to nourish were apparently cauterized from the mind by the reading of poems.

It was not for nothing that Confucius told his disciples that the three hundred and five songs of the Song-word Scripture could be boiled down to the commandment: "Have no twisty thoughts." You cannot have twisty thoughts if you are real and if you are thinking about real things. But if a mother is merely a biological event to you and if you yourself are merely a military event called an admiral, anything may happen: you may make your country ridiculous, humiliate a promising boy, and deprive the navy of a good officer, all in the twisted belief that you are being a wise man and a patriot.

One can see, not only in the three hundred and five songs, but in Chinese poetry of other periods, what Confucius meant. Consider two Chinese poems of the second century B.C. and the sixth of our era, both written by emperors. The first is a poem of grief—of the sense of loss of someone loved: a poem therefore of that inward world of feeling, of emotion, which seems to us most nearly ourselves and which, because it is always in flux, always shifting and changing and flowing away, is, of all parts of our experience of our lives, most difficult to know. We cannot know it through science. We cannot know it by knowing things *about* it—even the shrewdest and most intelligent things, helpful though they may be to us in other ways. We cannot know it either by merely feeling it—by uttering its passing urgencies, crying out "I love" meaning "I think of myself as loving" or sobbing "I grieve" meaning "I think of myself as grieving." How then can we know it?

The Emperor Wu-ti wrote (this is Arthur Waley's beautiful translation):

> The sound of her silk skirt has stopped.
> On the marble pavement dust grows.
> Her empty room is cold and still.
> Fallen leaves are piled against the doors.
>
> Longing for that lovely lady
> How can I bring my aching heart to rest?

Four images, one of sound, two of sight, one of feeling, each like a note plucked on a stringed instrument. Then a question like the chord the four would make together. And all at once we *know*. We know this grief which no word could have described, which any abstraction the mind is capable of would have destroyed. But we know more than this grief: we know our own—or will when it shall visit us—and so know something of ourselves.

The second is a poem of that emotion, that feeling, which is even more difficult to know than grief itself. The second is a poem of delight: youth and delight—the morning of the world—the emotion, of all emotions, most difficult to stop, to hold, to see. "Joy whose hand is ever at his lips bidding adieu." How would you *know* delight in yourself and therefore yourself delighting? Will the psychiatrists tell you? Is there a definition somewhere in the folios of abstraction by which we attempt to live which will capture it for you? The Emperor Ch'ien Wen-ti (again Waley's translation) knew that there is only one mirror which will hold that vanishing smile—the mirror of art, the mirror of the poem:

> A beautiful place is the town of Lo-yang:
> The big streets are full of spring light
> The lads go driving out with harps in their hands:
> The mulberry girls go out to the fields with their baskets
> Golden whips glint at the horses' flanks,
> Gauze sleeves brush the green boughs.
> Racing dawn the carriages come home—
> And the girls with their high baskets full of fruit.

In this world within, you see, this world which is ourselves, there is no possibility of knowing by abstracting the meaning out—or what we hope will be the meaning. There we must know things *as* themselves and it must be *we* who know them. Only art, only poetry, can bring about that confrontation, because only art, only poetry, can show us what we are and ourselves confronting it. To be ignorant of poetry is to be ignorant therefore of the one means of reaching the world of our experience of the world. And to be ignorant of *that* world is to be ignorant of who and what we are. And to be ignorant of who and what we are is to be incapable of reality no matter what tools we have, or what intelligence, or what skills. It is this incapacity, this impotence, which is the tragedy of the time we live in. We are spiritually impotent because we have cut ourselves off from the poem. And the crowning irony is that it is only in the poem that we can know how impotent we have become.

Why do we teach poetry in this scientific age? To present the great alternative not to science but to that knowledge by abstraction which science has imposed. And what is this great alternative? Not the "messages" of poems, their interpreted "meanings," for these are abstractions also—abstractions far inferior to those of science. Not the explications of poetic texts, for the explication of a poetic text which goes no farther ends only in abstraction.

No, the great alternative is the poem as itself, the poem as a poem, the poem as a work of art—which is to say, the poem in the context in which alone the work of art exists: the context of the world, of the man and of the thing, of the infinite relationship which is our lives. To present the great alternative is to present the poem not as a message in a bottle, and not as an object in an uninhabited landscape, but as an action in the world, an action in which we ourselves are actors and our lives are known.

### SUGGESTIONS FOR WRITING

1. Archibald MacLeish, about whom comment was made on p. 66, won the Pulitzer Prize for Poetry in 1933 and in 1953. He suggests here that poetry has special qualifications for being an effective agent to satisfactory knowledge. In other words, MacLeish says that poetry is a good way of knowing. What are the special qualifications? Choose a poem and indicate what it helps you to "know" and what characteristics and specific items in the poem led you to this "knowing."
2. MacLeish mentions the dominance of science today. Write the dialogue of a fictional encounter between a science major and a non-science major. What has science to offer? What has poetry to offer?
3. Archibald MacLeish has written, "A poem should not mean, but be." In the previous selection you were asked to apply that statement to John Ciardi's analytical method. Do you have a different feeling about the statement after reading MacLeish's article?
4. With which quotation at the beginning of this section would MacLeish most closely agree? disagree?

DYLAN THOMAS

## A Few Words of a Kind*

I am going to read aloud from the works of some modern British poets, and also read a few poems of my own. My own ones include some early ones, some fairly hurly-burly ones, very recent ones, reasoned, decent ones, lamenting ones and lamentable ones, together with a few comments whenever they may or may not be necessary.

I wondered what kind of words I should put down to introduce these laboriously churning poems of mine. Indeed, I thought, they want from me no introduction at all. Let them stand on their own feet, the little lyrical cripples. But I felt, too, that there must be

---

* From *Mademoiselle* (July, 1956). © 1956 by Street and Smith Publications, Inc. Reprinted by permission of Harold Ober Associates Incorporated.

a few words of a kind before or between the ranting of the poems. A whole hour of loud and unrelieved verse-speaking is, I imagine, hell to anyone except some brash antiseptic forty-two-toothed smilingly ardent young hunters of culture with net, notebook, poison bottle, pin and label, or to the dowager hunters of small seedy lions, stalking the metropolitan bush with legs and rifles cocked, or to the infernal androgynous literary ladies with three names who produce a kind of verbal ectoplasm to order as a waiter dishes up spaghetti. But to an ordinary audience—not that there's any such thing but only, like yourselves, bunches of eccentrics—there must be a hush between poems. And how was I going to fill that hush with harmless words until the next poem came woodenly booming along like a carved bee?

I couldn't, I knew, say much if anything about what the poems might mean. In a few cases, of course, I didn't anyway know myself —though that is true, I hope, only of certain of my earliest published poems, explosive bloodbursts of a boily boy in love with the shape and sound of words, death, unknown love and the shadows on his pillow. And for the rest of the poems, they are what they mean, however obscure, unsuccessful, sentimental, pretentious, ludicrous, rhetorical, wretched, ecstatic, plain bad. Or could I shove in autobiographical snippets saying where I lived and how, when I wrote this or that, indicating how I felt in heart and head at that particular time?

I could, for instance, talk about my education, which critics say I have not got. And that's true enough. But I do wish I had learned some other languages apart from English, BBC Third Program, and saloon. Then perhaps I could understand what some people mean when they say I have been influenced by Rimbaud.

My education was the liberty I had to read indiscriminately and all the time, with my eyes hanging out. I never could have dreamed there were such goings-on, such do's and argie-bargies, such ice blasts of words, such love and sense and terror and humbug, such and so many blinding bright lights breaking across the just awaking wits and splashing all over the pages, as they can never quite do again after the first revelation. In a million bits and pieces, all of which were words, words, words, and each of which seemed alive forever in its own delight and glory and right.

It was then, in my father's brown study before homework, usually the first botched scribblings of gauche and gawky heartchoked poems about black-bloomered nymphs, the jussive grave and the tall, improbable loves of the sardine-packed sky, poems never to be shown to anyone except on pain of death, that I began to know one kind of writing from another, one kind of badness, one kind of goodness. I wrote endless imitations, though I never at the time of writing thought them to be imitations but rather colossally original, things unheard of, like eggs laid by tigers, imitations of whatever I happened to be golloping then, Thomas Browne, Robert W. Service, Stevenson, De Quincey, Eskimo Nell, Newbolt, Blake, Marlowe, the Imagists, the boy's own paper, Keats, Poe, Burns, Dostoevsky, Anon. and Shakespeare. I tried my little trotters at every poetical form. How could I know the tricks of this trade unless I tried to do them myself? For the poets wouldn't soar from the grave and show me how their poems were done by mirrors, and I couldn't trust the critics then—or now. I learned that the bad tricks come easy and the good tricks, which help you to say what you think you wish to say in the most meaningful, moving way, naturally I am still learning—though in earnest company I must call these tricks by other, technical names. Nothing in those days was too much for me to try. If *Paradise Lost* had not already been written, I would have had a shot at it.

My early days, dear God! I never thought that one day I might be here or anywhere filling up time before, I'm afraid, a drone of poems by talking about my early days, just as though I were a man of letters. I used to think that once a writer became a man of letters, if only for ten minutes, he was done for. But I feel all right. I suppose I am suffering from one of the first pleasant injections of insidious corruption. "My early days" seems to me to suggest that I am responsible and established, that all the old doubts and worries are over. Now I need bother my head about nothing except birth, death, sex, money, politics and religion, that, jowled and wigged, aloof and branded as a bloodhound, sober as a judge in my bit of vermin, I can summon my juvenile literary delinquence before me and give it a long periodic sentence. For me to think of prefacing my poems by talking about my early days is to invite myself to indulge myself with a hundred tongue-picked, chopped and chiseled evocative shock phrases in a flamboyant rememoration of past and almost entirely fictitious peccadilloes of interest to nobody but me

and my guardian angel, who was, I believe, an unsuccessful psy-
choanalyist in this life and who is lolloping above me now, casebook in claw, a little seedy and down at wing and heel, in the gut-
tural consulting room of space. I am the kind of human dredger
that digs up the wordy mud of his own Dead Sea, a kind of pig that
roots for unconsidered truffles in the reeky wood of his past.

But still I gladly accept the fact that I first saw the light and
screamed at it in a loud lump of Wales. I'm only human, as the
man says who deep inside him refuses to believe it, and of course
my writing would not be what it is—always experimental and always completely unsatisfactory—if it had not been for the immortal
fry of the town in which I simmered up. Naturally, my early poems
and stories, two sides of an unresolved argument, came out of a
person who came willy-nilly out of one particular atmosphere and
environment, and are part and parcel, park and castle, lark and sea
shell, dark and school bell, muck and entrail, cock, rock and bub-
ble, accent and sea lap, root and rhythm of them. And that, so far as
I am concerned, is all there is to it. If I had been born and brought
up in an igloo and lived on whales, not in it, about the same would
be true, except that then it would have been extremely unlikely had
I become a writer. And "Goody!" cry my justified detractors.

Or I could preface this small reading by talking about poets. I
think they're pretty dull. It's a common failing to underestimate
the sheer ordinariness of the lives and characters of many dead
poets, and to overestimate that of living poets whom one might
come across. Indeed it is not unusual for people, after they have
met a more or less living poet, to wonder with hardly concealed
amazement how he could ever have produced the work he has. I
except certain oldish poets alive today who are made solemn and
unapproachable, not so much by their poetry or their strict religious
observance as by their judicial positions on the boards of eminent
publishers who may even then at one's time of meeting, be considering one's own first experimental novel of innocence lost and wisdom
catastrophically gained by the age of nineteen. The same kind of
amazement, the idol destroyed ("How *could* such a man have written such marvelous devotional poetry, I saw him fall downstairs
yesterday in his suspenders!"), might well have occurred to us had
we met many of the poets now dead. I think it was Logan Pearsall
Smith who remembered how, as a small boy, he saw of all people

Matthew Arnold in a restaurant, and Matthew Arnold talked and laughed much too loud.

I couldn't talk about poets, but I do wish that I was reading only the work of other modern poets now, and not my own at all. That is, I wish I were reading the work of modern poets I like, for I like to read only the poets I like. This means, of course, that I have to read a lot of poems I don't like before I find the ones I do, but when I do find the ones I do, then all I can say is, "Here they are," and read them aloud to myself or to anyone, like yourselves, voluntarily cornered. And when I read aloud the poems of modern poets I like very much, I try to make them alive from inside. I try to get across what I feel, however wrongly, to be the original impetus of the poem. I am a practicing interpreter, however much of a flannel-tongued one-night-stander.

But in my own poems I've had my say, and when I read them aloud I can only repeat it. When I read, for instance, my earliest poems aloud, my interpretation of them—though that's far too weighty a word just for reading them aloud—can't be considered as the final or original interpretation, performance or blare. I do not remember now the first impulse that pumped and drove those lines along, and that which is in them is for you more than for me, for you or for anyone, or of course for no one, to make what you or he will of them. In these poems I've had my say; now I'm only saying it again.

But what does it matter? Poetry is what in a poem makes you laugh, cry, prickle, be silent, makes your toenails twinkle, makes you want to do this or that or nothing, makes you know that you are alone and not alone in the unknown world, that your bliss and suffering is forever shared and forever all your own. All that matters about poetry is the enjoyment of it, however tragic it may be. All that matters is the eternal movement behind it, the great undercurrent of human grief, folly, pretension, exultation, and ignorance, however unlofty the intention of the poem.

Now I'm going to read some poems straight, without hindrance, for this isn't a lecture at all. It isn't about trends and impacts and the influence of someone on someone else. It isn't trying to prove anything by quotations, to groove one hypothetical school of poetry oilily into another, to jigsaw all the pieces that are poems into one improbable picture and then say, "Here it is, this is modern poetry." I am no gray and tepid don smelling of water biscuits. Only posterity can see the picture of the poetry of today as a whole, and the function of posterity is to look after itself. You can tear a poem apart to see what makes it technically tick, and say to yourself when the works are laid out before you, the vowels, the consonants, the rhymes and rhythms, Yes, this is it, this is why the poem moves me so. It is because of the craftsmanship. But you're back again where you began. The best craftsmanship always leaves holes and gaps in the works of the poem so that something that is not in the poem can creep, crawl, flash or thunder in. "Everything," Yeats said, though he was talking of the highest moments of the most exalted art, "everything happens in a blaze of light." Only the printed page or the interior monologue or the private discussion can give to each separate poem the full concentrated time that the poem is justified in asking for the assessment of its success or failure to demonstrate its own hypothesis. In public all I think that can be presented is the poem itself, and all that can be experienced in public is the realization of the immediacy or lack of immediacy through which the hypothesis, the central motive of the poem, affects the reader through his ear. The printed page is the place in which to examine the works of a poem, and the platform the place on which to give the poem the works.

You won't ask me any questions afterward, will you? I don't mind answering a bit, only I can't. Even to such simple questions as, "What is the relationship of the poet to society in a hydrogenous age?" I can only cough and stammer. And some of the questions I remember from the nightmare past—"Tell me, are the young English intellectuals really psychological?" "Is it absolutely essential, do you think, to be homosexual to write love poems to women?" "I always carry Kierkegaard in my pocket. What do you carry?"

SUGGESTIONS FOR WRITING

1. Dylan Thomas (1914-1953) was born in the Welsh seaport of Swansea. His formal education ended with the Swansea Grammar school; thereafter he was at various times a newspaper reporter, a hack writer, an odd-job man, and a documentary film scriptwriter. He visited the United States in 1950, 1952, and 1953. "I don't believe in New York," he said, "but I love Third Avenue." He used this essay to describe his feelings

when he gave a public performance reading his own poetry. He pretends that he needed something to fill the hush between poems, and he begins to talk about himself and his "early days." Finally, he defines poetry as something that "makes you know that you are alone and not alone in the unknown world, that your bliss and suffering is forever shared and forever all your own." Write an essay indicating the feelings and thoughts that come over you when you find a poem you like.

2. What does Thomas mean by the statement: "The best craftsmanship always leaves holes and gaps in the works of the poem so that something that is not in the poem can creep, crawl, flash or thunder in"? Illustrate his meaning by describing Frost's "Stopping By Woods on a Snowy Evening" (p. 299) or one of the other poems in this book.

3. Even without the reading of poetry, the preface itself is quite a performance. What kind of man was Dylan Thomas? There is abundant internal evidence here. Write as complete a portrait as possible, using only the clues in the above article. Who was he? What did he think about different subjects? How did he see himself? How did he think others saw him? Examine the evidence carefully, take notes, and write.

T. S. ELIOT

## Poetry Is a Superior Amusement*

Poetry is a superior amusement: I do not mean an amusement for superior people. I call it an amusement, an amusement *pour distraire les honnêtes gens,* not because that is a true definition, but because if you call it anything else you are likely to call it something still more false. If we think of the nature of amusement, then poetry is not amusing; but if we think of anything else that poetry may seem to be, we are led into far greater difficulties. Our definition of the use of one kind of poetry may not exhaust its uses; and will probably not apply to some other kinds; or if our definition applies to all poetry, it becomes so general as to be meaningless: It will not do to talk of "emotion recollected in tranquillity," which is only one poet's account of his recollection of his own methods; or to call it a "criticism of life," than which no phrase can sound more

---

* From *The Sacred Wood* by T. S. Eliot (London: Methuen and Co., Ltd., 1932). Copyright 1928 by Methuen and Co., Ltd., London. Reprinted by permission of the publishers. This material is from the Preface and the essay on Dante.

frigid to anyone who has felt the full surprise and elevation of a new experience of poetry. And certainly poetry is not the inculcation of morals, or the direction of politics; and no more is it religion or an equivalent of religion, except by some monstrous abuse of words. And certainly poetry is something over and above, and something quite different from, a collection of psychological data about the minds of poets, or about the history of an epoch; for we could not take it even as that unless we had already assigned to it a value merely as poetry.

Hence, in criticizing poetry, we are right if we begin, with what sensibility and what knowledge of other poetry we possess, with poetry as excellent words in excellent arrangement and excellent metre. That is what is called the technique of verse. But we observe that we cannot define even the technique of verse; we cannot say at what point "technique" begins or where it ends; and if we add to it a "technique of feeling," that glib phrase will carry us but little farther. We can only say that a poem, in some sense, has its own life; that its parts form something quite different from a body of neatly ordered biographical data; that the feeling, or emotion, or vision, resulting from the poem is something different from the feeling or emotion or vision in the mind of the poet.

On the other hand, poetry as certainly has something to do with morals, and with religion, and even with politics perhaps, though we cannot say what. If I ask myself (to take a comparison on a higher plane) why I prefer the poetry of Dante to that of Shakespeare, I should have to say, because it seems to me to illustrate a saner attitude towards the mystery of life. And in these questions, and others which we cannot avoid, we appear already to be leaving the domain of criticism of "poetry." So we cannot stop at any point. The best that we can hope to do is to agree upon a point from which to start, and that is, in part, the subject of this book. . . .

\*          \*          \*          \*

Dante's is the most comprehensive, and the most *ordered* presentation of emotions that has ever been made. Dante's method of dealing with any emotion may be contrasted, not so appositely with that of other "epic" poets as with that of Shakespeare. Shakespeare takes a character apparently controlled by a simple emotion, and analyses the character and the emotion itself. The emotion is split up into constituents—and perhaps destroyed in the process. The mind of Shakespeare was one of the most critical that has ever existed. Dante, on the other hand, does not analyse the emotion so much as he exhibits its relation to other emotions. You cannot, that is, understand the *Inferno* without the *Purgatorio* and the *Paradiso*. "Dante," says Landor's Petrarch, "is the great master of the disgusting." That is true, though Sophocles at least once approaches him. But a disgust like Dante's is no hypertrophy of a single reaction: it is completed and explained only by the last canto of the *Paradiso*.

> La forma universal di questo nodo,
>   credo ch'io vidi, perché più di'largo
>   dicendo questo, mi sento ch'io godo.

The contemplation of the horrid or sordid or disgusting, by an artist, is the necessary and negative aspect of the impulse toward the pursuit of beauty. But not all succeed as did Dante in expressing the complete scale from negative to positive. The negative is the more importunate. . . .

We are not here studying philosophy, we *see* it, as part of the ordered world. The aim of the poet is to state a vision, and no vision of life can be complete which does not include the articulate formulation of life which human minds make.

> Onde convenne legge per fren porre . . .

It is one of the greatest merits of Dante's poem that the vision is so nearly complete; it is evidence of this greatness that the significance of any single passage, of any of the passages that are selected as "poetry," is incomplete unless we ourselves apprehend the whole. . . .

The mystical experience is supposed to be valuable because it is a pleasant state of unique intensity. But the true mystic is not satisfied merely by feeling, he must pretend at least that he *sees,* and the absorption into the divine is only the necessary, if paradoxical, limit of this contemplation. The poet does not aim to excite—that is not even a test of his success—but to set something down; the state of the reader is merely that reader's particular mode of perceiving what the poet has caught in words. Dante, more than any other poet, has succeeded to dealing with his philosophy, not as a theory (in the modern and not the **Greek** sense of that word) or as something *per ceived*. When most of our modern poets confine themselves to what they had perceived, they produce for us, usually, only odds and ends of still life and stage properties; but that does not imply so much that the method of Dante is obsolete, as that our vision is perhaps comparatively restricted.

### SUGGESTIONS FOR WRITING

1. T. S. Eliot (1888-    ) is an American poet, critic, and essayist living in England. He received the Nobel Prize for Literature in 1948. Here he is represented by selections from two separate essays (divided by a line of asterisks). The first is taken from the preface, the second from an essay on Dante. In the first, he tells what poetry is (or is not); in the second, he illustrates what poetry is by discussing the qualities of Dante's poetry. Compare T. S. Eliot's definition with those at the beginning of this section and with Aiken's (page 324).

2. Each statement Eliot makes about poetry raises questions in his mind, until he says "we cannot stop at any point." Does this mean he believes poetry cannot be adequately defined? If so, why does he call poetry a superior amusement?

3. Why does Eliot prefer Dante's poetry?

4. Most students have read Eliot's "The Love Song of J. Alfred Prufrock." Compare the "vision of life" in that poem with Eliot's final statement here: "Modern poets . . . produce for us, usually, only odds and ends of still life and stage properties."

5. Eliot tries to define poetry by telling us chiefly what it is not. While it is possible to poke fun at such a method, it is also possible to see its serious advantages. Write a composition in which you define something by stating chiefly what it is not.

CONRAD AIKEN

## Poetry Is Excellence of Statement*

American poetry has been extensively anthologized; but so far as I am aware there has been no attempt hitherto to present in one

---

* From *A Comprehensive Anthology of American Poetry* edited by Conrad Aiken (New York: Random House, Inc., 1929). Copyright 1929, 1945 by Random House, Inc. Reprinted by permission of the publishers.

volume a selection which shall represent the whole range of it, from its beginnings down to the present day. In a few textbooks, it is true, one may find, along with prose selections also, a fairly adequate survey. But for some curious reason the notion of a compact, and comprehensive anthology of the verse alone has not found expression. That such a thing should be useful goes without saying. That it should be difficult is obvious, too—almost as obvious as that the editor who undertakes it will inevitably make mistakes in judgment and will inevitably be reproached for them. At the very outset he faces the formidable question of proportion. How much space shall he give to "early" American poetry—the poetry of the seventeenth and eighteenth centuries? How much, in this regard, shall he allow himself to be weighed upon by purely historical considerations? Should the Connecticut wits—for example—be represented, simply on the ground that they existed, and that they enjoyed for a time a kind of popularity? Or should he frankly admit to himself that their work was almost wholly without aesthetic value, and ruthlessly exclude them?

The present editor has felt that the aesthetic judgment (whatever that may be, and however we may define it) is the only sound basis for procedure; and if now and then he has momentarily compromised with this principle, admitting here and there a poem merely because it has achieved an immense popularity, he has, on the whole, done this reluctantly and seldom. American poetry, if one takes it as a whole, is not yet a great or rich poetry, though it has shown not infrequently the elements of greatness and richness; it has been provincial, uneven, tentative, brilliant; but if one cannot as yet say that it takes a very high place in the poetry of the world, as the expression of a national soul or culture, one can at least say emphatically that the time has come for a firm revision of our critical attitude toward it. We are too much accustomed, I fear, to what one might term a high protective tariff in this matter. We are a little too willing to suspend or modify judgment, on the ground that too much was not to be expected of a pioneer people in a new continent. Insensibly, we have got into the habit of accepting the second-best; and by closing our eyes to the best—by which I mean the best poetry of the world—have found it not too difficult to persuade ourselves of the excellence of the native product.

It is time, I think, to give up this rather childish habit, and to regard American poetry as severely as we would regard Greek or Chinese or English poetry. For if American poetry is not yet great, it has at least reached that point at which one may say that it is mature. It has a history of nearly three hundred years. In sheer quantity, if one keeps in mind all the minor poets and poetasters of the eighteenth and nineteenth centuries, it is enormous—few people, unless we except librarians, can have any idea of it. And if we admit cheerfully enough that the first two-thirds of its history is pretty barren, nevertheless one can also say with some assurance that it now comprises names of which no country need be ashamed, and that it is beginning to wear the dignity that goes with a tradition.

In view of this, it has been the present editor's intention to be somewhat severer with his material than his predecessors have been, in order that the process of clarification of this tradition might take a step forward. He has been rather hard on certain national favorites; it will be thought by some that he has been too drastic with Longfellow [five selections] * and Holmes [one selection—"The Last Leaf"] * and Whittier [three selections] * and Lowell [three selections] * and Lanier [two selections],* and that he has been too generous with Poe [eighteen] * and Whitman [nine] * and Dickinson [twenty-four] *; and that he has perhaps erred in proportion by giving to the poetry of the last twenty years so much more space than has been given to that of any preceding era. To such an objection he can only reply that in his opinion the poetry which begins roughly, with Emily Dickinson has been the richest which America has produced; and that our so-called classics have been very seriously overestimated. If he can disturb prevailing notions about these things, and set in motion a revaluation of American poetry, which will find perhaps a higher place for comparatively unknown poets like Anne Bradstreet or Thomas Chivers or Trumbull Stickney than for Longfellow or Lowell or Bryant—not, be it understood, in point of range, but in point of sheer excellence or intensity—he will consider that he has been of some small service to American criticism. He has tried to eliminate, as far as possible, those things which embody the faults which so cursed American poetry in the nineteenth century—excessive sentimentality, senten-

---

* Brackets added by editor.

tiousness, easy dactylic exoticism—in order that the present movement in American poetry toward severer outline, both in idea and
expression, might be more visible. If he has at all succeeded in this,
he will have made one degree easier the ultimate compilation of a
first-rate anthology by his successors.

Fifteen years have passed since this anthology was first published
—almost a literary generation; but in now revising and amplifying
it, and bringing it up to date, I have cast back even further than
that. Perspective changes; the critic's eye changes; poetry changes
too. One finds that one had too much of X, too little of Y, none at
all of Z—nor is it even as simple as that. For there arises also the
question of the relation of X with Y, and then, further, the relation
of each with the whole mass and current of his day. One's own
view of the mass and current, meanwhile, has been imperceptibly
changing with the changing times; the shadows and lights fall now
in other places; what seemed formerly only a tendency, and of the
vaguest and most tentative at that, now reveals itself as a quite
definite and accomplished direction; what formerly seemed to be
a direction has now become vestigal, stopped off: one of Nature's
little experiments which, alas, has failed.

But in adding (and to a very small extent subtracting) I believe
I have only sharpened, not changed the character of the book.
The aim, as before, has been to be rid of excess baggage, particularly of the more sentimental sort, even if (such are one's bad habits)
one cannot hope to be wholly successful. I have been blamed
by some anthologists for being too "abstract" in my taste; if by
this it is meant that I have tried to avoid the petty, on the one
hand, or the oratorical and politically tendentious, on the other, I
take it as a compliment. Sentiment, whether it is for privileged
classes, or for the flowers that bloom in the spring, can never excuse
inadequacy of statement. For if poetry can very nearly do without
meaning (witness the miracles of nonsense verse) it plainly cannot
do without excellence of statement. The "greatness" of a poet will,
of course, in the end, always depend, and precisely, on his range
and richness of meaning: do we perceive him as an island, a penin-
sula, a continent? But without that *first* prerequisite of poetry,
clarity and excellence of statement, he will never have been perceived by us at all, even as an islet.

It remains to add that every anthology, and this is no exception, is a collaboration, a collaboration between the anthologist, the poets and the public. It is also, however, a collaboration in experiment. Which way will taste go? Which way will poetry go? Will these yellows keep their luminosity, the reds turn gray? Even now new poets are working at this, competitively, and for survival; new ideas and fashions are competing too, if more bloodlessly, for a share in the evolving consciousness of man. The anthologist is an interpreter in all this, with perhaps a *little,* just a little, unconscious *parti pris;* and the public, the public awareness, itself grinding out its own conflicting complex of wants and fears, is the slow-working arbiter and perpetuator. The whole fascinating confusion, with its involved differentials, is simply a process of communal growing. . . . And no doubt, in another twenty years, we shall know into what.

SUGGESTIONS FOR WRITING

1. Conrad Aiken (1889-      ) is an American poet, critic, and novelist. He is introducing an anthology of poetry and justifying his choices. He reveals himself as a man sensitive to the meanings of words and the necessity of qualifying—constantly balancing and refining meanings. Perhaps he is too careful. He almost seems to be backing his anthology into a very tight parking space. What gives this piece its special tone? Analyze the first sentence carefully and reconstruct it so that it avoids its present tone.

2. The sentence structure, "If it is not X, at least it is Y," has been criticized as too pedantic. Cite two or three instances of Aiken's use of this structure and reveal what lies at the root of the criticism.

3. "Poetry is . . ." Compare Aiken's definition with those listed in the quotations at the beginning of this section. Formulate your own definition after discussing some of the others.

4. What is the relation between "clarity and excellence of statement" and "range and richness of meaning"? Aiken argues that the two qualities are compatible. Can you cite any poetry where they are not, e.g., where a deliberate ambiguity (preventing clarity of statement) fosters richness of meaning?

5. A typical college student lacks the experience to make judgments about what should go into an anthology of American poetry. What experience is necessary for this task? Must one be a poet? If a student cannot judge the *range* of poetry to be represented, he can at least judge single poems. Why?

# Literature

Three questions are essential to all just criticism: What is the author's object? How far has he accomplished it? How far is that object worthy of approbation?
—N. P. Willis, Preface to *Pencillings by the Way*, 1835

People take England on trust, and repeat that Shakespeare is the greatest of all authors. I have read him: there is nothing that compares with Racine or Corneille: his plays are unreadable, pitiful.
—Napoleon Bonaparte, *On St. Helena*, 1821

I am bound by my own definition of criticism: a disinterested endeavor to learn and propagate the best that is known and thought in the world.
—Matthew Arnold, *Functions of Criticism at the Present Time*, 1865

To criticise is to appreciate, to appropriate, to take intellectual possession, to establish in fine a relation with the criticised thing and make it one's own.
—Henry James, Preface to *Spoils of Poynton*, 1907

The artist, like the God of the creation, remains within or behind or beyond or above his handiwork, invisible, refined out of existence, indifferent, paring his fingernails.
—James Joyce, *Portrait of the Artist as a Young Man*, 1916

A man ought to read just as inclination leads him; for what he reads as a task will do him little good. A young man should read five hours in a day, and so may acquire a great deal of knowledge.
—Samuel Johnson, Boswell's *Life of Dr. Johnson*, 1791

Literature is a kind of intellectual light which, like the light of the sun, may sometimes enable us to see what we do not like.
—Samuel Johnson, *A Project for the Employment of Authors*, 1756

The difference between literature and journalism is that journalism is unreadable, and literature is not read.
—Oscar Wilde, *The Critic as Artist*, 1891

RALPH WALDO EMERSON

# Company of the Wisest Men*

It is easy to accuse books, and bad ones are easily found; and the best are but records, and not the things recorded; and certainly there is dilettantism enough, and books that are merely neutral and do nothing for us. In Plato's *Gorgias*, Socrates says: "The ship-master walks in a modest garb near the sea, after bringing his passengers from Ægina or from Pontus, not thinking he has done anything extraordinary, and certainly knowing that his passengers are the same, and in no respect better than when he took them on board." So is it with books, for the most part—they work no redemption in us. The bookseller might certainly know that his customers are in no respect better for the purchase and consumption of his wares. The volume is dear at a dollar, and, after reading to weariness the lettered backs, we leave the shop with a sigh, and learn, as I did, without surprise, of a surly bank director, that in bank parlors they estimate all stocks of this kind as rubbish.

But it is not less true that there are books which are of that importance in a man's private experience, as to verify for him the fables of Cornelius Agrippa, of Michael Scott, or of the old Orpheus of Thrace,—books which take rank in our life with parents and lovers and passionate experiences, so medicinal, so stringent, so revolutionary, so authoritative—books which are the work and the proof of faculties so comprehensive, so nearly equal to the world which they paint, that, though one shuts them with meaner ones, he feels his exclusion from them to accuse his way of living.

Consider what you have in the smallest chosen library. A company of the wisest and wittiest men that could be picked out of all

* From *Society and Solitude,* 1870.

civil countries, in a thousand years, have set in best order the results
of their learning and wisdom. The men themselves were hid and
inaccessible, solitary, impatient of interruption, fenced by etiquette;
but the thought which they did not uncover to their bosom friend
is here written out in transparent words to us, the strangers of another age.

We owe to books those general benefits which come from high
intellectual action. Thus, I think, we often owe to them the perception of immortality. They impart sympathetic activity to the moral
power. Go with mean people, and you think life is mean. Then read
Plutarch, and the world is a proud place, peopled with men of
positive quality, with heroes and demigods standing around us, who
will not let us sleep. Then, they address the imagination—only
poetry inspires poetry. They become the organic culture of the
time. College education is the reading of certain books which the
common sense of all scholars agrees will represent the science already accumulated. If you know that—for instance in geometry, if
you have read Euclid and Laplace—your opinion has some value;
if you do not know these, you are not entitled to give any opinion
on the subject. Whenever any sceptic or bigot claims to be heard
on the questions of intellect and morals, we ask if he is familiar
with the books of Plato, where all his pert objections have once for
all been disposed of. If not, he has no right to our time. Let him go
and find himself answered there.

Meantime the colleges, whilst they provide us with libraries,
furnish no professor of books; and, I think, no chair is so much
wanted. In a library we are surrounded by many hundreds of dear
friends, but they are imprisoned by an enchanter in these paper and
leathern boxes; and, though they know us, and have been waiting
two, ten, or twenty centuries for us—some of them—and are eager
to give us a sign, and unbosom themselves, it is the law of their
limbo that they must not speak until spoken to; and as the enchanter has dressed them, like battalions of infantry, in coat and
jacket of one cut, by the thousand and ten thousand, your chance
of hitting on the right one is to be computed by the arithmetical
rule of Permutation and Combination—not a choice out of three
caskets, but out of half a million caskets all alike. But it happens
in our experience, that in this lottery there are at least fifty or a
hundred blanks to a prize. It seems, then, as if some charitable soul,

after losing a great deal of time among the false books, and alighting upon a few true ones which made him happy and wise, would do a right act in naming those which have been bridges or ships to carry him safely over dark morasses and barren oceans, into the heart of sacred cities, into palaces and temples. This would be best done by those great masters of books who from time to time appear —the Fabricii, the Seldens, Magliabecchis, Scaligers, Mirandolas, Bayles, Johnsons, whose eyes sweep the whole horizon of learning. But private readers, reading purely for love of the book, would serve us by leaving each the shortest note of what he found.

There are books; and it is practicable to read them, because they are so few. We look over with a sigh the monumental libraries of Paris, of the Vatican, and the British Museum. In 1858, the number of printed books in the Imperial Library at Paris was estimated at eight hundred thousand volumes, with an annual increase of twelve thousand volumes; so that the number of printed books extant today may easily exceed a million. It is easy to count the number of pages which a diligent man can read in a day, and the number of years which human life in favorable circumstances allows to reading; and to demonstrate that, though he should read from dawn till dark, for sixty years, he must die in the first alcoves. But nothing can be more deceptive than this arithmetic, where none but a natural method is really pertinent. I visit occasionally the Cambridge Library, and I can seldom go there without renewing the conviction that the best of it all is already within the four walls of my study at home. The inspection of the catalogue brings me continually back to the few standard writers who are on every private shelf; and to these it can afford only the most slight and casual additions. The crowds and centuries of books are only commentary and elucidation, echoes and weakeners of these few great voices of Time.

The best rule of reading will be a method from nature, and not a mechanical one of hours and pages. It holds each student to a pursuit of his native aim, instead of a desultory miscellany. Let him read what is proper to him, and not waste his memory on a crowd of mediocrities. As whole nations have derived their culture from a single book—as the Bible has been the literature as well as the religion of large portions of Europe—as Hafiz was the eminent genius of the Persians, Confucius of the Chinese, Cervantes of the

Spaniards; so, perhaps, the human mind would be a gainer, if all
the secondary writers were lost—say, in England, all but Shakespeare, Milton, and Bacon—through the profounder study so drawn
to those wonderful minds. With this pilot of his own genius, let the
student read one, or let him read many, he will read advantageously.
Dr. Johnson said: "Whilst you stand deliberating which book your
son shall read first, another boy has read both: read anything five
hours a day, and you will soon be learned."

Nature is much our friend in this matter. Nature is always clari-
fying her water and her wine. No filtration can be so perfect. She
does the same thing by books as by her gases and plants. There is
always a selection in writers, and then a selection from the selection. In the first place, all books that get fairly into the vital air of
the world were written by the successful class, by the affirming and
advancing class, who utter what tens of thousands feel though they
cannot say. There has already been a scrutiny and choice from
many hundreds of young pens, before the pamphlet or political
chapter which you read in a fugitive journal comes to your eye. All
these are young adventurers, who produce their performance to
the wise ear of Time, who sits and weighs, and, ten years hence, out
of a million of pages reprints one. Again it is judged, it is win-
nowed by all the winds of opinion, and what terrific selection has
not passed on it before it can be reprinted after twenty years—and
reprinted after a century!—it is as if Minos and Rhadamanthus
had indorsed the writing. 'T is therefore an economy of time to
read old and famed books. Nothing can be preserved which is not
good, and I know beforehand that Pindar, Martial, Terence, Galen,
Kepler, Galileo, Bacon, Erasmus, More, will be superior to the
average intellect. In contemporaries, it is not so easy to distinguish
betwixt notoriety and fame.

Be sure, then, to read no mean books. Shun the spawn of the
press on the gossip of the hour. Do not read what you shall learn,
without asking, in the street and the train. Dr. Johnson said, "he
always went into stately shops"; and good travellers stop at the best
hotels; for, though they cost more, they do not cost much more, and
there is the good company and the best information. In like manner, the scholar knows that the famed books contain, first and last,
the best thoughts and facts. Now and then, by rarest luck, in some
foolish Grub Street is the gem we want. But in the best circles is

the best information. If you should transfer the amount of your reading day by day from the newspaper to the standard authors— but who dare speak of such a thing?

## SUGGESTIONS FOR WRITING

1. Emerson (1803-1882) is best known for his essays on ideals which are essentially American. In many of his essays, however, he ranged freely beyond American shores into the universal realms of the mind. His style is interesting and flinty—sometimes the steel of the mind strikes the flint and produces sparks and flashes, sometimes only the thud of steel on stone. Examine his style by using the second paragraph as a pattern for something you wish to say. Substitute the word "teachers" for "books" in the first sentence and continue to make substitutions where necessary in order that the subject of the paragraph will be teachers.

2. What book has been the most important to your "private experience"? Describe it and its effect on you.

3. "College education is the reading of certain books which the common sense of all scholars agrees will represent the science already accumulated." Make a list of at least twenty-five books you think should be part of a college education. Indicate after each title why it should be on your list.

4. In the fifth paragraph Emerson seems to be asking a jury of reputable people to send him that month's selection of their book club. Yet he would be the first to object to the "book-of-the-month-club" idea, preferring his own "wrong" choice to someone else's "right" choice. What are the alternatives for someone who wants to read most of the best books published each year? Which do you favor?

RICHARD WRIGHT

# One Book in the World*

One morning I arrived early at work and went into the bank lobby where the Negro porter was mopping. I stood at a counter and picked up the Memphis *Commercial Appeal* and began my

---

\* From *Black Boy* by Richard Wright (New York: Harper & Row, Publishers, 1945). Copyright 1945 by Richard Wright. Reprinted by permission of the publishers.

free reading of the press. I came finally to the editorial page and saw an article dealing with one H. L. Mencken. I knew by hearsay that he was the editor of the *American Mercury,* but aside from that I knew nothing about him. The article was a furious denunciation of Mencken, concluding with one, hot, short sentence: Mencken is a fool.

I wondered what on earth this Mencken had done to call down upon him the scorn of the South. The only people I had ever heard denounced in the South were Negroes, and this man was not a Negro. Then what ideas did Mencken hold that made a newspaper like the *Commercial Appeal* castigate him publicly? Undoubtedly he must be advocating ideas that the South did not like. Were there, then, people other than Negroes who criticized the South? I knew that during the Civil War the South had hated northern whites, but I had not encountered such hate during my life. Knowing no more of Mencken than I did at that moment, I felt a vague sympathy for him. Had not the South, which had assigned me the role of a non-man, cast at him its hardest words?

Now, how could I find out about this Mencken? There was a huge library near the riverfront, but I knew that Negroes were not allowed to patronize its shelves any more than they were the parks and playgrounds of the city. I had gone into the library several times to get books for the white men on the job. Which of them would now help me to get books? And how could I read them without causing concern to the white men with whom I worked? I had so far been successful in hiding my thoughts and feelings from them, but I knew that I would create hostility if I went about this business of reading in a clumsy way.

I weighed the personalities of the men on the job. There was Don, a Jew; but I distrusted him. His position was not much better than mine and I knew that he was uneasy and insecure; he had always treated me in an offhand, bantering way that barely concealed his contempt. I was afraid to ask him to help me to get books; his frantic desire to demonstrate a racial solidarity with the whites against Negroes might make him betray me.

Then how about the boss? No, he was a Baptist and I had the suspicion that he would not be quite able to comprehend why a black boy would want to read Mencken. There were other white men on the job whose attitudes showed clearly that they were Kluxers or sympathizers, and they were out of the question.

There remained only one man whose attitude did not fit into an anti-Negro category, for I had heard the white men refer to him as a "Pope lover." He was an Irish Catholic and was hated by the white Southerners. I knew that he read books, because I had got him volumes from the library several times. Since he, too, was an object of hatred, I felt that he might refuse me but would hardly betray me. I hesitated, weighing and balancing the imponderable realities.

One morning I paused before the Catholic fellow's desk.

"I want to ask you a favor," I whispered to him.

"What is it?"

"I want to read. I can't get books from the library. I wonder if you'd let me use your card?"

He looked at me suspiciously.

"My card is full most of the time," he said.

"I see," I said and waited, posing my question silently.

"You're not trying to get me into trouble, are you boy?" he asked, staring at me.

"Oh, no, sir."

"What book do you want?"

"A book by H. L. Mencken."

"Which one?"

"I don't know. Has he written more than one?"

"He has written several."

"I didn't know that."

"What makes you want to read Mencken?"

"Oh, I just saw his name in the newspaper," I said.

"It's good of you to want to read," he said. "But you ought to read the right things."

I said nothing. Would he want to supervise my reading?

"Let me think," he said. "I'll figure out something."

I turned from him and he called me back. He stared at me quizzically.

"Richard, don't mention this to the other white men," he said.

"I understand," I said. "I won't say a word."

A few days later he called me to him.

"I've got a card in my wife's name," he said. "Here's mine."

"Thank you, sir."

"Do you think you can manage it?"

"I'll manage fine," I said.

"If they suspect you, you'll get in trouble," he said.

That afternoon I addressed myself to forging a note. Now, what were the names of books written by H. L. Mencken? I did not know any of them. I finally wrote what I thought would be a foolproof note: *Dear Madam: Will you please let this nigger boy*—I used the word "nigger" to make the librarian feel that I could not possibly be the author of the note—*have some books by H. L. Mencken?* I forged the white man's name.

I entered the library as I had always done when on errands for whites, but I felt that I would somehow slip up and betray myself. I doffed my hat, stood a respectful distance from the desk, looked as unbookish as possible, and waited for the white patrons to be taken care of. When the desk was clear of people, I still waited. The white librarian looked at me.

"What do you want, boy?"

As though I did not possess the power of speech, I stepped forward and simply handed her the forged note, not parting my lips.

"What books by Mencken does he want?" she asked.

"I don't know, ma'am," I said, avoiding her eyes.

"Who gave you this card?"

"Mr. Falk," I said.

"Where is he?"

"He's at work, at the M—— Optical Company," I said. "I've been in here for him before."

"I remember," the woman said. "But he never wrote notes like this."

Oh, God, she's suspicious. Perhaps she would not let me have the books? If she had turned her back at that moment, I would have ducked out the door and never gone back. Then I thought of a bold idea.

"You can call him up, ma'am," I said, my heart pounding.

"You're not using these books, are you?" she asked pointedly.

"Oh, no, ma'am. I can't read."

"I don't know what he wants by Mencken," she said under her breath.

I knew now that I had won; she was thinking of other things and the race question had gone out of her mind. She went to the shelves. Once or twice she looked over her shoulder at me, as though she was still doubtful. Finally she came forward with two books in her hand.

"I'm sending him two books," she said. "But tell Mr. Falk to come in next time, or send me the names of the books he wants. I don't know what he wants to read."

I said nothing. She stamped the card and handed me the books. Not daring to glance at them, I went out of the library, fearing that the woman would call me back for further questioning. A block away from the library I opened one of the books and read a title: *A Book of Prefaces.* I was nearing my nineteenth birthday and I did not know how to pronounce the word "preface." I thumbed the pages and saw strange words and strange names. I shook my head, disappointed. I looked at the other book; it was called *Prejudices.* I knew what that word meant; I had heard it all my life. And right off I was on guard against Mencken's books. Why would a man want to call a book *Prejudices?* The word was so stained with all my memories of racial hate that I could not conceive of anybody using it for a title. Perhaps I had made a mistake about Mencken? A man who had prejudices must be wrong.

When I showed the books to Mr. Falk, he looked at me and frowned.

"That librarian might telephone you," I warned him.

"That's all right," he said. "But when you're through reading those books, I want you to tell me what you get out of them."

That night in my rented room, while letting the hot water run over my can of pork and beans in the sink, I opened *A Book of Prefaces* and began to read. I was jarred and shocked by the style, the clear, clean, sweeping sentences. Why did he write like that? And how did one write like that? I pictured the man as a raging demon, slashing with his pen, consumed with hate, denouncing everything American, extolling everything European or German, laughing at the weaknesses of people, mocking God, authority. What was this? I stood up, trying to realize what reality lay behind the meaning of the words. . . . Yes, this man was fighting, fighting with words. He was using words as a weapon, using them as one would use a club. Could words be weapons? No. It frightened me.

I read on and what amazed me was not what he said, but how on earth anybody had the courage to say it.

Occasionally I glanced up to reassure myself that I was alone in the room. Who were these men about whom Mencken was talking so passionately? Who was Anatole France? Joseph Conrad? Sinclair Lewis, Sherwood Anderson, Dostoevski, George Moore, Gustave Flaubert, Maupassant, Tolstoy, Frank Harris, Mark Twain, Thomas Hardy, Arnold Bennett, Stephen Crane, Zola, Norris, Gorky, Bergson, Ibsen, Balzac, Bernard Shaw, Dumas, Poe, Thomas Mann, O. Henry, Dreiser, H. G. Wells, Gogol, T. S. Eliot, Gide, Baudelaire, Edgar Lee Masters, Stendhal, Turgenev, Huneker, Nietzsche, and scores of others? Were these men real? Did they exist or had they existed? And how did one pronounce their names?

I ran across many words whose meanings I did not know, and I either looked them up in a dictionary or, before I had a chance to do that, encountered the word in a context that made its meaning clear. But what strange world was this? I concluded the book with the conviction that I had somehow overlooked something terribly important in life. I had once tried to write, had once reveled in feeling, had let my crude imagination roam, but the impulse to dream had been slowly beaten out of me by experience. Now it surged up again and I hungered for books, new ways of looking and seeing. It was not a matter of believing or disbelieving what I read, but of feeling something new, of being affected by something that made the look of the world different.

As dawn broke I ate my pork and beans, feeling dopey, sleepy. I went to work, but the mood of the book would not die; it lingered, coloring everything I saw, heard, did. I now felt that I knew what the white men were feeling. Merely because I had read a book that had spoken of how they lived and thought, I identified myself with that book. I felt vaguely guilty. Would I, filled with bookish notions, act in a manner that would make the whites dislike me?

I forged more notes and my trips to the library became frequent. Reading grew into a passion. My first serious novel was Sinclair Lewis's *Main Street*. It made me see my boss, Mr. Gerald, and identify him as an American type. I would smile when I saw him lugging his golf bags into the office. I had always felt a vast distance separating me from the boss, and now I felt closer to him, though still distant. I felt now that I knew him, that I could feel the very limits of his narrow life. And this had happened because I had read a novel about a mythical man called George F. Babbitt.

The plots and stories in the novels did not interest me so much as the point of view revealed. I gave myself over to each novel without reserve, without trying to criticize it; it was enough for me to see and feel something different. And for me, everything was something different. Reading was like a drug, a dope. The novels created moods in which I lived for days. But I could not conquer my sense of guilt, my feeling that the white men around me knew that I was changing, that I had begun to regard them differently.

Whenever I brought a book to the job, I wrapped it in newspaper —a habit that was to persist for years in other cities and under other circumstances. But some of the white men pried into my packages when I was absent and they questioned me.

"Boy, what are you reading those books for?"

"Oh, I don't know, sir."

"That's deep stuff you're reading, boy."

"I'm just killing time, sir."

"You'll addle your brains if you don't watch out."

SUGGESTIONS FOR WRITING

1. Richard Wright, (1909-   ) as the above piece from his autobiographical *Black Boy* (1945) indicates, is a self-educated Negro author. He was born and reared in Natchez, Mississippi. The *Oxford Companion to American Literature* says, "Since the publication of *Native Son* (1940), Wright has been considered the leading Negro author of the U.S." The experience that Wright reports in the above piece is not unique among people who have had a happy exposure to books. One finds an author who suddenly opens up a new world much as Mencken opened up Wright's world. If such an experience has happened to you, describe it.

2. Wright says that Mencken made the look of the world different, but to the majority of North Americans who read this passage, it is Wright himself who makes the look of the world different. How? What does a white person reading this passage see that he never saw or felt before? How does Wright drive home the message? His story is quite clearly an operational definition of racial prejudice at work. Write the story from the point of view of the white man who let Wright use his library card.

3. Define prejudice by showing it in operation, in other words, by revealing it at work in an encounter between two human beings.

VIRGINIA WOOLF

## They Have Loved Reading*

"We have only to compare"—with those words the cat is out of
the bag, and the true complexity of reading is admitted. The first
process, to receive impressions with the utmost understanding, is
only half the process of reading; it must be completed, if we are
to get the whole pleasure from a book, by another. We must pass
judgment upon these multitudinous impressions; we must make of
these fleeting shapes one that is hard and lasting. But not directly.
Wait for the dust of reading to settle; for the conflict and the questioning to die down; walk, talk, pull the dead petals from a rose,
or fall asleep. Then suddenly without our willing it, for it is thus
that Nature undertakes these transitions, the book will return, but
differently. It will float to the top of the mind as a whole. And the
book as a whole is different from the book received currently in
separate phrases. Details now fit themselves into their places. We
see the shape from start to finish; it is a barn, a pigsty, or a cathedral. Now then we can compare book with book as we compare
building with building. But this act of comparison means that our
attitude has changed; we are no longer the friends of the writer,
but his judges; and just as we cannot be too sympathetic as friends,
so as judges we cannot be too severe. Are they not criminals, books
that have wasted our time and sympathy; are they not the most insidious enemies of society, corrupters, defilers, the writers of false
books, faked books, books that fill the air with decay and disease?
Let us then be severe in our judgments; let us compare each book
with the greatest of its kind. There they hang in the mind the shapes
of the books we have read solidified by the judgments we have
passed on them—*Robinson Crusoe, Emma, The Return of the Native.* Compare the novels with these—even the latest and least of
novels has a right to be judged with the best. And so with poetry—
when the intoxication of rhythm has died down and the splendor

of words has faded a visionary shape will return to us and this must be compared with *Lear,* with *Phèdre,* with *The Prelude;* or if not with these, with whatever is the best or seems to us to be the best in its own kind. And we may be sure that the newness of new poetry and fiction is its most superficial quality and that we have only to alter slightly, not to recast, the standards by which we have judged the old.

It would be foolish, then, to pretend that the second part of reading, to judge, to compare, is as simple as the first—to open the mind wide to the fast flocking of innumerable impressions. To continue reading without the book before you, to hold one shadow-shape against another, to have read widely enough and with enough understanding to make such comparisons alive and illuminating—that is difficult; it is still more difficult to press further and to say, "Not only is the book of this sort, but it is of this value; here it fails; here it succeeds; this is bad; that is good." To carry out this part of a reader's duty needs such imagination, insight, and learning that it is hard to conceive any one mind sufficiently endowed; impossible for the most self-confident to find more than the seeds of such powers in himself. Would it not be wiser, then, to remit this part of reading and to allow the critics, the gowned and furred authorities of the library, to decide the question of the book's absolute value for us? Yet how impossible! We may stress the value of sympathy; we may try to sink our own identity as we read. But we know that we cannot sympathize wholly or immerse ourselves wholly; there is always a demon in us who whispers, "I hate, I love," and we cannot silence him. Indeed, it is precisely because we hate and we love that our relation with the poets and novelists is so intimate that we find the presence of another person intolerable. And even if the results are abhorrent and our judgments are wrong, still our taste, the nerve of sensation that sends shocks through us, is our chief illuminant; we learn through feeling; we cannot suppress our own idiosyncrasy without impoverishing it. But as time goes on perhaps we can train our taste; perhaps we can make it submit to some control. When it has fed greedily and lavishly upon books of all sorts—poetry, fiction, history, biography—and has stopped reading and looked for long spaces upon the variety, the incongruity of the living world, we shall find that it is changing a little; it is not so greedy, it is more reflective. It will begin to bring us not merely judgments on particular books, but it will tell us that there is a quality common to certain books. Listen, it will say, what shall we call *this*? And it will read us perhaps *Lear* and then perhaps the *Agamemnon* in order to bring out that common quality. Thus, with our taste to guide us, we shall venture beyond the particular book in search of qualities that group books together; we shall give them names and thus frame a rule that brings order into our perceptions. We shall gain a further and a rarer pleasure from that discrimination. But as a rule only lives when it is perpetually broken by contact with the books themselves—nothing is easier and more stultifying than to make rules which exist out of touch with facts, in a vacuum—now at last, in order to steady ourselves in this diffi-cult attempt, it may be well to turn to the very rare writers who are able to enlighten us upon literature as an art. Coleridge and Dryden and Johnson, in their considered criticism, the poets and novelists themselves in their unconsidered sayings, are often sur-prisingly relevant; they light up and solidify the vague ideas that have been tumbling in the misty depths of our minds. But they are only able to help us if we come to them laden with questions and suggestions won honestly in the course of our own reading. They can do nothing for us if we herd ourselves under their authority and lie down like sheep in the shade of a hedge. We can only understand their ruling when it comes in conflict with our own and vanquishes it.

If this is so, if to read a book as it should be read calls for the rarest qualities of imagination, insight, and judgment, you may perhaps conclude that literature is a very complex art and that it is unlikely that we shall be able, even after a lifetime of reading, to make any valuable contribution to its criticism. We must remain readers; we shall not put on the further glory that belongs to those rare beings who are also critics. But still we have our responsibilities as readers and even our importance. The standards we raise and the judgments we pass steal into the air and become part of the atmosphere which writers breathe as they work. An influence is created which tells upon them even if it never finds its way into print. And that influence, if it were well instructed, vigorous and individual and sincere, might be of great value now when criticism is necessarily in abeyance; when books pass in review like the proces-sion of animals in a shooting gallery, and the critic has only one second in which to load and aim and shoot and may well be pardoned if he mistakes rabbits for tigers, eagles for barndoor fowls, or misses altogether and wastes his shot upon some peaceful cow grazing in a further field. If behind the erratic gunfire of the press the author felt that there was another kind of criticism, the opinion of people reading for the love of reading, slowly and unprofessionally, and judging with great sympathy and yet with great severity, might this not improve the quality of his work? And if by our means books were to become stronger, richer, and more varied, that would be an end worth reaching.

Yet who reads to bring about an end however desirable? Are there not some pursuits that we practice because they are good in themselves, and some pleasures that are final? And is not this among them? I have sometimes dreamt, at least, that when the Day of Judgment dawns and the great conquerors and lawyers and statesmen come to receive their rewards—their crowns, their laurels, their names carved indelibly upon imperishable marble—the Almighty will turn to Peter and will say, not without a certain envy when He sees us coming with our books under our arms, "Look, these need no reward. We have nothing to give them here. They have loved reading."

SUGGESTIONS FOR WRITING

1. Virginia Woolf (1882-1941) is considered by some to be among the most important English novelists. Among her most interesting experimental works are *Jacob's Room* (1922), *Mrs. Dalloway* (1925), *Orlando* (1929), and *The Waves* (1931). In this piece from *The Second Common Reader* (1932) she speaks of a book floating "to the top of the mind as a whole. And the book as a whole is different from the book received currently in separate phrases." Describe the experience of finally getting an impression of "a total book."

2. Mrs. Woolf says, "Indeed, it is precisely because we hate and we love that our relation with the poets and novelists is so intimate that we find the presence of another person intolerable." Explain the meaning of this statement, illustrating it with your experience in reading a specific book.

3. Mrs. Woolf says of the best critics, "We can only understand their ruling when it comes in conflict with our own and vanquishes it." If you have had such an experience with literary critics, describe it, indicating how your opinion was changed. If you have not yet had this

experience with literature, consider another realm and indicate how
you changed your opinion of something after you heard what a critic
had to say.

4. At what stage in a lifetime of reading is a person sufficiently competent
to become a critic? What makes a critic? Describe the ideal characteristics of a critic.

SEAN O'FAOLAIN

# The Short Story*

We forget when enjoying the pleasure of any art, of music, poetry, painting or the theatre, that a very great part of our pleasure
has been dependent on convention. We are expected to forget it. In
the theatre we have all tacitly agreed to see nothing odd about a
room that, on the stage, has only three sides; or, in painting, it
does not seem odd to us that we see a view as if our heads were
held in a vice whereas in life we let our eyes wander east and west,
shift position a dozen times and see the landscape under fifty changing lights. The point is elementary; that is why it is so important;
because it is so very obvious it is constantly forgotten, and this
forgetting has, as I will show in this chapter, profound implications.
I will here barely hint at one of them by recalling how a humorous
philosopher once pointed to a cow in a field and said to me, 'What
do you see there?' I obligingly said that I perceived a cow. 'But
you do not,' he replied. 'You deduce a cow. All you see is the appearance of one-half of the outside of a cow. And when you look at
a portrait of your aunt all you see is a picture of the outside of one-
half of your aunt. You go through a series of lightning processes
before accepting this superficies as a portrait of your aunt, and
many critics (who examine those mental processes more carefully
than the rest of us) would probably deny that it comes anywhere
near being a portrait of your aunt. It is, for instance, the whole case
against Realism that it concentrates on giving us the outside of the
one-half of everything.' In other words the convention of realism

* From *The Short Story* by Sean O'Faolain (New York: The Devin-Adair Co.,
1951). Copyright 1951 by The Devin-Adair Co. Reprinted by permission of the
publishers.

depends for its success on our forgetting that realism is a convention. So does every other convention.

The chief purpose of these conventions is, of course, the simple purpose of communication. Every art has its own hieroglyphics. These are its language, its technique, its conventions. In the short story the speaker of this language is the writer; he has to learn its conventions, know what can be done with them, understand their limitations, adapt them to his own purpose, and often add to them. The listener to the language is the reader, and he, also, if he wants to get the most out of the art before him, has to familiarize himself with its conventions. The writer, however, must always presume that his reader is practised in these essential conventions; otherwise there can be no artistic communication at all. If therefore there is anything of a technical order which *can* be taught to would-be writers of the short story it is in this field of accepted conventions. As in Bridge.

Let us take an example. One of these conventions concerns the beginnings of stories. A thousand years ago—or today in places like the Irish or Scottish highlands where the folk mind is a thousand years old—a man could begin his story in this simple way, and nobody made the slightest demur:

> 'Once upon a time, in a distant land, there lived a giant. This giant dwelt in a great castle on top of a mountain. He was the most powerful and dreaded giant in all that land. He had six arms and he had eyes at the back of his head as well as at the front, and when he roared the villagers a hundred miles away looked at the sky and said, "The Thunder Giant is angry today." '

Even that 'once-upon-a-time' was a convention, which meant that people agreed to believe the most fantastic impossibilities provided they occurred long ago and far away enough; and they did so for the sufficient reason that it amused them to do it. We still do this. Today, a story may begin like this, and, again, nobody will make the slighest demur: 'The underworld shivered. Word had gone out that Two-gun Hawkeye had escaped from Dartmoor and was on the loose again. For Hawkeye was the man-eating spider at the centre of a vast network of criminal conspiracy that stretched from end to end of Europe. . . .' A business man who would refuse to pay fifteen shillings carriage on a gross of gentlemen's suspenders

until he saw the invoice, will roll himself up like a dormouse in an
armchair and swallow this whole, simply because it suits his pleasure.

As we become more sophisticated, however, we begin to nourish
the tendency to disbelieve, so that the author has to make it all seem
a little more plausible. We all know, for example, the story that
begins with a preamble in which the writer tells us how he came
into possession of the facts; for one of the natural concerns of every
author is not merely to make fiction seem like authentic fact but
to make us overlook his omniscience about it all, an omniscience
reaching even to the secret thoughts and desires of complete
strangers. He may begin, therefore, by telling us that he has found
an old diary in an old chest in an attic, and that his story is based
on that diary; or tell the whole story in the form of letters. Balzac's
*La Grande Bretèche* is pieced together from three conversations.
Another device is to tell it all in the first person. One of the very
loveliest short stories ever written is *Punin and Baburin* by Turgenev: it has the self-explanatory subtitle 'Piotr Petrovich's Story,'
and not until Turgenev has written away two hundred and fifty
precious words about his Piotr Petrovich do we come on the sentence, 'But I will begin my story consecutively and in proper order.'
Inevitably that story runs to thirty-thousand words and is really not
a short story at all.

Now one of the most successful inventions of the true modern
short story has been a convention which cuts out all that. Maupassant more than anybody else showed readers that if they were, as
we say colloquially, 'quick on the uptake,' they could dive into the
narrative without any explanations, preambles, elaborate introductions, apologies, or other notations as to place, time or occasion.
Thus *La Parure* bluntly opens: "She was one of those pretty and
charming girls who . . .' We take this abrupt 'she' for granted nowadays. The convention has been established. Or take this opening
to one of Thomas Hardy's short stories—it is in *Life's Little Ironies:*
'To the eyes of a man viewing it from behind, the nut-brown hair
was a wonder and a mystery . . .' In Defoe's time a reader would
have said, 'What *is* he talking about?' Today we should have no
difficulty in understanding a story that began at the end: e.g. 'The
first thing Mullins knew after that was the nurse saying, "Feeling
better now?" '

This is what I mean by the hieroglyphics of technique. It is short-hand, now an established device or convention, well-known to the merest amateur. Its main achievement is to shorten the preamble. 'Beginners,' says Chekov, 'have often to do this—fold in two and tear up the first half. One must write so that the reader should understand, without the author's explanations . . . what it is all about.'

## SUGGESTIONS FOR WRITING

1. Sean O'Faolain (1900-    ), who is one of the best short story writers now living, is also one of the best writers on short stories as a craft. His book, *The Short Story* (1951), from which this excerpt was taken, is a classic on the subject. He defines the role of convention in the short story. In a sense our lives are ruled by convention and, as O'Faolain points out, the conventions change from time to time. Note some conventions that have changed in your lifetime and describe the reaction of people some years ago to the now-changed conventions.

2. Examine a story and, without giving a detailed description of the plot or characterizations, reveal the "hieroglyphics of technique."

3. O'Faolain says, "It is . . . the whole case against Realism that it concentrates on giving us the outside of the one-half of everything." Write the dialogue of a debate between a conventional realist and a conventional impressionist in any art form. What is the major point of the realist and by what means of reasoning does he reach it? How does the impressionist counter this argument? How does he reach his own major point?

ARNOLD BENNETT

# Why a Classic Is a Classic*

The large majority of our fellow citizens care as much about literature as they care about archaeology or the program of the Legislature. They do not ignore it; they are not quite indifferent to it. But their interest in it is faint and perfunctory; or, if their

* From *Literary Taste* by Arnold Bennett (New York: Doubleday & Co., 1909). Copyright 1927 by Doubleday & Co., Inc. Reprinted by permission of the publishers and Jonathan Cape, Ltd.

interest happens to be violent, it is spasmodic. Ask the two hundred thousand persons whose enthusiasm made the vogue of a popular novel ten years ago what they think of that novel now, and you will gather that they have utterly forgotten it, and that they would no more dream of reading it again than of reading Bishop Stubb's *Select Charters*. Probably if they did read it again they would not enjoy it—not because the said novel is a whit worse now that it was ten years ago; not because their taste has improved—but because they have not had sufficient practice to be able to rely on their taste as a means of permanent pleasure. They simply don't know from one day to the next what will please them.

In the face of this one may ask: Why does the great and universal fame of classical authors continue? The answer is that the fame of classical authors is entirely independent of the majority. Do you suppose that if the fame of Shakespeare depended on the man in the street it would survive a fortnight? The fame of classical authors is originally made, and it is maintained, by a passionate few. Even when a first-class author has enjoyed immense success during his lifetime, the majority have never appreciated him so sincerely as they have appreciated second-rate men. He has always been reinforced by the ardor of the passionate few. And in the case of an author who has emerged into glory after his death the happy sequel has been due solely to the obstinate perseverance of the few. They could not leave him alone; they would not. They kept on savoring him, and talking about him, and buying him, and they generally behaved with such eager zeal, and they were so authoritative and sure of themselves, that at last the majority grew accustomed to the sound of his name and placidly agreed to the proposition that he was a genius; the majority really did not care very much either way.

And it is by the passionate few that the renown of genius is kept alive from one generation to another. These few are always at work. They are always rediscovering genius. Their curiosity and enthusiasm are exhaustless, so that there is little chance of genius being ignored. And, moreover, they are always working either for or against the verdicts of the majority. The majority can make a reputation, but it is too careless to maintain it. If, by accident, the passionate few agree with the majority in a particular instance, they will frequently remind the majority that such and such a reputation has been made, and the majority will idly concur: "Ah, yes. By the way, we must not forget that such and such a reputation exists." Without that persistent memory-jogging the reputation would quickly fall into the oblivion which is death. The passionate few only have their way by reason of the fact that they are genuinely interested in literature, that literature matters to them. They conquer by their obstinacy alone, by their eternal repetition of the same statements. Do you suppose they could prove to the man in the street that Shakespeare was a great artist? The said man would not even understand the terms they employed. But when he is told ten thousand times, and generation after generation, that Shakespeare was a great artist, the said man believes—not by reason, but by faith. And he too repeats that Shakespeare was a great artist, and he buys the complete works of Shakespeare and puts them on his shelves, and he goes to see the marvellous stage effects which accompany *King Lear* or *Hamlet,* and comes back religiously convinced that Shakespeare was a great artist. All because the passionate few could not keep their admiration of Shakespeare to themselves. This is not cynicism; but truth. And it is important that those who wish to form their literary taste should grasp it.

What causes the passionate few to make such a fuss about literature? There can be only one reply. They find a keen and lasting pleasure in literature. They enjoy literature as some men enjoy beer. The recurrence of this pleasure naturally keeps their interest in literature very much alive. They are forever making new researches, forever practising on themselves. They learn to understand themselves. They learn to know what they want. Their taste becomes surer and surer as their experience lengthens. They do not enjoy today what will seem tedious to them tomorrow. When they find a book tedious, no amount of popular clatter will persuade them that it is pleasurable; and when they find it pleasurable no chill silence of the street crowds will affect their conviction that the book is good and permanent. They have faith in themselves. What are the qualities in a book which give keen and lasting pleasure to the passionate few? This is a question so difficult that it has never yet been completely answered. You may talk lightly about truth, insight, knowledge, wisdom, humor, and beauty, but these comfortable words do not really carry you very far, for each of them has to be defined, especially the first and last. It is all very well for Keats in his airy manner to assert that beauty is truth, truth beauty, and that that is all he knows or needs to know. I, for one, need to know a lot more. And I shall never know. Nobody, not even Hazlitt nor Sainte-Beuve, has ever finally explained why he thought a book beautiful. I take the first fine lines that come to hand—

> The woods of Arcady are dead,
> And over is their antique joy—

and I say that those lines are beautiful, because they give me pleasure. But why? No answer! I only know that the passionate few will, broadly, agree with me in deriving this mysterious pleasure from those lines. I am only convinced that the liveliness of our pleasure in those and many other lines by the same author will ultimately cause the majority to believe, by faith, that W. B. Yeats is a genius. The one reassuring aspect of the literary affair is that the passionate few are passionate about the same things. A continuance of interest does, in actual practice, lead ultimately to the same judgments. There is only the difference in width of interest. Some of the passionate few lack catholicity, or, rather, the whole of their interest is confined to one narrow channel; they have none left over. These men help specially to vitalize the reputations of the narrower geniuses: such as Crashaw. But their active predilections never contradict the general verdict of the passionate few; rather they reinforce it.

A classic is a work which gives pleasure to the minority which is intensely and permanently interested in literature. It lives on because the minority, eager to renew the sensation of pleasure, is eternally curious and is therefore engaged in an eternal process of rediscovery. A classic does not survive for any ethical reason. It does not survive because it conforms to certain canons, or because neglect would not kill it. It survives because it is a source of pleasure, and because the passionate few can no more neglect it than a bee can neglect a flower. The passionate few do not read "the right things" because they are right. That is to put the cart before the horse.

"The right things" are the right things solely because the passionate few *like* reading them. Hence—and I now arrive at my point—the one primary essential to literary taste is a hot interest in literature. If you have that, all the rest will come. It matters nothing that at present you fail to find pleasure in certain classics. The driving impulse of your interest will force you to acquire experience, and experience will teach you the use of the means of pleasure. You do not know the secret ways of yourself: that is all. A continuance of interest must inevitably bring you to the keenest joys. But, of course, experience may be acquired judiciously or injudiciously, just as Putney may be reached via Walham Green or via Moscow.

## SUGGESTIONS FOR WRITING

1. Arnold Bennett (1867-1931) was an English author whose fame rests chiefly on *The Old Wives' Tale* (1908) and the *Clayhanger* series (1911-1925). In this essay he argues that people "simply don't know from one day to the next what will please them." In other words, most people do not have a developed sense of taste on which they can rely. If this is so, speculate on the reasons for it. Why do some books become best-sellers one year only to be forgotten the next? Is it the books themselves or a matter of popular taste that makes them best-sellers?

2. Is it true, as Bennett says, that the man on the street believes Shakespeare great only because he has been told "ten thousand times"? How do you view this "fact"? In matters of this sort is it reasonable for the man on the streeet to act out of faith and not out of personal judgment? What are your convictions about the views of the man on the street? Do you care how or where he gets his opinions? Is his lack of reasoning power in matters of literary concern simply a "fact" of human nature that can't be changed? If it can be changed, what method would you propose?

3. Bennett asks, "What are the qualities in a book which give keen and lasting pleasure to the passionate few?" Answer from your own experience.

4. "A classic is a work which gives pleasure to the minority which is intensely and permanently interested in literature." If such is always the case, how can one explain the Broadway play which receives bad notices but which becomes a box office success, or the badly received book which becomes a best-seller? Defend Bennett.

LIONEL TRILLING

## The Meaning of a Literary Idea*

The question of the relation which should properly obtain between what we call creative literature and what we call ideas is a matter of insistent importance for modern criticism. It did not always make difficulties for the critic, and that it now makes so many is a fact which tells us much about our present relation to literature.

Ever since men began to think about poetry, they have conceived that there is a difference between the poet and the philosopher, a difference in method and in intention and in result. These differences I have no wish to deny. But a solidly established difference inevitably draws the fire of our question; it tempts us to inquire whether it is really essential or whether it is quite so settled and extreme as at first it seems. To this temptation I yield perhaps too easily, and very possibly as the result of an impercipience on my part—it may be that I see the difference with insufficient sharpness because I do not have a proper notion either of the matter of poetry or of the matter of philosophy. But whatever the reason, when I consider the respective products of the poetic and of the philosophic mind, although I see that they are by no means the same and although I can conceive that different processes, even different mental faculties, were at work to make them and to make them different, I cannot resist the impulse to put stress on their similarity and on their easy assimilation to each other.

Let me suggest some of the ways in which literature, by its very nature, is involved with ideas. I can be quite brief because what I say will not be new to you.

The most elementary thing to observe is that literature is of its nature involved with ideas because it deals with man in society, which is to say that it deals with formulations, valuations, and decisions, some of them implicit, others explicit. Every sentient organism acts on the principle that pleasure is to be preferred to pain,

* From *The Liberal Imagination* by Lionel Trilling (New York: The Viking Press, Inc., 1950). Copyright 1949 by Lionel Trilling. Reprinted by permission of the publishers.

but man is the sole creature who formulates or exemplifies this as an idea and causes it to lead to other ideas. His consciousness of self abstracts this principle of action from his behavior and makes it the beginning of a process of intellection or a matter for tears and laughter. And this is but one of the innumerable assumptions or ideas that are the very stuff of literature.

This is self-evident and no one ever thinks of denying it. All that is ever denied is that literature is within its proper function in bringing these ideas to explicit consciousness, or ever gains by doing so. Thus, one of the matters of assumption in any society is the worth of men as compared with the worth of women; upon just such an assumption, more or less settled, much of the action of the *Oresteia* is based, and we don't in the least question the propriety of this—or not until it becomes the subject of open debate between Apollo and Athene, who, on the basis of an elaborate biological speculation, try to decide which is the less culpable, to kill your father or to kill your mother. At this point we, in our modern way, feel that in permitting the debate Aeschylus has made a great and rather silly mistake, that he has for the moment ceased to be *literary.* Yet what drama does not consist of the opposition of formulable ideas, what drama, indeed, is not likely to break into the explicit exposition and debate of these ideas?

This, as I say, is elementary. And scarcely less elementary is the observation that whenever we put two emotions into juxtaposition we have what we can properly call an idea. When Keats brings together, as he so often does, his emotions about love and his emotions about death, we have a very powerful idea and the source of consequent ideas. The force of such an idea depends upon the force of the two emotions which are brought to confront each other, and also, of course, upon the way the confrontation is contrived.

Then it can be said that the very form of a literary work, considered apart from its content, so far as that is possible, is in itself an idea. Whether we deal with syllogisms or poems, we deal with dialectic—with, that is, a developing series of statements. Or if the word "statements" seems to prejudge the question so far as literature is concerned, let us say merely that we deal with a developing series—the important word is "developing." We judge the value of the development by judging the interest of its several stages and the propriety and the relevance of their connection among themselves. We make the judgment in terms of the implied purpose of the developing series.

Dialectic, in this sense, is just another word for form, and has for its purpose, in philosophy or in art, the leading of the mind to some conclusion. Greek drama, for example, is an arrangement of moral and emotional elements in such a way as to conduct the mind— "inevitably," as we like to say—to a certain affective condition. This condition is a quality of personal being which may be judged by the action it can be thought ultimately to lead to.

We take Aristotle to be a better critic of the drama than Plato because we perceive that Aristotle understood and Plato did not understand that the form of the drama was of itself an idea which controlled and brought to a particular issue the subordinate ideas it contained. The form of the drama *is* its idea, and its idea *is* its form. And form in those arts which we call abstract is no less an idea than is form in the representational arts. Governments nowadays are very simple and accurate in their perception of this— much more simple and accurate than are academic critics and aestheticians—and they are as quick to deal with the arts of "pure" form as they are to deal with ideas stated in discourse: it is as if totalitarian governments kept in mind what the rest of us tend to forget, that "idea" in one of its early significations exactly means form and was so used by many philosophers.

It is helpful to have this meaning before us when we come to consider that particular connection between literature and ideas which presents us with the greatest difficulty, the connection that involves highly elaborated ideas, or ideas as we have them in highly elaborated systems such as philosophy, or theology, or science. The modern feeling about this relationship is defined by two texts, both provided by T. S. Eliot. In his essay on Shakespeare Mr. Eliot says, "I can see no reason for believing that either Dante or Shakespeare did any thinking on his own. The people who think that Shakespeare thought are always people who are not engaged in writing poetry, but who are engaged in thinking, and we all like to think that great men were like ourselves." And in his essay on Henry James, Mr. Eliot makes the well-known remark that James had a mind so fine that no idea could violate it.

In both statements, as I believe, Mr. Eliot permits his impulse to spirited phrase to run away with him, yielding too much to what he conceives to be the didactic necessities of the moment, for he has it in mind to offer resistance to the nineteenth-century way of looking at poetry as a heuristic medium, as a communication of knowledge. This is a view which is well exemplified in a sentence of Carlyle's: "If called to define Shakespeare's faculty, I should say superiority of Intellect, and think I had included all in that." As between the two statements about Shakespeare's mental processes, I give my suffrage to Carlyle's as representing a more intelligible and a more available notion of intellect than Mr. Eliot's, but I think I understand what Mr. Eliot is trying to do with his—he is trying to rescue poetry from the kind of misinterpretation of Carlyle's view which was once more common than it is now; he is trying to save for poetry what is peculiar to it, and for systematic thought what is peculiar to it.

As for Mr. Eliot's statement about James and ideas, it is useful to us because it gives us a clue to what might be called the sociology of our question. "Henry James had a mind so fine that no idea could violate it." In the context "violate" is a strong word, yet we can grant that the mind of the poet is a sort of Clarissa Harlowe and that an idea is a sort of Colonel Lovelace, for it is a truism of contemporary thought that the whole nature of man stands in danger of being brutalized by the intellect, or at least by some one of its apparently accredited surrogates. A specter haunts our culture —it is that people will eventually be unable to say, "They fell in love and married," let alone understand the language of *Romeo and Juliet,* but will as a matter of course say, "Their libidinal impulses being reciprocal, they activated their individual erotic drives and integrated them within the same frame of reference."

Now this is not the language of abstract thought or of any kind of thought. It is the language of non-thought. But it is the language which is developing from the peculiar status which we in our culture have given to abstract thought. There can be no doubt whatever that it constitutes a threat to the emotions and thus to life itself.

The specter of what this sort of language suggests has haunted us since the end of the eighteenth century. When he speaks of the mind being violated by an idea, Mr. Eliot, like the Romantics, is simply voicing his horror at the prospect of life being intellectualized out of all spontaneity and reality.

We are the people of the idea, and we rightly fear that the intellect will dry up the blood in our veins and wholly check the emotional and creative part of the mind. And although I said that the fear of the total sovereignty of the abstract intellect began in the Romantic period, we are of course touching here upon Pascal's opposition between two faculties of the mind, of which *l'esprit de finesse* has its heuristic powers no less than *l'esprit de géométrie,* powers of discovery and knowledge which have a particular value for the establishment of man in society and the universe.

But to call ourselves the people of the idea is to flatter ourselves. We are rather the people of ideology, which is a very different thing. Ideology is not the product of thought; it is the habit or the ritual of showing respect for certain formulas to which, for various reasons having to do with emotional safety, we have very strong ties of whose meaning and consequences in actuality we have no clear understanding. The nature of ideology may in part be understood from its tendency to develop the sort of language I parodied, and scarcely parodied, a moment ago.

It is therefore no wonder that any critical theory that conceives itself to be at the service of the emotions, and of life itself, should turn a very strict and jealous gaze upon an intimate relationship between literature and ideas, for in our culture ideas tend to deteriorate into ideology. And indeed it is scarcely surprising that criticism, in its zeal to protect literature and life from the tyranny of the rational intellect, should misinterpret the relationship. Mr. Eliot, if we take him literally, does indeed misinterpret the relationship when he conceives of "thinking" in such a way that it must be denied to Shakespeare and Dante. It must puzzle us to know what thinking is if Shakespeare and Dante did not do it.

SUGGESTIONS FOR WRITING

1. Lionel Trilling (1905-    ) is a literary critic who teaches at Columbia University. He has written short stories, a novel, *The Middle of the Journey* (1947), and critical essays on E. M. Forster and Matthew Arnold. In this essay he begins by assuming that there is a difference between the poet and the philosopher. He also makes an assumption (unstated) that one of the functions of a literary critic is to understand and reveal that difference. Write an essay explaining the difference between poets and philosophers.

2. Trilling says that we can call two emotions in juxtaposition an idea. He illustrates by pointing out Keats's frequent use of the emotions of love and death. Choose two different emotions and illustrate Trilling's point. In your essay define "emotion" carefully.

3. "The form of the drama *is* its idea, and its idea *is* its form." Read the articles by Rohden (p. 375) and Charles Morgan (p. 380), then illustrate the meaning of form and idea.

4. Why is the following statement a threat to the emotions? "Their libidinal impulses being reciprocal, they activated their individual erotic drives and integrated them within the same frame of reference." Must literature appeal to the emotions? Is it nonliterary if it appeals only to the mind? Compare what Matthew Arnold has to say in "The Value of Humane Letters" (p. 9).

# The Stage

Not to go to the theatre is like making one's toilet without a mirror.
—Schopenhauer, *Studies in Pessimism*, 1851

The writing of plays is a gréat matter, forming as it does the minds and affections of men in such sort that whatsoever they see done in show on the stage, they will presently be doing in earnest in the world, which is but a larger stage.
—George Bernard Shaw, *The Dark Lady of the Sonnets*, 1914

Probably more people have thought Hamlet a work of art because they found it interesting than have found it interesting because it is a work of art. It is the "Mona Lisa" of literature.
—T. S. Eliot, *The Sacred Wood*, 1920

The stage being the representation of the world and the actors in it, how can it be imagined that the picture of human life can be more exact than life itself is?
—Dryden, *The Rival Ladies*, 1664

Epic and tragic composition, also comedy, the writing of dithyrambs and most branches of flute- and harp-playing are all, if looked at as a whole, imitations.
—Aristotle, *Poetics*, c. 330 B.C.

The curtain is still down, the house-lights are still up, but we are in a theater and, if experience has not embittered us, are dreaming that this evening or another evening the beat of wings will grow louder in our silences, the supreme illusion will stoop down and gather us, the hosts will speak.
—Charles Morgan, *The Nature of Dramatic Illusion*, 1933

And, please . . . I beg the actors not to be afraid of remaining silent, for silence speaks more eloquently than do words in certain moments . . . If the actors know how to make silence speak.
—Pirandello, stage direction for *The Life I Gave You*, 1931

GEORGE BERNARD SHAW

# Theater Critic*

Somebody has sent me a cutting from which I gather that a pro-
posal to form a critics' club has reached the very elementary stage
of being discussed in the papers in August. Now clearly a critic
should not belong to a club at all. He should not know anybody:
his hand should be against every man, and every man's hand against
his. Artists insatiable by the richest and most frequent doses of
praise; entrepreneurs greedy for advertisement; people without
reputations who want to beg or buy them ready made; the rivals
of the praised; the friends, relatives, partisans, and patrons of the
damned: all these have their grudge against the unlucky Minos in
the stalls, who is himself criticized in the most absurd fashion.

People have pointed out evidences of personal feeling in my
notices as if they were accusing me of a misdemeanor, not knowing
that a criticism written without personal feeling is not worth reading. It is the capacity for making good or bad art a personal matter
that makes a man a critic. The artist who accounts for my dis-
paragement by alleging personal animosity on my part is quite
right: when people do less than their best, and do that less at once
badly and self-complacently, I hate them, loathe them, detest them,
long to tear them limb from limb and strew them in gobbets about
the stage or platform. (At the Opera, the temptation to go out and
ask one of the sentinels for the loan of his Martini, with a round or
two of ammunition, that I might rid the earth of an incompetent
conductor or a conceited and careless artist, has come upon me so

---

* From *Shaw on Music* edited by Eric Bentley (New York: Doubleday & Co.,
Inc., 1955). Reprinted by permission of the Public Trustee and the Society of
Authors.

strongly that I have been withheld only by my fear that, being no marksman, I might hit the wrong person and incur the guilt of slaying a meritorious singer.)

In the same way, really fine artists inspire me with the warmest personal regard, which I gratify in writing my notices without the smallest reference to such monstrous conceits as justice, impartiality, and the rest of the ideals. When my critical mood is at its height, personal feeling is not the word: it is passion: the passion for artistic perfection—for the noblest beauty of sound, sight, and action—that rages in me. Let all young artists look to it, and pay no heed to the idiots who declare that criticism should be free from personal feeling. The true critic, I repeat, is the man who becomes your personal enemy on the sole provocation of a bad performance, and will only be appeased by good performances. Now this, though well for art and for the people, means that the critics are, from the social or clubable point of view, veritable fiends. They can only fit themselves for other people's clubs by allowing themselves to be corrupted by kindly feelings foreign to the purpose of art, unless, indeed, they join Philistine clubs, wherein neither the library nor the social economy of the place will suit their nocturnal, predatory habits. If they must have a club, let them have a pandemonium of their own, furnished with all the engines of literary vivisection. But its first and most sacred rule must be the exclusion of the criticized, except those few stalwarts who regularly and publicly turn upon and criticize their critics. (No critics' club would have any right to the name unless it included—but the printer warns me that I have reached the limit of my allotted space.)


SUGGESTIONS FOR WRITING

1. George Bernard Shaw (1856-1950) wrote music and drama criticism before 1900, and afterwards turned to writing plays himself. His writing for the stage brought to people's attention his unorthodox turn of mind and his distrust of conventions and accepted institutions. Clearly, however, as the above piece indicates, he was a striking individualist almost from the beginning. A critic, says Shaw, "should not know anybody: his hand should be against every man, and every man's hand against his." Are you convinced? Explain what you think the role of a theater critic should be.

2. Shaw says, "A criticism written without personal feeling is not worth reading." Glance at a copy of the *Saturday Review* or your local newspaper's theater page. How often do you find personal feeling revealed? In an essay, indicate to what degree modern journalistic critics follow Shaw's advice.

3. Shaw feels that a critic need not worry about being just or impartial, so long as he chastises one who does less than his best and praises quality. Indicate circumstances under which Shaw's advice might not be appropriate.

4. Criticize a work of artistic endeavor by one of your colleagues in a manner Shaw would approve.


MAXWELL ANDERSON

# Tragedy in Modern Drama*

Anybody who dares to discuss the making of tragedy lays himself open to critical assault, for the theorists have been hunting for the essence of tragedy since Aristotle without entire success. There is no doubt that playwrights have occasionally written tragedy successfully, from Aeschylus on, and there is no doubt that Aristotle came very close to a definition of what tragedy is in his famous passage on catharsis. But why the performance of tragedy should have a cleansing effect on the audience, why an audience is willing to listen to tragedy, why tragedy has a place in the education of men, has never, to my knowledge, been convincingly stated. I have not solved the Sphinx's riddle which fifty generations of skillful brains have left in shadow. But I have one suggestion which I think might lead to a solution.

It was not until after I had fumbled my way through a good many successes and an appalling number of failures that I began to doubt the sufficiency of dramatic instinct and to wonder whether or not there were general laws governing dramatic structure which so poor a head for theory as my own might grasp and use. I shan't trouble you with the details of my search. But I reread Aristotle's

* From *Off Broadway* by Maxwell Anderson (New York: William Sloan Associates, 1947). Copyright 1939, 1947 by Maxwell Anderson. Reprinted by permission of the publishers.

*Poetics* in the light of some bitter experience, and one of his observations led me to a comparison of ancient and modern play-
writing methods. In discussing construction, he made a point of
the recognition scene as essential to tragedy.

The recognition scene, as Aristotle isolated it in the tragedies of
the Greeks, was generally an artificial device, a central scene in
which the leading character saw through a disguise, recognized as
a friend or as an enemy, perhaps as a lover or a member of his own
family, some person whose identity had been hidden. Iphigenia, for
example, acting as priestess in an alien country, receives a victim
for sacrifice and then recognizes her own brother in this victim.
There is an instant and profound emotional reaction; instantly her
direction in the play is altered. But occasionally, in the greatest of
the plays, the recognition turned on a situation far more convincing, though no less contrived. Oedipus, hunting savagely for the
criminal who has brought the plague upon Thebes, discovers that
he is himself that criminal. And since this discovery affects not only
the physical well-being and happiness of the hero but the whole
structure of his life, the effect on him and on the direction of the
story is incalculably greater than could result from the more superficial revelation made to Iphigenia.

Now scenes of exactly this sort are rare in the modern drama
except in detective stories adapted for the stage. But when I probed
a little more deeply into the memorable pieces of Shakespeare's
theater and our own, I began to see that though modern recognition scenes are subtler and harder to find, they are none the less
present in the plays we choose to remember. They seldom have to
do with anything so naïve as disguise or the unveiling of a personal
identity. But the element of discovery is just as important as ever.
For the mainspring in the mechanism of a modern play is almost
invariably a discovery by the hero of some element in his environment or in his own soul of which he has not been aware or which
he has not taken sufficiently into account. Here is the rule which I
formulated for my own guidance: A play should lead up to and
away from a central crisis, and this crisis should consist in a discovery by the leading character which has an indelible effect on his
thought and emotion and completely alters his course of action.
The leading character, let me say again, must make the discovery;

it must affect him emotionally; and it must alter his direction in the play.

Try that formula on any play you think worthy of study. The turning point of *The Green Pastures,* for example, is the discovery by God, who is the leading character, that a God who is to endure must conform to the laws of change. The turning point of *Hamlet* is Hamlet's discovery, in the play scene, that his uncle was unquestionably the murderer of his father. In *Abe Lincoln in Illinois,* Lincoln's discovery is that he has been a coward, that he has stayed out of the fight for the Union because he was afraid. In each case, you will note, the discovery has a profound emotional effect on the hero and gives an entirely new direction to his action in the play.

Now this prime rule has a corollary which is just as important as the rule itself. The hero who is to make the central discovery in a play must not be a perfect man. He must have some variation of what Aristotle calls a tragic fault; and the reason he must have it is that when he makes his discovery he must change both in himself and in his action, and he must change for the better. The fault can be a very simple one—a mere unawareness, for example—but if he has no fault he cannot change for the better but only for the worse, and, for a reason which I shall discuss later, it is necessary that he become more admirable and not less so at the end of the play. In other words, a hero must pass through an experience which opens his eyes to an error of his own. He must learn through suffering. In a tragedy he suffers death itself as a consequence of his fault or his attempt to correct it, but before he dies he has become a nobler person because of his recognition of his fault and the consequent alteration of his course of action. In a serious play which does not end in death, he discovers that fault during the course of the action, and he does what he can to rectify it at the end. In *The Green Pastures* God's fault was that he believed himself perfect. He discovered that he was not perfect, that he had been in error and must make amends. Hamlet's fault was that he could not make up his mind to act. He offers many excuses for his indecision until he discovers that there is no real reason for hesitation and that he has delayed out of cowardice. Lincoln, in *Abe Lincoln in Illinois,* has exactly the same difficulty. In the climactic scene it is revealed to him that he has hesitated to take sides through fear of the consequences to himself, and he then chooses to go ahead without regard for what may be in store for him. From the point of view of the playwright, then, the essence of a tragedy, or even of a serious play, is the spiritual awakening or regeneration of his hero.

When a playwright attempts to reverse the formula, when his hero makes a discovery which has an evil effect—or one which the audience interprets as evil—on his character, the play is inevitably a failure on the stage. In *Troilus and Cressida* Troilus discovers that Cressida is a light woman. He draws from her defection the inference that all women are faithless, that faith in woman is the possession of fools. As a consequence he turns away from life and seeks death in a cause as empty as the love he has given up, the cause of the strumpet Helen. All the glory of Shakespeare's verse cannot rescue the play for an audience, and save in *Macbeth* Shakespeare nowhere wrote so richly, so wisely, or with such a flow of brilliant metaphor.

For the audience will always insist that the alteration in the hero be for the better—or for what it believes to be the better. As audiences change, the standards of good and evil change, though slowly and unpredictably, and the meanings of plays change with the centuries. One thing only is certain: that an audience watching a play will go along with it only when the leading character responds in the end to what it considers a higher moral impulse than moved him at the beginning of the story, though the audience will of course define morality as it pleases and in the terms of its own day. It may be that there is no absolute up or down in this world, but the race believes that there is and will not hear of any denial.

And now at last I come to the point toward which I've been struggling so laboriously. Why does the audience come to the theater to look on while an imaginary hero is put to an imaginary trial and comes out of it with credit to the race and to himself? The theater originated in two complementary religious ceremonies, one celebrating the animal in man and one celebrating the god. Old Greek Comedy was dedicated to the spirits of lust and riot and earth, spirits which are certainly necessary to the health and continuance of the race. Greek tragedy was dedicated to man's aspiration, to his kinship with the gods, to his unending, blind attempt to lift himself above his lusts and his pure animalism into a world where there are other values than pleasure and survival. However unaware of it we may be, our theater has followed the Greek patterns with no change in essence, from Aristophanes and Euripides to our own day. Our more ribald musical comedies are simply our approximation of the Bacchic rites of Old Comedy. In the rest of our theater we sometimes follow Sophocles, whose tragedy is always an exaltation of the human spirit, sometimes Euripides, whose tragicomedy follows the same pattern of an excellence achieved through suffering. Our comedy is largely the Greek New Comedy, which grew out of Euripides' tragicomedy, and is separated from tragedy only in that it presents a happier scene and puts its protagonist through an ordeal which is less than lethal.

And since our plays, aside from those which are basically Old Comedy, are exaltations of the human spirit, since that is what an audience expects when it comes to the theater, the playwright gradually discovers that he must follow the ancient Aristotelian rule: he must build his plot around a scene wherein his hero discovers some mortal frailty or stupidity in himself and faces life armed with a new wisdom. He must so arrange his story that it will prove to the audience that men pass through suffering purified, that, animal though we are, despicable though we are in many ways, there is in us all some divine, incalculable fire that urges us to be better than we are.

It could be argued that what the audience demands of a hero is only conformity to race morality, to the code which seems to the spectators most likely to make for race survival. In many cases, especially in comedy and obviously in the comedy of Molière, this is true. But in the majority of ancient and modern plays it seems to me that what the audience wants to believe is that men have a desire to break the molds of earth which encase them and claim a kinship with a higher morality than that which hems them in. The rebellion of Antigone, who breaks the laws of men through adherence to a higher law of affection, the rebellion of Prometheus, who breaks the law of the gods to bring fire to men, the rebellion of God in *The Green Pastures* against the rigid doctrine of the Old Testament, the rebellion of Tony in *They Knew What They Wanted* against the convention that called on him to repudiate his cuckold child, the rebellion of Liliom against the heavenly law which asked him to betray his own integrity and make a hypocrisy of his affection, even the repudiation of the old forms and the affirmation of new by the heroes of Ibsen and Shaw, these are all instances to me of the groping of men toward an excellence dimly apprehended, seldom possible of definition. They are evidence to me that the theater at its best is a religious affirmation, an age-old rite restating and reassuring man's belief in his own destiny and his ultimate hope. The theater is much older than the doctrine of evolution, but its one faith, asseverated again and again for every age and every year, is a faith in evolution, in the reaching and the climb of men toward distant goals, glimpsed but never seen, perhaps never achieved, or achieved only to be passed impatiently on the way to a more distant horizon.

## SUGGESTIONS FOR WRITING

1. Maxwell Anderson (1888-    ) was awarded the Pulitzer Prize (1933) and has won the Drama Critics' Circle Award twice. His most notable plays are *What Price Glory* (1924) [written with Laurence Stallings], *Both Your Houses* (1933), *Winterset* (1935), *High Tor* (1936), and *Joan of Lorraine* (1946). In the above essay, writing from experience, he argues that "the audience will always insist that the alteration in the hero be for the better—or for what it believes to be the better." Exemplify this statement from your experience with plays. Can you find any exception to it?

2. Write an outline of a play or a sketch of the development of a main character which exemplifies Anderson's thesis. The theme should follow Anderson's rule for playwrights: "He must build his plot around a scene wherein his hero discovers some mortal frailty or stupidity in himself and faces life armed with a new wisdom."

3. "The theater at its best is a religious affirmation, an age-old rite restating and reassuring man's belief in his own destiny and his ultimate hope." In an essay, reveal how a movie you have seen fails to measure up to Anderson's definition of "theater at its best."

ROBERT BRUSTEIN

# The Glowering, Inarticulate Hero*

When a hitherto unknown actor named Marlon Brando . . .
years ago assumed the role of Stanley Kowalski, the glowering, inarticulate hero of Tennessee Williams' *A Streetcar Named Desire,*
few people realized the symbolic importance of that creation. For
Brando was to personify an entire postwar generation of troubled
spirits trying to find an identity. Today we find his Kowalski wherever we look, whether in our latest literature, our poetry, our painting, our movies, our popular music, or on our city streets. In one
guise or another he is the hero of the Beat Generation.

This new ideal image, as Brando first gave it dramatic form and
as tribal followers from coast to coast have adopted it, is that of
a man of much muscle and little mind, often surly and discontented,
prepared to offer violence with little provocation. He peers out at
the world from under beetling eyebrows, his right hand rests casually on his right hip. Walking with a slouching, shuffling gait, he
scratches himself often and almost never smiles. He is especially
identified by the sounds that issue from his mouth. He squeezes, he
grunts, he passes his hand over his eyes and forehead, he stares
steadily, he turns away, he scratches, then again faces his adversary,
and finally speaks—or tries to.

The new hero has cut himself off from cultural and social life
and now seems close to abdicating even from himself. Whether he
throws words on a page, like the San Francisco novelist Jack
Kerouac, or pigment onto a canvas like the "action" painter Franz
Kline, whether he mumbles through a movie or shimmies in the
frenetic gyrations of rock-'n-roll, he is a man belligerently exalting
his own inarticulateness. He "howls" when he has the energy, and
when he doesn't, sits around "beat" and detached, in a funk. He
is hostile to the mind, petulant toward tradition, and indifferent
to order and coherence. He is concerned chiefly with indulging his

* Originally titled "The Cult of Unthink"; from *Horizon, A Magazine of the
Arts* (September, 1959). © 1958 by American Heritage Publishing Co., Inc. Reprinted by permission of the publishers.

own feelings, glorifying his own impulses, securing his own "cool" kicks. His most characteristic sound is a stammer or a saxophone wail; his most characteristic symbol, a blotch and a glob of paint.

He exults in solitude and frequently speaks proudly of his "personal vision." Yet, while outwardly individualistic and antisocial, he is inwardly conformist. He travels in packs, writes collective manifestoes, establishes group heroes like the late movie star James Dean, and adheres to the ethics of the coterie. He is "existential" without having developed any substantial existence. If he has a coherent philosophy, it is one of simple negation without any purposeful individual rebellion to sustain it.

The novelists and poets now centering in San Francisco are the most striking examples of conformists masquerading as rebels. They travel together, drink together, "smoke pot" together, publish together, dedicate works to each other, share the same pony-tailed girls in faded blue jeans, wear a uniform costume, and take for their collective theme the trials and tribulations of their own troubled souls. "I saw the best minds of my generation destroyed by madness, starving hysterical naked," writes Allen Ginsberg, the most talented of the group, before launching into a description of the worst degradations to which the human animal can descend. The only horror not included in it is loneliness, for the Beat Generation suffers its degradations en masse.

It is significant that the heroes and saints of the Beat Generation are all death lovers and escapists. The junkies, the derelicts, the delinquents, the madmen, the criminals, and the Outsiders who people this literature have in common their paralysis in the face of all intelligible forms of behavior. In this they are counterparts of the personification created on the level of popular culture by Marlon Brando and aped by large numbers of Stanislavsky Method actors since. In *The Wild One,* for example, Brando played a "saintly motorcyclist," equipped with leather jacket, studded belt, and violent nature, of the type Ginsberg and Kerouac exalt in their writing. Brando, who has a strong social conscience, has expressed regret at his participation in this film and lately has even been attempting roles of a more articulate nature. But the success of his imitators—James Dean, Ralph Meeker, Ben Gazzara, Paul Newman, Rod Steiger, and countless others—testifies to the persistent popularity of a hero unlike any before seen in the movies.

Like the heroes of San Francisco literature, this hero is extremely withdrawn, but his subjectivity seems as much the result of the actor's technique as of the scenarist's concept. The famous Method of the Russian director Stanislavsky, as presently practiced in this country, exalts the actor's personality over the written word. That is, the actor imposes his experience on the part rather than—like, say, Sir Laurence Olivier—subordinates himself to it. The personality of many Method actors, however, rather than being an individual expression, is often a parody of Brando's playing of Stanley Kowalski. The result of this imitation is a culture hero with easily distinguishable traits. Important among them is that he is usually a delinquent of some kind and that—for all the dependence of his media on language—he cannot talk.

The hero's link with the Beat Generation is signified by the fact that he is invariably an outcast or a rebel who stands in a very uneasy relationship with society. His rebellion, like that of the San Francisco writers, is expressed as much through his costume (torn T shirt, leather jacket, blue jeans) as through his behavior, for in a world of suits and ties, a shabby, careless appearance is an open sign of alienation. Again as in the case of the San Franciscans, his rebellion seems to be unmotivated. It no longer has any political or social relevance, and it is obscured by his inability to describe it. Most often, he is a rebel without a cause, whose sense of grievance has turned inward on himself, making his grip on reality extremely uncertain. Although he often travels in groups, sometimes in juvenile gangs, he seems to be alienated even from his friends. He is a man whom nobody understands and who understands nobody. Toward the world of authority—his father, his teachers, and the police—he feels hostile and he seems to be submissive only with his girl friend. His confusion has isolated him within a self which he cannot comprehend and which, in consequence, causes him unspeakable pain. . . .

While the present school of Abstract Expressionist and "action" painters in America may at first glance seem far removed from the Brandos and Jimmy Deans and Kerouacs, they too have moved into private worlds. Their manifestoes are defiant repudiations of the world beyond the self and of any art concerned with representing something external to it. The Abstract Expressionist's attitude toward his surroundings is illustrated by the new function he gives his work: his painting is no longer a gate opening onto a world of forms and ideas but a wall on which he inscribes his personal state of mind. The frenzied arabesques of Jackson Pollock, the calligraphic images of Franz Kline and Robert Motherwell, the huge horizontal blocks of Mark Rothko, the frosty specters of Clyfford Still, the "bursts" and "blasts" of Adolph Gottlieb, are all concerned not with things or with people but with the artist's responses to his own mystic visions. In these "action" paintings we are confronted with the painter's dreams before he has reflected on them, sometimes before he even knows what they are. "When the painting is finished," writes one of their number, "the subject reveals itself."

In short, the Abstract Expressionists do not seem hostile to reality around them so much as completely indifferent to it. As far as these painters are concerned, the outside world might just as well not exist. They seek in their own souls for mystical states which they can transfer to canvas as "flux," "nonrational truths," and "personal myths." The painter no longer feels a need to describe or to reflect upon his subject but rather, like Grace Hartigan, to "distill it until I have its essence." When we hear more talk about "essences," we are on familiar territory. The spilled ink, the spattered paint, and the dripped pigment are expressions of "spontaneity," much like Kerouac's automatic writing. Drawing almost disappears, while color, with its exclusively emotional attack, becomes predominant. The intelligence is suspended in favor of intuitions, feelings, impulses.

One is hard put to test the validity of these feelings and impulses, since no one seems to know quite what they are. The latest abstract paintings deal with an "unknown realm of experience" and are therefore designed to suggest emotions unaccountable to reason. Since these emotions are nonrational, it becomes impossible to discourse about them. The painter Clyfford Still finds "demands for communication . . . both presumptuous and irrelevant." The painting is not to be explained or understood but rather *experienced*. Since the painting is now a feeling rather than an object, it can only call forth a subjective response. In fact, the spectator is expected to have a response to a response, ideally the same response as the artist. He is no longer to see through the painter's eyes but simply to vibrate in tune with his unconscious mind.

The result is a pictorial parallel to the mumbling Method performance and the stammering San Francisco novel—an exercise in noncommunication, which forces one to take the artist's "higher vision" on faith alone. The paintings no doubt have a certain validity, but validity of a very limited and relative kind, like a Rorschach test which conjures up different associations in each spectator. The Abstract Expressionist's reluctance to communicate concretely casts serious doubts on his insights. An artist is under no compulsion to communicate, but it is nonsense to assume that he is more profound if he cannot get through with his feelings and ideas.

In fact, in this new art it is often difficult to distinguish between self-expression and self-indulgence. The feeling most powerfully reflected in Pollock's work is aggression, while Still's paintings have the look of complete passivity. Like the San Francisco literati, these artists alternate between "mad" and "beat." These emotions prepare us for the familiar assault on all authority and tradition, both in art and society. Like the "disaffiliated" writer, each artist likes to think of himself as a "solitary," alone in a hostile world, free of all conditioning, protecting the supreme integrity of his achievement. The image of the artist maintaining his solitary vision in the face of indifference and misunderstanding attracts our sympathy, for it recalls the unhappy fact that many great artists of the past hundred years were scorned by their society and forced to stand alone. But in the Abstract Expressionist, this stance is more an affectation than a fact. Actually his rebellion radiates an aura of conformism. He, too, travels in "schools" and "colonies." Although we are told that each of the new paintings is a bid for "individual identity," what is depressing is that so many of them look as if they might have been done by the same person. Despite the intense subjectivity of the new painting, the "visions" seem to be collective rather than personal. Although this is sometimes justified as "unconscious collaboration," the psychology of the Abstract Expressionist seems to be more that of the coterie than of the solitary.

It is, finally, a little pretentious to talk about solitariness when Abstract Expressionism has received so much instantaneous critical acclaim and when it has become the source of such active commercial speculation. (Since his death, Pollock's works have fetched as much as $30,000 apiece.) Clearly, the new art is not in that state of rebellious isolation it pretends to be. As the critic Ernst Gombrich has observed, the days have passed when you could shock the critics or the public; they have not only become fully conditioned to shock but have begun to demand it. A declaration of rebellion in America today carries with it not obscurity and poverty but immediate attention and adulation. For the artist, the ready acceptance of new departures is a happier situation than was the old hostility to them, but it indicates that his new forms and new truths are neither very dangerous nor very piercing. Although they may baffle people, they do not upset them—as for instance the angry paintings of the German Expressionists did a generation or more ago, enraging viewers to the point of spitting on the canvases. The newest departures are too remote to shake anybody's complacency, too obscure to give any profound shocks to the soul.

Taken together in their inarticulateness, obscurity, and self-isolation, the assorted bearers of Beat Generation attitudes in the various arts in America show an increasing reluctance to come to grips with life. They seem to be engaged in a new kind of expatriation—this time more symbolic than geographic. Unlike the expatriates of the past, they are not moving toward what they see as culture and enlightenment, but away from it. Having abdicated the traditional responsibilities of the avant-garde—that of facing existing culture squarely and honestly if only to criticize, condemn, or demolish it —they seem determined to slough off all responsibility whatsoever. In this, the artists of the Beat Generation differ from Britain's Angry Young Men today, who not only have serious public and intellectual causes to fight for but are highly articulate about them. But we may take solace in the fact that America also has artists who are eloquent, individualistic, and above all sympathetic to the claims of the intelligence, and who no doubt will outlast the Kowalski cult of unthink.

SUGGESTIONS FOR WRITING

1. Robert Brustein (1927-     ) graduated from Amherst and Columbia, has taught at Cornell and Vassar, and is now a member of the English Department at Columbia University. He is also drama critic for the *New Republic* and has contributed many articles to leading magazines. Brustein writes as if the cult of unthink were well on the way

out. John Ciardi said as much in his provocative essay, "Epitaph for
the Dead Beats," *Saturday Review* (February 6, 1960). The echo returns
in the critical essays in Thomas Parkinson's *A Casebook on the Beat*
(1961). Is the movement over? Has "The Method" school of acting run
its course? Is the Beat Generation a dead issue? Write an essay considering these questions.

2. Are the Beats outwardly individualistic and inwardly conformist? Or
is this characteristic simply a human condition? Are we all inwardly
conformists? How is it possible to identify with a movement without
conforming to its institutions and characteristics? Write a theme on
this topic.

3. In his second paragraph, Brustein depicts the "hero" of the Method
school of acting. Is it possible to be annoyed at the excesses of that
school and yet find yourself fascinated by it? In other words, if you
enjoy the type of acting here associated with Marlon Brando, what are
the qualities which appeal to you?

4. Brustein talks about the group's urge to seek detachment, separation,
isolation, which the group calls "coolness." What is "cool"? What are
the varieties of meaning of the word? Describe someone who is "cool"
by showing him in the act of being "cool."

P . R . R O H D E N

# The Histrionic Experience*

What is it that distinguishes a person in a play from a "real"
person? It seems to be the fact that the former stands before our
eyes as a fully developed totality. We see our fellowmen only in a
fragmentary fashion, and the faculty of self-knowledge usually is so
much impaired by vanity and desire that it amounts to nothing.
What we call "dramatic illusion," therefore, is the paradoxical
phenomenon that we know better what is going on in the mind of
a Hamlet than what stirs our own minds. For Shakespeare, the
poet-actor, shows not only the act but also its motives, and in such
a comprehensive way as we never see them combined in real life.

This establishment of a rational connection between character

* From *Reflections on Art* translated by Susan K. Langer [originally from
*Der Schauspieler* by Ewald Geissler (Berlin, 1926)] (Baltimore: The Johns Hopkins Press, 1958). © 1958 by The Johns Hopkins Press. Reprinted by permission
of the author and publishers.

and fate transcends reality, even if it does not—as in Schiller—assume the specific form of "idealization," the heightening towards the moral normative. The "greatness" of an Oedipus or a Macbeth does not depend on the fact that they are better men than we, but on the integration of their actions and sufferings with a superindividual order of existence that lends them significance. The amoral deities of some religions go to prove that the longing of man may be directed towards a sheer increase in strength, just so it gives life some meaning that transcends the contingencies of mere empirical existence.

What, then, happens within the soul of the actor when he plays Hamlet? Some maintain that the performer only acts "as if" he were Hamlet; others, that he is "really" Hamlet. Both attempts at interpretation are inadequate. To "be" Hamlet, or even only to act as if one were Hamlet, presupposes that a Hamlet "reality" exists outside the histrionic creation. One can "imitate" only a given reality. However, the congruence of character and fate which Shakespeare established in his *Hamlet* exists only within the tragedy. Each representation of Hamlet is therefore a creation, not a reproduction. Even the poet participates only indirectly in the creative process on the stage. *Ad libitum* comedy shows to what a high degree the actor can emancipate himself from the dramatist. And it is but by a misconceived idealism, rooted in today's preponderance of the literary play, that an actor considers himself the "servant" of the poet. Certainly, anyone endowed with theatrical imagination can derive an approximate picture of the action by reading a Shakespearean drama, just as a musician can hear the melody and the rhythm when reading an orchestral score. But reading cannot replace actual presentation. If the poet really could transmit everything to the actor, then not only would anyone be able to play Hamlet, but there would also be only one correct Hamlet interpretation, whereas in fact each great performer plays Hamlet differently.

What the dramatist delivers is the words and ideograms of a psychic existence. It is left to the actor to integrate these words through speech melody, speech rhythm, and gesture into a unit which only then gives the full reality of "Hamlet." Whoever designates the histrionic art as reproductive, because it is tied to the "text," must logically deny the poet his creativity because *he* merely manipulates the language of his native land. But a stanza from *Iphigenie* is something different from the sum of its words subjected to a metric scheme; the same magic atmosphere that separates the work of the poet from the everyday concept elevates the actor's vitally intoned and embodied word-gesture above the poetic "verse-ideogram."

But how does this histrionic magic come about? Through an interaction between a surrender to the emotional current and a conscious drive towards form. Thomas Mann has pointed out to us in *Tonio Kröger* and in *Königliche Hoheit* that a sincere sentimental overflow is not sufficient to create a work of art. The disconcerted astonishment of the young prince, when for the first time he grasps the concept of artistic self-discipline, is one of the most delightful passages in the novel. The same holds true for the actor. If an actress playing Iphigenia were to permit herself to be so overcome by her emotion that she actually broke down in uncontrollable sobbing, she would force the director to break off the performance by quickly lowering the curtain. To "become absorbed" in the role without retaining a supervisory control over its performance would be the surest means of destroying the dramatic "illusion."

For this illusion is based on the very fact that the performer knows all about the character from the beginning; this makes it possible for him slowly to intensify his power, to reserve it for an apparently quite uncontrollable outburst, and then allow it gradually to ebb away again. Feeling and expression of feeling are, to be sure, sometimes connected, but they are subject to different laws. Even in daily life we notice that the expression of genuine emotions may at times assume forms of bad taste. Anyone used to self-observation has noted that a statement is the more convincing the more consciously its formulation is controlled.

The histrionic art, therefore, is not based on some sort of "repression": so that Wegener would have developed into a blue-bearded despot and Elisabeth Bergner into an ecstatic saint if only our present civilization admitted of such characters. The potentialities of those characters are transferred by the actor not into the reality of actual life, but to the stage. Between the several realms of reality there is only one bridge, that of analogy. A religious philosopher who speaks, for instance, of the wrath of God, is guilty of an anthropomorphism. He transfers a human characteristic to the deity, whereas he is really dealing with a simile. A like relation exists between real and artistically formulated emotion. The portrayer of Othello is not jealous, but "jealous"—insofar as we mean to express the ideogrammatic character of the affect by the quotation marks.

Even though, accordingly, we reject both the attempted definitions of the histrionic experience as, respectively, a "so-being" and a "so-acting," yet there lies in them a core of truth which language indicates in the ambiguity of the word "stage-play." For the "stage," the spectacle, is not only for the audience, but also means the inner vision (*Innenschau*) by which the actor gains access to his role. And according to the interrelation of "stage" and "play," i.e. surrender to the stage reality and control of this surrender, in the individual artist, two actor types may be distinguished. In the case of one, the "comedian," the primary factor is the joy in playing, the pleasure found in the change of character with its trappings of masks, costumes, and mummery. This type is very little ego-connected, but is the more ego-dependent. Since each part is for him only an opportunity to satisfy his urge for play and metamorphosis, his accomplishment is to a large degree independent of the poetic value of the play. An actress of this type is recognized by her preference for male parts, just as the comedian in general prefers character portrayals that are alien, if not opposite, to his role in private life. The best example is the melancholy of the clown, where psychical artistry is combined with physical acrobatics.

If this type is equated with man at large, it constitutes the ultimate refinement of the social phenomenon which we call "acting." He who acts aims at a kind of self-presentation which places his ego in the most favorable light. Hence he is not concerned with interpretation but with impression. Still, one must beware of judging the comedian only by the worst of his kind. Not only Possart but also Matkowsky was one of them. In postwar Germany this type is on the decline, just as generally speaking the most brilliant representatives belong to the Romance cultures. In the French drama, from Corneille to Rostand, there are parts which can be played only by comedians. Just consider the manner in which a Cid delivers his emotions front stage, or how a Cyrano de Bergerac plays catch ball with his feelings.

Hence it is no accident that we have to designate a Frenchwoman,

Sarah Bernhardt, as the most brilliant representative of this type. To the melancholy German and—as has been proved by guest performances of the Russians—to the Slavs, this type is alien. The German wants introspection rather than play and prefers the character actor in whom the surrender to the part outweighs the joy of metamorphosis. This type of actor, which since the time of Kainz and Eleonora Duse has found its most important representatives in Moissi, Werner Krauss, Klöpfer, George and Elisabeth Bergner, is the counterpart of the comedian. His psychological receptivity enables him to submerge himself to a much greater extent in the personality to be represented. He who personally knows actors of this sort must have noticed that they often carry the expression, and especially the look, of a character that they portrayed for hours after the performance. For the pain and the pleasure of a character whom they impersonate become real to them in a much more profound way than to a comedian, because they represent him empathically.

Thus representation becomes almost substitution, which in the case of the intensified excitability of the character actor can go so far as to produce a sympathetic emotional reaction from the sufferings of a part he is playing. Those who enjoy medical terminology may well speak of hysteria. In the case of such a neurotic actor we are dealing with a manic type in whom the borders between normality and derangement are often fluid. Even if the well-known story of the actor who plays Napoleon and then suddenly imagines he *is* Napoleon, is probably too crass ever to have occurred, even the slightest sign of depression during the withdrawal from a role into private life proves the danger of this kind of "ecstasy."

But precisely on the basis of this immediate link with the part can the lesser versatility of the ecstatic performer be explained. The number of roles that "suit" him are naturally limited. For he cannot artificially establish the experiential contact; above all, he cannot cover a mistake or a sudden disruption by his artistic skill. Floodlights and the smell of backdrops, the purple robe and the scepter have no magic power over him who derives his· art from his psyche and not from the props. Therefore each part is for him an experiment which necessitates a revision of his artistic resources. But whenever his stream of experience is permitted to flow unhampered the gain in depth compensates for the loss in breadth. Then there arise images of such compelling power as the Wallenstein of a Werner Krauss or the Saint Joan of an Elisabeth Bergner, where each intonation, each gesture has its immovable place; in short, creations of "such stuff as dreams are made on," and yet of such a consuming inner truth that they leave all reality behind, burst asunder the frame of the merely theatrical, and knock at the gates of cosmic existence.

## SUGGESTIONS FOR WRITING

1. Peter Rohden, a contemporary German critic, argues that each production of *Hamlet* is a creation, not a reproduction. In what sense is this true?
2. Why is artistic self-discipline on the part of the actor necessary to preserve the dramatic illusion?
3. Rohden speaks of two types of actors, those who "surrender" to the part, and those who, like the comedian, experience the joy of metamorphosis. He says the Germans prefer the actor who surrenders to the part. Which do you prefer, and why?
4. Do you believe a dramatic performer can "burst asunder the frame of the merely theatrical, and knock at the gates of cosmic existence"? The question assumes that the answer will provide definitions of (1) normal existence, (2) a theatrical existence, e.g., the existence of Hamlet, and (3) a cosmic (nonnormal, nontheatrical) existence above both.

CHARLES MORGAN

# The Nature of Dramatic Illusion*

It is true that art is rooted in imitation, and that, when it is cut off from that root and becomes decoration only or didacticism only, it dries up and withers. It is rooted in imitation—but in imitation of what? Do not let us say of ordinary life, for the phrase, though Aristotle himself uses it, has no precise meaning. Mr. Baldwin is said to be a representative Englishman; his life is presumably the

---

* From *Essays by Divers Hands* (*Transactions of the Royal Society of Literature*, N.S., Vol. XIII, 1933). Reprinted by permission of Hilda Morgan and Field, Roscoe & Co.

ordinary life of an English ex-Prime Minister; but I do not see him as you see him, nor do we see him as Shelley would have seen him. How, then, is art to imitate him? It cannot. It can imitate my view of him or yours or Shelley's, but in each of these imitations there will be more of Shelley or you or me than of the hypothetical ordinariness of Mr. Baldwin. All that art can do in the way of imitation of a given natural subject is, first, to negative a spectator's own preconceptions of that subject so that he lies open to imaginative acceptance of a different view, the artist's view, of it, and secondly, to impregnate him with this fresh, this alien understanding. Illusion is the impregnating force—in masterpieces permanently fruitful, in lesser works of art existent but without endurance, and from machine-made plays, however well made, absent. How often we say of a play that it was "a good story" or "an admirable entertainment"; that it was "cleverly constructed," or that its "characters were natural and alive"; and, having thus praised it, add with a vague sense of disappointment, "but there was nothing in it." What is the critical equivalent of that evasive phrase? The formalists have no answer; the impressionists have none. Does not the phrase mean that the play had no impregnating power? Though it had a thousand other virtues it was without illusion.

The lady of whom I have spoken believes that, in the photograph of her son, she has seen her own impression of him. Evidently she has done nothing of the kind. She has been persuaded to forget her view of him and to accept the camera's as her own. When she goes to a play, which seems to her exactly like life, she has been persuaded to abandon her own view of life and to accept the dramatist's. It is true that, when the dramatist is of her own imaginative and intellectual kin, the exchange is not revolutionary, but, when he is a man of genius and has power to persuade her to take his view of "A Doll's House" or to see with his eyes the lamp thrown at wife and mother by Strindberg's Father, the results are prodigious. That lamp of Strindberg's still hurtles through the domestic air, and by Nora a million feminine squirrels were converted into tigresses whose cubs still embarrass us.

And why? Not because the lady in the stalls had ever before thought of herself as resembling the lady of Strindberg's lamp; not because, if she was a squirrel, she had ever perceived, until Ibsen pointed it out to her, the limitations of her comfortable cage; not because these great plays were like life as she had formerly understood it; but because her own preconceptions were stilled and afterwards impregnated. What stirred her, what influenced her, was not delusion, which is of herself, but illusion—that divine essence above the battle—which is of the drama. . . . Dramatic art has, therefore, a double function—first to still the preoccupied mind, to empty it of triviality, to make it receptive and meditative; then to impregnate it. Illusion is the impregnating power. It is that spiritual force in dramatic art which impregnates the silences of the spectator, enabling him to imagine, to perceive, even to become, what he could not of himself become or perceive or imagine.

Inquiry, now, into the nature and origin of this impregnating force will expose the root of the theory. Illusion, as I conceive it, is form in suspense. The phrase is obscure and must be explained.

Analytical critics have all supposed that form is valuable in itself. They have based their judgments on a study of form, first establishing by general argument what they consider a perfect form for tragedy or comedy, then asking us to match particular plays with it. It is not surprising that they so often weary themselves in crying "This is not a play" when they encounter dramatic expression that does not correspond with their ideal form. Their confusion, and it is a confusion that has run through the ages, springs from their failure to perceive one plain truth—that in a play form is not valuable *in itself;* only the suspense of form has value. In a play, form is not and cannot be valuable in itself, because until the play is over form does not exist.

Form is *in itself* valuable only in those works of art into which the time factor does not enter, and which, therefore, come to us whole. Painting, sculpture and architecture come to us whole; they are directly formal arts. An epic poem does not come to us whole, but a short lyric or a particular line therein may almost be said to do this, so slight, by comparison with an epic, is the time factor involved. A play's performance occupies two or three hours. Until the end its form is latent in it. It follows that during the performance we are not influenced by the form itself, the completed thing, but by our anticipations of completion. We are, so to speak, waiting for the suspended rhyme or harmony, and this formal suspense has the greater power if we know beforehand, as the Greeks did, what the formal release is to be.

This suspense of form, by which is meant the incompleteness of a known completion, is to be clearly distinguished from common suspense—suspense of plot—the ignorance of what will happen, and I would insist upon this distinction with all possible emphasis, for suspense of plot is a structural accident, and suspense of form is, as I understand it, essential to the dramatic art itself. The desire to know what will happen, when it exists at all, is a quality of the audience's delusion; it springs from their temporary belief that they are witnessing, not art, but life; it is the product of deluded curiosity, and is often strongest in the weakest minds. It is obviously stronger in a housemaid watching a play by Mr. Edgar Wallace than in a cultivated spectator of the Aeschylean 'Prometheus,' and it would become progressively less strong even in the housemaid as by repeated visits to the theatre the designs of Mr. Wallace were made more familiar to her. I do not wish to speak contemptuously of suspense of plot, for it often contributes to the pleasure of play-going and reading; it has this value—that it keeps our eyes on stage or book. It may draw attention to a work of art and has been used by great artists for that purpose, but it is not essential to the art itself. Suspense of form, on the contrary, is one of those things without which drama is not.

It may be objected that without form there can be no suspense of form, and that to this extent a formal critic is justified. My argument is that he is wrong in insisting that particular dramatic forms are valuable in themselves. What rhyme is begun matters less than that the rhyme be completed; what harmony is used matters less than that it be resolved; what form is chosen, though it is true that some forms are more beautiful than others, matters less than that while the drama moves *a* form is being fulfilled.

Dramatic illusion, then, is the suspense of dramatic form, and is to be thought of as men think of divinity—an essence in which they may or may not partake, a power which may or may not visit them.

SUGGESTIONS FOR WRITING

1. Charles Morgan wrote this article in 1933, but there is still a freshness and timelessness in his approach. Except for his reference to ex-Prime Minister Baldwin, it might have been written today. And except for

the references to post-Aristotelian plays, it might have been written in Aristotle's day. The force and clarity of this selection is due partly to Morgan's way with words—his use of precise but unpedantic language—but it is also due to the thought itself. We read and we nod our heads in agreement. In this process are we not agreeing with our own experience in the theater?

2. To what extent is Morgan's concept of illusion applicable to other art forms (including literature)? What modifications would you make?

3. Choose a specific dramatic presentation (play, TV, movie) and reveal the nature of the dramatic illusion to which Morgan refers. In other words, change Morgan's definition by analysis and classification into an operational definition. Your definition should use the dramatic presentation only as an illustration. Avoid describing the plot in detail.


AGNES DE MILLE

# Pavlova*


Anna Pavlova! My life stops as I write that name. Across the daily preoccupation of lessons, lunch boxes, tooth brushings, and quarrelings with Margaret flashed this bright, unworldly experience and burned in a single afternoon a path over which I could never retrace my steps. I had witnessed the power of beauty, and in some chamber of my heart I lost forever my irresponsibility. I was as clearly marked as though she had looked me in the face and called my name. For generations my father's family had loved and served the theater. All my life I had seen actors and actresses and had heard theater jargon at the dinner table and business talk of box-office grosses. I had thrilled at Father's projects and watched fascinated his picturesque occupations. I took a proprietary pride in the profitable and hasty growth of "The Industry." But nothing in his world or my uncle's prepared me for theater as I saw it that Saturday afternoon.

Since that day I have gained some knowledge in my trade and I recognize that her technique was limited; that her arabesques were not as pure or classically correct as Markova's, that her jumps and

* From *Dance to the Piper* by Agnes De Mille (Boston: Little, Brown and Co., 1952). Copyright 1951, 1952 by Agnes De Mille. Reprinted by permission of Little, Brown and Co.—Atlantic Monthly Press.

*batterie* were paltry, her turns not to be compared in strength and number with the strenuous durability of Baronova or Toumanova. I know that her scenery was designed by second-rate artists, her music was on a level with restaurant orchestrations, her company definitely inferior to all the standards we insist on today, and her choreography mostly hack. And yet I say she was in her person the quintessence of theatrical excitement.

As her little bird body revealed itself on the scene, either immobile in trembling mystery or tense in the incredible arc which was her lift, her instep stretched ahead in an arch never before seen, the tiny bones of her hands in ceaseless vibration, her face radiant, diamonds glittering under her dark hair, her little waist encased in silk, the great tutu balancing, quickening and flashing over her beating, flashing, quivering legs, every man and woman sat forward, every pulse quickened. She never appeared to rest static, some part of her trembled, vibrated, beat like a heart. Before our dazzled eyes, she flashed with the sudden sweetness of a humming-bird in action too quick for understanding by our gross utilitarian standards, in action sensed rather than seen. The movie cameras of her day could not record her allegro. Her feet and hands photographed as a blur.

Bright little bird bones, delicate bird sinews! She was all fire and steel wire. There was not an ounce of spare flesh on her skeleton, and the life force used her body until she died of the fever of moving, gasping for breath, much too young.

She was small, about five feet. She wore a size one and a half slipper, but her feet and hands were large in proportion to her height. Her hand could cover her whole face. Her trunk was small and stripped of all anatomy but the ciphers of adolescence, her arms and legs relatively long, the neck extraordinarily long and mobile. All her gestures were liquid and possessed of an inner rhythm that flowed to inevitable completion with the finality of architecture or music. Her arms seemed to lift not from the elbow or the arm socket, but from the base of the spine. Her legs seemed to function from the waist. When she bent her head her whole spine moved and the motion was completed the length of the arm through the elongation of her slender hand and the quivering reaching fingers. Without in any way being sensual—being, in fact, almost sexless—she suggested all exhilaration, gaiety, and delight. She jumped, and we broke bonds with reality. We flew. We hung over the earth, spread in the air as we do in dreams, our hands turning in the air as in water—the strong forthright taut plunging leg balanced on the poised arc of the foot, the other leg stretched to the horizon like the wing of a bird. We lay balancing, quivering, turning, and all things were possible, even to us, the ordinary people.

I have seen two dancers as great or greater since, Alicia Markova and Margot Fonteyn, and many other women who have kicked higher, balanced longer, or turned faster. These are poor substitutes for passion. In spite of her flimsy dances, the bald and blatant virtuosity, there was an intoxicated rapture, a focus of energy, Dionysian in its physical intensity, that I have never seen equaled by a performer in any theater of the world. Also she was the *first* of the truly great in our experience.

I sat with the blood beating in my throat. As I walked into the bright glare of the afternoon, my head ached and I could scarcely swallow. I didn't wish to cry. I certainly couldn't speak. I sat in a daze in the car, oblivious to the grownups' ceaseless prattle. At home I climbed the stairs slowly to my bedroom and, shutting myself in, placed both hands on the brass rail at the foot of my bed; then, rising laboriously to the tips of my white buttoned shoes, I stumped the width of the bed and back again. My toes quivered with weakness. I repeated the exercise. The blessed, relieving tears stuck at last on my lashes. Only by hurting my feet could I ease the pain in my throat. . . .

Standing on Ninth Avenue under the El, I saw the headlines on the front page of the New York *Times*. It did not seem possible. She was in essence the denial of death. My own life was rooted to her in a deep spiritual sense, and had been during the whole of my growing up. It mattered not that I had only spoken to her once and that my work lay in a different direction. She was the vision and the impulse and the goal.

## SUGGESTIONS FOR WRITING

1. Agnes De Mille, the daughter of Cecil B. De Mille, became a choreographer in 1928. She is one of the outstanding choreographers in the United States. She first came to wide public attention for her choreographical work in the musical *Oklahoma!*. As the daughter of Cecil B.

De Mille, the movie producer, she spent her early days in an atmosphere of the theater. As she says in the above essay, "All my life I had seen actors and actresses and had heard theater jargon at the dinner table . . ." The theater world is a world of exaggeration. Nothing is simply good; it is great. Still, one senses in this essay something that reaches beyond the typical exaggeration of the theater. One senses a genuine enchantment. What gives the essay this tone? What specific words or phrases lift it above the average? Write an essay about your favorite theatrical person and, assuming you feel a genuine enchantment or a deeply felt reason for using superlatives, let your reader feel the depth of your wonder and amazement.

2. Agnes De Mille does not stop with generalizations; she describes specific movements of Pavlova and a specific dance, *The Swan*. But since she wants to convey her own reaction and not just the impression generally that Pavlova made, Miss De Mille gives us the details of a few key experiences. For example, she says, "Anna Pavlova! My life stops as I write that name. . . . everyone sat stricken. Death was upon each of us. . . . Standing on Ninth Avenue under the El, I saw the headlines on the front page of the New York *Times*." Using Miss De Mille's technique, convey your own reaction to the death of a famous theatrical person.

3. The fifth paragraph is crowded with details which describe Pavlova physically. Describe the physical features of someone to reveal how they contribute to that person's ability to perform.

# Music and Painting

Art is not an end in itself, but a means of addressing humanity.
—Modest Petrovich Mussorgsky, 1835-1881

Without music life would be a mistake.
—Nietzsche, *Maxims and Missiles,* 1888

Perpetual modernness is the measure of merit in every work of art.
—Emerson, 1803-1882

And if you, O poet, represent a story by depicting it with your pen, the painter with his brush will so render it as to be more easily satisfying and less tedious to understand. If you call painting "dumb poetry," then the painter may say of the poet that his art is "blind painting."
—Leonardo da Vinci, 1452-1519

No man ever forgot the visitations of that power to his heart and brain, which created all things new; which was the dawn in him of music, poetry, and art.
—Emerson, *Essays, First Series* (Love) 1841

Music is Love in search of a word.
—Sidney Lanier, *The Symphony,* 1877

The best, most beautiful, and most perfect way that we have of expressing a sweet concord of mind to each other is by music. When I would form, in my mind, ideas of a society in the highest degree happy, I think of them as expressing their love, their joy, and the inward concord, and harmony, and spiritual beauty of their souls, by sweetly singing to each other.
—Jonathan Edwards, *Miscellaneous Observations,* 1747

And the minute the words were out of his mouth somebody over in the crowd struck up the doxologer, and everybody joined in with all their might, and it just warmed you up and made you feel as good as church letting out. Music *is* a good thing; and after all that soul-butter and hogwash I never see it freshen up things so and sound so honest and bully.
—Mark Twain, *Huckleberry Finn,* 1884

*388*

B. H. HAGGIN

# The Meaning of Music*

Full many a glorious morning have I seen
Flatter the mountain-tops with sovereign eye,
Kissing with golden face the meadows green,
Gilding pale streams with heavenly alchymy;
Anon permit the basest clouds to ride
With ugly rack on his celestial face,
And from the forlorn world his visage hide,
Stealing unseen to west with this disgrace:
Even so my sun one early morn did shine,
With all-triumphant splendour on my brow:
But, out! alack! he was but one hour mine,
The region cloud hath mask'd him from me now.
   Yet him for this my love no whit disdaineth;
   Suns of the world may stain when heaven's sun staineth.

In the sonnet I quoted, or in one of Hamlet's soliloquies, we see a complex form of words embody and communicate a complex synthesis of thought and emotion. And if anyone were to ask "What thought, what emotion?" the answer would be "The thought and emotion expressed and defined by that form of words." One can say that the sonnet is concerned with the love which is given and then withheld; one can say further that this love is compared with the sun which lights the earth and then is hidden by clouds; but to do this is not to convey the rich overtones of sense and feeling that are expressed by

---

* From *Music for the Man Who En oys Hamlet* by B. H. Haggin (New York: Alfred A. Knopf, Inc., 1944). Copyright 1944, © 1960 by B. H. Haggin. Reprinted by permission of the author.

Full many a glorious morning have I seen
Flatter the mountain-tops with sovereign eye,
Kissing with golden face the meadows green,
Gilding pale streams with heavenly alchymy;

and the rest of the poem. The only way of conveying those overtones is to state the precise form of words that Shakespeare himself
devised for this purpose.

A painter, too, may be aware only of choosing a bit of paint and
placing it on the canvas in relation to a number of other bits; but
the choice, the placing, the relation involve exercise of judgment—
which is to say that they involve the whole man, the sum at that
moment of his experience, thought, emotion, insight. What is involved in the choices and uses of the bits of paint reveals itself
through them; and in the end the completed integrated arrangement of lines, colors, planes, masses, and forms is a visual embodiment and communication of a particular synthesis of that experience, thought, emotion, insight.

Roger Fry has described the process of a Cézanne still life, in
which bottles, pears, and apples, so commonplace as to have no
emotional associations in themselves, are "deprived of all those
specific characters by which we ordinarily apprehend their concrete
existence," and are "reduced to pure elements of space and volume"
which are then "coordinated and organized by the artist's sensual
intelligence." He refers to Cézanne's own conception that it was out
of these relations of formal elements that emotion was to emanate;
and he says: "One may wonder whether painting has ever aroused
graver, more powerful, more massive emotions than those to which
we are compelled by some of Cézanne's masterpieces in this genre."
And these emotions to which we are compelled—not by the subjects
of the paintings, but by the pictorial treatment of the subjects—
these grave, powerful, massive emotions are something we have no
way of knowing or defining or conveying, other than by those relations of formal elements on the canvas that were Cézanne's way.

So with the piece of music that is a formal organization of sound
—or sounds—in time. The sounds have no external references to
objects or ideas; what they have is the internal coherence of a kind
of grammar of their own; and the relations in which they are placed
—in a texture of horizontal lines of sounds in sequence (melody)

and vertical sounds in simultaneous combination (harmony), articulated by duration and stress (rhythm), and colored by the timbres of instruments or voices—are governed basically by this grammar, which is used in an individual style by each composer, in obedience to the laws of his own being. He too, that is, may be aware only of choosing a sound and placing it in relation to a number of others; but the choice, the placing, the relation, involving exercise of judgment as they do, involve the sum at that moment of his experience, thought, emotion, insight—of which a particular synthesis is finally embodied and communicated in the completed formal arrangement of sounds. If anyone were to ask about the second movement of Beethoven's Sonata Opus 111 "What thought, what emotion, what insight?" one could say, as I did earlier, "The sense of experience mastered, lessons learned, resignation, inner illumination achieved." But one would have to use the same words about the opening of Schubert's B flat Sonata, to describe experience mastered, lessons learned, resignation and illumination achieved that are different from Beethoven's and expressed in different musical terms. This demonstrates the inadequacy of the words, and the fact that here again we have no way of knowing or defining or conveying the synthesis of experience and emotion that is embodied in each piece of music, other than by the formal construction in sound that each man used for the purpose.

One might, for that matter, find no other words than "experience mastered, lessons learned, resignation and illumination achieved" for other pieces of music by Beethoven himself—that is, for the same synthesis of experience and emotion that embodies itself in different constructions of sound. From this we realize that in dealing with a work of art we are concerned not with meaning but with meaning as embodied in form. We read Shakespeare not merely for his profound insights, but for these insights as made explicit and affecting in his rich poetic forms; and so with Cézanne's powerful emotions, and the inner illumination and exaltation of Beethoven in his last years. We are, then, interested in each different formal construction on canvas from which we get the impact of the same powerful emotions, each different construction of sound which conveys to us the same inner illumination and exaltation.

I have gone into all this to get you to see that just as the way to understand Shakespeare's poem is to read it, and the way to understand Cézanne's still life is to look at it, so the way—the only way —to understand Beethoven's or Schubert's sonata movement is the one you have already used successfully with its opening passage— to listen to it. It was natural for you, when the music made no sense, to ask to be told what its sense was, and to ask to be told in words, since you were accustomed to think of sense as expressible in words. And it was necessary for you to learn to apprehend from a phrase of music a sense which was not definable by words—which was defined solely by the particular organization of sounds in that phrase of music. You may say that I did use words to describe it and help you apprehend it; but they did not really describe what in the end you had to apprehend from the music and would have apprehended even without my words; and you will discover, when you are accustomed to the medium, that the meaning of a phrase of Beethoven or Schubert is grasped immediately with the sounds, and that if there is any difficulty, what is needed is not explanation of the phrase in words but repeated hearing of it. And you cannot get a wrong idea by listening to Beethoven or Schubert himself, but you will get some very wrong ideas by listening to the people who undertake to speak for him. . . .

### SUGGESTIONS FOR WRITING

1. B. H. Haggin (1900-   ) has been music critic for *Nation* since 1936. Parts of his book, *Music for the Man Who Enjoys Hamlet* (1944), have appeared in many anthologies. One significant item in his essay has caused considerable thought and comment among music critics: must a person be able to read music to enjoy it? Some say, "Not necessarily." They claim that, as Haggin says, all one need do is expose himself to music and let it "have its way with him." Others contend that understanding of music cannot be complete without a technical knowledge of it. What do you think? Is this true of all knowledge and art? Must one be able to dissect a poem to enjoy it fully? Must one have a knowledge of strains and stresses to enjoy the beautiful architectural forms fully? Can any appreciation be complete? What is complete appreciation? Write an essay indicating how you feel about these questions.

2. Are biographical and historical material necessary for interpreting a work of art? If not, why is such material so frequently used? Can a work of art be interpreted in and of itself? Can it be approached as if it had simply come into the reviewer's presence in the morning mail?

What are the pros and cons of using historical and biographical material as an approach to a work of art?
3. Haggin speaks of "a sense which was not definable by words." Can such a sense exist? How can we know or what ways do we have of knowing about such a sense? How can such a sense be communicated if words cannot be used?

ROBERT HERRICK

## To Music, to Becalm His Fever (1648)

Charm me asleep, and melt me so
With thy Delicious Numbers;
That being ravisht, hence I goe
Away in easie slumbers.
   Ease my sick head,
   And make my bed,
Thou Power that canst sever
   From me this ill:
   And quickly still:
   Though thou not kill
    My fever.

Thou sweetly canst convert the same
From a consuming fire,
Into a gentle-licking flame,
And make it thus expire.
   Then make me weep
   My paines asleep;
And give me such reposes,
   That I, poore I,
   May think, thereby,
   I live and die
    'Mongst Roses.

Fall on me like a silent dew,
Or like those Maiden showrs,
Which, by the peepe of day, doe strew
A Baptime o'er the flowers.
   Melt, melt my paines,
   With thy soft straines;

That having ease me given,
With full delight,
I leave this light
And take my flight
For Heaven.

## SUGGESTIONS FOR WRITING

1. Robert Herrick (1591-1674) was an English poet who wrote in the language of his age. Transform it into twentieth-century prose and analyze the profound effect of poetic utterance in Herrick's statement.
2. What is the effect of music on human beings? Herrick claims it can bring about physical-psychological change, and today the therapeutic effect of music is universally recognized. Analyze the reasons for this.
3. Compare and contrast Herrick's statement with the quotation by Mark Twain at the beginning of this section.
4. B. A. Haggin, in the previous selection, speaks of the similarities between poetry and music. Analyze Herrick's poem to reveal the similarity of which Haggin speaks.

MARIO  CASTELNUOVO-TEDESCO

## Musical Manifestations of Man*

"But," one will ask, "what are the qualities of a poem requisite to its suitability for musical setting? What is the ideal poem?" Naturally, it is difficult to say. The answer depends especially upon the sensitivity of the composer, and also upon the *genre* he prefers: he may have a stronger leaning towards dramatic or lyric, gay or sentimental poetry. Just the same, I believe there are some necessary conditions common to all first, one that goes to the essence: the poem must have an "expressive core"; it should express a "state of soul," whatever the musician's preferences may cause the nature of that state to be; it should, in any case, be capable of awakening a "resonance" in the composer's soul; it should express the "core" in a perfect, simple and direct, clear, and harmonious

---

* From "Problems of a Song Writer" in *The Musical Quarterly.* Copyright 1944 by G. Schirmer, Inc. Reprinted by permission of the publishers.

form, rich, but without too many words. A certain "margin" should be left for the music: from this point of view, an intimate and re-strained poem is preferable to a too sonorous and decorative one. (I cite a typical case: the great Italian poet, Gabriele d'Annunzio, who, with his vast wealth of words, seems to have amused himself by creating a sort of overwhelming and flamboyant verbal music, is a real difficulty to the composer. That is why, I think, attempts to set his poetry have succeeded so rarely, with one notable exception: the admirable *I Pastori* of Pizzetti.)

There are also other conditions, those of dimensions, of form. The poem should not be too long (unless the song is for voice and orchestra, a type which, as I have said, offers other possibilities); nor, on the other hand, should it be too short (unless there are to be several songs in a cycle). From this point of view also, the Ro-mantic poets offered ideal texts to their musicians—texts not only expressive, varied, and harmonious, but of reasonable length. Great Italian poetry, however, presents many difficulties in this respect. One cannot set "The Divine Comedy" to music, and, among the smaller forms, the sonnet (a prime favorite of Italian poets) is most unadaptable to music—first, because of the content, which is often too philosophic and intellectual; next, because of its almost too strict a form; and finally, because of the difficulty of balancing quatrains and tercets into different musical periods. The less strict forms of the *canzone* and the *ballata* are generally preferable, or poems that are entirely free.

I have said that contemporary poetry does not frequently offer inducements to composers; but we have a great heritage from past centuries in the literatures of all countries and all languages. And when I speak of foreign languages, I have in mind original texts, not translations. Translations of poetry are almost always "be-trayals." (*Traduttore, traditore.*) Even if there is not a betrayal of the contents, there is a betrayal of rhythm or of form, and these are poetic elements too precious and essential to be neglected.

This leads us to another problem: the often discussed one of the "musicality" of the different languages. That quality doubtless differs in degree from one tongue to another; but each language has its own special expressive possibilities (at least according to the fairly wide experience that I have had), and they are worth the trouble of trying out.

If one asks me what the most musical language is, naturally I answer, "Italian!" First, because it is my own language; then, because it is universally recognized as the most agreeable and easy language to sing. Broad, expressive, sonorous, it lends itself admirably to song, and one can easily understand why Italy is considered the fatherland and even the source of *bel canto*. But my admiration and preference for my native language do not prevent me from recognizing the qualities of other languages also. French, doubtless less suitable for impassioned outbursts (and consequently for song), is nevertheless subtler and lends itself to more exquisite nuances. Spanish has certain characteristics similar to those of Italian, except for a hardness sometimes more severe (and also, in compensation, a softness sometimes more languorous). I shall not say much of Latin, the mother of all these languages, except to note that it is generally regarded as a language especially fitting for sacred purposes, as the language of prayer. One is apt to forget its rich secular literature. I recall that, in my first years of study in Florence, the Director of the Conservatory was scandalized because I composed choruses on the Eclogues of Vergil instead of choosing to write motets. I have never tried Greek (distant memory of my early studies!) and in Hebrew I have composed only one chorus. German is an admirably rich language, quite in a class by itself by virtue of the forcefulness of its declamation, which permits vocal leaps that would be quite inexplicable in other languages (and also explains why Wagner is untranslatable).

I have left English for the last, not because I consider it less musical, but, on the contrary, because I am surprised that its musicality is so often doubted. I must confess that I too approached it with certain misgivings, so unfavorably had I been conditioned. My first encounter with English was by way of Shakespeare. Dissatisfied with an Italian translation of "Twelfth Night," from which I was setting several songs to music, I wanted to know the original text, and I was overjoyed and surprised to discover its language to be not only of a perfect beauty, but also of astonishing "musicality." I could not rest until I had set to music all the songs I could find in the tragedies and comedies, and I was miserable when I had exhausted the supply. In Shakespeare I found my ideal, the human richness, the greatest psychological profundity, united with the most supple and varied poetry. I have often been asked whether, in setting Shakespeare to music, I had been preoccupied with historical considerations—that is to say, with composing music in the Elizabethan manner. The answer is "No," because Shakespeare has seemed to me the most alive and most modern, the most eternal and universal of all poets (more so even than Dante), and I feel him to be a "contemporary." After Shakespeare came Shelley, and then the others I have mentioned, up to the American Walt Whitman, that great fraternal soul. Certainly, the English of Shakespeare and Shelley was not that of the man in the street; their poetic language is of supreme musicality, and I believe that one can discover in the great English lyrics treasures similar to those the German Romantics offered to the composers of *Lieder*.

To be sure, English does present some remarkable difficulties to the songwriter. One, for example, is its great number of monosyllabic words, which it is difficult to distribute over a melody in an expressive fashion and, at the same time, with correct accentuation. But, on the other hand, it is perhaps just this—its very lack of "sonorous substance"—that lends English its charm, and makes it one of the most "spiritual" and transparent languages I know.

I have already mentioned "song," "melody," "accent"; and I shall now reconsider them briefly together with some other problems and difficulties that confront the composer.

What is "song"? It is difficult to define. Fundamentally, it is a "gift of God," a deliverance of the human soul. And I have often said that, if I were to envy some great musician of the past, it would not be Bach for his fugues, or Beethoven for his symphonies, or Wagner for his music dramas, but perhaps Schubert for some of the simplest of his *Lieder,* such as *Du bist die Ruh* or *Litanei,* miraculous flowers of the spirit, as consoling as a friendly smile or a gentle tear.

But if one refuses to be satisfied with a transcendent explanation, it will be possible to arrive at a more positive and satisfactory one by way of defining "accent." Accent is the expressive quality that results when one throws into relief, while creating a melody, certain syllables in a word, words in a phrase, and phrases in a sentence. This aspect of rhythm, this expressive relief, this correct prosody, is not all there is to a song; musical declamation (which sometimes can be very efficacious) is not yet song itself. Song, while incorporating it, must go beyond it—must be a synthesis, a sublimation. The placing of accent is a mechanical process, and every conscientious musician can accomplish it; a complete song, on the other hand, is a product of artistic creation, and its fashioning is reserved for artists of talent, for the fortunate few who are gifted with both sentiment and fantasy.

Another problem is that of having a knowledge of the singing voice, but it is a secondary problem that can be solved intuitively. Every musician who truly "feels" song writes well for the voice; those who write poorly for it are those who regard mastering its special requirements as a mechanical process. In any case, we must, in this connection, take into account the diverse natures of the various languages. As already pointed out, Italian possesses a greater sonorous expression; French and English (I believe) admit of a more limited emotional range; while German permits vocal leaps that would be absurd in other languages.

And now we come to the last problem, the practical problem— how actually to write a song. That is quite personal. And heaven forbid that I should try to promulgate cut-and-dried theories. Each system is good, provided it gives satisfactory results. It has often happened to me—and, I am sure, to my colleagues also—that the question is asked (especially on the part of women): "How do you compose your music?" or "How do you set a poem to music?" or even "How are you inspired?" Questions so difficult to answer! However, one can say something. For example, to the second of these questions, I am likely to reply that, when I find a poem that particularly interests me or arouses my emotion, I commit it to memory and, at the same time, naturally, I analyze its form, its character, its distribution of phrases, its possibilities for contrast, etc. After some time, when the poem has entered my blood, so to speak (this may take anywhere from a day to several months), I sing it quite naturally: the music is born. For me to love a poem is to *know* it, it is to sing it! So much for the vocal part. But in a song there is also the instrumental part, commonly called the "accompaniment," as though to impute to it a secondary character, even though it is by no means the least important portion of a song nor necessarily the easiest one to evolve. To produce it properly is a matter of finding the right atmosphere, the "background," the environment that surrounds and develops the vocal line. It is also a question of expressing through the instrument what the voice alone cannot express. Finally, it is a question of creating something that will combine with the vocal line to form a quite inseparable and complete unity. This something exists in the poetry too. One need only strike upon it. Just as the voice part is born of the poem, so is the accompaniment given rise by it also (through the medium of the composer's intuition as well as through analysis): it is latent in the poetry. I have already said that every poem for music must have, above all, an "expressive core"—which may be formed of one or several fundamental elements—a core that provides the key to the poem itself. It is this key, it is these elements, that one must discover and to which one must give utterance through almost "symbolic" musical means. I have said that song is a synthesis; accompaniment itself is a synthesis too (even if it grows partly out of analysis, which seems contradictory). What will these "symbolic" means be? They must be several and of rather different natures. But I believe I may state that the simplest will be the surest and most efficacious. I myself began, in my first songs, with accompaniments rather complicated in harmony and rhythm. Afterwards I always tried to simplify, rather, I must say, through instinct than through reason. I tried to express my thoughts by the simplest and most natural means, even if, to some, these might seem less "interesting." These different "symbols" (and the greatest composers of *Lieder* have supplied us with examples) may consist of a melodic element, a thematic cell (which is sometimes in the voice part too), a rhythm (which may likewise stem from the voice part, or may, on the contrary, be entirely opposed to it), an instrumental figuration (we have hundreds of celebrated examples; as for me, a simple *arpeggio* sufficed for my Shakespeare song, "Arise," a chromatic scale for my setting of André Gide's *Ballade des biens immeubles*) or, finally, some harmonic element—a series of chords or even a single chord. . . .

This discourse has been a great deal longer than I had intended. I must bring it to a close.

I began by saying that song was the first musical manifestation of man. I believe that it will also be the last. As long as humanity remains, it will sing. And I should like to imagine that its "farewell to life" will also be a song. In the meanwhile let our song be of life.

And let me express a hope: that English-speaking people (Americans especially) find in their admirable poetry—which has given so much joy to me, an Italian—a rich source of inspiration for their song literature, towards the furthering of happiness and fraternity among men, as their great poet Whitman would have wished.

SUGGESTIONS FOR WRITING

1. Mario Castelnuovo-Tedesco is a contemporary composer. He says that English is a "musical" language. What characteristics of English cause him to say this?
2. Illustrate Castelnuovo's definition of "accent" by commenting on the "syllables in relief" of a folk song which is part of America's national heritage.
3. Castelnuovo commits a poem to memory if he thinks it has possibilities for a song. As he does so, he subjects it to a special kind of analysis. Choose a poem to analyze by Castelnuovo's "song testing" method.
4. Why is a song likely to be, in Castelnuovo's words, both the first and the last musical manifestation of man? Write a composition in which you make a thoughtful analysis of the place of music in man's life.

WALTER PATER

# Mona Lisa (from *The Renaissance*) *

Hers is the head upon which all "the ends of the world are come," and the eyelids are a little weary. It is a beauty wrought out from within upon the flesh, the deposit, little cell by cell of strange thoughts and fantastic reveries and exquisite passions. Set it for a moment beside one of those White Greek goddesses or beautiful women of antiquity, and how would they be troubled by this beauty, into which the soul with all its maladies has passed! All the thoughts and experience of the world have etched and moulded there, in that which they have of power to refine and make expressive the outward form, the animalism of Greece, the lust of Rome, the mysticism of the middle age with its spiritual ambition and imaginative lovers, the return of the Pagan world, the sins of the Borgias.

---

* From *Studies in the History of the Renaissance,* 1873.

She is older than the rocks among which she sits; like the vampire, she has been dead many times, and learned the secrets of the
grave; and has been a diver in deep seas, and keeps their fallen day
about her; and trafficked for strange webs with Eastern merchants,
and, as Leda was the mother of Helen of Troy, and, as Saint Anne,
the mother of Mary; and all this has been to her but as the sound
of lyres and flutes, and lives only in the delicacy with which it has
moulded the changing lineaments, and tinged the eyelids and the
hands.

#### SUGGESTIONS FOR WRITING

1. Walter Pater (1839-1894) published his *Studies in the History of the
   Renaissance* in 1873, and it was this work that first brought him fame.
   This selection is a sensitive and famous prose statement about a painting. It has, in fact, found its way into *Bartlett's Familiar Quotations.*
   Pater is revealing his thoughts as he looks carefully at the *Mona Lisa.*
   Try the same technique. Examine the facial expression of someone in
   a painting you consider noteworthy. Reveal what the expression is
   saying to you and to the world.
2. What are the essential differences between Da Vinci's *Mona Lisa,* as
   Pater describes it, and Norman Rockwell's paintings, as Wright Morris
   describes them in the following piece?
3. Would your reaction to the above lines be different if they had been
   printed in verse form? Is there something within your mind that makes
   poetry what it is? Convert Pater's prose to verse (more than ten lines
   per paragraph) and then describe the difference between prose and poetry.

#### WRIGHT MORRIS

### Abuse of the Past: Norman Rockwell *

We can say, first, last, and always, that Norman Rockwell has
been true to his beginnings, to his trust in his own and American
sentiment. He is a genre painter; he uses graphic means to tell a

---

* From *The Territory Ahead* by Wright Morris (New York: Harcourt, Brace
& World, Inc., 1958). Copyright © 1957, © 1958, © 1961 by Wright Morris.
Originally published in the *Atlantic Monthly* (December, 1957). Reprinted by
permission of the publishers, author, and Atheneum House, Inc.

story. His technique may be described as the most perfect where it dissolves, imperceptibly, into anecdote. This anecdotal picture that tells a simple story is the father of the story that gives us the simple picture, the *same* picture, as a rule—an unadorned, unpretentious, photographically convincing portrayal of *real* life.

In a period of forty years Rockwell has supplied the *Post* with more than three hundred of its covers. He has taught a generation of Americans to see. They look about them and see, almost everywhere they look, what Norman Rockwell sees—the tomboy with the black eye in the doctor's waiting room; the father discussing the Facts of Life with his teen-age son; the youth in the dining car on his first solo flight from home; and the family in the car, headed for an outing, followed by the same family on the tired ride home.

The convincing *realism* of the details, photographic in its accuracy, is all subtly processed through a filter of sentiment. It is this sentiment that heightens the reality, making it, for some, an object of affection, for others—a small minority—an object of ridicule. It all depends on that intangible thing, the point of view.

Countless young men and women at the beginning of careers in art, have tried, and usually failed, to explain *their* point of view to a puzzled mother, a skeptical father. What can be wrong—Father would like to know—with Norman Rockwell, who is so obviously *good?* The answer is his very *goodness,* of course, but this usually ends the argument. Discussion leads nowhere. The two points of view go their different ways.

After considerable exposure to "modern" art, in museums, fashion magazines, the world of advertising, and everyday living, that mythic figure, the man in the street, will still go along with Norman Rockwell. And so—whenever they can get him—will the *Saturday Evening Post.* In that respect, the times have not changed. A vote for Norman Rockwell is a vote for the *real* America. It is the nature of his gift that his very technique appears to dissolve into the subject, leaving the deposit of sentiment we like, otherwise no trace. After we have recognized the figures as our neighbors, and the street they live on as our own, we are left precisely where we came in—at the beginning. It is the nature of the genre piece to limit itself to clichés.

But if this charge is leveled at Norman Rockwell, it is leveled in suspension and will never reach him. Norman Rockwell is not there. In the picture we attack there is only ourselves. This is why such an attack gets us fighting mad. That row of photographs we keep on the piano has been maligned. However, this will help to explain the almost total absence of transitional material between Grant Wood's "Iowa Gothic"—which is true to the Rockwell tradition—and the sort of painting that most young people are doing today. It was easier to leap directly into the arms of God or the Devil than fight across the no man's land of raw-material clichés. A clean break—on such a battlefield—was the only one possible.

The extent to which this gap remains—and will continue to remain, we can feel with assurance—is evident in Rockwell's painting of Jennifer Jones in *The Song of Bernadette.* When the movie was released, Twentieth Century-Fox turned to Norman Rockwell, the illustrator, rather than to the resources of the movie camera, to portray and advertise the star in the leading role. That the movie industry should choose Norman Rockwell is both a testimony to his craft and a revealing commentary on the prevailing American taste. Our *realistic* front still has its soft, yellow filter sky.

A more recent example, in the form of a tribute, were Rockwell's portraits of the Presidential candidates. It was left to Rockwell, in this sense, to reveal what the camera angles concealed, and to give the people—insofar as they were self-evident—the facts. Mr. Rockwell's Stevenson is the most instructive: we see the wit and intellectual cut down to our size, not cut down with malice, but, rather, with affection, as the neighbors of a "famous" man know him to be a simple, regular guy. Mr. Stevenson emerges as the man we usually find behind a drug counter, shrewd in his way, of independent mind, and willing to both take and give advice. He is one of us, not at all the sort of egghead we had heard about.

Scrutinized, held under the light that we find the most illuminating—the soft-sharp lens of Rockwell's craft—our raw material is seldom raw at all. It is hardly material. The clinical word for it is cliché. In the beginning, this credo reads, was the cliché. The raw-material effect is like the tinseled snow hung on the rootless trees at Christmas, stimulating the sensation without the embarrassment of the facts. . . .

In a series of 1957 calendar illustrations, entitled "The Four Seasons," Mr. Rockwell supplies us with a credo that lucidly sums up his function as an artist. This is his statement:

In a world that puts such importance on the pursuit of youth, it is good to consider, occasionally, the charms—and the comforts—of maturity. For whatever else may be said, maturity fosters familiarity which in turn gives feelings of security and understanding that are valuable in these days of continuing change. I have tried to show these feelings in the paintings for the new Four Seasons calendar.

My pictures show two people who, after living together for many years, have reached the stage of sympathy and compatibility for which all of us strive. They know their weaknesses and their strengths. They are comfortable and secure in their relationships with each other. And while Mother presumably takes Father's strong points for granted, she's still trying tolerantly to keep him on the straight and narrow when signs of frailty appear.

Paintings like these are fun to do. While they are humorous, they are also human, and the subtle touch of forbearance evident in each of them is something all of us can learn. I can only hope you'll enjoy looking at these pictures as much as I have enjoyed working on them.

Perhaps the reader can visualize the "subtle touch of forbearance" in these illustrations. It verges closely—in the words of a recent parody in *Punch*—on the Brighter Side of the Bubonic Plague. Maturity—whatever else may be said—seen through the forbearance of Mr. Rockwell seems to be an adolescent pipe dream of the genial aspects of senility. The pursuit of youth is made more visible, rather than less, in these gentle fuddy-duddies, Mom and Pop, and their pathetic inability to grow *up*. A certain aging has taken place, but such growth as we observe is downward and backward. That Mother takes Father's strong points for granted is obvious, desperately so—because Father's *strong* points are touchingly invisible. A genial pathos, sentimentally evoked, would seem to be the mortar that binds them together, and provides the comfort in what we describe as their "relationship." That hard-work marriage has given way to the slogans inscribed on the insurance posters, where the happy smiling couple are preserved, safe from *old* age, in the amber of leisure. Nothing will touch them but the postman, with his monthly retirement check.

All of the durable clichés we have already described are served up afresh in these four tableaux. "Winter" shows us the calendar being nailed to the wall, one that features a pin-up girl discreetly censored—not the sort of tempting dish that men or boys, if the distinction exists, pin up for real delectation. "Spring" finds Father down with a cold, lovingly wrapped up in Mother's patchwork quilt, his feet in a pan of water as she spoon-feeds him what is so obviously good for him. "Summer" finds him in the yard, in a state of collapse, after a tussle with the lawn mower, while Mother, with a compassionate gaze, stands waiting to pour him a glass of lemonade. In all these pictures a cat, symbol of the loving home, is conspicuously evident, and proves, in his kittenish ways, to be as young in heart as his masters.

The date beneath these illustrations is 1957—but they are daydreams from a timeless past: only Mother's somewhat battered leather moccasins indicate that the time is the present. Immortal moths escape from the holes in Father's pair of red flannels, indicating that with "Autumn" something called Winter is near. The mature round of life—American style—in this manner comes full cycle, leaving the reader prepared and expectant for the new calendar that will usher in the New Year. We are free to rest assured that Mother will keep Father on the straight and narrow path.

We might say that Mr. Rockwell's special triumph is in the conviction his countrymen share that this mythic world he evokes actually exists. This cloudland of nostalgia seems to loom higher on the horizon, as the horizon itself, the world of actual experience, disappears from view. The mind *soars off*—in the manner that highways, with new model cars, soar off into the future—leaving the drab world of commonplace facts and sensations behind. In soaring into the past, rather than the future, Mr. Rockwell is true to himself and his public, since that is where the true territory ahead actually lies. In knowing this he illustrates, with admirable fidelity, the American Land of Heart's Desire. . . .

Among our many native gifts, which are large, is one that is seldom singled out for comment. It is the faculty, one might say the intuition, we have by which we transform adult works of art, few as they are, into children's books. We transform them into books that are *safe*. *Moby Dick* and *Huckleberry Finn* are not merely safe for boys to read, but are even read by them. They are adventure stories, on the shelf with *Treasure Island* and *Tom Swift*. It would seem to be here, and here alone, that the transforming powers of the Helmet of Mambrino are part of our tradition. We transform the adult into a child. It is the converse of transforming the present into the past. In either case we get back to the beginnings, back to the innocence before it was corrupted, back to that time when the world and ourselves were young.

A boy's-eye view of the world, enchanted in *Tom Sawyer,* disenchanted in *Huckleberry Finn,* is wonderfully blended in the art of Norman Rockwell and seasoned to taste. Here we can often have it both ways. The grown-up world impinges on the past only to heighten its flavor, the purity of the enchantment, the sweet pathos of the light that failed. Old folks—people who once again are notoriously childlike—reappear to reaffirm, in their seasoned wisdom, the youthful dreams. At the extremities of our life, two aspects of the childlike meet. It is the childish dream—somewhat battered by the interlude of life—that once again, in its wisdom, dominates our lives. An old man's gnarled hand, one finger clutched by a boy's small hand, sums it all up. The beginning and the ending of the dream are thus made one.

Mark Twain, the one who didn't like books, would have seen eye to eye with Norman Rockwell, since it is Twain's eyes through which Rockwell customarily sees. It is the world of Tom Sawyer, Huck Finn, and Aunt Sally brought up to date. It is still the old battle of Aunt Sally and her civilizing ways, all of it under the watchful eyes of grownups who are still—bless their hearts—children at heart themselves. They have grown up, but we have no idea how they got that way. They are included in the picture to frame and heighten what came *first.* Childhood came first, of course, and young dreams, and all those promises that men fail to live by—but back then they were real, back *then* we believed in them. Whereas, if you look around you now—but of course we don't. *It's a joke, son.* It's much better to look, as we do, into the mythic past.

A world of beginnings, of exemplary firsts, is what we find, in various formations, in the works of Wolfe, Hemingway, Fitzgerald, and Faulkner. Their work spans, oddly enough, the period between Rockwell's first *Post* cover and his last. The battle is still the same old battle of Aunt Sally and her civilizing ways. It is nostalgia, in one form or another, that challenges the ability of each writer to function, as it determined the style and substance of Rockwell's craft. Here in America we begin, and occasionally we end, with the abuses of the past.

## SUGGESTIONS FOR WRITING

1. Wright Morris (1910-    ) won the National Book Award for his novel *The Field of Vision* (1956). The above essay is from *The Territory Ahead* (1958). He argues that not only Norman Rockwell, but other and greater American artists have been guilty of "abuses of the past." Rockwell's crime, according to Morris, is that he has taught generations of Americans to see the wrong things. Can Rockwell be charged with this crime? What is the artist's responsibility? Write an essay considering these questions.

2. Morris raises a questioning eyebrow at Norman Rockwell's paintings, but realizes he will have a hard time proving his thesis. "What can be wrong —Father would like to know—with Norman Rockwell, who is so obviously good? The answer is his very *goodness*, of course, but this usually ends the argument. Discussion leads nowhere. The two points of view go their different ways." Summarize the two points of view. Is it true that discussion *must* lead nowhere? Is there no common ground?

3. What, precisely, is Norman Rockwell's abuse of the past? What has he done to incur Morris's displeasure?

4. What does Morris mean when he says, "It is the nature of the genre piece to limit itself to clichés."? Write an essay illustrating your answer with a description of a cliché painting.

# Other Art Forms

Art is a jealous mistress, and, if a man have a genius for painting, poetry, music, architecture, or philosophy, he makes a bad husband, and an ill provider.
> —Emerson, *Conduct of Life,* 1860

Since it [architecture] is music in space, [it is] as it were frozen music.
> —Friedrich von Schelling, *Philosophie der Kunst,* 1797

Architecture, sculpture, painting, music, and poetry, may truly be called the efflorescence of civilized life.
> —Herbert Spencer, *Essays on Education,* 1861

The surest test of the civilization of a people—at least, as sure as any—afforded by mechanical art is to be found in their architecture, which presents so noble a field for the display of the grand and the beautiful, and which, at the same time, is so intimately connected with the essential comforts of life.
> —William H. Prescott, *The Conquest of Peru,* 1847

The imitator is a poor kind of creature. If the man who paints only the tree, or flower, or other surface he sees before him were an artist, the king of artists would be the photographer. It is for the artist to do something beyond this: in portrait painting to put on canvas something more than the face the model wears for that one day; to paint the man, in short, as well as his features.
> —James McNeill Whistler, *The Gentle Art of Making Enemies,* 1890

Frequent indifference to external fact, though regrettable, is still relatively unimportant, for portraiture is not photography.
> —Samuel Shellabarger, *The Chevalier Bayard,* 1928

A photographer has his style as an essayist has his. He will select his subjects with equal individuality. He will present them with equal manner. The sum total of what he has to say will be equally his own.
> —*Life,* April 26, 1937

E . M . F O R S T E R

## Art for Art's Sake*

I believe in art for art's sake. It is an unfashionable belief, and some of my statements must be in the nature of an apology. Fifty years ago I should have faced you with more confidence. A writer or a speaker who chose "Art for Art's Sake" for his theme fifty years ago could be sure of being in the swim, and could feel so confident of success that he sometimes dressed himself in aesthetic costumes suitable to the occasion—in an embroidered dressing gown, perhaps, or a blue velvet suit with a Lord Fauntleroy collar; or a toga, or a kimono, and carried a poppy or a lily or a long peacock's feather in his medieval hand. Times have changed. Not thus can I present either myself or my theme today. My aim rather is to ask you quietly to reconsider for a few minutes a phrase which has been much misused and much abused, but which has, I believe, great importance for us—has, indeed, eternal importance.

Now we can easily dismiss those peacock's feathers and other affectations—they are but trifles—but I want also to dismiss a more dangerous heresy, namely the silly idea that only art matters, an idea which has somehow got mixed up with the idea of art for art's sake, and has helped to discredit it. Many things, beside art, matter. It is merely one of the things that matter, and high though the claims are that I make for it, I want to keep them in proportion. No one can spend his or her life entirely in the creation or the appreciation of masterpieces. Man lives, and ought to live, in a complex world, full of conflicting claims, and if we simplified them

* From *Two Cheers for Democracy* by E. M. Forster (New York: Harcourt, Brace & World, Inc., 1951). Copyright 1949 by E. M. Forster. Reprinted by permission of the publishers, and Edward Arnold, Ltd.

down into the aesthetic, he would be sterilized. Art for art's sake
does not mean that only art matters, and I would also like to rule
out such phrases as "The Life of Art," "Living for Art," and "Art's
High Mission." They confuse and mislead.

What does the phrase mean? Instead of generalizing, let us take
a specific instance—Shakespeare's *Macbeth,* for example, and pronounce the words, *"Macbeth* for *Macbeth's* sake." What does that
mean? Well, the play has several aspects—it is educational, it
teaches us something about legendary Scotland, something about
Jacobean England, and a good deal about human nature and its
perils. We can study its origins, and study and enjoy its dramatic
technique and the music of its diction. All that is true. But *Macbeth*
is furthermore a world of its own, created by Shakespeare and
existing in virtue of its own poetry. It is in this aspect *Macbeth* for
*Macbeth's* sake, and that is what I intend by the phrase "art for
art's sake." A work of art—whatever else it might be—is a self-
contained entity, with a life of its own imposed on it by its creator.
It has internal order. It may have external form. That is how we
recognize it.

Take for another example that picture of Seurat's which I saw
two years ago in Chicago—*"La Grande Jatte."* Here again there is
much to study and to enjoy: the pointillism, the charming face of
the seated girl, the nineteenth-century Parisian Sunday sunlight,
the sense of motion in immobility. But here again there is something more: *"La Grande Jatte"* forms a world of its own, created by
Seurat and existing by virtue of its own poetry: *"La Grande Jatte"*
*l'art pour l'art.* Like *Macbeth* it has internal order and internal life.

It is to the conception of order that I would now turn. This is
important to my argument, and I want to make a digression, and
glance at order in daily life, before I come to order in art.

In the world of daily life, the world which we perforce inhabit,
there is much talk about order, particularly from statesmen and
politicians. They tend, however, to confuse order with orders, just
as they confuse creation with regulations. Order, I suggest, is something evolved from within, not something imposed from without;
it is an internal stability, a vital harmony, and in the social and
political category it has never existed except for the convenience of
historians. Viewed realistically, the past is really a series of *dis*orders,

succeeding one another by discoverable laws, no doubt, and certainly marked by an increasing growth of human interference, but disorders all the same. So that, speaking as a writer, what I hope for today is a disorder which will be more favorable to artists than is the present one, and which will provide them with fuller inspirations and better material conditions. It will not last—nothing lasts —but there have been some advantageous disorders in the past— for instance, in ancient Athens, in Renaissance Italy, eighteenth-century France, periods in China and Persia—and we may do something to accelerate the next one. But let us not again fix our hearts where true joys are not to be found. We were promised a new order after the first world war through the League of Nations. It did not come, nor have I faith in present promises, by whomsoever endorsed. The implacable offensive of Science forbids. We cannot reach social and political stability for the reason that we continue to make scientific discoveries and to apply them, and thus to destroy the arrangements which were based on more elementary discoveries. If Science would discover rather than apply—if, in other words, men were more interested in knowledge than in power—mankind would be in a far safer position, and the stability statesmen talk about would be a possibility, there could be a new order based on vital harmony, and the earthly millennium might approach. But Science shows no signs of doing this: she gave us the internal combustion engine, and before we had digested and assimilated it with terrible pains into our social system, she harnessed the atom, and destroyed any new order that seemed to be evolving. How can man get into harmony with his surroundings when he is constantly altering them? The future of our race is, in this direction, more unpleasant than we care to admit, and it has sometimes seemed to me that its best chance lies through apathy, uninventiveness, and inertia. Universal exhaustion might promote that Change of Heart which is at present so briskly recommended from a thousand pulpits. Universal exhaustion would certainly be a new experience. The human race has never undergone it, and is still too perky to admit that it may be coming and might result in a sprouting of new growth through the decay.

I must not pursue these speculations any further—they lead me too far from my terms of reference and maybe from yours. But I do want to emphasize that order in daily life and in history, order in the social and political category, is unattainable under our present psychology.

Where is it attainable? Not in the astronomical category, where it was for many years enthroned. The heavens and the earth have become terribly alike since Einstein. No longer can we find a reassuring contrast to chaos in the night sky and look up with George Meredith to the stars, the army of unalterable law, or listen to the music of the spheres. Order is not there. In the entire universe there seem to be only two possibilities for it. The first of them—which again lies outside my terms of reference—is the divine order, the mystic harmony, which according to all religions is available for those who can contemplate it. We must admit its possibility, on the evidence of the adepts, and we must believe them when they say that it is attained, if attainable, by prayer. "O thou who changest not, abide with me," said one of its poets. "*Ordina questo amor, o tu che m'ami,*" said another. "Set love in order, thou who lovest me." The existence of a divine order, though it cannot be tested, has never been disproved.

The second possibility for order lies in the aesthetic category, which is my subject here: the order which an artist can create in his own work, and to that we must now return. A work of art, we are all agreed, is a unique product. But why? It is unique not because it is clever or noble or beautiful or enlightened or sincere or idealistic or useful or educational—it may embody any of those qualities —but because it is the only material object in the universe which may possess internal harmony. All the others have been pressed into shape from outside, and when their mould is removed they collapse. The work of art stands up by itself, and nothing else does. It achieves something which has often been promised by society, but always delusively. Ancient Athens made a mess—but the *Antigone* stands up. Renaissance Rome made a mess—but the ceiling of the Sistine got painted. James I made a mess—but there was *Macbeth*. Louis XIV—but there was *Phèdre*. Art for art's sake? I should just think so, and more so than ever at the present time. It is the one orderly product which our muddling race has produced. It is the cry of a thousand sentinels, the echo from a thousand labyrinths; it is the lighthouse which cannot be hidden: *c'est le meilleur témoinage que nous puissions donner de notre dignité.*[1] *Antigone* for *Antigone's* sake, *Macbeth* for *Macbeth's,* *"La Grande Jatte"* pour *"La Grande Jatte."*

If this line of argument is correct, it follows that the artist will tend to be an outsider in the society to which he has been born, and that the nineteenth-century conception of him as a Bohemian was not inaccurate. The conception erred in three particulars: it postulated an economic system where art could be a full-time job, it introduced the fallacy that only art matters, and it overstressed idiosyncrasy and waywardness—the peacock feather aspect—rather than order. But it is a truer conception than the one which prevails in official circles on my side of the Atlantic—I don't know about yours: the conception which treats the artist as if he were a particularly bright government advertiser and encourages him to be friendly and matey with his fellow citizens, and not to give himself airs.

Estimable is mateyness, and the man who achieves it gives many a pleasant little drink to himself and to others. But it has no traceable connection with the creative impulse, and probably acts as an inhibition on it. The artist who is seduced by mateyness may stop himself from doing the one thing which he, and he alone, can do —the making of something out of words or sounds or clay or marble or steel or film which has internal harmony and presents order to a permanently disarranged planet. This seems worth doing, even at the risk of being called uppish by journalists. I have in mind an article which was published some years ago in the London *Times,* an article called "The Eclipse of the Highbrow," in which the "Average Man" was exalted, and all contemporary literature was censured if it did not toe the line, the precise position of the line being naturally known to the writer of the article. Sir Kenneth Clark, who was at that time director of our National Gallery, commented on this pernicious doctrine in a letter which cannot be too often quoted. "The poet and the artist," wrote Clark, "are important precisely because they are not average men; because in sensibility, intelligence, and power of invention they far exceed the average." These memorable words, and particularly the words "power

---

[1] It is the best proof we can give of our dignity. [Editor's note.]

of invention," are the Bohemian's passport. Furnished with it, he slinks about society, saluted now by a brickbat and now by a penny, and accepting either of them with equanimity. He does not consider too anxiously what his relations with society may be, for he is aware of something more important than that—namely the invitation to invent, to create order, and he believes he will be better placed for doing this if he attempts detachment. So round and round he slouches, with his hat pulled over his eyes, and maybe with a louse in his beard, and—if he really wants one—with the peacock's feather in his hand.

If our present society should disintegrate—and who dare prophesy that it won't?—this old-fashioned and *démodé* figure will become clearer: the Bohemian, the outsider, the parasite, the rat—one of those figures which have at present no function either in a warring or a peaceful world. It may not be dignified to be a rat, but many of the ships are sinking, which is not dignified either—the officials did not build them properly. Myself, I would sooner be a swimming rat than a sinking ship—at all events I can look around me for a little longer—and I remember how one of us, a rat with particularly bright eyes called Shelley, squeaked out, "Poets are the unacknowledged legislators of the world," before he vanished into the waters of the Mediterranean.

What laws did Shelley propose to pass? None. The legislation of the artist is never formulated at the time, though it is sometimes discerned by future generations. He legislated through creating. And he creates through his sensitiveness and his power to impose form. Without form the sensitiveness vanishes. And form is as important today, when the human race is trying to ride the whirlwind, as it ever was in those less agitating days of the past, when the earth seemed solid and the stars fixed, and the discoveries of science were made slowly, slowly. Form is not tradition. It alters from generation to generation. Artists always seek a new technique, and will continue to do so as long as their work excites them. But form of some kind is imperative. It is the surface crust of the internal harmony, it is the outward evidence of order.

My remarks about society may have seemed too pessimistic, but I believe that society can only represent a fragment of the human spirit, and that another fragment can only get expressed through art. And I wanted to take this opportunity, this vantage ground, to assert not only the existence of art, but its pertinacity. Looking back into the past, it seems to me that that is all there has ever been: vantage grounds for discussion and creation, little vantage grounds in the changing chaos, where bubbles have been blown and webs spun, and the desire to create order has found temporary gratification, and the sentinels have managed to utter their challenges, and the huntsmen, though lost individually, have heard each other's calls through the impenetrable wood, and the lighthouses have never ceased sweeping the thankless seas. In this pertinacity there seems to me, as I grow older, something more and more profound, something which does in fact concern people who do not care about art at all.

In conclusion, let me summarize the various categories that have laid claim to the possession of Order:

(1) The social and political category. Claim disallowed on the evidence of history and of our own experience. If man altered psychologically, order here might be attainable; not otherwise.

(2) The astronomical category. Claim allowed up to the present century, but now disallowed on the evidence of the physicists.

(3) The religious category. Claim allowed on the evidence of the mystics.

(4) The aesthetic category. Claim allowed on the evidence of various works of art, and on the evidence of our own creative impulses, however weak these may be, or however imperfectly they may function. Works of art, in my opinion, are the only objects in the material universe to possess internal order, and that is why, though I don't believe that only art matters, I do believe in Art for Art's sake.

SUGGESTIONS FOR WRITING

1. E. M. Forster, about whom comment is made on p. 82, indicates that a work of art has a life of its own. What does he mean? How can a work like Shakespeare's *Macbeth* exist as a self-contained entity?

2. Explain what Forster means by the statement: ". . . what I hope for today is a disorder which will be more favorable to artists than is the present one, and which will provide them with fuller inspirations and better material conditions."

3. The sentence, "The poet legislates through creating," is interesting and a bit romantic, but is there any sense in which it is true?
4. Why will artists tend to be "outsiders"? Is there something in the nature of art or in the nature of the impulse to create that resists pressures to conform? Must an artist be, in some sense, odd? Write a sketch of a fictional artist which will illustrate your views on these questions.


EDWARD  J.  STEICHEN

# The Living Joy of Pictures*

In speculating about the creation of art and the enjoyment of art, we have to begin by trying to understand the fundamentals. Let's start with the one form of creation about which there is no speculation or argument: the woman who conceives and bears a child. I sometimes wonder about the guy who stands out in the meadow with an easel or with a camera and sees the daisies nodding their heads and the wind blowing the clouds in the sky, and makes a picture of that and thinks he's created something. I wonder if he shouldn't have his head examined. I think we should stop and think of the original creative force that exists in all living organisms and that is so beautifully expressed in the Bible: "Be fruitful and multiply." I think we should visualize what goes on within a woman during the weeks and months when she's carrying a child, and then think of that wondrous moment when the baby is being born, and the triumph when all that happens. It's just a little difficult to put that kind of test up to any artist when we talk about "creation." There are not many artists who can measure up to that, and those are and have been, I think, the great artists of all time. Those artists go through the same pains and struggle in the production of a work of art, whether it's music or poetry or painting or photography. When the work has the quality which lives, there's been a terrific ordeal.

Down in the garden of the Museum of Modern Art here, we now have a statue of Balzac that Auguste Rodin made. When it was finished, the committee that had commissioned it said that it was

* From *Holiday* (March, 1956). © 1956 by Edward Steichen. Reprinted by permission of the author.

nothing but a head stuck on a sack, and turned it down. And a long, long time afterward, all of the mass of studies and the sketches that Rodin had made for that statue were unearthed, and you could see the struggle and travail that gave form to a masterpiece. I remember one of Matisse's greatest paintings, called *The Dance*. At that time I was seeing a great deal of him, and I watched that painting from the first outlines on the canvas right straight through to the finish. I saw the effort and turmoil and the changes and changes that he made. It was gradual, almost as gradual as the development of the baby that's under a woman's apron. And then came the final burst of passion. Within a few days he changed the whole painting; the figures became brilliant vermilion, the background a deep Prussian blue. It was a moment of exaltation—a child being born! A work of art being born!

## SUGGESTIONS FOR WRITING

1. Edward J. Steichen, whom some consider to be one of the world's greatest photographers, came to public attention with his book of photographs taken all over the world, *The Family of Man* (1945). In this essay he raises an interesting question about art. What is creation? Is there a difference between created art and manufactured art?

2. What happens in an artist's mind during what Steichen calls "the final burst of passion"? Is such a burst characteristic of artists who use a brush or a chisel? Is it also characteristic of poets, novelists, and photographers? Whence comes this burst? Write an essay in which you describe it happening. Reveal the workings of your inner mind on the matter of creation.

3. Steichen says, "When the work has the quality that lives, there's been a terrific ordeal." Consider some novels or poems which live in your memory or which, somehow, made the world come alive for you. Is there any evidence of a "terrific ordeal"? Look into the lives of the poets or novelists whose works you have chosen to see if what Steichen says is true. Write a theme describing what you have found.

4. Using Steichen's extended analogy as a model, write a theme explaining one thing in terms of something else.

HENRI CARTIER-BRESSON

# The Art of Photography*

. . . I always recognized Henri Cartier-Bresson on the Paris streets, his slight gray figure slipping anonymously through the crowd with a quick, supple gait. I knew the charm of his smile, the innocence of his blue eyes. I had noticed the freedom of his gestures, never impeded by his Leica camera which he carries with him everywhere. He has a rapt, concentrated expression of one who listens and carefully observes, at the same time pursuing a private dream.

I had heard him say to friends who had asked to see his work: "But are you sure it won't bore you?"—quite unlike the amateur who is all too ready to arrange an evening of showing color slides of his last summer vacation. Alert and curious, Henri Cartier-Bresson is always asking your opinion, always questioning. Yet behind his anxiety one feels that he is serene, like someone who doubts yet has a basic certainty. He talks little, and almost never about photography, to which he has devoted the major part of his life for the past thirty years.

I saw him again in Paris in the quiet atmosphere of his studio which opens onto the sky and the city's slate roofs. He had just returned from London and was taking a train that evening for Italy, not to return to France before September. As a reporter he travels a good deal, though he denies being a "globe-trotter."

"Of course I'm curious," he says, "and when I arrive in a place I like to see and understand what is happening around me. But I need to move slowly. I try not to travel by plane. A photographer should never run. He should be a tireless walker. That's the way to capture the special moment on the sidewalk, at the street corner, and in life.

"In this style of photography one should not impose one's preconceived notions of a country; rather, one should correct them.

---

* An interview by Yvonne Baby from *Harper's Magazine* (November, 1961), translated by Elizabeth Carmichael. © 1961 by Harper & Row, Publishers. Reprinted by permission of *Harper's Magazine* and *L'Express*, Paris.

To me the only strictly documentary photography is a catalogue. All other photography is never purely descriptive but a personal means of expression. Only if one forgets oneself in the process does the subject become all-important and the photograph gain in power. That's the only attitude to take if you want to get to the depth of things. I know there are camera wizards, and I know the illusions they can create. Still I'm convinced the comments of such wizards never really amount to a distinctive point of view about any member of mankind and his country. To me such methods are merely gimmicks. Things done fast disappear fast; only what is done with time will remain. 'Slowness is beauty,' said Rodin, I think. Or was it 'Beauty is slowness'?"

The staccato in Henri Cartier-Bresson's voice reveals his nervousness. Sometimes he gets caught on a word, then recovers himself quickly; or he comes back to a phrase, blinks, smiles, and says: "Do you understand?" He refuses to tell anecdotes or any details about his personal life, adding that his biography can be found at the Magnum Photos agency.

"With me," he says, "photography is a way of drawing. It is not philosophy, or literature, or music: it is a strictly visual medium, grasping at the evidence of reality. The camera helps to see mechanically and optically. (Who nowadays would reproach a painter for using a pistol spray instead of the traditional paintbrush?) A photograph is made on the spot and at once. One has no right to use tricks or to play around with reality. We are always struggling with time: whatever has gone has gone forever. The time element is the key to photography. One must seize the moment before it passes, the fleeting gesture, the evanescent smile. For it is impossible to 'start again.' That's why I'm so nervous—it's horrible for my friends—but it's only by maintaining a permanent tension that I can stick to reality.

"My photographs are variations on the same theme: Man and his destiny. No one is infinitely versatile; each one of us carries within himself a particular vision of the universe. It is this view which makes for the unity in our work and, ultimately, its style. To me liberty is a strict, self-imposed framework: the discipline of respect for reality. Within it, however, there are infinite variations. I weave around the subject like the referee in a boxing match. We are passive onlookers in a world that moves perpetually. Our only moment of creation is that 1/25 of a second when the shutter clicks, the signal is given, and the knife falls. We are like skilled shots who pull the trigger and hit their target.

"Thinking should be done beforehand and afterwards—never while actually taking a photograph. Success depends on the extent of one's general culture, on one's set of values, one's clarity of mind and vivacity. The thing to be feared most is the artificially contrived, the contrary to life." . . .

## Shun the Picturesque

INTERVIEWER: What relationship is there between painting and photography?

CARTIER-BRESSON: The same rules of composition apply to both painters and photographers; both are confronted with the same visual problems. Just as one can analyze the structure of a painting, so in a good photograph one can discover the same rules, the proportional mean, the square within the rectangle, the Golden Rule, etc. That's why I like the rectangular dimension of the Leica negative, 24 by 36mm. I have a passion for geometry. My greatest joy is the surprise of facing a beautiful organization of forms, the intuitive recognition of a spontaneous—not contrived—composition; naturally with a subject that moves. I think it's only when handled this way that a subject takes on its full significance.

I never crop a photograph. If it needs to be cropped I know it's bad and that nothing could possibly improve it. The only improvement would have been to have taken another picture, at the right place and at the right time. Distance also is very important: the distance at which the photograph as a whole is taken, and also the distance between one element in the picture and another. Such relationships vary as much as the tonality of a voice heard nearby or far away. Unlike the painter, however, who can work at length on a canvas, we have to work by instinct and intuition, within a split second. We have to catch the specific detail. Our procedure is analytical, whereas the painter achieves his effects through meditation and synthesis.

We have to situate ourselves with respect to the subject; we have to have a point of view, we have to absorb ourselves in it. To me the camera is a prolongation of my eye. The instantaneous combination of eye, heart, and head seems essential to me.

I'm not in favor of color photography because in its present state of development I can't control it completely. Dealing as we do with a world in perpetual motion, I don't see how it's possible to resolve the contradiction between dark and light values and the altogether different properties of color itself. And the engraving process distorts color invariably. I prefer to go on using black and white film, which merely transposes the subject. I never use a flash bulb—just as it would never occur to me to shoot off a pistol in the middle of a concert.

Some photographers are inventors, others are discoverers. Personally, I'm interested in discovery, not for experimental purposes but to come to grips with life itself. It's the "why" that interests me. I shun the dangers of the anecdotal and the picturesque. Such effects may be easy, but they are little better than sensationalism. Getting a "surprise" effect, completely out of context, seems to me a cheap technique. I believe photography has great evocative powers and shouldn't be used simply to record facts. We should be abstract but work from nature, *i.e.,* use a rigorous structure based on reality.

Anybody can take photographs. In the *Herald Tribune* I saw some pictures taken by a monkey who had managed to use a Polaroid quite as well as a number of camera owners. It's precisely because our profession is open to everybody that it remains, in spite of its fascinating easiness, a most difficult operation.

## SUGGESTIONS FOR WRITING

1. The introduction to this essay as it appeared in *Harper's* said, "Among photographers there is a consensus that Henri Cartier-Bresson is one of the great photographers of our time. . . . Recently the French journalist, Yvonne Baby, was granted a rare interview with him in Paris." The concept of the shy, retiring, modest man granting a rare interview is interesting to brood about, for it raises the question of the "better mousetrap" theory of art. If you are good enough, the world will beat a path to your door. Cartier-Bresson seems to say: "Give no thought to the posture of the artist or to posturing of any kind; just be yourself." Yet we live in an age of merchandizing, of advertising, of marketing the image of the product. The temptation to achieve success through these methods is, for the artist, genuine. He has a message for the world in which he lives, not necessarily for a world several generations later. If he hides his light under a basket, he will never com-

municate his message. It is not an artificial dilemma. What is an artist
to do? Write an essay.
2. Cartier-Bresson says, "To me the only strictly documentary photography
is a catalogue. All other photography is never purely descriptive but a
personal means of expression. . . . I know there are camera wizards, and
I know the illusions they can create. Still I'm convinced the comments
of such wizards never really amount to a distinctive point of view about
any member of mankind and his country." In what way can a camera
be "a personal means of expression" or a comment which amounts to a
"distinctive point of view about any member of mankind"?


FRANK   LLOYD   WRIGHT

## The Cardboard House*


Let us take for text on this, our fourth afternoon, the greatest of
all references to simplicity, the inspired admonition: *"Consider the
lilies of the field—they toil not, neither do they spin, yet verily I
say unto thee—Solomon in all his glory was not arrayed like one
of these."* An inspired saying—attributed to an humble Architect in
ancient times, called Carpenter, who gave up Architecture nearly
two thousand years ago to go to work upon its Source.

And if the text should seem to you too far away from our subject
this afternoon—

### "The Cardboard House"

—consider that for that very reason the text has been chosen. The
cardboard house needs an antidote. The antidote is far more important than the house. As antidote—and as practical example, too,
of the working out of an ideal of organic simplicity that has taken
place here on American soil, step by step, under conditions that are
your own—could I do better than to take apart for your benefit
the buildings I have tried to build, to show you how they were,
long ago, dedicated to the Ideal of Organic Simplicity? It seems to
me that while another might do better than that, I certainly could

---

* From *The Future of Architecture* by Frank Lloyd Wright (New York: Horizon Press, Inc., 1953). Copyright 1953 by Horizon Press, Inc. Reprinted by permission of the publishers.

not—for that is, truest and best, what I know about the Subject. What a man *does, that* he has.

When, "in the cause of Architecture," in 1893, I first began to build the houses, sometimes referred to by the thoughtless as "The New School of the Middle West" (some advertiser's slogan comes along to label everything in this our busy woman's country), the only way to simplify the awful building in vogue at the time was to conceive a finer entity—a better building—and get it built. The buildings standing then were all tall and all tight. Chimneys were lean and taller still, sooty fingers threatening the sky. And beside them, sticking up by way of dormers through the cruelly sharp, sawtooth roofs, were the attics for "help" to swelter in. Dormers were elaborate devices, cunning little buildings complete in themselves, stuck to the main roof slopes to let "help" poke heads out of the attic for air.

Invariably the damp sticky clay of the prairie was dug out for a basement under the whole house, and the rubblestone walls of this dank basement always stuck up above the ground a foot or more and blinked, with half-windows. So the universal "cellar" showed itself as a bank of some kind of masonry running around the whole house, for the house to sit up on—like a chair. The lean, upper house walls of the usual two floors above this stone or brick basement were wood, set on top of this masonry chair, clapboarded and painted, or else shingled and stained, preferably shingled and mixed, up and down, all together with mouldings crosswise. These overdressed wood house walls had cut in them—or cut out of them, to be precise—big holes for the big cat and little holes for the little cat to get in and out or for ulterior purposes of light and air. The house walls were becorniced or bracketed up at the top into the tall, purposely profusely complicated roof, dormers plus. The whole roof, as well as the roof as a whole, was scalloped and ridged and tipped and swanked and gabled to madness before they would allow it to be either shingled or slated. The whole exterior was bedeviled —that is to say, mixed to puzzle pieces, with corner boards, panel boards, window frames, corner blocks, plinth blocks, rosettes, fantails, ingenious and jigger work in general. This was the only way they seemed to have, then, of "putting on style." The scroll saw and turning lathe were at the moment the honest means of this fashionable mongering by the wood butcher and to this entirely "moral" end. Unless the householder of the period were poor indeed, usually an ingenious corner tower on his house eventuated into a candle snuffer dome, a spire, an inverted rutabaga or radish or onion or— what is your favorite vegetable? Always elaborate bay windows and fancy porches played "ring around a rosy" on this "imaginative" corner feature. And all this the building of the period could do equally well in brick or stone. It was an impartial society. All material looked pretty much alike in that day.

Simplicity was as far from all this scrap pile as the pandemonium of the barnyard is far from music. But it was easy for the Architect. All he had to do was to call: "Boy, take down No. 37, and put a bay window on it for the lady!"

So—the first thing to do was to get rid of the attic and, therefore, of the dormer and of the useless "heights" below it. And next, get rid of the unwholesome basement, entirely—yes, absolutely—in any house built on the prairie. Instead of lean, brick chimneys, bristling up from steep roofs to hint at "judgment" everywhere, I could see necessity for one only, a broad generous one, or at most, for two, these kept low down on gently sloping roofs or perhaps flat roofs. The big fireplace below, inside, became now a place for a real fire, justified the great size of this chimney outside. A real fireplace at that time was extraordinary. There were then "mantels" instead. A mantel was a marble frame for a few coals, or a piece of wooden furniture with tiles stuck in it and a "grate," the whole set slam up against the wall. The "mantel" was an insult to comfort, but the *integral* fireplace became an important part of the building itself in the houses I was allowed to build out there on the prairie. It refreshed me to see the fire burning deep in the masonry of the house itself.

Taking a human being for my scale, I brought the whole house down in height to fit a normal man; believing in no other scale, I broadened the mass out, all I possibly could, as I brought it down into spaciousness. It has been said that were I three inches taller (I am 5 feet 8½ inches tall), all my houses would have been quite different in proportion. . . . Now all this probably tedious description is intended to indicate directly in bare outline how thus early there *was* an ideal of organic simplicity put to work, with historical consequences, here in your own country. The main motives and indications were (and I enjoyed them all):

First—To reduce the number of necessary parts of the house and the separate rooms to a minimum, and make all come together as enclosed space—so divided that light, air and vista permeated the whole with a sense of unity.

Second—To associate the building as a whole with its site by extension and emphasis of the planes parallel to the ground, but keeping the floors off the best part of the site, thus leaving that better part for use in connection with the life of the house. Extended level planes were found useful in this connection.

Third—To eliminate the room as a box and the house as another by making all walls enclosing screens—the ceilings and floors and enclosing screens to flow into each other as one large enclosure of space, with minor subdivisions only.

Make all house proportions more liberally human, with less wasted space in structure, and structure more appropriate to material, and so the whole more liveable. *Liberal* is the best word. Extended straight lines or streamlines were useful in this.

Fourth—To get the unwholesome basement up out of the ground, entirely above it, as a low pedestal for the living portion of the home, making the foundation itself visible as a low masonry platform, on which the building should stand.

Fifth—To harmonize all necessary openings to "outside" or to "inside" with good human proportions and make them occur naturally—singly or as a series in the scheme of the whole building. Usually they appeared as "light screens" instead of walls, because all the "Architecture" of the house was chiefly the way these openings came in such walls as were grouped about the rooms as enclosing screens. The *room* as such was now the essential architectural expression, and there were to be no holes cut in walls as holes are cut in a box, because this was not in keeping with the ideal of "plastic." Cutting holes was violent.

Sixth—To eliminate combinations of different materials in favor of monomaterial so far as possible; to use no ornament that did not come out of the nature of materials to make the whole building clearer and more expressive as a place to live in, and give the conception of the building appropriate revealing emphasis. Geometrical or straight lines were natural to the machinery at work in the building trades then, so the interiors took on this character naturally.

Seventh—To incorporate all heating, lighting, plumbing so that these systems became constituent parts of the building itself. These service features became architectural and in this attempt the ideal of an organic architecture was at work.

Eighth—To incorporate as organic architecture—so far as possible—furnishings, making them all one with the building and designing them in simple terms for machine work. Again straight lines and rectilinear forms.

Ninth—Eliminate the Decorator. He was all curves and all efflorescence, if not all "period."

This was all rational enough so far as the thought of an organic architecture went. The particular forms this thought took in the feeling of it all could only be personal. There was nothing whatever at this time to help make them what they were. All seemed to be the most natural thing in the world and grew up out of the circumstances of the moment. Whatever they may be worth in the long run is all they are worth.

Now *simplicity* being the point in question in this early constructive effort, organic simplicity I soon found to be a matter of true coordination. And Beauty I soon felt to be a matter of the sympathy with which such coordination was affected. Plainness was not necessarily simplicity. Crude furniture of the Roycroft-Stickley-Mission Style, which came along later, was offensively plain, plain as a barn door—but never was simple in any true sense. Nor, I found, were merely machine-made things in themselves simple. To think "in simple," is to deal in simples, and that means with an eye single to the altogether. This, I believe, is the secret of simplicity. Perhaps we may truly regard nothing at all as simple in itself. I believe that no one thing in itself is ever so, but must achieve simplicity (as an Artist should use the term) as a perfectly realized part of some organic whole. Only as a feature or any part becomes an harmonious element in the harmonious whole does it arrive at the estate of simplicity. Any wild flower is truly simple, but double the same wild flower by cultivation, it ceases to be so. The *scheme* of the original is no longer clear. Clarity of design and perfect significance both are first essentials of the spontaneously born simplicity of the lilies of the field who neither toil nor spin, as contrasted with Solomon who had "toiled and spun"—that is to say, no doubt had put on himself and had put on his temple, properly "composed," everything in the category of good things but the cook-stove.

Five lines where three are enough is stupidity. Nine pounds where three are sufficient is stupidity. But to eliminate expressive words that intensify or vivify meaning in speaking or writing is not simplicity; nor is similar elimination in Architecture simplicity—it, too, may be stupidity. In Architecture expressive changes of surface, emphasis of line and especially textures of material, may go to make facts eloquent, forms more significant. Elimination, therefore, may be just as meaningless as elaboration, perhaps more often so. I offer any fool, for an example.

To know what to leave out and what to put in, just where and just how—Ah, *that* is to have been educated in knowledge of SIMPLICITY. . . .

Standing here, with the perspective of long persistent effort in the direction of an organic Architecture in view, I can again assure you out of this initial experience that Repose is the reward of true simplicity and that organic simplicity is sure of Repose. Repose is the highest quality in the Art of Architecture, next to integrity, and a reward for integrity. Simplicity may well be held to the fore as a spiritual ideal, but when actually achieved, as in the "lilies of the field," it is something that comes of itself, something spontaneously born out of the nature of the doing whatever it is that is to be done. Simplicity, too, is a reward for fine feeling and straight thinking in working a principle, well in hand, to a consistent end. Solomon knew nothing about it, for he was only wise. And this, I think, is what Jesus meant by the text we have chosen for this discourse—"Consider the lilies of the field," as contrasted, for beauty, with Solomon.

Now, a chair *is* a machine to sit in.

A home *is* a machine to live in.

The human body *is* a machine to be worked by will.

A tree *is* a machine to bear fruit.

A plant *is* a machine to bear flowers and seeds.

And, as I've admitted before somewhere, a heart *is* a suction pump. Does that idea thrill you?

Trite as it is, it may be as well to think it over because the *least* any of these things may be, *is* just that. All of them are that before they are anything else. And to violate that mechanical requirement in any of them is to finish before anything of higher purpose can happen. To ignore the fact is either sentimentality or the prevalent insanity. Let us acknowledge in this respect, that this matter of mechanics is just as true of the work of Art as it is true of anything else. . . .

Would you have again the general principles of the spiritual ideal of organic simplicity at work in our culture? If so, then let us reiterate: First, Simplicity is Constitutional Order. And it is worthy of note in this connection that 9 times 9 equals 81 is just as simple as 2 plus 2 equals 4. Nor is the obvious more simple necessarily than the occult. The obvious is obvious simply because it falls within our special horizon, is therefore easier for us to *see;* that is all. Yet all simplicity near or far has a countenance, a visage, that is characteristic. But this countenance is visible only to those who can grasp the whole and enjoy the significance of the minor part, as such, in relation to the whole when in flower. This is for the critics.

This characteristic visage may be simulated—the real complication glossed over, the internal conflict hidden by surface and belied by mass. The internal complication may be and usually is increased to create the semblance of and get credit for—simplicity. This is the Simplicity lie usually achieved by most of the "surface and mass" architects. This is for the young architect.

Truly ordered simplicity in the hands of the great artist may flower into a bewildering profusion, exquisitely exuberant, and render all more clear than ever. Good William Blake says exuberance is *beauty,* meaning that it is so in this very sense. This is for the Modern Artist with the Machine in his hands. False Simplicity —Simplicity as an affectation, that is Simplicity constructed as a Decorator's outside put upon a complicated, wasteful engineer's or carpenter's "Structure," outside or inside—is not good enough Simplicity. It cannot be simple at all. But that is what passes for Simplicity, now that startling Simplicity effects are becoming the *fashion.* That kind of Simplicity is *violent.* This is for "Art and Decoration."

Soon we shall want Simplicity inviolate. There is one way to get that Simplicity. My guess is, there is *only* one way really to get it. And that way is, on principle, by way of *Construction* developed as Architecture. That is for us, one and all.

SUGGESTIONS FOR WRITING

1. Frank Lloyd Wright (1869-1959) began his career as an architect in 1893 in Chicago. *An Autobiography—Frank Lloyd Wright* (1932, rev. 1943) tells of his life struggle to establish modern principles of architecture. In the above excerpt from his essay, "The Cardboard House," he attempts to make plain what he means by Simplicity. But *Simplicity,* it seems, is not so simple. Describe an architectural object that Wright would praise as simple.
2. Which of the various facets of Wright's "organic structure" do you find most appealing? What attracts you to this facet?
3. When an architect plans a house for you, he wants to know what kind of a person you are. Write an autobiographical report for an architect telling him how you live, how you want to live, what your dreams are, what your needs are, what your tastes in music and art are. Tell him whatever you think he will need to know to plan your "dream" house.

WILLIAM SAROYAN

## Love, Death, Sacrifice, and So Forth*

Tom Garner, in the movie, on the screen, a big broad-shouldered man, a builder of railroads, President of the Chicago & Southwestern, staggers, does not walk, into his room, and closes the door.

You know he is going to commit suicide because he has staggered, and it is a movie, and already a long while has passed since the picture began, and something's got to happen real soon, something big, gigantic, as they say in Hollywood, a suicide or a kiss.

You are sitting in the theatre waiting for what you know is going to happen.

Poor Tom has just learned that the male offspring of his second wife is the product of his grown son by his first wife. Tom's first wife committed suicide when she learned that Tom had fallen in love with the young woman who finally became his second wife.

---

This young woman was the daughter of the President of the Santa Clara Railroad. She made Tom fall in love with her so that her father would go on being President of the Santa Clara. Tom had bought the Santa Clara for nine million dollars. Tom's first wife threw herself beneath a streetcar when she found out about Tom's infatuation. She did it by acting, with her face, her eyes, and lips and the way she walked. You didn't get to see anything sickening, you saw only the motorman's frantic expression while he tried to bring the car to a stop. You heard and saw the steel wheel grinding, the wheel that killed her. You heard people screaming the way they do about violent things, and you got the idea. The worst had happened. Tom's wife Sally had gone to her Maker.

Sally met Tom when he was a trackwalker and she a teacher in a small country school. Tom confessed to her one day that he did not know how to read, write or do arithmetic. Sally taught Tom to read, write, add, subtract, divide and multiply. One evening after they were married she asked him if he wanted to be a trackwalker all his life, and he said that he did. Sally asked him if he didn't have at least a little ambition, and Tom said he was satisfied, trackwalking was easy work, they had their little home, and Tom got in a lot of fishing on the side. This hurt Sally, and she began to act. Tom saw that it would mean a lot to Sally if he became ambitious. Sitting at the supper table, he said that he would. A strange look came into his eyes, his face acquired great character. You could almost see him forging ahead in life.

Sally sent Tom to school in Chicago, and she did Tom's work as a trackwalker in order to have money with which to pay for his tuition, a great woman, an heroic wife. You saw her one winter night walking along a railroad track, packing tools and oil cans, snow and desolation all around her. It was sad. It was meant to be sad. She was doing it for Tom, so that he would be able to become a great man. The day Tom announced that he had been made foreman of the construction of the Missouri Bridge, Sally announced she was with child, and Tom said now they could never stop him. With Sally and his baby to inspire him Tom would reach the heights.

Sally gave birth to a son, and while Tom was walking to her bedside you heard symphonic music, and you knew that this was a great moment in Tom's life. You saw Tom enter the dimly lighted room and kneel beside his wife and baby son, and you heard him pray. You heard him say, Our father which art in heaven, thine the glory and the power, forever and forever. You heard two people in the theatre blowing their noses.

Sally made Tom. She took him from the track and sent him to the president's chair. Then Tom became infatuated with this younger and lovelier woman, and Sally threw herself beneath the streetcar. It was because of what she had done for Tom that the suicide was so touching. It was because of this that tears came to the eyes of so many people in the theatre when Sally destroyed herself.

But Sally's suicide did not have any effect on Tom's infatuation for the younger woman, and after a short while he married the girl, being a practical man part of the time, being practical as long as Hollywood wanted him to be practical. Tom's son, a young man just expelled from college for drunkenness, moved into Tom's house, and had an affair with Tom's second wife.

The result was the baby, a good healthy baby, born of the son instead of the father. Tom's son Tommy is an irresponsible but serious and well-dressed young man, and he really didn't mean to do it. Nature did it. You know how nature is, even in the movies. Tom had been away from home so much, attending to business, and his second wife had been so lonely that she had turned to her husband's son, and he had become her dancing partner.

You saw her holding her hand out to the young irresponsible boy, and you heard her ask him significantly if he would like to dance with her. It took him so long to take her hand that you understand the frightening implication instantly. And she was so maddeningly beautiful, extending her hand to him, that you knew you yourself would never have been able to resist her challenge, even under similar circumstances. There was something irresistible about the perfection of her face and figure, lips so kissable, stance so elegant, body so lovely, soul so needful.

It simply had to happen. Man is flesh, and all that.

So the big railroad builder, the man who always had his way, the man who broke the strike and had forty of his men killed in a riot, and a fire, has staggered into his room and closed the door.

And you know the picture is about to end.

The atmosphere of the theatre is becoming electrical with the apprehension of middle-aged ladies who have spent the better parts of their lives in the movies, loving, dying, sacrificing themselves to noble ideals, etc. They've come again to the dark theatre, and a moment of great living is again upon them.

You can feel the spiritual tenseness of all of these ladies, and if you are listening carefully you can actually hear them living fully.

Poor Tom is in there with a terrific problem and a ghastly obligation.

For his honor's sake, for the sake of Hollywood ethics, for the sake of the industry (the third largest in America, I understand), for God's sake, for your sake and my sake, Tom has got to commit suicide. If he doesn't, it will simply mean we have been deceiving ourselves all these years, Shakespeare and the rest of us. We know he'll be man enough to do it, but for an instant we hope he won't, just to see what will happen, just to see if the world we have made will actually smash.

A long while back we made the rules, and now, after all these years, we wonder if they are the genuine ones, or if, maybe, we didn't make a mistake at the outset. We know it's art, and it even looks a little like life, but we know it isn't life, being much too precise.

We would like to know if our greatness must necessarily go on forever being melodramatic.

The camera rests on the bewildered face of Tom's old and faithful secretary, a man who knew Tom as a boy. This is to give you the full implication of Tom's predicament and to create a powerful suspense in your mind.

Then, at a trot, with the same object in view, time hurrying, culminations, ultimates, inevitabilities, Tom's son Tommy comes to the old and faithful secretary and exclaims that he has heard Tom, his father, is ill. He does not know that his father knows. It is a Hollywood moment. You hear appropriate music.

He rushes to the door, to go to his father, this boy who upset the natural order of the universe by having a sexual affair with his father's young wife, and then, bang, the pistol shot.

You know it is all over with the President of the Chicago & Southwestern. His honor is saved. He remains a great man. Once again the industry triumphs. The dignity of life is preserved. Everything is hotsytotsy. It will be possible for Hollywood to go on making pictures for the public for another century.

Everything is precise, for effect. Halt. Symphonic music, Tommy's hand frozen on the doorknob.

The old and faithful secretary knows what has happened, Tommy knows, you know and I know, but there is nothing like seeing. The old and faithful secretary allows the stark reality of the pistol shot to penetrate his old, faithful and orderly mind. Then, since Tommy is too frightened to do so, he forces himself to open the door.

All of us are waiting to see how it happened.

The door opens and we go in, fifty million of us in America and millions more all over the earth.

Poor Tom. He is sinking to his knees, and somehow, even though it is happening swiftly, it seems that this little action, being the last one of a great man, will go on forever, this sinking to the knees. The room is dim, the music eloquent. There is no blood, no disorder. Tom is sinking to his knees, dying nobly. I myself hear two ladies weeping. They know it's a movie, they know it must be fake, still, they are weeping. Tom is man. He is life. It makes them weep to see life sinking to its knees. The movie will be over in a minute and they will get up and go home, and get down to the regular business of their lives, but now, in the pious darkness of the theatre, they are weeping.

All I know is this: that a suicide is not an orderly occurrence with symphonic music. There was a man once who lived in the house next door to my house when I was a boy of nine or ten. One afternoon he committed suicide, but it took him over an hour to do it. He shot himself through the chest, missed his heart, then shot himself through the stomach. I heard both shots. There was an interval of about forty seconds between the shots. I thought afterwards that during the interval he was probably trying to decide if he ought to go on wanting to be dead or if he ought to try to get well.

Then he started to holler. The whole thing was a mess, materially and spiritually, this man hollering, people running, shouting, wanting to do something and not knowing what to do. He hollered so loud half the town heard him.

This is all I know about regular suicides. I haven't seen a woman throw herself under a streetcar, so I can't say about that. This is the only suicide I have any definite information about. The way this man hollered wouldn't please anyone in a movie. It wouldn't make anyone weep with joy.

I think it comes to this: we've got to stop committing suicide in the movies.

## SUGGESTIONS FOR WRITING

1. William Saroyan (1908-      ) is a poet, essayist, dramatist, novelist, and short story writer. His play, *The Time of Your Life* won the Pulitzer Prize in 1940. He has frequently written about motion pictures. In this essay he treats movies with a satiric scorn. His technique—of imaginatively recreating the darkened movie theater and giving his response to the movie—is especially effective. Describe your reaction to a movie you have seen by using Saroyan's technique as a model.

2. The television play has reached a climax. The hero has two choices. If he goes one way, x will occur. If he goes another, y will occur. Eight minutes of viewing time remain. Result x cannot be shown in less than fifteen minutes. Therefore, no matter what his reasoning or what the complication of the plot, the viewer knows the decision before the hero decides. It will have to be that which can occur in eight minutes. Thus the technicality of the medium decides plot structure. Have you experienced the frustration described above? If so, write about it.

3. What does Saroyan really want the movies to do? If you have trouble determining the answer from the essay, answer it for yourself. What do you really want the movies to do? How far should realism go? To what degree should background music be used? Describe an ideal movie.

JOHN  KEATS

# Ode on a Grecian Urn

### I

Thou still unravish'd bride of quietness,
    Thou foster-child of silence and slow time,
Sylvan historian, who canst thus express
    A flowery tale more sweetly than our rhyme:
What leaf-fring'd legend haunts about thy shape
    Of deities or mortals, or of both,
        In Tempe or the dales of Arcady?
What men or gods are these? What maidens loth?

What mad pursuit? What struggle to escape?
What pipes and timbrels? What wild ecstasy?

## II

Heard melodies are sweet, but those unheard
Are sweeter; therefore, ye soft pipes, play on;
Not to the sensual ear, but, more endear'd,
Pipe to the spirit ditties of no tone:
Fair youth, beneath the trees, thou canst not leave
Thy song, nor ever can those trees be bare;
Bold Lover, never, never canst thou kiss,
Though winning near the goal—yet, do not grieve;
She cannot fade, though thou hast not thy bliss,
For ever wilt thou love, and she be fair!

## III

Ah, happy, happy boughs! that cannot shed
Your leaves, nor ever bid the Spring adieu;
And, happy melodist, unwearièd,
For ever piping songs for ever new;
More happy love! more happy, happy love!
For ever warm and still to be enjoy'd,
For ever panting, and for ever young;
All breathing human passion far above,
That leaves a heart high-sorrowful and cloy'd,
A burning forehead, and a parching tongue.

## IV

Who are these coming to the sacrifice?
To what green altar, O mysterious priest,
Lead'st thou that heifer lowing at the skies,
And all her silken flanks with garlands drest?
What little town by river or sea shore,
Or mountain-built with peaceful citadel,
Is emptied of its folk, this pious morn?
And, little town, thy streets for evermore
Will silent be; and not a soul to tell
Why thou art desolate, can e'er return.

## V

O Attic shape! Fair attitude! with brede
Of marble men and maidens overwrought,

With forest branches and the trodden weed;
 Thou, silent form, dost tease us out of thought
As doth eternity: Cold Pastoral!
When old age shall this generation waste,
 Thou shalt remain, in midst of other woe
Than ours, a friend to man, to whom thou say'st,
 "Beauty is truth, truth beauty,"—that is all
 Ye know on earth, and all ye need to know.


## SUGGESTIONS FOR WRITING

1. John Keats (1795-1821) was an English poet of the Romantic period. He wrote this poem in a language appropriate to the subject matter. Define Sylvan historian, Tempe, dales of Arcady, loth, timbrels, ditties, cloy'd, lowing, Attic shape, brede, trodden weed.

2. Why are "unheard" melodies sweeter?

3. The poet tells the lover not to grieve: "do not grieve;/She cannot fade, though thou hast not thy bliss." Could such a lover fail to grieve? The lines, though false to our sense of reality do not disturb the mood the poem has created. What elements in this poem contribute to this mood?

4. The "frame" of Keats' poem is a Grecian urn the poet is looking at. The poet talks partly to himself and partly to the man and woman he sees on the Grecian urn. Comment on the appropriateness of a Grecian urn (rather than a painting, a statue, or something else) as a "frame" for the poet's thoughts.

5. The theme is the permanence and intransigence of beauty, wherever it may be found. Contrast this theme with the theme of "Ozymandias" by Percy Bysshe Shelley (p. 535).

6. "Beauty is truth, truth beauty." This phrase is the final idea of the poem. Analyze the steps which led the poet to this idea. Then write a statement beginning with Keats' definition of beauty and reveal what he means by his definition. Is he really talking about the beauty of a particular Grecian urn? Beauty in general? Beauty in human relations? The beauty that man contemplates but never sees?

*Part Five*

# THE SEARCH

# FOR

# SIGNIFICANCE

# Purpose in Life

The wise only possess ideas; the greater part of mankind are possessed by them.

—Coleridge, *Defoe*, 1830

The first thing a child should learn is how to endure. It is what he will have most need to know.

—Rousseau, *Émile*, 1762

Distribute the earth as you will, the principal question remains inexorable—Who is to dig it? Which of us, in brief word, is to do the hard and dirty work for the rest, and for what pay? Who is to do the pleasant and clean work, and for what pay? Who is to do no work, and for what pay?

—Ruskin, *Sesame and Lillies*, 1865

"If God didn't exist, man would have to invent Him."—I am rarely satisfied with my lines, but I confess that I have a father's tenderness for that one.

—Voltaire, to M. Saurin, November 10, 1770

The question is this: Is man an ape or an angel? My lord, I am on the side of the angels. I repudiate with indignation and abhorrence the contrary view, which is, I believe, foreign to the conscience of humanity.

—Benjamin Disraeli, *Speech to the Oxford Diocesan Society*, November 25, 1864

Why may not a goose say: "I have an interest in all parts of the universe. The earth serves me to walk upon; the sun to light me; the stars influence me; I get advantage from the wind and the waters; the roof of Heaven looks down upon nothing more favorably than on me. I am the darling of nature. Man himself keeps, lodges and serves me."

—Montaigne, *Essays*, 1580

JOSÉ ORTEGA Y GASSET

# Human Reality*

A great man is dying. His wife is by his bedside. A doctor takes the dying man's pulse. In the background two more persons are discovered: a reporter who is present for professional reasons, and a painter whom mere chance has brought here. Wife, doctor, reporter, and painter witness one and the same event. Nonetheless, this identical event—a man's death—impresses each of them in a different way. So different indeed that the several aspects have hardly anything in common. What this scene means to the wife who is all grief has so little to do with what it means to the painter who looks on impassively that it seems doubtful whether the two can be said to be present at the same event.

It thus becomes clear that one and the same reality may split up into many diverse realities when it is beheld from different points of view. And we cannot help asking ourselves: Which of all these realities must then be regarded as the real and authentic one? The answer, no matter how we decide, cannot but be arbitrary. Any preference can be founded on caprice only. All these realities are equivalent, each being authentic for its corresponding point of view. All we can do is to classify the points of view and to determine which among them seems, in a practical way, most normal or most spontaneous. Thus we arrive at a conception of reality that is by no means absolute, but at least practical and normative.

As for the points of view of the four persons present at the

* From *The Dehumanization of Art and Other Writings on Art and Culture,* translated by Willard R. Trask (Princeton, N.J.: The Princeton University Press, 1948). Copyright 1948 by Princeton University Press. Reprinted by permission of the publishers.

deathbed, the clearest means of distinguishing them is by measuring one of their dimensions, namely the emotional distance between each person and the event they all witness. For the wife of the dying man the distance shrinks to almost nothing. What is happening so tortures her soul and absorbs her mind that it becomes one with her person. Or to put it inversely, the wife is drawn into the scene, she is part of it. A thing can be seen, an event can be observed, only when we have separated it from ourselves and it has ceased to form a living part of our being. Thus the wife is not present at the scene, she is in it. She does not behold it, she "lives" it.

The doctor is several degrees removed. To him this is a professional case. He is not drawn into the event with the frantic and blinding anxiety of the poor woman. However it is his bounden duty as a doctor to take a serious interest, he carries responsibility, perhaps his professional honor is at stake. Hence he too, albeit in a less integral and less intimate way, takes part in the event. He is involved in it not with his heart but with the professional portion of his self. He too "lives" the scene although with an agitation originating not in the emotional center, but in the professional surface, of his existence.

When we now put ourselves in the place of the reporter we realize that we have traveled a long distance away from the tragic event. So far indeed that we have lost all emotional contact with it. The reporter, like the doctor, has been brought here for professional reasons and not out of a spontaneous human interest. But while the doctor's profession requires him to interfere, the reporter's requires him precisely to stay aloof; he has to confine himself to observing. To him the event is a mere scene, a pure spectacle on which he is expected to report in his newspaper column. He takes no feeling part in what is happening here, he is emotionally free, an outsider. He does not "live" the scene, he observes it. Yet he observes it with a view to telling his readers about it. He wants to interest them, to move them, and if possible to make them weep as though they each had been the dying man's best friend. From his schooldays he remembers Horace's recipe: *"Si vis me flere dolendum est primum ipsi tibi"*—if you want me to weep you must first grieve yourself.

Obedient to Horace the reporter is anxious to pretend emotion, hoping that it will benefit his literary performance. If he does not "live" the scene he at least pretends to "live" it.

The painter, in fine, completely unconcerned, does nothing but keep his eyes open. What is happening here is none of his business; he is, as it were, a hundred miles removed from it. His is a purely perceptive attitude; indeed, he fails to perceive the event in its entirety. The tragic inner meaning escapes his attention which is directed exclusively toward the visual part—color values, lights, and shadows. In the painter we find a maximum of distance and a minimum of feeling intervention.

The inevitable dullness of this analysis will, I hope, be excused if it now enables us to speak in a clear and precise way of a scale of emotional distances between ourselves and reality. In this scale, the degree of closeness is equivalent to the degree of feeling participation; the degree of remoteness, on the other hand, marks the degree to which we have freed ourselves from the real event, thus objectifying it and turning it into a theme of pure observation. At one end of the scale the world—persons, things, situations—is given to us in the aspect of "lived" reality; at the other end we see everything in the aspect of "observed" reality.

At this point we must make a remark that is essential in aesthetics and without which neither old art nor new art can be satisfactorily analyzed. Among the diverse aspects of reality we find one from which all the others derive and which they all presuppose: "lived" reality. If nobody had ever "lived" in pure and frantic abandonment a man's death, the doctor would not bother, the readers would not understand the reporter's pathos, and the canvas on which the painter limned a person on a bed surrounded by mourning figures would be meaningless. The same holds for any object, be it a person, a thing, or a situation. The primal aspect of an apple is that in which I see it when I am about to eat it. All its other possible forms—when it appears, for instance, in a Baroque ornament, or on a still life of Cézanne's, or in the eternal metaphor of a girl's apple cheeks—preserve more or less that original aspect. A painting or a poem without any vestiges of "lived" forms would be unintelligible, i.e., nothing—as a discourse is nothing whose every word is emptied of its customary meaning.

That is to say, in the scale of realities "lived" reality holds a peculiar primacy which compels us to regard it as "the" reality. Instead of "lived" reality we may say "human" reality. The painter who impassively witnesses the death scene appears "inhuman." In other words, the human point of view is that in which we "live" situations, persons, things. And, vice versa, realities—a woman, a countryside, an event—are human when they present the aspect in which they are usually "lived."

As an example, the importance of which will appear later, let us mention that among the realities which constitute the world are our ideas. We use our ideas in a "human" way when we employ them for thinking things. Thinking of Napoleon, for example, we are normally concerned with the great man of that name. A psychologist, on the other hand, adopts an unusual, "inhuman" attitude when he forgets about Napoleon and, prying into his own mind, tries to analyze his idea of Napoleon as such idea. His perspective is the opposite of that prevailing in spontaneous life. The idea, instead of functioning as the means to think an object with, is itself made the object and the aim of thinking.

SUGGESTIONS FOR WRITING

1. José Ortega y Gasset (1883-1955) was a leading Spanish philosopher. He went into self-exile during the Spanish Civil War, and after living and teaching in South America for many years, returned to Spain in 1949. His *The Revolt of the Masses,* 1930, is perhaps his best known book. In *The Dehumanization of Art* (1948), from which this excerpt is taken, he presents an operational definition of *reality,* which is a very difficult word to define. He says that the wife was not really present at her husband's death. If this is true, are you then not really present at various times during the day? When you are not consciously attending to the noises and activities around you, are you "present" (as Ortega uses the word)? Write a theme describing yourself at these moments, telling how you feel and where you are.

2. Oliver Wendell Holmes says (in the Quotations section for "Man Thinking," p. 500) that each man is three persons. Ortega y Gasset seems to be saying that there are as many of you as there are people who respond to you. Describe yourself as seen by three or four different people, for example, a clergyman, an employer, a teacher, a parent, an aunt, a school chum.

3. Ortega y Gasset says: "A painting or a poem without any vestiges of 'lived' forms would be unintelligible, i.e., nothing—as a discourse is nothing whose every word is emptied of its customary meaning." How, then, can modern abstract paintings have any meaning?

WILLIAM SHAKESPEARE

## Sonnet Thirty

When to the sessions of sweet silent thought
I summon up remembrance of things past,
I sigh the lack of many a thing I sought,
And with old woes new wail my dear time's waste.
Then can I drown an eye, unused to flow,
For precious friends hid in death's dateless night,
And weep afresh love's long-since cancelled woe,
And moan the expense of many a vanished sight.
Then can I grieve at grievances foregone,
And heavily from woe to woe tell o'er
The sad account of fore-bemoaned moan,
Which I new pay as if not paid before.
    But if the while I think on thee, dear friend,
    All losses are restored, and sorrows end.

SUGGESTIONS FOR WRITING

1. William Shakespeare (1564-1616), English poet and dramatist, is probably the greatest of them all. His *Sonnet Thirty* is the story of a man who looks back on his life with regret. He was never able to accomplish what would bring him fulfillment. What man is? What, after all, can one man do on this earth? Write a theme revealing each of the items that the poet bewails. It is conceivable that you could have one paragraph for line three, one for lines four, six, and seven (maybe more than one paragraph on "love's long-since cancelled woe"), one for lines eight through twelve.

2. The last two lines of Shakespeare's sonnet are said by some critics to detract from the power of the poem. Do you think so? Analyze the poem and write an answer.

ALBERT CAMUS

# Man Is Stronger than His Rock*

The gods had condemned Sisyphus to ceaselessly rolling a rock to the top of a mountain, whence the stone would fall back of its own weight. They had thought with some reason that there is no more dreadful punishment than futile and hopeless labor.

If one believes Homer, Sisyphus was the wisest and most prudent of mortals. According to another tradition, however, he was disposed to practice the profession of highwayman. I see no contradiction in this. Opinions differ as to the reasons why he became the futile laborer of the underworld. To begin with, he is accused of a certain levity in regard to the gods. He stole their secrets. Ægina, the daughter of Æsopus, was carried off by Jupiter. The father was shocked by that disappearance and complained to Sisyphus. He, who knew of the abduction, offered to tell about it on condition that Æsopus would give water to the citadel of Corinth. To the celestial thunderbolts he preferred the benediction of water. He was punished for this in the underworld. Homer tells us also that Sisyphus had put Death in chains. Pluto could not endure the sight of his deserted, silent empire. He dispatched the god of war, who liberated Death from the hands of her conqueror.

It is said also that Sisyphus, being near to death, rashly wanted to test his wife's love. He ordered her to cast his unburied body into the middle of the public square. Sisyphus woke up in the underworld. And there, annoyed by an obedience so contrary to human love, he obtained from Pluto permission to return to earth in order to chastise his wife. But when he had seen again the face of this world, enjoyed water and sun, warm stones and the sea, he no longer wanted to go back to the infernal darkness. Recalls, signs of anger, warnings were of no avail. Many years more he lived facing the curve of the gulf, the sparkling sea, and the smiles of earth. A decree of the gods was necessary. Mercury came and seized the im-

---

* From *The Myth of Sisyphus and Other Essays,* translated by Justin O'Brien (New York: Alfred A. Knopf, Inc., 1955). © 1955 by Alfred A. Knopf, Inc. Reprinted by permission of the publishers.

pudent man by the collar and, snatching him from his joys, led him forcibly back to the underworld, where his rock was ready for him.

You have already grasped that Sisyphus is the absurd hero. He *is*, as much through his passions as through his torture. His scorn of the gods, his hatred of death, and his passion for life won him that unspeakable penalty in which the whole being is exerted toward accomplishing nothing. This is the price that must be paid for the passions of this earth. Nothing is told us about Sisyphus in the underworld. Myths are made for the imagination to breathe life into them. As for this myth, one sees merely the whole effort of a body straining to raise the huge stone, to roll it and push it up a slope a hundred times over; one sees the face screwed up, the cheek right against the stone, the shoulder bracing the clay-covered mass, the foot wedging it, the fresh start with arms outstretched, the wholly human security of two earth-clotted hands. At the very end of his long effort measured by skyless space and time without depth, the purpose is achieved. Then Sisyphus watches the stone rush down in a few moments toward that lower world whence he will have to push it up again toward the summit. He goes back down to the plain.

It is during that return, that pause, that Sisyphus interests me. A face that toils so close to stones is already stone itself! I see that man going back down with a heavy yet measured step toward the torment of which he will never know the end. That hour like a breathing space which returns as surely as his suffering, that is the hour of consciousness. At each of those moments when he leaves the heights and gradually sinks toward the lairs of the gods, he is superior to his fate. He is stronger than his rock.

If this myth is tragic, that is because its hero is conscious. Where would his torture be, indeed, if at every step the hope of succeeding upheld him? The workman of today works every day in his life at the same tasks, and this fate is no less absurd. But it is tragic only at the rare moments when it becomes conscious. Sisyphus, proletarian of the gods, powerless and rebellious, knows the whole extent of wretched condition: it is what he thinks of during his descent. The lucidity that was to constitute his torture at the same time crowns his victory. There is no fate that cannot be surmounted by scorn.

If the descent is thus sometimes performed in sorrow, it can also take place in joy. This word is not too much. Again I fancy Sisyphus returning toward his rock, and the sorrow was in the beginning. When the images of earth cling too tightly to memory, when the call of happiness becomes too insistent, it happens that melancholy rises in man's heart: this is the rock's victory, this is the rock itself. The boundless grief is too heavy to bear. These are our nights of Gethsemane. But crushing truths perish from being acknowledged. Thus, Œdipus at the outset obeys fate without knowing it. But from the moment he knows, his tragedy begins. Yet at the same moment, blind and desperate, he realizes that the only bond linking him to the world is the cool hand of a girl. Then a tremendous remark rings out: "Despite so many ordeals, my advanced age and the nobility of my soul make me conclude that all is well." Sophocles' Œdipus, like Dostoevsky's Kirilov, thus gives the recipe for the absurd victory. Ancient wisdom confirms modern heroism.

One does not discover the absurd without being tempted to write a manual of happiness. "What! by such narrow ways—?" There is but one world, however. Happiness and the absurd are two sons of the same earth. They are inseparable. It would be a mistake to say that happiness necessarily springs from the absurd discovery. It happens as well that the feeling of the absurd springs from happiness. "I conclude that all is well," says Œdipus, and that remark is sacred. It echoes in the wild and limited universe of man. It teaches that all is not, has not been, exhausted. It drives out of this world a god who had come into it with dissatisfaction and a preference *for* futile sufferings. It makes of fate a human matter, which must be settled among men.

All Sisyphus' silent joy is contained therein. His fate belongs to him. His rock is his thing. Likewise, the absurd man, when he contemplates his torment, silences all the idols. In the universe suddenly restored to its silence, the myriad wondering little voices of the earth rise up. Unconscious, secret calls, invitations from all the faces, they are the necessary reverse and price of victory. There is no sun without shadow, and it is essential to know the night. The absurd man says yes and his effort will henceforth be unceasing. If there is a personal fate, there is no higher destiny, or at least there is but one which he concludes is inevitable and despicable. For the rest, he knows himself to be the master of his days. At that subtle moment when man glances backward over his life, Sisyphus returning toward his rock, in that slight pivoting he contemplates that series of unrelated actions which becomes his fate, created by him, combined under his memory's eye and soon sealed by his death. Thus, convinced of the wholly human origin of all that is human, a blind man eager to see who knows that the night has no end, he is still on the go. The rock is still rolling.

I leave Sisyphus at the foot of the mountain! One always finds one's burden again. But Sisyphus teaches the higher fidelity that negates the gods and raises rocks. He too concludes that all is well. This universe henceforth without a master seems to him neither sterile nor futile. Each atom of that stone, each mineral flake of that night-filled mountain, in itself forms a world. The struggle itself toward the heights is enough to fill a man's heart. One must imagine Sisyphus happy.

## SUGGESTIONS FOR WRITING

1. Albert Camus (1913-1960) was born in Algeria, played a part in the French Resistance in World War II, and later became an editor and a director of a publishing house. He is the author of essays, plays, and novels. In 1957 he won the Nobel Prize for Literature. Three of his best known books are *The Stranger* (1946), *The Plague* (1948), and *The Fall* (1956). In the above essay, as in many of his novels and plays, he deliberates on the fate of man. What is fulfillment? What is worth the struggle? His thoughtful reflection almost leads in a circle. One struggles all his life and what does he get—a sense of the worth of the struggle, the knowledge that "the struggle itself toward the heights is enough to fill a man's heart." Why struggle? Because if you don't, life won't be worth living. Does this reasoning give you any perspective on your life? Does it give a different dimension to your dreams and goals? Write a theme considering these questions.

2. Camus says that myths are made for the imagination to breathe life into them, whereupon he breathes life into the Sisyphus myth. Take another myth and like Camus, breathe life into it. Use Camus as a pattern and say something of significance about the role of man on this earth.

3. Comment on the final sentence of the essay, "One must imagine Sisyphus happy."

ST. THOMAS AQUINAS

# On the Existence of God *

The existence of God can be proved in five ways.

The first and more manifest way is the argument from motion. It is certain, and evident to our senses, that in the world some things are in motion. Now what is moved is moved by another, for nothing can be moved except it is in potentiality to that toward which it is moved; whereas a thing moves inasmuch as it is in act. For motion is nothing else than the reduction of something from potentiality to actuality. But nothing can be reduced from potentiality to actuality, except by something in a state of actuality. Thus that which is actually hot, as fire, makes wood, which is potentially hot, to be actually hot, and thereby moves and changes it. Now it is not possible that the same thing should be at once in actuality and potentiality in the same respect, but only in different respects. For what is actually hot cannot simultaneously be potentially hot; but it is potentially cold. It is therefore impossible that in the same respect and in the same way a thing should be both mover and moved, *i.e.*, that it should move itself. Therefore whatever is moved must be moved by another; and that by another again. But this cannot go on to infinity, because then there would be no first mover and, consequently, no other mover, seeing that subsequent movers move only inasmuch as they are moved by the first mover, as the staff moves only because it is moved by the hand. Therefore it is necessary to arrive at a first mover, moved by no other, and this everyone understands to be God.

The second way is from the nature of efficient cause. In the world of sensible things we find there is an order of efficient causes. There is no case known (neither is it, indeed, possible) in which a thing is found to be the efficient cause of itself, for so it would be prior to itself, which is impossible. Now in efficient causes it is not possible to go on to infinity, because in all efficient causes following in order, the first is the cause of the intermediate cause, and the intermediate is the cause of the ultimate cause, whether the inter-

---

* From *The Summa Theologica,* Part I.

mediate cause be several or only one. Now to take away the cause is to take away the effect. Therefore if there be no first cause among efficient causes, there will be no ultimate, nor any intermediate, cause. But if in efficient causes it is possible to go on to infinity, there will be no first efficient cause, neither will there be any ultimate effect, nor any intermediate efficient causes, all of which is plainly false. Therefore it is necessary to admit a first efficient cause, to which everyone gives the name God.

The third way is taken from possibility and necessity, and runs thus: We find in nature things that are possible to be and not to be, since they are found to be generated and to be corrupted, and consequently it is possible for them to be and not to be. But it is impossible for these always to exist, for that which can not-be at some time is not. Therefore if everything can not-be, then at one time there was nothing in existence. Now if this were true, even now there would be nothing in existence, because that which does not exist begins to exist only through something already existing. Therefore if at one time nothing was in existence, it would have been impossible for anything to have begun to exist, and thus even now nothing would be in existence—which is absurd. Therefore not all beings are merely possible, but there must exist something the existence of which is necessary. But every necessary thing either has its necessity caused by another, or not. Now it is impossible to go on to infinity in necessary things which have their necessity caused by another, as has already been proved in regard to efficient causes. Therefore, we cannot but admit the existence of some being having of itself its own necessity and not receiving it from another, but rather causing in others their necessity. This all men speak of as God.

The fourth way is taken from the gradation to be found in things. Among beings there are some more or less good, true, noble, and the like. But *more* and *less* are predicated of different things according as they resemble in their different ways something which is the maximum, as a thing is said to be hotter according as it more nearly resembles that which is hottest; so there is something which is truest, something best, something noblest and, consequently, something that is most being, for those things that are greatest in truth are greatest in being. . . . Now the maximum in any genus is the cause of all in that genus, as fire, which is the maximum of heat, is the cause of all hot things. . . . Therefore there must also be something which is to all beings the cause of their being, goodness, and every other perfection, and this we call God.

The fifth way is taken from the governance of the world. We see that things which lack knowledge, such as natural bodies, act for an end, and this is evident from their acting always, or nearly always, in the same way, so as to obtain the best result. Hence it is plain that they achieve their end, not fortuitously, but designedly. Now whatever lacks knowledge cannot move towards an end, unless it be directed by some being endowed with knowledge and intelligence, as the arrow is directed by the archer. Therefore some intelligent being exists by whom all natural things are directed to their end, and this being we call God.

## SUGGESTIONS FOR WRITING

1. St. Thomas Aquinas (1225-1274) was educated by monks in his native province of Naples. He joined the Dominican order and continued his studies at the universities of Cologne and Paris. He spent the last nine years of his life on his greatest work, *The Summa Theologica*. The above essay is part of his attempt to achieve a reconciliation between the Aristotelian and Catholic doctrines. A question which occurs frequently in discussions of the reasoning of St. Thomas Aquinas is this: Has man's increased knowledge of the physical universe reduced the validity of his arguments? Or, can science replace faith? Define faith and show how it differs from "science" as a way of knowing.

2. St. Thomas lists five proofs of God. Are the five distinct? Are there more? Is faith a proof? What distinguishes a nonproof from a proof? What distinguishes proof from truth? Consider these questions and write.

3. Voltaire said in 1770, "If God didn't exist, man would have to invent him." What do you suppose he meant by that?

4. St. Thomas' method of argument here is to foresee objections and answer them. Write a theme in which you set out to prove a point and, following St. Thomas' method, foresee objections to your "proofs" and answer them.

ERICH FROMM

# Man Is Not a Thing*

The growing popularity of psychology is interpreted by many as a sign of our approach to the Delphic ideal: "Know Thyself." The idea of self-knowledge has its roots in the Greek and Judaeo-Christian tradition. It was part of the Enlightenment attitude. Men like James and Freud, deeply rooted in this tradition, helped to transmit it to us. But we must not ignore other aspects of contemporary psychology which are dangerous and destructive to human spiritual development. . . .

From the manipulation of the customer and the worker, the uses of psychology have spread to the manipulation of everybody, to politics. While the idea of democracy originally centered around the concept of clear thinking and responsible citizens, the practice of democracy becomes more and more distorted by the same methods of manipulation which were first developed in market research and "human relations."

While all this is well known, I want now to discuss a more subtle and difficult problem which is related to individual psychology and especially to psychoanalysis. The question is: *To which extent is psychology* (the knowledge of others and of myself) *possible?* What limitations exist to such knowledge? And what are the dangers if these limitations are not respected?

Undoubtedly the desire to know our fellow men and ourselves corresponds to a deep need in human beings. Man lives within a social context. He needs to be related to his fellow man lest he become insane. Man is endowed with reason and imagination; his fellow man and he himself are problems which he cannot help trying to solve. The endeavor to understand man by thought is called psychology, "the knowledge of the soul."

However, complete rational knowledge is possible only of *things*. Things can be dissected without being destroyed; they can be manipulated without damage to their nature; they can be repro-

---

* From *The Saturday Review* (March 16, 1957). © 1957 by *The Saturday Review*. Reprinted by permission of the publishers and author.

duced. *Man is not a thing.* He cannot be dissected without being destroyed. He cannot be manipulated without being harmed. And he cannot be reproduced artificially. Life in its biological aspects is a miracle and a secret, and man in his human aspects is an unfathomable secret. We know our fellow man and ourselves in many ways, yet we do not know him or ourselves fully because we are not things. The further we reach into the depth of our being, or someone else's being, the more the goal of full knowledge eludes us. Yet we cannot help desiring to penetrate into the secret of man's soul, into the nucleus of "he."

What, then, does it mean, that we know ourselves or that we know another person? To know ourselves means to overcome the illusions we have about ourselves. To know our neighbor means to overcome the "parataxic distortions" (transference) we have about him. We all suffer, in varying degrees, from illusions about ourselves. We are enmeshed in fantasies of omniscience and omnipotence which were experienced as quite real when we were children. We rationalize our bad motives in terms of benevolence, duty, or necessity. We rationalize weakness and fear in terms of "good causes," our unrelatedness in terms of others' unresponsiveness. With our fellow man we distort and rationalize just as much, except that usually we do so in the opposite direction. Our lack of love makes him appear as hostile when he is only shy. Our submissiveness transforms him into a dominating ogre when he only asserts himself. Our fear of spontaneity makes him out to be childish, when he is really childlike and spontaneous. To know more about ourselves means to do away with the many veils which hide us and our neighbor from our view. One veil after another is lifted, one distortion after another dispelled.

Psychology can show us what man is *not.* It cannot tell us what man, each one of us, *is.* The soul of man, the unique core of each individual, can never be grasped and described adequately. It can be "known" only inasmuch as it is not misconceived. The legitimate aim of psychology, as far as ultimate knowledge is concerned, is the *negative,* the removal of distortions and illusions, *not the positive,* full, and complete knowledge of a human being.

There is, however, another path to knowing man's secret. This path is not that of thought, but of *love.* Love is active penetration of the other person in which my desire to know is stilled by union.

In the act of fusion I know you, I know myself, I know everybody
—and I "know" nothing. I know in the only way in which knowledge of that which is alive is possible for man—by the experience
of *union,* not by any knowledge our thought can give. The only
way to full knowledge lies in the act of love; this act transcends
thought, it transcends words.

Psychological knowledge may be one condition for full knowledge
in the act of love. I have to know the other person and myself
objectively in order to be able to see his reality or, rather, in order
to overcome the illusions, the irrationally distorted pictures I have
of him. If I know a human being as he is, or rather if I know what
he is not, then I may know him in his ultimate essence in the act of
love.

Love is an achievement not easy to attain. How does the man who
cannot love try to penetrate the secret of his neighbor? There is, as
I have tried to show in "The Art of Loving," one other way, a
desperate one, to know the secret: it is that of complete power over
another person, the power which makes him do what I want, feel
what I want, think what I want, which transforms him into a
thing, *my* thing. The ultimate degree of this attempt to know lies
in the extremes of sadism, in the desire to make a human being
suffer, to torture him, to force him to betray his "secret" in his
suffering or eventually to destroy him. In the craving to penetrate
man's secret lies an essential motive for the depth and intensity of
cruelty and destructiveness. In a very succinct way this idea has been
expressed by the Russian writer Isaac Babel. He quotes a fellow
officer in the Russian Civil War who has just stamped a former
master to death as saying: "With shooting—I'll put it this way—
with shooting you only get rid of a chap. . . . With shooting you'll
never get at the soul, to where it is in a fellow and how it shows
itself. But I don't spare myself, and I've more than once trampled
an enemy for over an hour. You see, I want to get to know what
life really is, what life's like down our way."

While sadism and destructiveness are motivated by the desire to
force man's secret, it can never lead to the expected goal. By making
my neighbor suffer, the distance between him and myself grows to
a point where no knowledge is possible. Sadism and destructiveness
are perverted, hopeless, and tragic attempts to learn.

The problem of knowing man runs parallel to the theological

problem of knowing God. Negative theology postulates that I cannot make any positive statement about God. The only knowledge
of God is what He is not. As Maimonides put it, the more I know
about what God is not the more I know about God. Or as Meister
Eckhart put it: "Meanwhile man cannot know what God is even
though he be ever so well aware of what God is not." One consequence of such negative theology lies in mysticism. If I can have
no full knowledge of God in thought, if theology is at best negative,
the positive knowledge of God can be achieved only in the act of
union with God.

Translating this principle to man, we might speak of a "negative
psychology," and furthermore say that full knowledge of man by
thought is impossible and that full "knowledge" can occur only
in the act of love. Just as mysticism is a logical consequence of
negative theology, love is the logical consequence of negative
psychology.

Stating the limitations of psychology is to point to the danger
resulting from ignoring these limitations. Modern man is lonely,
frightened, and little capable of love. He wants to be close to his
neighbor, yet he is too unrelated and distant to be able to be close.
His marginal bonds to his neighbor are manifold and easily kept
up, but a deep "central relatedness" hardly exists. To find closeness
he seeks knowledge; and in search of knowledge he finds psychology. Psychology becomes a substitute for love, for intimacy, for
union with others and oneself; it becomes the refuge of the lonely,
alienated man instead of being a step toward the act of union.

Psychology as a surrogate becomes apparent in the phenomenon
of the popularity of psychoanalysis. Psychoanalysis can be most
helpful in undoing the parataxic distortions within ourselves and
about our fellow man. It can undo one illusion after another, and
free the way to the decisive act, which we alone can perform: the
"courage to be," the jump, the act of ultimate commitment. Man
after his physical birth has to go through a continuous process of
birth. Emerging from the mother's womb is the first act of birth;
from her breast is the second; from her arm the third. From here
on the process of birth can stop; a person can develop into a socially
adjusted and useful person and yet remain stillborn in a spiritual
sense. If he is to develop into what he potentially is as a human
being, he must continue to be born. That is, he must continue to

dissolve the primary ties of soil and blood. He must proceed from one act of separation to the next. He must give up certainty and defenses and take the jump into the act of commitment, concern, and love.

What happens so often in psychoanalytic treatment is that there is a silent agreement between therapist and patient which consists in the assumption that psychoanalysis is a method by which one can attain happiness and maturity and yet avoid the jump, the act, the pain of separation. To use the analogy of the jump a little further, the psychoanalytic situation looks sometimes like that of a man wanting to learn how to swim and yet intensely afraid of the moment when he has to jump into the water, to have faith in the water's buoyancy. The man stands at the edge of the pool and listens to his teacher explain to him the movements he has to make; that is good and necessary. But if we see him going on talking, talking, talking we become suspicious that the talking and understanding have become a substitute for the real swim. No amount or depth of psychological insight can take the place of the act, the commitment, the jump. It can lead to it, prepare for it, make it possible—and this is the legitimate function of psychoanalytic work. But it must not try to be a substitute for the responsible act of commitment, an act without which no real change occurs in a human being.

If psychoanalysis is understood in this sense, another condition must be met. The analyst must overcome the alienation from himself and from his fellow man which is prevalent in modern times. As I have said, modern man experiences himself as a *thing,* an embodiment of energies to be invested profitably on the market. He experiences his fellow man as a thing to be used for profitable exchange. Contemporary psychology, psychiatry, and psychoanalysis are involved in this universal process of alienation. The patient is considered as a thing, the sum of many parts. Some of these parts are defective and need to be "fixed," like the parts of an automobile. There is a defect here and a defect there, called symptoms. The psychiatrist considers it his function to fix them. He does not look at the patient as a unique totality.

For psychoanalysis to fulfil its real possibilities, the analyst must overcome his own alienation, be capable of relating himself to the patient from core to core, and in this relatedness to open the path for the patient's spontaneous experience, and thus for the "understanding" of himself. He must not look on the patient as an object, or even be only a "participant observer." He must become one with the patient, and at the same time retain his own separateness and objectivity so that he can formulate his experiences in the act of oneness and of separateness at the same time.

The final understanding cannot be expressed fully in words. It is not an "interpretation" which describes the patient as an object with its various defects, and their genesis, but it is an over-all intuitive grasp; it takes place first in the analyst and then, if the analysis is successful, in the patient. This grasp is sudden. It is an intuitive act which can be prepared by many cerebral insights but can never be replaced by them. If psychoanalysis is to develop in this direction it has still unexhausted possibilities for human transformation and spiritual change. If it remains enmeshed in the socially patterned defect of alienation it may remedy this or that defect, but it will become another tool for making man more automatized and adjusted to an alienated and basically "inhuman" society.

SUGGESTIONS FOR WRITING

1. Erich Fromm (1900-    ), born in Frankfurt, Germany, underwent the preparation and education for psychoanalysis at Munich and at the Psychoanalytical Institute in Berlin. He has been active as a consultant psychologist and theorist in the application of psychoanalytic theory to problems of culture and society. He is now a naturalized United States citizen. Among his books are *Escape from Freedom* (1941), *Man for Himself* (1947), *The Forgotten Language* (1951), *The Sane Society* (1955), and *The Art of Loving* (1957). In the above essay he discusses one of his favorite themes: the integrity of man. He says, "*Man is not a thing. He cannot be dissected without being destroyed. He cannot be manipulated without being destroyed.*" Whereas our culture and society condition us and make us the human beings that we are, to what extent are "conditioning" (as provided by our society) and "manipulating" (as operated by our society) two different things? Isn't everything we do manipulated in some sense? Write a theme considering these questions.

2. Psychology, according to Fromm, can tell us what man is not, but it cannot tell us what man is. What are the descriptions that reveal nonman? If it is possible to know what man is not, reveal what your insight and common sense tell you about nonman.

3. St. Thomas on p. 448 indicated five proofs of God. Are there any proofs of man? Is it possible to use the reverse of any of St. Thomas's five proofs to apply to man?

WILLIAM WORDSWORTH

## The World Is Too Much with Us

The world is too much with us; late and soon,
Getting and spending, we lay waste our powers:
Little we see in Nature that is ours;
We have given our hearts away, a sordid boon!
The sea that bares her bosom to the moon;
The winds that will be howling at all hours,
And are up-gathered now like sleeping flowers;
For this, for everything, we are out of tune;
It moves us not.—Great God! I'd rather be
A pagan suckled in a creed outworn.
So might I, standing on this pleasant lea,
Have glimpses that would make me less forlorn;
Have sight of Proteus rising from the sea;
Or hear old Triton blow his wreathed horn.

RALPH WALDO EMERSON

## Things Are in the Saddle and Ride Mankind *

The horseman serves the horse
The neatherd serves the neat,
The merchant serves the purse,
The eater serves his meat;

'Tis the day of the chattel,
Web to weave, and corn to grind:
Things are in the saddle,
And ride mankind.

---

* From *Ode* (Inscribed to W. H. Channing).

There are two laws discrete,
Not reconciled,—
Law for man, and law for thing:
The last builds town and fleet,
But it runs wild,
And doth the man unking.

'Tis fit the forest fall,
The steep be graded,
The mountain tunnelled,
The sand shaded,
The orchard planted,
The glebe tilled,
The prairie granted,
The steamer build.

Let man serve law for man;
Live for friendship, live for love,
For truth's and harmony's behoof;
The state may follow how it can,
As Olympus follows Jove.

## SUGGESTIONS FOR WRITING

1. William Wordsworth (1770-1850), English poet of the Romantic period, bemoans the fact that man is out of tune with nature. Explicate, that is, make clear the meaning of this line: "Getting and spending, we lay waste our powers." First, what did Wordsworth mean; second, what meaning can you give to this line by *showing* mankind laying waste its powers by getting and spending?

2. Ralph Waldo Emerson (1803-1882), American poet, essayist, and lecturer of the "Golden Age" of American literature, says in the above excerpt that man is not attending to his proper role. Explicate the meaning of these two lines: "Things are in the saddle,/And ride mankind." First, what did Emerson mean; second, what meaning can you give to these lines by *showing* mankind being ridden by things?

3. What is the essential difference between the meaning of the line by Wordsworth, "Getting and spending we lay waste our powers," and the lines by Emerson, "Things are in the saddle,/And ride mankind." Beware the easy answer that Wordsworth is talking about the natural world and Emerson the man-made world. Is there a more profound difference? Is there an essential similarity? Write an essay considering these questions.

KEN MACRORIE

## We Can No Longer Hear the Silence*

How would you like a radio station on your dial that would in one day charm you with a program of eighteenth-century chamber music; provoke you with C. S. Lewis talking on love; haunt you with recordings of F.D.R.'s speeches; delight you with pure singing jazz of the 1920's and a seventeenth-century burlesque—Beaumont and Fletcher's *The Knight of the Burning Pestle*—and Wagner's first opera, *Rienzi*; amaze you with a comparison of the rehabilitation of Mau Mau youth and American delinquents, a French-language version of a Kipling fable, as well as Vincent Hallinan's pro-Soviet political commentary; and teach you with several different readings of one poem intoned with different emphasis?

I would like that, but the day that FM station KPFA in Berkeley, California, broadcast those programs, I was expected at work and that night I had to go to a meeting. If I had been free to commit myself to my radio all day and night, I would probably have died —for the usual reason, an overdose. There are simply too many messages.

When I lived in Manhattan a few years ago, I enjoyed reading the New York *Times*—full reports of events, complete texts of Presidential press conferences, long articles on tennis championships, unexpected human-interest stories in the business pages. When I moved to East Lansing, Michigan, I kept up the daily *Times* but found less and less time to read it along with two local papers. When I moved to San Francisco about a year ago, I was pleased to find the New York *Times* cost forty cents, out of my range. I no longer had to feel guilty about not reading it when it came in the mail. Now I hear tell that the *Times* will soon publish a national edition available at regular prices on the West Coast.

Too many messages.

---

* From "Too Many Messages," *The Reporter* (July 20, 1961). Copyright © 1961 by The Reporter Magazine Company. Reprinted by the kind permission of the author.

And then television. Years ago in New York I discovered *Camera Three,* a Sunday program of variety and quality. It is carried by networks to Michigan and to California. It presents Katherine Anne Porter reading the poetry of W. B. Yeats and W. H. Auden, or those two authentic practitioners of the nineteenth-century cake-walk, Leon James and Al Nimms; or a series called "The Necessity for Solitude," or Saul Steinberg's drawings, or a sharp dramatic presentation of Henry James's short story "The Real Thing"; on and on, every week.

The fact that KQED, the listener-supported educational TV channel in San Francisco, regularly runs the superlative Robert Herridge Theatre and tapes of Pablo Casals teaching students the cello at the University of California does not surprise me, but that the networks should produce regular programs such as *CBS Reports* and the *NBC White Papers* is almost beyond belief. The *White Paper* on the U-2 affair spoke fairly but without softness. The *White Paper* "Railroads: The End of the Line" brought terrifyingly alive the America that refuses to confront its dying but needed rapid transit system and the blight on modern civilization caused by the automobile. I saw the roads eating our land and I felt the cars eating my nerves. I missed the CBS documentary "Harvest of Shame," which apparently had guts.

If you watch television rather than dismiss it, you can add your favorite programs to the list. I could go on: the high-style network production of parts of *Vanity Fair,* the gripping *Play of the Week* production of Turgenev's *A Month in the Country,* the satirical sketches of Ernie Kovacs or Sid Caesar. But I must stop.

Too many messages. Too many good messages.

Not to mention too many bad messages. When I twist the knob only hoping, not knowing from a schedule, I get Jack Daily's *Hypocrisy for a Day,* Deputy Dan's *Demoralization by Gunfire,* and Lawrence Bilk's music played inside Jell-o. Dozens and hundreds of them, surrounding the good, enveloping it, burying it.

Too many messages, good and bad. And at the damnedest times and in the damnedest places.

In *Playboy,* the magazine that carries the near-nude "Playmate of the Month," appeared Eric Bentley's "Letter to a Would-Be Playwright." This piece of dramatic criticism drew letters of praise from two distinguished theater directors and a Yale professor of drama.

And then some lumberjack tells me I must read *True,* the manly man's magazine, and I laugh. But there in *True* is a feature article on the American Civil Liberties Union, making the point that the Union's defense of the civil rights of "such unsavory types as Nazis, gangsters, filth merchants, and Communists" really buttresses the rights of the common citizen. You pick the most unlikely spot for what you like best and I'll find it there for you. One last example: Jules Feiffer's acerb dissection of our sicknesses in the Hearst newspaper every Sunday.

The good messages are there, in great number, but blindly strewn through vast marshes of bad. I don't have time to find them all. I could get help from the daily and Sunday newspaper television previews, the regional and national television guides, the new Bay Area television bulletin issued by four San Francisco stations, the new Bay Area FM listening guide, the reviews in the national news magazines. But I haven't time to read *them.*

I go to the paperbound bookstore: three thousand of the best paperbacks in print. I won't cite them. You know who's there— everybody who ever wrote a line, good or bad. Four times a year there is a syndicated *Paperback Review,* listing and reviewing choice new titles. Another message about messages. I took time once to read it and found it strong, opinionated, first-rate. Now I regret every new issue I haven't time to read.

And musical messages. All the sounds are on record; I can afford only a few. Couldn't listen to them anyway. And also on record are the satirists, the whole stable of horses who aren't supposed to exist in an age unable (so they always tell us) to laugh at itself: Jonathan Winters, Mort Sahl, Lenny Bruce, Bill Dana, Bob Newhart—and the list goes on.

Too many messages, and these are only the mass communications. My world stuffed with messages. They hurtle at my door and pile up on the stoop, swirling out with a gust of wind to litter the entrance. The entrances of my mind are littered, with bad and with good. Every message that comes in lessens the chance of every other message. I cannot stand the flood of print and sound and picture.

The "businessmen" go on manufacturing shoddy messages for

profit. The intellectuals go on raving about the "garbage" of the mass media. Neither have seen clearly the state of the message-drowned world. Its critical characteristic is not the dearth of high quality messages—or even the profusion of second-rate messages—but simply the profusion of all kinds of messages. Not only do they increasingly distract us from firsthand experience, but they scatter our brains. There are no large centers of sanity to which we can turn, no moments of space and quiet that restore our souls. We cannot discover the exit from our thruway. We speed along, the din of messages beating upon us as we sit in what we call the driver's seat. Of course the world of tree and stream and cloud is right there, but it blurs beyond the billboards as we drive by, and we can no longer hear its silence.

## SUGGESTIONS FOR WRITING

1. Ken Macrorie (1918-    ) graduated from Oberlin and Columbia and has taught at Michigan State, San Francisco State, and Western Michigan University. He is editor of a professional journal called *College Composition and Communication*. His job involves staying alert to the latest trends in communication, and, as he says in this essay, his job becomes more complicated daily. Many of us have experienced the frustration of too many messages, and the experience raises an interesting point. How many messages are too many? Where do we draw the line and say "Enough"? At what standard do we aim? And, finally, what is the solution?

2. Examine the pages of your newspaper and discover the number of "messages" you would like to give attention in a week. Look for plays, movies, television shows, radio programs, lectures, community events, athletic events. Indicate how you will decide which messages come first. Also indicate what you would do if you had no other duties than to listen to such messages.

3. What does Macrorie mean by the final statement, "The world . . . is right there, . . . and we can no longer hear its silence"?

4. Macrorie complains that good messages are mixed in with the bad. From the internal evidence of the essay, indicate what kinds of messages Macrorie considers good. Would Macrorie (or would you) approve of a sort of *Reader's Digest* of the good? Who would decide what is "good"?

# Knowledge for What?

We call that fire of the black thundercloud electricity, and lecture learnedly about it, and grind the like of it out of glass and silk: but *what* is it? What made it? Whence comes it? Whither goes it?

—Thomas Carlyle, *Heroes and Hero-Worship*, 1841

No matter of fact can be mathematically demonstrated, though it may be proved in such a manner as to leave no doubt on the mind.

—Richard Whately, *Logic*, 1826

Why does the statement of a new fact always leave us cold? Because our minds have to take in something which deranges our old ideas. We are all like that in this miserable world.

—Charcot, *De l'expectation en médecine*, 1857

The fact in itself is nothing. It is valuable only for the idea attached to it, or for the proof which it furnishes.

—C. Bernard, *Introduction à la médecine expérimentale*, 1865

Those who refuse to go beyond fact rarely get as far as fact.

—T. H. Huxley, *The Progress of Science*, 1887

I hate and fear science because of my conviction that, for long to come if not for ever, it will be the remorseless enemy of mankind. I see it destroying all simplicity and gentleness of life, all the beauty of the world; I see it restoring barbarism under a mask of civilization; I see it darkening men's minds and hardening their hearts.

—George Gissing, *The Private Papers of Henry Ryecroft*, 1903

Science? Pooh! Whatever good has science done the world? Damned bosh!

—George Moore, *To Philip Goose*, 1932

Banish me from Eden when you will, but first let me eat of the fruit of the tree of knowledge.

—R. G. Ingersoll, *The Gods and Other Lectures*, 1876

JAMES B. CONANT

# Guides to Human Action*

I venture to define science as a series of interconnected concepts and conceptual schemes arising from experiment and observation and fruitful of further experiments and observations. The test of a scientific theory is, I suggest, its fruitfulness—in the words of Sir J. J. Thomson, its ability "to suggest, stimulate, and direct experiment."

The fallacy underlying what some might call the eighteenth- and nineteenth-century misconceptions of the nature of scientific investigations seems to lie in a mistaken analogy. Those who said they were investigating the structure of the universe imagined themselves as the equivalent of the early explorers and map makers. The explorers of the fifteenth and sixteenth centuries had opened up new worlds with the aid of imperfect maps; in their accounts of distant lands, there had been some false and many ambiguous statements. But by the time everyone came to believe the world was round, the maps of distant continents were beginning to assume a fairly consistent pattern. By the seventeenth century, methods of measuring space and time had laid the foundations for an accurate geography. The increased success of empirical procedures in improving the work of artisans was already improving men's accuracy of observation. Therefore, by a series of successive approximations, so to speak, maps and descriptions of distant lands were becoming closer and closer to accurate accounts of reality. Why would not

* From Bampton Lecture at Columbia University, 1952, in *Modern Science and Modern Man* by James B. Conant (New York: Columbia University Press, 1953). Copyright 1952 by Columbia University Press. Reprinted by permission of the publishers.

the labors of those who worked in laboratories have the same outcome? No one doubted that there were real rivers, mountains, trees,
bays with tides, rainfall, snowfall, glaciers; one could doubt any
particular map or description, of course, but given time and patience, it was assumed the truth would be ascertained. By the same
token there must be a truth about the nature of heat, light, and
matter.

To be sure, the map makers had been observing gross objects like
rocks and trees, rivers and mountains, while, as science progressed,
the force of gravity and atoms and waves in the ether became the
preoccupation of the physicist. Still, tentative ideas played a similar
part in both enterprises; working hypotheses as to the nature of a
river valley, the source of a lake, or the frontier of a mountain
range seemed to be the equivalent of the caloric fluid or the early
corpuscular theory of light. The early geographers' methods of identification were essentially those of common sense. Any given set of
observations might be in error. Yet even erroneous assumptions
might serve, at times, a useful purpose. To have assumed the existence of a lake beyond a certain mountain range might prove fortunate; as a "working hypothesis," even if false, it might lead an
explorer to important goals.

Of course, the possibility of error exists in all surveys. Indeed,
one can image a situation where even in geography no final certainty is possible. Assume an island surrounded by reefs that make
direct access out of the question except with special equipment,
and assume an explorer without such equipment. He must content
himself for the time being with telescopic observations from several
angles; he can thus construct a map but with many uncertainties.
For example, are those highly colored areas due to rocks or to
vegetation? On his return with adequate equipment, he can land,
go to the colored areas and directly determine their composition.
If before he returns, the island disappears below the surface of the
ocean, that makes no difference as to the validity of his methods.
We are all sure that in principle he could have returned and determined the accuracy of his suppositions about the nature of the
terrain.

This use of the "in principle" argument, I have already pointed
out, was the basis for the nineteenth-century physicist's confidence
in his picture of a gas with its rapidly moving particles. Those who

still hold today with the idea that the universe has a structure which, like the geography of an island, can be discovered by successive approximations, must cling to the "in principle" argument. Confront them with the phlogiston theory, the caloric fluid, the luminiferous ether—all now obsolete (except for pedagogic purposes)—and they will say, "Yes, the first maps were imperfect, but in principle it is possible to find out what really is the structure of the universe."

On this basic issue there is far from complete agreement among philosophers of science today. You can, each of you, choose your side and find highly distinguished advocates for the point of view you have selected. However, in view of the revolution in physics, anyone who now asserts that science is an exploration of the universe must be prepared to shoulder a heavy burden of proof. To my mind, the analogy between the map maker and the scientist is false. A scientific theory is not even the first approximation to a map; it is not a creed; it is a policy—an economical and fruitful guide to action by scientific investigators.

But lest my skepticism distort the picture unduly, let me point out how little the new physics has altered some of the older conceptual schemes of physics and chemistry; let me emphasize what an excellent policy the new physics has proved to be in terms of experiments. What disturbs many people are the difficulties that arise if we accept the map-maker analogy. That two conceptual schemes should appear so dissimilar as the wave formulation of the laws governing the transmission of light, on the one hand, and the corpuscular theory of light emission, on the other, distresses those who have looked to the physical sciences for an ever increasing degree of explanation as to how matter is "really constructed." It almost seems as though the modern physicist were like an explorer who, uncertain as to whether the colored areas dimly seen from a distance were rocks or trees, found on landing they were both! But this is a false parallel; it would be far better to say that the physicist seems now to be in the position of an explorer who can never land on the distant island. In short, the whole analogy between a map and a scientific theory is without a basis.

One objection to the point of view I am advocating in these lectures may be considered briefly at this point. It is to the effect that if a scientific theory is not even an approximation to a map of a portion of the universe, the so-called advance of pure science is nothing but a game; from which it would follow, so the objection runs, that the justification of science is to be found only in the application of science to the practical arts. The answer to those who put forward arguments of this type is to remind them of the work of mathematicians, painters, poets, and musical composers. To my mind, the significance of the fabric of scientific theories that have been produced in the last three hundred and fifty years is the same as the significance of the art of the great periods in history, or the significance of the work of the musical composers. For most scientists, I think the justification of their work is to be found in the pure joy of its creativeness; the spirit which moves them is closely akin to the imaginative vision which inspires an artist. To some degree, almost all men today applaud the success of the past in the realm of creative work and do not measure the degree of success by material standards. So too, at some distant time, the advance of science from 1600 to 1950 may be regarded entirely as a triumph of the creative spirit, one manifestation of those vast potentialities of men and women that make us all proud to be members of the human race.

A second objection to the skepticism of those of us who regard all scientific theories as formulations of policy is that our view is only a transitory social phenomenon. One must admit that perhaps the children now in elementary school may in the middle life feel that a picture of the universe that seems no picture is quite a satisfactory model. To be sure, it took generations for people to become accustomed to the concept of a force of gravity acting at a distance without any medium to transmit the force. Certainly by the year 2052, relativity and quantum mechanics will occupy a different position in the total science of that day from that assigned to them at present. When these new ideas have been assimilated into the culture of the times, the idea of science as an inquiry into the structure of the universe may once again become firmly established in people's minds.

My bet as to the future, however, is on the other horse. It seems to me more likely that the average citizen will come to think of science in totally different terms from those employed in explaining science to lay audiences fifty years ago. If I am right, in order to assimilate science into the culture of our twentieth-century highly industrialized society, we must regard scientific theories as guides to human action and thus an extension of common sense. At all events, this is the point of view presented in these lectures.

## SUGGESTIONS FOR WRITING

1. James B. Conant (1893-    ), American scientist and educator, was formerly president of Harvard and Ambassador to the Republic of West Germany. He is the author of *The Chemistry of Organic Compounds* (1933), *Education and Liberty* (1953), *The Revolutionary Transformation of the American High School* (1959), and *Science and Common Sense* (1961). In the above essay (which was a Bampton Lecture at Columbia University in 1952) Conant presents the point of view that scientific theories are guides to human action and not simply inquiries into the structure of the universe. Shall the scientists tell us how to live? Isn't this one of the things that Emerson and Wordsworth were worrying about in the poems on p. 457? Yet, there is much that science can present to mankind, and shouldn't we use every instrument at hand to find guides to human action?

2. Conant is pointing out the same danger that Sir Charles P. Snow has emphasized in his books and lectures: the growing distance between the culture of science and the culture of the humanities. Conant says that we need "to assimilate science into the culture of our twentieth-century highly industrialized society." How is this to be done? Many scientists are unable to converse intelligently with those in the humanities; the reverse is also true. What is the solution to this dilemma? What do "science majors" and "humanities majors" have in common? As each becomes more specialized, how are they ever to integrate their disciplines and find common guides to human action? Write an essay considering these questions.

3. To what degree should the man in the street, assuming he is literate and possessed of common sense, have a voice in the direction in which scientific advances lead us? Should scientists have complete control of scientific instruments of destruction?

C.  P.  SNOW

# The Future of Man*

Auschwitz and Hiroshima. We have seen all that; in some of it we have acquiesced or helped. No wonder we are morally guilty. Men like ourselves have done such things—and at the same time men like ourselves, sometimes the same men who have taken a hand in the horrors, have been showing more concern for the unlucky round them than has ever been shown by a large society in human history. That is the moral paradox in which we have to live.

It is wrong to try to domesticate the horrors. The mass slaughter of the concentration camps was both the most awful and the most degrading set of actions that men have done so far. This set of actions was ordered and controlled by abnormally wicked men, if you like, but down the line the orders were carried out by thousands of people like the rest of us, civil servants, soldiers, engineers, all brought up in an advanced Western and Christian society. While it was people not like the rest of us but a great deal better, people who for imagination and morality, not to speak of intellect, stand among the finest of our race, people like Einstein, Niels Bohr and Franck, who got caught up in the tangle of events which led to Hiroshima and Nagasaki. The dropping of those bombs was of a lesser order of wickedness from what was done at Auschwitz. But Western man ought not to forget that he did it; Eastern man certainly won't.

At the same time we ought not to forget what there is to our credit. Some kinds of optimism about man's nature are dangerous—but so are some kinds of pessimism. Think of the care the Swedes and the Danes are taking of their old and poor, or of prisoners, or of social misfits. Nothing like that has been done at any period or in any place until our lifetime. We can congratulate ourselves in Britain, too. The Scandinavians have not made anything like a perfect society. In some ways we have not got as near to it as they

---

* From *The Nation* (September 13, 1958). © 1958 by *The Nation*. Reprinted by permission of the publishers.

have. But we have both made a better shot at it than anyone before us.

Britain is a much fairer and a much kinder society than the one I was born into in 1905. It may seem sentimental to have consciences troubled about capital punishment, about removing one life when Western man has recently eliminated twenty million: yet it is a sign of moral sensitivity. So is the attempt, however grudging, to treat women as though they were equal human beings. So is the feeling behind the Wolfenden Report.* So is the conviction—so urgent in the United States—that children have a special right to happiness.

Some of these feelings may lead to practical follies (I believe that the American one is making a mess of their education), but that is not the point. They are signs of a development of something very rare in the world up to now, which one might call moral kindness. I have no doubt that in Scandinavia, England, some, though not all, of the United States, and perhaps three or four other countries in the West, the amount of fairness, tolerance and effective kindness within the society would seem astonishing to any nineteenth-century man.

It would also seem astonishing to any nineteenth-century man how much we know. There is probably no one now alive as clever as Clerk Maxwell or Gauss; but thousands of people know more than Clerk Maxwell or Gauss, and understand more of those parts of the world that they spent their lives trying to understand. Put those two down, or even greater men, such as Newton and Archimedes, in front of what is now understood—and they would think it wonderful. So it is, and we can take pride and joy in it. It will go on; the search to understand is one of the most human things about us. Compared with our ancestors, there are some trivial physical differences. We are a good deal taller and heavier, we live much longer. But above all, we know more.

All this it would be reasonable to call progress, so long as we don't expect of progress more than it can give. In each of our individual lives there is, of course, something beyond human help. Each of us has to live part of his life alone: and he has to die alone. That part of our experience is right outside of time and history, and

---

* Report of the Committee on Homosexual Offenses and Prostitution, September, 1957.

progress has no meaning there. In this sense, the individual condition is tragic. But that is no excuse for not doing our best with the social condition.

To think otherwise, to take refuge in facile despair, has been the characteristic intellectual treachery of our day. It is shoddy. We have to face the individual condition: for good and evil, for pettiness and the occasional dash of grandeur, we have to know what men are capable of: and then we can't contract out. For we are part, not only of the privileged North European-British American *enclave* of progress, but of another progress which is altering the whole world.

I mean something brutally simple. Most people in Asia still haven't enough to eat: but they have a bit more than before. Most people in Asia are still dying before their time (on the average, Indians live less than half as long as Englishmen): but they are living longer than before. Is *that* progress? This is not a subject to be superior or refined or ingenious about, and the answer is: *of course it is.*

It is because Western man has grown too far away from that elemental progress that we can't get on terms with most of the human race. Through luck we got in first with the scientific-industrial revolution; as a result, our lives became, on the average, healthier, longer, more comfortable to an extent that had never been imagined; it doesn't become us to tell our Chinese and Indian friends that that kind of progress is not worth having.

We know what it is like to live among the shops, the cars, the radios, of Leicester and Orebro and Des Moines. We know what it is like to ask the point of it all, and to feel the Swedish sadness or the American disappointment or the English Welfare State discontent. But the Chinese and Indians would like the chance of being well-fed enough to ask what is the point of it all. They are in search of what Leicester, Orebro and Des Moines take for granted, food, extra years of life, modest comforts. When they have got these things, they are willing to put up with a dash of the Swedish sadness or American disappointment. And their determination to get them is likely in the next thirty years to prove the strongest social force on earth.

Will they get them? Will the social conditions everywhere reach within foreseeable time something like the standard of the privileged Western enclave? There is no technical reason why not. If it does, the level of moral kindness will go up in parallel. These ought to be realistic hopes. There seems only one fatality that might destroy them. That is, it goes without saying, an H-bomb war.

No one can pretend that it is not possible. For myself, I think that it won't happen—then though we have seen how good and conscientious men have become responsible for horrors, even though two atomic bombs have been dropped already, and by Western man. But I still think, partly as a guess, partly as a calculation, that we shall escape the H-bomb war—just as I think we shall escape the longer-term danger of Malthusian overpopulation.

It may easily be that I am letting hope run away with me about the H-bomb war. Some of the wisest disagree with me. Let us imagine that they are right and that the H-bombs go off. Is that going to be the end? I find it difficult to believe. In England a lot of us would be dead, our children with us. A lot of Americans and Russians would also be killed outright. No one knows how many would die afterwards through effects of radiation. But I don't believe that men have at present the resources to destroy the race.

If that is so, and if after an H-bomb war a viable fraction of the world population were left untouched (my guess is that it would be a large fraction, at least two-thirds), then we should all be amazed how soon hope of progress took possession again. The human species is biologically a very tough one, and tough in a sense no animal species can be, through its intelligence, its organization of knowledge, the capacity of its members not to be totally bound within the rapacious self. After the most hideous H-bomb war, the inhabitants of Africa and India and South America would have the strength of those qualities to build on. The material and scientific gap, left through the devastation of the West and Russia, would be filled up at a speed not flattering to Western or Russian self-esteem. What would the moral scar be?

I think we can already answer that question, for we too have, as I said at the beginning, witnessed horrors and assisted at them. Most of us don't live constantly in the presence of Hiroshima and Auschwitz: the memory doesn't prevent us getting morally concerned about the fate of one murderer or cross because a lonely and impoverished old man doesn't have enough calls from the District Visitor.

It would be just the same if the Northern hemisphere became more or less destroyed. Men elsewhere would not live under that shadow; they would be busy with their own societies. If those societies were less fair and morally sensitive than ours is now, they would soon catch up. Within a bizarrely short interval, after hundreds of millions of people had been incinerated by H-bombs, men in countries unaffected would be passionately debating capital punishment. It sounds mad, but it is the kind of madness which makes human beings as tough as they are, and as capable of behaving better than they have so far behaved.

So there remains a sort of difficult hope. As long as men continue to be men, individual man will perceive the same darkness about his solitary condition as any of us does now. But he will also feel occasional intimations that his own life is not the only one. In the midst of his egotisms, pettiness, power seekings, and perhaps the horrors these may cause, he will intermittently stretch a little beyond himself. That little, added to the intelligence and growing knowledge of the species, will be enough to make his societies more decent, to use the social forces for what, in the long sight of history, are good ends.

None of it will be easy. As individuals, each of us is almost untouched by this progress. It is no comfort to remember how short human history is. As individuals, that seems just an irony. But as a race, we have scarcely begun to live.

SUGGESTIONS FOR WRITING

1. Sir Charles Percy Snow (1905-    ), British novelist and scientist, received his Ph.D. in physics from Cambridge and became a Fellow of Corpus Christi College. His books include: *The Light and the Dark* (1948), *Time of Hope* (1950), *The Masters* (1951), *The New Men* (1954), *The Two Cultures and the Scientific Revolution* (1960), and *Science and Government* (1961). Here he argues that "the level of moral kindness [goes] up in parallel" with material progress. Have you been able to observe this in any of your experiences? Do you agree with Snow?

2. Snow's final statement, "as a race, we have scarcely begun to live," should provide a challenge to a developed imagination. As man casts about for his fulfillment, where will he turn next? How can the race

live a better life? What are the terms and conditions of "better"? What do you think man's future is?

3. Were scientists morally guilty of making the A- and H-bombs possible? Or is the guilt to be borne by governments? Or is the guilt that of Western man? Or is it mankind? Is it an example of man committing and suffering for his sins? Is the question theological, sociological, or scientific? Write an essay considering these questions.

J . R O B E R T   O P P E N H E I M E R

# Man's Future*

The words "prospects in the arts and sciences" mean two quite different things to me. One is prophecy: What will the scientists discover and the painters paint, what new forms will alter music, what parts of experience will newly yield to objective description? The other meaning is that of a view: What do we see when we look at the world today and compare it with the past? I am not a prophet; and I cannot very well speak to the first subject, though in many ways I should like to. I shall try to speak to the second, because there are some features of this view which seem to me so remarkable, so new and so arresting, that it may be worth turning our eyes to them; it may even help us to create and shape the future better, though we cannot foretell it.

In the arts and in the sciences, it would be good to be a prophet. It would be a delight to know the future. I had thought for a while of my own field of physics and of those nearest to it in the natural sciences. It would not be too hard to outline the questions which natural scientists today are asking themselves and trying to answer. What, we ask in physics, is matter, what is it made of, how does it behave when it is more and more violently atomized, when we try to pound out of the stuff around us the ingredients which only violence creates and makes manifest? What, the chemists ask, are those special features of nucleic acids and proteins which make life possi-

---

* "Prospects in the Arts and Sciences," an address delivered as part of the Columbia Bicentennial. Copyright © 1955 by Columbia University Press, trustees for the University in the city of New York. Reprinted by permission of Columbia University Press and Simon and Schuster, Inc.

ble and give it its characteristic endurance and mutability? What subtle chemistry, what arrangements, what reactions and controls make the cells of living organisms differentiate so that they may perform functions as oddly diverse as transmitting information throughout our nervous systems or covering our heads with hair? What happens in the brain to make a record of the past, to hide it from consciousness, to make it accessible to recall? What are the physical features which make consciousness possible?

All history teaches us that these questions that we think the pressing ones will be transmuted before they are answered, that they will be replaced by others, and that the very process of discovery will shatter the concepts that we today use to describe our puzzlement.

It is true that there are some who profess to see in matters of culture, in matters precisely of the arts and sciences, a certain macrohistorical pattern, a grand system of laws which determines the course of civilization and gives a kind of inevitable quality to the unfolding of the future. They would, for instance, see the radical, formal experimentation which characterized the music of the last half-century as an inevitable consequence of the immense flowering and enrichment of natural science; they would see a necessary order in the fact that innovation in music precedes that in painting and that in turn in poetry, and point to this sequence in older cultures. They would attribute the formal experimentation of the arts to the dissolution, in an industrial and technical society, of authority—of secular, political authority, and of the catholic authority of the church. They are thus armed to predict the future. But this, I fear, is not my dish.

If a prospect is not a prophecy, it is a view. What does the world of the arts and sciences look like? There are two ways of looking at it: One is the view of the traveler, going by horse or foot, from village to village to town, staying in each to talk with those who live there and to gather something of the quality of its life. This is the intimate view, partial, somewhat accidental, limited by the limited life and strength and curiosity of the traveler, but intimate and human, in a human compass. The other is the vast view, showing the earth with its fields and towns and valleys as they appear to a camera carried in a high-altitude rocket. In one sense this prospect will be more complete; one will see all branches of knowl-

edge, one will see all the arts, one will see them as part of the vastness and complication of the whole of human life on earth. But one
will miss a great deal; the beauty and warmth of human life will
largely be gone from that prospect.

It is in this vast high-altitude survey that one sees the general
surprising quantitative features that distinguish our time. This is
where the listings of science and endowments and laboratories and
books published show up; this is where we learn that more people
are engaged in scientific research today than ever before, that the
Soviet world and the free world are running neck and neck in the
training of scientists, that more books are published per capita in
England than in the United States, that the social sciences are pursued actively in America, Scandinavia, and England, that there are
more people who hear the great music of the past, and more music
composed and more paintings painted. This is where we learn that
the arts and sciences are flourishing. This great map, showing the
world from afar and almost as to a stranger, would show more: It
would show the immense diversity of culture and life, diversity in
place and tradition for the first time clearly manifest on a world-
wide scale, diversity in technique and language, separating science
from science and art from art, and all of one from all of the other.
This great map, worldwide, culture-wide, remote, has some odd
features. There are innumerable villages. Between the villages there
appear to be almost no paths discernible from this high altitude.
Here and there passing near a village, sometimes through its heart,
there will be a superhighway, along which windy traffic moves at
enormous speed. The superhighways seem to have little connection
with villages, starting anywhere, ending anywhere, and sometimes
appearing almost by design to disrupt the quiet of the village. This
view gives us no sense of order or of unity. To find these we must
visit the villages, the quiet, busy places, the laboratories and studies
and studios. We must see the paths that are barely discernible; we
must understand the superhighways and their dangers.

In the natural sciences these are and have been and are likely to
continue to be heroic days. Discovery follows discovery, each both
raising and answering questions, each ending a long search, and
each providing the new instruments for a new search. There are
radical ways of thinking unfamiliar to common sense and connected
with it by decades or centuries of increasingly specialized and un-

familiar experience. There are lessons of how limited, for all its variety, the common experience of man has been with regard to natural phenomena, and hints and analogies as to how limited may be his experience with man. Every new finding is a part of the instrument kit of the sciences for further investigation and for penetrating into new fields. Discoveries of knowledge fructify technology and the practical arts, and these in turn pay back refined techniques, new possibilities of observation and experiment.

In any science there is harmony between practitioners. A man may work as an individual, learning of what his colleagues do through reading or conversation; he may be working as a member of a group on problems whose technical equipment is too massive for individual effort. But whether he is a part of a team or solitary in his own study, he, as a professional, is a member of a community. His colleagues in his own branch of science will be grateful to him for the inventive or creative thoughts he has, will welcome his criticism. His world and work will be objectively communicable; and he will be quite sure that if there is error in it, that error will not long be undetected. In his own line of work he lives in a community where common understanding combines with common purpose and interest to bind men together both in freedom and in co-operation.

This experience will make him acutely aware of how limited, how inadequate, how precious is this condition of his life; for in his relations with a wider society, there will be neither the sense of community nor of objective understanding. He will sometimes find, in returning to practical undertakings, some sense of community with men who are not expert in his science, with other scientists whose work is remote from his, and with men of action and men of art. The frontiers of science are separated now by long years of study, by specialized vocabularies, arts, techniques, and knowledge from the common heritage even of a most civilized society; and anyone working at the frontier of such science is in that sense a very long way from home, a long way too from the practical arts that were its matrix and origin, as indeed they were of what we today call art.

The specialization of science is an inevitable accompaniment of progress; yet it is full of dangers, and it is cruelly wasteful, since so much that is beautiful and enlightening is cut off from most of the world. Thus it is proper to the role of the scientist that he not merely find new truth and communicate it to his fellows, but that he teach, that he try to bring the most honest and intelligible account of new knowledge to all who will try to learn. This is one reason—it is the decisive organic reason—why scientists belong in universities. It is one reason why the patronage of science by and through universities is its most proper form; for it is here, in teaching, in the association of scholars and in the friendships of teachers and taught, of men who by profession must themselves be both teachers and taught, that the narrowness of scientific life can best be moderated, and that the analogies, insights, and harmonies of scientific discovery can find their way into the wider life of man.

In the situation of the artist today there are both analogies to and differences from that of the scientist; but it is the differences which are the most striking and which raise the problems that touch most on the evil of our day. For the artist it is not enough that he communicate with others who are expert in his own art. Their fellowship, their understanding, and their appreciation may encourage him; but that is not the end of his work, nor its nature. The artist depends on a common sensibility and culture, on a common meaning of symbols, on a community of experience and common ways of describing and interpreting it. He need not write for everyone or paint or play for everyone. But his audience must be man; it must be man, and not a specialized set of experts among his fellows. Today that is very difficult. Often the artist has an aching sense of great loneliness, for the community to which he addresses himself is largely not there; the traditions and the culture, the symbols and the history, the myths and the common experience, which it is his function to illuminate, to harmonize, and to portray, have been dissolved in a changing world.

There is, it is true, an artificial audience maintained to moderate between the artist and the world for which he works: the audience of the professional critics, popularizers, and advertisers of art. But though, as does the popularizer and promoter of science, the critic fulfills a necessary present function and introduces some order and some communication between the artist and the world, he cannot add to the intimacy and the directness and the depth with which the artist addresses his fellow men.

To the artist's loneliness there is a complementary great and terrible barrenness in the lives of men. They are deprived of the illumination, the light and tenderness and insight of an intelligible interpretation, in contemporary terms, of the sorrows and wonders and gaieties and follies of man's life. This may be in part offset, and is, by the great growth of technical means for making the art of the past available. But these provide a record of past intimacies between art and life; even when they are applied to the writing and painting and composing of the day, they do not bridge the gulf between a society, too vast and too disordered, and the artist trying to give meaning and beauty to its parts.

In an important sense this world of ours is a new world, in which the unity of knowledge, the nature of human communities, the order of society, the order of ideas, the very notions of society and culture have changed and will not return to what they have been in the past. What is new is new not because it has never been there before, but because it has changed in quality. One thing that is new is the prevalence of newness, the changing scale and scope of change itself, so that the world alters as we walk in it, so that the years of man's life measure not some small growth or rearrangement or moderation of what he learned in childhood, but a great upheaval. What is new is that in one generation our knowledge of the natural world engulfs, upsets, and complements all knowledge of the natural world before. The techniques, among which and by which we live, multiply and ramify, so that the whole world is bound together by communication, blocked here and there by the immense synapses of political tyranny. The global quality of the world is new: our knowledge of and sympathy with remote and diverse peoples, our involvement with them in practical terms, and our commitment to them in terms of brotherhood. What is new in the world is the massive character of the dissolution and corruption of authority, in belief, in ritual, and in temporal order. Yet this is the world that we have come to live in. The very difficulties which it presents derive from growth in understanding, in skill, in power. To assail the changes that have unmoored us from the past is futile, and in a deep sense, I think, it is wicked. We need to recognize the change and learn what resources we have.

Again I will turn to the schools and, as their end and as their center, the universities. For the problem of the scientist is in this respect not different from that of the artist or of the historian. He needs to be a part of the community, and the community can only with loss and peril be without him. Thus it is with a sense of interest and hope that we see a growing recognition that the creative artist is a proper charge on the university, and the university a proper home for him; that a composer or a poet or a playwright or painter needs the toleration, understanding, the rather local and parochial patronage that a university can give; and that this will protect him from the tyranny of man's communication and professional promotion. For here there is an honest chance that what the artist has of insight and of beauty will take root in the community, and that some intimacy and some human bonds can mark his relations with his patrons. For a university rightly and inherently is a place where the individual man can form new syntheses, where the accidents of friendship and association can open a man's eyes to a part of science or art which he had not known before, where parts of human life, remote and perhaps superficially incompatible, can find in men their harmony and their synthesis.

These, then, in rough and far too general words, are some of the things we see as we walk through the villages of the arts and of the sciences and notice how thin are the paths that lead from one to another, and how little in terms of human understanding and pleasure the work of the villages comes to be shared outside.

The superhighways do not help. They are the mass media—from the loudspeakers in the deserts of Asia Minor and the cities of Communist China to the organized professional theater of Broadway. They are the purveyors of art and science and culture for the millions upon millions—the promoters who represent the arts and sciences to humanity and who represent humanity to the arts and sciences; they are the means by which we are reminded of the famine in remote places or of war or trouble or change; they are the means by which this great earth and its peoples have become one to one another, the means by which the news of discovery or honor and the stories and songs of today travel and resound throughout the world. But they are also the means by which the true human community, the man knowing man, the neighbor understanding neighbor, the schoolboy learning a poem, the women dancing, the individual curiosity, the individual sense of beauty are being blown dry and issueless, the means by which the passivity of the disengaged spectator presents to the man of art and science the bleak face of unhumanity.

For the truth is that this is indeed, inevitably and increasingly, an open and, inevitably and increasingly, an eclectic world. We know too much for one man to know much, we live too variously to live as one. Our histories and traditions—the very means of interpreting life—are both bonds and barriers among us. Our knowledge separates as well as it unites; our orders disintegrate as well as bind; our art brings us together and sets us apart. The artist's loneliness, the scholar despairing because no one will any longer trouble to learn what he can teach, the narrowness of the scientist—these are unnatural insignia in this great time of change.

For what is asked of us is not easy. The openness of this world derives its character from the irreversibility of learning; what is once learned is part of human life. We cannot close our minds to discovery; we cannot stop our ears so that the voices of far-off and strange people can no longer reach them. The great cultures of the East cannot be walled off from ours by impassable seas and defects of understanding based on ignorance and unfamiliarity. Neither our integrity as men of learning nor our humanity allows that. In this open world, what is there, any man may try to learn.

This is no new problem. There has always been more to know than one man could know; there have always been modes of feeling that could not move the same heart; there have always been deeply held beliefs that could not be composed into a synthetic union. Yet never before today have the diversity, the complexity, the richness so clearly defied hierarchical order and simplification; never before have we had to understand the complementary, mutually not compatible ways of life and recognize choice between them as the only course of freedom. Never before today has the integrity of the intimate, the detailed, the true art, the integrity of craftsmanship and the preservation of the familiar, of the humorous and the beautiful stood in more massive contrast to the vastness of life, the greatness of the globe, the otherness of people, the otherness of ways, and the all-encompassing dark.

This is a world in which each of us, knowing his limitations, knowing the evils of superficiality and the terrors of fatigue, will have to cling to what is close to him, to what he knows, to what he can do, to his friends and his tradition and his love, lest he be dissolved in a universal confusion and know nothing and love nothing. It is at the same time a world in which none of us can find hieratic prescription or general sanction for any ignorance, any insensitivity, any indifference. When a friend tells us of a new discovery we may not understand, we may not be able to listen without jeopardizing the work that is ours and closer to us; but we cannot find in a book or canon—and we should not seek—grounds for hallowing our ignorance. If a man tells us that he sees differently than we, or that he finds beautiful what we find ugly, we may have to leave the room, from fatigue or trouble; but that is our weakness and our default. If we must live with a perpetual sense that the world and the men in it are greater than we and too much for us, let it be the measure of our virtue that we know this and seek no comfort. Above all, let us not proclaim that the limits of our powers correspond to some special wisdom in our choice of life, of learning, or of beauty.

This balance, this perpetual, precarious, impossible balance between the infinitely open and the intimate, this time—our twentieth century—has been long in coming; but it has come. It is, I think, for us and our children, our only way.

This is for all men. For the artist and for the scientist there is a special problem and a special hope, for in their extraordinarily different ways, in their lives that have increasingly divergent character, there is still a sensed bond, a sensed analogy. Both the man of science and the man of art live always at the edge of mystery, surrounded by it; both always, as the measure of their creation, have had to do with the harmonization of what is new with what is familiar, with the balance between novelty and synthesis, with the struggle to make partial order in total chaos. They can, in their work and in their lives, help themselves, help one another, and help all men. They can make the paths that connect the villages of arts and sciences with each other and with the world at large the multiple, varied, precious bonds of a true and worldwide community.

This cannot be an easy life. We shall have a rugged time of it to keep our minds open and to keep them deep, to keep our sense of beauty and our ability to make it, and our occasional ability to see it in places remote and strange and unfamiliar; we shall have a rugged time of it, all of us, in keeping these gardens in our villages, in keeping open the manifold, intricate, casual paths, to keep these flourishing in a great, open, windy world; but this, as I see it, is the condition of man; and in this condition we can help, because we can love, one another.

SUGGESTIONS FOR WRITING

1.  J. Robert Oppenheimer (1904-   ) was director of the laboratory at Los Alamos (where the first atomic bomb was made) from 1943 to 1945. Later he became director of the Institute for Advanced Studies at Princeton. In this essay, first given as a radio talk in 1954 as part of Columbia University's Bicentennial, Oppenheimer claims that it is the proper role of the scientist "that he not merely find new truth and communicate it to his fellows, but that he teach, that he try to bring the most honest and intelligible account of new knowledge to all who will try to learn." Do you suppose that a time will come that the frontier of scientific knowledge will be so inaccessible to the layman that only a chosen few will be able to understand where the frontier is? Image a map so complicated that only seven years of intensive training will enable one to read it. As you understand the present state of science and its probable future, is this likely to happen? How, if it is true, will the selection of the chosen few occur? Write an essay considering these questions.

2.  "The superhighways do not help," says Oppenheimer. He explains that they are not of humanity. Write an essay using Oppenheimer's analogy of a walk through the country versus a trip on a superhighway. What view does the one afford in relation to the other? What do you miss on the superhighway? In your essay concern yourself not only with the quality of the road but with the direction in which it leads.

BERTRAND  RUSSELL

## "Useless" Knowledge*

Perhaps the most important advantage of "useless" knowledge is that it promotes a contemplative habit of mind. There is in the world much too much readiness, not only for action without adequate previous reflection, but also for some sort of action on occa-

---

* From *In Praise of Idleness* by Bertrand Russell (London: George Allen & Unwin, Ltd., 1935). Reprinted by permission of the publishers.

sions on which wisdom would counsel inaction. People show their bias on this matter in various curious ways. Mephistopheles tells the young student that theory is gray but the tree of life is green, and everyone quotes this as if it were Goethe's opinion, instead of what he supposes the devil would be likely to say to an undergraduate. Hamlet is held up as an awful warning against thought without action, but no one holds up Othello as a warning against action without thought. Professors such as Bergson, from a kind of snobbery towards the practical man, decry philosophy, and say that life at its best should resemble a cavalry charge. For my part, I think action is best when it emerges from a profound apprehension of the universe and human destiny, not from some wildly passionate impulse of romantic but disproportioned self-assertion. A habit of finding pleasure in thought rather than in action is a safeguard against unwisdom and excessive love of power, a means of preserving serenity in misfortune and peace of mind among worries. A life confined to what is personal is likely, sooner or later, to become unbearably painful; it is only by windows into a larger and less fretful cosmos that the more tragic parts of life become endurable.

A contemplative habit of mind has advantages ranging from the most trivial to the most profound. To begin with, there are minor vexations, such as fleas, missing trains, or cantankerous business associates. Such troubles seem hardly worthy to be met by reflections on the excellence of heroism or the transitoriness of all human ills, and yet the irritation to which they give rise destroys many people's good temper and enjoyment of life. On such occasions, there is much consolation to be found in out-of-the-way bits of knowledge which have some real or fancied connection with the trouble of the moment; or even if they have none, they serve to obliterate the present from one's thoughts. When assailed by people who are white with fury, it is pleasant to remember the chapter in Descartes' *Treatise on the Passions* entitled "Why those who grow pale with rage are more to be feared than those who grow red." When one feels impatient over the difficulty of securing international cooperation, one's impatience is diminished if one happens to think of the sainted King Louis IX, before embarking on his crusade, allying himself with the Old Man of the Mountain, who appears in the Arabian Nights as the dark source of half the wickedness in the world. When the rapacity of capitalists grows oppressive, one may be suddenly consoled by the recollection that Brutus, that exemplar of republican virtue, lent money to a city at 40 per cent, and hired a private army to besiege it when it failed to pay the interest.

Curious learning not only makes unpleasant things less unpleasant, but also makes pleasant things more pleasant. I have enjoyed peaches and apricots more since I have known that they were first cultivated in China in the early days of the Han dynasty; that Chinese hostages held by the great King Kaniska introduced them into India, whence they spread to Persia, reaching the Roman Empire in the first century of our era; that the word "apricot" is derived from the same Latin source as the word "precocious," because the apricot ripens early; and that the *a* at the beginning was added by mistake, owing to a false etymology. All this makes the fruit taste much sweeter.

About a hundred years ago, a number of well-meaning philanthropists started societies "for the diffusion of useful knowledge," with the result that people have ceased to appreciate the delicious savor of "useless" knowledge. Opening Burton's *Anatomy of Melancholy* at haphazard on a day when I was threatened with the mood, I learned that there is a "melancholy matter," but that, while some think it may be engendered of all four humors, "Galen holds that it may be engendered of three alone, excluding phlegm or pituita, whose true assertion Valerius and Menardus stiffly maintain, and so doth Fuscius, Montaltus, Montanus. How [say they] can white become black?" In spite of this unanswerable argument, Hercules de Saxonia and Cardan, Guianerius and Laurentius, are (so Burton tells us) of the opposite opinion. Soothed by these historical reflections, my melancholy, whether due to three humors or to four, was dissipated. As a cure for too much zeal, I can imagine few measures more effective than a course of such ancient controversies.

But while the trivial pleasures of culture have their place as a relief from the trivial worries of practical life, the more important merits of contemplation are in relation to the greater evils of life, death and pain and cruelty, and the blind march of nations into unnecessary disaster. For those to whom dogmatic religion can no longer bring comfort, there is need of some substitute, if life is not to become dusty and harsh and filled with trivial self-assertion. The world at present is full of angry self-centered groups, each incapable of viewing human life as a whole, each willing to destroy civilization rather than yield an inch. To this narrowness no amount of technical instruction will provide an antidote. The antidote, in so far as it is matter of individual psychology, is to be found in history, biology, astronomy, and all those studies which, without destroying self-respect, enable the individual to see himself in his proper perspective. What is needed is not this or that specific piece of information, but such knowledge as inspires a conception of the ends of human life as a whole, art and history, acquaintance with the lives of heroic individuals, and some understanding of the strangely accidental and ephemeral position of man in the cosmos—all this touched with an emotion of pride in what is distinctly human, the power to see and to know, to feel magnanimously and to think with understanding. It is from large perceptions combined with impersonal emotion that wisdom most readily springs.

Life, at all times full of pain, is more painful in our time than in the two centuries that preceded it. The attempt to escape from pain drives men to triviality, to self-deception, to the invention of vast collective myths. But these momentary alleviations do but increase the sources of suffering in the long run. Both private and public misfortune can only be mastered by a process in which will and intelligence interact: the part of will is to refuse to shirk the evil or accept an unreal solution, while the part of intelligence is to understand it, to find a cure if it is curable, and, if not, to make it bearable by seeing it in its relations, accepting it as unavoidable, and remembering what lies outside it in other regions, other ages, and the abysses of interstellar space.

## SUGGESTIONS FOR WRITING

1. Bertrand Russell, about whom comment has been made on p. 285, says that life should not resemble a cavalry charge. He favors a contemplative life, but not one without action. One difficulty of putting his philosophy into action is that it requires a mature judgment to know when to act. Vessels ready to sail at the tide may miss the tide if all is left to contemplation and reflection. To push Russell's argument to the extreme, it is conceivable that a person could never choose a college, for if he followed Russell's advice to the letter, he would have to investigate and reflect upon the offerings of several hundred colleges. If you disagree with this interpretation of Russell's essay, write an answer that puts the contemplative life in a different perspective. If you agree, continue the attack.

2. Does the world have a place for "useless" knowledge today? Write an essay in response to this question, taking care to give an operational definition of "useless" knowledge.

3. Russell says, "It is from large perceptions combined with impersonal emotion that wisdom most readily springs." What does he mean by that statement? What is wisdom? What are large perceptions and what is impersonal emotion? Can you put these terms into an operational definition?

ABRAHAM  FLEXNER

## The Usefulness of Useless Knowledge*

We may look at this question from two points of view: the scientific and the humanistic or spiritual. Let us take the scientific first. I recall a conversation which I had some years ago with Mr. George Eastman on the subject of use. Mr. Eastman, a wise and gentle farseeing man, gifted with taste in music and art, had been saying to me that he meant to devote his vast fortune to the promotion of education in useful subjects. I ventured to ask him whom he regarded as the most useful worker in science in the world. He replied instantaneously: "Marconi." I surprised him by saying, "Whatever pleasure we derive from the radio or however wireless and the radio may have added to human life, Marconi's share was practically negligible."

I shall not forget his astonishment on this occasion. He asked me to explain. I replied to him somewhat as follows:

"Mr. Eastman, Marconi was inevitable. The real credit for everything that has been done in the field of wireless belongs, as far as such fundamental credit can be definitely assigned to anyone, to Professor Clerk Maxwell, who in 1865 carried out certain abstruse and remote calculations in the field of magnetism and electricity. Maxwell reproduced his abstract equations in a treatise published in 1873. At the next meeting of the British Association Professor H. J. S. Smith of Oxford declared that 'no mathematician can turn over the pages of these volumes without realizing that they contain

---

* From *Harper's Magazine* (October, 1939). Copyright 1939 by Harper & Row, Publishers. Reprinted by permission of the Estate of Abraham Flexner.

a theory which has already added largely to the methods and resources of pure mathematics.' Other discoveries supplemented Maxwell's theoretical work during the next fifteen years. Finally in
1887 and 1888 the scientific problem still remaining—the detection
and demonstration of the electromagnetic waves which are the carriers of wireless signals—was solved by Heinrich Hertz, a worker
in Helmholtz's laboratory in Berlin. Neither Maxwell nor Hertz
had any concern about the utility of their work; no such thought
ever entered their minds. They had no practical objective. The
inventor in the legal sense was of course Marconi, but what did
Marconi invent? Merely the last technical detail, mainly the now
obsolete receiving device called coherer, almost universally discarded."

Hertz and Maxwell could invent nothing, but it was their useless
theoretical work which was seized upon by a clever technician and
which has created new means for communication, utility, and
amusement by which men whose merits are relatively slight have
obtained fame and earned millions. Who were the useful men? Not
Marconi, but Clerk Maxwell and Heinrich Hertz. Hertz and Maxwell were geniuses without thought of use. Marconi was a clever
inventor with no thought but use.

The mention of Hertz's name recalled to Mr. Eastman the Hertz-
ian waves, and I suggested that he might ask the physicists of the
University of Rochester precisely what Hertz and Maxwell had
done; but one thing I said he could be sure of, namely, that they
had done their work without thought of use and that throughout
the whole history of science most of the really great discoveries
which had ultimately proved to be beneficial to mankind had been
made by men and women who were driven not by the desire to be
useful but merely the desire to satisfy their curiosity.

"Curiosity?" asked Mr. Eastman.

"Yes," I replied, "curiosity, which may or may not eventuate in
something useful, is probably the outstanding characteristic of modern thinking. It is not new. It goes back to Galileo, Bacon, and to
Sir Isaac Newton, and it must be absolutely unhampered. Institutions of learning should be devoted to the cultivation of curiosity
and the less they are deflected by considerations of immediacy of
application, the more likely they are to contribute not only to human welfare but to the equally important satisfaction of intellectual

interest which may indeed be said to have become the ruling passion of intellectual life in modern times."

What is true of Heinrich Hertz working quietly and unnoticed
in a corner of Helmholtz's laboratory in the later years of the nineteenth century may be said of scientists and mathematicians the
world over for several centuries past. We live in a world that would
be helpless without electricity. Called upon to mention a discovery
of the most immediate and far-reaching practical use we might well
agree upon electricity. But who made the fundamental discoveries
out of which the entire electrical development of more than one
hundred years has come?

The answer is interesting. Michael Faraday's father was a blacksmith; Michael himself was apprenticed to a bookbinder. In 1812,
when he was already twenty-one years of age, a friend took him to
the Royal Institution where he heard Sir Humphry Davy deliver
four lectures on chemical subjects. He kept notes and sent a copy
of them to Davy. The very next year, 1813, he became an assistant
in Davy's laboratory, working on chemical problems. Two years
later he accompanied Davy on a trip to the Continent. In 1825,
when he was thirty-four years of age, he became Director of the
Laboratory of the Royal Institution where he spent fifty-four years
of his life.

Faraday's interest soon shifted from chemistry to electricity and
magnetism, to which he devoted the rest of his active life. Important
but puzzling work in this field had been previously accomplished
by Oersted, Ampère, and Wollaston. Faraday cleared away the difficulties which they had left unsolved and by 1841 had succeeded in
the task of induction of the electric current. Four years later a second and equally brilliant epoch in his career opened when he discovered the effect of magnetism on polarized light. His earlier discoveries have led to the infinite number of practical applications by
means of which electricity has lightened the burdens and increased
the opportunities of modern life. His later discoveries have thus far
been less prolific of practical results. What difference did this make
to Faraday? Not the least. At no period of his unmatched career
was he interested in utility. He was absorbed in disentangling the
riddles of the universe, at first chemical riddles, in later periods,
physical riddles. As far as he cared, the question of utility was never
raised. Any suspicion of utility would have restricted his restless

curiosity. In the end, utility resulted, but it was never a criterion to which his ceaseless experimentation could be subjected. . . .

In the domain of higher mathematics almost innumerable instances can be cited. For example, the most abstruse mathematical work of the eighteenth and nineteenth centuries was the "Non-Euclidean Geometry." Its inventor, Gauss, though recognized by his contemporaries as a distinguished mathematician, did not dare to publish his work on "Non-Euclidean Geometry" for a quarter of a century. As a matter of fact, the theory of relativity itself with all its infinite practical bearings would have been utterly impossible without the work which Gauss did at Göttingen.

Again, what is known now as "group theory" was an abstract and inapplicable mathematical theory. It was developed by men who were curious and whose curiosity and puttering led them into strange paths; but "group theory" is today the basis of the quantum theory of spectroscopy, which is in daily use by people who have no idea as to how it came about. . . .

I am pleading for the abolition of the word "use," and for the freeing of the human spirit. To be sure, we shall thus free some harmless cranks. To be sure, we shall thus waste some precious dollars. But what is infinitely more important is that we shall be striking the shackles off the human mind and setting it free for the adventures which in our own day have, on the one hand, taken Hale and Rutherford and Einstein and their peers millions upon millions of miles into the uttermost realms of space and, on the other, loosed the boundless energy imprisoned in the atom. What Rutherford and others like Bohr and Millikan have done out of sheer curiosity in the effort to understand the construction of the atom has released forces which may transform human life; but this ultimate and unforeseen and unpredictable practical result is not offered as a justification for Rutherford or Einstein or Millikan or Bohr or any of their peers. Let them alone. No educational administrator can possibly direct the channels in which these or other men shall work. The waste, I admit again, looks prodigious. It is not really so. All the waste that could be summed up in developing the science of bacteriology is as nothing compared to the advantages which have accrued from the discoveries of Pasteur, Koch, Ehrlich, Theobald Smith, and scores of others—advantages that could never have accrued if the idea of possible use had permeated their minds. These great artists—for such are scientists and bacteriologists—disseminated the spirit which prevailed in laboratories in which they were simply following the line of their own natural curiosity.

I am not criticizing institutions like schools of engineering or law in which the usefulness motive necessarily predominates. Not infrequently the tables are turned, and practical difficulties encountered in industry or in laboratories stimulate theoretical inquiries which may or may not solve the problems by which they were suggested, but may also open up new vistas, useless at the moment, but pregnant with future achievements, practical and theoretical.

With the rapid accumulation of "useless" or theoretic knowledge a situation has been created in which it has become increasingly possible to attack practical problems in a scientific spirit. Not only inventors, but "pure" scientists have indulged in this sport. I have mentioned Marconi, an inventor, who, while a benefactor to the human race, as a matter of fact merely "picked other men's brains." Edison belongs to the same category. Pasteur was different. He was a great scientist; but he was not averse to attacking practical problems—such as the condition of French grapevines or the problems of beer-brewing—and not only solving the immediate difficulty, but also wresting from the practical problem some far-reaching theoretic conclusion, "useless" at the moment, but likely in some unforeseen manner to be "useful" later. Ehrlich, fundamentally speculative in his curiosity, turned fiercely upon the problem of syphilis and doggedly pursued it until a solution of immediate practical use—the discovery of salvarsan—was found. The discoveries of insulin by Banting for use in diabetes and of liver extract by Minot and Whipple for use in pernicious anemia belong in the same category; both were made by thoroughly scientific men, who realized that much "useless" knowledge had been piled up by men unconcerned with its practical bearings, but that the time was now ripe to raise practical questions in a scientific manner.

Thus it becomes obvious that one must be wary in attributing scientific discovery wholly to any one person. Almost every discovery has a long and precarious history. Some one finds a bit here, another a bit there. A third step succeeds later and thus onward till a genius pieces the bits together and makes the decisive contribution. Science, like the Mississippi, begins in a tiny rivulet in the distant

forest. Gradually other streams swell its volume. And the roaring
river that bursts the dikes is formed from countless sources.

## SUGGESTIONS FOR WRITING

1. Abraham Flexner (1866-1959), American educator and physician, was
director of the Institute for Advanced Studies at Princeton from 1930
to 1939. Afterwards he was associated with the General Education
Board. In this essay he repeats the idea that many scientists worked
"without thought of use." If one takes this literally, it is not easy to
believe. Does any man work without hoping that someone may find his
work useful? Perhaps the work of Clerk Maxwell was concentrated exclusively on theory, but it is difficult to visualize a man like Clerk Maxwell living without hope of a better world and without the hope that he
may contribute to it by providing the theory others may find "useful."
Imagine a debate between yourself and a theoretical scientist and
record the dialogue.
2. Imagine the following situation and write about it: In 1939 a great
number of wealthy and influential men read Flexner's article in
*Harper's* and gave unlimited financial resources to universities and
institutes of advanced study for the pursuit of "useless" knowledge.
What fields of knowledge might have been more fully explored by now?
What changes might have occurred in the world? What would have been
the effect on American education?
3. In what ways do money, national prestige in a space race, the urgent
demands of medicine to save lives, and the cultural conditioning of a
materialistic civilization limit the freedom a theoretical scientist needs?
How essential is it to allow the opportunity for pure research and
the indulgence of trained curiosity in any direction? Write a theme
considering these questions and, without denying the importance of
free curiosity, point out the difficulties that lie in the way.

WILLIAM  BARRETT

# Science and Finitude*

[Existentialism] embodies the self-questioning of the time, seeking
to reorient itself to its own historical destiny. Indeed, the whole
problematic of existentialism unfolds from this historical situation.

* From *Irrational Man* by William Barrett (New York: Doubleday & Co., Inc.,
1958). © 1958 by William Barrett. Reprinted by permission of the publishers.

Alienation and estrangement; a sense of the basic fragility and contingency of human life; the impotence of reason confronted with the depths of existence; the threat of Nothingness, and the solitary and unsheltered condition of the individual before this threat. One can scarcely subordinate these problems logically one to another; each participates in all the others, and they all circulate around a common center. A single atmosphere pervades them all like a chilly wind: the radical feeling of human finitude. The limitless horizons into which man looked at the time of the Renaissance have at last contracted. Oddly enough, man's discovery that he himself is finite through and through—is so, one might say, from the inside out—comes at a time when there seem no longer to be any limits to his technological conquest of nature. But the truth about man is never to be found in one quality that opposes another, but in both qualities at once; and so his weakness is only one side of the coin, his power the other. A recognition of limits, of boundaries, may be the only thing that prevents power from dizzy collapse.

But, it might be argued, what makes Western civilization unique is its possession of science, and in science we find uniform and continuous progress without limits. Research goes on, its results are rich and positive, and these are brought together in ever wider and more inclusive systems. There would seem, in this process, to be no contracting of horizons either in fact or in possibility. In a certain sense this is true, and yet science in the twentieth century has come up with answers which make the ambitions of rationalism seem overweening, and which themselves suggest that man must redefine his traditional concept of reason. It would be unlikely if this were otherwise, for scientists too are men and therefore participate in the collective psyche as well as help fashion it. Religion, social forms, science, and art are modes in which man exists; and the more we come to recognize the temporal being of man the more we must recognize a unity within and behind all these modes in which that temporal existence finds its expression.

Science too—and within its own authentic sphere—has come up against the fact of human finitude. That this has happened within science itself, and not in the philosophizing about science, makes the discovery more authentic and momentous. The anthropological sciences, and particularly modern depth psychology, have shown us that human reason is the long historical fabrication of a creature, man, whose psychic roots still extend downward into the primeval soil. These discoveries of the irrational, however, lie outside reason itself; they are stubborn obstacles to the use of reason in our lives, but obstacles which the confirmed rationalist might still hope to circumvent by a cleverer use of that very tool, reason. The more decisive limitations are those that have shown up *within* the workings of reason, in the more rigorous sciences of physics and mathematics. The most advanced of Western sciences, physics and mathematics, have in our time become paradoxical: that is, they have arrived at the state where they breed paradoxes for reason itself. More than one hundred and fifty years ago the philosopher Kant attempted to show that there were ineluctable limits to reason; but the Western mind, positivistic to the core, could be expected to take such a conclusion seriously only when it showed up in the findings of science. Science has in this century, with the discoveries of Heisenberg in physics, and Godel in mathematics, at least caught up with Kant.

Heisenberg's Principle of Indeterminacy shows that there are essential limits to our ability to know and predict physical states of affairs, and opens up to us a glimpse of nature that may at bottom be irrational and chaotic—at any rate, our knowledge of it is limited so that we cannot know this not to be the case. This finding marks an end to the old dream of physicists who, motivated by a thoroughly rational prejudice, thought that reality must be predictable through and through. The figure of the Laplacian Demon was a very striking symbol of this: Imagine, says Laplace, a Being who knows the position and momentum of every particle in the universe, together with the laws of motion governing such particles; such a Being would be able to predict all subsequent states of the universe. Physicists can no longer operate on such cryptotheological faiths, but must take their predictability only where and to the extent that it exhibits itself in experience.

The situation in physics is made more paradoxical by Bohr's Principle of Complementarity, according to which the electron must be regarded both as a wave and as a particle, according to its context. The application of these contradictory designations would have seemed thoroughly illogical to a nineteenth-century physicist. Indeed, some physicists have suggested a new form of logic, from which the classic law of the Excluded Middle (either A or not A) would be dropped; and when new forms of logic are being constructed, one can only conclude that the nature of what is and what is not rational stands open to doubt. In practice, the Principle of Complementarity sets a rigorous limit upon the observations of physics: As one physicist, Von Pauli, puts it, *"I can choose to observe one experimental set-up, A, and ruin B, or choose to observe B and ruin A. I cannot choose not to ruin one of them."* Here the language is perfectly appropriate to the pathos of knowledge in every area in life; we know one thing at the cost of not knowing something else, and it is simply not the case that we can choose to know everything at once. What is remarkable is that here, at the very farthest reaches of precise experimentation, in the most rigorous of the natural sciences, the ordinary and banal fact of our human limitations emerges.

Godel's findings seem to have even more far-reaching consequences, when one considers that in the Western tradition, from the Pythagoreans and Plato onward, mathematics as the very model of intelligibility has been the central citadel of rationalism. Now it turns out that even in his most precise science—in the province where his reason had seemed omnipotent—man cannot escape his essential finitude: every system of mathematics that he constructs is doomed to incompleteness. Godel has shown that mathematics contains insoluble problems, and hence can never be formalized in any complete system. This means, in other words, that mathematics can never be turned over to a giant computing machine; it will always be unfinished, and therefore mathematicians—the human beings who construct mathematics—will always be in business. The human element here rises above the machine: mathematics is unfinished as is any human life.

But since mathematics can never be completed, it might be argued that Godel's finding shows us that there are no limits to mathematical knowledge. True, in one sense; but in another sense it sets a more drastic limitation upon mathematical knowledge, since mathematicians now know they can never, formally speaking, reach rock bottom; in fact, there is no rock bottom, since mathematics has no self-subsistent reality independent of the human activity that mathematicians carry on. And if human reason can never reach rock bottom (complete systematization) in mathematics, it is not likely to reach it anywhere else. There is no System possible for human existence, Kierkegaard said a century ago, differing with

Hegel, who wished to enclose reality within a completely rational structure; the System is impossible for mathematics, Godel tells us today. In practice, the fact that there is no rock bottom means that the mathematician can never prove the consistency of mathematics except by using means that are shakier than the system he is trying to prove consistent. Mathematics thus cannot escape finally the uncertainty that attaches to any human enterprise.

The situation is all the more vexing since mathematicians in the last half century have come up with some very troublesome paradoxes. Mathematics is like a ship in mid-ocean that has sprung certain leaks (paradoxes); the leaks have been temporarily plugged, but our reason can never guarantee that the ship will not spring others. This human insecurity in what had been the most secure of the disciplines of rationality marks a new turn in Western thinking. When the mathematician Hermann Weyl exclaims, "We have tried to storm Heaven, and we have only succeeded in piling up the tower of Babel," he is giving passionate expression to the collapse of human *hubris;* and we can be sure that mathematics has at last been returned to its rightful status as an activity or mode of being of finite man.

The concurrence of these various discoveries in time is extraordinary. Heidegger published his *Being and Time,* a somber and rigorous meditation on human finitude, in 1927. In the same year Heisenberg gave to the world his Principle of Indeterminacy. In 1929 the mathematician Skolem published a theorem which some mathematicians now think almost as remarkable as Godel's: that even the elementary number system cannot be categorically formalized. In 1931 appeared Godel's epoch-making discovery. When events run parallel this way, when they occur so close together in time, but independently of each other and in diverse fields, we are tempted to conclude that they are not mere "meaningless" coincidences but very meaningful symptoms. The whole mind of the time seems to be inclining in one direction.

What emerges from these separate strands of history is an image of man himself that bears a new, stark, more nearly naked, and more questionable aspect. The contradiction of man's horizons amounts to a denudation, a stripping down, of this being who has now to confront himself at the center of all his horizons. The labor of modern culture, wherever it has been authentic, has been a labor of denudation. A return to the sources; "to the things themselves," as Husserl puts it; toward a new truthfulness, the casting away of ready-made presuppositions and empty forms—these are some of the slogans under which this phase in history has presented itself. Naturally enough, much of this stripping down must appear as the work of destruction, as revolutionary or even "negative": a being who has become thoroughly questionable to himself must also find questionable his relation to the total past which in a sense he represents.

### SUGGESTIONS FOR WRITING

1. William Barrett, about whom comment is made on p. 528, seeks in his book, *Irrational Man,* to reveal how the philosophy of existentialism has pervaded all aspects of life. Science, he claims, has not escaped the influence of this philosophy; on the contrary, it has led man to see the attractiveness of existentialism. What does Barrett mean when he says science "has come up against the fact of human finitude"?
2. Barrett says: "Science has in this century, with the discoveries of Heisenberg in physics and Godel in mathematics, at least caught up with Kant." Comment on this statement.
3. What has Bohr's Principle of Complementarity to do with existentialism?
4. According to Barrett, "The whole mind of the time seems to be inclining in one direction." What is that direction?
5. Can man strip away everything and begin again, as Barrett implies? What conditions would be necessary?

# Man Thinking

One, with God, is always a majority, but many a martyr has been burned at the stake while the votes were being counted.

—Thomas B. Reed, *Speech in the House of Representatives,* 1885

Many demons are in the woods, in waters, in wildernesses, and in dark pooly places, ready to hurt and prejudice people; some are also in the thick black clouds, which cause hail, lightning and thunder, and poison the air, the pastures and grounds.

—Martin Luther, *Table-Talk,* 1569

Every student during his academic period ought to get up one bit of history thoroughly from the ultimate sources, in order to convince himself what history is not.

—William Graham Sumner, *Folkways,* 1907

There are three Johns: (1) the real John, known only to his Maker; (2) John's ideal John, never the real one, and often very unlike him; (3) Thomas's ideal John, never the real John, nor John's John, but often very unlike either.

—Oliver Wendell Holmes, *The Autocrat of the Breakfast-Table,* 1858

No man is an island entire of itself; every man is a piece of the continent, a part of the main; if a clod be washed away by the sea, Europe is the less, as well as if a promontory were, as well as if a manor of thy friends or of thine own were; any man's death diminishes me, because I am involved in mankind; and therefore never send to know for whom the bell tolls; it tolls for thee.

—John Donne, *Devotions* (Meditation 17), 1624

"What do you think?" Is there a more profoundly social question than that? It assumes that we are all living together and have within ourselves the power to sort things out and create a civilization.

—Brooks Atkinson, *Credo of a Critic,* 1949

LAWRENCE FERLINGHETTI

# Constantly Risking Absurdity*

Constantly risking absurdity
                    and death
            whenever he performs
                    above the heads
                            of his audience
        the poet like an acrobat
                    climbs on rime
                        to a high wire of his own making
    and balancing on eyebeams
                    above a sea of faces
            paces his way
                    to the other side of day
        performing entrechats
                    and slight-of-foot tricks
    and other high theatrics
                    and all without mistaking
            any thing
                    for what it may not be
    For he's the super realist
                who must perforce perceive
            taut truth
                    before the taking of each stance or step
    in his supposed advance
                    toward the still higher perch
    where Beauty stands and waits
                        with gravity
                    to start her death-defying leap
And he
        a little charleychaplin man
                    who may or may not catch
            her fair eternal form
                    spreadeagled in the empty air
            of existence.

SUGGESTIONS FOR WRITING

1. Lawrence Ferlinghetti, a wartime naval lieutenant commander and one of the more successful of the Beat Generation poets, has employed a number of effective figures in this poem. Choose one and explain its significance.

2. "The empty air of existence." Why empty? Is this the existentialist posture? Existentialism, in one guise or another, enters this anthology through several of the selections and it is the dominant concern of this section. In all, more than a third of the book touches upon the philosophical repercussions of existentialism. But one should hastily add the warning that once one begins to look for existentialism, he sees it everywhere. Three of the themes of existentialism which, by a broad interpretation, find a place in this book are "alienation and anxiety," "existence before essence," and "process, not finality."

   "Alienation and anxiety" refers to man's exultation of reason at the expense of his heart and soul and at the expense of a warm and human relation with anything else. Hence, when he finds that reason also fails, all his hopes are replaced by fear and terror, and he becomes lonely, independent, unpredictable—a man on the brink of nothingness. These ideas are examined in the articles by Panduro, Swarthout, T. B. Morgan, Gilbert, Fromm, Barrett (two selections), Sartre, Bigelow, and Shinn.

   "Existence before essence" means that a man can understand human life only in terms of his own particular life. A man, therefore, never *is* but is always *becoming,* because his own life is never complete. It follows that the uniqueness of his own experiences and impressions is the main thing to which he can make a commitment. The authors who examine this idea are Dewey, Thoreau, Whitman ("A Child Went Forth"), Riesman, Gallico, DeVoto, Brustein, and Rohden.

   "Process not finality" means that nothing is complete; everything is always becoming. The object of other philosophical systems is to provide an answer to all problems, to fill the beaker of life to the very top. Existentialism keeps pouring water into the beaker, but a small hole near the bottom prevents absolute fulfillment. Authors who represent this idea are MacLeish, LaFarge, Shaler, Barzun, Mencken (two selections), Stein, Woolf, Rapoport, Ciardi, Barr, Camus, and almost the whole section on "Learning to Write."

   Examine three or four selections in one of the above categories and reveal the elements of existentialism in each selection.

J E A N - P A U L   S A R T R E

# Existentialism*

What is meant by the term *existentialism?*

Most people who use the word would be rather embarrassed if they had to explain it, since, now that the word is all the rage, even the work of a musician or painter is being called existentialist. . . . It seems that for want of an advance-guard doctrine analogous to surrealism, the kind of people who are eager for scandal and flurry turn to this philosophy which in other respects does not at all serve their purposes in this sphere.

Actually, it is the least scandalous, the most austere of doctrines. It is intended strictly for specialists and philosophers. Yet it can be defined easily. What complicates matters is that there are two kinds of existentialist; first, those who are Christian, among whom I would include Jaspers and Gabriel Marcel, both Catholic; and on the other hand the atheistic existentialists, among whom I class Heidegger, and then the French existentialists and myself. What they have in common is that they think that existence precedes essence, or, if you prefer, that subjectivity must be the starting point.

Just what does that mean? Let us consider some object that is manufactured, for example, a book or a paper cutter: here is an object which has been made by an artisan whose inspiration came from a concept. He referred to the concept of what a paper cutter is and likewise to a known method of production, which is part of the concept, something which is, by and large, a routine. Thus, the paper cutter is at once an object produced in a certain way and, on the other hand, one having a specific use; and one can not postulate a man who produces a paper cutter but does not know

---

* From *Existentialism* translated by Bernard Frechtman (New York: Philosophical Library, 1947). Copyright 1949 by Philosophical Library, Inc. Reprinted by permission of the publishers.

what it is used for. Therefore, let us say that, for the paper cutter, essence—that is, the ensemble of both the production routines and the properties which enable it to be both produced and defined— precedes existence. Thus, the presence of the paper cutter or book in front of me is determined. Therefore, we have here a technical view of the world whereby it can be said that production precedes existence.

When we conceive God as the Creator, He is generally thought of as a superior sort of artisan. Whatever doctrine we may be considering, whether one like that of Descartes or that of Leibnitz, we always grant that will more or less follows understanding or, at the very least, accompanies it, and that when God creates He knows exactly what He is creating. Thus, the concept of man in the mind of God is comparable to the concept of paper cutter in the mind of the manufacturer, and, following certain techniques and a conception, God produces man, just as the artisan, following a definition and a technique, makes a paper cutter. Thus, the individual man is the realization of a certain concept in the divine intelligence. . . .

Atheistic existentialism, which I represent, is more coherent. It states that if God does not exist, there is at least one being in whom existence precedes essence, a being who exists before he can be defined by any concept, and that this being is man, or, as Heidegger says, human reality. What is meant here by saying that existence precedes essence? It means that, first of all, man exists, turns up, appears on the scene, and, only afterwards, defines himself. If man, as the existentialist conceives him, is indefinable, it is because at first he is nothing. Only afterward will he be something, and he himself will have made what he will be. Thus, there is no human nature, since there is no God to conceive it. Not only is man what he conceives himself to be, but he is also only what he wills himself to be after this thrust toward existence.

Man is nothing else but what he makes of himself. Such is the first principle of existentialism. It is also what is called subjectivity, the name we are labeled with when charges are brought against us. But what do we mean by this, if not that man has a greater dignity than a stone or table? For we mean that man first exists, that is, that man first of all is the being who hurls himself toward a future and who is conscious of imagining himself as being in the future. Man is at the start a plan which is aware of itself, rather than a patch of moss, a piece of garbage, or a cauliflower; nothing exists prior to this plan; there is nothing in heaven; man will be what he will have planned to be. Not what he will want to be. Because by the word "will" we generally mean a conscious decision, which is subsequent to what we have already made of ourselves. I may want to belong to a political party, write a book, get married; but all that is only a manifestation of an earlier, more spontaneous choice that is called "will." But if existence really does precede essence, man is responsible for what he is. Thus, existentialism's first move is to make every man aware of what he is and to make the full responsibility of his existence rest on him. And when we say that a man is responsible for himself, we do not only mean that he is responsible for his own individuality, but that he is responsible for all men.

The word subjectivism has two meanings, and our opponents play on the two. Subjectivism means, on the one hand, that an individual chooses and makes himself; and, on the other, that it is impossible for man to transcend human subjectivity. The second of these is the essential meaning of existentialism. When we say that man chooses his own self, we mean that every one of us does likewise; but we also mean by that that in making this choice he also chooses all men. In fact, in creating the man that we want to be, there is not a single one of our acts which does not at the same time create an image of man as we think he ought to be. To choose to be this or that is to affirm at the same time the value of what we choose, because we can never choose evil. We always choose the good, and nothing can be good for us without being good for all.

If, on the other hand, existence precedes essence, and if we grant that we exist and fashion our image at one and the same time, the image is valid for everybody and for our whole age. Thus, our responsibility is much greater than we might have supposed, because it involves all mankind. If I am a workingman and choose to join a Christian trade union rather than be a communist, and if by being a member I want to show that the best thing for man is resignation, and that the kingdom of man is not of this world, I am not only involving my own case—I want to be resigned for everyone. As a result, my action has involved all humanity. To take a more individual matter, if I want to marry, to have children; even if this marriage depends solely on my own circumstances or passion or wish, I am involving all humanity in monogamy and not merely myself. Therefore, I am responsible for myself and for everyone else. I am creating a certain image of man of my own choosing. In choosing myself, I choose man.

This helps us understand what the actual content is of such rather grandiloquent words as anguish, forlorness, despair. As you will see, it's all quite simple.

First, what is meant by anguish? The existentialists say at once that man is anguish. What that means is this: the man who involves himself and who realizes that he is not only the person he chooses to be, but also a lawmaker who is, at the same time, choosing all mankind as well as himself, can not help escape the feeling of his total and deep responsibility. Of course, there are many people who are not anxious; but we claim that they are hiding their anxiety, that they are fleeing from it. Certainly, many people believe that when they do something, they themselves are the only ones involved, and when someone says to them, "What if everyone acted that way?" they shrug their shoulders and answer, "Everyone doesn't act that way." But really, one should always ask himself, "What would happen if everybody looked at things that way?" There is no escaping this disturbing thought except by a kind of double-dealing. A man who lies and makes excuses for himself by saying "not everybody does that," is someone with an uneasy conscience, because the act of lying implies that a universal value is conferred upon the lie.

Anguish is evident even when it conceals itself. This is the anguish that Kierkegaard called the anguish of Abraham. You know the story: an angel has ordered Abraham to sacrifice his son; if it really were an angel who has come and said, "You are Abraham, you shall sacrifice your son," everything would be all right. But everyone might first wonder, "Is it really an angel, and am I really Abraham? What proof do I have?" . . .

Now, I'm not being singled out as an Abraham, and yet at every moment I'm obliged to perform exemplary acts. For every man, everything happens as if all mankind had its eyes fixed on him and were guiding itself by what he does. And every man ought to say to himself, "Am I really the kind of man who has the right to act in such a way that humanity might guide itself by my actions?" And if he does not say that to himself, he is masking his anguish.

There is no question here of the kind of anguish which would lead to quietism, to inaction. It is a matter of a simple sort of anguish that anybody who has had responsibilities is familiar with. For example, when a military officer takes the responsibility for an attack and sends a certain number of men to death, he chooses to do so, and in the main he alone makes the choice. Doubtless, orders come from above, but they are too broad; he interprets them, and on this interpretation depend the lives of ten or fourteen or twenty men. In making a decision he can not help having a certain anguish. All leaders know this anguish. That doesn't keep them from acting; on the contrary, it is the very condition of their action. For it implies that they envisage a number of possibilities, and when they choose one, they realize that it has value only because it is chosen. We shall see that this kind of anguish, which is the kind that existentialism describes, is explained, in addition, by a direct responsibility to the other men whom it involves. It is not a curtain separating us from action, but is part of action itself.

When we speak of forlornness, a term Heidegger was fond of, we mean only that God does not exist and that we have to face all the consequences of this. The existentialist is strongly opposed to a certain kind of secular ethics which would like to abolish God with the least possible expense. About 1880, some French teachers tried to set up a secular ethics which went something like this: God is a useless and costly hypothesis; we are discarding it; but, meanwhile, in order for there to be an ethics, a society, a civilization, it is essential that certain values be taken seriously and that they be considered as having an *a priori* existence. It must be obligatory, *a priori*, to be honest, not to lie, not to beat your wife, to have children, etc., etc. So we're going to try a little device which will make it possible to show that values exist all the same, inscribed in a heaven of ideas, though otherwise God does not exist. In other words—and this, I believe, is the tendency of everything called reformism in France—nothing will be changed if God does not exist. We shall find ourselves with the same norms of honesty, progress, and humanism, and we shall have made of God an outdated hypothesis which will peacefully die off by itself.

The existentialist, on the contrary, thinks it very distressing that God does not exist, because all possibility of finding values in a heaven of ideas disappears along with Him; there can no longer be an *a priori* Good, since there is no infinite and perfect consciousness to think it. Nowhere is it written that Good exists, that we must be honest, that we must not lie; because the fact is we are on a plane where there are only men. Dostoevski said, "If God didn't exist, everything would be possible." That is the very starting point of existentialism. Indeed, everything is permissible if God does not exist, and as a result man is forlorn, because neither within him nor without does he find anything to cling to. He can't start making excuses for himself.

If existence really does precede essence, there is no explaining things away by reference to a fixed and given human nature. In other words, there is no determinism, man is free, man is freedom. On the other hand, if God does not exist, we find no values or commands to turn to which legitimize our conduct. So, in the bright realm of values, we have no excuse behind us, no justification before us. We are alone, with no excuses.

That is the idea I shall try to convey when I say that man is condemned to be free. Condemned, because he did not create himself, yet, in other respects is free; because, once thrown into the world, he is responsible for everything he does. The existentialist does not believe in the power of passion. He will never agree that a sweeping passion is a ravaging torrent which fatally leads a man to certain acts and is therefore an excuse. He thinks that man is responsible for his passion.

The existentialist does not think that man is going to help himself by finding in the world some omen by which to orient himself. Because he thinks that man will interpret the omen to suit himself. Therefore, he thinks that man, with no support and no aid, is condemned every moment to invent man. Ponge, in a very fine article, has said, "Man is the future of man." That's exactly it. But if it is taken to mean that this future is recorded in heaven, that God sees it, then it is false, because it would really no longer be a future. If it is taken to mean that, whatever a man may be, there is a future to be forged, a virgin future before him, then this remark is sound. But then we are forlorn.

Actually, things will be as man will have decided they are to be. Does that mean that I should abandon myself to quietism? No. First, I should involve myself; then, act on the old saw, "Nothing ventured, nothing gained." Nor does it mean that I shouldn't belong to a party, but rather that I shall have no illusions and shall do what I can. For example, suppose I ask myself, "Will socialization, as such, ever come about?" I know nothing about it. All I know is that I'm going to do everything in my power to bring it about. Beyond that, I can't count on anything. Quietism is the attitude of people who say, "Let others do what I can't do." The doctrine I am presenting is the very opposite of quietism, since it declares, "There is no reality except in action." Moreover, it goes further, since it adds, "Man is nothing else than his plan; he exists only to the extent that he fulfills himself; he is therefore nothing else than the ensemble of his acts, nothing else than his life."

SUGGESTIONS FOR WRITING

1. Jean-Paul Sartre (1905-    ), French philosopher, playwright and novelist, studied under the German philosophers Husserl and Heidegger. Among his works are: *Nausea* (1938), *The Flies* (1943), *No Exit* (1944), *The Age of Reason* (1945), *The Reprieve* (1947), *Troubled Sleep* (1949), and *Being and Non-Being* (1956). Sartre is considered by many to be an outstanding leader of the existentialist school of philosophy. As Sartre defines it in this essay, existentialism is thinking that existence precedes essence. But what does that mean? Is there any way of making an operational definition of existentialism? Examine the ideas in Sartre's essay and write a theme showing existentialism in operation.

2. Sartre says that the starting point of existentialism is Dostoevski's statement, "If God didn't exist, everything would be possible." In what way is this true? What does Sartre mean? What would be possible? What is impossible if God exists? Write an essay considering these questions.

3. The Beat Generation addicts described in Brustein's article (p. 369) found comfort in those aspects of existentialism which stress full involvement in life. Would they want to accept the entire philosophy of existentialism as set forth in Sartre's article?

4. Consider the implications of Sartre's version of existentialism. If the criminal is morally responsible only to himself, what happens to civilization? On the other hand, to whom is the artist responsible if not to himself? Write an essay considering these questions.

GORDON BIGELOW

## A Primer of Existentialism*

For some years I fought the word by irritably looking the other way whenever I stumbled across it, hoping that like dadaism and some of the other "isms" of the French *avant garde* it would go away if I ignored it. But existentialism was apparently more than the picture it evoked of uncombed beards, smoky basement cafes, and French beatniks regaling one another between sips of absinthe with brilliant variations on the theme of despair. It turned out to be of major importance to literature and the arts, to philosophy and theology, and of increasing importance to the social sciences. To learn more about it, I read several of the self-styled introductions to the subject, with the baffled sensation of a man who reads a critical introduction to a novel only to find that he must read the novel before he can understand the introduction.

We should not run into trouble so long as we understand from the outset that the six major themes outlined below will apply in varying degrees to particular existentialists. A reader should be able to go from here to the existentialists themselves, to the more specialized critiques of them, or be able to recognize an existentialist theme or coloration in literature when he sees it.

A word first about the kinds of existentialism. Like transcendentalism of the last century, there are almost as many varieties of this *ism* as there are individual writers to whom the word is applied (not all of them claim it). But without being facetious we might group them into two main kinds, the *ungodly* and the *godly*. To take the ungodly or atheistic first, we would list as the chief spokesmen among many others Jean-Paul Sartre, Albert Camus, and Simone de Beauvoir. Several of this important group of French writers had rigorous and significant experience in the Resistance during the Nazi occupation of France in World War II. Out of the despair which came with the collapse of their nation during those terrible years they found unexpected strength in the single indomitable human spirit, which even under severe torture could maintain

* From *College English* (December, 1961). © 1961 by National Council of Teachers of English. Reprinted by permission of the author.

the spirit of resistance, the unextinguishable ability to say "No." From this irreducible core in the human spirit, they erected after the war a philosophy which was a twentieth-century variation of the philosophy of Descartes. But instead of saying "I think, therefore I am," they said "I can say No, therefore I exist." As we shall presently see, the use of the word "exist" is of prime significance. This group is chiefly responsible for giving existentialism its status in the popular mind as a literary-philosophical cult.

Of the godly or theistic existentialists we should mention first a mid-nineteenth-century Danish writer, Søren Kierkegaard; two contemporary French Roman Catholics, Gabriel Marcel and Jacques Maritain; two Protestant theologians, Paul Tillich and Nicholas Berdyaev; and Martin Buber, an important contemporary Jewish theologian. Taken together, their writings constitute one of the most significant developments in modern theology. Behind both groups of existentialists stand other important figures, chiefly philosophers, who exert powerful influence upon the movement—Blaise Pascal, Friedrich Nietzsche, Henri Bergson, Martin Heidegger, Karl Jaspers, among others. Several literary figures, notably Tolstoy and Dostoevski, are frequently cited because existentialist attitudes and themes are prominent in their writings. The eclectic nature of this movement should already be sufficiently clear and the danger of applying too rigidly to any particular figure the general characteristics of the movement which I now make bold to describe:

## 1. Existence Before Essence

Existentialism gets its name from an insistence that human life is understandable only in terms of an individual man's existence, his particular experience of life. It says that a man *lives* (has existence) rather than *is* (has being or essence), and that every man's experience of life is unique, radically different from everyone else's and can be understood truly only in terms of his involvement in life or commitment to it. . . .

## 2. Reason Is Impotent to Deal With the Depths of Human Life

There are two parts to this proposition—first, that human reason is relatively weak and imperfect, and second, that there are dark places in human life which are "non-reason" and to which reason scarcely penetrates. . . .

## 3. Alienation or Estrangement

One major result of the dissociation of reason from the rest of the psyche has been the growth of science, which has become one of the hallmarks of Western civilization, and an ever increasing rational ordering of men in society. As the existentialists view them, the main forces of history since the Renaissance have progressively separated man from concrete earthy existence, have forced him to live at ever higher levels of abstraction, have collectivized individual man out of existence, have driven God from the heavens, or what is the same thing, from the hearts of men. They are convinced that modern man lives in a fourfold condition of alienation: from God, from nature, from other men, from his own true self. . . .

## 4. "Fear and Trembling," Anxiety

At Stockholm when he accepted the Nobel Prize, William Faulkner said that "Our tragedy today is a general and universal physical fear so long sustained by now that we can even bear it. There are no longer problems of the spirit. There is only one question: When will I be blown up?" The optimistic vision of the Enlightenment which saw man, through reason and its extensions in science, conquering all nature and solving all social and political problems in a continuous upward spiral of Progress, cracked open like a melon on the rock of World War I. The theories which held such high hopes died in that sickening and unimaginable butchery. Here was a concrete fact of human nature and society which the theories could not contain. The Great Depression and World War II deepened the sense of dismay which the loss of these ideals brought, but only with the atomic bomb did this become an unbearable terror, a threat of instant annihilation which confronted all men, even those most insulated by the thick crust of material goods and services. Now the most unthinking person could sense that each advance in mechanical technique carried not only a chromium and plush promise of comfort but a threat as well. . . .

## 5. The Encounter with Nothingness

For the man alienated from God, from nature, from his fellow man and from himself, what is left at last but Nothingness? The testimony of the existentialists is that this is where modern man now finds himself, not on the highway of upward Progress toward a radiant Utopia but on the brink of a catastrophic precipice, below which yawns the absolute void, an uncompromised black Nothingness. . . .

### 6. Freedom

Sooner or later, as a theme that includes all the others, the existentialist writings bear upon freedom. The themes we have outlined above describe either some loss of man's freedom or some threat to it, and all existentialists of whatever sort are concerned to enlarge the range of human freedom.

For the avowed atheists like Sartre freedom means human autonomy. In a purposeless universe man is *condemned* to freedom because he is the only creature who is "self-surpassing," who can become something other than he is. Precisely because there is no God to give purpose to the universe, each man must accept individual responsibility for his own becoming, a burden made heavier by the fact that in choosing for himself he chooses for all men "the image of man as he ought to be." A man *is* the sum total of the acts that make up his life—no more, no less—and though the coward has made himself cowardly, it is always possible for him to change and make himself heroic. In Sartre's novel, *The Age of Reason*, one of the least likable of the characters, almost overwhelmed by despair and self-disgust at his homosexual tendencies, is on the point of solving his problem by mutilating himself with a razor, when in an effort of will he throws the instrument down, and we are given to understand that from this moment he will have mastery over his aberrant drive. Thus in the daily course of ordinary life must men shape their becoming in Sartre's world.

The religious existentialists interpret man's freedom differently. They use much the same language as Sartre, develop the same themes concerning the predicament of man, but always include God as a radical factor. They stress the man of faith rather than the man of will. They interpret man's existential condition as a state of alienation from his essential nature which is God-like, the problem of his life being to heal the chasm between the two, that is, to find salvation. The mystery and ambiguity of man's existence they attribute to his being the intersection of two realms. "Man bears within himself," writes Berdyaev, "the image which is both the

image of man and the image of God, and is the image of man as
far as the image of God is actualized." Tillich describes salvation
as "the act in which the cleavage between the essential being and
the existential situation is overcome." Freedom here, as for Sartre,
involves an acceptance of responsibility for choice and a *commitment* to one's choice. This is the meaning of faith, a faith like
Abraham's, the commitment which is an agonizing sacrifice of one's
own desire and will and dearest treasure to God's will.

A final word. Just as one should not expect to find in a particular writer all of the characteristics of existentialism as we have described them, he should also be aware that some of the most striking
expressions of existentialism in literature and the arts come to us
by indirection, often through symbols or through innovations in
conventional form. Take the preoccupation of contemporary writers
with time. In *The Sound and the Fury,* Faulkner both collapses
and expands normal clock time, or by juxtapositions of past and
present blurs time into a single amorphous pool. He does this by
using various forms of "stream of consciousness" or other techniques
which see life in terms of unique, subjective experience—that is,
existentially. The conventional view of externalized life, a rational
orderly progression cut into uniform segments by the hands of a
clock, he rejects in favor of a view which sees life as opaque, ambiguous, and irrational—that is, as the existentialist sees it. Graham
Greene does something like this in *The Power and the Glory.* He
creates a scene isolated in time and cut off from the rest of the
world, steamy and suffocating as if a bell jar had been placed over
it. Through this atmosphere fetid with impending death and human
suffering, stumbles the whiskey priest, lonely and confused, pursued
by a police lieutenant who has experienced the void and the death
of God.

Such expressions in literature do not mean necessarily that the
authors are conscious existentialist theorizers, or even that they
know the writings of such theorizers. Faulkner may never have read
Heidegger—or St. Augustine—both of whom attempt to demonstrate that time is more within a man and subject to his unique
experience of it than it is outside him. But it is legitimate to call
Faulkner's views of time and life "existential" in this novel because
in recent years existentialist theorizers have given such views a local
habitation and a name. One of the attractions, and one of the

dangers, of existential themes is that they become like Sir Thomas Browne's quincunx: once one begins to look for them, he sees them everywhere. But if one applies restraint and discrimination, he will find that they illuminate much of contemporary literature and sometimes the literature of the past as well.

### SUGGESTIONS FOR WRITING

1. Gordon Bigelow is a professor at the University of Florida and has spent a year at the University of Vienna on a Fulbright grant. His professional interests are American literature, and as the above essay indicates, philosophical aspects of the humanities. Bigelow explains the puzzlement that confronts every beginning student of existentialism. He says the feeling is like "a man who reads a critical introduction to a novel only to find that he must read the novel before he can understand the introduction." If you share his feeling, describe the source of your puzzlement in a theme. Are you unable to understand the words? Is there insufficient illustration? Is it contrary or different from philosophical theories which you know and which block your mind from receiving this one? Are the variations of the divergent "isms" too complex to grasp in a single reading?

2. Four of the six general characteristics which Bigelow describes are distinctly unpleasant: impotent reason, alienation, anxiety, the encounter with nothingness. Generally speaking, what is unpleasant is unattractive, yet it cannot be denied that many contemporary artists (poets, painters, novelists, playwrights) are attracted to this philosophy. Can you account for its attractiveness? What is the compelling nature of the philosophy? Write an essay considering these questions.

3. The above article is an excerpt from a longer piece which appeared in the December, 1961, issue of *College English*. A number of the illustrations have been left out of the excerpt. Can you provide your own illustrations? In your encounter with contemporary literature you have probably read something to which you can apply the six points made by Bigelow. Write an essay indicating how these qualities may be applied to a modern author.

ROGER SHINN

## Kierkegaard: The Disturbing Dane*

"That individual" is the epitaph Sören Kierkegaard proposed for himself. And "that individual" he was.

In a double sense he is the central figure in existentialism. First, he set the style of the movement in writings unforgettably fervent, glittering, tempestuous, witty, and devout. Second, he was the living existentialist, involved to the hilt in all that he wrote. Like ancient Socrates, who *talked* and *was* philosophy, Kierkegaard both *wrote* and *lived* existentialism.

It is tempting to examine his life. The materials are dramatic enough: his lonely oddity of appearance and character; his burden of his father's guilt and his own; his courtship and engagement to Regina; his agonizing break with her, due partly to inner conflicts, partly to a peculiar sense of vocation; his double life as a public "frivolous bird" and a private "penitent"; his prolific writings in a short career; his inner torment and experience of grace; his attack upon the Church in the name of faithfulness to Christ.

Furthermore, on Kierkegaard's own advice we should look at him. In true existentialist manner he derides the practice of separating the writing from the writer. He invites us to look at himself—so that he may make us look at ourselves. His own life he called "an epigram calculated to make people aware." Richard Niebuhr describes him in a vivid sentence. He shows us a "series of signs on the road, which read 'This way to the signpost' "; then "when we arrive at the signpost we will find a hand pointing nowhere except directly at us."

But this is a very short book. So, with a profound apology to Kierkegaard, I shall say little more of his career and get on to his writings. After a slow start—a Danish writer reaches few people at first—his works have come to reverberate through Europe and America. More than twenty volumes are available in English, all

* From *The Existentialist Posture* by Roger Shinn (New York: Association Press, 1959). © 1959 by the National Board of YMCA's. Reprinted by permission of the publishers.

published in a remarkable burst of energy since 1936 (eighty-one years after Kierkegaard's death). The disturbing Dane has found his audience.

It would be *absurd* (to use one of his favorite words) to sum up Kierkegaard's teachings. He does not lay out his ideas in orderly fashion. Anyone who puts them in order distorts them. Like a literary boxer, Kierkegaard jabs, feints, catches his reader off-balance. He drives you (for his writings are always directed at *you*) into a corner, pummels you, offers you a way out and dares you to take it. He makes you laugh as he turns his whiplike wit on someone, then agonize as the backlash catches you. He pours out sarcasms and invective, then instantaneously shifts to humble and reverent prayer.

Yet I shall try the risky business of describing a few of the themes that he infused into existentialism.

## The Critique of Rationalism

Everyone who dislikes the existentialists calls them *irrationalists*. That seems to end discussion. Actually, however, it only raises an issue.

Diderot, the French revolutionist, once wrote satirically: "Astray at night in an immense forest, I have only a small light to guide me. A stranger comes along and tells me: 'My friend, blow out your candle so as to see your way better.' This stranger is a theologian."

That is a devastating blow—if it connects. Perhaps it is a wild haymaker that misses most theologians (who, after all, make a career of *reasoning* about religion). But all the heirs of Diderot think that his punch hits squarely the existentialists. The existentialist has an answer. He says that Diderot's man in the woods can make a fool of himself in two ways. (1) He can blow out the light. (2) He can assume that his candle is a giant searchlight which illumines the whole woods and takes all the risk out of his adventure.

If error No. 1 is stupidity, error No. 2 is a crazed hallucination. The wise man will use all the light he has, without deceiving himself about how much he has. Pascal, years before Diderot, said that there is "nothing so conformable to reason" as a certain "disavowal of reason."

All the existentialists try to determine, as accurately as possible, the extent of reason's light. All reason as much as they can. But all refuse to deny experiences that they cannot explain (as I refuse to deny gravitation even though I cannot explain it). And, going further, they insist that reason can never remove from life the risk of personal decision.

Kierkegaard understands very well that objective reasoning about evidence is the only way to settle some questions. He knows that people trap themselves in their illusions, that detachment from factual reality is insanity. But, he continues, it is not enough that a man know the objective truth; he must himself be truthfully related to the objective reality. Kierkegaard makes the point with one of his characteristic stories.

A man escapes from an insane asylum. He decides to convince people that he is sane by talking rationally. Finding a ball on the ground, he puts it in the tail pocket of his coat. As he walks, the ball bounces against his rear end. And at every bounce, he says, "Bang, the earth is round." Though he tells *the objective truth,* he does not demonstrate his sanity. Now, says Kierkegaard, he would not do better to say that the earth is flat. Objective truth is better than objective falsity. But more important than both is *subjective truth*—that is, the truth of *a subject* (a person) rightly related to reality. That is the meaning of the repeated statements: "Truth is subjectivity." "Truth consists precisely in inwardness."

Consequently, says Kierkegaard, man can be related to God only "by virtue of the infinite passion of inwardness." The attempts to get at God by objective logical arguments are ridiculous. Although Kierkegaard sees the flaws which logicians have found in the "proofs" of God's existence, his major objection is something else. To stand apart from God and try to prove his reality is to remove oneself from the inward relation which alone makes possible any knowledge of God. With typically flamboyant rhetoric he says: "So rather let us sin, sin out and out, seduce maidens, murder men, commit highway robbery. . . ." God can still get at us. But when we coolly stand off from God and try to prove that he is there, he cannot reach us.

Rationalism, whether in theology or in general philosophy, has never quite recovered its old health since the battering of the early existentialists. But Kierkegaard's attack leaves two major problems:

Like all Christians since Paul, Kierkegaard sees the "offense" and the "foolishness" to our normal inclinations in the Gospel of God's act in Christ. Then he goes on to exult so much in the "absurdity" of faith that one must sometimes wonder what reason can do to distinguish truth from nonsense in religion.

Sometimes Kierkegaard suggests that it does not matter too much what a person believes so long as he believes it with passionate commitment. At other times he rejects any such "devilish" wisdom. This conflict he left to future existentialism. Today some existentialists put great importance in the *content* of belief; others think the *manner* of belief is the truly important thing.

### Self-Discovery

Existentialism, we have noticed, starts with the question: "Who am I? What does it mean for me to exist as a unique individual?" That turns out to be an impossibly difficult question. No one ever answers it. But to begin to answer it, even to ask it in all serious-ness, is a momentous event.

The great obstacle to an answer is that each of us fears to under-stand himself. Living by false self-images, we lack the nerve to explore ourselves without illusion. Personality is fiendishly elusive in its tricks of self-deception.

If we begin to get past the delusions, we discover at the core of selfhood a deep *anxiety*. (In everyday language the word *anxiety* has become so trivial that perhaps we should say *dread*.) Some peo-ple will not admit this; they are the cowards who manage to cover up. Those with the honesty to see themselves can discover this anxiety. Almost everybody has moments of insight when he catches this truth.

What causes such anxiety? The plainest answer is simply that *life is insecure*. And man can see beyond his own limitations just enough to crave the security he never attains. He finds tentative security in home or job or reputation. But, unless he is an expert in self-deception, he knows that these are all temporary, as he is himself temporary. Absolutely nothing in this world can satisfy his craving.

Furthermore, man has the dizzying privilege of choosing what he will be. Of course, heredity and environment enter in. But each of us does something with his heredity and environment. *Our deci-sions make ourselves.* Once in all time exists this specific self, able to do and be what no one else can do and be. This is the anxious, the "dreadful" responsibility of each self.

At this point many people ask: Is all this necessary? What good can such talk do? Of course, there is a lot of anxiety around. But doesn't talking about it simply ruin people's confidence? Isn't it more healthy to forget it and be moderately happy without such worries?

The existentialist answer, contrary to some rumors, is not a sour desire to see everybody turn morose. Existentialists can enjoy parties, friendship, sports. (Kierkegaard was a devotee of the theater.) But, says the existentialist, when you enjoy life, know what you are doing.

Yes, many people get along fairly well in a mediocre, conventional sort of life. As long as health and finances are favorable, the neighbors decent, the children out of trouble, and the nation out of war, they feel pretty secure.

But this security is an evasion. It is always vulnerable. A change of events (cancer, war, bad luck) can bring the roof crashing in at any moment, for life is basically insecure. Furthermore, this mediocrity settles for a subhuman level of living instead of genuine existence. It saves one from the awful anxiety of taking responsibility for the making of a self.

If Kierkegaard is right, our churches actually harm us when they develop cults of "peace of mind" and "positive thinking." They encourage evasion instead of honest self-searching. They would do better to tear away our illusions, until we see ourselves in our "sickness unto death." Only then will healing really be possible.

Kierkegaard tries to work past our normal tricks of deception in his famous description of the three stages of life. In the *aesthetic stage,* where we all have a yen to live, one takes life in terms of unfettered enjoyment. Like a stone skipping on the surface of the water, he gaily tastes the delights of life. But as the stone must sink, the aesthetic life must end in despair. Enjoyment without commitment cannot support it for long.

Despair then drives one to decision. In resolute choice one becomes a real person. Struggle and responsibility are the marks of real selfhood. But this *ethical stage* brings experiences of remorse and penitence. It is no use to say, with perhaps a sidelong glance at the Kinsey report, that one's behavior is as good as average, for ethical decision means commitment, and human beings are half-hearted in their commitments. Once again the result is despair.

Now the self must either revive the futile hopes that have already failed it—or drive on to the *religious stage*. Here one knows himself as a person responsible to God. He learns the meaning of sin and suffering, with all the cheap veils torn away. For sin is not just a nasty act. It is the fear and distrust that keep us away from God. But to know oneself as a suffering sinner is a gain. Suffering has a grandeur that was missing in the falsity of a life that kept trying not to suffer. And suffering may open the way to the knowledge of God's love, which brings joy and peace rather than despair. The aesthetic and ethical, not destroyed but dethroned, will then find their rightful place in true existence. But that outcome depends upon "the leap of faith."

## The Leap of Faith

The only answer to radical despair is radical trust. But we prefer not to be so radical. We like to move gradually into faith, without ever letting go of the old efforts at security. We aim to make the gap so easy that someone can cross it without ever realizing it. We are, says Kierkegaard, like a comic character in a Danish play, who "little by little, reached the point of assuming that almost having passed his examinations was the same as having passed them." Or we are like the poor swimmer who wants to keep a toe on the bottom rather than trust himself to the water. He is not really a swimmer until he "ventures far out," abandoning the support of the bottom for the support of the water. Faith is like lying on "70,000 fathoms of water," relying solely on the buoyancy of the sea.

It is important to notice that Kierkegaard is not describing the psychology of instantaneous conversion. A person usually struggles through a long period of time, just as he may very gradually learn to swim. Still there is the decisive difference between trusting the waves and trusting a foothold on the bottom. What Kierkegaard is saying is that there can be no Christianity without venturing, without dangerous trust in God. "Without risk there is no faith."

Hence faith requires a "leap." This leap is not, as is sometimes said, a kind of desperate lurch of the emotions that leaves the mind behind. It is a decision of the *whole* self—mind, will, feeling. But no one coasts into faith.

The real problem is not (as we like to think) doubt versus faith. If so, there might be any number of halfway points. One could move from doubt to probability to virtual certainty. But the actual conflict is despair and defiance versus trust. Here there are no halfway points.

SUGGESTIONS FOR WRITING

1. Roger Shinn has been on the faculties of Heidelberg College, Vanderbilt University, and Union Theological Seminary in New York City. He is the author of *Beyond This Darkness* (1953), *Life, Death and Destiny* (1957), and *The Existentialist Posture* (1959), from which the above chapter is taken. Shinn says, "If Kierkegaard is right, our churches actually harm us when they develop cults of 'peace of mind' and 'positive thinking.' They encourage evasion instead of honest self-searching." Is Kierkegaard right? What is wrong with "peace of mind" and "positive thinking"?

2. Write a theme on one of the following topics: "Enjoyment without commitment cannot support it for long." "Once in all time exists this specific self, able to do and be what no one else can do and be." "Objective truth is better than objective falsity. But more important than both is *subjective truth*." "Suffering has a grandeur that was missing in the falsity of a life that kept trying not to suffer." "Faith is like lying on '70,000 fathoms of water,' relying solely on the buoyancy of the sea."

3. Kierkegaard (1813-1855) was a Christian theologian who made existentialism a self-conscious movement and created much of its vocabulary. Account for the fact that Kierkegaard and Sartre, sharing a great number of basic premises, came to opposite conclusions about the existence of God.

WILLIAM BARRETT

## Existentialism in Art*

A great formal style in painting has never been created that did not draw upon the depths of the human spirit, and that did not,

---

\* From *Irrational Man* by William Barrett (New York: Doubleday & Co., Inc., 1958). © 1958 by William Barrett. Reprinted by permission of the publishers.

in its newness, express a fresh mutation of the human spirit. Cubism achieved a radical flattening of space by insisting on the two-
dimensional fact of the canvas. This flattening out of space would
seem not to be a negligible fact historically if we reflect that when,
once before in history, such a development occurred but in the
opposite direction—when the flatness of the Gothic or primitive
painters passed over into the solidity, perspective, and three-dimensional style of early Renaissance painting—it was a mark that man
was turning outward, into space, after the long period of introspection of the Middle Ages. Western man moved out into space
in his painting, in the fourteenth century, before he set forth into
actual physical space in the age of exploration that was to follow.
Thus painting was prophetic of the new turn of the human spirit
which was eventually to find expression in the conquest of the
whole globe. Have we the right, then, to suggest that the flattening
of painting in our own century portends a turning inward of the
human spirit, or at any rate a turning away from that outer world
of space which has hitherto been the ultimate arena of Western
man's extroversion? With Cubism begins that process of detachment
from the object which has become the hallmark of modern art.
Even though Cubism is a classical and formal style, the artist nevertheless asserts his own subjectivity by the freedom with which he
cuts up and dislocates objects—bottles, pitchers, guitars—as it
pleases him for the sake of the picture, which is now no longer
held up to us as a representation of those objects but as a visual
image with its own independent value alongside that of nature.
The subjectivity that is generally present in modern art is a psychological compensation for, sometimes a violent revolt against, the
gigantic externalization of life within modern society. The world
pictured by the modern artist is, like the world meditated upon by
the existential philosopher, a world where man is a stranger.

When mankind no longer lives spontaneously turned toward God
or the supersensible world—when, to echo the words of Yeats, the
ladder is gone by which we would climb to a higher reality—the
artist too must stand face to face with a flat and inexplicable world.
This shows itself even in the formal structures of modern art. Where
the movement of the spirit is no longer vertical but only horizontal,
the climactic elements in art are in general leveled out, flattened.
The flattening of pictorial space that is achieved in Cubism is not

an isolated fact, true only of painting, but is paralleled by similar changes in literary techniques. There is a general process of flattening, three chief aspects of which may be noted:

(1) *The flattening out of all planes* upon the plane of the picture. Near and far are pushed together. So in certain works of modern literature time, instead of space, is flattened out upon one plane. Past and present are represented as occurring simultaneously, upon a single plane of time. James Joyce's *Ulysses,* T. S. Eliot's *The Waste Land,* and Ezra Pound's *Cantos* are examples; and perhaps the most powerful use of the device was made by Faulkner in his early novel *The Sound and the Fury.*

(2) More important perhaps is *the flattening out of climaxes,* which occurs both in painting and literature. In traditional Western painting there is a central subject, located at or near the center of the picture, and the surrounding space in the picture is subordinate to this. In a portrait the figure is placed near the center, and the background becomes secondary to it, something to be blended as harmoniously as possible with the figure. Cubism abolished this idea of the pictorial climax: the whole space of the picture became of equal importance. Negative spaces (in which there are no objects) are as important as positive spaces (the contours of physical objects). If a human figure is treated, it may be broken up and distributed over various parts of the canvas. Formally speaking, the spirit of this art is anticlimactic.

When we turn to observe this same deflation or flattening of climaxes in literature, the broader human and philosophic questions involved become much clearer. The classical tradition in literature, deriving from Aristotle's *Poetics,* tells us that a drama (and consequently any other literary work) must have a beginning, middle, and end. The action begins at a certain point, rises toward a climax, and then falls to a dénouement. One can diagram a classical plot of this kind by means of a triangle whose apex represents the climax with which everything in the play has some logical and necessary connection. The author subordinates himself to the requirements of logic, necessity, probability. His structure must be an intelligible whole in which each part develops logically out of what went before. If our existence itself is never quite like this, no matter; art is a selection from life, and the poet is required to be selective. However, it is important to note that this canon of intelligible literary structure—beginning, middle, and end, with a well-defined climax—arose in a culture in which the universe too was believed to be an ordered structure, a rational and intelligible whole.

What happens if we try to apply this classical Aristotelian canon to a modern work like Joyce's *Ulysses,* 734 pages of power and dullness, beauty and sordidness, comedy and pathos, where the movement is always horizontal, never ascending toward any crisis, and where we detect not the shadow of anything like a climax, in the traditional sense of that term? If Joyce's had been a disordered mind, we could dismiss all this as a sprawling chaos; but he was in fact an artist in superb control of his material, so that the disorder has to be attributed to his material, to life itself. It is, in fact, the banal gritty thing that we live that Joyce gives us, in comparison with which most other fiction is indeed fiction. This world is dense, opaque, unintelligible; that is the datum from which the modern artist always starts. The formal dictates of the well-made play or the well-made novel, which were the logical outcome of thoroughly rational preconceptions about reality, we can no longer hold to when we become attentive "to the things themselves," to the facts, to existence in the mode in which we do exist. If our epoch still held to the idea, as Western man once did, that the whole of reality is a system in which each detail providentially and rationally is subordinated to others and ultimately to the whole itself, we could demand of the artist that his form imitate this idea of reality, and give us coherence, logic, and the picture of a world with no loose ends. But to make such a demand nowadays is worse than an impertinence: it is a travesty upon the historical being of the artist. . . .

(3) The last and most important aspect of what we have called the process of flattening in modern art is *the flattening out of values.* To understand this one can begin at the simplest level in painting, where it means merely that large and small objects are treated as of equal value. Cézanne paints apples with the same passionate concentration as he paints mountains, and each apple is as monumental as a mountain. Indeed, in some of Cézanne's still lifes, if one covers up all of the picture except a certain patch of folded tablecloth, one might very well be looking at the planes and peaks of his Mont St. Victoire. For Cézanne the painting dictates its own values: little and

big, high and low, sublime and ordinary outside the painting are
of equal importance if in a given painting they play the same
plastic role. . . . Following Cézanne, the Cubists took as subjects
for their most monumental paintings ordinary objects like tables,
bottles, glasses, guitars. Now the painter dispenses with objects altogether: the colored shape on his canvas is itself an absolute reality,
perhaps more so than the imaginary scene, the great battle, which
in a traditional canvas it might serve to depict. Thus we arrive at
last at *l'art brut* (raw, crude, or brute art), which seeks to abolish
not only the ironclad distinction between the sublime and the banal
but that between the beautiful and the ugly as well. . . .

The deflation, or flattening out, of values in Western art does not
necessarily indicate an ethical nihilism. Quite the contrary; in
opening our eyes to the rejected elements of existence, art may lead
us to a more complete and less artificial celebration of the world.
In literature, again, the crucial example is Joyce's *Ulysses*. It was not
a literary critic but a psychologist, C. G. Jung, who perceived that
this book was non-Western in spirit; he sees it as Oriental to such
an extent that he recommends it as a much-needed bible to the
white-skinned races. For *Ulysses* breaks with the whole tradition of
Western sensibility and Western aesthetics in showing each small
object of Bloom's day—even the objects in his pocket, like a cake
of soap—as capable at certain moments of taking on a transcendental importance—or in being, at any rate, equal in value to those
objects to which men usually attribute transcendental importance.
Each grain of sand, Joyce seems to be saying (as the Oriental says),
reflects the whole universe—and the Irish writer was not in the
least a mystic; he simply takes experience as it comes, in the course
of the single day he depicts in the novel. Any such break with
tradition, where a serious reversal of values is involved, is of course
dangerous, for the artist runs the risk of losing the safeguards that
the experience of the past has erected for him. A good deal of
modern art has clearly succumbed to this danger, and the result is
disorder in the art and the artist; but the danger is the price that
must be paid for any step forward by the human spirit. . . .

Through modern art our time reveals itself to itself, or at least
to those persons who are willing to look at their own age dispas-
sionately and without the blindness of preconceptions, in the looking glass of its art. In our epoch existential philosophy has appeared

as an intellectual expression of the time, and this philosophy exhibits numerous points of contact with modern art. The more closely
we examine the two together, the stronger becomes the impression
that existential philosophy is the authentic intellectual expression
of our time, as modern art is the expression of the time in terms of
image and intuition. . . .

There is a painful irony in the new image of man that is emerging, however fragmentarily, from the art of our time. An observer
from another planet might well be struck by the disparity between
the enormous power which our age has concentrated in its external
life and the inner poverty which our art seeks to expose to view.
This is, after all, the age that has discovered and harnessed atomic
energy, that has made airplanes that fly faster than the sun, and
that will, in a few years (perhaps in a few months), have atomic-
powered planes which can fly through outer space and not need to
return to mother earth for weeks. What cannot man do! He has
greater power now than Prometheus or Icarus or any of those daring
mythical heroes who were later to succumb to the disaster of pride.
But if an observer from Mars were to turn his attention from these
external appurtenances of power to the shape of man as revealed
in our novels, plays, painting, and sculpture, he would find there
a creature full of holes and gaps, faceless, riddled with doubts and
negations, starkly finite.

However disconcerting this violent contrast between power and
impoverishment, there is something a little consoling in it for anyone who is intimidated by excessive material power, as there is in
learning that a dictator is a drunkard or marked by some other
ordinary failing which makes him seem a trifle more human. If we
are to redeem any part of our world from the brute march of power,
we may have to begin as modern art does by exalting some of the
humble and dirty little corners of existence. On another level, however, this violent contrast is frightening, for it represents a dangerous
lagging of man behind his own works; and in this lag lies the terror
of the atomic bomb which hangs over us like impending night.
Here surely the ordinary man begins to catch a fleeting glimpse of
that Nothingness which both artist and philosopher have begun in
our time to take seriously. The bomb reveals the dreadful and total
contingency of human existence. Existentialism is the philosophy of
the atomic age.

SUGGESTIONS FOR WRITING

1. William Barrett (1913-    ) is a professor of philosophy at New York University. He was the youngest man (nineteen) ever to receive a doctor's degree in philosophy at Columbia. For several years he was editor of *Partisan Review,* and was among the first to introduce European existentialism to America. In the above essay from his book, *Irrational Man* (1958), Barrett is more approving and positive than Robert Brustein (p. 369) as a critic of modern trends. He sees an affirmation in the paradox of looking at "the rejected elements of existence." It will lead, he hopes, to "a more complete and less artificial celebration of the world." Is this what art should do, celebrate the world? Was not Whitman celebrating the world more than one hundred years ago? Must there be a new expression of celebration for each age?

2. Suppose Barrett were to evaluate and criticize "the method" school of acting. Would he, in contrast to Brustein (p. 369), find it a new means of "celebrating the world"?

3. Barrett speaks of Bloom's day in James Joyce's *Ulysses*. He says that each small object—even a cake of soap—in Bloom's daily experience may take on "a transcendental importance." Is such a thing possible? Choose an object—perhaps something you are wearing—and write of a fictional incident in which the object can, for you, take on a transcendental importance.

4. Barrett implies that the purpose of art is not necessarily to enlighten or entertain or please the sensibilities. Its purpose, as he says in the last paragraph, is to redeem "our world from the brute march of power . . . by exalting some of the humble and dirty little corners of existence." True? If you have another theory, write about it. If not, explain and illustrate what Barrett means.

L .   A .   G .   S T R O N G

## The Pleasures of Ignorance\*

The other morning I found myself suddenly awake some minutes before my time. Just as suddenly, and without premeditation, I found myself reviewing the extent of my knowledge and, before it

---

\* From *Personal Remarks* by L. A. G. Strong (London: Peter Nevill, Ltd., 1953). Reprinted by permission of A. D. Peters.

was time to get up, I had come to the conclusion that I knew practically nothing about anything.

This conclusion was not reached in any spirit of self-abasement,
or even of modesty. The time was not two-thirty a.m., but seven
forty-five. I woke from no nightmare, but was in calm and contented
possession of my faculties. I experienced a very definite pleasure
from the fact that I might remain for several minutes where I was.
The conviction of my own ignorance was a sane, happy, and (I
think) irrefutable conviction. It did not depress me because there
appeared to be good reasons why I need do nothing about it; good
reasons, in fact, for thinking that I am better as I am.

First of all, what is the positive extent of my knowledge? Apart
from immediate personal experiences, such as the fact that it is
unwise to take hold of the little door in front of a coal range in
one's fingers (learnt at the age of seven), that a mixture of sherbet
and milk chocolate in equal parts produces disconcerting results
(discovered at eight), and that it is socially inexpedient to make
jokes about false teeth (impressed on me a little later), the number
of things which I can positively say I know is very limited. I know
the genitive singular of a number of Latin words and a much smaller
number of Greek ones. I know, with less certainty, a few things that
happened during a certain limited period of English history; though
even these depend upon data which I am personally unable to
verify. I know a few mathematical formulae, impressed upon me
by trial—and error—in relation to my banking account. I can play,
with a dubious proportion of success, the game of applying to English
thoughts and objects the names under which similar thoughts and
objects seem to be known in France. I can inform a German that
the mountain is bedecked with snow, and a Spaniard that his
brother's hat is in the warehouse. I can tell an Italian railway porter
that his tiny hand is frozen. Still, as opportunities for imparting
such information occur but seldom, the knowledge is not much use
to me. I know who wrote a limited number of plays and poems and
pieces of music, and can in certain cases even give a sketchy account
of what they contain. I know, very roughly, the views held by the
various rival practitioners of a science which is as yet so tentative
that no two of them use the same term in the same way. I know the
words and tunes of a few songs. I can repeat several anecdotes.

The acquisition of this inconsiderable store has cost me fifty-six

years and my parents a good deal of money. Compared with all that
I do not know, it seems, to say the least, an inadequate return. I
do not understand the major phenomena of the world around me.
I do not understand half the contrivances which I use, such as
wireless, and the telephone. I am unable to repair an electric bell.
I have a very imperfect knowledge of my own personal mechanism.
What is worse, I am not particularly curious about these things.
When I put three pennies into an automatic machine, and receive
a ticket to Tottenham Court Road, I am not devoured by any desire
to know how the miracle is worked. I am simply grateful to be
saved standing in a queue at the booking office. I am so unob-
servant that I cannot even draw an accurate picture of the outside
of the house in which I am living. I do not think I could draw a
bus, or the outline of Big Ben, without going first to look at it. In
fact, as I said, outside the range of my own immediate experience,
and such deductions of cause and effect as seem to be constant when
I come into contact with them, I know next to nothing—and that
at the end of an elaborate and costly education.

It sounds tragic, and I suppose that as a civilized human being I
ought to be depressed. Yet I was not depressed as I lay comfortably
in bed that morning, and I am not depressed now. After all, when
we put theories aside, and come down to brass tacks, why should
I be? My ignorance does me no harm. Why should I bother how
automatic machines work, so long as they give me my ticket? What
does it matter how my voice is carried to Dorset, provided it reaches
the person I want to talk to? Why should my limited understanding
be tossed about on long and short waves, provided I can switch
over from the program I don't want to the one I do?

What does it matter if I do not know the facts involved in a book
which I have to review? I can look them up in a textbook or in the
encyclopedia, and they will then be accurate, whereas my memory
might deceive me. As long as one is aware of it, ignorance can be
the greatest help to one. Not long ago, I made an appalling howler
through satisfaction at my own knowledge. I had to review a book
on a technical subject. "Aha," I thought, "he ought to have included
such-and-such": and so pleased was I with my own erudition that I
omitted to do more than hastily survey the list of contents before
expressing my dignified surprise that the author had neglected, etc.
etc. etc. By a quite undeserved stroke of good luck, I discovered

a couple of days later to my horror that the author had not neglected, etc. etc. etc. He had dealt very fully with the matter. A burst
of telephoning at the last minute, and the error was corrected just
in time. Phew! Give me ignorance!

The happily ignorant man, the man aware of his own ignorance,
and perfectly content with it, does not misquote. He does not confuse William with Henry James, mix up the Strausses, or joyfully
praise W. B. Yeats as the author of *Berry & Co.* He invests his money
with caution, and only bets on certainties. He consults his lawyer
before he gives rein to his just indignation. He is not knowledge-
able enough to fall victim to the confidence trickster. In fact, such
a premium has our civilization put upon ignorance, he gets along
very comfortably indeed.

This, of course, is what it has come to. Knowledge is at a discount. Why need I bother to learn this, that, and the other thing,
when a walk to my bookcase, or, at the worst, to the nearest reference
library, will tell me all I want? Why should I be ashamed of my
ignorance, when in the nature of things I can only know a very
little about a very little? Since that early morning enlightenment,
when I realized the true extent of my ignorance, I have gone my
way serene and happy. I need not bother. It is all done for me.
Sometimes I need hardly walk as far as my bookcase. I can sit in my
chair, and listen to a broadcast talk upon the very subject about
which I desire information. The gentleman who gives the talk is
persuasive and kind. He knows infinitely more than I. It would be
downright discourteous to oppose to his discourse the obstacle of
any previous knowledge. We can leave all the knowing to him. It is
his business to—

A horrible thought has struck me. I myself stand on platforms
and give lectures. I myself broadcast. Am I just (I must be, surely)
am I just a surreptitious, disgraceful exception to a rule of enlightenment? Am I the only one who does not know? . . . I mean, are
all the others? . . . Is it possible that some of them, too. . . ?

I had better stop, before my newly won content evaporates.

### SUGGESTIONS FOR WRITING

1. L. A. G. Strong (1896-1958) was born near Plymouth, England, and
spent his boyhood summers in Dublin, which led him to the realiza-

tion that he had the two cultural backgrounds he refers to in the essay. He was a prolific writer of poems, plays, essays, and novels. Strong says in the above essay, "the number of things which I can positively say I know is very limited." How is Strong using the term "know"? How much do you know and when and where did you learn it? Write an essay revealing the extent of what you "know."

2. Are there pleasures for you in your ignorance? Is there a possibility of some sort of blessing occurring because of your ignorance?

3. Describe an individual who is unaware of his own ignorance, revealing his serene pompousness.

4. Discuss the view that Strong's thesis is fit only for an age of specialization, with experts for everything. In such a society, difficult questions arise: Who is to do the voting? Who is to understand how to vote? Who is to curb the force of corruption? Who is to press for progress?


P L A T O

# The Cave (A Free Translation) *

Let me offer you an analogy. Suppose a race of men who were born and brought up all their lives in a movie, who have never taken their eyes off the screen. All they have ever seen are the pictures, and all they have ever heard, except each other, is the sound track. That, and only that, is their world.

I am not concerned with what sort of picture they see. My point is that all they see, all they have ever seen, are pictures on a screen; and that those pictures are all the reality they know.

Now suppose that one of them is taken out; forcibly, because he is being taken away from everything he has been used to, from everything he regards as his world and his life. He is taken out into the sunlight, and the sunlight blinds him. The glitter and dazzle hurt him, and he cannot see any of the things he is shown, the things we now tell him are real.

He would have to get slowly used to these real things, perhaps by looking sideways at them at first, or at their shadows, or by looking

---

* From *The Practical Cogitator* by Charles P. Curtis and Ferris Greenslet (Boston: Houghton Mifflin Company, 1963). © 1962 by Houghton Mifflin Company. Reprinted by permission of the publishers.

at the stars or at the moon, before he could look at things by the light of the sun, let alone the sun itself.

What would he think, when he was finally able to look at these real things? He would know at last that it is the sun that relates the seasons and the courses of time, and that the sun is the reason behind all that he and his comrades used to see on the screen. He would remember his old companions and their opinions. And would he not be happy over what had happened to him and sorry for them, even a little contemptuous?

Now suppose he went back into the movie, suddenly out of the sunshine and into the dark. Wouldn't his old friends laugh at him? For he would not be able to see the shadows on the screen. He would take a long time to get used again to the darkness. And they would laugh at anyone who had been out and come back with his sight nearly gone; and as for the person who had taken him up and might force another of them up, and set others free of their darkness, would they not want to kill him?

Yes, they would.

This is the analogy I wanted to make. Our visible world is the inside of the movie house, and the light of the projector corresponds to the sun. Coming out of the movie into the sunlight is the soul's ascent into regions of intelligence. God knows if that is a true simile. But so it seems to me. In the visible world, where only things can be known and scarcely understood, this idea of the Good which we are seeking is the last thing to be understood, and that darkly. But once it is seen and understood, it is obvious to all that it is the very cause of all that is right and all that is beautiful. To the eye, it is the sun giving light and the lord of light, at once the seeing and the seen. To the mind and intelligence, it is the lord and very truth itself, both the understanding and the understood. And for anyone to act with wisdom, whether in private or in public affairs, he must have seen it and understood it, this idea of the Good.

No wonder that those who have seen and understood want nothing to do with the affairs of men. Naturally enough, their souls strike upwards toward that other world. I think this, too, lies in our analogy. And no wonder, too, that our man coming down among the miseries of mankind again feels out of place and clumsy, and appears rather ridiculous. Let him, still blind, not yet used to the dark, have to appear in a court or some such place and have to wrangle over the shadows of justice with men who have never seen justice itself as he has seen it.

A man who understands would not laugh when he saw our man clumsy and confused. He would know that our man had just come out of the light into darkness, and not out of the darkness into light. He would know which way the man's soul had been turned.

For, as such a man would know, our eyes can be turned to the light as well as toward the dark. If our whole soul is turned away from this visible world toward the bright regions, then our eyes can become able to understand the Good.

There must be some way, some technique of doing this. Do you not believe that it is a turning round of the soul into the right direction so that the eyes may see? For we all have eyes, though we do not know where to look. Untaught we cannot look in the right direction. There are mean men with keen eyes, small men, but smart, bad men, who are quick to discern what concerns them. They see only the things in the way they are looking. If their souls were turned round and pointed in the other direction, then that same keen vision would be as quick to see the Good as our man whom we have forced out into the sunlight and forced to turn his soul toward the Good.

Thus, I think, we draw toward a conclusion, and I believe it is this. Men whose souls have never been turned and who have never had sight of the Good and thereby experience of the truth cannot govern us. They lack that single illuminated purpose toward which all they do must be directed. And I conclude likewise that the others cannot be allowed to go on to the end they seek. Such men must be made to turn back, though it brings them back from the Isles of the Blessed, where they think they are already abiding.

Yes, I said, we are the founders of this state and we must compel the best of our citizens to reach what we think is the greatest understanding, to see the Good, and to climb the heights. But then, as soon as they have seen enough, we must refuse to let them linger there. They must go back again and share the labors and the honors of those who are the darkness inside.

We must do them this wrong. We must lay the worse life upon them, though they are capable of the best. For we are not concerned to make any one class in our state happy. We are trying to make our commonwealth happy as one whole, uniting them all in a harmony which we shall secure partly by compulsion, partly by persuasion. We shall require each to contribute what each can, and if we force a man into the sun and teach him to see the Good, we may not allow him to go his own way. We must likewise force him down and make him bind the state together in the common good and to a common end.

SUGGESTIONS FOR WRITING

1. Plato (427-347 B.C.) offered the analogy of the cave in Book VII of *The Republic*. In the above adaptation, the cave becomes a movie theater, a concept of Charles P. Curtis and Ferris Greenslet, authors of *The Practical Cogitator*. Plato was trying to describe the perfect state and, in the above chapter, was chiefly concerned with the education of the guardians or leaders of the state. He says, ". . . we must compel the best of our citizens to reach what we think is the greatest understanding, to see the Good, and to climb the heights." How would a modern American translate that passage into action? What is the best education one can have for leadership? Write a theme describing that education.
2. "We must force a man into the sun and teach him to see the Good," says Plato. Since he is using analogy all through this section, we need to translate the terms. What does "force a man into the sun" mean? In what ways do we now force students into the sun? Who, ideally, ought to do the forcing? If the answer is, "Those who have already seen the sun, how can we know who these men are? The teacher tests the student, but who tests the teacher? Many of our teachers disagree with each other. Which are we to follow? Write a theme considering these questions.
3. In terms of Plato's analogy, what is the duty of a teacher? What is the duty of a student? To whom are these duties owed? For whom does the state exist?

PERCY BYSSHE SHELLEY

# Ozymandias

I met a traveler from an antique land,
Who said: Two vast and trunkless legs of stone
Stand in the desert. Near them, on the sand,
Half sunk, a shattered visage lies, whose frown,
And wrinkled lip, and sneer of cold command,

Tell that its sculptor well those passions read,
Which yet survive, stamped on these lifeless things,
The hand that mocked them, and the heart that fed:
And on the pedestal these words appear:
"My name is Ozymandias, King of Kings:
Look on my works, ye Mighty, and despair!"
Nothing beside remains. Round the decay
Of that colossal wreck, boundless and bare,
The lone and level sands stretch far away.


SUGGESTIONS FOR WRITING

1. Percy Bysshe Shelley (1792-1822) is an English poet of the Romantic
   era. His poem "Ozymandias" is a famous expression of the imper-
   manence of the life of one human being. The strict pattern imposed by
   the sonnet form (fourteen lines), the use of iambic pentameter (five
   stressed syllables per line), and an intricately interwoven rhyme
   scheme (abab, acdc, ede, fef) have enhanced his expression rather than
   hindering it. Notice that the punctuation of the poem makes three
   sentences of it, and that two of the sentences end in mid-line. All of
   this points to a notable achievement of poetic excellence. There is an
   irony in the fact that Shelley's poem may endure longer than the stones
   of Ozymandias. Paraphrase the three sentences of the poem.

2. Packed into the poem is the essence of a dialogue between the poet
   and a traveler-friend. Imagine the circumstances of their meeting, the
   topic that led them to discuss the irony of life, and the actual dialogue
   between them.

3. Shelley has tried to say something enduring about the inability of man
   to leave a permanent mark or even to find complete fulfillment in life.
   In your own search for significance you have probably brooded on the
   same theme. Is man entitled to leave a permanent mark? Are all such
   attempts futile? (Was Shelley's?) What is to be said for dignity, integrity,
   and the process of making the search for achievement?

# Alternate Plan of Study

# DEFINITION

# DESCRIPTION

## PERSONAL EXPERIENCE

## EVALUATION

## COMPARISON AND CONTRAST

## ANALOGY

## ANALYSIS BY CLASSIFICATION

## POETRY

## HUMOR

# Index of Authors